THE LITERATURE OF ROCK, III
1984–1990
With Additional Material
for the Period 1954–1983

by
FRANK HOFFMANN AND
B. LEE COOPER

ress, Inc.
& London

The So5
Metr

British Library Cataloguing-in-Publication Data available

Library of Congress Cataloging-in-Publication Data

Hoffmann, Frank W., 1949–
  The literature of rock, III, 1984–1990 : with additional
material for the period 1954–1983 / by Frank Hoffmann and
  Cooper.
    p.   cm.
  Incaphy: p.
  ISBN bibliographical references and index.
    1. Roc 8-2762-X (acid-free paper)
  Cooper, B. —History and criticism—Bibliography.   I.
  1984–1990. II. Title.   III. Title : Literature of rock, 3,
  ML128.R6H
  016.78166—d

                                                    93-36263

CONTENTS

Introduction   v

Introductory Note and Subject Headings   xiii

ANNOTATED BIBLIOGRAPHY OF ROCK
LITERATURE   1

Appendixes

    A.   References/Book Stock List   885

    B.   A Basic Collection of Essential Rock
        Recordings   957

    C.   Journals Included in the Bibliography   963

Index   973

About the Authors   1002

INTRODUCTION

As noted in the previous volumes, rock music has made the recorded sound industry one of the greatest success stories in the history of show business. This success is due in no small part to the fact that the industry is a truly democratic one open to anyone with talent, savvy, and/or something that is saleable. Whereas "indie" labels in the early 1950s were signing up unknown regional artists and releasing 45 r.p.m. singles, beginning acts today are recording cassettes and videos of their work and marketing and distributing them through a host of channels. Such exciting grass roots activity contrasts greatly with the corporate controls rigorously guiding the movie, television, etc., sectors of the entertainment world. Most important of all, the music continues to strike a responsive chord with its intended audience, one that covers virtually the entire globe thanks to the all-pervasiveness of the mass media.

The literature of rock reflects the insatiable appetite of the public for any kind of information relating to the music and its leading figures. Print coverage in the early days of rock 'n' roll was comparatively limited in scope. This coverage was often biased in approach; it tended to be concerned with r&r either as a means of economic profit or as a morally degenerate form of expression (with much criticism of song lyrics). The aftermath of the British Invasion and the ascendancy of Bob Dylan stimulated the appearance of a vital press following who not only took rock seriously as an art form but also took a professional pride in defining, evaluating, and reporting the developments of the field to an increasingly wide audience. The 1970s brought even further diversifications as publishers became aware of the potential here for a profitable return on their investments.

The chief types of publications in which rock journalism is presently found include:

(1) *fanzines.* These vary in quality from the professionalism of expensively produced periodicals such as *Creem* to privately published titles, which often feature highly amateurish work. Both serious research and slavish hero worship can be found in this class of publication.

(2) *underground journals.* A fine line often separates these publications from the fanzine. However, the most noteworthy specimens of this genre (e.g., the *L.A. Free Press*, the *Village Voice*) tend to set forth an anti-establishment rhetoric that transcends the treatment of rock music for its own sake.

(3) *music trade magazines.* This category—which includes *Billboard*, *Cash Box*, and *Variety*—generally covers the economic side of the music industry.

(4) *serious music journals.* They are concerned primarily with the discussion of music as an art form, although titles such as *Rolling Stone* and *Spin* often attempt to treat rock as a sociological phenomenon as well as including purely political coverage. More conservative journals such as *Stereo Review* and *High Fidelity* also devote much

space to classical music and surveying reproduction equipment.

(5) *newspapers.* They usually include articles and reviews of rock music, particularly in Sunday editions.

(6) *general interest magazines.* In seeking a high readership, many of these publications (e.g., *Time*, *Newsweek*, *Saturday Review*) include contributions on rock music and its attendant subculture.

(7) *books and monographs.* Authoritatively written histories and critical anthologies of rock have appeared regularly in this format for approximately two decades.

Despite the existence of vast quantities of source material pertaining to rock music, a great deal of it slips past the attention of many researchers and other interested readers. Others, faced with a seemingly uncontrollable mass of printed matter, are at a loss as to how to efficiently locate the specific information they are looking for. These problems have served as the impetus for the creation of this work. In it, we propose the following:

(1) to bring together, in one bibliography, a diverse array of sources related to rock music.

(2) to arrange these sources in a meaningful manner while promoting ease of access to them.

(3) to evaluate the utility of these sources.

More specifically, the book aims at functioning as a pathfinder in the study of rock for both the serious student (an increasing number of colleges and universities are adding this subject to their course offerings) and the interested enthusiast who simply desires to know more about the topic in order to satisfy his/her own curiosity.

The book has been organized so as to achieve optimum utility as a reference source. This introduction explains how to use the book. The bibliography, which constitutes the bulk of the work, is a selective (occasionally annotated) listing of books, periodical articles, etc., concerned with rock music. It is arranged according to a historical outline of the genre. Additional topics of a relevant nature have been appended to the historical scheme developed by the authors. Top priority has been assigned to informative, authoritative publications possessed of nationwide distribution in recognition of (1) the need to provide limitations in view of the vast body of literature available, and (2) the need to cite sources readily accessible to the majority of users in order to maximize its potential effectiveness as a reference tool. Appendix A provides a list of books and monographs cited in the bibliography. Appendix B sets forth a basic stock list of rock recordings (updated from the previous volume). Appendix C provides a listing of periodicals, both past and present, that include notable coverage of rock music. An index citing artists, genres, concepts, and trends that appear in the bibliography completes the work.

How To Use The Work

The listings under each subject heading are generally divided into two primary parts: first, a listing of works dealing with the topic in general terms and, second, the inclusion of artists and other personalities (arranged alphabetically) that best exemplify the concept. The works themselves within each subheading have been arranged alphabetically by main entry (usually the author).

The main headings (and some of the larger subheadings) also are subdivided by lesser topics; for example, "Rhythm and Blues" includes "Clubs" and "Songwriters" as further divisions. The Index represents an important first step in the search process so as to assure that all desired citations can be located.

The process of categorizing the artists has proved to be one fraught with pitfalls. It would have been ideal to place each musician within one particular category; however, the diversified activities of many of them have rendered this a near impossibility. It was decided—in order to minimize the diffuseness that would have resulted from placing the writings on a given artist under its most appropriate heading—that all of the literature concerning a personality/group entity should be located in the category where he/she/they made an initial impression. For cxample, the Beatles—while having contributed to progressive rock, satirical humor, psychedelia, and the r&b revival, among other things—are best remembered as progenitors of the British Invasion. Its First Wave was given flight on the wings of Beatlemania. Accordingly, few exceptions (e.g., an artist making roughly the same impact in two categories) have been made to this rule.

Also in the interests of simplification, group members turning later to a solo career have been included under the group moniker, except in cases where an individual went on to make a far greater (or at least comparable) name for himself/herself than his/her band ever enjoyed. Cross-references within the bibliography and in the index are meant to assist in minimizing any confusion arising out of this procedure of categorization.

Some sources cited in this bibliography have only an abbreviated title preceded by "In:" Full bibliographical data on these sources can be found in the References section (Appendix A).

This bibliography is selective in nature; it has sought to be representative of the best in rock literature. Additional material of value has been excluded in the interests of space and organization. The quality of the material included has not been directly addressed (even in those cases where annotations exist; these have been employed primarily to clarify content to a greater extent than has been possible by means of title description alone). Inclusion itself in the listing was meant to imply either (1) authoritative writing, research, reporting, etc., or (2) that nothing of higher quality on a given topic could be found. In addition, certain titles have been included in view of their unique perspective (e.g., various insiders' accounts of the lives of stars). Record reviews and the more superficial news briefs have also been excluded due to limitations of space.

Abbreviations Employed

bibl.	Bibliography
bio	Biography
disc.	Discography
il.	Illustrations, photographs, etc.
int.	Interview
pap.	Paperback edition

Changes In The Third Installment Of The Series

Following on the heels of the watershed 1979–1983 years, the balance of the 1980s witnessed the continued fragmentation of styles, aided by the diversity of media packaging rock music for the public: AM and FM radio, cable (including separate pay channels) and network TV, home video (both tape and disc formats), concerts and festivals, the various print formats, etc. At present, it would be fairly typical to find that any two randomly selected rock fans are completely unfamiliar with each other's preferred genres.

The major developments of the 1984–1990 period appear to have been:

(1) the meteoric rise of the compact disc—which almost single-handedly pulled the recorded sound industry out of the severe depression of the early 1980s—and subsequent decline of the vinyl, long-playing record;

(2) the continued proliferation of video clips on broadcast TV;

(3) the substantial increase in the number of rock titles in the home video market;

(4) the rise of rap music as a major force on both the aesthetic and economic fronts;

(5) a revival of censorship comparable to the birth of rock 'n' roll in the mid-1950s;

(6) an upsurge in charity projects aimed at fighting poverty, political tyranny, pollution, etc.; and

(7) the return of old acts geared primarily to take advantage of a growing wave of nostalgia as the first generation or two of rock fans harked back to their roots.

The present volume in this series has attempted to keep step with these myriad developments by expanding both its subject headings and coverage of them. The advantages of hindsight have resulted in the reassignment of certain artists/concepts to new headings. And, of course, many artists/concepts appear for the first time. In addition, this volume has endeavored to fill in some of the gaps of the earlier installments by including some entries from the 1954–1983 period not included previously. Duplication of entries from the first two installments in the series has been studiously avoided; in effect, this volume builds upon the literature base begun by these works.

—F.W.H. and B.L.C.

INTRODUCTORY NOTE AND
SUBJECT HEADINGS

The scheme of subject headings utilized in the bibliography was developed with the aim of providing users with a clearer picture of the rock genre. It is primarily a historical outline, with relevant topics not amenable to a chronological pattern appended at the end. The headings are as follows (with pagination from text in order to facilitate easy reference):

1. Development of Rock and Roll Out of Its
    Stylistic Antecedents (1954–1956)   1
    A. Rhythm and Blues   7
    B. Rockabilly   44
    C. European Pop Tradition   93

2. The Beat Era (1956–1958)   108

3. Doo-Wop (1954–1957)   143

4. Neo-Doo-Wop (1958–   )   166

5. Brill Building Era (1959–1965)   172
    A. Teen Idols and the *American Bandstand*
        Phenomenon   179
    B. Dance Crazes (1960–1964)   181
    C. Instrumentals   182
    D. Novelty Songs   185

E. Payola Scandal (1959–1960) 186
F. Commercial Folk 186
  (1) Jamaican Sound: Calypso, Ska, Rock
      Steady 186
G. The Spector Sound (1958–1966) 187
H. Girl Groups (1960–1965; 1988–) 188

6. British Invasion (1964–) 189
A. British Scene Before 1964 189
B. First Wave (1964–1965) 190
C. Second Wave (1966–1970) 207
D. Third Wave (1971–1975) 214
E. Commonwealth Contributions 215

7. American Renaissance (1965–) 230
A. California Sound 230
  (1) The Surf Sound (1962–1964) 230
  (2) Car Songs (1963–1964) 232
  (3) Los Angeles Sound 233
B. Folk Rock (1965–1966) 233
  (1) British Folk Rock 237
  (2) Protest Songs 240

8. Soul Music 242
A. Chicago Sound (1958–) 244
B. Motown Sound (1960–) 245
C. Memphis Sound (1961–) 254
D. Muscle Shoals Sound (1966–) 256
E. The Philadelphia Sound (1970–) 257
F. Blue-Eyed Soul 257

9. Other Regional Styles 264
A. New Orleans Sound (1954–) 264
B. Cajun Rock 266

C. Zydeco 267
D. Tex-Mex (1956–) 268
E. Detroit Sound (1966–) 269
F. San Francisco Sound (1966–) 270
G. Bosstown Sound (1967–1969) 274
H. Sounds of the South (1970–) 274
I. Reggae (1970–) 276
J. Salsa 281
K. Junkanoo 284

10. Hybrid Children of Rock 285
A. Christian Rock/Christian Contemporary
Music 285
B. Punk Rock (1966–) 285
C. Acid Rock/Psychedelia (1966–1968) 286
D. Symphonic Rock/Classical Rock (1967–) 288
E. Progressive Rock (1967–) 291
F. Latin Rock (1969–) 305
G. Big Band Rock (1969–) 305
H. Afro-Rock (1972–) 306
I. Glitter Rock/Glam Rock (1972–1976) 309
J. Pub Rock (1971–1975) 314
K. Heavy Metal (1969–) 314
L. Speed Metal 348
M. Jazz-Rock Fusion (1970–) 351
N. Euro-Pop/Euro-Rock (1973–) 361

11. Nostalgia 368
A. Rock and Roll Revival (1969–) 368
B. Blues Revival (1960–) 368
C. Rhythm and Blues Revival 377
D. English Rhythm and Blues Revival 380
E. Neo-Rockabilly 381

12. Bubblegum   382

13. The Country Connection   390
     A.   Country Rock (1968–   )   390
     B.   Country Crossovers   395

14. Singer/Songwriter Tradition (1970–   )   399

15. Soft Rock   420
     A.   Middle-of-the-Road   422
     B.   Pop Stylists   425
     C.   Pop-Rock   426

16. AOR   436

17. Funk   453
     A.   Funk-Punk   459
     B.   Funk Metal   465

18. Disco   467
     A.   Dance-Oriented Rock (DOR)   470
     B.   Alternative Dance Music   477
     C.   Acid House   488
     D.   House Music   489
     E.   Ambient House   493

19. New Wave   495
     A.   Punk   495
     B.   Hardcore   505
     C.   Thrash   509
     D.   Oi   510
     E.   Post Punk   511
     F.   Industrial/Material Music   522

	G.	White Noise	524
	H.	Industrial Dance	526
	I.	New Wave Proper	527
	J.	Athens Sound	543
	K.	Goth Rock	546
	L.	Neo-Psychedelia	554
	M.	New Romantics/Blitz	563
	N.	Power Pop	570
	O.	Ska/Bluebeat Revival	573
	P.	Techno-Pop/Synth-Pop	575
20.		Avant-Garde	586
	A.	Electronic Music	592
	B.	Experimental	594
21.		Black Contemporary	598
	A.	Go-Go	619
	B.	Rap/Hip Hop	620
22.		New Age	644
	A.	Space Music	648
	B.	Ambient	648
23.		Alternative Rock	651
	A.	Postmodern	670
	B.	Manchester (Manc) Sound	737
24.		Roots Rock	741
25.		World Beat	748
26.		Related Topics	750
		—Advertising	750

—Archives   750
—Art   751
—Awards   752
—Censorship   753
—Charity   770
—Charts   782
—Clubs and Concert Venues   783
—Concerts, Festivals, Touring, etc.   784
—Copyright   788
—Counterfeiting, Bootlegging, etc.   789
—Drugs   790
—Economics and Marketing   791
—Education   792
—Fans, Audiences, etc.   793
—Fashion   793
—Films   793
—Formats   795
—Health   815
—History   815
—Humor   815
—Instruments   816
—Lyrics, Song   819
—Managers   819
—Mass Media   819
—Nostalgia   874
—Politics   875
—Posters   876
—Public Relations   876
—Record Album Covers   876
—Religion   877
—Retailing   877
—Sociology   878
—Songwriters   880
—Violence   884

Appendix A: References for *The Literature of Rock, III,*
1984–1990   885

Appendix B: A Basic Collection of Essential Rock
Recordings   957

Appendix C: Journals Included in the Index   963

Index   973

About the Authors   1002

1. DEVELOPMENT OF ROCK AND ROLL OUT OF ITS STYLISTIC ANTECEDENTS (1954–1956)

General Sources

Becker, Bart. *'Til The Cows Come Home: Rock 'N' Roll Nebraska.* Seattle: Real Gone Books, 1985. il.

Belz, Carl. "The Beginnings of Rock: 1954 Through 1956," In: *The Story of Rock.* pp. 16–59. il.

Cohn, Nik. "Roots," In: *Ball the Wall.* pp. 54–60. il.

Edwards, Don. "Rock 'N' Roll, Lexington Not a Perfect Match in '55," *Lexington (Kentucky) Herald-Leader.* (July 7, 1985) 12A.

Edwards, Joseph, comp. *Top 10's and Trivia of Rock and Roll and Rhythm and Blues, 1950–1980.* pp. 3–150.

Elrod, Bruce C., comp. *Your Hit Parade and American Top Ten Hits, 1958–1984.* pp. 1–390.

Gillett, Charlie. "The Sound Begins," In: *The Sound of the City: The Rise of Rock and Roll.* pp. 1–27. il.

Griggs, Bill. "The Rock 'N' Roll Era (or What Makes the 1950s so Unique?)," *Rockin' 50s.* n1 (August 1986) 3–5. il.

Hogan, Richard. "Twenty-Five Years of Rock 'N' Roll," In: *Contemporary Music Almanac, 1980/81,* comp. by Ronald Zalkind. pp. 81–94.

Kamin, Jonathan. "Parallels in the Social Reactions to Jazz and Rock," *Journal of Jazz Studies.* II (December 1974) 95–125.

Kamin, Jonathan. "The White R&B Audience and the Music Industry, 1952–1956," *Popular Music and Society.* VI (1978) 150–167.

Loder, Kurt. "The Music That Changed the World," *Rolling Stone.* n467 (February 13, 1986) 49–50. il.

Middleton, Richard. "Rock 'N' Roll, In: *Pop Music and the Blues: A Study of the Relationship and Its Significance.* pp. 148–161.

O'Neill, William O. "The Rise of Rock and Roll," In: *American High: The Years of Confidence, 1945–1960.* pp. 266–269.

Postol, Todd. "Reinterpreting the Fifties: Changing Views of a 'Dull' Decade," *Journal of American Culture.* VIII (Summer 1985) 39–45.

"The Rock and Roll Hall of Fame—Forefathers," *Rolling Stone.* n467 (February 13, 1986) 48. il.

Scheurer, Timothy E. "Country, Folk, and the Roots of Rock 'N' Roll," In: *American Popular Music—Volume Two: The Age of Rock.* pp. 9–12.

Shaw, Arnold. "Popular Music From Minstrel Songs to Rock

and Roll," In: *One Hundred Years of Music in America.* pp. 140–168. il.

Shaw, Arnold. "The Rock Revolution," *The Sonneck Society Newsletter.* IV (Spring 1978) 16–17.

Silver, Peter. *A Left Hand Like God.* London: Quartet, 1988.

Szatmary, David P. "The Blues, Rock 'N' Roll, and Racism," In: *Rockin' in Time: A Social History of Rock and Roll.* pp. 1–28. il.

Freed, Alan

Blackburn, Richard. "Alan Freed May Have Invented Rock 'N' Roll Radio—But He Had Help: The Amazing Stories of Dr. Hepcat, Professor Bop, Groover Boy, and Jack the Cat," *Waxpaper.* IV (May 4, 1979) 20–23, 37–38. il.

Blackburn, Richard. "Rock 'N' Roll Disc Jockeys," In: *Contemporary Music Almanac, 1980/81,* comp. by Ronald Zalkind. pp. 116–124. il.

Cotton, Lee. "Alan Freed," In: *Shake, Rattle and Roll—The Golden Age of American Rock 'N' Roll: Volume One, 1952–1955.* pp. 270–272. il.

Fanselow, Julie. "Alan Freed—Mr. Rock 'N' Roll Remembered," *The (Cleveland) Plain Dealer.* (September 6, 1985) sec. B, 3, 14.

Garofalo, Reebee, and Steve Chapple. "From ASCAP to Alan Freed: The Pre-history of Rock 'N' Roll," In: *American Popular Music—Volume Two: The Age of Rock.* pp. 63–72. il.

Jackson, John. "Spotlight on Alan Freed," *Rockin' 50s.* n1 (August 1986) 8–15. il.

Markey, S. "Remember Alan Freed Concert With 20 Cleveland Happenings," *Variety.* 322 (March 26, 1986) 92.

Marsh, Dave. "American Grandstand: Alan Freed Wept," *The Record.* II (October 1983) 15.

Millar, Bill. "Mr. Rock 'N' Roll," In: *The History of Rock.* n11 (1982) 215–217. il.

Ochs, Ed. " 'Rock' of Ages: Born Freed," *Billboard.* LXXXI (December 27, 1969) 110.

Rathbun, Keith. "Alan Freed's Defense Plea," *Scene.* XVII (March 20–26, 1986) 11.

Rutledge, Jeffrey. "Alan Freed: The Fall From Grace of a Forgotten Hero," *Goldmine.* n118 (February 1, 1985) 22, 54, 57. il.

Scott, Jane. "When 'Moon Dawg' Howled in Cleveland," *The (Cleveland) Plain Dealer.* (September 6, 1985) sec. B, p. 3.

Shaw, Arnold. "Rock 'N' Roll's Superpromoter," In: *The Rockin' Fifties.* pp. 104–11. il.

Smith, Wes. "The Moon Dog," In: *The Pied Pipers of Rock 'N' Roll: Radio Deejays of the '50s and '60s.* pp. 163–219. il.

Stambler, Irwin. "Freed, Alan," In: *The Encyclopedia of Pop, Rock and Soul.* pp. 242–244. il.

Haley, Bill

Belz, Carl. "Early Rock: The Contribution of Bill Haley," In: *The Story of Rock.* pp. 33–38. il.

"Bill Haley," *The Golden Age.* n5 (February 1987) 12–31. il.

Cohn, Nik. "Bill Haley," In: *Ball the Wall.* pp. 61–64.

Cotten, Lee. "Bill Haley and His Comets," In: *Shake, Rattle, and Roll—The Golden Age of American Rock 'N' Roll: Volume One, 1952–1955.* pp. 256–259.

Doggett, Peter. "Bill Haley," *Record Collector.* n38 (October 1982) 12–18.

Edwards, Don. "Haley an Unlikely Founding Father of Rock," *Lexington (Kentucky) Herald-Leader.* (July 7, 1985) 1A.

"15 Elected to Hall of Fame," *Billboard.* 98 (October 18, 1986) 101.

Finnis, Rob. "The Haley Story," *The History of Rock.* n2 (1982) 24–28.

Gilbert, Adrian. "Rock Around the Clock," *The History of Rock.* n2 (1982) 21–23.

Gleason, Ralph J. "Perspectives: Milt Gabler's Sound," *Rolling Stone.* n169 (September 12, 1974) 14.

Gregoire, Denise. "Bill Haley: The Orfeon Years," *Goldmine.* n47 (April 1980) 146–147. il.

Gregoire, Denise. "Spotlight on Bill Haley," *Rockin' 50s.* n4 (February 1987) 8–15. il.

Hirschberg, Dave. "Calling All Comets! The Reunion of Bill Haley's Comets—Part One," *Now Dig This.* n63 (June 1988) 18–22. il.

Hirschberg, Dave. "Calling All Comets! The Reunion of Bill Haley's Comets—Part Two," *Now Dig This.* n64 (July 1988) 24–26. il.

Jahn, Mike. "1955: Into the Public Eye," In: *Rock: From Elvis Presley to the Rolling Stones.* pp. 12–17. il.

"Jodimars Alias the Comets," *The Golden Age.* n5 (February 1987) 32–33.

McNutt, Randy. "Origins of Rock," In: *We Wanna Boogie: An Illustrated History of the American Rockabilly Movement.* pp. 19–30. il.

Petzke, Kenn. "Bill Haley: Personal Memories," *Goldmine.* n112 (November 9, 1984) 24–27, 34. il.

Petzke, Kenn. "Memories of Bill Haley," *Rockin' 50s.* n4 (November 1987) 3–5. il.

"Rock Hall of Fame to Induct 15 Acts," *Variety.* 234 (October 8, 1986) 147.

Shaw, Arnold. "Rock Around the Clock," In: *The Rockin' Fifties.* pp. 136–153. il.

Stambler, Irwin. "Haley, Bill," In: *The Encyclopedia of Pop, Rock and Soul.* pp. 275–276. il.

Stidom, Larry. "Joey Welz: The Return of Haley's 'Comet'," *Goldmine.* n149 (April 11, 1986) 72–76. il.

Taylor, Kevin, and John Marshall. "Bill Haley Discography," *Big Beat of the 50's.* n22 (November 1979) 12–14. il., disc.

Taylor, Kevin, and John Marshall. "Bill Haley: The Decca Years and Later," *Big Beat of the 50's.* n27 (May 1981) 4–15. il.

Tosches, Nick. "Young Bill Haley: The Lounge Act That Transcendeth All Knowing," In: *Unsung Heroes of Rock 'N' Roll.* pp. 73–77. il.

White, Timothy. "Bill Haley," In: *Rock Stars.* pp. 86–89. il.

Whitesell, Rick, and Stan Mayo. "Bill Haley Discography," *Record Exchanger.* n20 (1975) 9. disc.

A. RHYTHM AND BLUES

General Sources

Anderson, Clive. "Gospel," *The History of Rock.* n8 (1982) 158–162. il.

Barson, Michael, comp. *Rip It Up: Postcards From the Heyday of Rock 'N' Roll.* New York: Pantheon, 1989. il.

Berry, Jason, Jonathan Foose, and Tad Jones. *Up From the Cradle of Jazz.* Athens, Georgia: University of Georgia Press, 1986.

Brown, Ashley. "From Star to Superstar," *The History of Rock.* n24 (1982) 461–463. il.

Brown, Ashley. "The Roots of Soul," *The History of Rock.* n17 (1982) 321–322. il.

Brown, Geoff. "Black Voices," *The History of Rock.* n4 (1982) 61–63. il.

Choice, Wally. "History of Warner Brothers R&B," *Waxpaper.* III (July 7, 1978) 17–19. il.

Cooper, B. Lee. "Promoting Social Change Through Audio Repetition: Black Musicians as Creators and Revivalists, 1953–1978," *Tracking: Popular Music Studies.* II (Winter 1989) 26–46. il.

Cotten, Lee. *Shake, Rattle, and Roll—The Golden Age of American Rock 'N' Roll: Volume One, 1952–1955.* Ann Arbor, MI: Pierian, 1989. il.

George, Nelson. "Rhythm & Blues: How—and Why—This Section Got Its Name," *Billboard.* 98 (November 29, 1986) 23.

George, Nelson. "Rhythm & Blues: 'Retronuevo'— Appreciating the Past Without Repeating It," *Billboard.* 98 (June 28, 1986) 21.

Gibbs, Vernon. "The Superstar: Much More Than Just the Music," *Billboard.* 94 (June 5, 1982) BM-2, BM-14. il.

Gibbs, Vernon. "Veteran Hitmakers Span the Generations," *Billboard.* 95 (June 4, 1983) 33ff.

Gillett, Charlie. *The Sound of the City: The Rise of Rock and Roll.* New York: Pantheon, 1983. il.

Greig, Charlotte. "Tonight's the Night," In: *Will You Still Love Me Tomorrow? Girl Groups From the 50s On.* pp. 10–31. il.

Grendysa, Peter. "'50s R&B Stars Helped Cheat Themselves By Signing Poorly Negotiated Contracts," *Record Collector's Monthly.* n17 (February 1984) 1, 3, 10. il.

Grendysa, Peter. "Making Tracks Chicago Style: The Four Clefs, Five Breezes, Four Bluejackets, and The Aristo-Kats," *Goldmine.* n116 (January 4, 1985) 20–24. il.

Grendysa, Peter. "West Coast R&B," *Goldmine.* n123 (April 12, 1985) 26–28, 68–70. il.

Groia, Philip. "How It All Began," "Gospel on the Stoops of New York," and "The Kingdom of Rhythm and Blues," In: *They All Sang on the Corner.* pp. 15–30; 31–38; 95–106.

Guralnick, Peter. "The War is Over: Around the World and Home Again," In: *Listener's Guide to the Blues.* pp. 72–88. il.

Hansen, Barry. "Rhythm and Gospel," In: *The Rolling Stone Illustrated History of Rock and Roll,* ed. by Jim Miller. pp. 26–29. il.

Haskins, Jim. *The Cotton Club*. New York: Random House, 1977. il.

Hatch, David, and Stephen Millward. *From Blues to Rock: An Analytical History of Pop Music*. Manchester, U.K.: Manchester University Press, 1989 (c1987).

Hirshey, Gerri. *Nowhere to Run: The Story of Soul Music*. New York: Penguin, 1984.

Leichter, Albert, comp. *Discography of Rhythm and Blues and Rock 'N' Roll, Circa 1946–1964: A Reference Guide*. Staunton, VA: A. Leichter, 1975. il., disc.

Longstreet, Stephen. *Storyville to Harlem: Fifty Years in the Jazz Scene*. New Brunswick, NJ: Rutgers University Press, 1986. il.

McCourt, Tom. "Bright Lights, Big City: A Brief History of Rhythm and Blues, 1945–1957," In: *American Popular Music—Volume Two: The Age of Rock,* ed. by Timothy E. Scheurer. pp. 46–62. il.

McCutcheon, Lynn Ellis. *Rhythm and Blues: An Experience and Development*. Arlington, VA: Beatty, 1971. il.

McGowan, James A. *Here Today! Here To Stay! A Personal History of Rhythm and Blues*. St. Petersburg, FL: Sixth House, 1983.

Marcus, Greil. *Mystery Train*. Revised and expanded edition. New York: E.P. Dutton, 1982.

Maultsby, Portia K. "Rhythm and Blues, 1945–1955: A Survey of Styles," In: *Black American Popular Music:*

Rhythm and Blues, 1945–1955, comp. by B.J. Reagon. pp. 6–23. il.

Millar, Bill. "Rhythm and Blues," *The History of Rock.* n2 (1982) 29–32. il.

Pavlow, Al, comp. *Big Al Pavlow's The Rhythm 'N' Blues Book: A Disc-History of Rhythm 'N' Blues.* Providence: Music House, 1983. il.

Redd, Lawrence N. *Rock Is Rhythm and Blues: The Impact of Mass Media.* East Lansing, MI: Michigan State University Press, 1974.

Redd, Lawrence N. "Rock! It's Still Rhythm and Blues," *Black Perspective in Popular Music.* XIII (Spring 1985) 31–47.

Rowe, Mike. "Chicago R&B Hits, 1945–1959," In: *Chicago Breakdown.* pp. 217–218. il.

Ruppli, Michel, and Bill Daniels, comps. *The King Labels: A Discography.* Westport, CT: Greenwood, 1985. il., disc.

Russell, Tony. "Music Unlimited," *The History of Rock.* n17 (1982) 338–341. il.

Shaw, Arnold. *Black Popular Music in America: From the Spirituals, Minstrels, and Ragtime to Soul, Disco, and Hip-Hop.* New York: Schirmer, 1986. il.

Sigerson, Davitt. "A Quarter Century of R&B," *Rolling Stone.* n467 (February 13, 1986) 75–78. il.

Smith, Wes. *The Pied Pipers of Rock 'N' Roll: Radio Deejays of the '50s and 60s.* Marietta, GA: Longstreet, 1989.

Stidom, Larry. "Izatso?", *Goldmine.* n33 (January 1979) 6.

Stierle, Wayne. "Remember Yesterday Tomorrow," *Record Exchanger.* n31 (1983) 30.

Tagg, Philip. "Open Letter—'Black Music', 'Afro-American Music', and 'European Music'," *Popular Music.* VIII (October 1989) 285–298.

Tosches, Nick. *Unsung Heroes of Rock 'N' Roll: The Birth of Rock 'N' Roll in the Dark and Wild Years Before Elvis.* New York: Scribner, 1984. il.

Whitburn, Joel, comp. *Top Rhythm and Blues Singles, 1942–1988.* Menomonee Falls, WI: Record Research, 1988.

Clubs—The Apollo Theatre

Cassata, Mary Anne. "Motown Returns to the Apollo," *Song Hits.* n237 (November 1985) 32–33. il.

Fox, Ted. *Showtime at the Apollo.* New York: Holt, Rinehart, and Winston, 1983. il.

George, Nelson. "Relighting the Apollo at 50: New Luster for Harlem Landmark," *Billboard.* 97 (June 15, 1985) BM-6. il.

Riley, Clayton. "We Thought It Was Magic: Harlem's Apollo Theater," *New York Times Magazine.* (November 7, 1976) 36–38. il.

Schiffman, Jack. *Harlem Heyday: A Pictorial History of Modern Black Show Business and the Apollo Theatre.* New York: Prometheus, 1984. il.

Schiffman, Jack. *Uptown: The Story of Harlem's Apollo Theatre.* New York: Cowles, 1971. il.

Thomashefsky, Steve. "The Apollo Theater," *Living Blues.* n27 (May–June 1976) 12–17. il.

Walker, Jessie. *The Apollo Theater Story.* New York: Apollo Operations, 1966. il.

Record Companies

APOLLO THEATRE RECORDS

Nunziata, Susan. "N.Y.'s Apollo Theatre Launching 4 Record Labels," *Billboard.* 102:11 (March 17, 1990) 8, 91.

ATCO

Schulman, Derek. "Building for the Future," *Billboard.* 102:26 (June 30, 1990) W-8. il.

ATLANTIC

Ertegun, Ahmet M., and Doug Morris. "The Challenge of the '90s," *Billboard.* 102:26 (June 30, 1990) W-9. il.

CHESS

DiMartino, Dave. "MCA Says Chess Reissues are What the Fans Ordered," *Billboard.* 101 (August 26, 1989) 10ff.

Record Company Executives—Nesuhi Ertegun (See also: Mass Media)

"Ertegun, Lopez to Run WEA Intl.," *Variety.* 319 (May 8, 1985) 171.

"Ertegun Named IFPI President," *Billboard.* 97 (June 29, 1985) 72.

"Ertegun Says Fund Shortage Hampering IFPI Operations," *Billboard.* 98 (February 22, 1986) 76.

"Ertegun: WEA Not Seeking Partner," *Billboard.* 97 (February 16, 1985) 3ff.

Goodman, Fred. "Nesuhi Ertegun Dead at 71," *Rolling Stone.* n560 (September 7, 1989) 22–23. il.

Ace, Johnny

Cotton, Lee. "Johnny Ace," In: *Shake, Rattle, and Roll.* pp. 61–62. il.

Duncan, Robert. "Johnny Ace: The Games People Play," In: *Only the Good Die Young.* pp. 11–15.

Escott, Colin. "Johnny Ace: The First Rock 'N' Roll Casualty," *Goldmine.* n165 (November 21, 1986) 16–17. il.

Grendysa, Peter. "Johnny Ace: The 'Ace' of Duke," *Goldmine.* n187 (September 25, 1987) 28, 91. il.

"Johnny Ace Discography," *Shout.* n45 (July 1969) 6–7. disc.

Tosches, Nick. "Johnny Ace: Number One With a Bullet," In: *Unsung Heroes of Rock 'N' Roll.* pp. 133–138. il.

Adams, Faye

Cotten, Lee. "Faye Adams," In: *Shake, Rattle, and Roll.* pp. 126–128. il.

Grendysa, Peter. "Faye Adams: It Made Her Cry," *Goldmine.* n189 (October 23, 1987) 22–25. il.

Alexander, Arthur

Nickols, Pete. "Arthur Alexander," *Record Collector.* n66 (February 1985) 45–47. il., disc.

Baker, LaVern

Davis, Hank. "LaVern Baker: A Recollection," *Goldmine.* n125 (May 10, 1985) 50.

Grendysa, Peter. "Spotlight on LaVern Baker: Her Soulful Ballads and Novelty Hits Inspired Adulation and Blatant Imitation," *Record Collector's Monthly.* n19 (April 1984) 1, 8–9. il.

"LaVern Baker," *The Golden Age.* n4 (January 1987) 6–15. il.

Nickols, Pete. "LaVern Baker," *Record Collector.* n61 (September 1984) 35–39. il, disc.

Belvin, Jesse

Atkins, Jim. "Jesse Belvin's Death," *Goldmine.* n114 (December 7, 1984) 4.

Dawson, Jim. "Jesse Belvin: Bridge Between Cool Urban Blues

and Rough-Edged Rock," *Goldmine.* n166 (December 5, 1986) 12, 16–17. il.

Dawson, Jim. "Remembering an 'Across the Track' Artist," *Los Angeles Times.* (February 6, 1983) n.p.

Big Maybelle

Grendysa, Peter. "Big Maybelle: The Biggest of Them All," *Goldmine.* n192 (December 4, 1987) 28, 35. il.

Bland, Billy

Grendysa, Peter. "Billy Bland," *Goldmine.* n220 (December 30, 1988) 7. il.

Bland, Bobby "Blue"

Hannusch, J. "The Blues Belong to Bobby Bland," *Billboard.* 98 (October 18, 1986) 26.

Porter, B. "Brief Encounters," *Jazz Times.* (December 1985) 25.

Stambler, Irwin. "Bland, Bobby 'Blue', In: *The Encyclopedia of Pop, Rock and Soul.* pp. 59–60.

The Bobbettes

Grendysa, Peter. "The Bobbettes," *Goldmine.* n220 (December 30, 1988) 8. il.

Tamarkin, Jeff. "The Bobbettes," In: *Goldmine.* n64 (September 1981) 7–8.

Brenston, Jackie (See also: Ike and Tina Turner)

Tosches, Nick. "Jackie Brenston: To the Package Store in Style," In: *Unsung Heroes of Rock 'N' Roll.* pp. 106–111. il.

Brown, Buster

"Buster Brown," *The Golden Age.* n10 (July 1987) 4–7. il.

Wood, Dave. "Buster Brown," *New Kommotion.* II (Autumn 1976) 7.

Brown, Charles

Grendysa, Peter. 'Charles Brown: Mr. Black Night," *Goldmine.* n250 (February 23, 1990) 34. il.

Brown, James (See also: Rap)

Booth, Dave. "Daddy Cool," "Conversation With James Brown—Kitchener, Ontario on July 11, 1984," *Soul Survivor.* I (January 1985) 4–8. il., int.

Bowles, Billy. "Soul Singer James Brown Has A Flip-Side Record," *Detroit Free Press.* (October 16, 1988) 1A, 14A.

Brown, James, with Bruce Tucker. *James Brown: The Godfather of Soul.* New York: Macmillan, 1986. il.

Considine, J.D. "Calling Mr. Dynamite," *Record.* 4 (November 1984) 64. il.

Courtney, Ron. "James Brown Meets the Nine Nobles," *Goldmine.* n151 (May 9, 1986) 20–22. il.

Gambaccini, Paul. "James Brown," In: *Track Records*. pp. 145–152. il.

George, Nelson. "Rhythm and Blues: J.B. Rated Top R&B Act by New Tome," *Billboard*. 101 (January 14, 1989) 21.

George, Nelson. "Rhythm and Blues: The Godfather of Soul's Legacy Continues," *Billboard*. 100 (December 17, 1988) 22.

Goldberg, M. "James Brown Sentenced," *Rolling Stone*. n544 (January 26, 1989) 13.

Grein, Paul. "Hartman to Produce James Brown Album," *Billboard*. 98 (April 5, 1986) 20.

Guralnick, Peter. "James Brown: How It Is To Be Free," *Blues World*. n31 (June 1970) 11–13. il.

Guralnick, Peter. "Papa's Got a Brand New Bag," In: *Sweet Soul Music*. pp. 220–245. il.

Halbersberg, Elianne. "James Brown," *Song Hits*. n247 (September 1986) 36–37. il.

Hinckley, D. "Lost Someone," *Rock & Roll Confidential*. n64 (January 1989) 2.

Hirshey, Gerri. "James Brown," *Rolling Stone*. n585 (August 23, 1990) 98–102. il.

Hirshey, Gerri. "Superbull, Superbad," In: *Nowhere to Run*. pp. 265–293. il.

Hirshey, Gerri. " 'We Sang Like Angels'," In: *Nowhere to Run*. pp. 54–63. il.

"James Brown's U.S. Releases," *Record Collector.* n60 (August 1984) 21–25. il., disc.

Jeske, Lee. "James Brown: Still Sweating After All These Years," *Cash Box.* (March 21, 1987) 24, 27. il., int.

Johnson, Jon E., and Jerry Osborne, comps. "A Year in the Life of James Brown," *DISCoveries.* II (January 1989) 102.

Mack, B., and John Brodie. "Nobody Knows the Trouble I've Seen: James Brown Discography of Crime," *Spin.* 4 (December 1988) 36–37ff. il.

Marsh, Dave. "The Return of Mr. Dynamite (and Other Great Hits)," In: *Fortunate Son.* pp. 290–300. il.

Newman, M. "James Brown Faces Charges in 2 States," *Billboard.* 101 (January 14, 1989) 75.

"News," *Melody Maker.* 65 (January 7, 1989) 5. il. Brown found guilty of aggravated assault.

"News," *Melody Maker.* 65 (January 21, 1989) 5. il. Brown faces more legal problems.

"The Rock and Roll Hall of Fame: James Brown," *BMI.* n1 (1986) 25. il., bio.

Scott, Steve. "James Brown: Godfather of Soul," *Record Collector.* n40 (December 1982) 13–20. il., disc.

Silverman, Phil. "Latinized Funk and Raw Soul Herald a James Brown Revival," *Record Collector's Monthly.* n14 (November 1983) 15.

Stambler, Irwin. "Brown, James," In: *The Encyclopedia of Pop, Rock and Soul*. pp. 81–83.

"Ten Pioneers of Rock Selected for Induction to New Hall of Fame," *Variety*. 321 (November 27, 1985) 139.

Vare, E.A. "Brown's Career Has Punch Thanks to Stallone," *Billboard*. 98 (November 8, 1986) 22.

White, Cliff. "The Classic Soul of James Brown," *Let It Rock*. n32 (August 1975) 24–28. il.

White, Cliff, comp. "Discography," In: *James Brown: The Godfather of Soul*, by James Brown with Bruce Tucker. pp. 269–326. disc.

White, Timothy. "James Brown," In: *Rock Stars*. pp. 76–81. il.

White, Timothy. "James! The Power of Positive Badness," *Musician*. n90 (April 1986) 50–61. il.

Woodbridge, J. "The Politics of Dancing," *Melody Maker*. 60 (June 15, 1985) 15. il.

Brown, Nappy

Cotten, Lee. "Nappy Brown," In: *Shake, Rattle, and Roll*. pp. 246–247. il.

Jancik, Wayne. "Nappy Brown," *Goldmine*. n244 (December 1, 1989) 14. il.

Price, Mike, and Les Quinn. "Nattering With Nappy," *Now Dig This*. n52 (July 1987) 3–4. il.

Brown, Roy

Hannusch, Jeff. "Roy Brown: The Good Rockin' Man," In: *I Hear You Knockin'.* pp. 71–82. il.

Tosches, Nick. "Roy Brown: Good Rockin' Tonight," In: *Unsung Heroes of Rock 'N' Roll.* pp. 56–59. il.

Brown, Ruth

Cotton, Lee. "Ruth Brown," In: *Shake, Rattle, and Roll.* pp. 32–33. il.

Grendysa, Peter. "Hello, Ruth! The Ruth Brown Story," *It Will Stand.* n12/13 (198?) 4–6. il.

Jeske, Lee. "Ruth Brown," *Rolling Stone.* n576 (April 19, 1990) 79–83. il., int.

Nickols, Pete. "Ruth Brown," *Record Collector.* n65 (January 1985) 46–49. il., disc.

"Ruth Brown," *The Golden Age.* n4 (January 1987) 16–33. il.

Shaw, Arnold. "Interview With Ruth Brown," In: *Honkers and Shouters.* pp. 398–409. il., int.

Charles, Ray

Albertson, Chris. "Ray Charles," *Stereo Review.* LI (February 1986) 55–59. il., disc., bio.

Cotton, Lee. "Ray Charles," In: *Shake, Rattle, and Roll.* pp. 233–235. il.

Doggett, Pete. "Ray Charles," *Record Collector.* n45 (May 1983) 40–46. il., disc.

Etheredge, Jivin' Johnny. "Ray Charles: A Performer of Nearly Mythical Stature," *Goldmine*. n134 (September 13, 1985) 12, 14, 16, 18. il.

Jeske, Lee. "Ray Charles Unchains His Greatest Hits," *Cash Box*. (November 21, 1987) 8–9, 43. int.

Katz, Robin. "Brother Ray," *The History of Rock*. n17 (1982) 323–329. il.

Levenson, J. "What'd I Say—a Conversation with Ray Charles," *Down Beat*. 56 (January 1989) 4, 16–19. il., int., disc.

Martin, Guy. "Blue Genius: Brother Ray Charles Sings the Gospel Truth. Listen Up, Honey," *Esquire*. (May 1986) 92–102. il., int.

Rader, Dotson. "Ray Charles Sees the Beauty," *Parade Magazine*. (August 7, 1988) 4–6. il.

Ritz, David, comp. "Discography and Notes," In: *Brother Ray: Ray Charles' Own Story*, by Ray Charles and David Ritz. pp. 343–366. il.

"The Rock and Roll Hall of Fame: Ray Charles," *BMI*. n1 (1986) 23. il., bio.

White, Timothy. "Ray Charles," In: *Rock Stars*. pp. 48–51. il.

Cooke, Sam

Anderson, Clive. "Twistin' the Night Away," *The History of Rock*. n17 (1982) 333–335. il.

Duncan, Robert. "Sam Cooke: Saints and Sinners," In: *Only the Good Die Young.* pp. 21–26. il.

Funk, Ray. "SAR Records: Sam Cooke's Soul Label," *Goldmine.* n211 (August 26, 1988) 86–88. il.

Gambaccini, Paul. "Sam Cooke," In: *Masters of Rock.* pp. 27–33. il.

George, Nelson. " 'New' Sam Cooke Songs on the Way," *Billboard.* 97 (June 29, 1985) 48.
Re. the *Radio M.U.S.C. Man* l.p.

George, Nelson. "The Rhythm and the Blues," *Billboard.* 96 (December 22, 1984) 54.

George, Nelson. "Sam Cooking on British Single Chart," *Billboard.* 98 (April 12, 1986) 28.

Guralnick, Peter. "Prologue to Soul: Sam Cooke, Ray Charles, and the Business of Music," In: *Sweet Soul Music.* pp. 21–75. il.

Hirshey, Gerri. "Lady, You Shot Me," In: *Nowhere to Run.* pp. 99–116. il.

Martin, D. "Gospel Caravan," *Jazz Magazine.* n336 (February 1985) 28.

McEwen, Joe. *Sam Cooke: A Biography In Words and Pictures.* New York: Sire/Chappell, 1977.

"Nine Selected For Induction Into Songwriters Hall of Fame," *Billboard.* 98 (December 27, 1968) 8.

Palmer, Joanne. "Sam Cooke: Still Strong 30 Years After 'You
Send Me' Hits #1," *Goldmine.* n168 (January 2, 1987)
8–12. il.

Richmond, Norman. "Late Soul Kings Deaths Still Shrouded
in Mystery," *Soul Survivor.* n2 (Spring 1985) 29.

"The Rock and Roll Hall of Fame: Sam Cooke," *BMI.* n1
(1986) 24. il., bio.

Scott, Steve. "Sam Cooke," *Record Collector.* n44 (April 1983)
35–40. il., disc.

"Sony Hall of Fame Names 9 Inductees," *Variety.* 325 (December 31, 1986) 62.

Stambler, Irwin. "Cooke, Sam," In: *The Encyclopedia of Pop, Rock
and Soul.* pp. 142–143.

"Ten Pioneers of Rock Selected for Induction to New Hall of
Fame," *Variety.* 321 (November 27, 1985) 139.

Waller, Don. "Sam Cooke—Alive Again," *Los Angeles Times.*
(June 2, 1985) 50.

White, Timothy. "Sam Cooke," In: *Rock Stars.* pp. 72–75. il.

Covay, Don

Young, Jon. "Don Covay: The Quality of Mercy, Mercy,"
Musician. n125 (March 1989) 11.

Crudup, Arthur

Leadbitter, Mike. "Big Boy Crudup," *Blues Unlimited.* n75
(September 1970) 18–19. il.

Naylor, Bob. "Forefathers of Rock No. 4: Arthur Crudup," *Now Dig This.* n57 (December 1987) 29–30. il.

Day, Bobby

Aynsley, Steve. "Bobby Day: A Class Performer—Over and Over," *Now Dig This.* n77 (August 1989) 11. il.

Jackson, John. "Bobby Day: Sorting Out the Bobby Day Mystery," *Goldmine.* n166 (December 5, 1986) 34, 82. il.

McGarvey, Seamus. "Over and Over Again: It's Bobby Day— Part One," *Now Dig This.* n82 (January 1990) 22–25. il.

Stafford, John. "Rockin' With Robin," *Now Dig This.* n61 (April 1988) 3–5.

Tamarkin, Jeff. "Bobby Day: His Mysterious Recording History," *Goldmine.* n152 (May 23, 1986) 10–16. il.

Diddley, Bo (r.n.: Otha Elias Bates)

Cotton, Lee. "Bo Diddley," In: *Shake, Rattle, and Roll.* pp. 251–252. il.

Courtney, Ron. "Bo Diddley: Spending a Night With 'The Man'," *Goldmine.* n128 (June 21, 1985) 68, 78. il.

DeYoung, Bill. "Hey Bo Diddley," *Backstage Magazine.* I (August 3–16, 1988) 6–8. il.

Evans, Mike. "Hey, Bo Diddley! Who Put the Bom-Bom-de-Bom- Bom?," *Let It Rock.* n33 (September 1975) 27. il.

Hannusch, Jeff. "Bo Diddley is a Gunslinger," *Guitar Player.* XVIII (June 1984) 62–70. il.

Jones, Wayne. "Bo Diddley," In: *Rockin', Rollin', and Rappin'.* pp. 13–15. il.

Krutnik, Frank. "Bo Diddley," *Record Collector.* n46 (June 1983) 15–20. il., disc.

Loder, Kurt. "Bo Diddley: The Rolling Stone Interview," *Rolling Stone.* n493 (February 12, 1987) 76–80, 98–100. il., int.

Lydon, Michael, and Ellen Mandel. "Bo Diddley," In: *Boogie Lightning.* pp. 50–78. il.

Mandel, Howard. "Bo Diddley: Still Boppin'," *Guitar World.* XVIII (July 1984) 45–50. il.

"Music," *Playboy.* XXIII (April 1976) 30.

Ralabate, Bud. "Bo Diddley Defies Stereotyping: The 'Gunslinger' Takes on Fickle Fans, Record Companies, Radio Playlists, and Acid Rock," *Record Collector's Monthly.* n17 (February 1984) 46–47. il.

"Rock Perspectives: Chuck and Bo," *Modern Drummer.* 13 (January 1989) 46–47. mus.

Ruhlmann, William. "Bo Diddley Rocks the Bottom Line," *Goldmine.* n95 (March 16, 1984) 46–47. il.

Shepherd, Brian. "Bo Diddley Sings a Little Baby to Sleep," *Now Dig This.* n65 (August 1988) 28. il.

Stambler, Irwin. "Diddley, Bo," In: *The Encyclopedia of Pop, Rock and Soul.* pp. 178–179. il.

Tucker, Neely. "Bo Diddley; Most Any Way You Figure It, Bo Diddley Ought to be Playing the Blues," *Living Blues.* n77 (December 1987) 16–21. il., bio., disc.

Wilmer, Val. "Hey! Bo Diddley," *The History of Rock.* n30 (1982) 590–591. il.

Dillard, Varetta

Cotton, Lee. "Varetta Dillard," In: *Shake, Rattle, and Roll.* pp. 111–112. il.

Grendysa, Peter. "Varetta Dillard: Life in the Shadows," *Goldmine.* n204 (May 20, 1988) 10, 64–65. il.

Dixon, Willie

Baker, Cary. "Willie Dixon: The Blues Catalyst Finds Peace," *Goldmine.* n68 (January 1982) 6–9. il.

"Dixon Sues Led Zep Over Hit Records," *Variety.* 317 (January 30, 1985) 78. "Whole Lotta Love" allegedly plagiarized from his "You Need Love."

Eder, Bruce. "Willie Dixon: Living Blues," *Goldmine.* n250 (February 23, 1990) 8–15. il.

Flanagan, Bill. "Willie Dixon," In: *Written in My Soul.* pp. 66–75. il.

Guralnick, Peter. "Willie Dixon," *Musician.* n119 (September 1988) 20–26, 115. il.

"On the Scene," *BMI.* (Fall 1988) 3. il.

Stix, John. "Willie Dixon On Songwriting," *Guitar Blues Classics Collector's Yearbook—Volume One.* (Summer 1989) 56.

Wasserman, R. "Willie Dixon: Blues Bass With Punch," *Frets.* 8 (January 1986) 26–27ff. il., bio., int.

Domino, Fats (See also: New Orleans Sound)

Hannusch, J. "Fats Rocks Back on Tour and HBO," *Billboard.* 98 (July 19, 1986) 26.

Morthland, John. "The 'Toot-Toot' Wars," *Village Voice.* 30 (August 6, 1985) 39–41. il.

"The Rock and Roll Hall of Fame," *BMI.* n1 (1986) 30. il., bio.

Stambler, Irwin. "Domino, Antoine 'Fats'," In: *The Encyclopedia of Pop, Rock and Soul.* pp. 183–185. il.

"Ten Pioneers of Rock Selected for Induction to New Hall of Fame," *Variety.* 321 (November 27, 1985) 139.

Don and Dewey

Hess, Norbert. "Don Harris and Dewey Terry Discography," *Shout.* n102 (April 1975) 5–10. il., disc.

Hinckley, Dave, and Marv Goldberg. "Don and Dewey and . . . the Squires," *Yesterday's Memories.* n10 (1977) 4–5. il.

Raper, Jim. "Don and Dewey: An Appreciation," *Now Dig This.* n37 (April 1986) 2–3. il.

Don and Juan

Grendysa, Peter. "Don and Juan," *Goldmine*. n220 (December 30, 1988) 12. il.

Forrest, Jimmy

Cotton, Lee. "Jimmy Forrest," In: *Shake, Rattle, and Roll.* pp. 26–27. il.

Fulson, Lowell

Dahl, Bill. "Lowell Fulson," *Goldmine*. n250 (February 23, 1990) 30. il.

Driver, Dave. "Lowell Fulson," *Now Dig This*. n19 (October 1984) 7. il.

Gant, Cecil

Tosches, Nick. "Cecil Gant: Owl Stew, and All That," In: *Unsung Heroes of Rock 'N' Roll.* pp. 49–51. il.

Gene and Eunice

Propes, Steve. "Gene and Eunice: 'Ko Ko Mo'—R&B's Most Covered Song?," *Goldmine*. n207 (July 1, 1988) 20, 78, 80. il.

Gordon, Roscoe

Cotten, Lee. "Roscoe Gordon," In: *Shake, Rattle, and Roll.* pp. 20–21. il.

Hamilton, Roy

Cotten, Lee. "Roy Hamilton," In: *Shake, Rattle, and Roll.* pp. 163–164. il.

Grendysa, Peter. "The Roy Hamilton Story: Never Walking Alone," *Soul Survivor.* n5 (Summer 1986) 8–12. il.

Harris, Thurston

Brown, Pete. "Thurston Harris," *Now Dig This.* n15 (June 1984) 3–4. il.

Dawson, Jim. "Thurston Harris: Over and Over," *Goldmine.* n206 (June 17, 1988) 18, 25. il.

"Thurston Harris," *The Golden Age.* n8 (May 1987) 31–34. il.

Harris, Wynonie

Tosches, Nick. "Wynonie Harris: The Man Who Shook Down the Devil," In: *Unsung Heroes of Rock 'N' Roll.* pp. 37–43. il.

Waxie Maxie. "Wynonie (Mr. Blues) Harris," *Record Collector.* n12 (August 1980) 10–12. il., disc.

Harrison, Wilbert

Grendysa, Peter. "Wilbert Harrison Discography," *Goldmine.* n37 (January 1979) 24. disc.

Propes, Steve. "Wilbert Harrison: His Favorite Cities—Kansas City, Newark, and Miami," *Goldmine.* n181 (July 3, 1987) 20, 85. il.

Hawkins, Screamin' Jay

Hirshey, Gerri. "Sympathy for the Devil," In: *Nowhere to Run.* pp. 3–22. il.

Newman, Ralph M. "Screamin' Jay Hawkins," *Bim Bam Boom.* n7 (September 1972) p. 36. il.

"Screamin' Jay Hawkins Discography," *Goldmine.* n30 (November 1978) 9. il., disc.

Smith, Brian. "The Wit and Wisdom of Screamin' Jay Hawkins," *Now Dig This.* n78 (September 1989) 18–21. il.

Topping, Ray, and Kurt Mohr. "Screamin' Jay Hawkins: Discography," *Shout.* n56 (June 1970) 2–6. il., disc.

Tosches, Nick. "Screamin' Jay Hawkins: Horror and the Foot-Shaped Ashtray," In: *Unsung Heroes of Rock 'N' Roll.* pp. 120–127. il.

Hendricks, Bobby

Goldberg, Marv, and Mike Redmond. "The Bobby Hendricks Story," *Yesterday's Memories.* n12 (1977) 18–20. il.

Propes, Steve. "Bobby Hendricks: An Itchy Twitchy Feeling," *Goldmine.* n176 (April 24, 1987) 10, 20. il.

Russell, Wayne. "Bobby Hendricks: Itchy Twitchy Feeling," *Now Dig This.* n47 (February 1987) 3. il.

Hooker, John Lee

DeCurtis, Anthony. "Generations of Blues; John Lee Hooker

and His Boogie Chillum Make a Powerful New Album,"
Rolling Stone. n564 (November 2, 1989) 28. il., int.

Horne, Lena

Haskins, James, with Kathleen Benson. *Lena: A Personal and Professional Biography of Lena Horne.* New York: Stein and Day, 1984. il.

Howard, Brett. *Lena.* Los Angeles: Holloway House, 1981. il.

Reilly, Peter. "Lena Horne: Interview," *Stereo Review.* XLVII (February 1982) 82–83. il., int.

Isley Brothers

Bianco, David. "Isley Brothers," In: *Heat Wave.* pp. 39–41. il.

Doggett, Peter. "The Isley Brothers," *Record Collector.* n31 (March 1982) 54–60. il., disc.

Gonzalez, Fernando L., comp. "The Isley Brothers Discography," *Goldmine.* n63 (August 1981) 16–17. il., disc.

Pelletier, Paul, comp. "The Isley Brothers Complete U.K. Discography," *Record Collector.* n31 (March 1982) 60–61. il., disc.

Jackson, Bullmoose

Grendysa, Peter. "Moose Captures Pittsburgh," *Goldmine.* n113 (November 23, 1984) 56, 62, 64, 66. il.

Grendysa, Peter. "Musin' With the Moose: Bullmoose Jackson," *Goldmine.* n42 (November 1979) 16–17. il.

James, Etta

Alpert, Bob. "Etta James Owns the Blues," *Waxpaper.* III (April 7, 1978) 8–9, 42. il.

Booth, Dave "Daddy Cool". "Etta James," *Soul Survivor.* n3 (Autumn 1985) 4–8. il.

Cotten, Lee. "Etta James," In: *Shake, Rattle, and Roll.* pp. 240–241. il.

Nickols, Pete. "Etta James," *Record Collector.* n58 (June 1984) 36–41. il., disc.

Nickols, Pete. "Etta James: An Appreciation," *Now Dig This.* n19 (October 1984) 11–13. il.

John, Little Willie

Millar, Bill. "Free at Last," *The History of Rock.* n17 (1982) 336–337. il.

Propes, Steve. "Little Willie John: King of Detroit Soul Music," *Goldmine.* n171 (February 13, 1987) 22. il.

Johnson, Marv

Bianco, David. "Marv Johnson," In: *Heat Wave.* pp. 48–51. il.

Gonzalez, John D. "Motown Pioneer Will Crank Out Soulful Sounds at Festival," *Lansing (Michigan) State Journal.* (August 19, 1988) 1D, 3D. il.

Keegan, Kevin. " 'Move Two Mountains': Marv Johnson,"

Record Profile Magazine. n6 (July 1984) 10–13, 40–43, 48, 53,59,63. il.

Jordan, Louis

Cotten, Lee. "Louis Jordan," In: *Shake, Rattle, and Roll.* pp. 197–198. il.

Tosches, Nick. "Louis Jordan: Hep to the Art of Alto Sax Repair," In: *Unsung Heroes of Rock 'N' Roll.* pp. 33–36. il.

White, Cliff. "Louis Jordan," *The History of Rock.* n2 (1982) 33–35. il.

Knight, Sonny

Hill, Randal C. "Sonny Knight: His 'Confidential' Days Recounted," *Goldmine.* n94 (March 2, 1984) 22, 40, 42, 44ff. il.

Liggins, Joe

Grendysa, Peter, and Chris Beachlery. " 'Doin' the Cadillac Boogie With the Honeydripper': The Liggins Family Album," *It Will Stand.* n21 (198?) 14–17. il.

Mabon, Willie

Cotten, Lee. "Willie Mabon," In: *Shake, Rattle, and Roll.* pp. 80–81. il.

Grendysa, Peter. " 'Big Willie' Mabon: Chess Pianist, Dead at 60," *Goldmine.* n129 (July 5, 1985) 75–76. il.

McGhee, Stick

Tosches, Nick. "Stick McGhee: Spo-Dee-O-Dee—How to Get It, How to Use It," In: *Unsung Heroes of Rock 'N' Roll.* pp. 70–72. il.

McKinley, Mitchell

Pruter, Robert. "McKinley Mitchell: Down-Home Rhythm 'N' Blues," *Goldmine.* n133 (August 30, 1985) 30, 67, 78–79. il.

McNeely, Big Jay

Dawson, Jim. "Big Jay McNeely: The Man Who Blew Reveille at the Dawn of Rock and Roll," *Now Dig This.* n63 (June 1988) 4–6. il.

Dawson, Jim. "Big Jay McNeely: An Original Rock 'N' Roll Honker," *Goldmine.* n140 (December 6, 1985) 14–16, 30. il.

McPhatter, Clyde (See also: The Dominoes; The Drifters)

"Clyde McPhatter Atlantic Discography," *Big Beat of the 50's.* n27 (May 1981) 23–25. il., disc.

Doggett, Peter. "Clyde McPhatter," *Record Collector.* n102 (February 1988) 54–55. il., disc.

Escott, Colin. *Clyde McPhatter: A Biographical Essay.* Vollersode, West Germany: Bear Family, 1987. disc.

Garbutt, Bob. "Clyde McPhatter: The Forgotten Hero,"
Goldmine. n85 (June 1983) 22–28. il.

Millar, Bill. "Clyde McPhatter," *The History of Rock.* n4 (1982)
74–75. il.

Nickols, Pete. "Clyde McPhatter," *Record Collector.* n76 (December 1985) 25–28. il., disc.

Stambler, Irwin. "McPhatter, Clyde," In: *The Encyclopedia of
Pop, Rock and Soul.* pp. 457–458.

Topping, Ray, comp. "Clyde McPhatter Discography," *Shout.*
n78 (July 1972) 5–10. il., disc.

Weize, Richard, comp. "Clyde McPhatter Discography," *Now
Dig This.* n67 (October 1988) 12–14. il., disc.

Weize, Richard, comp. "A Preliminary Clyde McPhatter
Discography," In: *Clyde McPhatter: A Biographical Essay,*
by Colin Escott. pp. 80–100. disc.

Mickey and Sylvia

Grendysa, Peter. "Mickey and Sylvia: Life is Strange,"
Goldmine. n182 (July 17, 1982) 28, 77. il.

Milburn, Amos

"Amos Milburn Discography," *It Will Stand.* n3 (1979) 5. disc.

"Amos Milburn Discography," *The Golden Age.* n16 (1988)
4–11. il., disc.

Cotten, Lee. "Amos Milburn," In: *Shake, Rattle, and Roll.* pp. 90–91. il.

Grendysa, Peter. "Amos Milburn: Texas Boogie King," *Goldmine.* n202 (April 22, 1988) 12, 25. il.

"Interview With the 'One Scotch, One Bourbon' . . . Guy: Amos Milburn," *It Will Stand.* n3 (1977) 4–5. il.

Tosches, Nick. "Amos Milburn: The Chicken Shack Factor," In: *Unsung Heroes of Rock and Roll.* pp. 52–55. il.

Moore, Johnny

Dahl, Bill. "Johnny Moore: Turning Back the Hands of Time," *Goldmine.* n188 (October 9, 1987) 24, 88. il.

Otis, Johnny

Cotten, Lee. "Johnny Otis," In: *Shake, Rattle, and Roll.* pp. 106–107. il.

Gray, Brian, and Wouter Keesing, comps. "Johnny Otis Discography, 1953–1962," *The Golden Age.* n16 (1988) 12–22. il., disc.

Propes, Steve. "Johnny Otis—The Rock 'N' Roll Years: Doin' That Crazy Hand Jive," *Goldmine.* n200 (March 25, 1988) 8–12, 22. il.

Shaw, Arnold. "Interview With Johnny Otis," In: *Honkers and Shouters.* pp. 158–168. il., int.

Sweeney, Michael J., comp. "Johnny Otis Discography," *Goldmine.* n200 (March 25, 1988) 12. disc.

Welding, Pete. "Johnny Otis: The History of Rhythm and Blues," *Rolling Stone Interviews—Volume Two.* pp. 295–322. il., int.

Phillips, (Little) Esther

Garland, Phyl. "Little Esther Phillips," *Stereo Review.* L (July 1985) 69.

Hess, Norbert, et al., comps. "Esther Phillips Discography," *Shout.* n96 (June 1974) 5–11. il., disc.

Phillips, Phil(, and the Twilights)

Jancik, Wayne. "Phil Phillips," *Goldmine.* n244 (December 1, 1989) 36. il.

Teddy and the Twilights

Horner, Charlie, and Steve Applebaum. "Teddy and the Twilights," *Yesterday's Memories.* n9 (1976) 20–23. il.

Teen Queens

Bates, Lucille. "The Teen Queens," *Now Dig This.* n52 (July 1987) 23. il.

Thornton, Willie Mae "Big Mama"

Cotten, Lee. "Willie Mae Thornton," In: *Shake, Rattle, and Roll.* pp. 95–96. il.

Dahl, Bill. "Big Mama Thornton: They Call Me Big Mama," *Goldmine.* n228 (April 21, 1989) 99, 106. il.

Etheredge, Jivin' Jimmy. "Big Mama Thornton—Willie Mae Thornton," *Goldmine.* n89 (October 1983) 139–141. il.

Haskins, James. "Big Mama Thornton Dies of Heart Attack," *Rolling Stone.* n430 (September 13, 1984) 43.

McGraw, Carol. "Goodbye Blues," *Los Angeles Times.* (August 1, 1984) 1–2. il.

Treniers

Tosches, Nick. "The Treniers: Their God Wore Shoes," In: *Unsung Heroes of Rock and Roll.* pp. 65–69. il.

"The Treniers," *The Golden Age.* n20 (1989) 8–18. il.

Turner, Ike (See also: Jackie Brenston; Tina Turner)

"Ike Turner," *The Golden Age.* n20 (1989) 18–28. il.

Kiersh, Edward. "Ike's Story," *Spin.* I (August 1985) 38–43, 71. il.

Propes, Steve. "I Like Ike: The Ike Turner Interview," *Goldmine.* (November 3, 1989) 22–28, 94. il., int.

Stambler, Irwin. "Turner, Ike and Tina," In: *The Encyclopedia of Pop, Rock and Soul.* pp. 698–700. il.

Turner, (Big) Joe

Balliett, Whitney. "Majesty," *New Yorker.* LII (November 29, 1976) 80–97.

"Big Joe Turner Dies at 74," *Billboard.* 97 (December 7, 1985) 10.

"Big Joe Turner: 1911–1985," *Rolling Stone.* n465 (January 16, 1986) 14. il.

Cotten, Joe. "Joe Turner," In: *Shake, Rattle, and Roll.* pp. 137–138. il.

"Doc Pomus Remembers," *Living Blues.* n69 (1986) 12–13. il.

Driver, Dave. "They Called Him 'The Boss of the Blues'," *Now Dig This.* n33 (December 1985) 2–3. il.

"15 Elected to Hall of Fame," *Billboard.* 98 (October 18, 1986) 101.

Giddins, Gary. "Big Joe Turner: 1911–1985," *Village Voice.* 30 (December 3, 1985) 3, 71. il.

Giddins, Gary. "Joe Turner: Unmoved Mover," *Rhythm-A-Ning.* 92–94. il.

Grendysa, Peter. "Joe Turner, 1911–1985," *Goldmine.* n143 (January 17, 1986) 12, 64. il.

McGarry, T.W. "Blues Shouter Joe Turner Dies; 'Grandfather of Rock 'N' Roll'," *Los Angeles Times.* (November 25, 1985) 1–2. il.

(Obituary), *Cadence.* 12 (January 1986) 91.

(Obituary), *Down Beat.* 53 (March 1986) 13.

(Obituary), *Jazz Podium.* 35 (January 1986) 33. il.

(Obituary), *Jazz Times.* (January 1986) 25.

(Obituary), *Living Blues.* n68 (1986) 36.

(Obituary), *Melody Maker.* 60 (December 7, 1985) 8. il.

(Obituary), *Music Times.* 127 (March 1986) 162.

(Obituary), *Variety.* 321 (November 27, 1985) 158.

"Rock Hall of Fame to Induct 15 Acts," *Variety.* 324 (October 8, 1986) 147.

Rodrigues, D.A. (Obituary), *Jazz Forum.* n98 (1986) 33.

Stambler, Irwin. "Turner, Joe," In: *The Encyclopedia of Pop, Rock and Soul.* pp. 700–701.

Tosches, Nick. "Big Joe Turner: Steak for Breakfast, Gal Meat on a Rainy Day," In: *Unsung Heroes Of Rock and Roll.* pp. 20–25. il.

Voce, S. "Obituary," *Jazz Journal International.* 39 (February 1986) 20. il.

Weinstock, R. "Big Joe Turner: 1911–1985," *Living Blues.* n69 (1986) 11–12. il.

Wieseltier, L. "The Mind's Eye: Standin' in the Back Door Cryin'," *Vanity Fair.* 49 (April 1986) 42ff.

Waters, Muddy (r.n.: McKinley Morganfield)

"15 Elected to Hall of Fame," *Billboard.* 98 (October 18, 1986) 101.

O'Neal, Jim, and A. O'Neal. "Muddy Waters," *Living Blues.* n64 (March/April 1985) 15–40. il., int.

"Rock Hall of Fame to Induct 15 Acts," *Variety.* 324 (October 8, 1986) 147.

Stambler, Irwin. "Waters, Muddy," In: *The Encyclopedia of Pop, Rock and Soul.* pp. 731–733. il.

Willis, Chuck

"Chuck Willis," *The Golden Age.* n8 (May 1987) 27–31. il.

Cotten, Lee. "Chuck Willis," In: *Shake, Rattle, and Roll.* pp. 116–117. il.

Grendysa, Peter. "Chuck Willis: King of the Stroll," *Goldmine.* n225 (March 10, 1989) 25, 27, 30. il.

Grendysa, Peter, comp. "Chuck Willis' Singles Discography," *Record Collector's Monthly.* n16 (January 1984) 5. disc.

Wilson, Jackie (See also: The Dominoes)

Cordell, John A., comp. "Jackie Wilson Discography," *Record Profile Magazine.* n4 (February–March 1984) 61–62. il., disc.

Giddins, Gary. "Jolson's Greatest Heir," In: *Rhythm-A-Ning.* pp. 146–152. il.

Jacobs, Dick, as told to Tim Holmes. "Jackie Wilson—Taking

It Higher: A Producer Remembers 'Mr. Excitement'," *Musician.* n111 (January 1988) 21–26, 97–98. il.

Joyce, Frank. "Jackie Wilson: Lonely Teardrops," In: *The First Rock and Roll Confidential Report,* by Dave Marsh, et al. pp. 40–41. il.

Keegan, Kevin. "Above Jacob's Ladder: A Tribute to Jackie Wilson," *Record Profile Magazine.* n4 (February–March 1984) 8–11, 26–27, 59–61. il.

Loder, Kurt. "Jackie Wilson: 1934–1984," *Rolling Stone.* n417 (March 15, 1984) 44. il.

Nickols, Pete. "Jackie Wilson," *Record Collector.* n56 (April 1984) 15–18. il.

Nickols, Pete, and Paul Pelletier, comps. "Jackie Wilson Complete U.K. Discography," *Record Collector.* n56 (April 1984) 18. disc.

Pruter, Robert. "Jackie Wilson: His Chicago Years," *Goldmine.* n192 (December 4, 1987) 30, 34. il.

Richardson, Clive. "Hot Gospel," *The History of Rock.* n17 (1982) 330–332. il.

Settle, Ken. "Jackie Wilson: The 'Showman' is Laid to Rest," *Goldmine.* 94 (March 2, 1984) 7–8. il.

Settle, Ken. "Jackie Wilson: A Celebration of Dignity," *Goldmine.* n182 (July 17, 1982) 79. il.

Stambler, Irwin. "Wilson, Jackie," In: *The Encyclopedia of Pop, Rock and Soul.* pp. 742–743.

B. ROCKABILLY

General Sources

Baker, Cary. "Rockabilly Rebellion '81: The Big Beat is Boppin' Again," *Country Style.* n69 (August 1981) 41–43ff. il.

Baker, Chuck. *The Rockin' Fifties: A Rock and Roll Scrapbook.* Woodland Hills, CA: Avanco, 1973. il.

Becker, Bart. *'Til the Cows Come Home: Rock 'N' Roll Nebraska.* Seattle: Real Gone, 1986. il.

Blackburn, Richard, comp. *Rockabilly: A Comprehensive Discography of Reissues.* n.p.: R. Blackburn, 1975. disc.

Bruno, Bill. "The Preservation of Rock and Roll: Rockabilly Bonanza," *Music World.* n3 (March 1981) 52–54. il.

Clark, Alan. *Rock and Roll in the Movies—Number One.* West Covina, CA: Alan C. Lungstrum, 1987. il.

Clark, Alan. *Rock and Roll in the Movies—Number Two.* West Covina, CA: Alan C. Lungstrum, 1987. il.

Clark, Alan. *Rock and Roll in the Movies—Number Three.* West Covina, CA: Alan C. Lungstrum, 1988. il.

Clark, Alan. *Rock and Roll Legends—Number Three.* West Covina, CA: Leap Frog Productions, 1982. il.

Clark, Alan. *Rock and Roll Legends—Number Four.* West Covina, CA: Leap Frog Productions, 1983. il.

Clark, Alan. *Rock and Roll Legends—Number Five.* West Covina, CA: Leap Frog Productions, 1984. il.

Clark, Alan. *Rock and Roll Memories—Number One.* West Covina, CA: Alan C. Lungstrum, 1987. il.

Clark, Alan. *Rock and Roll Memories—Number Two.* West Covina, CA: Alan C. Lungstrum, 1987. il.

Clark, Alan. *Rock-A-Billy and Country Legends—Number One.* West Covina, CA: Alan Clark Productions, 1986. il.

Colman, Stuart. *They Kept on Rockin': The Giants of Rock 'N' Roll.* Poole, Dorset, U.K.: Blandford, 1982. il.

Coppage, Noel. "Rockabilly Stars," *Stereo Review.* XLVII (May 1982) 86.

Dickerson, P.J., and M.A. Gordon. *Rare 45 R.P.M. Records of the Rockin' Rollin' Fifties.* London: Vintage Record Centre, 1986. il.

Elson, Howard. *Early Rockers.* New York: Proteus, 1982. il.

Forte, Dan. "The Pioneers of the Rock Guitar," *Musician.* n43 (May 1982) 32–36. il.

Forte, Dan. "The Pioneers of Rock and Roll Guitar," *Guitar Player.* 18 (June 1984) 60.

Forte, Dan. "Roots of Rockabilly," *Guitar Player.* 17 (December 1983) 67–70, 96–98. il.

Gordon, Mike. "Fifty Collectable Rockabilly Records," *Record Collector.* n13 (September 1980) 31–32. disc.

Gordon, Mike. "Rockabilly," *Record Collector*. n13 (September 1980) 29–32. il.

Grevatt, Ren, and Merrill Pollack. "It All Started With Elvis," *Saturday Evening Post*. 232 (September 26, 1959) 26–27, 92–94. il.

Guralnick, Peter. "Rockabilly," *The Rolling Stone Illustrated History of Rock and Roll*, ed. by Jim Miller. pp. 61–65. il.

Hull, Robert A., and J. Sasfy. "B-I Bickey-i, Bo-Bo-Go: Rockabilly's Rabid Movement," *Creem*. 11 (February 1980) 30–31ff. il.

Isler, Scott. "Rockabilly: A Historical Overview," *Country Style*. n69 (August 1981) 10–12. il.

Jackson, John. "1950's Visual: 'Roots of Rock and Roll—Chapter One: The Early Years, 1955–1958'," *Rockin' 50s*. n13 (August 1988) 8.

Johnson, B.D. "Rock 'N' Roll Unearths Its Own Roots," *Macleans*. 96 (February 28, 1983) 53. il.

Kinder, Bob. *The Best of the First: The Early Days of Rock and Roll*. Chicago: Adams, 1986. il.

Kirsch, Don. "Collecting Rockabilly for Fun and Profit," *Goldmine*. n142 (January 3, 1986) 75. il.

Kirsch, Don. "Rare, Expensive, and Some Common 45s," *Goldmine*. n132 (August 16, 1985) 76. il.

Kirsch, Don, comp. *Rock 'N' Roll Obscurities—Volume One*. Tacoma, WA: D. Kirsch, 1977. il.

Kirsch, Don. "Rockabilly Compilation Albums: Part Two," *Goldmine.* n138 (November 8, 1985) 80. il.

Kirsch, Don. "Rockabilly EPs and LPs," *Goldmine.* n153 (June 6, 1986) 63–64. il.

Kirsch, Don. "Rockabilly 45s: Counterfeits and Reissues," *Goldmine.* n160 (September 12, 1986) 63. il.

Kirsch, Don. "Rockabilly Roots of Major Country Stars," *Goldmine.* n120 (March 1, 1985) 32, 80. il.

Kirsch, Don. "Those Rockabilly Ladies and Their Collectability," *Goldmine.* n124 (April 26, 1985) 75. il.

Kirsch, Don. "U.S. Rockabilly Regional Guide," *Goldmine.* n164 (November 7, 1986) 73. il.

McNutt, Randy. *We Wanna Boogie: An Illustrated History of the American Rockabilly Movement.* Fairfield, OH: Hamilton Hobby, 1988. il.

Millar, Bill. "In the Farms and on the Forecourts: The Short-Lived Heyday of Rockabilly," *The History of Rock.* n6 (1982) 112–113. il.

Millar, Bill. "Rockabilly Liberation," *Melody Maker.* 53 (October 21, 1978) 57–61. il.

Millar, Bill. "Rockabilly: Was This the Purist Style in Rock?," *The History of Rock.* n6 (1982) 101–103.

Miller, John, comp. "South Florida Rockabilly Discography," *Music World.* n87 (July 1981) 18–19. il., disc.

Mollica, Gary. "Rock 'N' Roll Revivalists" and "Rockabilly and 50s Rock 'N' Roll," In: *Vintage Rock 'N' Roll Catalog, 1986.* pp. 4–35; 89–92.

Morris, Chris. "Thirty Years Later . . . It Was A Very Good Year for Good Old Rock 'N' Roll," *Billboard.* 99 (December 26, 1987) 11, 45, 47.

Morthland, John. "Rockabilly," In: *The Best of Country Music: A Critical and Historical Guide to the 750 Greatest Albums.* pp. 239–279. disc.

Nooger, Dan. "Supplemental Listing to Major Label Coverage," *Goldmine.* n141 (December 20, 1985) 94. disc.

Oermann, Robert K., with Douglas B. Green. "Rockabilly," In: *The Listener's Guide to Country Music.* pp. 84–89. il.

"Rockabilly: A Fusion of Country and Rock 'N' Roll," *Billboard.* 75 (November 2, 1963) 1, 40.

Russell, Wayne. *Footsoldiers and Kings.* Brandon, Manitoba, Canada: Leech Print, n.d.

Russell, Wayne. *Footsoldiers and Kings—Volume Two.* Brandon, Manitoba, Canada: Leech Print, n.d.

Scott, Frank, et al., comps. "Rockabilly and '50s Rock 'N' Roll" and "Rockabilly Revival and European Artists," In: *Vintage Rock 'N' Roll Catalogue—1983.* pp. 3–26, 49–53. disc.

Szatmary, David P. "Elvis and Rockabilly," In: *Rockin' in Time: A Social History of Rock and Roll.* pp. 29–50. il.

Tosches, Nick. "Loud Covenants," In: *Country: Living Legends and Dying Metaphors in America's Biggest Music.* pp. 25–101. il.

White, Cliff. "The Breakthrough," In: *The Encyclopedia of Rock,* ed. by Tony Russell. pp. 22–37. il.

Adkins, Hasil

Tamarkin, Jeff. "Hasil Adkins: Hooray for Hasil!," *Goldmine.* n165 (November 21, 1986) 12, 22. il.

Bennett, Boyd

"Boyd Bennett," *The Golden Age.* n5 (February 1987) 8–12. il.

Bond, Eddie

Komorowski, Adam, and Dick Grant. *The Eddie Bond Story.* n.p.: Misty Mountain Music/Enkay Productions, 1982. il.

McNutt, Randy. "Eddie Bond," In: *We Wanna Boogie.* pp. 205–206. il.

Raiteri, Charles. "Eddie Bond: A Reluctant Rockabilly Rocker Remembers," *Goldmine.* n157 (August 1, 1986) 5–8. il., int.

Thompson, Gary. "Eddie Bond Discography," *Goldmine.* n30 (November 1978) 25. disc.

Bowen, Jimmy

Caviness, Jim. "My Visit to KDDD Radio," *Rockin' 50s.* n19 (August 1989) 14–15. il.

Chapados, Jean Pierre, comp. "Jimmy Bowen Singles Discography," *New Kommotion.* n13 (Autumn 1976) 25. disc.

Burgess, Sonny

McNutt, Randy. "Sonny Burgess," In: *We Wanna Boogie.* pp, 209–212. il.

Burlison, Paul (See also: Sam Phillips and Sun Records; Johnny Burnette)

Escott, Colin. "The Sun Rhythm Section: Still Burnin'," *Goldmine.* n234 (July 14, 1989) 70–72. il.

McNutt, Randy. "Paul Burlison," In: *We Wanna Rock.* pp. 213–214. il.

Burnette, Dorsey (See also: Johnny Burnette)

Newcombe, Jim. "An Interview With Dorsey Burnette," *Now Dig This.* n58 (January 1988) 5–7. il., int.

Stambler, Irwin. "Burnette, Dorsey," In: *The Encyclopedia of Pop, Rock and Soul.* pp. 88–89.

Burnette, Johnny(, Rock 'N' Roll Trio) (See also: Dorsey Burnette)

Bowman, Robert, and Ross Johnson. "Train Started Rollin': A Conversation With Paul Burlison of the Rock 'N' Roll Trio," *Journal of Country Music.* 11 (1986) 16–25. il., int.

Bowman, Robert, and Ross Johnson. "Train Kept A-Rollin': A Conversation With Paul Burlison of the Rock 'N' Roll Trio," *Journal of Country Music.* 13 (1987) 12–21. il., int.

Burlison, Paul. "The Slap Bass Sound," *Guitar Player.* 13 (December 1983) 70.

Cajiao, Trevor. "Johnny Burnette Discography," *Now Dig This.* n46 (January 1987) 18–22. il., disc.

Cajiao, Trevor. "Johnny Burnette: The Releases Keep A-Rollin'," *Now Dig This.* n77 (August 1989) 9.

Harris, Paul, and Trevor Cajiao. "Tear It Up! An Interview With Paul Burlison," *Now Dig This.* n37 (April 1986) 6–9. il., int.

Hilborne, Alison. "The Unpublished Johnny Burnette," *Now Dig This.* n71 (February 1989) 4–6. il.

Hilborne, Alison. "The Unpublished Johnny Burnette," *Now Dig This.* n72 (March 1989) 8–10. il.

"Johnny Burnette," *The Golden Age.* n2 (November 1986) 9–10. il.

Jones, Pete. "The Johnny Burnette R&R Trio: Details From the Coral Session Files," *New Kommotion.* n9 (Spring–Summer 1975) 16–17. il.

Millar, Bill. "The Burnettes: Heavyweight Recording Artists of the Rock 'N' Roll Trio," *The History of Rock.* n6 (1982) 114–115. il.

Raphael, Judy. "The Burnette 'Billies: Sons Carry on the Family Tradition," *Country Style.* n69 (August 1981) 48–50. il.

Smart, Peter, and Bob Westfall. "Johnny Burnette on Disc," *New Kommotion.* n8 (Winter 1975) 6–8. il.

Burton, James (See also: Rick Nelson)

Bradley, Tim. "Burton for Certain," *Guitar World.* 4 (November 1983) 65–67, 74–75. il.

Fishell, Steve. "James Burton: First Call for the Royalty of Rockabilly," *Guitar Player.* 18 (June 1984) 88–101. il.

Kienzle, Rich. "James Burton," In: *Great Guitarists: The Most Influential Players in Blues, Country Music, Jazz, and Rock.* pp. 192–197. il.

Tobler, John. "James Burton Discography," *Zig Zag.* n59 (April 1976) 21. disc.

Byrne, Jerry

Gray, Brian, and Adam Komorowski, comps. "Jerry Byrne," *The Golden Age.* n14 (1988) 9–10. il.

Wallis, Ian. "The Jerry Byrne Story," *Now Dig This.* n47 (February 1987) 5. il.

Campbell, Jo Ann

Griggs, Bill. "Jo Ann Campbell: The Blonde Bombshell," *Rockin' 50s.* n15 (December 1988) 18–20. il.

"Jo Ann Campbell," *The Golden Age.* n3 (December 1986) 33–36. il.

Campi, Ray

Cajiao, Trevor. "Ramblin' Ray: The Ray Campi Story—Part One," *Now Dig This.* n31 (October 1985) 17–19. il., bio.

Cajiao, Trevor. "Ray's Best Yet," *Now Dig This.* n66 (September 1988) 3–4. il.

Drust, Greg. "Ray Campi Discography," *Goldmine.* n15 (March–April 1977) 10–11. il., disc.

McNutt, Randy. "Ray Campi," In: *We Wanna Boogie.* pp. 215–216. il.

Clark, Sanford

Jancik, Wayne. "Sanford Clark's Collectible Discs," *Goldmine.* n140 (December 6, 1985) 84–86. il., disc.

"Sanford Clark Discography," *The Golden Age.* n15 (1988) 5–9. il., disc.

"Sanford Clark: 'The Fool'," *The Golden Age.* n15 (1988) 4. il.

Clement, Jack

Newcomb, Jim. "An Interview With Jack Clement," *Now Dig This.* n62 (May 1988) 24–27. il., int.

Collins Kids

Russell, Wayne. "The Collins Kids: Hop, Skip, and Jump," *Goldmine.* n192 (December 4, 1987) 28–34. il.

Curtis, Mac

"Mac Curtis," *The Golden Age.* n7 (April 1987) 4–10. il.

McNutt, Randy. "Mac Curtis," In: *We Wanna Boogie.* pp. 222–225. il.

Millar, Bill. "Mac Curtis: Hot Rock," *Goldmine.* n89 (October 1983) 42, 56, 58. il.

Curtis, Sonny

Cockburn, Howard, and Trevor Cajiao. "Sonny Curtis: Talk Right Back—Part One," *Now Dig This.* n59 (February 1988) 10–13. il.

McNutt, Randy. "Sonny Curtis," In: *We Wanna Boogie.* pp. 226–228. il.

Donner, Ral

Helsinki, Jack. "Ray Donner: 'I Didn't Figure on Him,' " *Goldmine.* n184 (August 1987) 22–24. il.

Komorowski, Adam. "You Don't Know What You've Got Until You Lose It: The Real Donner Story," *New Kommotion.* n21 (1979) 4–9. il., bio.

Raper, Jim. "Ray Donner: The Great Pretender," *Now Dig This.* n15 (June 1984) 21–22. il.

Wilson, Terry. "Ray Donner: Chicago's Elvis," *Kommotion.* n8 (Winter 1975) 23. il.

Dorman, Harold

Escott, Colin. "Harold Dorman," *Goldmine.* n213 (September 23, 1988) 23, 72. il.

Downing, Big Al

Cajiao, Trevor. "Oh Babe! An Interview With Big Al Downing—Part One," *Now Dig This.* n45 (December 1986) 6–7. il., int.

Cajiao, Trevor. "Oh Babe! An Interview With Big Al Downing—Part Two," *Now Dig This.* n46 (Janaury 1987) 24–25. il., int.

Millar, Bill. "Big Al Downing and the Poe-Kats: The Story Behind the Story," *New Kommotion.* n24 (1980) 4–7, 33. il., bio.

Topping, Ray. "Big Al Downing Discography," *Shout.* n86 (June 1973) 2–4. il., disc.

Ellis, Jimmy (See also: Orion)

"Jimmy Ellis Discography," *DISCoveries.* 1 (May–June 1988) 25. il., disc.

Feathers, Charlie

Escott, Colin. "Charlie Feathers," *Goldmine.* n238 (September 8, 1989) 26–28. il.

Escott, Colin. "Charlie Feathers: Rockabilly Enigma," *Goldmine.* n199 (March 11, 1988) 12, 119. il.

"The Greatest Rocker of All Time . . . Charlie Feathers," *Bim Bam Boom.* n13 (August–September 1974) 42. il.

McNutt, Randy. "Charlie Feathers," In: *We Wanna Boogie.* p. 229. il.

Fontaine, Eddie

Cajiao, Trevor. "Eddie Fontaine: Still Shakin'," *Now Dig This.* n48 (March 1987) 18–23. il.

McNutt, Randy. "Eddie Fontaine," In: *We Wanna Boogie.* p. 234. il.

Fontana, D.J. (See also: Elvis Presley)

Cajiao, Trevor. "The D.J. Fontana Interview," *Now Dig This.* n61 (April 1988) 18–25. il., int.

Jones, Wayne. "D.J. Fontana Interview," *Goldmine.* n56 (January 1981) 11. il., int.

McNutt, Randy. "Looking for a Cool Spot," In: *We Wanna Boogie.* pp. 115–118. il.

Mikelbank, Peter. "D.J. Fontana: Elvis' Drummer Capsulizes the King's Career," *Goldmine.* n184 (August 14, 1987) 12–14, 30. il., bio.

Oksanen, Dave. "A Legendary Drummer: D.J. Fontana," *Music World.* n88 (August 1981) 40–45. il.

Glenn, Glen

John, Barry. "The Glen Glenn Story: The Era of a Hollywood Rockabilly," *Now Dig This.* n48 (March 1987) 3–6. il.

McNutt, Randy. "Glen Glenn," In: *We Wanna Boogie.* p. 235. il.

Gunter, Hardrock

Tosches, Nick. "Hardrock Gunter: The Mysterious Pig-Iron Man," *Journal of Country Music.* 10 (1985) 36–39. il.

Hall, Roy

Cajiao, Trevor. "Roy Hall," *Now Dig This.* n15 (June 1984) 11–12. il.

Hawkins, Martin. "Roy Hall: Tracks of the 'Hounds'," *Goldmine.* n96 (March 30, 1984) 59, 64, 66. il.

Tosches, Nick. "Roy Hall: See, We Was All Drunk," *Unsung Heroes of Rock 'N' Roll.* pp. 78–82. il.

Hawkins, Dale

McNutt, Randy. "Oh! Suzy-Q: Dale Hawkins," In: *We Wanna Boogie.* pp. 236–237. il.

Jackson, Wanda

Lay, Rip. "Wanda Jackson: The Early Years (1955–1963)," *Who Put the Bomp.* n9 (Spring 1972) 16–21. il., bio.

McNutt, Randy. "Wild, Wild Wimmen," In: *We Wanna Boogie.* pp. 185–191. il.

Nunn, Roger. "The Wanda Jackson Story—Part One," *Now Dig This.* n54 (September 1987) 17–19. il., bio.

Nunn, Roger. "The Wanda Jackson Story—Part Three," *Now Dig This*. n56 (November 1987) 26–30. il., bio.

Nunn, Roger. "The Wanda Jackson Story—Part Two," *Now Dig This*. n55 (October 1987) 25–28. il., bio.

Oermann, Robert K. "Those Wild, Wild Women," *Country Style*. n69 (August 1981) 38–40. il.

"Rockin' Girls," *The Golden Age*. n3 (December 1986) 4–6, 37–38. il.

Tamarkin, Jeff. "Wanda Jackson: That Happy Country Gospel Rockabilly Party Gal," *Goldmine*. n178 (May 22, 1987) 6–9. il.

Tamarkin, Jeff. "Wanda Jackson: That Happy Country Gospel Rockabilly Party Gal—Part Two," *Goldmine*. n179 (June 5, 1987) 20.

Tosches, Nick. "Wanda Jackson: Laced By Satan, Unlaced by the Lord," In: *Unsung Heroes of Rock 'N' Roll*. pp. 128–132. il.

"Wanda Jackson," *The Golden Age*. n3 (December 1986) 7–30. il.

Janes, Roland

Bowman, Robert, and Ross Johnson. "Roland Janes: Behind the Scenes at Sun," *Journal of Country Music*. 10 (1985) 14–27.

Cajiao, Trevor. "Roland Janes: Whole Lotta Shakin' Goin'

On—Part One," *Now Dig This.* n81 (December 1989) 4–8. il.

Cajiao, Trevor. "Roland Janes: Whole Lotta Shakin' Goin' On—Part Two," *Now Dig This.* n82 (January 1990) 4–8. il.

Kesler, Stan (See also: Sam Phillips and Sun Records)

Bowman, Rob, and Ross Johnson. "Stan Kesler: The Flip Side of Sun—Part Two," *Journal of Country Music.* 13 (1989) 20–29. il.

Newcombe, Jim. "An Interview With Stan Kesler," *Now Dig This.* n62 (May 1988) 4–6. il., int.

Knox, Buddy

Cain, Robert. "Buddy Knox: The 'Party Doll' Man," *Goldmine.* n94 (March 2, 1984) 36, 50, 53–55. il.

Caviness, Jim "Spotlight on Buddy Knox," *Rockin' 50s.* n19 (August 1989) 8–14. il.

Garbutt, Bob, comp. "Buddy Knox Discography," *Goldmine.* n94 (March 2, 1984) 56. disc.

Hill, Randal C. "Buddy Knox: Partyin' in the Haystack," *Goldmine.* n189 (October 23, 1987) 38, 42. il.

Komorowski, Adam. "Buddy Knox," *New Kommotion.* n23 (1980) 8–12. il.

Millar, Bill. "The Happy Rockabilly," *The History of Rock.* n10 (1982) 192–193. il.

LaBeef, Sleepy

Humphrey, Mark. "Sleepy LaBeef: 30 Years on the Rockabilly Road," *Guitar Player.* 17 (December 1983) 84–89, 154. il.

McNutt, Randy. "Sleepy LaBeef," In: *We Wanna Boogie.* p. 243.

Smith, Lynn, and Dick Grant. "Sleepy LaBeef: The Early Days," *Now Dig This.* n55 (October 1987) 4–7. il., bio.

Tamarkin, Jeff. "Sleepy LaBeef: A Constant Paid Vacation," *Goldmine.* n201 (April 8, 1988) 14, 27. il.

Lind, Bob

Eng, Steve. "Bob Lind: A Fleeting Glimpse," *Goldmine.* n191 (November 20, 1987) 14, 38. il.

Lou, Bonnie

McNutt, Randy. "Bonnie Lou," In: *We Wanna Boogie.* pp. 201–203. il.

Luman, Bob

"Bob Luman," *The Golden Age.* n21 (1989) 4–16. il.

Cockburn, Howard. "The Bob Luman Story—Part One," *Now Dig This.* n58 (January 1988) 18–22. il., bio.

Cockburn, Howard. "The Bob Luman Story: 'Let's Think About Living'—Part Two," *Now Dig This.* n59 (February 1988) 16–17. il., bio.

Escott, Colin. "Bob Luman: Red Cadillac and a Black Mustache," *Goldmine.* n238 (September 8, 1989) 35. il.

Green, Douglas B. "Remembering . . . Bob Luman (1937–1978)," *Country Style.* n69 (August 1981) 35. il.

Grimes, John L. "Bob Luman: A Friend Remembered," *DIS-Coveries.* 2 (February 1989) 36–40. il.

Maddox, Rose

McNutt, Randy. "Rose Maddox: Miss Boogie," In: *We Wanna Boogie.* pp. 192–193. il.

Mann, Carl

Cajiao, Trevor. "Carl Mann Interview," *Now Dig This.* n20 (November 1984) 2–5. il., int.

Escott, Colin. "Carl Mann: The 'Mona Lisa' Story and More," *Goldmine.* n176 (April 24, 1987) 10. il., bio.

Komorowski, Adam. "Mann Made Hits," *New Kommotion.* n14 (Winter 1977) 24–26. il.

McNutt, Randy. "Carl Mann," In: *We Wanna Boogie.* pp. 248–251. il.

Martin, Janis

"Janis Martin," *The Golden Age.* n3 (December 1986) 30–32. il.

Mitchell, Guy

Foster, Ivan. "Guy Mitchell," *Record Collector.* n53 (January 1984) 20–23. il., disc.

Mizell, Hank

McAuliffe, Jon. "The Resurrection of Hank Mizell," *Music World.* n85 (May 1981) 54–60. il.

Thompson, Gary. "Hank Mizell," *Goldmine.* n76 (September 1982) 25. il.

Moore, Scotty (See also: Elvis Presley)

Green, Douglas. "Scotty Moore—Perhaps the First Rock and Roll Guitarist," In: *Rock Guitarists.* pp. 128–130. il.

Guralnick, Peter. "Scotty Moore: Elvis, Scotty, and Bill—A Sidelong View of History," In: *Lost Highway: Journeys and Arrivals of American Musicians.* pp. 96–105. il.

Moore, Sparkle

Russell, Wayne. "Sparkle Moore," *Now Dig This.* n49 (April 1987) 3. il.

Orion (See also: Jimmy Ellis)

Craig, Dondra. "Orion," *Inside Country Music.* 1 (July 1983) 42–43. il.

Oksanen, Dave. "Orion: The Star Shines on Boston," *Music World.* 87 (July 1981) 9–13. il.

Stidom, Larry. "Orion/Jimmy Ellis," *Goldmine.* n127 (June 7, 1985) 18–26. il.

Perkins, Carl

"All Perkins Wanted Was His 'Blue Suede Shoes'," *Variety.* 322 (February 5, 1986) 142.

Cajiao, Trevor. "Carl Perkins Born to Rock," *Now Dig This.* n77 (August 1989) 4–5. il.

Cajiao, Trevor. "Carl Perkins: The Man Behind the Music— Part One," *Now Dig This.* n54 (September 1987) 4–7. il.

Cajiao, Trevor. "Carl Perkins: The Man Behind the Music— Part Three," *Now Dig This.* n56 (November 1987) 10–11. il.

Cajiao, Trevor. "Carl Perkins: The Man Behind the Music— Part Two," *Now Dig This.* n55 (October 1987) 11–12. il.

Carr, Patrick. "Carl Perkins, Livin' Legend," *Country Music.* 2 (September 1973) 65–71. il.

Clee, Ken. "Carl Perkins Discography," *Goldmine.* n49 (June 1980) 10. il., disc.

Escott, Colin, and Martin Hawkins. "Blue Suede Shoes: One Song Rocketed Carl Perkins to Stardom," *The History of Rock.* n6 (1982) 109–111. il.

"15 Elected to Hall of Fame," *Billboard.* 98 (October 18, 1986) 101.

Flanagan, Bill. "Carl Perkins," *Musician.* n67 (May 1984) 22–28. il.

Goldsmith, T. "Carl Perkins," *BMI.* n4 (1985) 22–23. il.

Jarvis, Jeff. "A Rockabilly Session," *People Weekly.* 25 (January 6, 1986) 17. il.

Kienzle, Rich. "Carl Perkins," In: *Great Guitarists.* pp. 225–230. il.

Komorowski, Adam. "Boppin' the Blues—Part Two," *New Kommotion.* 2 (Spring 1977) 18–19. il.

Lydon, Michael. "Carl Perkins," In: *Rock Folk: Portraits From the Rock 'N' Pantheon.* pp. 24–45. il.

McGee, Dave. "Carl Perkins," *Rolling Stone.* n576 (April 19, 1990) 73–77, 124. il., int.

McNutt, Randy. "Rocking Guitar Man," In: *We Wanna Boogie.* pp. 88–96. il.

Newcombe, Jim. "Carl Perkins in Toronto," *Now Dig This.* n67 (October 1988) 15. il.

"Perkins, McDill Inducted into NSAI Hall of Fame," *Variety.* 321 (November 13, 1985) 119.

Reinhart, Charles. "Carl Perkins and His Jam With George and Ringo," *Goldmine.* n148 (March 28, 1986) 90. il.

"Rock Hall of Fame to Induct 15 Acts," *Variety.* 324 (October 8, 1986) 147.

Scott, Steve. "Carl Perkins," *Record Collector.* n73 (September 1983) 41–44. il., disc.

Shaw, R. "Whole Lotta Promotion for Rock Veterans' New Album," *Billboard.* 98 (June 7, 1986) 24ff.

Slevigen, Jan. "Carl Perkins: Still Boppin' the Blues," *Now Dig This.* n47 (February 1987) 19–22. il.

"Songwriters, DJs Honor Their Own," *Billboard.* 97 (October 26, 1985) 62.

Stambler, Irwin. "Perkins, Carl," In: *The Encyclopedia of Pop, Rock and Soul.* pp. 515–516.

Theroux, Gary. "Carl Perkins: A Legend in Blue Suede Shoes," *Goldmine.* n161 (September 26, 1986) 5–12. il.

Treude, Helmut. "Carl Perkins: Country Music With Colored Beat," *Country Corner.* n52 (December 1976) 12–15, il.

Waxie Maxie. "Carl Perkins," *Record Collector.* n12 (August 1980) 24–26. il., disc.

Westfall, Bob. "Carl Perkins on Disc," *Kommotion.* n8 (Winter 1975) 13–15. il.

Phillips, Sam, and Sun Records

Becker, Robert J. "The Sun Sound," *Record Exchanger.* 3 (February 1972) 12–14. il.

Bream, Terry. "The Million Dollar Quartet Sessions," *Goldmine.* n211 (August 26, 1988) 26, 30. il.

Cain, Robert. "Sun Records Today: An Interview With Shelby Singleton," In: *Whole Lotta Shakin' Goin' On: Jerry Lee Lewis.* pp. 103–108. il.

Cajiao, Trevor. "31 Years Ago This Month . . . Million Dollar Confusion," *Now Dig This.* n57 (December 1987) 6–7. il.

Clark, Alan. *Legends of Sun Records.* West Covina, CA: Alan Clark Productions, 1986. il.

Clark, Alan. *Sun Photo Album.* West Covina, CA: National Rock and Roll Archives, 1986. il.

Davis, Hank, and Colin Escott. "Sam Phillips—America's Other Uncle Sam," *Goldmine.* n183 (July 31, 1987) 12–14. il.

Davis, Hank, and Colin Escott. "Sam Phillips—America's Other Uncle Sam: Part Three—Sunset," *Goldmine.* n185 (August 28, 1987) 24–25. il.

Davis, Hank, and Colin Escott. "Sam Phillips—America's Other Uncle Sam: Part Two—Golden Sam," *Goldmine.* n184 (August 14, 1987) 16–20. il.

Doggett, Peter. "The Sun Label in Britain," *Record Collector.* n54 (February 1984) 31–34. il., disc.

Doggett, Peter. "Sun Records: The Golden Years," *Record Collector.* n92 (April 1987) 24–25. il., disc.

Escott, Colin. "The Million Dollar Quartet: What Really Happened," *Goldmine.* n236 (August 11, 1989) 10–16. il.

Escott, Colin, and Martin Hawkins, comps. *Sun Records: The Discography.* Vollersode, West Germany: Bear Family, 1987. disc.

Escott, Colin, and Martin Hawkins. "What They Did and Where They Are Now," In: *Sun Records: The Brief History of the Legendary Record Label.* pp. 141–157. il.

Finnis, Robert. "The Rise and Set of Sun," *Rock.* 11 (December 14, 1970) 9–10, 31. il.

Guralnick, Peter. "Million Dollar Memories," *New Kommotion.* n25 (1981) 7–12. il.

Guralnick, Peter. "The Million Dollar Quartet," *The New York Times Magazine.* (March 25, 1979) 28–30ff. il.

Hall, Claude. "Phillips, Presley, Cash, and Sun," *Billboard.* 81 (December 27, 1969) 11. il.

Hawkins, Martin. "The Sun Records Archives," *Record Collector.* n108 (August 1988) 19–22. il.

Hawkins, Martin. "The Sun Story," *The History of Rock.* n3 (1982) 44–47. il.

Kaye, Elizabeth. "The Rolling Stone Interview: Sam Phillips," *Rolling Stone.* n467 (February 13, 1986) 53–58, 85–88. il., int.

Koda, Cub. "The Rockin' Sun Years: Sumpin' For Cool-in-the-Know Folks," *Goldmine.* n182 (July 17, 1982) 78–79. il.

Koda, Cub. "The Sun Blues Box: A Killer By Any Standard," *Goldmine.* n151 (May 9, 1986) 68, 70. il.

McNutt, Randy. "The Rise of Sun," In: *We Wanna Boogie.* pp. 50–64.

Ochs, Ed. "Tomorrow," *Billboard.* 81 (August 30, 1969) 6, 78.

Oermann, Robert K. "Sunrise to Sunset," *Country Style.* n69 (August 1981) 33–34. il.

Pugh, John. "The Rise and Fall of Sun Records," *Country Music.* 2 (November 1973) 26–32. il.

"Rockabilly: A Fusion of Country and Rock 'N' Roll," *Billboard's World of Country Music*. 75 (November 2, 1963) 1–40. il.

Sasfy, Joe. "Sunrise at Memphis," *Musician*. n88 (February 1986) 96–100, 110. il.

Sharp, Larry G. "Interviewers Soft on Sam," *Goldmine*. n189 (October 23, 1987) 29. il.

Sims, Barbara. "Sun Records: An Insider's View," *JEMF Quarterly*. 12 (1976) 119–121. il.

"Sun Record Company Discography," *Mean Mountain Music*. 4 (1979) 15–21. il., disc.

Pittman, Barbara

Davis, Hank. "Barbara Pittman: Sun's Teen Queen," *Goldmine*. n234 (July 14, 1989) 30–33, 77. il.

McNutt, Randy. "Barbara Pittmann," In: *We Wanna Boogie*. pp. 194–197. il.

Poovey, Groovey Joe

McNutt, Randy. "Groovey Joe Poovey," In" *We Wanna Boogie*. pp. 255–256. il.

Porter, Royce

Sturm, Adrian. "Royce Porter: Rockabilly Turned Nashville Songwriter," *Goldmine*. n89 (October 1983) 48, 66, 76ff.

Powers, Johnny

Loren, Dennis. "Johnny Powers," *Record Profile Magazine.* n11 (October–November 1985) 14–17. il.

Whitall, Susan. "Utica's Rockabilly Export," *Detroit News.* (January 20, 1988) 1D, 7D. il.

Presley, Elvis (See also: Sam Phillips and Sun Records; Films)

Almost Slim. "Louisiana Hayride," *Wavelength.* n30 (April 1983) 14–17. il.

Archer, Jules. "Is This Unassuming Rocker America's New Rebel?," *DISCoveries.* 1 (January–February 1988) 14–18. il.

"August 31, 1957—The Night Elvis Rocked Vancouver," *Now Dig This.* n53 (August 1987) 25–27. il.

Bangs, Lester. "Graceland Uber Alles," In: *Complete Elvis,* ed. by Martin Torgoff. pp. 130–133. il.

Banney, Howard, ed. "Jay Thompson's Interview With Elvis Presley," *Goldmine.* n56 (January 1981) 12–13. il., int.

Banney, Howard, comp. *Return to Sender: The First Complete Discography of Elvis Tribute and Novelty Records, 1956–1986.* Ann Arbor, MI: Pierian, 1987. disc.

Barbin, Lucy de, and Dary Matera. *Are You Lonesome Tonight? The Untold Story of Elvis Presley's One True Love—and the Child He Never Knew.* New York: Villard, 1987. il., bio.

Belz, Carl. "Early Rock: The Contribution of Elvis Presley," *The Story of Rock.* pp. 38–45. il.

Booth, Stanley. "A Hound Dog, To the Manor Born," In: *Complete Elvis,* ed. by Martin Torgoff. pp. 4–69. il.

Booth, Stanley. "The King is Dead! Hang the Doctor!," In: *Complete Elvis,* ed. by Martin Torgoff. pp. 70–85. il.

Bream, Terry. "Elvis on TV: His '50s Appearances," *Goldmine.* n196 (January 29, 1988) 14, 16. il.

Bream, Terry. "Elvis on TV—Part Two: His '60s and '70s Appearances," *Goldmine.* n211 (August 26, 1988) 8–12, 16. il.

Brewer-Giorgio, Gail. *Is Elvis Alive?* New York: Tudor, 1988. il.

"Briefings," *Saturday Review.* 11 (September–October 1985) 20. il.
Report on the sale of a Presley photograph.

Brock, Van K. "Images of Elvis, the South, and America," In: *Elvis,* ed. by Jac L. Tharpe. pp. 87–122. il.

Burke, Bill E. *Elvis: A 30-Year Chronicle.* Tempe, AZ: Osbourne Enterprises, 1985. il., bio.

Cabaj, Janice. *The Elvis Image.* Smithtown, NY: Exposition, 1982. il.

Cajiao, Trevor. "September 1956—One Helluva' Month!," *Now Dig This.* n53 (August 1987) 6–8. il.

Carr, Roy, and Mick Farren. *Elvis: The Illustrated Record.* New York: Harmony, 1982. il., disc.

Carsch, Henry. "The Protestant Ethic and the Popular Idol in America: A Case Study," *Social Compass.* 15 (1968) 45–69.

Chernikowski, Stephanie. "A Real Gone Cat," In: *Complete Elvis,* ed. by Martin Torgoff. pp. 104–107. il.

Clark, Alan. *The Elvis Presley Photo Album.* West Covina, CA: Alan Clark Productions, 1981. il.

Cohn, Nik. "Elvis Presley," In: *Ball the Wall.* pp. 65–71. il.

Columbus, Maria. "A Decade of Elvis in Print," *DISCoveries.* 1 (July–August 1988) 34–36. il., bibl.

Columbus, Maria. "Elvis and the Press," *Goldmine.* n196 (January 29, 1988) 8–10, 41. il.

Corliss, Richard, and Elizabeth L. Bland. "The King is Dead—or Is He?," *Time.* (October 10, 1988) 90–91. il.

Cotten, Lee. *All Shook Up: Elvis Day-By-Day, 1954–1977.* Ann Arbor, MI: Pierian, 1985. il., bio.

Cotten, Lee. "Elvis in the Fifties: A Look Back," In: *Long Lonely Highway,* comp. by Ger Rijff. pp. ix–xv. il.

Cotten, Lee, and Howard A. DeWitt. *Jailhouse Rock: The Bootleg Records of Elvis Presley, 1970–1983.* Ann Arbor, MI: Pierian, 1983. disc.

Covey, Maureen, Todd Slaughter, and Michael Wells. *Elvis for*

the Record: The Story of Elvis Presley in Words and Pictures.
Knutsford, U.K.: Stafford Pemberton, 1982. il.

Deen, Jeannie. "A Young Girl's Fancy," In: *Elvis,* ed. by Jac L.
Tharpe. pp. 169–172. il.

DeWitt, Howard A. "Elvis Presley and Memphis: The Obscure
Years, 1948–1952," *Record Profile Magazine.* n3 (December 1983–January 1984) 16–17, 65, 69. il., bio.

DeWitt, Howard A. "Elvis Presley and Memphis: The Obscure
Years, 1948–1952—Part Three," *Record Profile Magazine.*
n6 (July 1984) 39, 62. il., bio.

DeWitt, Howard A. "Elvis Presley and Memphis: The Obscure
Years, 1948–1952—Part Two," *Record Profile Magazine.*
n4 (February–March 1984) 13, 18. il., bio.

Doggett, Peter. "Elvis: A Golden Celebration," *Record Collector.*
n67 (March 1985) 18–22. il.

Doggett, Peter. "Elvis in the 60's," *Record Collector.* n113
(January 1989) 3–6. il.

Doggett, Peter. "Elvis Presley on CD," *Record Collector.* n98
(October 1987) 6–9. il., disc.

Doggett, Peter. "Elvis Presley: The Final Decade," *Record
Collector.* n96 (August 1987) 3–10. il., disc.

Doggett, Peter. "Elvis Presley: The Sun Years," *Record Collector.*
n105 (May 1988) 3–6. il., disc.

Doggett, Peter. "Elvis Presley's U.K. Singles," *Record Collector.*
n47 (July 1983) 18–21. il., disc.

Doggett, Peter. "Elvis' 25th Anniversary Set," *Record Collector.* n14 (October 1980) 16–20. il.

Doggett, Peter. "Elvis' U.K. LPs," *Record Collector.* n18 (February 1981) 4–10. il., disc.

Doole, Kerry. "Rock Me, Eternally—Elvis," *Rock Express.* 11 (September–October 1987) 20–26. il.

Dowling, Paul. "Elvis Presley: His Rare Worldwide Jackets and Sleeves," *Goldmine.* n184 (August 14, 1987) 26, 30. il., disc.

Duncan, Robert. "Elvis Presley: Rust Never Sleeps," In: *Only the Good Die Young.* pp. 159–168. il.

Dundy, Elaine. *Elaine and Gladys: The Genesis of the King.* New York: Macmillan, 1985. il.

"Dutch court backs piracy charges; Presley recordings deemed illegal," *Billboard.* 99 (September 12, 1987) 75.

Edwards, Michael, and Ellis Amburn. *Priscilla, Elvis, and Me: In the Shadow of the King.* New York: St. Martin's 1988. il.

Elvis Presley Records Checklist, 1954–1977. Jacksonville, IL: Ladd, 1977. disc.

Finnis, Rob. "The Elvis Presley Followers: Copying the King," *The History of Rock.* n7 (1982) 135–137. il.

Fitzgerald, Jim, with art by Al Kilgore. *Elvis: The Paper Doll Book.* New York: St. Martin's, 1982. il.

Flans, R. "Reminiscing WIth D.J. Fontana," *Modern Drummer.* 9 (May 1985) 22–25ff. il.

Foerster, Fred, ed. *Elvis—Just For You: A Special Goldmine Anthology.* Iola, WI: Goldmine, 1987. il.

Fricke, David, et al. "Elvis Presley: 'Elvis' on NBC-TV on December 3, 1968," *Rolling Stone.* n501 (June 4, 1987) 53–54, 143. il.

Gambaccini, Paul. "Elvis Presley," In: *Masters of Rock.* pp. 212–221. il.

Gates, David. "Elvis Statue Found on Mars! (Or, Just Your Average Week on the Elvis Watch," *Newsweek.* (October 3, 1988) 63. il.

Geller, Larry, and Jess Stearn. *The Truth About Elvis.* New York: Jove, 1980. il.

Gilbert, Adrian. "Memphis, Tennessee," *The History of Rock.* n3 (1982) 41–43. il.

Glade, Emory. *Elvis: A Golden Tribute.* Wauwatosa, WI: Robus, 1984. il.

Goldman, Albert. "Down at the End of Lonely Street," *Life.* 13 (June 1990) 96–104. il.
The author theorizes that Presley committed suicide.

Greene, Bob. "American Beat: Greetings from Graceland," *Esquire.* (December 1987) 53–54. il.

Greene, Bob. "American Beat: The Nixon-Presley Papers," *Esquire.* (October 1988) 63–65. il.

Griffith, Ashley, and Kerrin L. Griffith. "Elvis Presley," *Stereo Review.* 37 (July 1976) 76–80. il.

Guralnick, Peter. "Elvis Emerging: A Year of Innocence and Experience," *Journal of Country Music.* 12 (1989) 44–48, 65–72. il.

Guralnick, Peter. "Faded Love," *Country Music.* 8 (January–February 1980) 42–44. il.

Haining, Peter. *Elvis in Private.* London: Hale, 1987. il.

Hammontree, Patsy Guy. "Audience Amplitude: The Cultural Phenomenon of Elvis Presley," In: *Elvis,* ed. by Jac L. Tharpe. pp. 52–60. il.

Hammontree, Patsy Guy. *Elvis Presley: A Bio-Bibliography.* Westport, CT: Greenwood, 1985. il., bio., bibl.

Helinski, Jack. "Elvis—What's in the Can?," *Goldmine.* n92 (January 1984) 6, 11, 16, 18, 20, 22ff. il.

Helinski, Jack. "Elvis—What's in the Can?, Part Two—An Update," *Goldmine.* n189 (October 23, 1987) 36–37. il.

Helinski, Jack. "Joan Deary: Her Job is Listening to Unreleased Elvis Tunes," *Goldmine.* n80 (January 1983) 10. il.

"Hy Gardner Callin'!," *Now Dig This.* n53 (August 1987) 16–17. il.

"In the Beginning . . . Early Memories of the Presley Legend," *Now Dig This.* n53 (August 1987) 4–5. il.

"An Interview With Don Wardell: RCA's Man in Charge of Elvis," *Goldmine.* n236 (August 11, 1989) 38, 108. il., int.

Jones, Linda. "Elvis Presley Radio Shows: The Man, The Music, and the Legend," *Goldmine.* n236 (August 11, 1989) 30, 36. il.

Jones, Peter. "Elvis: The Early Years," *The History of Rock.* n3 (1982) 48–54. il., bio.

Jones, Randall, comp. "An Elvis Discography," *Record Exchanger.* n25 (1977) 16–19. il., disc.

Jorgensen, Ernst, Erik Rasmussen, and Johnny Mikkelsen. *Reconsider Baby: The Definitive Elvis Sessionography, 1954– 1977.* Reprint ed., with additions. Ann Arbor, MI: Pierian, 1986. il.

Kanchanawan, Nitaya. "Elvis, Thailand, and I," In: *Elvis,* ed. by Jac L. Tharpe. pp. 162–168. il.

Kaye, Lenny. "If Elvis Had Lived," In: *Complete Elvis,* ed. by Martin Torgoff. pp. 126–129. il.

Kellom, Debbie. "Sam Phillips Authenticates Presley Acetate: Negotiations Continue Over Record Rights," *Goldmine.* n218 (December 2, 1988) 27. il.

Kendall, William C. "And Now, Direct to You From Hillbilly Heaven," In: *Elvis,* ed. by Jac L. Tharpe. pp. 61–64. il.

Kent, David. "Elvis at the Louisiana Hayride: A Legitimate Search for Illegitimate Records," *Goldmine.* n105 (August 3, 1984) 18–20. il., disc.

Kiefer, Kit. "Elvis' Rarest Recording?," *Goldmine.* n211 (August 26, 1988) 7, 83. il.

Kiefer, Kit. "Elvis' Rarest Recording! New Evidence May Authenticate Presley Acetate," *Goldmine.* n213 (September 23, 1988) 18–19. il.

Kiley, P. "Behind the Walls of Heartache," *Melody Maker.* 60 (August 3, 1985) 39. il., int.w/A. Bleasdale. Coverage of the play, *Are You Lonesome Tonight?*

Kirkby, Joan. "The Memphis Faun: A View From Australia," In: *Elvis,* ed. by Jac L. Tharpe. pp. 11–26. il.

Loder, Kurt. "The King Is Gone But Not Forgotten," *Rolling Stone.* n506 (August 13, 1987) 29–33. il. Features rare pictures taken by photographer Jay Leviton in August 1956.

Malone, Bill C. "Elvis, Country Music, and the South," In: *Elvis,* ed. by Jac L. Tharpe. pp. 123–134. il.

Marcus, Greil. "Antihero," *Spin.* 3 (August 1987) 64–66. il.

Marcus, Greil. "Playing House With Elvis, and Other Likely Stories: A Multi-Media Update on the State of a Legend," *Journal of Country Music.* 11 (Winter 1986) 84–90. il.

Marsh, Dave. "How Great Thou Art," In: *Fortunate Son.* pp. 303 306. il.

Marsh, Dave. "The Secret Life of Elvis Presley," In: *Fortunate Son.* pp. 78–83. il.

Martin, Bob. "Elvis Under the Counter: A Look at the Current Elvis Presley Bootleg Industry," *Goldmine.* n189 (October 23, 1987) 29. il.

Matthew-Walker, Robert. *Heartbreak Hotel: The Life and Music of Elvis Presley.* London: Archway, 1988. il.

McAlister, Marshall. "The Complete Elvis CD Catalog," *DISCoveries.* 2 (January 1989) 96–97. disc.

McAuliffe, Jon. "The Alpha and Omega of Elvis Presley," *Music World.* n88 (August 1981) 60–63. il.

McCutchan, Ann. "No End to Elvis," *Battle Creek (Michigan) Enquirer.* (January 5, 1988) 1B. il.

McNutt, Randy. "Elvis Presley: 'I Have to Move'," In: *We Wanna Boogie.* pp. 78–83. il.

Middleton, Richard. "All Shook Up? Innovation and Continuity in Elvis Presley's Vocal Style," In: *Elvis,* ed. by Jac L. Tharpe. pp. 151–161. il.

Miller, Jim. "Forever Elvis," *Newsweek.* (August 3, 1987) 48–55. il.

Minto, Gordon. "Extend Presley," *Now Dig This.* n53 (August 1987) 23–24. il.

Moline, Karen. "A Letter to Elvis," In: *Complete Elvis,* ed. by Martin Torgoff. pp. 98–103. il.

Moody, Raymond A., Jr. *Elvis After Life: Unusual Psychic Experiences Surrounding the Death of a Superstar.* Atlanta: Peachtree, 1987. il.

"More Money Raised for Tokyo Statue of Presley," *Billboard.* 98 (February 22, 1986) 77.

Morris, E. "Presley's Executors Fight Tax Assessment," *Billboard.* 98 (May 10, 1986) 6.

Morthland, John. "Elvis Has Left the Building," *Stereo Review.* 40 (January 1978) 108–109. il.

Morthland, John. "Producing the King," *Country Music.* 7 (December 1977) 31ff. il.

Nelson, Pete. *King! When Elvis Rocked the World.* New York: Proteus, 1985. il.

Newman, Bob. "Elvis Presley: His Private Meeting With President Nixon," *Goldmine.* n169 (January 16, 1987) 16, 18. il.

"No Canadian Airplay for Elvis If He Was Starting Out Today," *Variety.* 323 (June 4, 1986) 124.

O'Brien, Glenn. "Anagrams," In: *Complete Elvis,* ed. by Martin Torgoff. pp. 10–17. il.

Osborne, Jerry. "Collecting Elvis: His Rarest," *DISCoveries.* 1(January–February 1988) 21–25, 127ff. il., disc.

Osborne, Jerry, comp. *Elvis—Like Any Other Soldier.* Port Townsend, WA: Osborne Enterprises, 1989. il., disc.

Osborne, Jerry. "Elvis LPS: His Most Collectible U.S. Records," *Goldmine.* n196 (January 29, 1988) 18, 20. il., disc.

Osborne, Jerry. "The 1956 Little Rock Interview," *DISCoveries.* 1 (November 1988) 110. il., int.

Osborne, Jerry, comp. *Presleyana: Elvis Presley Record Price Guide.* Second ed. Phoenix: O'Sullivan and Woodside, 1983. il., disc.

Osborne, Jerry, Perry Cox, and Joe Lindsay, comps. *The Official Price Guide to Elvis Presley and the Beatles.* New York: Ballantine, 1988. il., disc.

Osborne, Jerry, and Randall Jones, comps. *The Complete Elvis.* Great Neck, NY: Funky Angel Productions, 1977. il., disc.

Osborne, Jerry, and Ed Leek. "Elvis' First Recordings: Update," *DISCoveries.* 2 (January 1989) 18–21. il., disc.

Patrick, Gary F. "The Elvis Novelty Records," *Goldmine.* n80 (January 1983) 16–20. il., disc.

"Pay TV Goes All Out for Presley Birthday in Jan.," *Variety.* 317 (January 9, 1985) 183.

Paytress, Mark. "Elvis Presley: Books and Memorabilia," *Record Collector.* n120 (August 1989) 3–8. il.

Paytress, Mark. "Elvis Presley: The Las Vegas Years," *Record Collector.* n125 (January 1990) 3–7. il., disc.

Peters, Richard. *Elvis: The Golden Anniversary Tribute.* London: Pop Universal/Souvenir, 1984. il.

Pielke, Robert G. "Elvis and the Negation of the Fifties," In:

You Say You Want a Revolution. Chicago: Nelson-Hall, 1986. pp. 139–156. il.

Pratt, Linda Ray. "Elvis, or the Ironies of a Southern Identity," In: *Rock Music in America,* ed. by Janet Podell. pp. 23–34. il.

Presley, Priscilla. "He Saved Me for so Long," *People Weekly.* 24 (September 16, 1985) 108–119. il. Excerpts of the book *Elvis and Me* (Putnam, 1985).

Presley, Priscilla Beaulieu, with Sandra Harmon. *Elvis and Me.* New York: G.P. Putnam, 1985. il.

"Presley Enterprises Fights Back in Court," *Billboard.* 97 (August 24, 1985) 6.

"Presley Estate Sues RCA Over Royalties on *Golden Collection* LP," *Variety.* 318 (March 6, 1985) 373.

Ricci, James. "The Elvis Cult: Devotion is Alive 10 Years After His Death," *Detroit Free Press.* (July 26, 1987) 1F, 6F. il.

Rijff, Ger, comp. *Long Lonely Highway: A 1950's Elvis Scrapbook.* Reprint ed., with additions. Ann Arbor, MI: Pierian, 1987. il.

Roblin, A. "Elvis Presley Cosmetics Line Get 'Love Me Tender' Label," *Billboard.* 98 (February 8, 1986) 63.

Roblin, A. "Elvis Tribute Week Inspires Fans—and Sales," *Billboard.* 99 (September 12, 1987) 37–38.

"The Rock and Roll Hall of Fame," *BMI.* n1 (1986) 27. il., bio.

Roy, Samuel. *Elvis: Prophet of Power*. Brookline Village, MA: Branden, 1985. il.

Ruhlmann, William. "Elvis Lives (At Least His Record Company Thinks So): The Posthumous Releases, 1977–1989," *Goldmine*. n236 (August 11, 1989) 22–24, 28, 95. il.

Ruhlmann, William. "Elvis Lives: The Book, the Tape, and the Story That Swept the Talk Shows," *Goldmine*. n211 (August 26, 1988) 68, 78. il.

Russell, Wayne, and Trevor Cajiao. "Red West Stars In—Red: What Happened?," *Now Dig This*. n79 (October 1989) 16–18. il.

Saitta, Jim. "RCA Versus Elvis," *Goldmine*. n117 (January 18, 1985) 14, 18. il.

Santelli, Robert. "Elvis Presley: Four Greats Talk About the 'King'," *Goldmine*. n133 (August 30, 1985) 20–30. il, int.

Savers, Wendy, comp. *Elvis Presley—A Complete Reference: Biography, Chronology, Concerts List, Filmography, Discography, Vital Documents, Bibliography, and Index*. Jefferson, NC: McFarland, 1984. il., bio., disc., bibl.

Scheurer, Timothy E. "Elvis Presley and the Myth of America," In: *American Popular Music—Volume Two: The Age of Rock*. pp. 102–112. il.

Scott, Steve. "The Elvis Legacy," *Record Collector*. n91 (March 1987) 3–8. il., disc.

Scott, Steve. "Elvis Presley: The Early Years," *Record Collector.* n80 (April 1986) 3–8. il., bio.

Scott, Steve. "Elvis Presley's U.K. EPs: A Collector's Guide to Extended Play Releases From 1956 to 1982," *Record Collector.* n36 (August 1982) 21–27. il., disc.

Scott, Steve. "From Elvis in Memphis: A Complete Guide to Elvis' Memphis Recording Sessions," *Record Collector.* n27 (November 1981) 12–16. il., disc.

Silverman, Phil. "LP of Unreleased Presley Tracks Due From RCA in October," *Record Collector's Monthly.* n12 (September 1983) 17.

Simpson, Trevor. "E.P.'s EPs: The Complete Elvis Presley British EP Discography, 1957–1982," *Goldmine.* n80 (January 1983) 11–13. il., disc.

Skjoldhoj, Ole. "Facts Behind the 'Elvis Recordings Sessions'," *Goldmine.* n149 (April 11, 1986) 81. il.

Spedding, Chris. "Elvis and Dino: Was the King of Rock 'N' Roll a Copy Cat?," *Musician.* n136 (February 1990) 129–130. il.

Stambler, Irwin. "Presley, Elvis," In: *The Encyclopedia of Pop, Rock and Soul.* pp. 533–537. il.

Stanley, David. *Life With Elvis.* Old Tappan, NJ: Fleming H. Revell, 1987. il.

Stearn, Jesse. *Elvis: His Spiritual Journey.* Norfolk, VA: Donning Press, 1982. il.

Stern, Michael. *Elvis World.* New York: Knopf, 1987. il.

Stuller, Jay "Legends That Will Not Die," *Saturday Evening Post.* (July–August 1985) 42–49. il.

Tamarkin, Jeff. "Elvis Presley: Good Readin' Tonight—A Guide to Books About Elvis," *Goldmine.* n133 (August 30, 1985) 24–28. il., bibl.

Tamarkin, Jeff. "Elvis Presley: Reshaping the Elvis Catalog— A Talk With RCA's Gregg Geller," *Goldmine.* n133 (August 30, 1985) 8–12. il.

Taylor, Roger G., ed. *Elvis in Art.* London: Elm Tree, 1987. il.

"Ten Pioneers of Rock Selected for Induction to New Hall of Fame," *Variety.* 321 (November 27, 1985) 139.

Tharpe, Jac L. "Will the Real Elvis Presley . . . ?," In: *Elvis,* ed. by Jac L. Tharpe. pp. 3–10. il.

Tobler, John, and Richard Wootton. *Elvis: The Legend and the Music.* London: Optimum, 1983. il.

Toivonen, Timo, and Antero Laiho. " 'You Don't Like Crazy Music': The Reception of Elvis Presley in Finland," *Popular Music and Society.* 13 (Summer 1989) 1–22.

Torgoff, Martin. "A–Z: Life, Music, Films, People, Places, and Things," In: *Complete Elvis,* ed. by Martin Torgoff. pp. 134–251. il.

Torgoff, Martin. "After the Flood: Elvis and His Literary Legacy," In: *Complete Elvis,* ed. by Martin Torgoff. pp. 18–19. il.

Tosches, Nick. "Elvis: Getting the Ink, 1954–1955," *Goldmine.* n68 (January 1982) 14. il.

Tosches, Nick. "Elvis Presley—The Death of Elvis," *Goldmine.* n92 (January 1984) 7–8. il.

Tosches, Nick. "Elvis: The Shocking Hillbilly Cat," *Country Style.* n69 (August 1981) 14–21. il.

Tosches, Nick. "The Million Dollar Quartet: Marked Down," *Goldmine.* n56 (January 1981) 10. il.

Tosches, Nick. "Nashville Babylon—Loud Covenants II: Elvis, the Parter of Seas and Lips," *Creem.* 9 (April 1978) 52–55. il.

Townson, John, Gordon Minto, and George Richardson. *Elvis U.K.: The Ultimate Guide to Elvis Presley's British Record Releases, 1956–1986.* Poole, Dorset, England: Blandford, 1987. il., disc.

Tucker, Stephen R. "Visions of Elvis: Changing Perceptions in National Magazines, 1956–1965," In: *Elvis,* ed. by Jac L. Tharpe. pp. 27–39. il.

Umphred, Neal. "Elvis Lives! On CD, on Video, and in Print," *Goldmine.* n221 (January 13, 1989) 16–24, 67, 72–75. il.

Umphred, Neal, comp. "Elvis Presley Compact Disc Discography and Price Guide," *Goldmine.* n221 (January 13, 1989) 72–75. disc.

Umphred, Neal. "Elvis Presley Radio Programs: Discography and Price Guide," *Goldmine.* n236 (August 11, 1989) 32–36. il.

Umphred, Neal. "From Elvis in Memphis: New Information About the Sun Recordings," *Goldmine.* n211 (August 26, 1988) 17–18. il.

Van Hollebeke, Jim. "Elvis Presley: Big Record News," *Goldmine.* n117 (January 18, 1985) 14, 18. il.

Van Hollebeke, Jim. "Elvis: The Legend is Far From Dead," *Goldmine.* n133 (August 30, 1985) 5. il.

Van Hollebeke, Jim. "Mandatory Additions to the Elvis Bookpile," *Goldmine.* n133 (August 30, 1985) 79–80. il., bibl.

Vellenga, Dirk, with Mick Farren. *Elvis and the Colonel.* New York: Delacorte, 1988. il.

Walker, John. "The Bootleg Elvis," In: *Complete Elvis,* ed. by Martin Torgoff. pp. 92–97. il.

West, Red, Sonny West, and Dave Hebler, as told to Steve Dunleavy. *Elvis: What Happened?* New York: Ballantine, 1977. il.

White, Timothy. "Elvis Presley," In: *Rock Stars.* pp. 56–61. il.

Whitesell, Rick. "Making the Legend Human Again," *Goldmine.* n44 (January 1980) 11–12. il.

Wolfe, Charles. "Presley and the Gospel Tradition," In: *Elvis,* ed. by Jac L. Tharpe. pp. 135–150. il.

Worth, Fred L., and Steve D. Tamerius, comps. *Elvis: His Life From A to Z.* Chicago: Contemporary Books, 1988. il.

Zuckerman, F. "Cable Shows Mark Presley's Birthday," *Billboard.* 97 (January 5, 1985) 33.
Coverage of a tour of Graceland.

Preston, Johnny

Hill, Randal C. "Johnny Preston: A Genuine (Dove) Soap Opera," *Goldmine.* n216 (November 4, 1988) 72–81. il.

Stafford, John. "Feelin' Fine—That's Johnny Preston," *Now Dig This.* n73 (April 1989) 4–5. il.

Rainwater, Marvin

Grant, Dick, comp. "Marvin Rainwater Singles Discography," *Now Dig This,* n55 (October 1987) 30. il., disc.

"Marvin Rainwater," *The Golden Age.* n2 (November 1986) 15–27. il.

Millar, Bill. "Marvin Rainwater: Whole Lotta Marvin," *Goldmine.* n52 (September 1980) 24–25. il.

Rich, Charlie

Burton, Charlie. "The Ups and Downs in the Life of a Sun Legend: Charlie Rich," *Country Music.* 1 (February 1973) 40–44. il.

Doggett, Peter. "Charlie Rich," *Record Collector.* n50 (October 1983) 30–33. il., disc.

Eron, Judy, and Geoffrey Morgan. *Charlie Rich.* Mankato, MN: Creative Education, 1975. il.

Escott, Colin. "Charlie Rich: Before Closed Doors," *Goldmine.* n170 (January 30, 1987) 16, 64. il.

Guralnick, Peter. "Silver Fox at Bay," *Country Music.* 5 (June 1976) 22–26, 62. il.

Stambler, Irwin. "Rich, Charlie," In: *The Encyclopedia of Pop, Rock and Soul.* pp. 568–570.

Windeler, Robert. "The Long, Hard Road of Charlie Rich," *Stereo Review.* 34 (January 1975) 62–63. il.

Riley, Billy Lee

Koda, Cub. "Billy Lee Riley: Super Outrageously Cool Comp," *Goldmine.* n143 (January 17, 1986) 62. il.

McNutt, Randy. "Story of a Rocker," In: *We Wanna Boogie.* pp. 134–138. il.

Newcomb, Jim. "Still Red Hot!," *Now Dig This.* n56 (November 1987) 30–31. il.

Palmer, Robert. "Billy Lee Riley's Red-Hot Return," *Rolling Stone.* n268 (June 2, 1978) 19–20. il.

Tamarkin, Jeff. "Billy Lee Riley: Red Hot Sun Rocker," *Goldmine.* n169 (January 16, 1987) 14. il.

Thompson, Gary, and Don Ezell, comps. "Billy Lee Riley Discography," *Goldmine.* n28 (September 1978) 14. il.

Ryan, Charlie

McNutt, Randy. "Hot Rod Charlie," In: *We Wanna Boogie.* pp. 258–260. il.

Scott, Jack

Cajiao, Trevor. "Jack Scott Talks to *Now Dig This*—Part One," *Now Dig This.* n72 (March 1989) 17–22. il., int.

Cajiao, Trevor. "Jack Scott Talks to *Now Dig This*—Part Three," *Now Dig This.* n74 (May 1989) 24–26. il., int.

Cajiao, Trevor. "Jack Scott Talks to *Now Dig This*—Part Two," *Now Dig This.* n73 (April 1989) 22–24. il., int.

Collis, John. "Rockabilly From Michigan," *The History of Rock.* n24 (1982) 468–469. il.

"Jack Scott," *The Golden Age.* n19 (1989) 4–5. il.

Thompson, Gary. "Jack Scott is Back," *Goldmine.* n12 (September–October 1976) 33. il.

Scott, Ray

McNutt, Randy. "Ray Scott," In: *We Wanna Boogie.* pp. 261–262. il.

Turner, Big Al. "He's the One That Done It: The Ray Scott Story," *Now Dig This.* n56 (November 1987) 3–5. il.

Self, Ronnie

McNutt, Randy. "Mr. Frantic," In: *We Wanna Boogie.* p. 162. il.

Russell, Wayne. "Ronnie Self," *Goldmine.* n75 (August 1982) 158. il.

Simmons, Gene

Cajiao, Trevor. "Memories of a Sun Rockabilly . . . ," *Now Dig This.* n62 (May 1988) 16–17. il.

McNutt, Randy. "Rockabilly Soul," In: *We Wanna Boogie.* pp. 157–161. il.

Smith, Ray

Komorowski, Adam. "Ray Smith," *New Kommotion.* n22 (1979) 20–24. il.

Sturm, Adri. "The Ray Smith Story," *Record Exchanger.* n30 (1982) 10–15. il.

Smith, Warren

Escott, Colin. "Warren Smith: Rock and Roll Ruby," *Goldmine.* n188 (October 9, 1987) 22. il.

Komorowski, Adam. "Warren Smith," *New Kommotion.* n22 (1979) 48–53. il.

Starr, Andy

Russell, Wayne. "Andy Starr," *Now Dig This.* n45 (December 1986) 9. il.

Summers, Gene

"Gene Summers," *The Golden Age.* n7 (April 1987) 16–25. il.

Parker, Richard. "Gene Summers: Texas Rockabilly Rebel," *Goldmine.* n69 (February 1982) 26–27. il.

Sun Rhythm Section (See also: Sam Phillips and Sun Records)

Cajiao, Trevor. "Smoochy Speaks! Smoochy Smith, Piano Pounder With the Sun Rhythm Section," *Now Dig This.* n76 (July 1989) 18–21. il.

Newcombe, Jim. "Keeping the Sun Shining," *Now Dig This.* n62 (May 1988) 18. il.

Thompson, Hayden

Grant, Dick. "Hayden Thompson: Your Mama Don't Dance," *Now Dig This.* n18 (September 1984) 14–15. il.

Komorowski, Adam, and Dick Grant. *The Hayden Thompson Story.* il.

McNutt, Randy. "Hayden Thompson," In: *We Wanna Boogie.* pp. 266–268. il.

Thompson, Gary, comp. "Hayden Thompson Discography," *Goldmine.* n41 (October 1979) 16. disc.

Twitty, Conway

Carr, Patrick, and Marshall Fallwell. "Introducing Harold Jenkins," *Country Music.* 2 (May 1974) 24–32. il.

"Conway Twitty," *Song Hits.* n221 (July 1984) 46–47. il.

"Conway Twitty," *Song Hits Yearbook.* 13 (Fall 1985) 50–51. il.

"Conway Twitty: 'Rock 'N' Roll Years'," *Record Collector.* n82 (June 1986) 13–15. il., disc.

Cross, Wilbur, and Michael Kosser. *The Conway Twitty Story: An Authorized Biography.* Garden City, NY: Doubleday, 1986. il., bio.

Escott, Colin. *Conway Twitty: Rock 'N' Roll Years.* Bremen, West Germany: Bear Family, 1985. il., bio.. disc.

Garbutt, Bob. "Conway Twitty," *Goldmine.* n82 (March 1983) 16–18. il.

McNutt, Randy. "Lonely Blues Boy," In: *We Wanna Boogie.* pp. 99–102. il.

Ryan, Jack. "Conway Twitty: Rockabilly to Country," *Record Profile Magazine.* n10 (July–August 1985) 22–25. il.

Weize, Richard, comp. "A Preliminary Conway Twitty Discography," In: *Conway Twitty,* by Colin Escott. pp. 59–80. il., disc.

Van Eaton, James

Cajiao, Trevor. "James Van Eaton: Whole Lotta Shakin' Goin' On—Part One," *Now Dig This.* n81 (December 1989) 4–7. il.

Davis, Hank, and Colin Escott. "Jimmy Van Eaton: The Driving Force Behind Jerry Lee," *Goldmine.* n234 (July 14, 1989) 27–28. il.

Van Story, Marcus

McNutt, Randy. "Marcus Van Story," In: *We Wanna Boogie.* p. 270. il.

Yelvington, Malcolm

Cajiao, Trevor. "Yakety Yak," *Now Dig This.* n68 (November 1988) 19–21. il.

Cajiao, Trevor. "Yakety Yak," *Now Dig This.* n69 (December 1988) 8–10. il.

Hawkins, Martin. "Malcolm Yelvington," *New Kommotion.* n22 (1979) 39–40. il.

McNutt, Randy. "No Regrets," In: *We Wanna Boogie.* pp. 151–156. il.

York, Rusty

McNutt, Randy. " 'Sugaree' Revisited," In: *We Wanna Boogie.* pp. 129–133. il.

C. EUROPEAN POP TRADITION

General Sources

Brooks, Elston. *I've Heard Those Songs Before: The Weekly Top Ten Tunes For the Past Fifty Years.* New York: Morrow Quill, 1981.
One ex-journalist's own revisionist charting of popular music singles for the period, 1930–1980. Extreme bias favoring MOR material.

Brahms, Caryl, and Ned Sherrin. *Song By Song: The Lives and Work of Fourteen Great Lyric Writers.* Bolton, Lancs., U.K.: Ross Anderson, 1984.

Cohen, Norm. "Tin Pan Alley's Contribution to Folk Music," *Western Folklore*. 29 (September 1970) 9–20.

Cohen-Stratyner, Barbara, ed. *Popular Music, 1900–1919: An Annotated Guide to American Popular Songs*. Detroit: Gale, 1988.

Colbert, Warren E. *Who Wrote That Song? Or, Who the Hell is J. Fred Coots? An Informal Survey of American Popular Songs and Their Composers*. New York: Revisionist Press, 1975.

Craig, Warren. *The Great Songwriters of Hollywood*. San Diego: Barnes, 1980.

Craig, Warren. *Sweet and Lowdown: America's Popular Song Writers*. Metuchen, NJ: Scarecrow, 1978.

Goldberg, Isaac. *Tin Pan Alley*. New York: Ungar, 1961. il.

Hamm, Charles. "The Music of Tin Pan Alley," In: *Music in the New World*. pp. 339–372. il.

Hamm, Charles. "Top Forty: The Most Often Recorded Songs in America, 1900–1950," In: *Yesterdays: Popular Song in America*. pp. 487–488. il.

Hamm, Charles. "The Top Songs on 'Your Hit Parade', 1935–1958," In: *Yesterdays*. pp. 493–494. il.

Hamm, Charles. "*Variety* Magazine's Golden 100 Tin Pan Alley Songs, 1918–1935," In: *Yesterdays*. pp. 489–492. il.

Jasen, David A. *Tin Pan Alley: The Composers, The Performers, and Their Times—The Golden Age of American Popular Music From 1886 to 1956*. New York: Donald I. Fine, 1988. il.

Kimler, Walter. *Not Fade Away: A Comparison of Jazz Age With Rock Era Pop Song Composers.* Ann Arbor, MI: Pierian, 1984. il.

Lees, Gene. *Singers and the Song.* New York: Oxford University Press, 1987. il.

Leibowitz, Alan, comp. "Composers and Lyricists," In: *The Record Collector's Handbook.* pp. 120–122. il.

Moore, MacDonald Smith. *Yankee Blues: Musical Culture and American Identity.* Bloomington, IN: Indiana University Press, 1985.

Pessen, Edward. "The Great Songwriters of Tin Pan Alley's Golden Age: A Social, Occupational, and Aesthetic Inquiry," *American Music.* 3 (Summer 1985) 180–197.

Scheurer, Timothy E. "The Tin Pan Alley Years (1890–1950)," In: *American Popular Music—Volume One: The Nineteenth Century and Tin Pan Alley.* pp. 87–91. il.

Shapiro, Nat, and Bruce Pollock, eds. "Lyricists and Composers Index," In: *Popular Music, 1920–1979—A Revised Cumulation: Volume Three.* pp. 2167–2598.

Shepherd, John. *Tin Pan Alley.* London: Routledge and Kegan Paul, 1982. il.

Tawa, Nicholas E. *Serenading the Reluctant Eagle: American Musical Life: 1925–1945.* New York: Schirmer, 1984. il.

Tawa, Nicholas E. *The Way to Tin Pan Alley: American Popular Song, 1866–1910.* New York: Schirmer, 1990. il.

Tyler, Don. *Hit Parade: An Encyclopedia of the Top Songs of the Jazz, Depression, Swing, and Sing Eras.* New York: Quill, 1985. il.

Whitburn, Joel, comp. *Pop Memories, 1890–1954: The History of American Popular Music.* Menomonee Falls, WI: Record Research, 1986. disc.

Whitcomb, Ian. *Irving Berlin and Ragtime America.* London: Century, 1987. il.

Whitcomb, Ian. *Tin Pan Alley: A Pictorial History, 1919–1939.* New York: Continents, 1975. il.

White, Mark. *"You Must Remember This . . .": Popular Songwriters, 1900–1980.* New York: Scribner, 1985. il.

Wilder, Alec. *American Popular Song: The Great Innovators, 1900–1950,* ed. by James T. Maher. New York: Oxford University Press, 1972. il.

Wilk, Max. *They're Playing Our Song: From Jerome Kern to Stephen Sondheim.* New York: Atheneum, 1973. il.

Cover Recordings (See also: Otis Williams)

Ackerman, Paul. "R&B Tunes' Boom Relegates Pop Field to Cover Activity," *Billboard.* 67 (March 26, 1955) 18, 22.

Belz, Carl. "Early Rock: Crossovers and Covers," In: *The Story of Rock.* pp. 25–30. il.

Chapple, Steve, and Reebee Garofalo. "Black Roots/White Fruits: Racism in the Music Industry," In: *Rock and Roll is Here to Pay.* pp. 231–267. il.

Cohen, John. "The Folk Music Interchange: Negro and White," In: *The American Folk Scene: Dimensions of the Folksong Revival,* ed. by Devid A. DeTurk amd A. Poulin, Jr. pp. 59–66. il.

Cooper, B. Lee. "The Black Roots of Popular Music," In: *Images of American Society in Popular Music.* pp. 111–123.

Cooper, B. Lee. "Promoting Social Change Through Audio Repetition: Black Musicians as Creators and Revivalists, 1953–1978," *Tracking: Popular Music Studies.* 2 (Winter 1989) 26–46. il.

Cotten, Lee. "Cover Records," In: *Shake, Rattle, and Roll.* pp. xxiv–xxx. il.

"Covers of the Songs of Buddy Holly—Part One," *Music World and Record Digest.* 2 (April 25, 1979) 8.

DeWitt, Howard A. "Chuck Berry's Songs: Some Sources" and "Cover Record," In: *Chuck Berry: Rock 'N' Roll Music.* pp. 249–250; 251–264. il.

Griggs, Bill. "Spotlight on Cover Songs: What Were They and Why Did We Have Them?," *Rockin' 50s.* n20 (October 1989) 8–14. il.

"Kicking Off the Covers," *DISCoveries.* 2 (January 1989) 40–42. il.

Komorowski, Adam, Bill Millar, and Ray Topping. "Elvis: The Original Versions and Other Notes," *New Kommotion.* n17 (Autumn 1977) 4–9. il., disc.

McNutt, Randy. "Go, Cats, Go! But Please Don't Cover My Cover," In: *We Wanna Boogie.* pp. 76–77. il.

Moonoogian, George A. "Deja-Vu (With Records, Too)," *Goldmine.* n33 (February 1979) 24–25. il.

Shaw, Arnold. "Sh-Boom," In: *The Rockin' 50s.* pp, 73–79. il.

Snyder, Robert. "Cover Records: What? When? Why?," In: *Out Best to You—From Record Digest,* comp. by Jerry Osborne. pp. 77–85. il.

Stierle, Wayne. "Let Us Count the Elvis Cover Records (Wait a Minute! There Aren't Any!)," *DISCoveries.* 2 (January 1989) 38–39. disc.

Vance, Joel. "Rock-'N'-Roll Roots on Savoy Records," *Stereo Review.* 39 (November 1977) 112.

Bennett, Tony

Giddins, Gary. "Tony Bennett Without Fear," In: *Rhythm-A-Ning: Jazz Tradition and Innovation in the '80s.* pp. 65–68. il.

Jasper, Tony. *Tony Bennett.* London: W.H. Allen, 1984. il.

Rowland, Mark. "Tony Bennett," *Musician.* n98 (December 1986) 17–22. il.

Benton, Brook

DeCurtis, Anthony. "Brook Benton: 1931–1988," *Rolling Stone.* n526 (May 19, 1988) 18.

Boone, Pat

Barnard, Stephen. "Rock to Religion," *The History of Rock.* n16 (1982) 313–315. il.

Boone, Pat. *Together.* Nashville: Thomas Nelson, 1979. il.

Jones, Peter. "Pat Boone," *Record Collector.* n19 (March 1981) 31–36. il., disc.

Ressner, Jeffrey. "Pat Boone," *Rolling Stone.* n576 (April 19, 1990) 89–91, 124. il., int.

Carter, Mel

Eberwein, Eric. "Mel Carter: Still a Boy in Love With Pop Music," *Goldmine.* n121 (March 15, 1985) 12–16. il.

Chordettes

Tamarkin, Jeff. "The Chordettes: Four Girls, a Sandman, and a Lollipop," *Goldmine.* n171 (February 13, 1987) 22, 30. il.

Cole, Nat "King"

Doggett, Peter. "Nat King Cole," *Record Collector.* n66 (February 1985) 21–28. il., disc.

Haskins, James, with Kathleen Benson. *Nat King Cole.* New York: Stein and Day, 1984. il.

Pelletier, Paul, comp. "Nat King Cole Complete U.K. Discography," *Record Collector.* n66 (February 1985) 23–28. il., disc.

Teubig, Klaus. *Straighten Up and Fly Right: A Chronology/ Discography of Nat 'King' Cole Jazz Recordings From 1936– 1950.* Berlin, West Germany: K. Teubig, 1987. il., disc.

Tosches, Nick. "Nat King Cole: Beyond Pink Cadillacs," In: *Unsung Heroes of Rock 'N' Roll.* pp. 26–32. il.

Crew-Cuts (See also: Cover Recordings)

Kearney, Mark, and Randy Ray. "The Crew-Cuts: Bridging the Gap," *Goldmine.* n212 (September 9, 1988) 18, 67. il.

Crosby, Bing

Crosby, Kathryn. *My Life With Bing.* Wheeling, IL: Collage, 1983. il., bio.

Giddins, Gary. "Bing For the Millions," In: *Riding on a Blue Note.* pp. 14–21. il.

Koening, Joseph. *Bing.* New York: Dell, 1977. il., bio.

Morgereth, Timothy A., comp. *Bing Crosby: A Discography, Radio Program List, and Filmography.* Jefferson, NC: McFarland, 1987. il., disc.

O'Connor, Sheldon, with Gord Atkinson. *Bing: A Voice for all Seasons.* Tralee, Kerry, Ireland: Kerryman, 1984. il.

Thomas, Bob. *The One and Only Bing.* New York: Grosset and Dunlap, 1977. il., bio.

Crosby, Gary (See also: Bing Crosby)

Crosby, Gary, and Ross Firestone. *Going My Own Way.* Garden City, NY: Doubleday, 1983. il., bio.

Fisher, Eddie

Fisher, Eddie. *Eddie: My Life, My Loves.* New York: Harper, 1981. il., bio.

Greene, Myrna. *You Gotta Have Heart: The Eddie Fisher Story.* New York: Eriksson, 1978. il., bio.

Four Freshmen

Ashley, Dennis. "The Four Freshmen," *Classic Wax.* n3 (May 1981) 7–9. il.

Linder, Mark. "The Four Freshmen: Forty Years and Going Strong," *Goldmine.* n193 (January 1, 1988) 14, 102. il.

Four Lads

Kearney, Mark, and Randy Ray. "The Four Lads: They Had Moments to Remember," *Goldmine.* n205 (June 3, 1988) 24, 79. il.

Hilltoppers

Stierle, Wayne. "The Hilltoppers: From Hit Pop Act to Vanishing Act," *Goldmine.* n190 (November 9, 1987) 24, 133. il.

Laine, Frankie

Arnold, Thomas K. "Frankie Laine: Still Going Strong at 70," *Goldmine.* n90 (November 1983) 16–17, 34, 36ff. il.

Jones, Peter. "Frankie Laine," *Record Collector.* n27 (November 1981) 36–43. il., disc.

Lanson, Snooky

Elrod, Bruce. "Snooky Lanson Interviewed," *DISCoveries.* 1
(November 1988) 107. il., int.

Lee, Peggy

Falzarano, Gina. "30 Years of Fever," *DISCoveries.* 1 (July–
August 1988) 19–22. il., bio.

Lennon Sisters

Paquette, Rene E. "The Lennon Sisters: Thirty Years of
Beautiful Harmony," *Goldmine.* n141 (December 20,
1985) 18–20. il., bio.

Liberace

"Liberace: 40 Glittering Years in Show Business," *Billboard.* 97
(March 30, 1985) L1–20. il., bio.

Thomas, Bob. *Liberace: The True Story.* New York: St. Martin's,
1987. il., bio.

London, Julie

Bogart, Charles H. "Julie London: Julie is Her Name,"
Goldmine. n92 (January 1984) 25, 140, 146. il.

Pelletier, Paul. "Julie London," *Record Collector.* n45 (May
1983) 31–34. il., disc.

Mancini, Henry

Caps, John. "Henry Mancini: On Scoring and Recording," In:
Motion Picture Music, ed. by Lue Van de Ven. pp. 89–91. il.

Upton, Rich. "Henry Mancini: Where Were the Real Scores?," *Goldmine.* n152 (May 23, 1986) 73. il.

Mathis, Johnny

Barnett, Dave. "Johnny Mathis," *Record Collector.* n106 (June 1988) 61–66. il., disc.

Jasper, Tony. *Johnny: The Authorized Biography of Johnny Mathis.* London: Comet, 1984. il., disc., filmog. Originally published by W.H. Allen (1983).

Kanakaris, Alex. "A Portrait of . . . Johnny Mathis," *Classic Wax.* n2 (January 1981) 3–5. il.

McGuire Sisters

"New Acts," *Variety.* 320 (August 7, 1985) 77.

Miller, Mitch

Fox, Ted. "Mitch Miller," In: *In the Groove.* pp. 25–71. il.

Page, Patti

Bowling, Angela. "Patti Page: For 40 Years 'The Singing Rage'," *Goldmine.* n164 (November 7, 1986) 18, 22–23. il.

Page, Patti. *Once Upon a Dream.* New York: Popular Library, 1960. il.

Paul, Les, and Mary Ford (r.n.: Lester William Polfus)

Fink, Stu. "Les Paul: Inventor, Innovator, Hit Musician . . . Redhead," *Goldmine.* n193 (December 18, 1987) 8–10, 26. il.

Flippo, Chet. "I Sing the Body Electric: The Rolling Stone Interview With Les Paul," *Rolling Stone.* n180 (February 13, 1975) 44–52, 54–55. il., int.

Griggs, Bill. "The Wizard of Waukesa: An Interview With Les Paul," *Rockin' 50s.* n18 (June 1989) 21–23. il., int.

Jeske, Lee. "Les Paul: The Man, the Guitar, the Legend," *Cash Box.* LI:44 (May 7, 1988) 6–7, 18. int.

Kienzle, Rich. "Les Paul," In: *Great Guitarists.* pp. 142–147.

Ray, Johnnie

Hodenfield, Chris. "Johnnie Ray: The Tears Have Dried," *Rolling Stone.* n108 (May 11, 1972) 10.

Parker, Brian, and Peter Jones. "The Johnnie Ray Story," *Record Collector.* n18 (February 1981) 30–34. il., disc.

Reese, Della

Shaw, Arnold. "Della Reese Interview," In: *The Rockin' 50s.* pp. 201–205. il., int.

Sinatra, Frank

Adler, Bill. *Sinatra: The Man and the Myth; An Unauthorized Biography.* New York: New American Library, 1987. il., bio.

Barnes, Ken, ed. *Sinatra and the Great Song Stylists.* London: Allan, 1972. il.

Brown, Leigh. "Frank Sinatra: The Swoon Years (1942–1946)," *Goldmine.* n234 (July 14, 1989) 76–77. il., bio.

Doggett, Peter. "Frank Sinatra's EPs and Early Singles," *Record Collector.* n90 (February 1987) 45–47. il., disc.

Frank, Alan. *Sinatra.* London: Hamlyn, 1984, c1978. il., bio.

Gehman, Richard. *Sinatra and His Rat Pack.* New York: Belmont, 1961. il., bio.

Giddins, Gary. "Frank Sinatra," In: *Rhythm-A-Ning.* pp. 225–235. il.

Giddins, Gary. "The Once and Future Sinatra," In: *Rising on a Blue Note.* pp. 62–70. il.

Giddins, Gary. "The One and Only Frank Sinatra," *Stereo Review.* 48 (February 1984) 52–58. il.

Goddard, Peter. *Frank Sinatra: The Man, the Myth, and the Music.* Canada: Greywood, 1973. il., bio.

Home, Robin D. *Sinatra.* London: Michael Joseph, 1962. il., bio.

Jewell, Derek. *Frank Sinatra: A Celebration.* Boston: Little, Brown, 1985. il.

Kelley, Kitty. *His Way: The Unauthorized Biography of Frank Sinatra.* New York: Bantam, 1986. il., bio.

Pelletier, Paul, comp. "Complete U.K. Discography of Frank Sinatra's EPs and Early Singles," *Record Collector.* n90 (February 1987) 46–47. il., disc.

Pelletier, Paul. "Frank Sinatra's U.K. Singles," *Record Collector.* n51 (November 1983) 30–35. il., disc.

Peters, Richard. *The Frank Sinatra Scrapbook: His Life and Times in Words and Pictures—Incorporating the Sinatra Sessions.* New York: St. Martin's, 1983. il., bio.

Rockwell, John. *Sinatra: An American Classic.* New York: Rolling Stone, 1984. il.

Sciacca, Tony. *Sinatra.* New York: Pinnacle, 1976. il., bio.

Sinatra, Nancy. *Frank Sinatra: My Father.* New York: Pocket, 1985. il., bio.

Turner, John Frayn. *Frank Sinatra: A Personal Portrait.* Tunbridge Wells, U.K.: Midas, 1984. il., bio.

Weisman, Eric Robert. "Wine, Women, and Song: Frank Sinatra and the Rhetoric of Whoopee," *Pennsylvania Speech Communication Annual.* 32 (1976) 67–79.

Sinatra, Frank, Jr. (See also: Frank Sinatra)

Turkington, Gregg. "Frank Sinatra, Jr.: His Way," *Goldmine.* n211 (August 26, 1988) 72, 76–77. il., bio.

Starr, Kay

Brown, Leigh. "Kay Starr: The Great Starr," *Goldmine.* n168 (January 2, 1987) 6, 20. il.

Storm, Gale

Storm, Gale. *I Ain't Down Yet.* Indianapolis: Bobbs-Merrill, 1981. il., autobio.

Vaughan, Sarah

Giddins, Gary. "Divine and Mortal," In: *Riding on a Blue Note.* pp. 48–56. il.

Giddins, Gary. "Sarah Vaughan," In: *Rhythm-A-Ning.* pp. 26–34. il.

Lee, Richard. "Sarah Vaughan: Cool, Calm, and Classic," *After Dark.* 9 (September 1976) 28–30. il.

Washington, Dinah

Beachley, Chris, and Carolyn Horne. "Dinah Washington: The Queen of the Blues," *It Will Stand.* n8/9 (198?) 4–6. il.

Cotten, Lee. "Dinah Washington," In: *Shake, Rattle, and Roll.* pp. 203–204. il.

Haskins, James. *Queen of the Blues: A Biography of Dinah Washington.* New York: William Morrow, 1987. il., bio.

Welk, Lawrence

Coakley, Mary L. *Mister Music Maker: Lawrence Welk.* Garden City, NY: Doubleday, 1958. il., bio.

Schwienher, William K. *Lawrence Welk: An American Institution.* Chicago: Nelson-Hall, 1980. il., bio.

Wilson, Nancy

Pike, Jon R. "Nancy Wilson: She Did It Her Way," *Goldmine.* n248 (January 26, 1990) 32, 74. il.

2. THE BEAT ERA (1956–1958)

General Sources

Baker, Chuck. *The Rockin' Fifties: A Rock and Roll Scrapbook; A Fast Encounter With the General That Spawned Rock and Roll and Student Unrest, Howdy Doody and Revolution, Elvis Presley and Flights in Space!* Woodland Hills, CA: Avanco, 1973. il., bibl., disc.
Brief text, complemented by photos depicting U.S. society during that era.

Bane, Michael. *White Boy Singin' the Blues: The Black Roots of White Rock.* New York: Penguin, 1982. il.

Belz, Carl. *The Story of Rock.* Second Edition. New York: Harper and Row, 1972. il.

Busnar, Gene. *It's Rock 'N' Roll: A Musical History of the Fabulous Fifties.* New York: Wanderer, 1979. il.

Carter, Tom. "Rock Rolled Into Lexington Via Records, Radio, Clubs," *Lexington (Kentucky) Herald-Leader.* (July 7, 1985) 1D, 3D. il.

Cohn, Nik. "Classic Rock," In: *Ball the Wall.* pp. 72–91. il.

Colman, Stuart. *They Kept on Rockin': The Giants of Rock 'N' Roll.* Poole, Dorset, U.K.: Blandford, 1982. il., bio.

Cooper, B. Lee. " 'Just Let Me Hear Some of That . . . ': Discographies of Fifty Classic Rock Era Performers," *JEMF Quarterly*. n74 (Fall 1983/Winter 1984) 100–116. disc.

Curtis, James M. *Rock Eras: Interpretations of Music and Society, 1954–1984.* Bowling Green, OH: Bowling Green State University Popular Press, 1987. il.

"Deep South R&R Hassle," *Billboard.* 68 (April 7, 1956) 20.

Edwards, Don. "Rock 'N' Roll, Lexington Not a Perfect Match in '55," *Lexington (Kentucky) Herald-Leader.* (July 7, 1985) 12A.

Elson, Howard. *Early Rockers.* New York: Proteus, 1982. il.

Ewen, David. "The Rock Revolution" and "Rock Around the Clock . . . ," In: *All the Years.* pp. 552–569; 611–639. il.

Gillett, Charlie. "Five Styles of Rock 'N' Roll," In: *The Sound of the City.* pp. 29–44. il.

"Great Rock and Roll Controversy . . . ," *Look.* 20 (June 26, 1956) 40–48. il.

Griggs, Bill. "The Rock 'N' Roll Era (or What Makes the 1950's so Unique?)," *Rockin' 50s.* n1 (August 1986) 3–5. il.

Guralnick, Peter. "Rock 'N' Roll Music: Going Up and Coming Down," In: *Feel Like Going Home.* pp. 2–19. il.

Hamm, Charles. " 'Rock Around the Clock'; or, the Rise of Rock 'N' Roll," In: *Yesterdays.* pp. 391–424. il.

Hibbard, Don J., and Carol Kaleiahoha. "In the Beginning," In: *The Role of Rock*. pp. 7–21. il.

Kamin, Jonathan. "The White R&B Audience and the Music Industry, 1952–1956," *Popular Music and Society*. 4 (1975) 170–187.

Kelly, William P. "Running on Empty: Reimaging Rock and Roll," *Journal of American Culture*. 4 (Winter 1981) 152–159.

Kinder, Bob. *The Best of the First: The Early Days of Rock and Roll*. Chicago: Adams, 1986. il.

Loder, Kurt. "The Music That Changed the World," *Rolling Stone*. n467 (February 13, 1986) 49–50. il.

Middleton, Richard. "Rock 'N' Roll," In: *Popular Music and the Blues*. pp. 148–161. il.

Morris, Chris. "Thirty Years Later . . . It Was a Very Good Year For Good Old Rock 'N' Roll," *Billboard*. 99 (December 26, 1987) Y-11, Y-45, Y-47.

O'Neill, William O. "The Rise of Rock and Roll," In: *American High: The Years of Confidence, 1945–1960*. pp. 266–269. il.

Palmer, Robert. "Rock Begins," In: *The Rolling Stone Illustrated History of Rock and Roll*. pp. 3–14. il.

Postol, Todd. "Reinterpreting the Fifties: Changing Views of a 'Dull' Decade," *Journal of American Culture*. 8 (Summer 1985) 39–45.

Robinson, Red, and Peggy Hodgins. *Rockbound: Rock 'N' Roll Encounters, 1955–1969.* Surrey, British Columbia, Canada: Hancock House, 1983. il.

Samuels, Gertrude. "Why They Rock 'N' Roll—and Should They?," *New York Times Magazine.* (January 12, 1958) 19. il.

Scheurer, Timothy E. "Country, Folk, and the Roots of Rock 'N' Roll," In: *American Popular Music—Volume Two: The Age of Rock.* pp. 9–12. il.

Shaw, Arnold. "Popular Music From Minstrel Songs to Rock and Roll," In: *One Hundred Years of Music in America,* ed. by Paul Henry Lang. pp. 140–168. il.

Shaw, Arnold. "The Rock Revolution," *Sonneck Society Newsletter.* 4 (Spring 1978) 16–17.

Shaw, Arnold. "When It Started: Rockabilly, Haley, and Presley," In: *The Rock Revolution.* pp. 19–25. il.

Szatmary, David P. "The Blues, Rock 'N' Roll, and Racism," In: *Rockin' in Time.* pp. 1–28. il.

Willoughby, Larry. "Rock 'N' Roll," In: *Texas Rhythm/Texas Rhyme.* pp. 83–95. il.

Songwriters

BLACKWELL, OTIS

Giddings, Gary. "Just How Much Did Elvis Learn From Otis Blackwell?," In: *Riding on a Blue Note.* pp. 28–38. il.

Hinkley. D. "Profile: Otis Blackwell," *BMI.* n2 (1986) 24. il.

Kenton, Gary. "Otis Blackwell: Handy Man on the Comeback Trail," *Record Profile Magazine.* n8 (December 1984) 6–8. il.

Russell, Tom. "Otis Blackwell: Don't Be Cruel," *Goldmine.* n183 (July 31, 1987) 16, 28. il.

Topping, Ray, comp. "Otis Blackwell Discography," *Goldmine.* n85 (June 1983) 18. disc.

BRYANT, BOUDLEAUX, AND FELICE

"Felice and Boudleaux Bryant," *BMI.* n1 (1986) 61. il., bio.

Flippo, Chet. "Boudleaux Bryant 1920–1987: a Remembrance," *BMI.* (Fall 1987) 16–19.

"Hall of Fame Inductees," *Variety.* 321 (November 27, 1985) 139.

Loder, Kurt. "Obituary: Boudleaux Bryant: 1920–1987," *Rolling Stone.* n506 (August 13, 1987) 14. il.

(Obituary), *Notes.* 44:4 (1988) 697.

Oermann, Bob. "Boudleaux Bryant," *BMI.* n4 (1982) 26–27. il.

Pollock, Bruce. "Felice and Boudleaux Bryant," In: *In Their Own Words.* pp. 135–146. il.

LEIBER, JERRY, AND MIKE STOLLER

Fricke, David. "Leiber & Stoller," *Rolling Stone.* n576 (April 19, 1990) 97–100. il., int.

Pruter, Robert. "Edith Piaf: She Borrowed from the Leiber-Stoller Songbook," *Goldmine.* n193 (December 18, 1987) 18, 30. il.

Zimmerman, K. "Leiber-Stoller Says: Don't Be Cruel, Dismiss Spector-Klein Lawsuit," *Variety.* 334 (January 25, 1989) 4.

Bell, Freddie, and the Bellboys

Russell, Wayne. "Freddie Bell and the Bellboys: Rockin' Was Their Business," *Goldmine.* n181 (July 3, 1987) 20, 85. il.

Berry, Chuck

Aletti, Vince. "Chuck Berry Tells All—Sort of: The Rock Legend Sits for a Candid Film Portrait and Writes His Own Life Story," *Rolling Stone.* n514 (December 3, 1987) 71–74. il., int.

Aronoff, K. "Rock Perspectives: Chuck and Bo," *Modern Drummer.* 13 (January 1989) 46–47. mus.

Belz, Carl. "Chuck Berry: Folk Poet of the Fifties," In: *The Story of Rock.* pp. 61–66. il.

Berry, Chuck. *Chuck Berry: The Autobiography.* New York: Harmony, 1987. il., autobio.

"Berry Gets $$ in Sugar Hill Dispute," *Billboard.* 97 (July 27, 1985) 72.

Briggs, David. "Oh, What a Thrill!," *Now Dig This.* n66 (September 1988) 16–17. il.

Cajiao, Trevor. "21 Little-Known Facts About Chuck Berry," *Now Dig This.* n60 (March 1988) 18–19. il.

Christgau, Robert. "Chuck Berry: Eternal Rock and Roller," In: *Any Old Way You Choose It.* pp. 140–148. il.

"Chuck Berry," *The Golden Age.* n12 (September 1987) 8–33. il., bio.

"Chuck Berry Discography—Part One: Singles," *R-O-C-K.* n4 (1981) 8–27. il., disc.

Clee, Ken, comp. "Chuck Berry Discography," *Goldmine.* n42 (November 1979) 8. disc.

Cook, Phil. "Chuck Berry," *Record Collector.* n19 (March 1981) 4–10. il., disc.

Cooper, B. Lee. "Chuck Berry and the American Motor Car," *Music World.* n86 (June 1981) 18–23. il.

Cooper, B. Lee. " 'Nothin' Outrun My V-8 Ford': Chuck Berry and the American Motor Car, 1955–1979," *JEMF Quarterly.* 16 (Spring 1980) 18–23.

Corliss, Richard. "Still Reelin', Still Rockin'," *Time.* (October 19, 1987) 84. il., int.

Cotten, Lee. "Chuck Berry," In: *Shake, Rattle, and Roll.* pp. 264–266. il.

DeWitt, Howard A. *Chuck Berry: Rock 'N' Roll Music.* Second Edition. Ann Arbor, MI: Pierian, 1985. il.

"Discography—Chuck Berry (1955–1963)," *Record Finder.* n53 (January 1984) 12–16. disc.

"Feedback," *The Golden Age.* n14 (1988) 25–28. il.

Flanagan, Bill. "Chuck Berry," In: *Written in My Soul.* pp. 76 85. il.

Furek, Maxim. "Spotlight on Chuck Berry," *Rockin' 50s.* n8 (October 1987) 9–16. il.

Gambaccini, Paul. "Chuck Berry," In: *Masters of Rock.* pp. 73–80. il.

Gray, Susan. "Chuck Berry—Bio," *The Golden Age.* n12 (September 1987) 4–7. il., bio.

Greene, Bob. "Rock 'N' Roll in Outer Space," *San Francisco Chronicle.* (December 7, 1980) 2. il.

Hilburn, Robert. "Still Rockin' at 60," *Detroit News.* (October 29, 1986) 1D, 6D. il.

Huffhines, Kathy. "Chuck Berry is Ready to Talk," *Detroit Free Press.* (October 18, 1987) 1E, 4E. il.

Jelot-Blanc, Jean-Jacques. *Chuck Berry.* Paris: Horus, 1980. il.

Kienzle, Rich. "Chuck Berry," In: *Great Guitarists*. pp. 182–185. il.

Lydon, Michael. "Chuck Berry," In: *Rock Folk*. pp. 1–23. il.

McCullaugh, J. "Stars Sign on for Filmed Tribute to Chuck Berry," *Billboard*. 98 (August 23, 1986) 94. Re: *Chuck Berry: Hail! Hail! Rock 'N' Roll.*

"Medley: Unadulterated Berry," *High Fidelity/Musical America*. 36 (July 1986) 54.

Moonoogian, George A. "The Earliest Chuck Berry Recordings?," *DISCoveries*. 1 (October 1988) 14–15. il.

Moonoogian, George A. "Walking Down Broadway," *DISCoveries*. 1 (December 1988) 42.

Murry, Charles Shaar. "Chuck Berry," *The History of Rock*. n4 (1982) 64–68. il.

Neely, Kim. "Berry Faces Drug, Child-Abuse Charges," *Rolling Stone*. n586 (September 6, 1990) 30.

Neely, Kim. "DEA Targets Chuck Berry," *Rolling Stone*. n585 (August 23, 1990) 34. il.

Reff, Morten, comp. "The Chuck Berry Discography," In: *Chuck Berry: Rock 'N' Roll Music*. pp. 175–274. il., disc.

Reff, Morten. "Chuck Berry Discography—Part Two," *Whole Lotta Rockin'*. n9 (February 1974) 23. disc.

Reff, Morten. "Chuck Berry—Words and Music," *Rockin' 50s*. n8 (October 1987) 22–23. il.

"The Rock and Roll Hall of Fame: Chuck Berry," *BMI.* n1 (1986) 32. il., bio.

"Rocky Birthday for Chuck Berry," *Detroit Free Press.* (October 19, 1986) 1F, 6F. il.

Roth, Arlen. "Hot Guitar: The Flash of Chuck Berry," *Guitar Player.* 18 (June 1984) 118.

Shaw, Arnold. "Chuck Berry," In: *The Rockin' 50s.* pp. 144–147. il.

Simels, Steve. "Chuck Berry's Rock-and-Roll," *Stereo Review.* 51 (September 1986) 110.

Stambler, Irwin. "Berry, Chuck," In: *The Encyclopedia of Pop, Rock and Soul.* pp. 50–52. il.

"Starspot: Chuck Berry," *Video Review.* (May 1988) 14. il., int.

"Ten Pioneers of Rock Selected for Induction to New Hall of Fame," *Variety.* 321 (November 27, 1985) 139.

Topping, Ray, comp. "Chuck Berry Discography," *Goldmine.* n90 (November 1983) 20–21. il., disc.

Vito, Rick. "The Chuck Berry Style: A Modern Rocker Pays Tribute to the Master," *Guitar Player.* 18 (June 1984) 72–75. il., int.

Wheeler, Tom. "Chuck Berry: The Interview," *Guitar Player.* 22 (March 1988) 56–63. il., int.

Wheeler, Tom. "Chuck Berry: The Records," *Guitar Player.* 22 (March 1988) 64–67. disc.

Wheeler, Tom. "Chuck Berry: The Story," *Guitar Player.* 22 (March 1988) 50–54. il., bio.

White, Timothy. "Chuck Berry," In: *Rock Stars.* pp. 42–47. il.

Cochran, Eddie

Barrett, Tony. "Remembering Eddie Cochran," *Now Dig This.* n49 (April 1987) 18–21. il.

Beard, Will. "Eddie Cochran: British E.P. Discography," *New Rockpile.* n11 (Summer 1974) 2. disc.

Bush, Willaim J. "Eddie Cochran: The Legend Lives On," *Guitar Player.* 17 (December 1983) 71–79. il.

Cohn, Nik. "Eddie Cochran," In: *Rock: From the Beginning.* pp. 44–46. il.

Doggett, Peter. "Eddie Cochran," *Record Collector.* n21 (May 1981) 36–42. il., disc.

Doggett, Peter. "Eddie Cochran," *Record Collector.* n79 (March 1986) 9–14. il., disc.

"Eddie Cochran—Discography (Part One)," *The Golden Age.* n17 (1988) 12–16. disc.

"Eddie Cochran—The Early Years," *The Golden Age.* n17 (1988) 10–11. il.

"Eddie Cochran Recording File: Part One," *New Kommotion.* n19 (Spring 1978) 49–50. il.

"Eddie Cochran Recording File: Part Two," *New Kommotion.* n20 (Summer 1978) 21.

Eder, Bruce. "Eddie Cochran: Somethin' Else," *Goldmine.* n238 (September 8, 1989) 16–18, 22–24. il.

Lassman, David P. "Spotlight on Eddie Cochran," *Rockin' 50s.* n12 (June 1988) 10–16. il.

Leigh, Spencer. "Eddie Cochran: The Final Tour!," *Record Collector.* n107 (July 1988) 32–34. il.

Pugash, Mark. "Cochran: Adept Musician and Strong Songwriter," *Goldmine.* n132 (August 16, 1985) 78. il.

Stambler, Irwin. "Cochran, Eddie," In: *The Encyclopedia of Pop, Rock and Soul.* pp. 135–136.

Umphred, Neal. "Eddie Cochran Discography and Price Guide," *Goldmine.* n238 (September 8, 1989) 20, 24. disc.

Comstock, Bobby

Jones, Wayne. "Bobby Comstock," In: *Rockin', Rollin', and Rappin'.* pp. 22–24. il.

The Crickets (See also: Buddy Holly)

Bell, Argyle. "Joe B. Mauldin," *Goldmine.* n223 (February 10, 1989) 8–9. il.

Fink, Stu. "The Show Must Go On: Bobby Vee, Dion, and Tommy Allsup on the Days After the Crash," *Goldmine.* n223 (February 10, 1989) 20–22. il.

Firminger, John. "The Crickets," *Record Collector.* n128 (April 1990) 42–46. il., disc.

Firminger, John. "The Crickets in Alphabetical Order! Part Eight," *Now Dig This.* n76 (July 1989) 24–25. il.

Firminger, John. "The Crickets in Alphabetical Order! Part Eleven," *Now Dig This.* n79 (October 1989) 14. il.

Firminger, John. "The Crickets in Alphabetical Order! Part Five," *Now Dig This.* n73 (April 1989) 16–17. il.

Firminger, John. "The Crickets in Alphabetical Order! Part Four," *Now Dig This.* n72 (March 1989) 13. il.

Firminger, John. "The Crickets in Alphabetical Order! Part Nine," *Now Dig This.* n77 (August 1989) 10. il.

Firminger, John. "The Crickets in Alphabetical Order! Part One," *Now Dig This.* n69 (December 1988) 13. il.

Firminger, John. "The Crickets in Alphabetical Order! Part Seven," *Now Dig This.* n75 (June 1989) 24. il.

Firminger, John. "The Crickets in Alphabetical Order! Part Six," *Now Dig This.* n74 (May 1989) 13. il.

Firminger, John. "The Crickets in Alphabetical Order! Part Ten," *Now Dig This.* n78 (September 1989) 15. il.

Firminger, John. "The Crickets in Alphabetical Order! Part Thirteen," *Now Dig This.* n81 (December 1989) 16–17. il.

Firminger, John. "The Crickets in Alphabetical Order! Part Three," *Now Dig This.* n71 (February 1989) 8. il.

Firminger, John. "The Crickets in Alphabetical Order! Part Twelve," *Now Dig This.* n80 (November 1989) 28. il.

Firminger, John. "The Crickets in Alphabetical Order! Part Two," *Now Dig This.* n70 (January 1989) 13. il.

Griggs, Bill. "Spotlight on the Crickets," *Rockin' 50s.* n7 (August 1987) 9–16. il.

Miller, W.F. "Rock Pioneer," *Modern Drummer.* 9 (June 1985) 20–23ff. il., bio., int. w/Jerry Allison.

Stidom, Larry. "John Pickering and the Picks: Behind the Crickets Sound—Part One," *Goldmine.* n107 (August 31, 1984) 22–33. il.

Stidom, Larry. "John Pickering and the Picks: Behind the Crickets Sound—Part Two," *Goldmine.* n108 (September 14, 1984) 34–40. il.

Esquerita (r.n.: Eskew Reeder)

Carter, Johnny. "Who Was Esquerita?," *Rockin' 50s.* n6 (June 1987) 23. il.

Topping, Ray, comp. "Esquerita Discography," *New Kommotion.* n21 (1979), 15–16. disc.

White, Chas. "Esquerita is Dead," *Now Dig This.* n49 (April 1987) 37. il.

Everly Brothers (See also: John Fogerty)

Arblaster, Roy, and Clive Leah, comps. "The Everly Brothers Complete U.K. EPs and LPs Discography," *Record Collector.* n49 (September 1983) 6–7. disc.

Arblaster, Roy. "The Everly Brothers Solo Releases," *Record Collector.* n63 (November 1984) 15–18. il., disc.

Arblaster, Roy. "The Everly Brothers' U.K. Albums," *Record Collector.* n49 (September 1983) 3–7. il.

Baker, Glenn A. "Promoter Inexperience Cited in Everlys Tour Shortful," *Billboard.* 98 (January 11, 1986) 9.

Berman, Jay. "Spotlight on the Everly Brothers," *Rockin' 50s.* n3 (December 1986) 9–17. il.

Bleiel, Jeff. "Phil Everly: Living Alone," *Goldmine.* n211 (August 26, 1988) 73, 77. il.

Booth, Dave "Daddy Cool". "The Everly Brothers," *Goldmine.* n94 (March 2, 1984) 14–15, 18, 24, 28ff. il.

Doggett, Peter. "The Everly Brothers: Their U.K. Singles," *Record Collector.* n31 (March 1982) 13–19. il., disc.

"Don and Phil," *Now Dig This.* n55 (October 1987) 18–21. il.

"Don (Everly) to John (Fogerty) Brother to Brother," *Musician.* n93 (July 1986) 42–44. il.

Firminger, John. "It's Everly Time!," *Now Dig This.* n19 (October 1984) 26. il.

Hosum, John, comp. *Living Legends: The History of the Everly Brothers on Record—An Illustrated Discography.* Seattle: Foreverly, 1985. il., disc.

Isler, Scott. "The Everlys: Brothers in Arms," *Musician.* n93 (July 1986) 38–48, 104. il.

Karpp, Phyllis. *Ike's Boys: The Story of the Everly Brothers.* Ann Arbor, MI: Pierian, 1988. il., bio., disc.

Keele, Linda, Colin Escott, and Dave "Daddy Cool" Booth, comps. "Everly Brothers Discography," *Goldmine.* n94 (March 2, 1984) 28, 30. disc.

Loder, Kurt. "The Everly Brothers: The Rolling Stone Interview," *Rolling Stone.* n473 (May 8, 1986) 61–64, 84–90. il., int.

McKenna, Kristine. "Don 'N' Phil Sing Bye Bye Breakup," *Los Angeles Times.* (January 15, 1984) 54, 56. il.

Miller, Billy. "The Beat 'N' Sound of the Everly Brothers," *Kicks.* n1 (Spring 1979) 5–13. il.

Naylor, Bob. "The Everly Brothers Story: Part One," *Now Dig This.* n31 (October 1985) 9–11. il., bio.

Naylor, Bob. "The Everly Brothers Story: Part Three," *Now Dig This.* n33 (December 1985) 8–10. il., bio.

Naylor, Bob. "The Everly Brothers Story: Part Two," *Now Dig This.* n32 (November 1985) 9–11. il., bio.

Roblin, A. "Everlys Making Headway With New Single," *Billboard.* 98 (May 17, 1986) 28.

"The Rock and Roll Hall of Fame: The Everly Brothers," *BMI.* n1 (1986) 31. il., bio.

Ryan, Jack. "The Everly Brothers: Together Again," *Record Profile Magazine.* n8 (December 1984) 22–24. il.

Savers, Joan. *The Everly Brothers Rock 'N' Roll Odyssey.* New
    York: Putnam, 1986. il., bio.

Schwed, Mark. "On the Road Again," *The (Columbia, South
    Carolina) State.* (July 5, 1984) 1B, 5B. il.

Sokoloff, Vicky. "The Everly Brothers: Their Solo Careers,"
    Goldmine. n236 (August 11, 1989) 97–100, 108. il.

Stambler, Irwin. "The Everly Brothers," In: *The Encyclopedia of
    Pop, Rock and Soul.* pp. 220–222.

"Ten Pioneers of Rock Selected for Induction to New Hall of
    Fame," *Variety.* 321 (November 27, 1985) 139.

White, Roger. *Walk Right Back: The Story of the Everly Brothers.*
    London: Plexus, 1984. il., bio.

Gracie, Charlie

Aynsley, Steve. "The Fabulous Charlie Gracie: Once a Legend,
    Now a Friend," *Now Dig This.* n18 (September 1984)
    16–21. il.

"Charlie Gracie Discography," *Goldmine.* n24 (March 1978)
    18–19. il., disc.

Hawkins, (Screamin') Jay

Cohen, Scott. "Living Poets Society: Screamin' Jay Hawkins,"
    Spin. 6:1 (April 1990) 98. il., int.

Hawkins, Ronnie

Escott, Brian, and Wile Willie Jeffrey. "Rockin' With Ron-
    nie," *New Kommotion.* n18 (Winter 1978) 4–8. il.

Leigh, Spencer. "Ronnie Hawkins," *Record Collector.* n89 (January 1987) 36–39. il.

Maxie, Waxie. "The Ronnie Hawkins Story," *Record Collector.* n16 (December 1980) 40–43. il., bio., disc.

Melhuish, Martin. "The Rockabilly Rebel: Rompin' Ronnie Hawkins," In: *Heart of Gold: 30 Years of Canadian Pop Music.* pp. 21–25. il.

Yorke, Ritchie. "Ronnie Hawkins," In: *Axes, Chops, and Hot Licks.* pp. 65–71. il.

Holden, Ron

Propes, Steve. "Ron Holden: From Fingerprints to Fame," *Goldmine.* n186 (September 11, 1987) 22, 78. il.

Holly, Buddy (See also: The Crickets)

Beecher, John. "The Buddy Holly Story," *The History of Rock.* n10 (1982) 184–189. il., bio.

Beecher, John. "New Mexican Music," *The History of Rock.* n10 (1982) 190–191. il.

Beecher, John. *Remembering Buddy.* London: Pavilion, 1987. il., bio.

Beecher, John. "The Unreleased Buddy Holly," *Record Collector.* n88 (December 1986) 28–30. il., disc.

Black, Jim. "Buddy Holly Select Price Guide," *Goldmine.* n107 (August 31, 1984) 43–45. il., disc.

Black, Jim, and Bill Griggs. "The Essential Buddy Holly: A Collector's Price Guide," *Goldmine.* n107 (August 31, 1984) 40–42. il., disc.

Booth, Dave "Daddy Cool", and Colin Escott. "Norman Petty: In the Studio With Buddy Holly," *Goldmine.* n107 (August 31, 1984) 14–20. il., int.

Dallas, Karl. "They Died Young," *The History of Rock.* n10 (1982) 194–195. il.

Dawson, Jim. " 'Lost' Holly Tapes Ready for Release," *Goldmine.* n123 (April 12, 1985) 6, 8. il.

Dean, Johnny. "Buddy Holly: A Great Innovator of the 50s," *Record Collector.* n56 (April 1984) 2. il.

Doggett, Peter. "Buddy Holly," *Record Collector.* n56 (April 1984) 3–7. il., disc.

Doggett, Peter. "Buddy Holly," *Record Collector.* n101 (January 1988) 3–9. il., disc.

Doggett, Peter. "Buddy Holly, 1936–1959," *Record Collector.* n114 (February 1989) 37–40. il.

Duncan, Robert. "Buddy Holly: Angel Without Wings," In: *Only the Good Die Young.* pp. 16–20. il.

Everett, Todd. "Buddy Holly: The True Story," In: *Our Best to You—From Record Digest,* ed. by Jerry Osborne. pp. 139–140. il., bio.

Fink, Stu. "Buddy Holly: For Those Who Knew Him," *Goldmine.* n156 (July 18, 1986) 12–18. il.

Fink, Stu. "Buddy Holly: For Those Who Knew Him—Part Two," *Goldmine.* n159 (August 29, 1986) 12–16. il.

Fink, Stu. "Lubbock Festival Remembers Holly," *Goldmine.* n163 (October 24, 1986) 6.

Finkelstein, Stu. "Lubbock 1984: Holly's Legend Lives On," *Goldmine.* n111 (October 26, 1984) 63–64. il.

Firminger, John. "Britain Remembers Buddy Holly," *Now Dig This.* n72 (March 1989) 24. il.

Firminger, John. "Food for Thought," *Now Dig This.* n19 (October 1984) 6. il.

Flippo, Chet. "The Buddy Holly Story," *Rolling Stone.* n274 (September 21, 1978) 49–51. il.

Fong–Torres, Ben. "The Gary Busey Story," *Rolling Stone.* n274 (September 21, 1978) 48, 52–53. il.

Friedman, Kinky. "Buddy Holly's Texas," *Rolling Stone.* n576 (April 19, 1990) 103–106. il.

Glubke, Mark. "February 3, 1959: The Day the Legend Began," *Battle Creek (Michigan) Enquirer.* (February 3, 1989) 1B–2B. il.

Goldrosen, John, and John Beecher. *Remembering Buddy: The Definitive Biography of Buddy Holly.* New York: Penguin, 1986. il., bio.

Griggs, Bill. "Buddy Holly: Beyond the Buddy Holly Boxed Set," *Goldmine.* n202 (April 22, 1988) 12, 28. il.

Griggs, Bill. "The Buddy Holly Legend: Separating Fact From Fiction," *DISCoveries.* 1 (January–February 1988) 26–29. il.

Griggs, Bill. "An Interrupted Bus Trip: New Facts About Buddy Holly's Last Tour," *Goldmine.* n223 (February 10, 1989) 10. il.

Griggs, Bill. "Spotlight on February 3, 1959," *Rockin' 50s.* n16 (February 1989) 6–14. il.

Griggs, Bill. "Who Was 'Ivan'," *Rockin' 50s.* n4 (February 1987) 16–17. il.

"Hall of Fame Inductees," *Variety.* 321 (November 27, 1985) 139.

Hamilton, Bruce. "Lightning Struck Twice That Day," In: *Our Best to You—From Record Digest,* ed. by Jerry Osborne. Prescott, Arizona:*Record Digest, 1979, 213.*

Harris, Paul. "Buddy's Buddies," *Now Dig This.* n67 (October 1988) 18–22. il.

Heatley, Michael. "Not Fade Away," *The History of Rock.* n10 (1982) 181–183. il.

Helene, Kathryn. "Buddy Holly: The Iowa Connection," *The Palimpsest.* 63 (September–October 1982) 150–159. il.

Hepcat, Henry. "Not Fade Away," *Time Barrier Express.* 3 (1979) 15–18. il.

Ingman, John. "New Discoveries," *Now Dig This.* n19 (October 1984) 6.

Ingman, John. "Norman Petty Productions," *Now Dig This.* n19 (October 1984) 3–5. il.

Kelly, Eddie. "Norman Petty Interview," *New Kommotion.* n27 (1983) 35. int.

Kerns, William D. "Buddy Holly Tribute Concert Planned," *Music World and Record Digest.* n58 (August 15, 1979) 8.

Kerns, William D. "Friends of Buddy Holly Gather for Tribute," *Music World and Record Digest.* n63 (September 19, 1979) 8–9. il.

Laing, Dave. *Buddy Holly.* New York: Collier, 1971. il., bio.

Larson, Don. "Report From Clear Lake: 25 and Still Alive," *Goldmine.* 101 (June 8, 1984) 20–21. il.

"Lubbock 1984," *Goldmine.* n107 (August 31, 1984) 39.

"Lubbock 1986," *Goldmine.* n156 (July 18, 1986) 57.

MacNeish, Jerry. "Norman Petty: Setting His Record Labels Straight," *Goldmine.* n156 (July 18, 1986) 20–22, 56. il.

McNutt, Randy. "Buddy Holly," In: *We Wanna Boogie.* pp. 84–87. il.

"MMA Cites Holly, Elects President." *BMI.* n3 (1980) 13.

"Pop Music Academy Adds New Members," *Variety.* 322 (March 12, 1986) 151.

"The Rock and Roll Hall of Fame: Buddy Holly," *BMI.* n1 (1986) 28. il., bio.

Scott, Steve. "Buddy Holly," *Record Collector.* n22 (June 1981) 10–17. il., disc.

Sousa, Lisa M., comp. "Buddy Holly: A Compendium," *One-TwoThreeFour.* (1985) 79–83. il.

"Ten Pioneers of Rock Selected for Induction to New Hall of Fame," *Variety.* 321 (November 27, 1985) 139.

" 'That'll Be the Day' When Putative Cleffers Win Money From MPL," *Variety.* 324 (August 13, 1986) 108.

Tobler, John. *The Buddy Holly Story.* London: Plexus, 1979. il., bio.

Umphred, Neal, comp. "Buddy Holly U.S. Discography and Price Guide," *Goldmine.* n223 (February 10, 1989) 77–78. disc.

Lewis, Jerry Lee (See also: Little Richard; Sam Phillips and Sun Records)

Cajiao, Trevor. "The Jerry Lee Lewis Boxing Match," *Now Dig This.* n79 (October 1989) 22–25. il.

Cocks, Jay. "A Few Rounds With the Killer," *Time.* 121 (March 14, 1983) 98. il.

Cooper, B. Lee. "In Search of Jerry Lee Lewis," *JEMF Quarterly.* 18 (Fall 1982–Winter 1983) 192–193.

Cooper, B. Lee. "Jerry Lee Lewis and Little Richard: Career Parallels in the Lives of the Court Jesters of Rock 'N' Roll," *Music World and Record Digest.* n46 (May 23, 1979) 6.

Cooper, B. Lee. "Jerry Lee Lewis: Rock and Roll's Living Legend," *Fire-Ball Mail.* 19 (May–June 1982) 9–12. il.

Cooper, B. Lee, and James A. Creeth. "Present at the Creation: The Legend of Jerry Lee Lewis on Record, 1956–1963," *Fire-Ball Mail.* 22 (May–June 1984) 9–12. il., disc.

Davis, Hank. "The Jerry Lee Lewis Sun Sound," *Goldmine.* n234 (July 14, 1989) 14.

Escott, Colin. "Jerry Lee Lewis: Huey P. Meaux and the 'Southern Roots' Sessions," *Goldmine.* n196 (January 29, 1988) 38, 40. il.

Escott, Colin. "Jerry Lee Lewis: The Ferriday Wild Man," *Goldmine.* n234 (July 14, 1989) 7–12. il.

Escott, Colin. *Jerry Lee Lewis: The Killer, 1963–1968.* Bremen, West Germany: Bear Family, 1986. il., bio.

Escott, Colin. *Jerry Lee Lewis: The Killer, 1969–1972.* Bremen, West Germany: Bear Family, 1986. il., bio.

Escott, Colin. *Jerry Lee Lewis: The Killer, 1973–1977.* Bremen, West Germany: Bear Family, 1987. il., bio.

Forte, Dan. "Kenny Lovelace: Two Decades With Jerry Lee Lewis," *Guitar Player.* 17 (December 1983) 81–82, 154. il., int.

Gambaccini, Paul. "Jerry Lee Lewis," In: *Track Records.* pp. 93–100. il.

Gamblin, Barrie. "Jerry Lee Lewis: A Post-1970 Discography," *New Kommotion.* n6 (Summer 1974) 22–23. disc.

Gollubier, Bruce. "Spotlight on Jerry Lee Lewis," *Rockin' 50s.* n21 (December 1989) 8–16. il.

Grissim, John. "Jerry Lee Lewis: Higher Than Most...And Getting Higher," *Rolling Stone.* n66 (September 17, 1970) 30–33. il.

Guralnick, Peter. "Jerry Lee Lewis: The Greatest Rocker of Them All," *Fire-Ball Mail.* 22 (January–February 1984) 10–11. il.

Hubner, John. "Jerry Lee Lewis: The Killer at 45," *Goldmine.* n62 (July 1981) 23–25. il.

Humphrey, Mark. "Jerry Lee Lewis: Where the Lord and the Devil Both Have Their Way," *Quarter Notes.* (June 1982) 106–108. il., bio.

Lefebvre, Tania A. *Jerry Lee Lewis: The Killer's Story.* Paris: Horus, 1980. il., bio.

Lewis, Myra, With Murray Silver. *Great Balls of Fire! The Uncensored Story of Jerry Lee Lewis.* New York: St. Martin's, 1989, c1982.

McAuliffe, Jon. "Jerry Lee Lewis: Another Place, Another Time—The Smash Years," *Goldmine.* n176 (April 24, 1978) 16. il.

McNutt, Randy. "Mr. Pumping Piano," In: *We Wanna Boogie.* pp. 103–105. il.

"The Rock and Roll Hall of Fame: Jerry Lee Lewis," *BMI.* n1 (1986) 26. il., bio.

Scott, Steve. "Jerry Lee Lewis," *Record Collector.* n41 (January 1983) 20–26. il., disc.

Seay, David. "The King and the Killer," In: *Stairway to Heaven.* pp. 45–69. il.

Shaw, Arnold. "Jerry Lee Lewis Interview," In: *The Rockin' 50s.* pp. 190–193. il., int.

Tamarkin, Jeff. "Great Balls of Fire! Producer Adam Fields Talks About the New Jerry Lee Lewis Film Biography," *Goldmine.* n234 (July 14, 1989) 16–20. il., int.

"Ten Pioneers of Rock Selected for Induction to New Hall of Fame," *Variety.* 321 (November 27, 1985) 139.

Tosches, Nick. "Behold a Shaking: Jerry Lee Lewis, 1953–1956," *Journal of Country Music.* 9 (October 1981) 4–11. il.

Tosches, Nick. "The Coming of Jerry Lee Lewis," *Journal of Country Music.* 9 (1982) 16–25. il.

Tosches, Nick. "Jerry Lee Lewis: The Smash/Mercury Years," *Goldmine.* n112 (November 9, 1984) 6–22. il.

Tosches, Nick, comp. "Jerry Lee Lewis: The Smash/Mercury Years—Part Two," *Goldmine.* n113 (November 23, 1984) pp. 30–38. il., disc.

Tosches, Nick. "Loud Covenants," In: *Country: The Biggest Music in America.* pp. 23–97. il.

Tosches, Nick. "Whole Lotta Shakin' Goin' On," *Goldmine.* n76 (September 1982) 19. il.

Umphred, Neal, comp. "Jerry Lee Lewis U.S. Sun Records Discography and Price Guide," *Goldmine.* n234 (July 14, 1989) 22–24. disc.

Weize, Richard, comp. "A Preliminary Jerry Lee Lewis Discography," In: *Jerry Lee Lewis: The Killer, 1963–1968,* by Colin Escott. pp. 81–127. disc.

Weize, Richard, comp. "A Preliminary Jerry Lee Lewis Discography," In: *Jerry Lee Lewis: The Killer, 1969–1972,* by Colin Escott. pp. 65–120. disc.

Weize, Richard, comp. "A Preliminary Jerry Lee Lewis Discography (Revised Edition)," In: *Jerry Lee Lewis: The Killer, 1973–1977,* ed. by Colin Escott. pp. 65–120. disc.

White, Timothy. "Jerry Lee Lewis," In: *Rock Stars.* pp. 66–71. il.

Woodford, Chris. "He Is What He Is," *Now Dig This.* n82 (January 1990) 28. il.

Woodford, Chris. "Jerry Lee Lewis Meets the Press," *Now Dig This.* n62 (May 1988) 12–13. il.

Woodford, Chris. "*Still* the Greatest Live Show on Earth," *Now Dig This.* n50 (May 1987) 9–10. il.

Little Richard

Alexander, Alice. "Little Richard: No Rock 'N' Roll, Just Rock of Ages," *Philadelphia Inquirer.* (April 30, 1979) 8A, 10A. il.

Beeson, Frank. "Charles Connor: The Big Beat Behind Little Richard," *Goldmine.* n175 (April 10, 1987) 16–18. il.

Bowen, Pete. "Little Richard—The Specialty Years," *Now Dig This.* n80 (November 1989) 4–8. il.

Clerk, Carol. "Bible Basher," *Melody Maker.* 61 (October 25, 1986) 14. il., int.

Collier, Aldore. "Little Richard Tells How He Got What He Wanted, But Lost What He Had," *Jet.* 67 (November 26, 1984) 60–63. il., int.

Cooper, B. Lee. "Dr. Rock on Little Richard: Speculating on a Long–Awaited Biography," *Record Profile Magazine.* n4 (February–March 1984) 21–22, 25. il.

Cooper, B. Lee, comp. "Selected International Discography of Little Richard Albums, 1952–1983," *Record Profile Magazine.* n4 (February–March 1984) 24–27. disc.

Courtney, Ron. "The Midnight Call to Little Richard," *Record Profile Magazine.* n4 (February–March 1984) 20–25. il.

Doggett, Peter. "Little Richard," *Record Collector.* n69 (May 1985) 32–36. il., disc.

Doggett, Peter. "Little Richard: The Specialty Sessions," *Record Collector.* n125 (January 1990) 62–65. il.

Garodkin, John, Comp. *Little Richard Special.* Second Edition. Praesto, Denmark: Mjolner, 1984. il.

"Guitar Center's Rock Walk Honors Little Richard," *Music Trades.* 134 (December 1986) 50.

Hampshire, Baz. "Dr. Rock and the Georgia Peach," *Now Dig This.* n18 (September 1984) 22–23. il.

Hilburn, Robert. "Chart Full of Miracles for Richard," *Los Angeles Times.* (October 25, 1985) 1, 14. il.

Hirshey, Gerri. "Tooty, Fruity," *Rolling Stone.* n426/427 (July 19–August 2, 1984) 41, 43. il.

Holdship, Bill. "The Quasar Speaks," *Creem.* 16 (January 1985) 44–45. il., int.

Johnstone, Damien. "The Big Show—Rockin' Australia 1957," *Now Dig This.* n37 (April 11, 1986) 16–23. il.

Koda, Cub. "Little Richard and Old Town Doo-Wop Greats," *Goldmine.* n149 (April 11, 1986) 82. il.

Lhamon, W.T., Jr. "Little Richard as a Folk Performer," *Studies in Popular Culture.* 8 (1985) 7–17.

"Little Richard Museum," *Variety.* 318 (April 17, 1985) 231.

McGarvey, Seamus. "Charles Connor: That New Orleans Rhythm Man! Part One," *Now Dig This.* n70 (January 1989) 6–9. il.

McGarvey, Seamus. "Charles Connor: That New Orleans Rhythm Man! Part Two," *Now Dig This.* n71 (February 1989) 9–11. il.

Moonoogian, George A. "Blues Classics Revisited," *Whiskey, Women, and....* n3 (1972) 17–18. il.

Newcombe, Jim. "Toronto Rock 'N' Roll," *Now Dig This.* n78 (September 1989) 16–17. il.

Norman, Philip, with photographs by Annie Leibovitz. "Rocker of Ages," *The (London) Sunday Times Magazine.* (March 3, 1985) 22–29. il.

Puterbaugh, Parke. "Little Richard," *Rolling Stone.* n576 (April 19, 1990) 50–54, 126. il., int.

Raper, Jim. "Classic Cuts: *Here's Little Richard* (1957)," *Now Dig This.* n59 (February 1988) 18–19. il.

"The Rock and Roll Hall of Fame: Little Richard," *BMI.* n1 (1986) 29. il., bio.

Smith, Gary. "Before There Was Michael, There Had to be a . . . Little Richard," *People Weekly Extra.* n26 (November–December 1984) 50–53. il.

Tamarkin, Jeff. "Little Richard Leaves a Message," *Goldmine.* n175 (April 10, 1987) 10–14, 18. il.

"Ten Pioneers of Rock Selected for Induction to New Hall of Fame," *Variety.* 321 (November 27, 1985) 139.

Watts, Michael. "His Majesty," *The History of Rock.* n8 (1982) 148–152. il.

White, Charles. "Excerpts from *The Life and Times of Little Richard: The Quasar of Rock*," *Rolling Stone.* n426/427 (July 19–August 2, 1984) 43–49, 112. il.

White, Chas. "Dr. Rock and the Georgia Peach—Part One," *Now Dig This.* n18 (September 1984) 22–23. il.

White, Chas. "Dr. Rock and the Georgia Peach—Part Three," *Now Dig This.* n20 (November 1984) 22–23. il.

White, Chas. "Dr. Rock and the Georgia Peach—Part Two," *Now Dig This.* n19 (October 1984) 24–25. il.

White, Chas. "Little Richard in Merry England," *Now Dig This.* n33 (December 1985) 24. il.

White, Chas. "Little Richard Update," *Now Dig This.* n71 (February 1989) 31.

White, Timothy. "Little Richard," In: *Rock Stars.* pp. 52–55. il.

Winner, Langdon. "Little Richard," In: *The Rolling Stone Illustrated History of Rock and Roll,* ed. by Jim Miller. pp. 48, 53. il.

Valens, Ritchie

Ebsen, Ragnar, and Gerd Muesfeldt, comps. "Ritchie Valens Discography," *Goldmine.* n168 (January 2, 1987) 59. disc.

Eder, Bruce. "Ritchie Valens," *Goldmine.* n223 (February 10, 1989) 14–18. il.

Griggs, Bill, and Jim Black, comps. "A U.S. Discography of Ritchie Valens," In: *Buddy Holly: A Collector's Guide.* pp. 84–85. il., disc.

"Hackford, Sill Plan Biopic on Valens; Stars Play Mentors," *Variety.* 323 (July 16, 1986) 116. Re. *La Bamba* (film).

Hawkins, Martin. "Ritchie Valens," *The History of Rock.* n10 (1982) 196–197. il.

Mendheim, Beverly A. "Ritchie Valens; Remembering 'The 17-Year-Old Recording Sensation'," *Goldmine.* n168 (January 2, 1987) 22, 59–60. il.

Mendheim, Beverly A. *Ritchie Valens: The First Latino Rocker.* Tempe, AZ: Bilingula Review Press, 1987. il.

Mendheim, Beverly A. "Spotlight on Ritchie Valens," *Rockin' 50s.* n6 (June 1987) 9–16. il.

Pelletier, Paul. "Ritchie Valens," *Record Collector.* n76 (December 1985) 54–56. il., disc.

"Ritchie Valens," *The Golden Age.* n13 (October 1987) 4–9. il.

Umphred, Neal, comp. "Ritchie Valens U.S. Discography and Price Guide," *Goldmine.* n223 (February 10, 1989) 78. disc.

Vincent, Gene

Aynsley, Steve. "Death of a Guitar Hero," *Now Dig This.* n68 (November 1988) 26–27. il.

Aynsley, Steve. "Important Words," *Now Dig This.* n82 (January 1990) 18–21. il.

Cajiao, Trevor, Steve Aynsley, Harry Dodds, and Roger Nunn, comps. "Gene Vincent Discography," In: *I Remember Gene Vincent,* by Alan Vince. pp. 44–50. disc.

Carpenter, John, comp. "Gene Vincent and the Blue Caps—'56 Sessions," *Now Dig This.* n19 (October 1984) 16–19. il.

Clark, Alan. *Gene Vincent: The Screaming End.* West Covina, CA: Leap Frog Productions, 1984. il., bio.

Cook, Phil, and Steve Scott. "Gene Vincent," *Record Collector.* n20 (April 1981) 12–17. il., disc.

Davis, Hank. "Gene Vincent: Race With the Devil," *Goldmine.* n238 (September 8, 1989) 8–10, 14, 111. il.

Dodds, Harry. "The Legendary Guitarists of Gene Vincent," *Now Dig This.* n70 (January 1989) 5–7. il.

Doggett, Peter. "Gene Vincent," *Record Collector.* n70 (June 1985) 25–29. il., disc.

Erskine, Robert. "Spotlight on Gene Vincent," *Rockin' 50s.* n2 (October 1986) 9–15. il.

Finnis, Rob. "Gene Vincent: Powerful, Intense, and Dangerous," *The History of Rock.* n6 (1982) 104–108. il.

Forte, Dan. "Cliff Gallup of Gene Vincent's Blue Caps: Rockabilly Virtuoso," *Guitar Player.* 17 (December 1983) 90–94. il.

"Gene Vincent," *The Golden Age.* n2 (November 1986) 30–32. il.

"Gene Vincent," *The Golden Age.* n13 (October 1987) 10–24. il.

"Gene Vincent—Discography (Part Three)," *The Golden Age.* n17 (1988) 17–25. il., disc.

"Gene Vincent: The Capitol Years," *Record Collector.* n103 (March 1988) 28–31. il., disc.

Hagarty, Britt. *The Day the World Turned Blue: A Biography of Gene Vincent.* Vancouver, Canada: Talon, 1983. il., bio.

Kinder, Bob. "Gene Vincent—1959," In: *The Best of the First.* pp. 9–15. il.

Kirsch, Don. "Jerry Merritt: The Rockin' Guitar Behind Gene Vincent," *Goldmine.* n146 (February 28, 1986) 18–20, 58. il.

McNutt, Randy. "Be-Bop-A-Vincent," In: *We Wanna Boogie.* pp. 97–98. il.

Nunn, Roger. "The Blue Caps are Back!," *Now Dig This.* n67 (October 1988) 8–9. il.

Rowbotham, Cliff. "Gene Vincent on Record, A–Z," *Not Fade Away.* n6 (March 1975) 12–18. il.

Simons, Paul, comp. "Gene Vincent Discography," *Big Beat of the 50's.* n31 (May 1982) 19–24. il., disc.

Stafford, Stafford. "An Original Blue Cap Talks to *Now Dig This,*" *Now Dig This.* n67 (October 1988) 8–9. il.

Umphred, Neal, comp. "Gene Vincent Discography and Price Guide," *Goldmine.* n238 (September 8, 1989) 12, 14. disc.

Vince, Alan. *I Remember Gene Vincent.* Tyne and Wear, U.K.: Now Dig This Special Publications, 1985. il.

Weiser, Ron. "Ahead of His Time: Gene Vincent's Influence in Rock 'N' Roll," *Who Put the Bomp.* n9 (Spring 1972) 9–14. il.

Williams, Larry

Gari, Brian. "Larry Williams: an Infectious Bad Boy," *Goldmine.* n172 (February 27, 1987) 78, 82. il.

Janick, Wayne. "Collectibles of Lucas, Williams, and Others," *Goldmine.* n122 (March 29, 1985) 132. il.

Woodford, Chris. "The Larry Williams Story—Part Five," *Now Dig This.* n61 (April 1988) 14–16. il., bio.

Woodford, Chris. "The Larry Williams Story—Part Four: The British Connection," *Now Dig This.* n60 (March 1988) 25–27. il., bio.

Woodford, Chris. "The Larry Williams Story—Part One," *Now Dig This.* n57 (December 1987) 8–9. il., bio.

Woodford, Chris. "The Larry Williams Story—Part Three: The Great Days," *Now Dig This.* n59 (February 1988) 5–7. il., bio.

Woodford, Chris. "The Larry Williams Story—Part Two," *Now Dig This.* n58 (January 1988) 8–9. il., bio.

Woodford, Chris, and Trevor Cajiao, comps. "Larry Williams Discography," *Now Dig This.* n63 (June 1988) 16–17. disc.

3. DOO-WOP (1954–1957)

General Sources

Brown, Ashley. "The Alchemists," *The History of Rock.* n15 (1982) 281–283. il.

Brown, Geoff. "Doo-Wop," *The History of Rock.* n4 (1982) 69–73. il.

Cooper, B. Lee. "The Black Roots of Popular Music," In: *Images of American Society in Popular Music.* pp. 111–123.

Cummings, Tony. "Doo-Wop: The Streetcorner Harmonisers," In: *The Sound of Philadelphia.* pp. 24–33. il.

Groia, Philip. *They All Sang on the Corner: A Second Look at New York City's Rhythm and Blues Vocal Groups.* Rev. ed. West Hempstead, NY: Phillie Dee Enterprises, 1984.

Hansen, Barry. "Doo-Wop," In: *The Rolling Stone Illustrated History of Rock and Roll,* ed. by Jim Miller. pp. 82–91. il.

Javna, John, comp. *The Doo-Wop Sing-Along Songbook.* New York: St. Martin's, 1986. il.

Larsen, Laurie. "Group Harmony Thrives Despite Downsized Stage," *Record Collector's Monthly.* n16 (January 1984) 8. il.

Nickols, Pete. "Doo-Wop," *Record Collector.* n87 (November 1986) 24–27. il., disc.

Nickols, Pete. "Doo-Wop," *Record Collector.* n88 (December 1986) 45–49. il., disc.

Pruter, Robert. "The Great Debate: R&B Harmony vs. Modern Harmony," *Goldmine.* n53 (October 1980) 173. il.

Redmond, Mike, and Marv Goldberg. "The Doo-Wah Sound: Black Pop Groups of the 1950's," *Yesterday's Memories.* n1 (1975) 22–24, 26. il.

Sicurella, Joe (Moonglow). "Collecting Young Male Tenor-Led Groups," *Goldmine.* n127 (June 7, 1985) 87. il.

Tamarkin, Jeff. "Ambient Sound Records: Group Harmony in the '80s," *Goldmine.* n70 (March 1982) 20, 22–23. il.

Acappella

Geberer, Raanan. "Acappella—in the Mid-1960s," *Goldmine.* n90 (November 1983) 174, 180, 182, 188. il.

Tamarkin, Jeff. "Acappella in the '80s: It's Not Just Doo-Wop Anymore," *Goldmine.* n210 (August 13, 1988) 22, 79. il.

Andrews, Lee, and the Hearts

Clee, Ken, comp. "Lee Andrews and the Hearts Discography," *Music World.* n86 (June 1981) 14–15. disc.

Stafford, John. "Lee Andrews—Interviewed," *Now Dig This.* n72 (March 1989) 26–27. il., int.

Tancredi, L. Carl. "Lee Andrews and the Hearts," *Yesterday's Memories.* n1 (1975) 4–12. il., disc.

Tancredi, L. Carl. "Lee Andrews and the Hearts—Part Two," *Yesterday's Memories.* n3 (1975) 10–12. il.

Ballard, Hank, and the Midnighters; The Royals

Cotten, Lee. "The Midnighters," In: *Shake, Rattle, and Roll.* pp. 173–175. il.

Dawson, Jim. "The Twist: Around and Around and Up and Down," *Goldmine.* n219 (December 16, 1988) 96. il.

Goldberg, Marv. "The Midnighters," *Big Town Review.* n3 (July–August 1972) 48. il.

"Goldmine Value Guide: Hank Ballard and the Midnighters," *Goldmine.* n127 (June 7, 1985) 82.

Grendysa, Peter. "The Royals: Ballard Blows Away the Ballads," *Goldmine.* n210 (August 13, 1988) 29, 77. il.

"Hank Ballard," *The Golden Age.* n8 (May 1987) 7–26. il.

McGarvey, Seamus. "Working With Annie: The Hank Ballard Interview—Part One," *Now Dig This.* n47 (February 1987) 6–7. il., int.

McGarvey, Seamus. "Working With Annie: The Hank Ballard Interview—Part Two," *Now Dig This.* n49 (April 1987) 4–6. il., int.

Nickols, Pete. "It's Finger Poppin' Time: Hank Ballard and

the Midnighters," *Now Dig This.* n3 (October 1985) 28–29. il.

Pruter, Robert. "Hank Ballard: The Original Twist," *Goldmine.* n210 (August 13, 1988) 30, 79. il.

Stambler, Irwin. "Ballard, Hank," In" *The Encyclopedia of Pop, Rock and Soul.* pp. 29–30.

Topping, Ray. "The Midnighters Discography," *Shout.* n62 (January 1971) 5–7. il., disc.

Tosches, Nick. "The Midnighters: From the Sins of Annie to the Twist," In: *Unsung Heroes of Rock 'N' Roll.* pp. 112–115. il.

White, Cliff. "Midnight Man," *The History of Rock.* n25 (1982) 494–495. il.

Brown Dots (See also: 4 Tunes)

Goldberg, Marv. "The Brown Dots and the 4 Tunes," *DISCoveries.* 2 (February 1989) 46–49. il.

Cadets (See: Jacks)

Cadillacs

Gendron, Bernard. "Theodor Adorno Meets the Cadillacs," In: *Studies in Entertainment,* ed. by Tania Modleski.

Newcombe, Jim. "Go, Speedo, Go," *Now Dig This.* n70 (January 1989) 23–25. il.

Cardinals

Grendysa, Peter. "The Cardinals: Birds of a Different Feather," *Goldmine.* n253 (April 6, 1990) 20, 31. il.

Channels (featuring Earl Lewis)

McGarvey, Seamus. "The Channels: Earl Lewis Interviewed," *Now Dig This.* n67 (October 1988) 5–7. il., int.

Chords

Cotten, Lee. "The Chords," In: *Shake, Rattle, and Roll.* pp. 191–192. il.

Goldberg, Marv, and Mike Redmond. "The Chords," *Yesterday's Memories.* n7 (1976) 4–6. il.

Propes, Steve. "The Chords: Hello Again to 'Sh Boom'," *Goldmine.* n180 (June 19, 1987) 6, 12. il.

Clovers

"The Clovers," *The Golden Age.* n6 (March 1987) 27–33. il.

Dallman, Jerry. "From the Clovers to the Classics With Bill Harris," *Guitar Player.* 9 (May 1975) 10, 33, 35, 37–39. il.

Stambler, Irwin. "The Clovers," In: *The Encyclopedia of Pop, Rock and Soul.* pp. 133–134.

Tosches, Nick. "The Clovers: Absalom, Absalom! Doo-wah, Doo-wah!," In: *Unsung Heroes of Rock and Roll.* pp. 96–100. il.

Coasters

"The Coasters," *The Golden Age.* n18 (1988) 12–20. il.

"Coasters Moniker Dropped by Perry in Court Settlement," *Variety.* 319 (June 26, 1985) 91.

Cramlington, Tom, comp. "The Coasters on London Records," *Now Dig This.* n16 (July 1984) 8. il.

Doggett, Peter. "The Coasters," *Record Collector.* n26 (October 1981) 13–18. il., disc.

"15 Elected to Hall of Fame," *Billboard.* 98 (October 18, 1986) 101.

Millar, Bill. "At Smokey Joe's Cafe," *The History of Rock.* n15 (1982) 294–297. il.

"Rock Hall of Fame to Induct 15 Acts," *Variety.* 324 (October 8, 1986) 147.

Stambler, Irwin. "The Coasters," In: *The Encyclopedia of Pop, Rock and Soul.* 134–135.

Crows

Cotten, Lee. "The Crows," In: *Shake, Rattle, and Roll.* p. 169. il.

Gart, Galen. "The Crows: 'Gee', It's a Hit," *Goldmine.* n201 (April 8, 1988) 14, 29. il.

Propes, Steve. "Gee—Part Two: The West Coast Girlfriend," *Goldmine.* n215 (October 21, 1988) 28, 100. il.

Del-Vikings

"New Acts," *Variety.* 324 (October 15, 1986) 178.

Stambler, Irwin. "The Del-Vikings," In: *The Encyclopedia of Pop, Rock and Soul.* pp. 167–168.

Dells

Jones, Wayne, and Robert Pruter. "The Dells—Part One: The Early Years, 1952–1959," *Goldmine.* n100 (May 25, 1984) 30–33. il.

Pruter, Robert. "The Dells—Part Three: The 1970s and 1980s," *Goldmine.* n105 (August 3, 1984) 28–38. il.

Pruter, Robert, with assistance from Wayne Jones. "The Dells—Part Two: The Soul Years in Chicago, 1960–1972," *Goldmine.* n104 (July 20, 1984) 15–26. il.

Dominoes; Billy Ward and the Dominoes (See also: Clifton Chenier; The Drifters; Clyde McPhatter; Jackie Wilson)

Beckman, Jeff. "Bill Ward and the Dominoes," *Big Town Review.* n1 (February–March 1972) 18.

Giddins, Gary. "Placing the Dominoes," In: *Riding on a Blue Note.* pp. 22–27. il.

Stambler, Irwin. "The Dominoes," In: *The Encyclopedia of Pop, Rock and Soul.* pp. 185–186.

Tosches, Nick. "The Dominoes: The Glory of Bubbonia," In: *Unsung Heroes of Rock and Roll.* pp. 101–105. il.

Drifters (See also: Dominoes; Ben E. King; Clyde McPhatter)

Beachley, Chris, and Marv Goldberg. "The Drifters—Let Their Music Play: Part Three," *It Will Stand.* n7 (1979) 4–8. il.

Cotten, Lee. "Clyde McPhatter and the Drifters," In: *Shake, Rattle, and Roll.* pp. 133–134. il.

Davis, Jim. "The Bill Pinkney Story," *Yesterday's Memories.* n5 (1976) 22. il.

Gambaccini, Paul. "The Drifters," In: *Masters of Rock.* pp. 142–150. il.

Ginsburg, David D. "On LP: Clyde McPhatter and the Drifters," *Record Profile Magazine.* n10 (July–August 1985) 43.

Goldberg, Marv, and Mike Redmond. "Starring the Original Drifters," *Record Exchanger.* 4 (December 1974) 4–25. il.

"Hall of Fame Elects New Members," *Rolling Stone.* n514 (December 3, 1987) 15.

Hirshey, Gerri. "Uptown, Saturday Night," In: *Nowhere to Run.* pp. 31–41. il.

Kinder, Bob. "Rudy Lewis and the Drifters," In: *Best of the First.* pp. 63–65. il.

Krutnik, Frank. "The Drifters," *Record Collector.* n39 (November 1982) 50–56. il., disc.

Matthews, Herb. "The Drifters—an Update," *It Will Stand.* n24/25 (198?) 20–23. il.

Matthews, Herb. "You Haven't the Right: The Never Ending Saga of the Drifters," *It Will Stand.* n26 (198?) 26–27. il.

Millar, Bill. *The Drifters: The Rise and Fall of the Black Vocal Group.* New York: Collier, 1981. il., bio.

Millar, Bill. "Under the Boardwalk," *The History of Rock.* n15 (1982) 290–293. il.

Stambler, Irwin. "The Drifters," In: *The Encyclopedia of Pop, Rock and Soul.* pp. 192–193. il.

McPHATTER, CLYDE

"15 Elected to Hall of Fame," *Billboard.* 98 (October 18, 1986) 101.

"Rock Hall of Fame to Induct 15 Acts," *Variety.* 324 (October 8, 1986) 147.

Dubs

McGarvey, Seamus. "New York Rock 'N' Roll and Doo-Wop: The Dubs—'Could This Be Magic'," *Now Dig This.* n78 (September 1989) 10–12. il.

Earls

Jancik, Wayne. "Larry Chance and the Earls," *Record Profile Magazine.* n11 (October–November 1985) 18–20. il.

Tamarkin, Jeff. "Larry Chance: The Earls 'Remember Then' and Now," *Goldmine.* n135 (September 27, 1985) 68–70. il.

Tamarkin, Jeff, comp. "Goldmine Value Guide Discography for Larry Chance and the Earls," *Goldmine.* n140 (December 6, 1985) 89. disc.

El Dorados (See also: Kool Gents)

Galgano, Bob. "El Dorados and Kool Gents," *Bim Bam Boom.* n2 (October–November 1971) 8. il.

Hinckley, Dave, and Marv Goldberg. "The El Dorados," *Yesterday's Memories.* n13 (1979) 35–36. il.

Pruter, Robert. "The El Dorados," *Goldmine.* n244 (December 1, 1989) 20. il.

Elegants

Hill, Randal C. "The Elegants," *Goldmine.* n220 (December 30, 1988) 12. il.

Falcons

Keegan, Kevin. " 'Standing on Guard': A Tribute to James Gibson," *Record Profile Magazine.* n6 (July 1984) 6, 63. il.

Fiestas

Jancik, Wayne. "The Fiestas," *Goldmine.* n244 (December 1, 1989) 24–25. il.

Five Chances

Pruter, Robert. "The Five Chances and Their World of Chicago R&B," *Goldmine.* n253 (April 6, 1990) 18–19, 33. il.

Five Keys

"The Five Keys," *Shout.* n105 (October–November 1975) 13–16. il.

Grendysa, Peter. "The Five Keys," *Goldmine.* n211 (August 26, 1988) 71, 76. il.

5 Royales

Cotten, Lee. "The '5' Royales," In: *Shake, Rattle, and Roll.* pp. 85–86. il.

Five Satins

Galgano, Bob, et al., comps. "The Five Satins Discography," *Bim Bam Boom.* n3 (December 1971–January 1972) 6. disc.

Grendysa, Peter. "The Five Satins: In the Still of the Nite . . . on Guard Duty," *Goldmine.* n193 (January 1, 1988) 14, 25. il.

Lumpkin, Doug. "Spotlight on the Five Satins," *Rockin' 50s.* n22 (February 1990) 8–14. il.

Nassar, Ray, comp. "Discography," *Paul's Record Magazine.* 2 (September 1975) 11–12. disc.

Five Sharps

Grendysa, Peter. "The Five Sharps and 'Stormy Weather'," *Goldmine.* n218 (December 2, 1988) 29, 85. il.

Flairs

Goldberg, Marv, and Rick Whitesell. "The Flairs," *Yesterday's Memories.* n10 (1977) 6–10. il.

Propes, Steve. "The Flairs: The L.A. Doo-Wop Tradition Begins," *Goldmine.* n144 (January 31, 1986) 54. il.

Flamingos

Pruter, Robert. "The Flamingos: The Chicago Years," *Goldmine.* n253 (April 6, 1990) 28–30, 108, 116. il.

Tancredi, L. Carl. "Chance Recordings of the Flamingos," *Bim Bam Boom.* n4 (February–March 1972) 6. il.

Four Blazes

Grendysa, Peter. "The Four Blazes: Hotter Than Hades!," *Goldmine.* n96 (March 30, 1984) 70–72. il.

Four Buddies

Goldberg, Marv, and Mike Redmond. "Heart and Soul: The Story of the Four Buddies," *Record Exchanger.* 3 (1972) 14–15. il.

Four Coins

Janusek, Carl, and Nancy Janusek. "The Four Coins: Pop's Answer to Coin Collecting," *Goldmine.* n178 (May 22, 1987) 10–12. il.

Janusek, Carl, and Nancy Janusek. "The Four Coins: Pop's Answer to Coin Collecting," *Goldmine.* n179 (June 5, 1987) 16. il.

Four Tunes (See also: Brown Dots)

Cotten, Lee. "The Four Tunes," In: *Shake, Rattle, and Roll.* pp. 147–148. il.

Grendysa, Peter. "The Four Tunes: Almost a Legend," *Goldmine.* n222 (January 27, 1989) 59, 62. il.

Fuqua, Harvey (See: Moonglows; Motown Sound)

Harptones

Ardolina, Art. "Harptones Singles," *Shout.* n93 (February 1974) 4–5. il., disc.

Marcus, Ed. "The Harptones," *Stormy Weather.* n3 (January 1970) 7. il.

Vance, Marcia, and Steve Flam. "The Harptones Discography," *Bim Bam Boom.* n2 (October–November 1971) 6. disc.

Hollywood Flames (See also: Bobby Day)

Byrd, Bobby. "The Flames," *Yesterday's Memories.* n3 (1975) 4–8. il.

Goldberg, Marv. "The Flames (Rekindled)," *Yesterday's Memories.* n5 (1976) 24–25. il.

Grendysa, Peter. "The Hollywood Flames," *Goldmine.* n244 (December 1, 1989) 26. il.

Impalas

Grendysa, Peter. "The Impalas," *Goldmine.* n244 (December 1, 1989) 28. il.

Jones, Wayne. "The Impalas: An Interview With Joe 'Speedo' Frazier," *Goldmine.* n75 (August 1982) 24, 29. il.

Jacks

Fileti, Donn, and Marv Goldberg. "The Jacks/Cadets," *Yesterday's Memories.* n2 (1975) 4–9. il.

Goldberg, Marv, and Donn Fileti. "Yesterday's Memories: The Jacks/Cadets," *DISCoveries.* 2 (April 1989) 34–35. il.

Johnnie and Joe

Fuchs, Aaron. "Johnnie and Joe: The J&S Records Story," *Goldmine.* n81 (February 1983) 10–12. il.

Kool Gents (See also: El Dorados)

Hinckley, Dave, and Marv Goldberg. "The Kool Gents," *Yesterday's Memories.* n13 (1979) 42. il.

Pruter, Robert. "The Dee Clark Story," *Goldmine.* n60 (May 1981) 19–21. il.

Laddins

Tamarkin, Jeff. "The Laddins: A New York Story," *Goldmine*. n253 (April 6, 1990) 10–12. il.

Larks

Grendysa, Peter. "Eugene Mumford: How He Left Those Prison Walls," *Goldmine*. n253 (April 6, 1990) 26, 116. il.

Propes, Steve. "The Larks and the Jerk: Jerked Around and Still a Hit," *Goldmine*. n211 (August 26, 1988) 72, 76. il.

Little Anthony and the Imperials

Day, Jack. "I'm on the Inside (Looking Out): Little Anthony Interviewed," *DISCoveries*. 2 (March 1989) 28–30. il., int.

Stambler, Irwin. "Little Anthony and the Imperials," In: *The Encyclopedia of Pop, Rock and Soul*. pp. 407–408.

Little Caesar and the Romans

Gagnon, Rick, and Dave Gnerre. "Little Caesar and the Romans: Still Singin' Those Oldies But Goodies," *Goldmine*. n210 (August 13, 1988) 12, 14, 16. il.

Lymon, Frankie, and the Teenagers

"Frankie Lymon," *The Golden Age*. n6 (March 1987) 11–23. il.

Groia, Phil. "Frankie Lymon and the Teenagers," *Bim Bam Boom*. n12 (1974) 17–18. il.

Hyde, Bob. "Frankie Lymon and the Teenagers: A Sessionography of George Goldner, 1955–1961," *Now Dig This.* n66 (September 1988) 18–22. il.

Koda, Cub. "Frankie Lymon and the Teenagers: Murray Hill's Finest Moment Yet," *Goldmine.* n177 (May 8, 1987) 63, 65, 67. il.

Millar, Bill. "Teenage Tragedy," *The History of Rock.* n4 (1982) 76–77. il.

Nassar, Ray. "I Can Explain," In: *Our Best to You—From Record Digest,* comp. by Jerry Osborne. pp. 11–18. il.

Sicurella, Joe, comp. "Discography," *Big Town Review.* 1 (July–August 1972) 14–15. il.

Stambler, Irwin. "The Teenagers," In: *The Encyclopedia of Pop, Rock and Soul.* pp. 671–672.

Lymon, Lewis, and the Teenchords

Goldblatt, David. "A Talk With Lewis Lymon," *Goldmine.* n80 (January 1983) 24–25. il.

"Lewis Lymon," *The Golden Age.* n6 (March 1987) 23. il.

Marathons (See also: Olympics)

Propes, Steve. "The Marathons," *Goldmine.* n244 (December 1, 1989) 30, 33. il.

McPhatter, Clyde (See: Dominoes; Drifters)

Mello-Kings

Grendysa, Peter. "The Mello-Kings," *Goldmine.* n220 (December 30, 1988) 14. il.

Monotones

Stierle, Wayne. "The Monotones: They Wrote the Book of Love," *Goldmine.* n210 (August 13, 1988) 18, 20. il.

Moonglows

Bianco, David. "Harvey Fuqua," In: *Heat Wave.* pp. 26–27. il.

Cotten, Lee. "The Moonglows," In: *Shake, Rattle, and Roll.* pp. 226–229. il.

Fuchs, Aaron, and Dan Nooger. "Harvey Fuqua: The Motown Days," *Goldmine.* n121 (March 15, 1985) 18–24. il.

Mohr, Kurt, comp. "Moonglows Discography," *Shout.* n73 (January 1972) 2–3. disc.

"The Moonglows Discography," *Rocking Regards.* n15 (June 1979) 7–9. disc.

Stambler, Irwin. "The Moonglows," In: *The Encyclopedia of Pop, Rock and Soul.* pp. 471–472.

Nutmegs

Grendysa, Peter. "The Nutmegs: The Untold Story," *Goldmine.* n183 (July 31, 1987) 16, 28. il.

"Nutmegs Discography," *Record Digest.* 2 (April 15, 1979) 12. disc.

Olympics (See also: Marathons)

Hinckley, Dave, and Marv Goldberg. "The Olympics," *Yesterday's Memories.* 3 (1977) 14–16. il.

Orioles (featuring Sonny Til)

Cotten, Lee. "The Orioles," In: *Shake, Rattle, and Roll.* pp. 120–122. il.

Stambler, Irwin. "The Orioles," In: *The Encyclopedia of Pop, Rock and Soul.* pp. 501–502.

Penguins

Cotten, Lee. "The Penguins," In: *Shake, Rattle, and Roll.* pp. 221–223. il.

Fields, Tom. "Doo-Wopp Beach—The West Coast Meets the East Coast: The Story of the Penguins," *It Will Stand.* n14/15 (1980) 14–15. il., bio.

Fields, Tom, comp. "Penguins Discography," *It Will Stand.* n14/15 (1980) 15. disc.

Goldberg, Marv, and Mike Redmond. "The Penguins," *Record Exchanger.* n6 (Fall 1972) 14–16. il.

Groia, Phil, et al., comps. "The Penguins," *Bim Bam Boom.* n7 (September 1972) 9, 57. il.

McGarvey, Seamus. "Earth Angel: Cleve Duncan of the Penguins," *Now Dig This.* n73 (April 1989) 12–14. il.

Propes, Steve. "The Penguins," *Goldmine.* n244 (December 1, 1989) 35. il.

Stambler, Irwin. "The Penguins," In: *The Encyclopedia of Pop, Rock and Soul.* pp. 514–515.

Platters

Baker, G.A. "Buck Ram's Platters Stir Controversy Down Under," *Billboard.* 98 (August 9, 1986) 67.

Beachley, Chris. "The Buck Ram Platters and the Great Pretenders," *It Will Stand.* n17/18 (1980) 7–8. il.

Beachley, Chris. "The Platters: Their Magic Touch Remains," *It Will Stand.* n17/18 (1980) 4–5. il.

Cotten, Lee. "The Platters," In: *Shake, Rattle, and Roll.* pp. 281–282. il.

Fanning, Mary. "The Man With the Magic Touch: An Interview With Buck Ram," *Now Dig This.* n64 (July 1988) 3–5. il., int.

Leigh, Spencer. "The Platters," *Record Collector.* n49 (September 1983) 30–33. il.

Millar, Bill. "Golden Platters," *The History of Rock.* n15 (1982) 298–300. il.

"Platters' Ox Tour Almost Ruined by Minister's Shortsighted Ruling," *Variety.* 324 (July 30, 1986) 76.

Roth, Steve. "The Sonny Turner Story," *It Will Stand.* n17/18
(198?) 5–7. il.

Stambler, Irwin. "The Platters," In: *The Encyclopedia of Pop,
Rock and Soul.* pp. 525–526.

Stierle, Wayne. "They All Copied the Tony Williams Style,"
DISCoveries. 2 (February 1989) 110–111. il.

Stierle, Wayne. "Tony Williams: Absolutely the Greatest Lead
Vocalist in History," *DISCoveries.* 2 (February 1989)
108–109. il.

Wasserman, Steve, comp. "The Platters Discography," *Bim
Bam Boom.* n6 (July 1972) 11. disc.

Ravens

Grendysa, Peter. "The Ravens: Early Birds," *Goldmine.* n179
(June 5, 1987) 22, 82. il.

Stambler, Irwin. "The Ravens," In: *The Encyclopedia of Pop, Rock
and Soul.* pp. 556–557.

Royals (See: Hank Ballard and the Midnighters)

Shields

Hinckley, Dave. "The Shields," *Yesterday's Memories.* n10
(1977) 3. il.

Silhouettes

Grendysa, Peter. "The Silhouettes," *Goldmine.* n220 (December
30, 1988) 74. il.

"The Silhouettes," *The Golden Age.* n10 (July 1987) 8–10. il.

Skyliners

Bleiel, Jeff. "The Skyliners: Setting a Standard With 'Since I Don't Have You'," *Goldmine.* n187 (September 25, 1987) 28, 91. il.

Cajiao, Trevor. "The Skyliners," *Now Dig This.* n20 (November 1984) 15–16. il.

Clee, Ken, and Fernando L. Gonzalez, comps. "The Skyliners Discography," *Goldmine.* n64 (September 1981) 8–9. il., disc.

Spaniels

Cotten, Lee. "The Spaniels," In: *Shake, Rattle, and Roll.* pp. 180–181.

Lee, Alan, and Donna Hennings. "The Spaniels," *Yesterday's Memories.* n6 (1976) 4–7. il.

Stambler, Irwin. "The Spaniels," In: *The Encyclopedia of Pop, Rock and Soul.* p. 631.

Starlighters

Oates, Max. "The Starlighters: D.C. Vocal Harmony," *Goldmine.* n213 (September 23, 1988) 23, 72. il.

Strong, Nolan, and the Diablos

Grendysa, Peter. "The Diablos: A Profile," *Goldmine.* n142 (January 3, 1986) 20, 26. il.

Grendysa, Peter, comp. "Nolan Strong and the Diablos Discography," *Goldmine.* n142 (January 3, 1986) 14. disc.

Koda, Cub. "Nolan Strong: An Appreciation of the Original Sound of the Motor City," *Goldmine.* n142 (January 3, 1986) 12–20. il.

Til, Sonny (See: Orioles)

Turbans

Grendysa, Peter. "The Turbans," *Goldmine.* n244 (December 1, 1989) 97. il.

Velours

McGarvey, Seamus. "New York Doo-Wop: The Velours Story—Part One," *Now Dig This.* n58 (January 1988) 25–27. il.

McGarvey, Seamus. "New York Doo-Wop: The Velours Story—Part Two," *Now Dig This.* n59 (February 1988) 25–26. il.

Williams, Maurice, and the Zodiacs; Gladiolas

Beachley, Chris. "The Gladiolas/The Zodiacs," *Yesterday's Memories.* n3 (1975) 13–17. il.

Beachley, Chris. "The Gladiolas/The Zodiacs," *It Will Stand.* n2 (1978) 12–13. il.

Beachley, Chris, comp. "The Gladiolas/Zodiacs Discography," *Yesterday's Memories.* n3 (1975) 16. disc.

Fuchs, Aaron. "Maurice Williams: A Founding Father of Beach Music," *Goldmine.* n95 (March 16, 1984) 37–45. il.

McGarvey, Seamus. "Stay! Just a Little Bit Longer, Little Darlin': The Gladiolas and the Zodiacs—The Maurice Williams Story," *Now Dig This.* n79 (October 1989) 4–9. il., bio.

Stambler, Irwin. "Maurice Williams," In: *The Encyclopedia of Pop, Rock and Soul.* p. 741.

Topping, Ray, comp. "Maurice Williams and the Zodiacs Discography," *Goldmine.* n95 (March 16, 1984) 45. disc.

Williams, Otis, and the Charms

Cotten, Lee. "The Charms," In: *Shake, Rattle, and Roll.* pp. 208–209. il.

Italinao, Ronnie. "Otis Williams and His Many Charms," *Time Barrier Express.* n18 (August–September 1976) 8–13. il.

Willows

Grendysa, Peter. "The Willows: Hello Hello Again," *Goldmine.* n212 (September 9, 1988) 18, 26. il.

4. Neo-Doo-Wop (1958–)

Barry and the Tamerlanes

Fink, Stu. "Barry and the Tamerlanes," *Goldmine.* n244 (December 1, 1989) 12. il.

Belmonts (See: Dion)

Black, Jay (See: Jay and the Americans)

Capris

Grendysa, Peter. "The Capris," *Goldmine.* n244 (December 1, 1989) 16. il.

"Interview: The Capris," *Record Exchanger.* n5 (November–December 1970) 14–16. il., int.

Crests

Glenister, Derek, and Ray Topping. "Crests," *New Kommotion.* 2 (Autumn 1976) 24–25. il.

Jones, Wayne. "Johnny Maestro," In: *Rockin', Rollin', and Rappin'.* pp. 19–21. il.

Lumpkin, Doug. "Spotlight on the Crests," *Rockin' 50s.* n11 (April 1988) 10–14. il.

Danny and the Juniors

Griggs, Bill. "Danny and the Juniors: Rock and Roll is Here to Stay," *Rockin' 50s.* n21 (December 1989) 22–23. il.

Stambler, Irwin. "Danny and the Juniors," In: *The Encyclopedia of Pop, Rock and Soul.* pp. 160–161.

Stidom, Larry. "The Juniors: Rock 'N' Roll is Here to Stay," *Goldmine.* n151 (May 9, 1986) 16–18, 22. il.

Diamonds

"Diamonds' Title Disputed," *Variety.* 324 (August 6, 1986) 78ff.

Kearney, Mark, and Randy Ray. "The Diamonds: Shining Brightly in the '50s," *Goldmine.* n179 (June 5, 1987) 22–36. il.

Tamarkin, Jeff, comp. "The Diamonds Selected Singles Discography," *Goldmine.* n179 (June 5, 1987) 36. disc.

Dion; Dion and the Belmonts

Bowen, Pete, comp. "Dion: The American Chart Hits, 1958–1968," *Now Dig This.* n78 (September 1989) 6. disc.

Bowen, Pete. "Dion: The Wanderer Returns," *Now Dig This.* n78 (September 1989) 4–7. il.

DiMucci, Dion, with Davin Seay. *The Wanderer: Dion's Story.* New York: Beech Tree/William Morrow, 1988. il., bio.

Errigo, Angie. "Street–Corner Sounds," *The History of Rock.* n21 (1982) 408–409. il.

Leigh, Spencer. "Dion," *Record Collector.* n57 (May 1984) 9–14. il., disc.

Leigh, Spencer, comp. "Dion and the Belmonts Complete U.K. Discography," *Record Collector.* n57 (May 1984) 14. disc.

McDowell, Mike, comp. "Belmonts Discography," *Blitz.* n29 (November–December 1978) 21–23. il., disc.

Sculatti, Gene. "The Necessarily Incomplete Dion Primer," *Waxpaper.* n6 (June 25, 1976) 14–15. il.

Stambler, Irwin. "Dion," In: *The Encyclopedia of Pop, Rock and Soul.* pp. 179–181.

Tamarkin, Jeff. "Dion: The Return of the Wanderer," *Goldmine.* n185 (August 28, 1987) 8–16. il.

Tamarkin, Jeff, comp. "Dion Discography," *Goldmine.* n185 (August 28, 1987) 10. disc.

Enchanters (See also: Garnet Mimms)

Gross, Martin. "The Enchanters," *Record Profile Magazine.* n2 (September 1983) 38–39. il.

Esquires

Pruter, Robert. "Get on Up . . . and Get Away: The Esquires," *It Will Stand.* n26 (1982) 6–9. il.

Essex

Hill, Randal C. "The Essex," *Goldmine.* n244 (December 1, 1989) 24. il.

Four Seasons (featuring Frankie Valli)

Bleiel, Jeff. "The Four Seasons: '70s," *Goldmine.* n251 (March 9, 1990) 38, 125. il.

Fisher, Bob. "Valli's Evergreens: Why the Four Seasons Were Perennial Chart-Toppers," *The History of Rock.* n29 (1982) 570–573. il.

"Four Seasons' Award From Quality Records Reduced to $400,000," *Variety.* 320 (August 7, 1985) 70.

Ingram, George. "The Four Seasons," *Record Collector.* n33 (May 1982) 14–22. il., disc.

Jay and the Americans

Bordowitz, Hank. "Kenny Vance: Behind-the-Scenes Look at Jay and the Americans and Eddie and the Cruisers," *Goldmine.* n157 (August 1, 1986) 10. il.

McConnell, E. "Jay vs. Jay in $1 Mil Suit," *Billboard.* 101 (January 7, 1989) 78.

Jive Five

Stierle, Wayne. "The Jive Five: A True New York Story," *Goldmine.* n210 (August 13, 1988) 10, 14. il.

Johnson, General

"Interview With General Norman Johnson," *It Will Stand.* n1 (1978) 4–5. il., int.

Lewis, Huey, and the News (See: AOR)

Manhattan Transfer (See also: Jazz-Rock Fusion)

Tamarkin, Jeff. "The Manhattan Transfer: Tim Hauser Remembers Group Harmony Then and Now," *Goldmine.* n103 (July 1984) 32–38. il.

Marvelows

Pruter, Robert. "The Marvelows," *Goldmine.* n244 (December 1, 1989) 32. il.

Pruter, Robert. "The Marvelows," *Goldmine.* 3 (1979) 19–22. il.

Mystics

Clee, Ken, comp. "Mystics Discography," *Goldmine.* n90 (November 1983) 71. disc.

Nylons (See: Commonwealth Contributions—Canada)

Originals

Towne, Steve. "Freddie Gorman and the Originals," *Goldmine.* n64 (September 1981) 23–25. il.

Persuasions

Cooper, B. Lee. "Repeating Hit Tunes, A Cappella Style: The Persuasions as Song Revivalists, 1967–1982," *Popular Music and Society.* 13 (Fall 1989) 17–27.

Sha Na Na

Jones, Wayne. "Jon 'Bowser' Bauman of Sha Na Na," *Goldmine.* n63 (August 1981) 140–141. il.

Stambler, Irwin. "Sha Na Na," In: *The Encyclopedia of Pop, Rock and Soul.* pp. 610–611.

Tams

Jancik, Wayne. "The Tams," *Goldmine.* n244 (December 1, 1989) 40, 96. il.

Tee, Willie

Clifton, Michael. "Willie Tee," *Soul Survivor.* n8 (Winter 1987/1988) 26. il.

"Interview With 'The Real' Willie Tee," *It Will Stand.* n2 (1978) 4–5. il.

5. BRILL BUILDING ERA (1959–1965)

Songwriters

GENERAL SOURCES

Goodman, Fred. "The New Brill Building: Professional Song-writers Reclaim a Place in Rock & Roll," *Rolling Stone.* n522 (March 24, 1988) 17–21. il., int.

"Heart Throbs: Where the Girls Are," *Esquire.* (May 1990) 122–125. il., int. Recounts stories behind the genesis of the following hit songs: "Runaround Sue," "Peggy Sue," "Donna," and "Cathy's Clown."

BACHARACH, BURT

Sutherland, Sam. "Bacharach and Sager Set Sights on Produc-ing," *Billboard.* 98 (August 16, 1986) 24.

Stambler, Irwin. "Bacharach, Burt," In: *The Encyclopedia of Pop, Rock and Soul.* pp. 25–27.

GOFFIN, GERRY, AND CAROLE KING (See also: CAROLE KING)

"Nine Selected for Induction into Songwriters Hall of Fame," *Billboard.* 98 (December 27, 1986) 8.

"Song Hall of Fame Names 9 Inductees," *Variety*. 325 (December 31, 1986) 62.

GREENWICH, ELLIE

Hoerburger, R. "Greenwich Seeks More Support for *Leader (of the Pack)*," *Billboard*. 97 (June 15, 1985) 48. int.

Stambler, Irwin. "Greenwich, Ellis," In: *The Encyclopedia of Pop, Rock and Soul*. pp. 269–271.

KING, CAROLE (See also: GERRY GOFFIN)

Grein, Paul. "Carole King Reaches Silver Screen in *Murphy's Romance*," *Billboard*. 98 (February 1, 1986) 44.

Stambler, Irwin. "King, Carole," In: *The Encyclopedia of Pop, Rock and Soul*. pp. 370–371.

MANN, BARRY, AND CYNTHIA WEIL

"Nine Selected for Induction into Songwriters Hall of Fame," *Billboard*. 98 (December 27, 1986) 8.

Robinson, Julius. "Songwriter's Spotlight—Mann and Weil," *Cash Box*. LI:48 (June 6, 1988) 4, 16. il., int.

"Song Hall of Fame Names 9 Inductees," *Variety*. 325 (December 31, 1986) 62.

Christie, Lou (r.n.: Lugee Sacco)

Christie, Lou. "Commentary: It's More Than Just Nostalgia," *Billboard*. 97 (July 20, 1985) 10.

Riegel, R. "Lou Strikes Twice," *Creem.* 16 (February 1985) 16.
il.

Darin, Bobby

Stambler, Irwin. "Darin, Bobby," In: *The Encyclopedia of Pop,
Rock and Soul.* pp. 161–162.

Francis, Connie

Stambler, Irwin. "Francis, Connie," In: *The Encyclopedia of Pop,
Rock and Soul.* pp. 238–239.

King, Ben E. (See also: Drifters)

Stambler, Irwin. "King, Ben E.," In: *The Encyclopedia of Pop,
Rock and Soul.* pp. 368–370.

Lee, Brenda (r.n.: Mae Tarpley)

"Brenda Lee," *The Golden Age.* n11 (August 1987) 7–35. il.

Garbutt, Bob. "Brenda Lee: The Early Years," *New Kommotion.*
n18 (Winter 1978) 31.

Hawkins, Martin. "Little Miss Dynamite," *The History of Rock.*
n16 (1982) 318–320.

Hill, Randal C. "Brenda Lee: Sweet Somethin's," *Goldmine.*
n185 (August 28, 1987) 26, 78. il.

Jones, Peter. "The Brenda Lee Story," *Record Collector.* n23 (July
1981) 13–18. il., bio.

Knight, K. "Brenda Lee: The Consummate Entertainer!," *Cash Box.* 53 (August 19, 1989) 20. il.

Newcombe, Jim. "Little Miss Dynamite," *Now Dig This.* n52 (July 1987) 24–25. il.

Smith, John, III. "Spotlight on Brenda Lee," *Rockin' 50s.* n5 (April 1987) 9–17. il.

Lee, Dickey

Escott, Colin, and Richard Weize. "Dickey Lee: Surviving in Style," *Country Sounds.* 1 (June 1986) 22–23. il.

McNutt, Randy. "Teen Rockabilly," In: *We Wanna Boogie.* pp. 144–150. il.

McDaniel, Gene

Stambler, Irwin. "McDaniel, Gene," In: *The Encyclopedia of Pop, Rock and Soul.* pp. 454–455.

Orbison, Roy

Barnard, Stephen. "Only the Lonely," *The History of Rock.* n21 (1982) 412–416. il.

Booth, Dave "Daddy Cool", and Colin Escott. "Roy Orbison: A Cadillac and a Diamond Ring," *Goldmine.* n118 (February 1, 1985) 6–12. il.

Bream, Terry. "Roy Orbison: The Early Years," *Goldmine.* n218 (December 2, 1988) 29, 85. il., bio.

Clayson, Alan. *Only the Lonely: Roy Orbison's Life and Legacy.*
New York: St. Martin's, 1989. il., bio.

Clee, Ken. "Roy Orbison Discography," *Goldmine.* n41 (October 1979) 8. disc.

Cochburn, Howard. "A Fan Remembers . . . To Howard From
Roy Orbison," *Now Dig This.* n70 (January 1989) 18–21.
il.

Cochburn, Howard, comp. "Roy Orbison Discography," *Now
Dig This.* n71 (February 1989) 18–22. il., disc.

Cochburn, Howard. "Roy Orbison: One Year On," *Now Dig
This.* n62 (May 1988) 10.

Cochburn, Howard. "Roy Orbison: The Early Years," *Now Dig
This.* n62 (May 1988) 9–11. il.

"Crying," *Rock & Roll Confidential.* n64 (January 1989) 1–2.
Tribute to recently deceased star.

Daniels, Bill, Leo Kolijn, and Colin Escott. "Roy Orbison
Discography," *Goldmine.* n118 (February 1, 1985) 6–12.
il., disc.

Doggett, Peter. "Roy Orbison," *Record Collector.* n43 (March
1983) 25–32. il.

Escott, Colin. "Roy Orbison: The Early Years," *Record Collector.*
n117 (May 1989) 43–47. il., bio.

Escott, Colin. "Roy Orbison: The Early Years," *Goldmine.* n229
(May 5, 1989) 16–19. il., bio.

Escott, Colin. "Roy Orbison: The M-G-M Years, 1965–1973," *Goldmine.* n229 (May 5, 1989) 20–21.

"15 Elected to Hall of Fame," *Billboard.* 98 (October 18, 1986) 101.

Folkhart, Burt A. "Rock 'N' Roll's Roy Orbison Dies," *Los Angeles Times.* (December 8, 1988) 3, 32. il.

Fremer, Michael. "Bill Porter: The Engineer Behind the Orbison Sound," *Goldmine.* n229 (May 5, 1989) 18–19. il.

Fricke, David. "Roy Orbison Remembered," *Rolling Stone.* n544 (January 12, 1989) 44–46ff.

Goodman, Fred. "Rock Legend Roy Orbison Dead at 52," *Rolling Stone.* n543 (January 12, 1989) 15.

Hawkins, Martin, and Colin Escott. "Roy Orbison—The Sun Days," *Time Barrier Express.* 3 (July–August 1977) 35–37. il.

Hilburn, Robert. "Roy Orbison's Pop Legacy of Greatness," *Los Angeles Times.* (December 8, 1988) 1, 14. il.

Isler, Scott. "It's Over," *Musician.* n124 (February 1989) 88–90. il.

Nash, Alanna. "Living in Dreams," *Stereo Review.* 54 (May 1989) 114.

"Opryland Purchases Acuff-Rose Group; Orbison Suit Over," *Variety.* 319 (June 19, 1985) 89.

Pond, Steve. "Roy Orbison," In: *The Rolling Stone Interviews: The 1980s,* ed. by Sid Holt. pp. 331–339. il.

Pond, Steve. "Roy Orbison 1936–1988," *Rolling Stone.* n544 (January 26, 1989) 22–25ff. il., int., bio.

"Rock Hall of Fame to Induct 15 Acts," *Variety.* 324 (October 8, 1986) 147.

"Roy Orbison: An Interviewer's Dream (Excerpts from a 1979 Conversation)," *Goldmine.* n229 (May 5, 1989) 9–10, 23. il., int.

Stambler, Irwin. "Orbison, Roy," In: *The Encyclopedia of Pop, Rock and Soul.* pp. 499–501.

Stierle, Wayne. "Roy Orbison: When the Legend Began," *DISCoveries.* 2 (April 1989) 24–25. il.

Tamarkin, Jeff. "Roy Orbison: A Tribute, 1936–1988," *Goldmine.* n220 (December 30, 1988) 81. il.

Umphred, Neal. "Roy Orbison: U.S. Discography and Price Guide," *Goldmine.* n229 (May 5, 1989) 12–14, 22. il., disc.

Whitall, Susan. "Orbison's Legacy: Three Decades of Rock's Finest Moments," *Detroit News.* (December 8, 1988) 1A, 12A.

Pitney, Gene

Stambler, Irwin. "Pitney, Gene," In: *The Encyclopedia of Pop, Rock and Soul.* pp. 524–525.

Roe, Tommy

Stambler, Irwin. "Roe, Tommy," In: *The Encyclopedia of Pop, Rock and Soul.* pp. 579–580.

Royal, Billy Joe

"Billy Joe Royal," *Cash Box.* (October 31, 1987) 10, 35. il., int.

Shannon, Del (r.n.: Charles Westover)

Goldberg, Michael. "Del Shannon: 1934–1990," *Rolling Stone.* n574 (March 22, 1990) 20, 124. il.

Stambler, Irwin. "Shannon, Del," In: *The Encyclopedia of Pop, Rock and Soul.* p. 612.

Vinton, Bobby

Stambler, Irwin. "Vinton, Bobby," In: *The Encyclopedia of Pop, Rock and Soul.* pp. 721–722.

A. TEEN IDOLS AND THE *AMERICAN BANDSTAND* PHENOMENON

American Bandstand; Dick Clark, MC

Stambler, Irwin. "Clark, Dick," In: *The Encyclopedia of Pop, Rock and Soul.* pp. 124–125.

Anka, Paul

Stambler, Irwin. "Anka, Paul," In: *The Encyclopedia of Pop, Rock and Soul.* pp. 11–12.

Avalon, Frankie

Stambler, Irwin. "Avalon, Frankie," In: *The Encyclopedia of Pop, Rock and Soul.* pp. 21–22.

Blane, Marcie

Shannon, Bob, and Jeff Tamarkin. "Marcie Blane," *Goldmine.* n220 (December 30, 1988) 8. il.

Duke, Patty

Gari, Brian. "Patty Duke," *Goldmine.* n244 (December 1, 1989) 20. il.

Fabian (r.n.: F. Forte)

Stambler, Irwin. "Fabian," In: *The Encyclopedia of Pop, Rock and Soul.* pp. 222–223.

Nelson, Rick(y) (r.n.: Eric Hilliard Nelson)

"15 Elected to Hall of Fame," *Billboard.* 98 (October 18, 1986) 101.

Grein, Paul. "Rick Nelson: TV's First Rock Star Singer, Dead at 45, Reached the Charts Via the Tube," *Billboard.* 98 (January 11, 1986) 6.

Kirby, Kip. "Nashville Scene: Some Friends Remember Rick Nelson's Legacy, the New Year's Tribute," *Billboard.* 98 (January 18, 1986) 37.

"Lonesome Town," *Creem.* 17 (April 1986) 6. Tribute to the recently deceased star.

(Obituary), *International Musician.* 84 (February 1986) 11.

(Obituary), *Melody Maker.* 61 (January 11, 1986) 5. il.

(Obituary), *Musician.* n89 (March 1986) 24.

(Obituary), *Variety.* 321 (January 8, 1986) 247.

Obrecht, Jas. "Ricky Nelson, 1940–1985," *Guitar Player.* 20 (March 1986) 12. il.

"Rock Hall of Fame to Induct 15 Acts," *Variety.* 324 (October 8, 1986) 147.

Selvin, Joel. *Ricky Nelson: Idol for a Generation.* New York: Contemporary Books, 1990. il., bio.

Stambler, Irwin. "Nelson, Rick," In: *The Encyclopedia of Pop, Rock and Soul.* pp. 480–482.

Vee, Bobby (See also: Crickets; Buddy Holly)

Stambler, Irwin. "Vee, Bobby," In: *The Encyclopedia of Pop, Rock and Soul.* pp. 715–716.

B. DANCE CRAZES (1960–1964)

Bonds, Gary U.S.

Stambler, Irwin. "Bonds, Gary U.S.," In: *The Encyclopedia of Pop, Rock and Soul.* pp. 71–72.

Checker, Chubby (r.n.: Ernest Evans)

Bowermaster, J. "Chubby Checker," *Record.* 4 (December 1985) 46–48ff. il., bio., int.

Stambler, Irwin. "Checker, Chubby," In: *The Encyclopedia of Pop, Rock and Soul.* p. 115.

C. INSTRUMENTALS

General Sources

Forte, Dan. "Instrumental Rock: The '80s Revival," *Guitar Player.* 19 (November 1985) 49.

Forte, Dan, and others. "Instrumental Rock Guitarists: The Unsung Heroes," *Guitar Player.* 19 (October 1985) 60–62ff. il.

Alpert, Herb(, and the Tijuana Brass)

Stambler, Irwin. "Alpert, Herb," In: *The Encyclopedia of Pop, Rock and Soul.* pp. 8–10.

Black, Bill, Combo (See also: Elvis Presley)

Escott, Colin. "Bill Black: Elvis, Scotty, and Who?," *Goldmine.* n211 (August 26, 1988) 14–16. il.

Jancik, Wayne. "The Bill Black Combo," *Goldmine.* n58 (March 1981) 16–17. il.

Booker T and the M.G.s (See also: Memphis Sound)

Stambler, Irwin. "Booker T and the M.G.s," In: *The Encyclopedia of Pop, Rock and Soul.* pp. 72–74.

Eddy, Duane

DeMuir, H. "Newbeats: The Twang Shall Meet," *Creem.* 19 (December 1987) 66. il.

Jenkins, M. "Gunn Law," *Melody Maker.* 61 (March 29, 1986) 10–11. il., int.

Stambler, Irwin. "Eddy, Duane," In: *The Encyclopedia of Pop, Rock and Soul.* pp. 209–210.

Mack, Lonnie (See also: Stevie Ray Vaughan)

Faull, Trev. "Lonnie Mack," *Record Collector.* n81 (May 1986) 42–45.

Kienzle, Rich. "Lonnie Mack," In: *Great Guitarists.* pp. 211–214. il.

Ruhlmann, William. "Lonnie Mack: That 'Memphis' Man Strikes Like Lightning," *Goldmine.* n138 (November 8, 1985) 20, 70. il.

Sandmel, Ben. "Big Mack Attack: Rock Pioneer Lonnie Mack in Session With Stevie Ray Vaughan," *Guitar Player.* 19 (April 1985) 32–42. il., bio.

Sandmel, Ben. "Lonnie Mack is Back on the Track," *Guitar World.* 5 (May 1984) 55–61.

Santoro, Gene. "Double Whammy," *Guitar World.* 7 (January 1986) 32–36. il.

Raybeats

Forte, Dan. "The Raybeats: '60s Music for '80s People," *Guitar Player.* 19 (November 1985) 51–55ff. il., bio. of member Jody Harris.

Milkowski, B. "Profile," *Down Beat.* 51 (July 1984) 59ff. il., int., bio. of member Jody Harris.

Satriani, Joe

Morris, Chris. "Joe Satriani Set for 'Surfing' Tour; Guitarist's Album Climbs the Pop Chart," *Billboard.* 100:21 (May 21, 1988) 31–32. int.

Obrecht, Jas. "Triple Crown Winner: Joe Satriani," *Guitar Player.* 23 (January 1989) 22–24ff. il., int. Wins "Best Overall Guitarist," "Best New Talent" and "Best Guitar Album" from *Guitar Player*'s 19th Annual Readers Poll.

Ventures

Stambler, Irwin. "The Ventures," In: *The Encyclopedia of Pop, Rock and Soul.* pp. 716–718.

Wray, Link

Bradford, Rob. "Link Wray," *Record Collector.* n85 (September 1986) 36–39. il., disc.

Kienzle, Rich. "Link Wray," In: *Great Guitarists.* pp. 235–236. il.

Koda, Cub. "Link Wray: Godfather of the Power Chord," *Time Barrier Express.* n26 (September–October 1979) 32–38. il.

"Link Wray," In: *Rock Guitarists.* pp. 169–170. il.

Millar, Bill. "Link Wray," *Goldmine.* n56 (January 1981) 164–165. il.

Westfall, Bob, and Cub Koda, comps. "Wray Family Discography," *Time Barrier Express.* n26 (September–October 1979) 36–38. il., disc.

Zito, Tom. "The 'Rumble' Man Comes Back," *Rolling Stone.* n86 (July 8, 1971) 12.

D. NOVELTY SONGS

Answer Songs

Cooper, B. Lee. "Sequel Songs and Response Recordings: The Answer Record in Modern American Music, 1950–1985," *International Journal of Instructional Media.* 13:3 (1986) 227–239.

Cooper, B. Lee, and Wayne S. Haney. *Response Recordings: An Answer Song Discography, 1950–1990.* Metuchen, NJ: Scarecrow, 1990.

Dees, Rick

"Rick Dees in the Clear on 'Sonny Sniffs Glue' Parody Record Single," *Variety.* 323 (July 16, 1986) 1ff.

Demento, Dr. (Disc Jockey)

Liveton, S. "Newbeats: Demented to Meet You," *Creem.* 17 (April 1986) 75. il.

New Vaudville Band

Tamarkin, Jeff. "The New Vaudeville Band," *Goldmine.* n220 (December 30, 1988) 15. il.

One-Hit Wonders

McConie, Stuart. "One for the Money," *New Musical Express.*
(February 24, 1990) 18–19. il. Survey of artists infamous
for having had only one hit.

E. THE PAYOLA SCANDAL (1959–1960) (See: PAYOLA)

F. COMMERCIAL FOLK

Baez, Joan

Baez, Joan. *Daybreak.* London: Panther, 1971. Original pub.:
London: MacGibbon & Kee, 1970. A collection of vi-
gnettes concerned with her growth as both an individual
and artist.

Swan, Peter. *Joan Baez, a Bio-disco-bibliography: Being a Selected
Guide to Material in Print, on Record, on Cassette and on Film,
With a Biographical Introduction.* Brighton, U.K.: Noyce,
1977. il., bio., disc., bibl.

Highwaymen

Frankel, David. "Where are They Now? The Highwaymen,"
Rolling Stone. n508 (September 10, 1987) 62. il., int.
w/Stephen Trott.

Jamaican Sound: Calypso, Ska, Rock Steady

Hill, D.R. "Trinidad's Calypso and the Phonograph Record,"
Record Research. n217/218 (October 1985) 4–5. il.

Rowland, M. "Are Trinidad Trends Heading North?," *Billboard.* 97 (April 6, 1985) 50–51.

"Top Calypso Acts Honored," *Billboard.* 100 (August 5, 1989) 32. Coverage of the first Calypso and Steelband Music Awards.

BELAFONTE, HARRY

Stewart, Al. "Harry Belafonte Is Back," *Billboard.* 100:21 (May 21, 1988) 77. int.

G. THE SPECTOR SOUND (1958–1966)

"Phil Spector's 'To Know Him Is to Love Him': BMI's Most Performed Country Song of the Year," *BMI.* (Fall 1988) 20–21. il.

Puterbaugh, Parke. "The Wall of Sound," *Rolling Stone.* n585 (August 23, 1990) 113–114. il., int. w/Spector associates.

Stambler, Irwin. "Spector, Phil," In: *The Encyclopedia of Pop, Rock and Soul.* pp. 631–632.

Crystals

Stambler, Irwin. "The Crystals," In: *The Encyclopedia of Pop, Rock and Soul.* pp. 157–158.

Ronettes

Stambler, Irwin. "The Ronettes," In: *The Encyclopedia of Pop, Rock and Soul.* pp. 583–584.

Soxx, Bob B., and the Blue Jeans

Stambler, Irwin. "Bob B. Soxx and the Blue Jeans," In: *The Encyclopedia of Pop, Rock and Soul.* p. 629.

H. GIRL GROUPS (1960–1965; 1988–)

Light, Alan. "The New Girl Groups," *Rolling Stone.* n581 (June 28, 1990) 15–16. il. Notes acts such as Seduction, Sweet Sensation, The Good Girls, Pajama Party, Expose, and 3-5-7. Includes sidebar, "Girl Groups Back on the Charts."

Big Trouble

DeSavia, Tom. "Big Trouble," *Cash Box.* (February 6, 1988) 12. il., int. w/Bobbi Eakes.

En Vogue

Stern, Perry. "Sound Check: En Vogue; Fast Parties," *Me Music Express Magazine.* 14:148 (June 1990) 21. il., int. w/Cindy Herron.

Mint Juleps

Giles, Jeff. "Mint Juleps Mix It Up," *Rolling Stone.* n565 (November 16, 1989) 33. il., int.

Shirelles

Stambler, Irwin. "The Shirelles," In: *The Encyclopedia of Pop, Rock and Soul.* p. 613.

6. BRITISH INVASION (1964–)

Holland, Bill. "Visa Requirements Tighten—Young British Bands Affected," *Billboard.* 97 (November 23, 1985) 1ff.

A. BRITISH SCENE PREVIOUS TO 1964

General Sources

Ellis, Royston. *The Big Beat Scene.* London: Four Square, 1961. il.

Gardner, Graham. *Then and Now.* Shepperton, Middlesex, U.K.: Graham Gardner, 1981. il., int. w/twelve British recording artists of the late 1950s and early 1960s.

Leslie, Peter. *FAB: The Anatomy of a Phenomenon.* London: MacGibbon & Kee, 1965. il. Analysis of the relationship between popular music, fashion and teen culture. Includes case histories of leading artists from that era.

Steele-Perkins, Chris, and Richard Smith. *The Teds.* London: Travelling Light/Exit, 1979. il.

Dene, Terry

Wooding, Dan. *I Thought Terry Dene Was Dead.* London: Coverdale House, 1974. il. pap.

Faith, Adam

Faith, Adam. *Adam, His Fabulous Year.* London: Picture Story
Publications, 1960. il. pap. Aimed at teen fans; uncritical
and patronizing in tone.

Faith, Adam. *Poor Me.* London: Four Square/Souvenir, 1961. il.
pap.

Shadows

Geddes, George. "Jet Harris and Tony Meehan," *Record Collector.* n74 (October 1985) 17–20. il., disc.

Storm, Rory, and the Hurricanes (See also: Ringo Starr)

Leigh, Spencer. "Rory Storm and the Hurricanes," *Record
Collector.* n99 (November 1987) 28–32. il.

Vaughan, Frankie

Vaughan, Frankie. *The Frankie Vaughan Story.* London: Penrow,
1957. il., autobio.

B. FIRST WAVE (1964–1965)

General Sources

Barnes, Richard, comp. *Mods.* London: Eel Pie, 1979. il.
Collage of photos, press clippings and ads—largely from
1964—devoted to the Mod subculture.

Cross, Colin, with Paul Kendall and Mick Farren, comps.

Encyclopedia of British Beat Groups and Solo Artists of the Sixties. London: Omnibus, 1981. il.

May, Chris, and Tim Phillips. *British Beat.* London: Socion, 1974. il.

Animals; Eric Burdon and the Animals (See also: Eric Burdon)

Stambler, Irwin. "The Animals," In: *The Encyclopedia of Pop, Rock and Soul.* pp. 10–11. il.

Beatles (See also: Michael Jackson)

"Beatle City to Shutter," *Variety.* 318 (March 27, 1985) 95.

"Beatles' Apple Records lawsuit vs. Capitol Draws Press Barbs," *Variety.* 323 (June 11, 1986) 75.

"Beatles Exhibit Heads for London," *Billboard.* 97 (December 21, 1985) 54.

"Beatles Fail to Snare More Back Royalties from English Court," *Variety.* 323 (May 14, 1986) 86.

"Beatles' Firm Sues Apple Computer Over Trademark Use," *Variety.* 334 (March 1, 1989) 69.

"Beatles Suing Capitol-EMI Again for Licensing 'Revolution' to Nike," *Variety.* 328 (August 5, 1987) 63ff.

"Beatles, Yoko Lose Bid in EMI Royalties Action," *Billboard.* 98 (April 19, 1986) 92.

Buchanan, R. "Radio Kings: Ad Rock," *Rolling Stone.* n508 (September 10, 1987) 58. il.

"Can't Buy Me Love, But . . . ; Beatles Items Fetch $300,000," *Billboard.* 98 (September 13, 1986) 78.

"Capitol Moves to Pull American Edition Beatles LPs from the Shelves," *Cash Box.* 49:24 (November 23, 1985) 36.

Cocks, Jay, with Elizabeth L. Bland and Elaine Dutka. "Wanna Buy a Revolution? The Beatles Shill for Sneak as Mad. Ave. Rocks Out," *Time.* 129 (May 18, 1987) 78.

DeCurtis, Anthony. "Beatles Sue Over Nike Commercial," *Rolling Stone.* n508 (September 10, 1987) 15. Re. the use of the song, "Revolution."

DeCurtis, Anthony. "Beatles Sue Over Nike Commercial," *Rolling Stone.* n508 (September 10, 1987) 15. int. w/Paul McCartney and band associates.

DiMauro, P. "Beatles Win Round in Suit vs. Capitol Over Back Royalties," *Variety.* 324 (August 6, 1986) 79–80.

Goldberg, M. "Beatles: Court Fights Rage On," *Rolling Stone.* n529 (June 30, 1988) 15. Re. two similar albums featuring twenty-five-year-old demo recordings.

Grein, Paul. "Beatles' British Albums Will Replace U.S. Versions," *Billboard.* 97 (December 7, 1985) 84.

Guzek, Arnot. *Beatles Discography.* Alphen aan de Rijn: Beatles Unlimited, 1978. pap.

Harry, Bill. *Paperback Writers: The History of the Beatles in Print.* London: Virgin, 1984. il., bibl. Exhaustive listing—including books, magazines, fanzines, and music collections—pervaded by strong British (and, to a lesser extent, European) bias.

"Helmers to Make Sgt. Pepper Clips for Documentaries," *Variety.* 323 (April 30, 1986) 136ff.

Jeske, Lee. "Beatles Collector Offers $750,000 Collection to Start Fab Four Museum," *Cash Box.* (December 27, 1986) 14, 35.

Jones, P. "Beatles Officially Hit Soviet Marketplace," *Billboard.* 98 (April 12, 1986) 65.

Kassan, Brian. "Beatles for Sale: Retailers Cautiously Anticipate CD-Mania," *Cash Box.* (March 7, 1987) 5, 13.

"L.A. Judge Decides Beatlemania Prod. Must Stand Trial," *Variety.* 320 (October 2, 1985) 3ff.

Mendelssohn, John. "Eleganza. Time Marches On!," *Creem.* 18 (December 1986) 24ff.

"Menon, Martin Comment on Beatles CDs," *Cash Box.* (March 7, 1987) 5, 10, 13. int. w/EMI Music Worldwide chairman and famed Beatles producer.

Morris, Chris, and M. Newman. "RIAA, Capitol Team to Hunt Beatles Bootleggers," *Billboard.* 101 (March 25, 1989) 4ff.

"A New Beatles Album?," *Musician.* n81 (July 1985) 32. Re. unissued recordings.

"Nike Denies Its Ad Showed Disrespect for Beatles' Music,"
    Variety. 328 (August 12, 1987) 91.

"No New Probe for Beatles Coin," *Variety.* 322 (April 2, 1986)
    82.

Pielke, Robert. "The Beatles and the Affirmation of the
    Sixties," In: *You Say You Want a Revolution.* Chicago:
    Nelson-Hall, 1986. pp. 157–182. il.

"RIAA Launches Special Probe of Beatles' Bootlegs," *Variety.*
    334 (March 15, 1989) 53.

Reck, D. "Beatles Orientalis: Influences from Asia in a Popular
    Song Tradition," *Asian Music.* 16:1 (1985) 83–149.

Ressner, Jeffrey. "New Beatles LPs Due?," *Rolling Stone.* n571
    (February 8, 1990) 28.

"Rhino Execs Fined for Bootleg Disks," *Variety.* 321 (October
    30, 1985) 88.

Robertshaw, N. "Beatles Sue to Stop Beer Campaign;
    Heineken U.K. Pushes Tape Offer," *Billboard.* 98 (Au-
    gust 16, 1986) 62A.

Schipper, H. "Beatles Awarded $10,000,000 in Judgment
    Against Beatlemania," *Variety.* 323 (June 11, 1986) 75.

Schipper, H. "Lincoln Slipped Past Potato Chips, Chicken and
    Lotsa Other Suitors to Win Beatles' Song For Blurb,"
    Variety. 319 (July 10, 1985) 79ff. Re. "Help."

" 'Something' Used in Ad," *Rolling Stone.* n519 (February 11,
    1988) 23.

Soocher, Stan. "You Never Give Me My Money," *Rolling Stone.* n570 (January 25, 1990) 14–15. il.

Spencer, P. "Set Works for GCSE—The Beatles: *Help!*," *Music Teacher.* 68 (January 1989) 27ff. il., music.

Stambler, Irwin. "The Beatles," In: *The Encyclopedia of Pop, Rock and Soul.* pp. 37–40. il.

"Tarnished Image of Liverpool Kills Beatles Museum," *Variety.* 321 (January 22, 1986) 2ff.

Terry, Ken. "Beatles Lawyer Charges Capitol Diverted Albums," *Variety.* 325 (December 24, 1986) 1ff.

Terry, Ken. "McCartney Deserts Other Beatles in Legal Fight vs. Capitol/EMI; Damages Upped to $80–mil.," *Variety.* 321 (January 22, 1986) 73ff.

Terry, Ken. "2 Ex-Beatles Win 1, Lose 1 in Lawsuits vs. Capitol, EMI," *Billboard.* 100 (June 4, 1988) 76.

Wiener, Jon. "Beatles Buy-Out," *New Republic.* n3773 (May 11, 1987) 13–14.
Report on Nike's use of "Revolution" in its TV ad campaign.

HARRISON, GEORGE

DeCurtis, Anthony. "George Harrison," *Rolling Stone.* n512 (November 5, 1987. 47–50. il., int.

Giuliano, Geoffrey. *Dark Horse: The Private Life of George Harrison.* New York: Dutton, 1990. il.

Kordosh, J. "Fab! Gear! The George Harrison Interview," *Creem.* 19 (December 1987) 42–44ff. il., int.

Stambler, Irwin. "Harrison, George," In: *The Encyclopedia of Pop, Rock and Soul.* pp. 281–283.

LENNON, JOHN

"Beatles Pair Honored," *Billboard.* 98 (September 27, 1986) 3ff.

Gates, David, and others. "Lennon: The Battle Over His Memory," *Newsweek.* (October 17, 1988) 64–73. il. Includes sidebar, "Yoko Ono: A Widow Guards Her Husband's Legacy," by Cathleen McGuigan.

Hunter, N. "U.K.'s PRS Withholds Lennon Prize in Light of Poor Entries," *Billboard.* 101 (August 12, 1989) 70.

Jeske, Lee. "Live Lennon Recording Released Fourteen Years After Concert," *Cash Box.* XLIX:35 (February 15, 1986) 10.

"Nine Selected for Induction into Songwriters Hall of Fame," *Billboard.* 98 (December 27, 1986) 8.

Ressner, Jeffrey. "Concert Marks John Lennon's Birthday," *Rolling Stone.* n577 (May 3, 1990) 26.

Robbins, Janet Lund. "Flash: Working Class Hero; In Homage to Her Late Husband, Yoko Ono Has Opened a Gallery in New York City to Exhibit John Lennon's Lesser-Known Artwork," *Spin.* 5:7 (October 1989) 28. il.

Seideman, T. "*Lennon Live* is the First Music Title to Ship Gold," *Billboard.* 98 (March 22, 1986) 39.

Stambler, Irwin. "Lennon, John, and Ono, Yoko," In: *The Encyclopedia of Pop, Rock and Soul.* pp. 396–399. il.

Tabor, L. "Rock On," *International Musician.* 84 (November 1985) 6. Strawberry Fields dedicated in Central Park.

McCARTNEY, PAUL

DeCurtis, Anthony. "Paul McCartney," *Rolling Stone.* n512 (November 5, 1987) 39–44. il., int.

Fricke, David. "One for the Road; Backstage With Paul McCartney for His First World Tour in More Than a Decade," *Rolling Stone.* n571 (February 8, 1990) 42–48. il., int.

Gett, S. "Paul McCartney Presses on With a Harder Edge," *Billboard.* 98 (September 6, 1986) 19. Re. *Press to Play.*

Grein, Paul. "McCartney Resumes Tie With Capitol," *Billboard.* 97 (November 9, 1985) 3ff.

Iorio, Paul. "Paul McCartney Furthers a Great Capitol Tradition With 'Press to Play'," *Cash Box.* (August 30, 1986) 11. il.

"McCartney Re-signs With Capitol Label; Single is Due Soon," *Variety.* 321 (November 6, 1985) 85ff.

Neely, Kim. "McCartney: Visa Deal No Sellout," *Rolling Stone.* n569 (January 11, 1990) 20.

"News: On the Long and Winding Road Again," *Spin.* 5:8 (November 1989) 28. il.

"Paul McCartney to Receive Special Award," *Billboard.* 98 (January 18, 1986) 65.
Re. American Music Awards, "Award of Merit."

Salewicz, C. "Tug of War: Paul McCartney Wants to Lay His Demons to Rest," *Musician.* n96 (October 1986) 56–60ff. il.

Stambler, Irwin. "McCartney, Paul," In: *The Encyclopedia of Pop, Rock and Soul.* pp. 452–454. il.

Sweeting, Adam. "Yesterday and Today," *Rolling Stone.* n565 (November 16, 1989) 22. il., int.

STARR, RINGO (r.n.: RICHARD STARKEY)

Aronoff, Kenny. "Ringo Starr: The Early Period," *Modern Drummer.* 11 (October 1987) 102–103. il.

Flans, R. "Ringo," *Modern Drummer.* 5 (December 1981–January 1982) 10–13ff. il.

Garbarini, V. "Ringo," *Musician Player & Listener.* n40 (February 1982) 44–53. il., int.

Stambler, Irwin. "Starr, Ringo," In: *The Encyclopedia of Pop, Rock and Soul.* pp. 640–641.

Wild, David. "A Starr is Reborn," *Rolling Stone.* n559 (August 24, 1989) 104–106ff. il.

Big Three

Leigh, Spencer. "The Big Three," *Record Collector.* n83 (July 1986) 14–18. il., disc.

Burdon, Eric (See also: Animals)

Stambler, Irwin. "Burdon, Eric," In: *The Encyclopedia of Pop, Rock and Soul.* pp. 86–87.

Chad and Jeremy (r.n.: C. Stuart and J. Clyde)

Stambler, Irwin. "Chad and Jeremy," In: *The Encyclopedia of Pop, Rock and Soul.* pp. 107–108.

Clark, Dave, Five

Stambler, Irwin. "Dave Clark Five, The," In: *The Encyclopedia of Pop, Rock and Soul.* pp. 122–124.

Clark, Petula

Kon, Andrea. *This is My Song: Biography of Petula Clark.* London: Comit, 1984. il., bio. pap.

Stambler, Irwin. "Clark, Petula," In: *The Encyclopedia of Pop, Rock and Soul.* pp. 125–126.

Faithfull, Marianne

Considine, J.D. "As Tears Go By," *Buzz.* 3:2 (December 1987) 24–29. il., int.

Milkowski, Bill. "Marianne Faithfull," *Down Beat.* (November 1987) 15. il., int.

Stambler, Irwin. "Faithfull, Marianne," In: *The Encyclopedia of Pop, Rock and Soul*. pp. 224–225.

Freddie and the Dreamers

Stambler, Irwin. "Freddie and the Dreamers," In: *The Encyclopedia of Pop, Rock and Soul*. pp. 241–242.

Gerry and the Pacemakers

Stambler, Irwin. "Gerry & the Pacemakers," In: *The Encyclopedia of Pop, Rock and Soul*. p. 256.

Herman's Hermits

Stambler, Irwin. "Noone, Peter," In: *The Encyclopedia of Pop, Rock and Soul*. pp. 491–493.

Hollies (See also: Crosby, Stills and Nash)

The Hollies, as told to Anne Nightingale. *How to Run a Beat Group*. London: Daily Mirror, 1964. il. The compact book (100 pages) provides a bird's-eye view of life on the road. It has continued to retain value due to its perspective on the British Beat Era.

Stambler, Irwin. "The Hollies," In: *The Encyclopedia of Pop, Rock and Soul*. pp. 292–293.

The Kinks

Iorio, Paul. "Everything You Wanted To Know About the Kinks But Were Afraid to Read: The *Cash Box* Interview With Ray Davies," *Cash Box*. (February 14, 1987) 13, 28–29. il., int.

Lababedi, I., and B. Nevin. Ray Davies: Face to Face With the Lost Decade," *Creem.* 18 (June 1987) 46–47. il., int.

Rogan, Johnny. *The Kinks: The Sound and the Fury.* London: Elm Tree, 1984. il., bio.

Santelli, R. "Knowing the Job," *Modern Drummer.* 9 (February 1985) 18–21 ff. il., int. w/Mick Avory.

Savage, Jon. *The Kinks: The Official Biography.* London: Faber, 1984. il., bio., disc.

Stambler, Irwin. "The Kinks," In: *The Encyclopedia of Pop, Rock and Soul.* pp. 374–376.

DAVIES, RAY

McCullaugh, J. "Heavy Marketing Push for Davies' *Return to Waterloo,*" *Billboard.* 97 (July 13, 1985) 26.

Sullivan, J. "Why is This Man Smiling? Ray Davies Bounces Back," *Record.* 4 (April 1985) 32ff. il.

Kramer, Billy J, and the Dakotas

Stambler, Irwin. "Kramer, Billy J & the Dakotas," In: *The Encyclopedia of Pop, Rock and Soul.* p. 388.

Manfred Mann; Manfred Mann's Earth Band

Stambler, Irwin. "Mann, Manfred," In: *The Encyclopedia of Pop, Rock and Soul.* pp. 440–442.

Moody Blues (See also: Symphonic Rock)

Stambler, Irwin. "Moody Blues," In: *The Encyclopedia of Pop, Rock and Soul.* pp. 470–471.

Peter and Gordon (r.n.: P. Asher and G. Waller)

Stambler, Irwin. "Peter & Gordon," In: *The Encyclopedia of Pop, Rock and Soul.* pp. 516–517.

Rolling Stones

Coppola, Vincent. "Rock Grows Up," *Newsweek.* (December 19, 1983) 90–93. il.

Davis, Ancil. "Rolling Stones Said Negotiating With Pepsi on U.S. Tour," *Amusement Business.* (May 11, 1985) 1ff.

DeCurtis, Anthony. "The Rolling Stones: Artist of the Year," *Rolling Stone.* n573 (March 8, 1990) 24–29. il., int. w/Jagger and Richards.

DeCurtis, Anthony. " 'Steel Wheels' Tour Rolls," *Rolling Stone.* n563 (October 19, 1989) 11–14. il.

Dowley, Tim. *Mick Jagger and the Stones.* Tunbridge Wells, Kent, England: Midas, 1982. il.

Fricke, David. "Satisfaction?," *Rolling Stone.* n560 (September 7, 1989) 36–44, 82. il., int.

German, Bill. " 'Steel Wheels' Tour Rolls on in Japan," *Rolling Stone.* n576 (April 19, 1990) 25. il.

Gigies, Nancy. "Stones May Rock for Pepsi," *Advertising Age.* (March 25, 1985) 1ff.

Goldberg, Michael. "Rich Stones Want to Roll On," *Rolling Stones.* n569 (January 11, 1990) 17.

Goldberg, Michael. " 'Steel Wheels' Spawns New Deals. How Much Money do the Rolling Stones Need?," *Rolling Stone.* n563 (October 19, 1989) 16.

Isler, Scott. "New Summary: Stones Drummer Denies Breakup," *Musician.* n107 (September 1987) 15–16ff. il., int. w/Watts.

Jagger, Chris. "Backstage Confidential," *Rolling Stone.* n573 (March 8, 1990) 32, 117.

Kirby, Fred. "Stones Settle Suit vs. Abkco; Public Retains Most Rights," *Variety.* 314 (April 25, 1984) 85ff.

Lahr, John. "Exiles on Easy Street: The Decadent Career of the Rolling Stones," *New Republic.* (December 24, 1984) 26–30. il.

Lichtman, Irv. "Volvo Pulls 'Stones' Ad," *Billboard.* 98 (May 17, 1986) 84.

Robinson, Lisa. "On the Road Again," *Spin.* 5:9 (December 1989) 50–59. il., int.

Slater, Andrew. "Stones Headed for CBS; $25 Million Deal in Works," *Rolling Stone.* (September 28, 1983) 59.

Stambler, Irwin. "The Rolling Stones," In: *The Encyclopedia of Pop, Rock and Soul.* pp. 580–583. il.

"Volvo Yanks Ad With Stones Song; ABKCO Asks Blood,"
Variety. 323 (May 7, 1986) 535–536.

JAGGER, MICK (See also: DAVID BOWIE)

Armbruster, G. "Hancock, Hammer, Leavell, and 6 Others
Gather No Moss on Jagger's New Solo Album," *Keyboard
Magazine.* 11 (May 1985) 12ff. Re. *She's the Boss.*

Bockris, V. "The Worst Dinner Party I Ever Gave," *Village
Voice.* 31 (April 15, 1986) 42. il., int.

Connelly, Christopher. "Stepping Out! Mick Jagger Releases a
Solo Album But Says It's Not the End of the Stones—
Yet," *Rolling Stone.* (February 14, 1985) 18ff. il., int.

Gilmore, Mikal. "Mick Jagger," *Rolling Stone.* n512 (November 5, 1987) 30–35. il., int.

Goodman, Fred. "Jagger Wins Court Battle: Case Focused on
Authorship of 'Just Another Night'," *Rolling Stone.* n527
(June 2, 1988) 23. il., int.

Hunter, M. "Big Boss Man," *Record.* 4 (May 1985) 24–25ff. il.

Irwin, C. "Boss Cat," 60 (February 16, 1985) 20–21ff. il., int.

Jamaican Artist Sues Jagger Over 'Just Another Night' Single," *Variety.* 322 (January 29, 1986) 79.

Lovece, F. "Jagger Release Mines New Territory," *Billboard.* 98
(November 15, 1986) 66. Re. long-form video, *Running
Out of Luck.*

McCullaugh, J. "Jagger Shows Market Savvy With New Film," *Billboard.* (September 6, 1986) 48ff. Re. *Running Out of Luck.*

McInernay, Jay. "Jagger—Watching; A Week Around Town With Mick," *Esquire.* (May 1985) 209ff. il.

"Mick Jagger: Candid Talk About Music, Videos and Tapes He Won't Let His Kids Watch!," *Video Review.* (December 1986) 65–67, 176. il., int.

"Reggae Musician Says Jagger Stole 'Just Another Night'," *Billboard.* 98 (January 11, 1986) 80.

RICHARDS, KEITH

DeCurtis, Anthony, and Kurt Loder. "Keith Richards Set to Record First Solo LP," *Rolling Stone.* n508 (September 10, 1987) 15. il., int.

Loder, Kurt. "Keith Richards," *Rolling Stone.* n512 (November 5, 1987) 64–67. il., int.

STEWART, IAN

Fricke, David. "Ian Stewart: 1938–1985: 'The Sixth Stone' Dies in London," *Rolling Stone.* (January 30, 1985) 19. il., obit.

"Ian Stewart," *Variety.* (December 18, 1985) 99. obit.

WOOD, RON (See also: JEFF BECK GROUP; FACES)

Flanagan, Bill. "The Nine Lives of Ron Wood," *Musician.* n95 (September 1986) 61–63, 106, 113. il.

Wood, Ron. *Ron Wood.* New York: Harper, 1987. il., autobio.

WYMAN, BILL

McCarthy, Todd. "Stones Bassist Goes Public With $1–Mil. Film About Private Life," *Variety.* 312 (October 19, 1983) 2ff.

Mendelssohn, John. "Eleganza: The World's Boredest Man," *Creem.* 18 (June 1987) 26ff. il.

Sutherland, Sam. "Wyman's Production Firm Offers Him Starring Role," *Billboard.* 95 (May 7, 1983) 49.

Who

Farber, Celia. "A Fan's Notes," *Spin.* 5:6 (September 1989) 40–42, 102. il.

Goldberg, M. "The Who by Numbers," *Rolling Stone.* n559 (August 24, 1989) 28.

Stambler, Irwin. "The Who," In: *The Encyclopedia of Pop, Rock and Soul.* pp. 738–741. il.

DALTREY, ROGER

Welch, Chris. "Roger Daltrey," *Creem.* 17 (March 1986) 16–17ff. il.

Yardumian, Rob. "Roger Daltrey is Back Back on Track," *Cash Box.* (August 15, 1987) 11, 33. il., int.

MOON, KEITH

Wittet, T.B. "Keith Moon Remembered," *Modern Drummer.* 6 (June 1982) 14–17ff. il., bio.

PHILLIPS, SIMON

Goodwin, S., and W.G. Miller. "Simon Phillips," *Modern Drummer.* 10 (December 1986) 16–21ff. il., int.

TOWNSHEND, PETE

Dobrin, Gregory. "Pete Townshend Releases *White City* Album and Video," *Cash Box.* XLIX:24 (November 23, 1985) 35.

Fricke, David. "Pete Townshend," *Rolling Stone.* n512 (November 5, 1987) 179–183. il., int.

Yardbirds (See also: Jeff Beck; Eric Clapton; Cream)

Stambler, Irwin. "The Yardbirds," In: *The Encyclopedia of Pop, Rock and Soul.* pp. 755–757.

C. SECOND WAVE (1966–1970)

Beck, Jeff; Jeff Beck Group; Beck, Bogart and Appice (See also: Yardbirds; Ron Wood)

Drozdowski, Ted. "Guitar Slingers Shoot It Out," *Rolling Stone.* n566 (November 30, 1989) 28. il. Covers tour featuring the headliner collaboration of Beck and Stevie Ray Vaughan.

Fish, S.K., and B. Cioffi. "Creem Showcase," *Creem.* 17 (February 1986) 68–69. il.

Fricke, David. "Jeff Beck—Number One With a Slow Bullet: Confessions of a Reluctant Guitarist," *Musician.* n79 (May 1985) 40–46ff. il.

Obrecht, Jas. "Beck on Beck," *Guitar Player.* 19 (November 1985) 84–87ff. il., int., disc.

Obrecht, Jas. "Jeff Beck Gallery," *Guitar Player.* 19 (November 1985) 88–89. il.

Obrecht, Jas. "Jeff Beck's Odyssey," *Guitar Player.* 19 (November 1985) 87ff.

Pond, Jeff. "Alone Together: Guitar Gurus Jeff Beck and Stevie Ray Vaughan Take to the Road," *Rolling Stone.* n570 (January 25, 1990) 45–47, 56. il., int.

Stambler, Irwin. "Beck, Jeff," In: *The Encyclopedia of Pop, Rock and Soul.* pp. 42–44.

Stern, C. "Faces," *Musician Player & Listener.* n30 (February 1981) 48–49. il.

Stix, John. "Jeff Beck: The Ultimate," *Guitar.* (May 1990) 14–28. il., int. covering his career output.

Bee Gees

Billboard Salutes the Bee Gees. Los Angeles: Billboard Publications, 1978. il. pap. Minimal text; high quality graphics and pictures throughout the 117 pages.

Gett, S. "The Beat: Brothers Gibb Are Back in Big Way," *Billboard.* 99 (September 19, 1987) 26.

Gett, S. "Bee Gees Ready to Win Again," *Billboard.* 99 (September 12, 1987) 21.

Pryce, Larry. *The Bee Gees.* St. Albans, U.K.: Panther, 1979. il. pap.

Stambler, Irwin. "The Bee Gees," In: *The Encyclopedia of Pop, Rock and Soul.* pp. 44–46. il.

Tatham, Dick. *The Incredible Bee Gees.* London: Futura, 1979. disc. pap.

White, Adam. "Bee Gees Hope to Break 'Fever' Grip," *Rolling Stone.* n562 (October 5, 1989) 32–33. il., int.

Clapton, Eric (See also: Cream; Yardbirds)

Fish, S.K., B. Cioffi. "Creem Showcase," *Creem.* 17 (February 1986) 67–68. il.

Guitar Player. 19 (July 1985) il., bio., bibl., disc. Special issue devoted entirely to Clapton.

Peisch, J. "The Slowhand of God: Sittin' in With Eric Clapton," *Record.* 4 (July 1985) 30–34ff. il., int.

Pidgeon, John. *Eric Clapton: A Biography.* St. Albans: Panther, 1976. il., disc. pap.

Stambler, Irwin. "Clapton, Eric," In: *The Encyclopedia of Pop, Rock and Soul.* pp. 121–122. il.

Turner, Steve. *Conversations With Eric Clapton.* London: Abacus, 1976. il., disc. pap.

White, Timothy. "Rollin' & Tumblin'," *Spin.* 5:12 (March 1990) 32–39. il., int.

Dave Dee, Dozy, Beaky, Mick and Tich

Clayson, Alan. "Dave Dee, Dozy, Beaky, Mick, and Tich," *Record Collector.* n41 (January 1983) 54–58. il., disc.

Woodard, Rex. "Dave Dee, Dozy, Beaky, Mick and Tich: Zabadak," *Goldmine.* n215 (October 21, 1988) 10–14, 20. il., disc.

Faces (See also: Jeff Beck; Humble Pie; Rod Stewart)

Stambler, Irwin. "The Faces," In: *The Encyclopedia of Pop, Rock and Soul.* pp. 223–224.

LANE, RONNIE (See also: ARMS)

Goodman, Fred. "MS Trust Begun by Rocker is Placed in Receivership," *Billboard.* 98 (June 7, 1986) 98.

LeQuang, J.A. "Lane's [sic] Foundation into Receivership; Charges Forseen," *Variety.* 323 (May 14, 1986) 2ff.

Reavis, Dick J. "The Faulty Cure," *Texas Monthly.* (September 1986) 124–127, 192, 200–208. il., int., bio.

Fleetwood Mac

Clarke, Tina. "Rock Notes: Back to the Blues," *Me Music Express Magazine.* 14:148 (June 1990) 13. il., int. w/Stevie Nicks.

Gett, Steve. "Fleetwood Mac Looks Ahead," *Billboard.* 99 (October 10, 1987) 21.

Kordosh, J. "Fleetwood Mac Return Without Leaving," *Creem.* 19 (September 1987) 32–35. il.

Stambler, Irwin. "Fleetwood Mac," In: *The Encyclopedia of Pop, Rock and Soul.* pp. 228–231. il.

Strauss, D. "Simplicity as a Way of Life," *Record.* 4 (November 1984) 16–17ff. il.

Frampton, Peter (See also: Humble Pie)

Coffi, B. "Tech Talk: Frampton Comes to Terms With Himself," *Creem.* 19 (October 1987) 50–51. il.

Humble Pie (See also: Peter Frampton)

Stambler, Irwin. "Humble Pie," In: *The Encyclopedia of Pop, Rock and Soul.* pp. 301–302.

Idle Race (See also: Electric Light Orchestra)

Baker, Glenn A. "The Idle Race: The Lewis Carroll World of Intelligent Fantasy," *Goldmine.* n137 (October 25, 1985) 66, 68. il.

John, Elton (r.n.: Reginald Kenneth Dwight; See also: Copyright)

Baker, Glenn A. "Elton Hits New Heights," *Billboard.* 98 (December 6, 1986) 75.

John, Elton. *The Elton John Tapes: Elton John in Conversation With Andy Peebles.* London: BBC Publications, 1981. il. pap.

"John to Avoid S. Africa While Apartheid Lasts," *Variety.* 321 (January 1, 1986) 127ff.

"John Tour of Oz With Orchestra to Break Even; High Overhead," *Variety.* 325 (December 10, 1986) 92.

Jones, P. "Settlement Reached in Elton John/Dick James Case," *Billboard.* 97 (December 14, 1985) 70.

Stambler, Irwin. "Elton John," In: *The Encyclopedia of Pop, Rock and Soul.* pp. 341–344.

COOPER, RAY

Goodwin, S. "Ray Cooper: Energy and Discipline," *Modern Percussion.* 2:2 (1986) 14–17ff. il., int.

OLSSON, NIGEL

Flans, R. "The Heart of Nigel Olsson," *Modern Drummer.* 9 (February 1985) 26–29ff. il., bio., int.

John's Children

Thompson, Dave. "John's Children," *Record Collector.* n58 (June 1984) 30–34. il., disc.

Proby, P.J. (r.n.: James Marcus Smith)

"45 Revelations," *Creem.* 17 (May 1986) 33.

Scaffold

Leigh, Spencer. "Scaffold," *Record Collector.* n54 (February 1984) 22–26. il., disc.

Small Faces (See: Faces)

Spooky Tooth

Hoog, Brian. "Spooky Tooth," *Record Collector.* n82 (June 1986) 30–34. il., disc.

Tortelli, Joseph. "Spooky Tooth: The Last Puff," *Goldmine.* n218 (December 2, 1988) 30, 87. il.

Stewart, Rod (See also: Jeff Beck; Faces)

Stambler, Irwin. "Stewart, Rod," In: *The Encyclopedia of Pop, Rock and Soul.* pp. 649–651. il.

Traffic

Stambler, Irwin. "Traffic," In: *The Encyclopedia of Pop, Rock and Soul.* pp. 693–695.

WINWOOD, STEVE

Morris, Chris. "Winwood on a Roll With New Disk," *Bill-board.* 100 (August 27, 1988) 33ff.

Stambler, Irwin. "Winwood, Steve," In: *The Encyclopedia of Pop, Rock and Soul.* pp. 744–745.

D. THIRD WAVE (1971–1975)

General Sources

Van der Kiste, John. *Roxeventies: Popular Music in Britain 1970–1979.* Torpoint, Cornwall, U.K.: Kawabata, 1982. il., disc.

Arrows

Harry, Bill. *Arrows: The Official Story.* London: Everest, 1976. il., bio.

Stardust, Alvin

Leigh, Spencer. "Alvin Stardust," *Record Collector.* n60 (August 1984) 28–32. il., disc.

Thin Lizzy

Irwin, C. "Phil Lynott, 1951–1986," *Melody Maker.* 61 (January 11, 1986) 3. il.

(Obituary), *Creem.* 17 (April 1986) 6.

(Obituary), *Musician.* n89 (March 1986) 24.

(Obituary), *Variety.* 321 (January 15, 1986) 245.

"Phil Lynott, Ex of Thin Lizzy Dies in London at Age 35," *Billboard.* 98 (January 18, 1986) 4.

E. COMMONWEALTH CONTRIBUTIONS

Australia/New Zealand (See also: Counterfeiting)

GENERAL SOURCES

Baker, Glenn A. "Australia Music Biz Study Points to a Lack of Government Support," *Billboard.* 99 (October 17, 1987) 77.

Stafford, P., and others. "International Spotlight: Australia," *Billboard.* 101 (January 28, 1989) A2ff. il.

ANGEL; ANGEL CITY

Fricke, David. "Angels Finally Fly," *Rolling Stone.* n573 (March 8, 1990) 56. il., int. w/vocalist Doc Neeson.

EASYBEATS

Baker, Glenn A. "Vanda & Young," *Apra Journal.* 2:10 (1982) 38–39.

"Easybeats Regroup for an Aussie Tour," *Variety.* 324 (September 3, 1986) 121.

FINN, TIM

Baker, Glenn A. "Tim Finn," *Apra Journal.* 4:2 (1986) 56–57.

KELLY, PAUL

Yardumian, Rob. "New Faces to Watch: Paul Kelly," *Cash Box.* (October 3, 1987) 11. il., int.

LITTLE RIVER BAND; LRB

Baker, Glenn A. "Little River Band—First Under the Wire," *Apra Journal.* 2:10 (1982) 10–12.

"Glenn Wheatley Waxes Optimistic Over Little River's Future Course," *Variety.* 323 (April 30, 1986) 115–116.

Vare, E.A. "New Lineup, New Director for LRB," *Billboard.* 97 (February 2, 1985) 66. int.

MEN AT WORK (See also: JAMES COLIN HAY)

Coupe, S. "Men at Work," *Apra Journal.* 3:1 (1983) 2–5. il.

"Men at Work Tour of China Postponed; Docu, LP Planned," *Variety.* 320 (October 9, 1985) 116.

HAY, JAMES COLIN (See also: MEN AT WORK)

Iorio, Paul. "Colin James Hay: Man at Work Goes Solo," *Cash Box.* (April 18, 1987) 11, 25. il., int.

STIFF LITTLE FINGERS

"Sidelines: Stiff Little Fingers," *Melody Maker.* 63 (December 12, 1987) 13. il., int. w/Jake Burns. Re. reunion tour.

WA WA NEE

Yardumian, Rob. "Wa Wa Nee," *Cash Box.* (November 14, 1987) 8. il., int. w/lead vocalist and keyboardist Paul Gray.

Canada

GENERAL SOURCES

Collie, Ashley. Music Marketing: Canadian Rockers Cozy Up to Corporate America With Mixed Results," *Music Scene.* n350 (July–August 1986) 14–15.

Jennings, Nicholas. "Vancouver's Rock 'n' Roll Explosion," *Maclean's.* (March 21, 1988) 62–63. il.

ADAMS, BRYAN (See also: JIM VALLANCE)

"Adams Sets Sales Record for a Canadian Artist," *Variety.* 321 (January 1, 1986) 127.

Bateman, J. "Adams and Vallance: The Secrets of Association," *Music Scene.* n346 (November–December 1985) 8–9. il.

"Bryan Adams Hard at Work," *Canadian Musician.* 7:2 (1985) 11. il.

Burley, T. "The Awakening of Bryan Adams," *Canadian Musician.* 9:4 (1987) 5, 7. il.

Fissinger, L. "Bryan Adams," *Record.* 4 (December 1985) 20–22ff. il., int.

Harrison, T. "Bryan Adams: From Frying Pan, *Into the Fire,*" *Canadian Musician.* 9:4 (1987) 44–45ff. il., int.

Jennings, Nicholas. "The Superstar," *Maclean's.* (July 6, 1987) 32–35. il., int. w/Adams and associates.

Mehler, M. "Reckless Disregard: Rock 'n' Roll Misfit Bryan Adams Tries Hard to be a Nice Guy. No Cigar," *Record.* 4 (May 1985) 12–14. il.

"*Reckless* Nears Record," *Billboard.* 96 (September 14, 1985) 89. The album is reported to be likely to become the top-selling album of all time by a Canadian artist.

"Top PRO Award Goes to Adams, Vallance for *Reckless* Album," *Variety.* 320 (October 9, 1985) 116.

APRIL WINE

"A Brighter Horizon for April Wine With New Band and Outside Writers," *Canadian Composer.* n204 (October 1985) 36–37.

BLONDES (See also: PLATINUM BLONDE)

Sharp, Keith. "Sound Check: The Blondes; Self-Satisfying," *Me Music Express Magazine.* 14:148 (June 1990) 17. il., int.

BLUE RODEO

"Blue Rodeo: Raiders of a Lost Art," *Canadian Musician.* 11:4 (1989) 48–52. il.

Goldberg, Michael. "New Faces: Blue Rodeo," *Rolling Stone.* n562 (October 5, 1989) 29. il.

Levy, Joe. "New Faces to Watch: Blue Rodeo," *Cash Box.* (April 9, 1988) 11. il., int. w/Greg Keelor.

BOULEVARD

Sharp, Keith. "Sound Check: Boulevard; Street Talk," *Me Music Express Magazine.* 14:148 (June 1990) 17. il., int.
BOX

Collie, A. "The Box," *Canadian Musician.* 7:2 (1985) 34–35. il.

DOA

O'Day, E. "DOA: Canada's Premier Punks," *Music Scene.* n342 (March–April 1985) 16–17. il.

Wiggins, P. "Spotlight on Vancouver: Crisis Music for Crisis Times," *Canadian Musician.* 7:5 (1985) 52.

THE DEVICE

Burman, T. "Breaking in and Breaking out With Cover Bands," *Canadian Musician.* 8:4 (1986) 50ff.

Doerschuk, Bob. "Hit Songwriter Holly Knight Unleashes Her Keyboard Chops on Device's 22B3," *Keyboard Magazine.* 12 (April 1986) 16.

Gett, Steve. "Holly Knight's Band Sees Light of Day," *Billboard.* 98 (May 24, 1986) 27.

DOUG AND THE SLUGS

"Doug and the Slugs go for the Gold," *Canadian Composer.* n203 (September 1985) 44–45. Re. *Propaganda.*

EIGHT SECONDS

LaPointe, K. "Eight Seconds Has a Hit," *Billboard.* 98 (November 29, 1986) 58.

Merritt, J. "Eight Seconds: Countdown to Success," *Music Scene.* n345 (September–October 1985) 18. il.

54–40

"New Faces to Watch: 54–40," *Cash Box.* (August 16, 1986) 10. il., int.

FROZEN GHOST

Atherley, Ruth. "Seeking Pop's Promised Land: Frozen Ghost," *Maclean's.* (July 6, 1987) 37. il.

GLASS TIGER

Bessman, Jim. "Glass Tiger Succeeds South of Canada's Border," *Billboard.* 98 (November 22, 1986) 1ff.

LaPointe, K. "Glass Tiger Roars onto Canadian Scene," *Billboard.* 98 (July 5, 1986) 70.

"New Faces to Watch: Glass Tiger," *Cash Box.* (June 21, 1986) 12. il., int. w/drummer Michael Hanson.

Stern, P. "A Marketing Dream Come True: Glass Tiger," *Canadian Musician.* 8:3 (1986) 44–45.

GUESS WHO

Stambler, Irwin. "The Guess Who," In: *The Encyclopedia of Pop, Rock and Soul.* pp. 271–272.

HART, COREY

"Corey Hart Wins Popularity Poll," *Canadian Composer.* n213 (September 1986) 37–38.

"Hart Crew Heads Home After Tour," *Canadian Composer.* n207 (January 1986) 44–45.

Hazan, D. "Corey Hart," *Canadian Musician.* 7:3 (1985) 24–25. il.

LaPointe, K. "Corey Hart Second to Mine CRIA Diamond," *Billboard.* 98 (March 29, 1986) 63. Re. "Boy in the Box."

LaPointe, K. "Hart Hits Diamond Figure," *Billboard.* 98
    (February 22, 1986) 63–64.

Moleski, L. "Hart is Beside Himself," *Billboard.* 98 (November
    22, 1984) 32.

"A Music Industry Party," *Canadian Composer.* n205 (Novem-
    ber 1985) 22. il. Re. Juno Awards.

"Summer Tour is SRO for Hart," *Canadian Composer.* n203
    (September 1985) 42–43. il.

HAYWIRE

Allen, B. "Recording: Producing Haywire to Sound Competi-
    tive at Less Than Standard Cost," *Canadian Musician.* 8:4
    (1986) 92ff.

Stern, P. "Everything's Gone Haywire for East Coast Band,"
    Canadian Musician. 8:3 (1986) 15. il.

HEADPINS

Harrison, T. "Spotlight on Vancouver: Headpins: Surviving the
    Hiatus," *Canadian Musician.* 7:5 (1985) 50–51. il., int.

"Hot 10 Profiles: New Generation of Canadian Talent Bub-
    bling Behind Long-Time Successes," *Billboard.* 97 (Feb-
    ruary 2, 1985) C3ff. il.

O'Day, E. "Headpins: The Year of Living Patiently," *Music
    Scene.* n347 (January–February 1986) 12–13.

HELIX

Heague, K. "Sound & Lighting: On the Road With Helix Over 12 Years," *Canadian Composer.* 8:5 (1986) 71.

"Hot 10 Profiles: New Generation of Canadian Talent Bubbling Behind Long-Time Successes," *Billboard.* 97 (February 2, 1985) C3ff.

Treumuth, T. "Recording: Producing Helix, Honeymoon Suite and Smash Palace," *Canadian Musician.* 8:2 (1986) 76.

HONEYMOON SUITE (See also: HELIX)

Betts, Dave. "Honeymoon Suite Records With Ted Templeman," *Canadian Musician.* 9:5 (1987) 74.

Collie, A. "The Making of Honeymoon Suite," *Canadian Musician.* 7:4 (1985) 32–33ff. il., int.

"European Debut for Suite's *Big Prize,*" *Billboard.* 98 (January 18, 1986) 52.

Graham, D. "Live and Studio Setups for Honeymoon Suite," *Canadian Musician.* 9:6 (1987) 68. il.

Halbersberg, Elianne. "Honeymoon Suite," *Song Hits.* n250 (December 1986) 16–17. il.

"Hot 10 Profiles: New Generation of Canadian Talent Bubbling Behind Long-Time Successes," *Billboard.* 97 (February 2, 1985) C3ff.

Moleski, L. "The Honeymoon Isn't Over," *Billboard.* 98 (May 10, 1986) 27.

Norton, M.J., and H. Rabinowitz. "Honeymoon Suite, eh?," *Creem.* 17 (June 1985) 18. il.

Prendergast, S. "Business: The Evolution of Honeymoon Suite," *Canadian Musician.* 8:2 (1986) 76–77; 8:3 (1986) 74–75.

Stern, P. "Honeymoon Suite: The Ted Templeman Experience," *Canadian Musician.* 10:3 (1988) 5, 32–33ff. il.

IDLE EYES

Clinton, B.J. "Idle Eyes: The Heat is On," *Music Scene.* n345 (September–October 1985) 18–19.

Druckman, H. "Spotlight on Vancouver: Idle Eyes on Bruce Allen: 'He's the Star, Not Us'," *Canadian Musician.* 7:5 (1985) 47.

LaPointe, K. "Idle Eyes Keep It Low-Key; New Group's Campbell is in No Hurry," *Billboard.* 97 (August 27, 1985) 62A.

JURY

Einarson, John S. "The Jury: Winnipeg's Forgotten '60s Success Story," *Goldmine.* n167 (December 19, 1986) 12, 14. il., disc.

LOVERBOY

Harrison, T. "Loverboy: On the Wild Side," *Canadian Musician.* 9:6 (1987) 5, 36–37ff. il., int.

Harrison, T. "Loverboy: Return from the Big Black Hole," *Canadian Musician.* 8:1 (1986) 40–41. il., int. w/Mike Reno and Paul Dean.

LaPointe, K. "Loverboy is Powered by Producer Bruce Fairbairn," *Billboard.* 99 (September 26, 1987) 77.

McBride, Murdock. "Na-na-na-na Nationwide—With Loverboy," *Cash Box.* (October 10, 1987) 8. il., int. w/singer Mike Reno and guitarist Paul Dean.

Stambler, Irwin. "Loverboy," In: *The Encyclopedia of Pop, Rock and Soul.* pp. 420–422.

MADAME

"A Busy Summer for Madame," *Canadian Composer.* n202 (July–August 1985) 42–43.

"An Unexpected Evolution," *Canadian Composer.* n205 (November 1985) 10–13. il.

McGARRIGLE SISTERS; McGARRIGLES

Blanks, T. "To Feed the Folk: The McGarrigles Resurface," *Canadian Musician.* 8:2 (1986) 10.

Kiefer, Kit. "Kate and Anna McGarrigle," *Goldmine.* n248 (January 26, 1990) 72, 74. il.

NEXUS

Mattingly, R. "Nexus," *Modern Percussion.* 1:3 (1985) 8–13ff. il., bio., int.

NYLONS

Atherley, Ruth. "Seeking Pop's Promised Land: The Nylons," *Maclean's.* (July 6, 1987) 37. il.

Gross, J. "Canadian Musicians and Their Money," *Canadian Musician.* 8:4 (1986) 44–45ff. il.

"Music in Canada," *Music Scene.* n341 (January–February 1985) 14. il.

"Nylons Scheduled to be First Canadian Pop Artists to Perform in China," *Canadian Composer.* n203 (September 1985) 44–45.

PARACHUTE CLUB

Atherley, Ruth. "Seeking Pop's Promised Land: The Parachute Club," *Maclean's.* (July 6, 1987) 36. il.

"CAPAC Members in the News," *Canadian Composer.* n200 (April 1985) 46–47. il. Re. *At the Fest of the Moon.*

Druckman, H. "Queen Street Philly Soul," *Canadian Musician.* 8:6 (1986) 46–47ff. il., int.

Galardi, S. "Medley: Canadian Club," *Hi Fi/Musical America.* 35 (July 1985) 50.

"Hot 10 Profiles: New Generation of Canadian Talent Bubbling Behind Long-Time Successes," *Billboard.* 97 (February 2, 1985) C3ff. il.

LaPointe, K. "Parachute Club is Feeling Its Oates," *Billboard.* 98 (December 6, 1986) 66.

"New Acts," *Variety.* 317 (January 9, 1985) 187.

PARTLAND BROTHERS

Atherley, Ruth. "Seeking Pop's Promised Land: Partland Brothers," *Maclean's.* (July 6, 1987) 37. il.

Jeske, Lee. "New Faces to Watch: Partland Brothers," *Cash Box.* (May 23, 1987) 10. il., int.

PIN-UPS

Burman, T. "Breaking in and Breaking out With Cover Bands," *Canadian Musician.* 8:4 (1986) 50ff.

PLATINUM BLONDE

Collie, A. "Notes: Labatt's Backs CPI Challenger," *Canadian Musician.* 7:5 (1985) 14.

Gross, J. "Canadian Musicians and Their Money," *Canadian Musician.* 8:4 (1986) 47. il.

Hazan, D. "Platinum Blonde," *Canadian Musician.* 6:6 (1984) 32–33ff.

"Hot 10 Profile: New Generation of Canadian Talent Bubbling Behind Long-Time Successes," *Billboard.* 97 (February 2, 1985) C3ff. il.

LaPointe, K. "Blonde Garners Quintuple Platinum With *Alien Shores* Releases," *Billboard.* 98 (February 22, 1986) 63.

LaPointe, K. "Platinum Blonde Becomes the Hottest Thing in Canada," *Billboard.* 97 (September 28, 1985) 47.

Littlejohn, M.A. "Kenny MacLean Reveals All! 'My Life as a Blonde'," *Music Scene.* n349 (May–June 1986) 16–17.

ROCK AND HYDE

Atherley, Ruth. "Seeking Pop's Promised Land: Rock and Hyde," *Maclean's.* (July 6, 1987) il., bio.

RUSH

Fish, S.K. "Neil Peart," *Modern Drummer.* 10 (January 1986) 16–17ff. il., int.

Keewen, N. "Surviving With Rush; Drummer-Lyricist Neil Peart Looks Forward," *Canadian Composer.* n210 (April 1986) 4–9ff. il., int.

Mulhern, T. "Geddy Lee of Rush: Rock's Leading Bassist," *Guitar Player*. 20 (April 1986) 84–86ff. il., int., disc.

Peart, Neil. "Notes on the Making of *Moving Pictures*," *Modern Drummer*. 6 (December 1982) 56–57.

Stambler, Irwin. "Rush," In: *The Encyclopedia of Pop, Rock and Soul*. pp. 592–594.

Stern, P. "Rush: Baroque Cosmologies in Their Past, the Boys Focus on the Perfect Song," *Canadian Musician*. 7:6 (1985) 28–31. il., int. w/Geddy Lee.

7. AMERICAN RENAISSANCE (1965–)

Lewis, Gary, and the Playboys

Stambler, Irwin. "Lewis, Gary," In: *The Encyclopedia of Pop, Rock and Soul.* p. 401.

Revere, Paul, and the Raiders

Stambler, Irwin. "Revere, Paul, and the Raiders; Paul Revere and the Raiders Starring Mark Lindsay; The Raiders," In: *The Encyclopedia of Pop, Rock and Soul.* pp. 567–568.

A. CALIFORNIA SOUND

The Surf Sound

GENERAL SOURCES

Forte, Dan. "Hollywood's Assemblyline Hitmakers," *Guitar Player.* 19 (October 1985) 63ff.

Forte, Dan, and others. "Instrumental Rock Guitarists: The Unsung Heroes," *Guitar Player.* 19 (October 1985) 69–70ff.

BEACH BOYS (See also: PARENTS MUSIC RESOURCE CENTER)

Arnold, T.K. "Surf's Up Again for Beach Boys," *Billboard.* 97 (May 25, 1985) 46ff.

"Beach Boys Claim Love's Brother Stole Bucks from Trust Fund," *Variety.* 321 (January 1, 1986) 127.

Hines, G. "The Beach Boys Schizophrenia," *Musician Player & Listener.* n32 (April 1981) 18ff. il.

Morris, C. "Suit: Beach Boys Made False Claims," *Billboard.* 98 (July 19, 1986) 87. Re. July 4th Capitol Mall concerts.

Pankau, R. "Beach Boys Inspire Sports Fans During Opening of Olympic Fest," *Variety.* 324 (July 30, 1986) 71.

Ressner, J. "*Pet* Project Due on CD, But the Beach Boys' Long-Awaited *Smile* Disc is Shelved Indefinitely," *Rolling Stone.* n548 (March 23, 1989) 23. il.

Shaw, R. "Sunkist Backs Splashy Beach Boys Tour," *Billboard.* 98 (April 12, 1986) 25–26.

"Sidelines," *Melody Maker.* 65 (August 12, 1989) 14. il.

Stambler, Irwin. "The Beach Boys," In: *The Encyclopedia of Pop, Rock and Soul.* pp. 35–37. il.

White, Timothy. "The King of Summer Comes Home: Brian Wilson," *Musician.* n82 (April 1985) 42–48ff. il.

—WILSON, BRIAN

Pond, Steve. "Brian Wilson," *Rolling Stone.* n512 (November 5, 1987) 174–176. il., int.

Ressner, Jeffrey. "Personal Controversy Marks Brian Wilson's Return," *Rolling Stone.* n524 (April 21, 1988) 16. il.

JAN AND DEAN

Schipper, H. "Jan & Dean's Tour of China Part of Larger U.S. Deal," *Variety.* 325 (November 19, 1986) 2ff.

Stambler, Irwin. "Jan and Dean," In: *The Encyclopedia of Pop, Rock and Soul.* pp. 326–327.

SURFARIS

Tannenbaum, Rob. "Where are They Now? The Surfaris," *Rolling Stone.* (September 10, 1987) 66. il., int. w/Jim Fuller and Jim Pash.

TRADEWINDS

Gari, Brian. "The Tradewinds: New York Surfer Boys," *Goldmine.* n184 (August 14, 1987) 107, 111. il., disc.

Car Songs

Kornheiser, Tony. "Radio Daze," *Life.* (n.d.) 89–95. il.

Los Angeles Sound

LITTLE FEAT (FEATURING LOWELL GEORGE)

Stambler, Irwin. "Little Feat," In: *The Encyclopedia of Pop, Rock and Soul.* pp. 408–410.

LOGGINS AND MESSINA (r.n.: KENNY L. AND JIM M.) (See also: BUFFALO SPRINGFIELD)

Stambler, Irwin. "Loggins and Messina," In: *The Encyclopedia of Pop, Rock and Soul.* pp. 416–417.

RONSTADT, LINDA

Rosenbaum, Ron. "Melancholy Baby," *Esquire.* (October 1985) 100–108. il., int.

TOTO

Stambler, Irwin. "Toto," In: *The Encyclopedia of Pop, Rock and Soul.* pp. 691–693.

ZEVON, WARREN (See: SINGER/SONGWRITER TRADITION)

B. FOLK ROCK (1965–1966)

Balancing Act

Kassan, Brian. "New Faces to Watch: The Balancing Act," *Cash Box.* (February 21, 1987) 12. il., int. w/Jeff Davis and Steve Wagner.

Buffalo Springfield (See also: Crosby, Stills and Nash; Loggins and Messina; Neil Young)

Stambler, Irwin. "Buffalo Springfield," In: *The Encyclopedia of Pop, Rock and Soul.* pp. 84–86. il.

Byrds (See also: Crosby, Stills and Nash)

Fricke, David. "Roger McGuinn," *Rolling Stone.* n585 (August 23, 1990) 107–110, 146. il., int.

Stambler, Irwin. "The Byrds," In: *The Encyclopedia of Pop, Rock and Soul.* pp. 92–95.

Dylan, Bob (r.n.: Bob Zimmerman)

"ASCAP Honors Dylan," *Variety.* 322 (April 2, 1986) 80. Re. Founder Award.

"Bob D Schlepped Here," *Spin.* 4 (January 1989) 16. il. Childhood home is put up for sale.

"Hall of Fame Elects New Members," *Rolling Stone.* n514 (December 3, 1987) 15.

Jones, Allan, and David Fricke. "Blood on the Tracks; The Legend of Bob Dylan," *Melody Maker.* 66 (February 3, 1990) 29–36. il., bio. Includes assessments by contemporary U.K. acts.

Levy, O. "Dylan-Petty Tour Plays E. Berlin After Slow West German Sales," *Variety.* 328 (September 30, 1987) 128.

"Live Album, But No Touring Plans for Dylan," *Billboard.* 97 (January 12, 1985) 36.

Loder, Kurt. "Bob Dylan," *Rolling Stone.* n512 (November 5, 1987) 301–303. il., int.

Loder, Kurt. "Dylan Stirs Controversy in Israel," *Rolling Stone.* n511 (October 22, 1987) 15.

Mellers, W. "God, Modality and Meaning in Some Recent Songs of Bob Dylan," *Popular Music.* n1 (1981) 142–157.

Shalett, M. "On Target: Dylan's, Taylor's Audiences Differ," *Billboard.* 98 (September 13, 1986) 50–51.

Stambler, Irwin. "Dylan, Bob," In: *The Encyclopedia of Pop, Rock and Soul.* pp. 197–201. il.

Wolcott, J. "Mixed Media: Bob Dylan Beyond Thunderdome," *Vanity Fair.* 48 (October 1985) 22ff. il., bio.

Fugs

Pollock, Bruce. "Tuli Kupferberg and Essra Mohawk," In: *When the Music Mattered*, by Bruce Pollock. New York: Holt, Rinehart, and Winston, 1983. pp. 170–191. il.

Goodman, Steve

McGee, D. "The Steel Rail Ain't Heard the News," *Record.* 4 (December 1984) 80. il.

Havens, Richie

Hennessey, M. "Richie Havens Sees Acoustic Renaissance," *Billboard.* 97 (March 23, 1985) 38ff. int.

Obrecht, D.J. "Pro's Reply—Richie Havens: Playing in Open D," *Guitar Player.* 21 (October 1987) 20. il.

Holy Modal Rounders

Cresser, Wayne. "The Holy Modal Rounders: An Unholy Alliance," *Goldmine.* n189 (October 23, 1987) 39, 42. il., disc.

Ian and Sylvia

Browne, David. "Where are They Now? Ian and Sylvia," *Rolling Stone.* n508 (September 10, 1987) 55. il., int.

Indigo Girls

McCormick, Moira. "Indigo Girls: Two for the Road," *Rolling Stone.* n561 (September 21, 1989) 24. il., int.

Lovin' Spoonful

Stambler, Irwin. "The Lovin' Spoonful," In: *The Encyclopedia of Pop, Rock and Soul.* pp. 422–423.

Mamas and the Papas

Stambler, Irwin. "The Mamas and the Papas," In: *The Encyclopedia of Pop, Rock and Soul.* pp. 429–431.

Near, Holly

Nash, Alanna. "Holly Near," *Stereo Review.* (January 1988) 86–87. il., int., bio.

Rush, Tom

Ruhlmann, William. "Tom Rush: The '60s Folkie Meets the '80s Businessman," *Goldmine.* n181 (July 3, 1987) 22, 85. il., disc.

Simon and Garfunkel (r.n.: Paul S. and Art G.)

Stambler, Irwin. "Simon and Garfunkel," In: *The Encyclopedia of Pop, Rock and Soul.* pp. 613–616.

Trip Shakespeare

Azerrad, Michael. "New Faces: Trip Shakespeare," *Rolling Stone.* n585 (August 23, 1990) 36. il., int. w/lead guitarist Matt Wilson.

Turtles

Michael, S., and M. Newman. "Turtles' Flo & Eddie Sue De La Soul Over Sampling," *Billboard.* 101 (August 26, 1989) 10ff.

Owen, Frank. "Bite This," *Spin.* 5:8 (November 1989) 35–36. il.

Stambler, Irwin. "The Turtles," In: *The Encyclopedia of Pop, Rock and Soul.* pp. 703–704.

Wild, David. "Still Happy Together," *Rolling Stone.* n508 (September 10, 1987) 61. il., int. w/Mark Volman and Howard Kaylan.

Washington Squares

Tamarkin, Jeff. "The Washington Squares: Folk for the '80s," *Goldmine.* n100 (May 25, 1984) 68–70, 74. il.

1. BRITISH FOLK ROCK

Black Velvet Band

Ressner, Jeffrey. "New Faces: Black Velvet Band," *Rolling Stone.* n563 (October 19, 1989) 17. il., int. w/singer Kieran Kennedy.

Bloom, Luka

Fox, Marisa. "New Faces: Luka Bloom," *Rolling Stone.* n576 (April 19, 1990) 29. il., int.

Dexy's Midnight Runners

McIlheney, B. "Burning the Midnight Oil," *Melody Maker.* 60 (November 2, 1985) 18–19ff. il., int. w/Keith Rowland.

Fairport Convention (See also: Ian Matthews; Richard Thompson)

Fricke, David. "Dave Mattacks' Uncommon Modesty," *Musician.* n67 (May 1984) 72–77. il., int.

Incredible String Band

Parry, Neil. "The Incredible String Band," *Record Collector.* n93 (May 1987) 52–58. il., disc.

Martyn, John

Bacon, Tony. "John Martyn," *History of Rock.* n29 (1982) 581. il.

Matthews, Ian; Matthews' Southern Comfort (See also: Fairport Convention)

Stambler, Irwin. "Southern Comfort," In: *The Encyclopedia of Pop, Rock and Soul.* pp. 626–627.

Pogues

"All I Want for Christmas," *Melody Maker.* 60 (December 21/28, 1985) 14–15. il., int. w/MacGowan.

"Cait's Away," *Melody Maker.* 61 (November 15, 1986) 3. Bassist O'Riordan finally replaced by Darryl Hunt.

Cocks, Jay. "Eight Lads Putting on Airs," *Time.* (August 21, 1989) 56. il.

Grabel, R. "It's Really Pogue, Man," *Creem.* 18 (September 1986) 42–44. il.

Hendelman, David. "Under the Influence," *Rolling Stone.* n565 (November 16, 1989) 175–178. il., int.

Jarvis, Tim. "Down Under the Influence," *New Musical Express.* (March 30, 1990) 12–13. il.

McIlheney, Barry. It's a Long Way from Tipperary," *Melody Maker.* 60 (May 11, 1985) 16–17. il., int.

"Pogue Sticks," *Melody Maker.* 61 (March 15, 1986) 3. Cait O'Riordan has left and rejoined the same week.

Robbins, Ira. "The Pogues," *Musician.* n91 (May 1986) 11–14, 22. il.

Thompson, Dave. "The Pogues," *Record Collector.* n105 (May 1988) 10–14. il., disc.

Steeleye Span

Stambler, Irwin. "Steeleye Span," In: *The Encyclopedia of Pop, Rock and Soul.* pp. 641–643.

Thompson, Richard; Richard and Linda Thompson (See also: Fairport Convention)

Carbonara, Peter. "Love, Death, Guitars, etc.," *Spin.* 2 (November 1986) 52–54. il.

Flanagan, Bill. "Richard Thompson: Constant in the Darkness

. . . Where's That At?," *Musician.* n98 (December 1986) 94–102. il., int.

Forte, Dan. "Richard Thompson: England's Acoustic/Electric Eclectic," *Guitar Player.* 19 (June 1985) 8–9ff. il., int., disc.

Irwin, Chris. "The Thompsons: An Everyday Story of Country Folk," *Melody Maker.* 60 (June 8, 1985) 18–19. il., int.

Loder, Kurt. "Linda Thompson: Scenes from a Rock & Roll Marriage," *Rolling Stone.* n447 (May 9, 1985) 3, 20ff. il.

Padgett, Stephen. "Richard Thompson, the Daring Adventurer," *Cash Box.* (October 18, 1986) 10. int.

Pond, Steve. "Why Richard Thompson may be the Best Guitarist in Rock and Roll and Why You may not Have Heard of Him," *Rolling Stone.* n447 (May 9, 1985) 3, 16–17ff. il., int., bio.

Santoro, G. "Rockin' Guitar in the Celt Tradition," *Down Beat.* 52 (February 1985) 20–22. il., int., bio.

Tamarkin, Jeff. "Richard Thompson Downplays Studio Work," *Billboard.* 97 (March 30, 1985) 47. int.

2. PROTEST SONGS

General Sources

Cocks, Jay, with Cathy Booth and Denise Worrell. "Songs from the High Ground," *Time.* (October 7, 1985) 78–79. il

Ian, Janis (r.n.: Janis Fink)

Stambler, Irwin. "Janis Ian," In: *The Encyclopedia of Pop, Rock and Soul.* pp. 306–307.

Sloan, P.F.

Tamarkin, Jeff. "P.F. Sloan: on the Eve of Correction," *Goldmine.* n137 (October 25, 1985) 12–19. il., disc.

8. SOUL MUSIC

General Sources

Hoare, Ian. ed. *The Soul Book.* London: Eyre Methuen, 1975. il., disc. Also published by Delta (New York, 1975).

Petrie, Gavin, ed. and designer. *Black Music.* London: Hamlyn, 1974. il.

Burke, Solomon

Stambler, Irwin. "Burke, Solomon," In: *The Encyclopedia of Pop, Rock and Soul.* pp. 87–88.

Flack, Roberta

Stambler, Irwin. "Flack, Roberta," In: *The Encyclopedia of Pop, Rock and Soul.* pp. 227–228.

Hathaway, Donny

Stambler, Irwin. "Hathaway, Donny," In: *The Encyclopedia of Pop, Rock and Soul.* pp. 283–284.

Jackson, Chuck

Pruter, Robert. "The Independents: The Chuck Jackson and

Marvin Yancy, Jr. Brainchild," *Goldmine.* n195 (January 15, 1988) 16, 43. il.

LaBelle, Patti

Stambler, Irwin. "LaBelle, Patti," In: *The Encyclopedia of Pop, Rock and Soul.* pp. 390–392. il.

Maxwell, Holly

Pruter, Robert. "Holly Maxwell: From Opera to Soul," *Goldmine.* n193 (January 1, 1988) 100, 106–107. il., disc.

Peaches and Herb

Stambler, Irwin. "Peaches and Herb," In: *The Encyclopedia of Pop, Rock and Soul.* pp. 512–513.

Simtec and Wylie

Pruter, Robert. "Simtec and Wylie," *Soul Survivor.* n9 (Summer 1988) 24–26. il.

Sly and the Family Stone

Stambler, Irwin. "Sly and the Family Stone," In: *The Encyclopedia of Pop, Rock and Soul.* pp. 620–621.

Thomas, Irma

Barry, L. "Music: Baby, Baby," *Village Voice.* 31 (August 12, 1986) 68. il.

Whispers

Stambler, Irwin. "The Whispers," In: *The Encyclopedia of Pop, Rock and Soul.* pp. 736–738.

Wright, Betty

"Wright's Wit is Selling," *Cash Box.* LII:3 (July 16, 1988) 20.
 il., int.

A. CHICAGO SOUND (1958–)

Butler, Jerry (See also: Curtis Mayfield)

Stambler, Irwin. "Jerry Butler," In: *The Encyclopedia of Pop, Rock and Soul.* pp. 89–91.

Chandler, Gene (a.k.a. the "Duke of Earl"; r.n.: Eugene Dixon)

Stambler, Irwin. "Chandler, Gene," In: *The Encyclopedia of Pop, Rock and Soul.* pp. 108–109.

Chi-Lites

Stambler, Irwin. "Chi-Lites," In: *The Encyclopedia of Pop, Rock and Soul.* pp. 120–121.

Mayfield, Curtis (See also: Jerry Butler)

George, Nelson. "The Rhythm & the Blues: Curtis Mayfield Returns to Recording," *Billboard.* 97 (June 15, 1985) 53.

Stambler, Irwin. "Mayfield, Curtis," In: *The Encyclopedia of Pop, Rock and Soul.* pp. 448–450.

B. MOTOWN SOUND (1960–) (See also: RECORD COMPANIES)

General Sources

Licks, Doctor. "Standing in the Shadows—the Guitars of Motown," *Guitar Player.* 22 (December 1988) 26–34ff. il., disc., music.
Features Robert White, Eddie Willis, Joe Messina, Wah-Wah Watson, Dennis Coffey.

"Motown Memories," *Rolling Stone.* n585 (August 23, 1990) 79–83. il.
Photo album from the 1960s.

Motown (Record Label)

Robinson, Julius. "Motown Sold to MCA, Boston Ventures," *Cash Box.* LII:2 (July 9, 1988) 5.

GORDY, BERRY (LABEL PRESIDENT)

Goldberg, Michael. "Berry Gordy," *Rolling Stone.* n585 (August 23, 1990) 66–77, 146. il., int.

"Rock and Roll Hall of Fame: Berry Gordy Jr. (Includes Testimonial by Smokey Robinson)," *Rolling Stone.* n519 (February 11, 1988) 65. il.

Music Publishing House

Kirby, Kip. "Music Row Greets Jobete," *Billboard.* 97 (October 12, 1985) 64.

Sutherland, Sam. "Motown Publishing Arm Gets New Look," *Billboard.* 98 (April 12, 1986) 4.

Songwriters

Robinson, Julius. "NAS Honors Holland-Dozier-Holland," *Cash Box.* (July 23, 1988) 13.

Four Tops

Bessman, Jim. "Four Tops Turn Back to Their Roots," *Billboard.* 98 (April 12, 1986) 25–26.

Hoerburger, R. "Four Tops Hope to Recapture 'Magic'; Group Readies Second Album Since Rejoining Motown," *Billboard.* 97 (April 20, 1985) 44.

Stambler, Irwin. "The Four Tops," In: *The Encyclopedia of Pop, Rock and Soul.* pp. 237–238.

Gaye, Marvin

"15 Elected to Hall of Fame," *Billboard.* 98 (October 18, 1986) 101.

George, Nelson. "The Rhythm and the Blues: Will Motown Bring Gaye's Life to the Screen," *Billboard.* 97 (June 29, 1985) 48.

Holland, B. "Four Artists Win Washington Awards," *Billboard.* 97 (October 12, 1985) 52.
Re. Washington Area Music Awards.

"Marvin Gaye Tape Due From Sony," *Billboard.* 97 (February

2, 1985) 35. Re. recording made during his exile in Belgium.

"Motown Wins Auction for Film Rights to Gaye's Life," *Billboard.* 97 (September 21, 1985) 50.

(Obituary), *Black Perspective in Music.* 12:2 (1984) 275–276.

"Rock Hall of Fame to Induct 15 Acts," *Variety.* 324 (October 8, 1986) 147.

Schipper, H. "Motown Acquires Gaye Catalog for 35G; Ex-Manager Protests," *Variety.* 320 (September 18, 1985) 77.

Schipper, H. "Motown Wins at Auction for Gaye Film & TV Rights," *Variety.* 320 (September 4, 1985) 4ff.

Stambler, Irwin. "Gaye, Marvin," In: *The Encyclopedia of Pop, Rock and Soul.* pp. 250–252. il.

Stevens, A. (Obituary), *Crescendo International.* 22 (June–July 1985) 38.

Jackson Five/Jacksons

The Jackson Five. Hitchin: B.C. Enterprises/New English Library, 1972. il. pap.

Pitts, Leonard, Jr. *Papa Joe's Boys: The Jacksons' Story.* Cresskill, NJ: Sharon Publications, 1983. il., disc. pap.

Stambler, Irwin. "The Jacksons," In: *The Encyclopedia of Pop, Rock and Soul.* pp. 318–321.

JACKSON, JERMAINE

"Family Affair," *Melody Maker.* 61 (April 12, 1986) 33. il., int.

JACKSON, MICHAEL (See also: BEATLES; CHARITY; MUSIC PUBLISHERS)

Blackwell, Mark. "Flash: Driving Mr. Jackson," *Spin.* 6:4 (July 1990) 20. il.

DeCurtis, Anthony. "Michael Jackson to Hit the Road for Limited American Tour," *Rolling Stone.* n519 (February 11, 1988) 23. ,il.

DeSavia, Tom. "Michael Jackson," *Cash Box.* (January 16, 1988) 10. il.

Garland, Phyl. *Michael in Concert.* London: Pan, 1984. il. pap. Large format collection of live action photos accompanied by brief commentary.

Gilmore, Mikal. "The Invisible Man Returns: Michael Jackson Comes Face to Face With His Public on His Solo Tour," *Rolling Stone.* n526 (May 19, 1988) 35–37, 170–171. il., int. w/manager Frank Dileo.

Goodman, Fred. "Jackson LP: Early Sales for Bad are Good," *Rolling Stone.* n510 (October 8, 1987) 15.

Grein, Paul. "Prince, Jackson Top NARM List; 'Gift of Music' Sales Award Nominees," *Billboard.* 97 (February 16, 1985) 6ff.

Iorio, Paul. "Michael Jackson Becomes a Pepsi Recording Artist (Again)," *Cash Box.* 49:48 (May 17, 1986) 14.

Iorio, Paul. "Retailers Prepare for Michael Jackson Mania," *Cash Box.* (August 29, 1987) 10. il., int. w/assorted retailers.

"Jackson Singles: Mixed Reception," *Rolling Stone.* n508 (September 10, 1987) 15. Re. "I Just Can't Stop Loving You."

"Jackson Wins NAACP's Top Image Award," *Billboard.* 101 (January 21, 1989) 29.

"Jackson's Pepsi Deal the Sweetest," *Billboard.* 98 (May 17, 1986) 6.

McGuigan, Cathleen. "Michael Jackson's Newest Thriller," *Newsweek.* (August 3, 1987) 69. il.

"Michael Jackson Does Good: Provides 40 UNCF Scholarships," *Cash Box.* (September 5, 1987) 6.

"Michael to Paul: Beat It," *Newsweek.* (August 26, 1985) 48. il.

Morris, C. "Michael Jackson Film Makes Debut," *Billboard.* 98 (September 27, 1986) 4.

"Music Stamps," *Down Beat.* 53 (February 1986) 12.

"Pepsi to Sponsor Jackson to Tune of $10–Million," *Variety.* 323 (May 7, 1986) 535–536.

Regan, Stewart. *Michael Jackson.* Guildford, Surrey: Colour Library, 1984. il.
   Collection of photos, both portrait and action shots.

Ressner, Jeffrey. "Jackson Boosting the Beatles," *Rolling Stone.* n522 (March 24, 1988) 35–37. int. w/Jackson associates.

Stambler, Irwin. "Michael Jackson," In: *The Encyclopedia of Pop, Rock and Soul.* pp. 316–318. il.

Sutherland, Sam. "Jackson Stars in 3–D Film for Disney," *Billboard.* 97 (August 3, 1985) 4ff.

Martha and the Vandellas

Stambler, Irwin. "Martha and the Vandellas," In: *The Encyclopedia of Pop, Rock and Soul.* pp. 444–445.

Marvelettes

Stambler, Irwin. "The Marvelettes," In: *The Encyclopedia of Pop, Rock and Soul.* pp. 445–446.

McDowell, Carrie

DeSavia, Tom. "New Faces to Watch: Carrie McDowell," *Cash Box.* (September 12, 1987) 11. il., int.

Robinson, Smokey

DeSavia, Tom. "Smokey Robinson," *Cash Box.* (September 12, 1987) 10. il., int.

Goldberg, Michael. "Smokey Robinson," *Rolling Stone.* n512 (November 5, 1987) 61–62. il., int.

Stambler, Irwin. "Smokey Robinson," In: *The Encyclopedia of Pop, Rock and Soul.* pp. 577–579.

Ross, Diana (See also: Supremes)

Stambler, Irwin. "Diana Ross," In: *The Encyclopedia of Pop, Rock and Soul.* pp. 586–587.

Supremes (See also: Diana Ross)

"Singer Wilson Sues Gordy Over Coin from Supremes," *Variety.* 336 (August 9, 1989) 64.

Stambler, Irwin. "The Supremes," In: *The Encyclopedia of Pop, Rock and Soul.* pp. 660–663.

Temptations

Ivory, S., and L. Pitts, Jr. "The Temptations 25th," *Billboard.* 98 (May 3, 1986) T2–3ff. il.

Stambler, Irwin. "The Temptations," In: *The Encyclopedia of Pop, Rock and Soul.* pp. 672–674. il.

KENDRICK, EDDIE (See also: HALL AND OATES)

Grein, Paul. "Ruffin, Kendrick Return to Spotlight," *Billboard.* 91 (September 21, 1985) 41.

RUFFIN, DAVID (See also: HALL AND OATES; EDDIE KENDRICK)

White, Adam. "Singer David Ruffin Arrested on Drug Charge," *Rolling Stone.* n526 (May 19, 1988) 17. il.

Walker, Jr., and the All Stars

Stambler, Irwin. "Jr. Walker and the All Stars," In: *The Encyclopedia of Pop, Rock and Soul.* pp. 724–725.

Wells, Mary

Stambler, Irwin. "Mary Wells," In: *The Encyclopedia of Pop, Rock and Soul.* pp. 734–736.

Wonder, (Little) Stevie

"Anomaly Unearthed in Ban on Wonder's Music," *Variety.* 319 (June 19, 1985) 89.

"Cleffers Sue Wonder for Allegedly Stealing Song," *Variety.* 320 (October 9, 1985) 117.
Re. "I Just Called to Say I Love You."

Doerschuk, Bob. "Frenzy and Finesse Backstage at the Grammys With Wonder, Hancock, Dolby & Jones," *Keyboard Magazine.* 11 (June 1985) 10ff. il.

George, Nelson. "The Rhythm & the Blues: Wonder Speaks Out on South Africa," *Billboard.* 97 (May 25, 1985) 62.

Gleeson, M. "S. African B'casting's Ban on Stevie Wonder Draws Legislators' Fire," *Variety.* 319 (May 15, 1985) 1ff.

Goldberg, Michael. "The Timeless World of Wonder," *Rolling Stone.* n471 (April 10, 1986) 38–40ff. il., int.

Grein, Paul. "Cancer Society Honors Wonder," *Billboard.* 97 (October 26, 1985) 48.
Re. Allan K. Jones Life Achievement Award. ·

Grein, Paul. "Prince, Wonder Honored by Motion Picture Academy," *Billboard.* 97 (April 6, 1985) 6.
Re. "I Just Called to Say I Love You" the best original song.

"Monster Mash," *Melody Maker.* 61 (June 28, 1986) 22–23. il., int.

Ressner, Jeffrey. "Stevie Wonder Releases 'Characters'; New Album is Part of an Ongoing Multimedia Project," *Rolling Stone.* n513 (November 19, 1987) 15. int. w/ Wonder and associate producer Gary Olazabal.

"S. Africa May End Stevie Wonder Ban," *Variety.* 319 (July 17, 1985) 46.

Stambler, Irwin. "Stevie Wonder," In: *The Encyclopedia of Pop, Rock and Soul.* pp. 749–751.

"Stevie Wonder Rejects White House Invitation for Keys to Motown," *Variety.* 321 (December 25, 1985) 1ff.

"Wonder Called Plagiarist," *Billboard.* 97 (October 26, 1985) 6.
Re. "I Just Called to Say I Love You."

"Wonder Plagiarism Suit Bounced After One Plaintiff Splits, But...," *Variety.* 324 (August 27, 1986) 95.
Re. "I Just Called to Say I Love You."

"Wonder's Oscar Speech Riles S. African Radio," *Variety.* 318 (April 3, 1985) 70.

"Wonder's Records Back on S. African Radio," *Variety.* 320 (October 2, 1985) 143.

C. MEMPHIS SOUND (1961–)

Stax Records

Palmer, Robert. "Southern Soul," *Rolling Stone.* n585 (August 23, 1990) 77. il.

BOOKER T AND THE M.G.s (See: INSTRUMENTALS)

HAYES, ISAAC

Stambler, Irwin. "Hayes, Isaac," In: *The Encyclopedia of Pop, Rock and Soul.* pp. 284–286.

REDDING, OTIS

Stambler, Irwin. "Redding, Otis," In: *The Encyclopedia of Pop, Rock and Soul.* pp. 558–560. il.

SAM AND DAVE (r.n.: S. MOORE AND D. PRATER)

Goodman, Fred. "Dave Prater Killed in Car Crash," *Rolling Stone.* n526 (May 19,1988) 16. int. w/Sam Moore.

"New 'Sam & Dave' Prohibited from Using That Name," *Variety.* 321 (November 13, 1985) 118.

"Sam Aiming at Dave for Singing With Sam," *Variety.* 319 (July 17, 1985) 107.

Sippel, J. "Judge: 'Sam & Dave' Aren't; New Single, Album Enjoined," *Billboard.* 97 (August 31, 1985) 91.

Stambler, Irwin. "Sam and Dave," In: *The Encyclopedia of Pop, Rock and Soul.* pp. 597–598.

THOMAS, CARLA

Stambler, Irwin. "Thomas, Carla," In: *The Encyclopedia of Pop, Rock and Soul.* p. 681.

THOMAS, RUFUS

Stambler, Irwin. "Thomas, Rufus," In: *The Encyclopedia of Pop, Rock and Soul.* pp. 681–682.

Box Tops/Big Star/Alex Chilton

Cavanagh, David. "Back in Black," *Sounds.* (February 17, 1990) 15. il., int.

Fricke, David. "Catch a Fallen Star," *Melody Maker.* 60 (March 16, 1985) 34. il., bio., int.

"Sidelines: Alex Chilton," *Melody Maker.* 63 (October 10, 1987) 20. il., int.

Green, Al

Stambler, Irwin. "Green, Al," In: *The Encyclopedia of Pop, Rock and Soul.* pp. 267–269.

D. MUSCLE SHOALS SOUND (1966–) (See also: STAX RECORDS)

Franklin, Aretha

"15 Elected to Hall of Fame," *Billboard.* 98 (October 18, 1966) 101.

George, Nelson. "The Rhythm and the Blues: Who Needs to Tour? Not the Queen of Soul," *Billboard.* 97 (December 7, 1985) 62. il.

Grein, Paul. "Producer Walden Zooms to New Heights," *Billboard.* 97 (November 23, 1985) 49–50.

Miller, Jim, with Linda Tibbetts. "Cruising the Freeway of Love," *Newsweek.* (August 26, 1985) 69. il.

Nathan, A. "Aretha Returns to Roots," *Billboard.* 99 (September 5, 1987) 24–25.

"Rock Hall of Fame to Induct 15 Acts," *Variety.* 324 (October 8, 1986) 147.

Stambler, Irwin. "Franklin, Aretha," In: *The Encyclopedia of Pop, Rock and Soul.* pp. 240–241. il.

Pickett, Wilson

Stambler, Irwin. "Pickett, Wilson," In: *The Encyclopedia of Pop, Rock and Soul.* pp. 521–522.

Tex, Joe

Stambler, Irwin. "Tex, Joe," In: *The Encyclopedia of Pop, Rock and Soul.* pp. 675–676.

Wexler, Jerry (See: Rhythm and Blues)

E. THE PHILADELPHIA SOUND (1970–)

Delfonics

Stambler, Irwin. "Delfonics," In: *The Encyclopedia of Pop, Rock and Soul.* p. 168.

Melvin, Harold, and the Blue Notes (featuring Teddy Pendergrass) (See also: Teddy Pendergrass)

Stambler, Irwin. "Melvin, Harold, and the Blue Notes," In: *The Encyclopedia of Pop, Rock and Soul.* pp. 460–461.

O'Jays

Stambler, Irwin. "The O'Jays," In: *The Encyclopedia of Pop, Rock and Soul.* pp. 497–499. il.

Stylistics

Stambler, Irwin. "The Stylistics," In: *The Encyclopedia of Pop, Rock and Soul.* p. 656.

F. BLUE-EYED SOUL

Average White Band

Stambler, Irwin. "Average White Band," In: *The Encyclopedia of Pop, Rock and Soul.* pp. 22–23.

Tolleson, R. "Not Your Average Drummer," *Modern Drummer.* 9 (May 1985) 14–17ff. il., bio., int. w/Steve Ferrone.

Breathe

Robinson, Julius. "New Faces to Watch: Breathe," *Cash Box.* LI:44 (May 7, 1988) 7. int. w/lead singer David Glasper.

Cavaliere, Felix (See: Rascals)

DeVille, Willy/Mink DeVille (r.n.: Willy Borsey)

Jeske, Lee. "Willy DeVille: Ready to Shed the Mink," *Cash Box.* XLIX:39 (May 15, 1986) 14.

Stambler, Irwin. "DeVille, Willy," In: *The Encyclopedia of Pop, Rock and Soul.* pp. 173–175.

Wilner, R. "DeVille Files for Bankruptcy," *Billboard.* 98 (March 1, 1986) 77.

Hall, Daryl, and John Oates

Armbruster, G. "Daryl Hall: Keyboard Confessions of a Rock Troubador," *Keyboard Magazine.* 11 (April 1985) 54–56ff. il., bio., disc., int.

Armbruster, G. "Technician Mike Klvana on the Hall & Oates Keyboards," *Keyboard Magazine.* 11 (April 1985) 59ff.

DeCurtis, Anthony. "Phases in Stages: At the Signpost Up Ahead, Another Left Turn for Daryl Hall and John Oates," *Record.* 4 (June 1985) 22–24ff. il., int.

Fricke, David. "Keeping in Touch," *Melody Maker.* 60 (July 20, 1985) 38–39ff. il., int.

Santoro, G. "With Hall & Oates: G.E. Smith," *Guitar Player.* 20 (February 1986) 50–54ff. il.

Stambler, Irwin. "Hall and Oates," In: *The Encyclopedia of Pop, Rock and Soul.* pp. 276–279.

Trakin, R. "Daryl Hall & John Oates," *Creem.* 16 (April 1985) 22–24ff. il.

CURRY, MICKEY

Flans, R. "The Man Behind the *Bim Bam Boom*," *Modern Drummer.* 9 (June 1985) 16–19ff. il., bio., int.

Fogerty, E. "Up and Coming," *Modern Drummer.* 6 (June 1982) 100–101. il., bio., int.

HALL, DARYL

Gett, S. "Hall: Solo Stint Won't Have Snappy Ending," *Billboard.* 98 (October 25, 1986) 28.

"Hall, Foster Get Top BMI Awards for Songwriters," *Variety.* 323 (May 21, 1986) 91ff.
Re.: "Every Time You Go Away."

Lichtman, Irv. "BMI Honors Daryl Hall, David Foster," *Billboard.* 98 (May 24, 1986) 3ff.

Head, Roy

Knerr, Sharon. "Where are They Now? Roy Head," *Rolling Stone.* n508 (September 10, 1987) 66. il., int.

Rare Earth

Stambler, Irwin. "Rare Earth," In: *The Encyclopedia of Pop, Rock and Soul.* p. 552.

Rascals

Stambler, Irwin. "The Rascals," In: *The Encyclopedia of Pop, Rock and Soul.* pp. 552–554.

CAVALIERE, FELIX

Baird, Jock. "Felix Cavaliere: The Soulful Saga of the Rascals— and Beyond," *Musician.* n78 (April 1985) 62–64ff. il.

Righteous Brothers

Stambler, Irwin. "The Righteous Brothers," In: *The Encyclopedia of Pop, Rock and Soul.* pp. 574–576.

Scaggs, Boz

Stambler, Irwin. "Scaggs, Boz," In: *The Encyclopedia of Pop, Rock and Soul.* pp. 600–602.

Sharkey, Feargal

"New Faces to Watch: Feargal Sharkey," *Cash Box.* XLIX:44 (April 19, 1986) 10. il., int.

Simply Red

Dery, Mark. "Kellett & McIntyre: Keyboard Drivers on Simply Red's Soul Train," *Keyboard Magazine.* 13 (October 1987) 21.

Mico, Ted. "Red Souls in the Sunset," *Melody Maker.* 60 (August 31, 1985) 24–25ff. il., int. w/lead singer Mick Hucknall.

"New Face of the Year: Simply Red," *Cash Box.* (December 27, 1986) 14. il., int. w/Hucknall.

"New Faces to Watch: Simply Red," *Cash Box.* LXIX:45 (April 26, 1986) 10. il., int. w/Mick Hucknall.

"Shrink Rap," *Melody Maker.* 61 (March 22, 1986) 13. il., int. w/Hucknall.

Southside Johnny and the Asbury Jukes

Stambler, Irwin. "Southside Johnny and the Asbury Jukes," In: *The Encyclopedia of Pop, Rock and Soul.* pp. 627–629.

Stansfield, Lisa

Cohen, Scott. "Affectionately Yours," *Spin.* 6:3 (June 1990) 52–55. il., int.

Hardy, Ernest. "Grooving Globally: The 'World' of Lisa Stansfield," *Cash Box.* LIII:38 (April 14, 1990) 8. il., int.

Mayer, Dana. "Affectionately Yours," *Me Music Express Magazine.* 14:145 (March 1990) 16–18. il., int.

Tannenbaum, Rob. "Lisa Stansfield: Thanks to this New British Diva, 'Disco' May No Longer be a Dirty Word," *Rolling Stone.* n582/583 (July 12/26, 1990) 78–80, 132. il., int.

Vannelli, Gino

Stern, P. "Gino Vannelli: Looking for Right Formula to Follow-Up *Black Cars*," *Canadian Musician.* 8:2 (1986) 12. il.

Walker Brothers

Clayson, Alan. "The Walker Brothers," *Record Collector.* n47 (July 1983) 22–25. il., disc.

Winwood, Steve (See also: Traffic)

DeCurtis, Anthony. "Steve Winwood: From Mr. Fantasy to Mr. Entertainment," *Rolling Stone.* n540 (December 1, 1988) 46–47ff. il.

Kassan, Brian. "Steve Winwood: Living the High Life," *Cash Box.* (January 24, 1987) 11, 22. il., int.

Stambler, Irwin. "Winwood, Steve," In: *The Encyclopedia of Pop, Rock and Soul.* pp. 744–745.

Young, Paul

"Bad Memories," *Melody Maker.* 60 (October 12, 1985) 3. il. Ex-Q-Tips claim plagiarism of "Song in My Pocket."

Barol, Bill. "Soul With a British Accent," *Newsweek.* (August 19, 1985) 66. il.

Ginsberg, M. "The Secret of Paul Young's Success," *Rolling Stone.* n456 (September 12, 1985) 16–17. il., int.

Irwin, C. "On His Majesty's Secret Service," *Melody Maker.* 60 (April 6, 1985) 24–26. il., int.

Reis, N. "Paul Young Adds Songwriting to His Many Talents," *Billboard.* 98 (December 13, 1986) 18.

Simmons, S. "Paul Young: U.K. Soul Man," *Creem.* 17 (October 1985) 32–33ff. il., int.

Stambler, Irwin. "Young, Paul," In: *The Encyclopedia of Pop, Rock and Soul.* pp. 760–761.

9. OTHER REGIONAL STYLES

A. NEW ORLEANS SOUND (1954–)

Dirty Dozen Brass Band

Birnbaum, L. "The Dirty Dozen Brass Band: Funkifying the New Orleans Tradition," *Down Beat.* 52 (August 1985) 26–28. il., int.

Cook, E. "The Modern Sound of New Orleans: The Dirty Dozen," *Jazz Journal International.* 38 (November 1985) 12–13. il., int. w/Gregory Davis.

"Faces: New Orleans' Revenge," *Musician.* n66 (April 1984) 31.

Spedale, R., Jr. "Dirty Dozen Brass Band: Stepping Out in Another Direction," *Jazz Times.* (April 1985) 9ff. il., int.

Dr. John (r.n.: Mac Rebennack)

Stambler, Irwin. "Dr. John, the Night Tripper," In: *The Encyclopedia of Pop, Rock and Soul.* pp. 182–183.

Domino, Fats (See: The Beat Era)

Dorsey, Lee

Hannusch, J., and Fred Goodman. "Lee Dorsey Dead at 59," *Billboard.* 98 (December 13, 1986) 6ff.

(Obituary), *Second Line.* 40 (Fall 1988) 35.

(Obituary), *Variety.* 325 (December 10, 1986) 110.

GUITAR SLIM (r.n.: EDWARD JONES)

Gibbons, B. "Ten Great Guitarists (You May Have Never Heard Of)," *Guitar Player.* 20 (March 1986) 71. il.

Jones, Joe

Grendysa, Peter. "Joe Jones," *Goldmine.* n220 (December 30, 1988) 73. il.

Neville Brothers/Meters

McCormick, Moira. "Neville Brothers Spread the News," *Billboard.* 97 (August 31, 1985) 58.

Palmer, D. "The Neville Brothers' R&B Dynasty," *Down Beat.* 52 (March 1985) 20–22. il., bio.

Stambler, Irwin. "The Meters," In: *The Encyclopedia of Pop, Rock and Soul.* pp. 462–463.

NEVILLE, AARON

Kirk, K. "Neville Ending Story," *Melody Maker.* 61 (August 2, 1986) 13. il., int.

Price, Lloyd

Stambler, Irwin. "Price, Lloyd," In: *The Encyclopedia of Pop, Rock and Soul.* pp. 537–538.

Radiators

Hannusch, Jeff. "The Radiators Finally Get Hot," *Rolling Stone.* n522 (March 24, 1988) 26. il., int.

Tamarkin, Jeff. "The Radiators: Gone Fishin'," *Goldmine.* n196 (January 29, 1988) 27, 32. il.

Smith, Huey "Piano"

Berry, J., and others. "Huey 'Piano' Smith and Guitar Slim," *Living Blues.* n72 (1986) 14–22. il.

B. CAJUN ROCK

General Sources

Adcock, M. "Alright Bayou," *Folk Roots.* 9 (September 1987) 15ff. il.

DiMauro, P. "Louisiana's Music is Beginning to Draw Some National Interest," *Variety.* 320 (August 7, 1985) 2ff.

Hannusch, J. "Down on the Bayou; Slumping Sales are Boosted by Local Acts," *Billboard.* 98 (May 10, 1986) 49.

Beausoleil

Hokannen, N. "Louisiana Fiddler Michael Doucet: The Beausoleil Band Founder Leads a Cajun Music Revival," *Frets.* 9 (September 1987) 44–45ff. il., disc., music.

Pond, Steve. "Michael Doucet: The Art of Cajun Cooking," *Rolling Stone.* n528 (June 16, 1988) 21ff. il.

Kershaw, Nik

"New Acts," *Variety.* 319 (May 1, 1985) 496.

Vare, E.A. "For Nik Kershaw, It Paid to Advertise; British Artist Got His Manager Through *Melody Maker*," *Billboard.* 97 (June 8, 1985) 50.

Rockin' Sidney

Morthland, John. "The 'Toot-Toot' Wars," *Village Voice.* 30 (August 6, 1985) 39–41.

Storm, Warren

Boyat, Bernard. "Warren Storm: Cajun Crooner," *Goldmine.* n124 (April 26, 1985) 22–24. il., disc.

C. ZYDECO

General Sources

Fox, T. "Zydeco Music: Hot as a Pepper," *Audio.* 70 (September 1986) 42–49.

Hannusch, Jeff. "Louisiana's Zydeco Sounds Reaching New Listeners," *Billboard.* 97 (September 14, 1985) 75.

Patoski, Joe Nick. "The Big Squeezy," *Texas Monthly.* (August 1988) 98–103, 126–127. il.

Chenier, Clifton

Ancelet, B.J. (Obituary), *Living Blues.* n79 (March/April 1988) 51–52. il.

Caron, D. "Zydeco Guitar," *Guitar Player.* 19 (August 1985) 42–47ff. il., disc., int. w/Paul Senegal.

Doerschuk, Bob. "Clifton Chenier 1925–1987," *Keyboard Magazine.* 14 (March 1988) 31. il.

(Obituary), *Notes.* 44:4 (1988) 697.

(Obituary), *Variety.* 329 (December 16, 1987) 95.

Dural, Buckwheat (r.n.: Stanley Dural)

Doerschuk, Bob. "Zydeco Crossover Star Buckwheat Dural," *Keyboard Magazine.* 13 (December 1987) 67, 82ff. il., soundsheet.

Queen Ida

Ross, J. "Queen Ida: Zydeco Royalty," *Sing Out.* 32:1 (1986) 2–9. il., bibl.

D. TEX-MEX (1956–)

General Sources

Morthland, John. "Bands Across the Water," *Texas Monthly.* (November 1985) 138.
Notes that Texas Music appears to be more popular in Europe than in America.

Los Lobos

Iorio, Paul. "East Coastings," *Cash Box.* (April 4, 1987) 11. il., int. w/Louie Perez.

McCormick, Moira. "Los Lobos Move into the '80s; Mexican-American Rockers Update Sound on *Wolf,*" *Billboard.* 97 (February 9, 1985) 39.

Santoro, G. "Los Lobos: Hour of the Wolves," *Down Beat.* 52 (April 1985) 20–22. il., disc., int.

Meyers, Augie

"The Augian Way," *Texas Monthly.* 15:12 (December 1987) 104. il., int.

Tamarkin, Jeff. "Augie Meyers: Squeezing Out Sparks," *Goldmine.* n202 (April 22, 1988) 81–83. il., disc.

Raunch Hands

"New Faces to Watch: The Raunch Hands," *Cash Box.* XLIX:32 (February 25, 1986) 8. il., int. w/Mike Chandler and Mike Mariconda.

E. DETROIT SOUND (1966–)

MC5

Cary, M.D. *The Rise and Fall of the MC5: Rock Music and Counterculture Politics in the Sixties.* Ph.D. dissertation, 1985. Available from Dissertation Abstracts International University Microforms International.

Seger, Bob/Bob Seger System/Bob Seger and the Silver Bullet Band

Stambler, Irwin. "Seger, Bob," In: *The Encyclopedia of Pop, Rock and Soul.* pp. 605–608.

F. SAN FRANCISCO SOUND (1966–)

General Sources

Anthony, Gene. *The Summer of Love: Haight Ashbury at Its Highest.* Millbrae, CA: Celestial Arts, 1980. il.

Goldberg, Michael. "The San Francisco Sound," *Rolling Stone.* n585 (August 23, 1990) 91–96. il., int. w/big names of that scene (e.g., Grace Slick, Country Joe, Mickey Hart).

Country Joe (and the Fish)

McDonough, J. "Country Joe Comes Back," *Billboard.* 97 (May 4, 1985) 43.

Dinosaurs (See also: Jefferson Airplane; Quicksilver Messenger Service)

Miller, Warren. "The Dinosaurs: Back for the First Time," *Goldmine.* n87 (August 1983) 50, 52ff.

Grateful Dead

Bessman, Jim. "Dead's Popularity Nudges Arista's Home Vid Launch," *Billboard.* 99 (October 3, 1987) 49–50.

Dawes, A. "The Grateful Dead Rises [sic] to Platinum; Jackson Goes Gold," *Variety*. 328 (October 14, 1987) 217–218.

"Dead Show at Saratoga Sparks Controversy Over Rock Tix There," *Variety*. 319 (July 24, 1985) 70.

DiMartino, Dave. "Dead Get Injunction on Sale of Album," *Billboard*. 99 (September 26, 1987) 87.
Re. *Wake of the Flood*.

Goodman, Fred. "Brent Mydland: 1952–1990; Grateful Dead Keyboard Player and Songwriter is Found Dead in His Northern California Home," *Rolling Stone*. n586 (September 6, 1990) 17. il., int. w/Mydland and his songwriting partner, John Barlow.

Goodman, Fred. "The End of the Road?," *Rolling Stone*. n585 (August 23, 1990) 21–26, 147. il.

Goodman, Fred. "The Rolling Stone Interview: Jerry Garcia," *Rolling Stone*. n566 (November 30, 1989) 66–74, 118. il., int.

Iero, C., and C. Perry. "The Grateful Dead's Billy Kreutzmann & Mickey Hart," *Modern Drummer*. 5 (August/September 1981) 10–13ff. il., int.

McDonough, J. "The Dead are Anything But," *Billboard*. 98 (June 21, 1986) 22ff.

"News: Long Strange Trip," *Spin*. 5:8 (November 1989) 28.

"Sidelines," *Melody Maker*. 63 (October 3, 1987) 28. il., int.

Stambler, Irwin. "The Grateful Dead," In: *The Encyclopedia of Pop, Rock and Soul*. pp. 264–267. il.

Sutherland, Steve. "Grateful Dead: Bone Idols," *Melody Maker*. (October 27, 1990) 50–51. il., int. w/Garcia.

Great Society (See also: Jefferson Airplane)

Hogg, Brian. "The Great Society," *Record Collector*. n125 (January 1990) 68–69. il., int.

Jefferson Airplane/Jefferson Starship/Starship (See also: Dinosaurs; Great Society; KBC Band)

Dobrin, Gregory. "Jefferson's Gone But the Starship Still Flies High," *Cash Box*. XLIX:33 (February 1, 1986) 13. il., int. w/Grace Slick and Mickey Thomas.

Goldberg, Michael. "Jefferson Airplane Mulls Reunion," *Rolling Stone*. n524 (April 21, 1988) 17. il.

Pond, Steve. "On the Charts: Starship: It's Not Over Yet," *Rolling Stone*. n509 (September 24, 1987) 28. il.

Scoppa, Bud. "Back to the Future," *Spin*. 5:7 (October 1989) 80–81. il., int.

Stambler, Irwin. "Jefferson Airplane; Jefferson Starship; Starship; KBC Band," In: *The Encyclopedia of Pop, Rock and Soul*. pp. 328–331. il.

Joplin, Janis

"Life After Janis," *Texas Monthly*. 16:3 (March 1988) 72–74.

Stambler, Irwin. "Joplin, Janis," In: *The Encyclopedia of Pop, Rock and Soul.* pp. 350–351. il.

Weitzman, Steve. "Unreleased Janis Joplin Recording Surfaces," *Rolling Stone.* n513 (November 19, 1987) 24.

KBC Band (See also: Jefferson Airplane)

McDonough, J. "Kantner, Balin, Casady Take Off With New Band," *Billboard.* 97 (November 2, 1985) 47.

Schipper, H. "Airplane Alumni Form New Band, Plan Summer Tour," *Variety.* 319 (June 5, 1985) 73.

Miller, Steve(, Band)

Forte, Dan. "Steve Miller," *Musician.* n48 (October 1982) 48–53. il., bio., int.

Stambler, Irwin. "Miller, Steve," In: *The Encyclopedia of Pop, Rock and Soul.* pp. 465–466.

Quicksilver (Messenger Service) (See also: Dinosaurs)

Fricke, David. "John Cipollina's Pictorial Guitar: A Seminal Psychedelic Axeman Trips On," *Musician.* n66 (April 1984) 92. il.

Hogg, Brian. "Quicksilver Service," *Record Collector.* n68 (April 1985) 44–47. il., disc.

Skidmore, Mick. "Quicksilver Messenger Service: Happy Trails in Psychedelic Music," *Goldmine.* n135 (September 27, 1985) 12–22. il.

Sopwith Camel

Goldberg, Michael. "Where are They Now? Sopwith Camel," *Rolling Stone.* n508 (September 10, 1987) 54. il., int.

G. BOSSTOWN SOUND (1967–1969)

Beacon Street Union

Tortelli, Joseph. "Beacon Street Union: The Dream Died in Bosstown," *Goldmine.* n193 (December 18, 1987) 20, 28. il.

H. SOUNDS OF THE SOUTH (1970–)

Allman Brothers Band (See also: Dickey Betts)

DeCurtis, Anthony. "Chuck Leavell's Mixmaster," *Musician.* n75 (January 1985) 72ff.

Stambler, Irwin. "The Allman Brothers," In: *The Encyclopedia of Pop, Rock and Soul.* pp. 6–8. il.

Betts, Dickey/Great Southern (See also: Allman Brothers Band)

Kirby, Kip. "Sullivan Accents 'Personal' in Management," *Billboard.* 98 (March 29, 1986) 31–32.

Obrecht, Jas. "Dickey Betts, 1989," *Guitar Player.* 23 (August 1989) 35ff. il., int.

Dixon, Don

Bessman, Jim. "Don Dixon in Solo Debut," *Billboard.* 98 (December 20, 1986) 22ff.

Iorio, Paul. "Hit Producer Don Dixon Steps Out on His Own," *Cash Box.* (December 20, 1986) 10, 28. il., int.

Smith, M. "Smooth Operator," *Melody Maker.* 61 (April 5, 1986) 33. il., int.

Yardumian, Rob. "Don Dixon: Workin' Hard or Hardly Workin'?," *Cash Box.* (November 7, 1987) 8–9, 35. il., int.

Fetchin' Bones

Bessman, Jim. "Fetchin' Rattles Some Bones," *Billboard.* 98 (December 27, 1986) 34ff.

Gordon, Robert. "Flash: South by Southwest," *Spin.* 5:8 (November 1989) 14–15. il., int. w/lead singer Hope Nicholls.

Kentucky Headhunters

Tannenbaum, Rob. "New Faces: Kentucky Headhunters," *Rolling Stones.* n575 (April 5, 1990) 28. il., int.

Lynyrd Skynyrd (See also: Festivals...)

Ressner, Jeff. "Estates Seek to Block Use of Skynyrd Name," *Rolling Stone.* n536 (October 6, 1988) 29.

Stambler, Irwin. "Lynyrd Skynyrd," In: *The Encyclopedia of Pop, Rock and Soul.* pp. 425–427.

.38 Special

Altman, B. "Hats Off to Donnie: .38 Special," *Creem.* 18 (December 1986) 34–35. il.

Moleski, L. ".38 Special Shooting for New Image," *Billboard.* 98 (June 7, 1986) 40.

I. REGGAE (1970–) (See also: AFRO-ROCK)

General Sources

Barrett, Leonard E. *The Rastafarians: The Dreadlocks of Jamaica.* Kingston, Jamaica: Sangster's Book Stores Ltd./ London: Heinemann Educational, 1977. il.

Boot, Adrian, and Michael Thomas. *Jamaica: Babylon on Thin Wire.* London: Thames and Hudson, 1976. il.

Cashmore, Ernest. *Rastaman: The Rastafarian Movement in England.* London: Allen & Unwin, 1980. bibl.

Clark, Sebastian. *Jah Music.* London: Heinemann Educational, 1980. il.

Coleman, B. "Hot Rap/Reggae Fusion Catches on in U.S., U.K.," *Billboard.* 99 (December 12, 1987) 25.

Coore, C. "An Insider's View of Jamaican Reggae," *Guitar Player.* 19 (September 1985) 72–74.

Goodman, Fred. "Grass Route," *Billboard.* 97 (December 7, 1985) 71.

Harper, L. "Commentary: Reggae: Co-opted, Diluted, Ignored," *Billboard.* 98 (May 31, 1986) 9.

Kallyndyr, Rolston, and Henderson Dalrymple. *Reggae: A*

People's Music. Sudbury, Middlesex, U.K.: Carib-Arawak, 1977. il.

Owen, Frank. "Nineties in Effect; Dancehall Styles," *Spin.* 5:11 (February 1990) 56. il.
Survey of genre on dance floors and radio stations of New York City.

Owens, Joseph. *Dread: The Rastafarians of Jamaica.*
Introduction by Rex Nettleford. London/Kingston, Jamaica/ Port of Spain, Trinidad: Heinemann, 1979.

Sheridan, M. "Reggae Makes a Comeback in Jamaica," *Billboard.* 98 (August 16, 1986) 62A.

Thomas, Michael, and Adrian Boot. *Jah Revenge: Babylon Revisited.* London: Eel Pie, 1982. il.

Weinger, H. "Tour Aims to Lift Level of Reggae; Sunsplash USA Package," *Billboard.* 97 (April 27, 1985) 55ff.

Wexler, Paul. "Jamaica's Dancehall Style Takes Hold," *Rolling Stone.* n573 (March 8, 1990) 60. il.

And Why Not?

Sullivan, Caroline. "Sidelines: And Why Not?," *Melody Maker.* (July 28, 1990) 11. il.

Aswad

Owen, F. "Winds of Change," *Melody Maker.* 61 (July 5, 1986) 32. il., int.

Black Uhuru

Cordery, M. "Roots Rebellion," *Melody Maker.* 61 (May 24, 1986) 10. il., int.

"Fast Forward," *Melody Maker.* 60 (March 23, 1985) 4. Michael Rose is replaced by Junior Reid.

Boney M

Shearlaw, John, and David Brown. *Boney M.* Feltham, Middlesex, England: Hamlyn, 1979. il. pap.

Carlos, Don

"New Acts," *Variety.* 323 (May 14, 1986) 93.

Cliff, Jimmy (r.n.: James Chambers)

"Cliff Sues Lawyer, Manager, Alleging Conflict of Interest," *Variety.* 321 (November 6, 1985) 87.

Dread Zeppelin

Clarke, Tina. "Rock Notes: Reggae From Heaven?," *Me Music Express Magazine.* 14:148 (June 1990) 13. il., int. w/singer Tortelvis.

Daly, Steve. "Flash: Dazed and Confused," *Spin.* 6:3 (June 1990) 16. il., int.

Smith, Mat. "Dread Zeppelin: Un-Physical Graffiti," *Melody Maker.* (August 25, 1990) 7. il., int.

Smith, Mat. "Sidelines: Dread Zeppelin," *Melody Maker.* (July 21, 1990) 11. il., int. w/lead singer Tortelvis.

Dunbar, Sly

Mathur, P. "Hand in Glove," *Melody Maker.* 60 (August 10, 1985) 37. il., int.

Santelli, Robert. "Sly Dunbar," *Modern Drummer.* 9 (April 1985) 8–13ff. il., int.

Santelli, Robert. "Sly Dunbar," *Modern Drummer.* 10 (January 1986) 28–29ff. il., int.

Strauss, D. "Sly & Robbie: No Breaks," *Record.* 5 (January/ February 1986) 8. il.

Grant, Eddy

Jones, A. "Caribbean Sunsets," *Melody Maker.* 61 (November 22, 1986) 30–31. il., int.

Kirk, K. "Curtain Call," *Melody Maker.* 61 (January 11, 1986) 30–31ff. il., int.
Re. Hungarian tour.

Marley, Bob(, and the Wailers) (See also: Peter Tosh)

Dalrymple, Henderson. *Bob Marley: Music, Myth & the Rastas.* Sudbury, Middlesex, U.K.: Carib-Arawak, 1976. il. pap.

Goldman, Vivien, and Adrian Boot. *Bob Marley: Soul Rebel— Natural Mystic.* London: Eel Pie/Hutchinson, 1981. il., disc. pap.

Stambler, Irwin. "Marley, Bob," In: *The Encyclopedia of Pop, Rock and Soul.* pp. 442–444. il.

Marley, Ziggy(, and the Melody Makers)

DeCurtis, Anthony. "Ziggy Marley: Reggae's Heir Apparent; Bob Marley's Son Claims His Father's Throne," *Rolling Stone.* n522 (March 24, 1988) 92–98. il.

Lane, Daisann. "The Hard Line According to Ziggy Marley," *Spin.* 5:7 (October 1989) 44–47, 113. il., int.

Leland, J. "On Record: Melody Makers: Just Folks," (December 1985) 12. il., int.

"New Faces to Watch: Melody Makers," *Cash Box.* XLIX:15 (September 21, 1985) 10. il., int. w/Marley.

Shakespeare, Robbie (See: Sly Dunbar)

Third World

Jackson, A. "World in Action," *Melody Maker.* 60 (March 23, 1985) 33. il., int.

Tosh, Peter (r.n.: Winston Hubert McIntosh; See also: Bob Marley)

Beuttler, B. "Peter Tosh, 1944–87," *Down Beat.* 54 (December 1987) 11.

(Obituary), *Melody Maker.* 63 (September 19, 1987) 3. il.

(Obituary), *Melody Maker.* 63 (December 19/26, 1987) 50. il.

"Peter Tosh, Friend Slain at Home; Reggae Star Bore Marley's Torch," *Variety*. 328 (September 16, 1987) 108.

Sheridan, M. "Peter Tosh Shot, Killed," *Billboard*. 99 (September 26, 1987) 6ff.

Stambler, Irwin. "Tosh, Peter," In: *The Encyclopedia of Pop, Rock and Soul*. pp. 689–691.

UB40

DiPerna, Alan. "Reggae Rules from a Rock–Steady Stylist," *Musician*. n142 (August 1990) 72–76. il., int. w/Earl Falconer.

"Rock Notes: Reggae Redefined," *Me Music Express Magazine*. 14:145 (March 1990) 15. il., int. w/James Brown.

Stambler, Irwin. "UB40," In: *The Encyclopedia of Pop, Rock and Soul*. pp. 706–707.

Yellowman

Trakin, R. "Yellowman: Reggae's Clown Prince," *Creem*. 16 (January 1985) 15. il.

J. SALSA

General Sources

Boggs, Vernon W., and R. Meyersohn. "The Profile of a Bronx Salsero: Salsa's Still Alive!," *Popular Music & Society*. 12:4 (1988) 59–67. bibl.

Duany, J. "Popular Music in Puerto Rico: Toward an Anthro-
pology of Salsa," *Latin American Music Review.* 5:2 (1984)
186–216.
Includes appendix of the texts of three songs by Ruben
Blades.

Walsh, Michael, and Christina Garcia. "Shake Your Body,"
Time. (July 11, 1988) 50–52. il.

Bandera

Agudelo, C. "Notas: The Estefans Paved the Way for the New
Crossover Crop," *Billboard.* 101 (August 19, 1989) 61.

Blades, Ruben

Agudelo, C. "Notas: No Other Latin Act Matches the Chops of
Ruben Blades," *Billboard.* 100 (December 17, 1988) 49.

Barol, Bill. "Salsa With a Political Spin," *Newsweek.* (September 9, 1985) 97. il., int.

Bloom, Pamela. "Backbeat: A Ruben Blades Close–Up," *High
Fidelity.* (April 1986) 75–76, 87. il., int., disc.

Cocks, Jay, and Denise Worrell. "Of Ghosts and Magic," *Time.*
(July 11, 1988) 52. il., int.

Goodman, Fred. "English LP Due from Ruben Blades," *Rolling
Stone.* n522 (March 24, 1988) 29.

Charanga 76

Fernandez, E. "Notas: Charanga 76 Cuts 1st Salsa All–Digital,
DMM Album," *Billboard.* 98 (July 5, 1986) 38.

Miami Sound Machine/Estefan, Gloria, and the Miami Sound Machine

Dobrin, Gregory. "Make No Mistake—MSM Is Making It on Their Own Turf," *Cash Box.* XLIX:36 (February 22, 1986) 11. il., int. w/Gloria Estefan.

Dobrin, Gregory. "The World Gets the Rhythm of Gloria Estefan and Miami Sound Machine," *Cash Box.* (June 27, 1987) 13. il., int.

Fernandez, E. "Latin Notas," *Billboard.* 97 (March 30, 1985) 39.

Fernandez, E. "The Miami Sound," *Village Voice.* 31 (January 28, 1986) 49–50. il.

Fernandez, E. "Notas: Miami Sound Machine Invades Mainstream Market," *Billboard.* 98 (August 9, 1986) 41.

Fernandez, E. "Notas: Miami Sound Machine Tour Gets Pepsi Sponsorship," *Billboard.* 98 (November 8, 1986) 59.

Levy, Joe. "Gloria Estefan and Miami Sound Machine," *Cash Box.* (February 13, 1988) 7, 35. il., int.

Lounges, Tom. "The Bi-Cultural Fusion of the Miami Sound Machine," *Song Hits.* n249 (November 1986) 22–24. il.

Lounges, Tom. "Gloria Estefan and Miami Sound Machine," *Song Hits.* n262 (April 1988) 22–23. il.

"New Faces to Watch: Miami Sound Machine," *Cash Box.* XLIX:25 (November 30, 1985) 12. il., int. w/lead singer Gloria Estefan.

"Top Prize to Miami Sound Machine at Tokyo Music Fest,"
  Variety. 322 (April 9, 1986) 115.

Vega, L. "Sound Machine Has U.S. Hit," *Billboard.* 98 (February 15, 1986) 46.

ESTEFAN, GLORIA

Estefan, Gloria, as told to Kathryn Casey. "My Miracle," *Ladies
  Home Journal.* CVII:8 (August 1990) 99–101, 152–155.
  il.

Newman, M. "Gloria Days Here for MSM," *Billboard.* 101
  (August 5, 1989) 30ff.

K. JUNKANOO

Buffett, Jimmy

Shalett, M. "On Target," *Billboard.* 98 (August 2, 1986) 44.

Wood, G. "Nashville: Buffett Makes Bucks With Margari-
  taville Mart," *Billboard.* 98 (November 22, 1986) 36.

Wood, G. "Nashville Scene: Jimmy Buffett Comes Home to
  Music City," *Billboard.* 98 (September 13, 1986) 33.

K.C. and the Sunshine Band

Stambler, Irwin. "K.C. and the Sunshine Band," In: *The
  Encyclopedia of Pop, Rock and Soul.* pp. 358–361.

10. HYBRID CHILDREN OF ROCK

A. CHRISTIAN ROCK/CHRISTIAN CONTEMPORARY MUSIC

Woodward, Kenneth L., and others. "The New Christian Minstrels," *Newsweek.* (August 19, 1985) 70–71. il.

Taylor, Steve

"New Faces to Watch: Steve Taylor," *Cash Box.* XLIX:40 (March 22, 1986) 10. il.

B. PUNK ROCK (1966–)

Count Five

Tamarkin, Jeff. "The Count Five," *Goldmine.* n220 (December 30, 1988) 9.

Furys

Shaw, Greg. " 'Have Louie, Will Travel'—The Furys: Story of a Northwest Band," *R.P.M.* n5 (May 1984) 68–71. il.

Leaves

Hogg, Brian. "The Leaves," *Record Collector.* n89 (January 1987) 41–42. il., disc.

Music Machine

Hogg, Brian. "The Music Machine," *Record Collector.* n87
(November 1986) 20–22. il., disc.

Tamarkin, Jeff. "Music Machine," *Goldmine.* n159 (August 29,
1986) 5–10. il., disc.

Seeds/Sky Saxon Blues Band

Beeson, Frank. "Sky Saxon/The Seeds: A Web of Sound,"
Goldmine. n179 (June 5, 1987) 8–10. il., disc.

Hogg, Brian. "The Seeds," *Record Collector.* n86 (October 1986)
30–32. il., disc.

C. ACID ROCK/PSYCHEDELIA (1966–1968)

Creation

Eggett, Paul. "The Creation," *Record Collector.* n33 (May 1982)
60–63. il., disc.

Electric Prunes

Hogg, Brian. "The Electric Prunes," *Record Collector.* n85
(September 1986) 42–43. il., disc.

Fever Tree

Freeman, Stewart. "Fever Tree: A Little Bit of Frisco in Texas,"
Goldmine. n202 (April 22, 1988) 14, 25. il., disc.

Hawkwind

Thomas, Dave. "Hawkwind," *Record Collector.* n70 (June 1985) 46–51. il., disc.

Love

Hickey, Stewart. "Love: Arthur Lee's L.A. Lysergia," *Goldmine.* n171 (February 13, 1987) 24, 30. il.

Hogg, Brian. "Love," *Record Collector.* n29 (January 1982) 47–52. il., disc.

Nazz (See also: Todd Rundgren)

Hogg, Brian. "The Nazz," *Record Collector.* n59 (July 1984) 8–9. il., disc.

13th Floor Elevators/Roky Erickson

Anderson, T., and P. Buck. "On the Road With Roky & Pete," *Creem.* 17 (March 1986) 46.

Ortman, Jack, comp. "Roky Erickson Solo Discography," *Goldmine.* n173 (March 13, 1987) 93. disc.

Ortman, Jack, comp. *The Roky Erickson Story.* Austin, TX: Media Price, 1986. il., bio., disc.

Ortman, Jack, and Norm Silverman. "Roky Erickson and the 13th Floor Elevators: You're Gonna Miss Me," *Goldmine.* n173 (March 13, 1987) 8–10, 93. il., disc.

Yellow Balloon

Rogers, Don. "The Yellow Balloon: An Interview With Don Braught," *R.P.M.* n11 (October/November 1985) 34–35. il., int.

D. SYMPHONIC ROCK/CLASSICAL ROCK (1967–)

General Sources

"Art Rock," *Rolling Stone.* n509 (September 24, 1987) 71–75.

Duxbury, J.R. *Rockin' the Classics and Classicizin' the Rock: A Selectively Annotated Discography.* Westport, CT: Greenwood, 1985. disc.

Kozinn, Allan. "The Role of Rock," *Symphony.* (January/February 1990) 48–52, 67. il.

Carlos, Wendy/Walter Carlos

Diliberto, John. "Wendy Carlos D.A. (After Digital)," *Down Beat.* (March 1987) 20–22, 61. il., disc., int.

Milano, D. "Wendy Carlos," *Keyboard Magazine.* 12 (November 1986) 50–51ff. il., disc., soundsheet, int.

Curved Air

Heatley, Michael. "Curved Air: The Classical–Rock Way," *Goldmine.* n200 (March 25, 1988) 18, 37. il.

Paytress, Mark. "Curved Air," *Record Collector.* n102 (February 1988) 48–52. il., disc.

Dead Can Dance

Shelley, J. "Love and Death," *Melody Maker.* 61 (July 12, 1986) 32–33. il., int.

Sutherland, Sam. "Back to the Future," *Melody Maker.* 61 (January 4, 1986) 14–15. il., int.

Dream Academy

"New Faces to Watch: The Dream Academy," *Cash Box.* XLIX:24 (November 23, 1985) 12. il., int. w/Nick Laird–Clowes & Gilbert Gabriel.

Schlosberg, K. "The Academy Imperiled: Is This the Dream?," *Creem.* 17 (May 1986) 8–9. il.

Sutherland, Sam. "Dream Academy Hit is a Haze of 60s Influences," *Billboard.* 98 (February 8, 1986) 36ff.

Electric Light Orchestra

Bevan, Bev. *The Electric Light Orchestra Story.* Ed. by Garth Pearce. London: Mushroom, 1980. il., disc. cased and pap. eds.
A compilation of Bevan's diaries beginning with his membership in The Move in the late 1960s.

Bevan, Bev. "Taking Care of Business: Rock Touring, Then and Now," *Modern Drummer.* 9 (May 1985) 30ff. il.

Emerson, Lake and Palmer/Emerson, Lake and Powell (See also: Moody Blues)

DiMartino, D. "Emerson, Lake & Powell: Rockin' Dudes or Art-Rock Mofos?," *Creem.* 18 (October 1986) 44–46. il.

Doerschuk, Bob. "Classic Instruments & High-Tech Join Forces in Emerson's Nre Setup," *Keyboard Magazine.* 12 (July 1986) 40ff.

Doerschuk, Bob. "Keith Emerson: The Phoenix Rises from the Ashes of Progressive Rock," *Keyboard Magazine.* 12 (July 1986) 38–40ff. il.

"ELP Need Somebody," *Melody Maker.* 60 (February 16, 1985) 4. Carl Palmer replaced by Cozy Powell.

Stambler, Irwin. "Emerson, Lake and Palmer; Emerson, Lake and Powell," In: *The Encyclopedia of Pop, Rock and Soul.* pp. 214–215.

EMERSON, KEITH

Doerschuk, Bob. "Keith Emerson: The King of Progressive Rock Returns With a New Band and a Streamlined Style," *Keyboard Magazine.* 14 (April 1988) 82–87ff. il., disc., int.

"Profile: Career Update," *Keyboard Magazine.* 12 (January 1986) 24.

Moody Blues

Gett, S. "Moody Blues, ELP Enjoy Renewed Success," *Billboard.* 98 (September 13, 1986) 30ff.

"Moody Blues Capture Top Video Honors," *Billboard.* 98 (December 6, 1986) 1ff.

Simmons, S. "The Moody Blues Are Older Than You," *Creem.* 18 (December 1986) 45–46ff.

Stambler, Irwin. "The Moody Blues," In: *The Encyclopedia of Pop, Rock and Soul.* pp. 470–471.

EDGE, GRAEME

Larcombe, K. "Update," *Modern Drummer.* 13 (January 1989) 10. il.

HAYWARD, JUSTIN

Price, June. "Justin Hayward: Songwriter," *Goldmine.* n240 (October 6, 1989) 24, 26. il.

Renaissance

Pike, Jon R. "Renaissance...and Other Stories," *Goldmine.* n218 (December 2, 1988) 31, 89. il.

Shelleyan Orphan

Iorio, Paul. "New Faces to Watch: Shelleyan Orphan," *Cash Box.* (August 8, 1987) 10–11. il., int.

E. PROGRESSIVE ROCK (1967–)

General Sources

McAleer, Richard. *A Progressive Rock Portfolio.* Syracuse, New York: Central New Yorker, 1970. il.

Rock Opera

"*Chess* LP Selling Big in Europe, Rice to Produce Show in London," *Variety.* 318 (March 13, 1985) 117ff.

Davis, Lorrie, and Rachel Gallagher. *Letting Down My Hair.* London: Paul Elek, 1974. il. Orig. pub.: New York: Arthur Fields, 1973.
One of the stars of the Broadway production describes the experience. The overall tone is one of disillusionment.

Baker('s), Ginger, Air Force (See also: Jack Bruce; Eric Clapton; Cream)

Puterbaugh, Parke, and others. "Where are They Now? Ginger Baker," *Rolling Stone.* n558 (August 10, 1989) 54–55. il.

Saccone, T. "Update," *Modern Drummer.* 10 (October 1986) 6. il.

Barclay James Harvest

Domone, Keith. "Barclay James Harvest," *Record Collector.* n111 (November 1988) 70–73. il., disc.

Heatley, Michael. "Barclay James Harvest," *Goldmine.* n251 (March 9, 1990) 36, 122. il., disc.

Belew, Adrian (See also: Bears; David Bowie; Talking Heads; Frank Zappa)

McCormick, Moira. "*Creem* Showcase: Adrian Belew: Setting Free the Bears," *Creem.* 18 (September 1986) 62–63. il., int.

Santoro, G. "Adrian Belew: Twang Bar King," *Down Beat.* 53 (December 1986) 25–27. il., disc.

Bruford, Bill (See also: Genesis)

Kassan, Brian. "Bill Bruford: Exploring Jazz Elements With Earthworks," *Cash Box.* (May 16, 1987) 10, 31. il.

Mattingly, R. "Update," *Modern Drummer.* 9 (December 1985) 114.

Reed, T. "Control Zone: Talking Drums," *Melody Maker.* 63 (September 5, 1987) 46. il., int.

Stewart, D. "Rock Keyboards: The Two-Headed Keyboardist/ Drummer Hybrid," *Keyboard Magazine.* 13 (February 1987) 104. music.

Tolleson, R. "Pro Session: Instructional Drum Videos," *Down Beat.* 53 (July 1986) 56–57.

Buckingham, Lindsey (See also: Fleetwood Mac)

Agnelli, L.E. "Lindsey Buckingham," *Creem.* 16 (February 1985) 32–33ff. il.

McCullaugh, J. "Buckingham Not 'Insane' Over Clips," *Billboard.* 97 (September 28, 1985) 40–41. int.

Ressner, J. "Lindsey Buckingham Leaves Fleetwood Mac," *Rolling Stone.* n509 (September 24, 1987) 15ff.

"Rock 'n' Roll News: Kind of a Drag Now That Buckingham's Gone," *Creem.* 19 (December 1987) 4. il.

Strauss, D. "Simplicity as a Way of Life," *Record.* 4 (November 1984) 16–17ff. il.

Burnett, T-Bone (r.n.: J. Henry Burnett)

Kalogerakis, George. "T-Bone Burnett Steps Out," *Rolling Stone.* n522 (March 24, 1988) 34. il., int.

Law, M. "Two of a Kind," *Melody Maker.* 60 (July 27, 1985) 16–17. il., int.

Butcher, Jon(, Axis)

Adelson, Dave. "Jon Butcher Finds Happiness With New Producer, Label," *Cash Box.* (August 31, 1985) 7, 38.

Caravan

Moran, Mike. "Caravan," *Record Collector.* n83 (July 1986) 52–55. il., disc.

Coyne, Kevin

Jennings, Dave. "Kevin Coyne," *Melody Maker.* (March 3, 1990) 13. il.

Doors

Dobrin, Gregory. "The Morrison Legacy," *Cash Box.* (December 20, 1986) 10. il.
Report on poetry by the late singer which recently came to light.

Sugerman, Danny. *Wonderland Avenue: Tales of Glamour and Excess.* New York: Morrow, 1989.

Autobiography built around Sugarman's fixation for the band.

Family

Hogg, Brian. "Family," *Record Collector.* n84 (August 1986) 52–55. il., disc.

GTR

"GTR," *Super Song Hits.* n49 (Winter 1987) 46–47. il.

Sutton, Rich. "GTR: The Making of a Supergroup," *Song Hits.* n249 (November 1986) 16–17. il.

Gabriel, Peter (See also: Genesis)

Brogan, D. "Peter Gabriel and the Politics of Amnesty," *Creem.* 18 (November 1986) 38–39. il.

Dupler, Steven. "Gabriel's 'Sledgehammer' Sweeps MTV Awards," *Billboard.* 99 (September 26, 1987) 61.

Padgett, Stephen. "Peter Gabriel: From Genesis to Revelation," *Cash Box.* (August 2, 1986) 9, 30. il., int.

"Peter Gabriel on Manu Katche," *Modern Drummer.* 11 (December 1987) 21. il.

Shalett, M. "On Target: Genesis, Gabriel Fans Contrasted," *Billboard.* 98 (December 6, 1986) 41.

Shelley, J. "Floating Back to Happiness," *Melody Maker.* 61 (June 7, 1986) 10–11. il., int.

Stambler, Irwin. "Gabriel, Peter, In: *The Encyclopedia of Pop, Rock and Soul.* pp. 247–248. il.

Gamma

"Gamma," *Super Song Hits.* n33 (Fall 1982) 38–39. il.

Genesis (See also: Phil Collins; Peter Gabriel; Steve Hackett; Mike and the Mechanics)

Lake, S. "Face the Press," *Melody Maker.* 60 (March 30, 1985) 14–15. il., int. w/Phil Collins.

Milkowski, B. "Phil Collins: Genesis of a Drummer," *Down Beat.* 51 (July 1984) 20–22. il.

Simmons, S. "The Mechanics of Genesis," 18 (November 1986) 32–35. il.

Stambler, Irwin. "Genesis," In: *The Encyclopedia of Pop, Rock and Soul.* pp. 253–256.

Welch, Chris. "Genesis, in Defense of Genesis," *Creem.* 19 (October 1987) 44–45. il.

BANKS, TONY

Greenwald, Ted. "Tony Banks," *Keyboard Magazine.* 13 (February 1987) 50–57. il., int.

Gentle Giant (See also: Derek Shulman)

Dawson, Michael P. "Gentle Giant: Power and Glory," *Goldmine.* n212 (September 9, 1988) 20, 25–26. il., disc.

Golden Palominos

Kendall, D. "Oldies But Goodies," *Melody Maker.* 61 (May 31, 1986) 16. il., int. w/Anton Fier.

Smith, R.J. "N.Y. Rocker: Anton Fier Drums Up the Downtown Music Scene," *Village Voice.* 31 (November 11, 1986) 21–26ff. il.

Stubbs, D. "New Horizons," *Melody Maker.* 63 (September 12, 1987) 38. il., int. w/Fier.

STRAW, SYD

Passantino, Rosemary. "Golden Girl," *Spin.* 5:6 (September 1989) 59–60. il., int.

Ressner, Jeffrey. "New Faces: Syd Straw," *Rolling Stone.* n561 (September 21, 1989) 25. il., int.

Hackett, Steve (See also: Genesis)

Sutherland, Steve. "Guitar Heroes Enter the Synthesizer Age," *Billboard.* 98 (May 24, 1986) 24.

Harper, Roy

Cunliffe, Pete. "Roy Harper," *Record Collector.* n95 (July 1987) 34–38. il., disc.

Hendrix, Jimi(, Experience)

Goodman, Fred. "Redding: Be $$ and Cents; Hendrix Bassist Learned the Hard Way," *Billboard.* 98 (August 9, 1986) 66ff.

"Hendrix' Father Sues Over Videocassette of Son's Performance," *Variety.* 323 (July 9, 1986) 82.
Re. *Rainbow Bridge.*

McCullaugh, J. "Vintage Hendrix Out," *Billboard.* 98 (November 1, 1986) 50.
Video release.

"PPX Enterprises Files 2d Suit Protecting Its Hendrix Product Rights," *Variety.* 329 (December 2, 1987) 94.

Stambler, Irwin. "Hendrix, Jimi," In: *The Encyclopedia of Pop, Rock and Soul.* pp. 290–291. il.

Tarshis, Steve. *Original Hendrix.* London: Wise, 1982. il., disc. pap.

Holdsworth, Allan

Baird, Jock. "Allan Holdsworth: The Innocent Abroad," *Musician.* n64 (February 1984) 78–80, 98, 110. il., int.

Hedges, D. "*Creem* Showcase: Allan Holdsworth: His Weight, in Gold," *Creem.* 17 (August 1986) 62–63. il., int.

Milkowski, Bill. "Allan Holdsworth's New Horizons," *Down Beat.* (November 1985) 19–21. il., bio., disc., int.

Mulhern, T. "Synth Axe," *Guitar Player.* 20 (June 1986) 109–111. il., int.

Hunter, Ian

Clerk, Carol. "Hunter/Ronson; Holding Back the Years,"

Melody Maker. 66:5 (February 3, 1990) 44–45. il., int. w/the duo.

Jethro Tull

Puterbaugh, Parke. "Tull: Living in the Present," *Rolling Stone.* n566 (November 30, 1989) 44. il.

Rosenbluth, Jean. "Tull Test: Resorting to Knavery," *Rolling Stone.* n513 (November 19, 1987) 16. il., int.

Stambler, Irwin. "Jethro Tull," In: *The Encyclopedia of Pop, Rock and Soul.* pp. 333–334.

Kaleidoscope

Hogg, Brian. "Kaleidoscope," *Record Collector.* n109 (September 1988) 74–76. il., disc.

Wilson, Jordan. "Kaleidoscope," *Record Collector.* n125 (January 1990) 92–95. il., disc.

Man

Heatley, Michael. "Man: The Welsh Connection," *Goldmine.* n180 (June 19, 1987) 20, 67. il.

Marillion (See also: Fish)

Alexander, S. "Marillion's Ian Moseley," *Modern Drummer.* 10 (November 1986) 38–39. il.

Greenwald, T., and Bob Doerschuk. "Q: Are We Not Progressive? A: We are Marillion!," *Keyboard Magazine.* 12 (July 1986) 19.

Holdship, Bill. "Will Marillion Conquer America?; or, the Incredible Mr. Limpet Floats Again!," *Creem.* 17 (July 1986) 44–46ff. il., int.

"New Faces to Watch: Marillion," *Cash Box.* (August 24, 1985) 10. il.

Wall, Mick. *Market Square Heroes: The Authorized Story of Marillion.* London: Sidgwick and Jackson, 1987. il., bio.

Mike and the Mechanics (See also: Genesis)

Doerschuk, Bob. "Creative Sampling—Hassles = Success on Mike & the Mechanics," *Keyboard Magazine.* 12 (June 1986) 16.

Vare, E.A. "Veterans Become a Brand New Dinosaur," *Billboard.* 98 (February 1, 1986) 41ff.

Nelson, Bill

Diliberto, J. "Profile," *Down Beat.* 53 (May 1986) 44–46. il., bio., int.

Oldfield, Mike

Doerschuk, Bob. "Soundpage Exclusive: Elusive Visionary Michael Oldfield Emerges From the Mist," *Keyboard.* (January 1988) 83–88. il., int.

Parks, Van Dyke

Fricke, David. "Without Fame or Fortune," *Rolling Stone.* n586 (September 6, 1990) 24. il., int.

Parsons, Alan, Project

Aiken, J., and Bob Doerschuk. "Alan Parsons Project; The Essence of Studio Rock," *Keyboard Magazine.* 12 (August 1986) 66–67ff. il., disc., int.

Vare, E.A. "Other Managers Face CD Royalty Disputes; Retailer Urged to Stockpile Parson Project Product," *Billboard.* 98 (February 15, 1986) 3.

Vare, E.A. "Will Royalty Hassle Remove Parsons' CDs from Market?," *Billboard.* 98 (February 8, 1986) 1ff.

Pink Floyd

Dickie, Mary. "Rock Notes: Another Brick from the Wall," *Me Music Express Magazine.* 14:148 (June 1990) 13. il., int. w/Roger Waters.

Ferrar, Ann. "Pink Floyd," *Stereo Review.* (March 1988) 63–65. il., int. w/David Gilmour.

"Floyd No More," *Melody Maker.* 61 (November 15, 1986) 4. Split confirmed.

Fricke, David. "Pink Floyd: The Inside Story," *Rolling Stone.* n513 (November 19, 1987) 44–54. il., int.

Gett, Steve. "Pink Floyd's Success Endures," *Billboard.* 99 (October 31, 1987) 21ff. int.

Jones, P. "It's the Final Cut: Pink Floyd to Split Officially," *Billboard.* 98 (November 22, 1986) 70.

Miles. *Pink Floyd.* London: Omnibus, 1981. Rev. ed. il. pap.

Stambler, Irwin. "Pink Floyd," In: *The Encyclopedia of Pop, Rock and Soul.* pp. 522–524. il.

WATERS, ROGER

Cohen, S. "Treading Waters," *Spin.* 3 (September 1987) 64–67. il., int.

Ronson, Mick (See: David Bowie; Ian Hunter)

Rotary Connection

Tamarkin, Jeff. "Rotary Connection: Turn Me On," *Goldmine.* n206 (June 17, 1988) 20, 25, 76. il., disc.

Rude Buddha

Farber, Celia. "Flash: Refined Chaos," *Spin.* 5:7 (October 1989) 22. il., int.

Rundgren, Todd

Jenkins, Mark. "Todd Rundgren Goes 'Up Against It'," *Rolling Stone.* n570 (January 25, 1990) 23. il., int.

Steely Dan

Rowland, M. "Walter Becker: Dr. Wu Goes Hawaiian—Steely Dan's Mystery Man Reappears," *Musician.* n83 (September 1985) 23ff. il., int.

Stambler, Irwin. "Steely Dan," In: *The Encyclopedia of Pop, Rock and Soul.* pp. 643–645.

Sutherland, Sam. "Producer Profile: Becker Puts Himself in a 'Crisis' Situation," *Billboard.* 97 (August 17, 1985) 33ff. int.

Supertramp

Robinson, Julius. "Supertramp," *Cash Box.* (February 6, 1988) 12–13, 26. il., int. w/John Helliwell.

Vare, E.A. "Supertramp *Bound* for Turning Point; Back to 'Art Rock' Without Hodgson," *Billboard.* 97 (May 11, 1985) 40ff.

Tribe

Kehoe, Christopher. "Babes in Toyland," *Spin.* 5:10 (January 1990) 20. il., int.

Wood, Roy/Roy Wood's Wizzard/Wizzard

Fitzgerald, H. "Christmas Crackers," *Melody Maker.* 61 (December 6, 1986) 21. int.

Van Der Kiste, John. "Roy Wood and Wizzard," *Record Collector.* n80 (April 1986) 34–38. il., disc.

Wyatt, Robert

Hogg, Brian. "Robert Wyatt," *Record Collector.* n80 (April 1986) 46–50. il., disc.

Yes

Bessman, Jim. "Charles Says 'Yes' to Long-Form Project,"
    Billboard. 97 (May 25, 1985) 33.
    Re.: video, *9012 Live.*

Dupler, Steven. "Atco Says 'No' to Arista 'Yes'," *Billboard.* 101
    (January 14, 1989) 82ff.

Stambler, Irwin. "Yes," In: *The Encyclopedia of Pop, Rock and
    Soul.* pp. 757–758.

"Yes Concert Video Designed to Sell Without LP Help,"
    Variety. 319 (May 15, 1985) 83.

HOWE, STEVE

Sutherland, Sam. "Guitar Heroes Enter the Synthesizer Age,"
    Billboard. 98 (May 24, 1986) 24.

RUBIN, TREVOR

Mulhern, T. "Trevor Rabin: Taking Yes by Force," *Guitar
    Player.* 19 (January 1985) 14ff. il., int.

WHITE, ALAN

Santelli, R. "Alan White," *Modern Drummer.* 9 (January 1985)
    8–13ff.

F. LATIN ROCK (1969–)

Feliciano, Jose

Feliciano, Jose. "Viva Puerto Rico!: Jose Feliciano: 'Latin Pop is Making Its Own Statement'," *Billboard.* 98 (May 24, 1986) P12ff. il.

Santana

"Santana Reunion," *BMI.* (Fall 1988) 5. il.

Stambler, Irwin. "Santana," In: *The Encyclopedia of Pop, Rock and Soul.* pp. 599–600.

Sly Fox

"New Faces to Watch: Sly Fox," *Cash Box.* 49:39 (March 15, 1986) 14. il., int.

G. BIG BAND ROCK (1969–)

Blood, Sweat and Tears

Arnold, T.K. "Clayton-Thomas Sheds Tears Name," *Billboard.* 97 (March 15, 1985) 42ff. int.

Stambler, Irwin. "Blood, Sweat and Tears," In: *The Encyclopedia of Pop, Rock and Soul.* pp. 64–66.

SOLOFF, LEW

Bourne, Mike. "Lew Soloff: Big Band Brass Man," *Down Beat.* 54 (September 1987) 4, 24–26. il., bio., disc., int.

Brass Construction

Sutton, Rich. "Brass Construction—'Fast Food Success'," *Song Hits.* n227 (January 1985) 60–61. il.

Chicago (See also: Peter Cetera)

Grein, Paul. "Chicago Sustaining Comeback Momentum," *Billboard.* 97 (January 26, 1985) 6ff. il.
Re. Grammy record of the year nominee, "Hard Habit to Break."

Stambler, Irwin. "Chicago," In: *The Encyclopedia of Pop, Rock and Soul.* pp. 117–120.

H. AFRO-ROCK (1972–) (See also: WORLD BEAT)

General Sources

"African Beat," *Melody Maker.* 60 (February 9, 1985) 36.

Gore, J. "Global Guitar: Afrobeat Guitar," *Guitar Player.* 23 (January 1989) 101. music.

Roberts, John Storm. *Black Music of Two Worlds.* London: Allen Lane, 1973. bibl., disc.

Juju

Waterman, C.A. *Juju: The Historical Development, Socioeconomic Organization, and Communicative Functions of a West African Popular Music.* Ph.D. thesis, 1986. Available from UMI.

Ade, King Sunny

Migaldi, R. "Here Comes the King," *Creem.* 16 (February 15, 1985) 15. il.

Clegg, Johnny

Freedman, Samuel G. "Johnny Clegg's War on Apartheid," *Rolling Stone.* n574 (March 22, 1990) 58–65, 120–122. il., int.

Miller, J. "S.A. Musicians Get Organized," *Billboard.* 98 (July 5, 1986) 68.

Miller, J. "S. African Musician's Release is Banned," *Billboard.* 98 (August 9, 1986) 70.
Re. *Asimbonanga.*

Rogers, S. "Native Son," *Gentlemen's Quarterly.* 60 (May 1990) 87–88. il.

Fela (r.n.: Fela Anikulapo-Kuti)

"Fela for UK," *Melody Maker.* 61 (November 1, 1986) 3. Provides background on his prison commutation.

"Fela Kuti Released," *Melody Maker.* 61 (May 3, 1986) 4. il. Freed from remainder of jail sentence.

"Label Spearheads Campaign to Free Fela from Prison," *Variety.* 319 (June 12, 1985) 75.

Morris, C. "Fela Looks to Fall U.S. Tour," *Billboard.* 98 (July 12, 1986) 20ff. il.

Ladysmith Black Mambazo

Iorio, Paul. "America Discovers Ladysmith Black Mambazo,"
    Cash Box. (May 23, 1987) 12, 15. int. w/Joseph Shabalala.

Makeba, Mariam (See: Hugh Masekela)

Mapfumo, Thomas

Mapp, Ben, with Saki Mafundikwa. "Nineties in Effect; The
    Struggle Continues," *Spin*. 5:11 (February 1990) 54–55.
    il.

Masekela, Hugh

Berman, L. "Medley—The Fela in Masekela," *Hi Fi/Musical
    America*. 35 (October 1985) 62.

Bordowitz, H., and W. W. Kinnally. "Songs of Exile,"
    American Visions. 5 (April 1990) 30–34. il.

Obey, Chief Ebenezer

Poet, J. "And a Time to Dance," *Musician*. n91 (May 1986) 25.

Okosuns, Sonny

"Okosuns Blasts Jive Diskery for Alleged South African Ties,"
    Variety. 320 (September 4, 1985) 79.

Olatunji, Babatunde

Comer, B.S. "Around the World," *Modern Percussion*. 1:2
    (1985) 48–50. il., bio., int.

I. GLITTER ROCK/GLAM ROCK (1972–1976)

Bowie, David (r.n.: David Robert Jones; Hunter and Ronson)

Cann, Kevin. *David Bowie: A Chronology.* London: Vermilion, 1983. il., bibl., disc., filmography.

Cavanagh, David. "Everything's Hunky Dory, Says Dave," *Sounds.* (February 3, 1990) 9. il., int.

"Dunhill to Bow Bowie Picture CD," *Cash Box.* (March 5, 1988) 26.

Howard, P. "CD News," *Rolling Stone.* n559 (August 24, 1989) 125.
Re. Bowie's Rykodisc CD retrospective, *Sound + Vision.*

Juby, Kerry. *David Bowie.* London: Midas, 1982. il., disc.

Maslin, Janet. "Making Movies—The Long Jump from MTV," *Record.* 4 (September 1985) 21–24. il.

Miles. *The David Bowie Black Book.* Designed by Pearce Marchbank. London: Omnibus, 1981. il., disc. pap.

Morris, C. "David Bowie Pops Up on Another Iggy Album," *Billboard.* 98 (September 27, 1986) 20.

Murray, C.S. "On the Set With Bowie," *Record.* 4 (December 1984) 23–25ff. il.

"News," *Melody Maker.* 63 (October 31, 1987) 3.
American grand jury to decide what action will be taken following rape allegations.

Norman, P. "Beginners' Luck," *Vanity Fair.* 49 (January 1986) 58–65. il.

Ressner, Jeff. "Bowie's Bicoastal Blitz," *Rolling Stone.* n558 (August 10, 1989) 24. il.

Robbins, J. "Music Motions Scrambles to Get 'Streets' Clip into Sites for Aid to Africa," *Variety.* 320 (August 21, 1985) 7ff.

Seideman, T. "Bowie/Jagger Vidclip Heads for Movie Screens," *Billboard.* 97 (August 24, 1985) 1ff. Re. "Dancing in the Street."

Stambler, Irwin. "Bowie, David," In: *The Encyclopedia of Pop, Rock and Soul.* pp. 77–80. il.

Staunton, Terry. "Phone Dave for Your Fave," *New Musical Express.* (February 3, 1990) 5. il.

Sutherland, Steve. "David Bowie; A Pressing Engagement," *Melody Maker.* 66:5 (February 3, 1990) 8–9. il.

Udovitch, Mim. "You are the D.J.," *Spin.* 6:1 (April 1990) 18. il.
News about current touring plans.

Cooper, Alice (r.n.: Vincent Furnier)

"Cooper's New Home is MCA," *Billboard.* 98 (November 1, 1986) 22ff.

McIlheney, B. "Return of the Living Dead," *Melody Maker.* 61 (September 27, 1986) 41. il., int.

McNeil, Legs. "The 3 Faces of Alice," *Spin.* 5:8 (November 1989) 46–51, 118. il., int.

"Sidelines: Alice Cooper," *Melody Maker.* 65 (August 12, 1989) 14. il.

Stambler, Irwin. "Cooper, Alice," In: *The Encyclopedia of Pop, Rock and Soul.* pp. 144–146. il.

Stud Brothers. "Splatter Platter," *Melody Maker.* 63 (October 3, 1987) 40–41. il., int.

Glitter, Gary

Tremlett, George. *The Gary Glitter Story.* London: Futura, 1974. il. pap.

Goodbye Mr. Mackenzie

Jennings, Dave. "Sidelines: Goodbye Mr. Mackenzie," *Melody Maker.* 66:23 (June 9, 1990) 14. il., int. w/Martin Metcalfe.

Kiss

Blackwell, Mark. "Flash: Critic's Choice: Half as Old as Rock Itself, is Kiss Just a Joke? Laughing all the Way to the Bank," *Spin.* 6:6 (September 1990) 18. il., int. w/Gene Simmons and Paul Stanley.

Duncan, Robert. *Kiss.* Manchester, U.K.: Savoy/New English Library, 1980. il. pap.

Grein, Paul. "Goldberg's Spaceship Takes Off," *Billboard.* 97 (June 29, 1985) 39–40.

Kalodner, J.D., and others. "Kiss: 15 Years," *Billboard.* 101 (January 21, 1989) KISS8ff. il.

Simmons, S. "Give Us a Kiss!," *Creem.* 16 (March 1985) 41–43ff. il., int.

Stambler, Irwin. "Kiss," In: *The Encyclopedia of Pop, Rock and Soul.* pp. 376–378. il.

Swenson, John. *Kiss.* Feltham, U.K.: Hamlyn, 1979. il., disc. pap.

New York Dolls

Morrissey, Steve. *New York Dolls.* Manchester, U.K.: Babylon, 1980. il. pap.

JOHANSEN, DAVID (a.k.a.: BUSTER POINDEXTER)

"Johansen Wins 7 N.Y. Music Awards," *Variety.* 322 (April 2, 1986) 79.

"Shrink Rap," *Melody Maker.* 60 (March 2, 1985) 12. il., int.

Stambler, Irwin. "David Johansen," In: *The Encyclopedia of Pop, Rock and Soul.* pp. 339–341.

Tamarkin, Jeff. "Johansen Tops N.Y. Awards," *Billboard.* 98 (April 12, 1986) 85. il.

Pop, Iggy (a.k.a.: Iggy Stooge)

Roberts, Chris. "Iggy Pop: Bricks & Mortars," *Melody Maker.* (July 7, 1990) 34–35. il., int.

Stambler, Irwin. "Iggy Pop," In: *The Encyclopedia of Pop, Rock and Soul.* pp. 532–534.

Queen B

Push. "Sidelines: Queen B," *Melody Maker.* 66:4 (January 27, 1990) 14. il., int.

Wells, Steven. "B-Hive Yourself," *New Musical Express.* (February 3, 1990) 30. il., int. w/vocalist Belinda Lee and guitarist Ray "the Boy."

Wilkinson, Roy. "Some Like It Hot," *Sounds.* (February 3, 1990) 20. il., int.

Roxy Music (See also: Bryan Ferry)

Balfour, Rex. *The Bryan Ferry Story.* London: Michael Dempsey, 1976. il., disc. pap.

T. Rex/Tyrannosaurus Rex

Bessman, Jim. "Jem, Warner Bros. Team for T. Rex," *Billboard.* 97 (December 7, 1985) 39.

Bramley, John and Shan. *Marc Bolan: The Illustrated Discography.* London: Omnibus, 1982. il., disc. pap.
Includes British and American releases as well as some bootlegs.

Marc Bolan: Songs, Photos, Lyrics, Interviews, Memorabilia, Letters, Notes, Snapshots, Memories . . . a Tribute, comp. and ed. by Ted Dicks and Paul Platz. London: Essex, 1981. il., disc. Orig. pub.: Essex/Springwood, 1978.

A collection of reminiscences of Bolan's associates and friends.

Stambler, Irwin. "T. Rex," In: *The Encyclopedia of Pop, Rock and Soul.* p. 663.

Tremlett, George. *The Marc Bolan Story.* London: Futura, 1975. il. pap.

J. PUB ROCK (1971–1975)

Parker, Graham(, and the Rumour)

Givens, Ron. "Graham Parker," *Stereo Review.* (August 1988) 58–59. il., int.

Stambler, Irwin. "Parker, Graham," In: *The Encyclopedia of Pop, Rock and Soul.* pp. 507–509.

K. HEAVY METAL (1969–) (See also: Censorship)

General Sources

Bashe, Philip, and others. "Heavy Metal," *Billboard.* 98 (May 10, 1986) H1ff. il.

Billard, Mary. "Heavy Metal Goes on Trial," *Rolling Stone.* n582/583 (July 12/26, 1990) 83–88, 132. il. Includes sidebar, "Ozzy: Read My Lyrics."

Crockett, J. "From the Publisher: Heavy Metal Grammies," *Guitar Player.* 19 (May 1985) 4.
Re. inadequate instrumental categories.

Frost, D. "White Noise: How Heavy Metal Rules," *Village Voice.* 30 (June 18, 1985) 46–48ff. il.

Graham, J. "Heavy Metal on the Outs at MTV," *Rolling Stone.* n445 (April 11, 1985) 15.

Halfin, Ross. *The Power Age.* London: Eel Pie, 1982. il.
Minimal text accompanying collection of photos of genre's leading stars.

"Heavy Metal Manager: I Want My MTV," *Billboard.* 97 (July 20, 1985) 37.

Ivany, J.S. "Commentary: Lowering the Boom on Heavy Metal," *Billboard.* 97 (July 6, 1985) 10.

McClary, E. "In Plain Sight," *Rock & Roll Confidential.* n63 (December 1988) 5–6.
Heavy metal charged with promoting suicide.

Miller, D.S. *Youth, Popular Music, and Cultural Controversy: The Case of Heavy Metal.* Ph.D thesis, 1989. Available from UMI.

Pond, Steve. "Full-Metal Racket," *Rolling Stone.* n506 (August 13, 1987) 41, 58. il.
The popularity of the genre reaches a new high.

Ressner, Jeffrey. "Head Bangers: Learning to Earn," *Rolling Stone.* n565 (November 16, 1989) 33.

"Rock Promoter Sues N.H. Town for Okay of Heavy Metal Concert," *Variety.* 319 (July 24, 1985) 47.

Shalett, M. "On Target: Half the Audience at a Metal Concert Didn't Buy the LP," *Billboard.* 98 (February 15, 1986) 24.

Shalett, M. "On Target: Heavy Metal is 'Cool' Again, and Its Fans are Buying Records," *Billboard.* 97 (July 6, 1985) 22.

Straw, W. "Characterizing Rock Music Cultures: The Case of Heavy Metal," *Canadian University Music Review.* n5 (1984) 104–122. bibl.

Tannenbaum, Rob. "Church Assails Heavy Metal," *Rolling Stone.* n576 (April 19, 1990) 32.

Vare, E.A. "Heavy Metal: Pounding It Out!," *Billboard.* 97 (April 27, 1985) HM1ff.

Young, R. "Spotlight on Texas: San Antonio: Heavy Metal Stomping Ground Welcomes New Music Upstarts," *Billboard.* 97 (July 20, 1985) T18ff. il.

Economic Factors

Freeman, K. "Pioneering Indies Undaunted by Majors' Stripmining of Heroes and Profits," *Billboard.* 97 (April 27, 1985) HM3ff. il.

McCormick, Moira. "Merchandise Doing Whip-Snapping Business," *Billboard.* 97 (April 27, 1985) HM6ff.

Ptacek, G. "Majors Return to Nuts and Bolts of Pre-MTV Metal Marketing Days," *Billboard.* 97 (April 27, 1985) HM3ff. il.

AC/DC

Baker, Glenn A. "AC/DC: It's a Long Way to the Top, But It's Worth It," *APRA Journal.* 2:10 (1982) 6–9. il.

Bunton, Richard. *AC/DC: Hell Ain't No Bad Place to Be.* London: Omnibus, 1982. il., disc.

Dobrin, Gregory. "AC/DC: The Patriarchs of Metal Continue the Tradition," *Cash Box.* (August 24, 1985) 11. il.

Robinson, Julius. "AC/DC," *Cash Box.* (February 20, 1988) 9, 23. il., int. w/Angus Young.

"Shrink Rap," *Melody Maker.* 61 (February 1, 1986) 14. il., int. w/Angus Young.

Accept

Moleski, L. "Accept Expects Success from Touring," *Billboard.* 98 (July 26, 1986) 21.

Aerosmith

Cohen, Scott. "Living Poets Society: Steven Tyler," *Spin.* 5:9 (December 1989) 72–73. il., int.

Eddy, C. "This Aerosmith Species," *Creem.* 19 (October 1987) 6–9. il.

Levy, Joe. "Aerosmith," *Cash Box.* (December 19, 1987) 10. il., int. w/Steve Tyler.

"Perry Sues Managers of Aerosmith Over His Back Royalties," *Variety.* 319 (June 19, 1985) 89ff.

"Sidelines: Aerosmith," *Melody Maker.* 63 (October 17, 1987) 21. il., int.

Sippel, J. "Promoter's Suit Hits Aerosmith Members," *Billboard.* 98 (February 8, 1986) 80.

Vare, E.A. "Aerosmith Taking Care of Business; Concert Tour, Geffen Contract Give Rockers New Life," *Billboard.* 97 (October 5, 1985) 38ff.

Wild, David. "The Band That Wouldn't Die," *Rolling Stone.* n575 (April 5, 1990) 44–48, 74. il., int.

PERRY, JOE

Stix, John. "Joe Perry," *Guitar.* (May 1990) 10, 136. int. re. Perry's opinions on the classic recordings in the guitar-rock genre.

Almighty

Henderson, Alex. "New Faces: The Almighty," *Cash Box.* (May 26, 1990) 6. il., int. w/lead singer Ricky Warwick.

Spencer, Mr. "All Power to the Almighty," *Sounds.* (February 17, 1990) 20–21. il., int.

Angel City

Vare, E.A. "Australia's Angels Take Flight via MCA; Hard

Rockers Pinning Hopes on U.S./Canada Tour," *Billboard.* 97 (March 30, 1985) 47.

Bad News

Sutherland, Steve. "Metallic K.O.," *Melody Maker.* 63 (October 31, 1987) 42–43. il., int.

Beauvoir, Jean

Gett, Steve. "Beauvoir's Career Heats Up," *Billboard.* 98 (August 16, 1986) 24–25.

Smith, M. "Wild Child," *Melody Maker.* 61 (May 3, 1986) 36. il., int.

Tamarkin, Jeff. "Newbeats: Jean Beauvoir: The Dude Jams Man," *Creem.* 18 (December 1986) 67. il.

Beyond

Wilkinson, Roy. "A World Apart," *Sounds.* (February 24, 1990) 21. il., int. w/drummer Neil Cooper and guitar Andy Gatford.

Black Oak Arkansas (See: Lord Tracy)

Black Sabbath (See also: Ozzy Osbourne)

"Shrink Rap," *Melody Maker.* 61 (May 17, 1986) 10. il., int. w/Tony Iommi.

Vare, E.A. "Sabbath's *Seventh Star* Spotlights Iommi," *Billboard.* 98 (March 8, 1986) 47.

Blue Oyster Cult

Arnold, T.K. "Underbelly Hits the Road; Low Profile for Blue Oyster Cult," *Billboard.* 97 (January 26, 1985) 41ff. int. w/Eric Bloom.

Blur

Ngaire. "Sidelines: Blur," *Melody Maker.* (July 7, 1990) 12. il., int. w/singer Damon.

Bon Jovi(, Jon)

"Bon Jovi," *Super Song Hits.* n47 (Spring 1986) 10–12. il.

Bon Jovi, Jon. "Let Freedom Ring," *Spin.* 5:8 (November 1989) 56–60, 115. il.
   Firsthand account of his part in the Moscow Music Peace Festival.

Clerk, Carol. "Overnight Sensation," *Melody Maker.* 61 (September 13, 1986) 23. il., int. w/Jon Bon Jovi.

Eddy, C. "Music: Whitesnake Can Eat Puke," *Village Voice.* 32 (October 27, 1987) 83ff.

Fujita, S. "Bon Jovi Album Sets Record; 300,000 Units Sold in 6 Weeks in Japan," *Billboard.* 100 (December 17, 1988) 54.
   Re. *New Jersey.*

Gett, Steve. "Bon Jovi Album Slides Toward Platinum Mark," *Billboard.* 98 (September 20, 1986) 20.

Halbersberg, Elianne. "Bon Jovi," *Song Hits.* n253 (March 1987) 8–10. il.

Heatley, Michael. "Bon Jovi: Livin' on a Prayer," *Goldmine.* n189 (October 23, 1987) 41–42. il.

Iorio, Paul. "Jon Bon Jovi Talks About Slippery and Going Platinum," *Cash Box.* (September 27, 1986) 11. il., int.

Neilson, J. "A Slab o' Life With Bon Jovi," *Creem.* 17 (August 1985) 28–29ff. il.

O'Brien, Glenn. "Bon Vivant," *Spin.* 3 (April 1987) pp. 46–51, 98–99. il.

Rabbitt, Linda. "Bon Jovi," *Record Collector.* 3 (November 1988) 12–16. il., disc.

Santelli, Robert. "Bon Jovi Comes Home," *Rolling Stone.* n536 (October 6, 1988) 17. il.

Sherman, L. "Profile: Shooting Through the Key: Bon Jovi's David Bryan," *Keyboard Magazine.* 13 (August 1987) 18. il.

Sutton, Rich. "Bon Jovi," *Song Hits.* n227 (January 1985) 30–31. il.

Sutton, Rich. "Bon Jovi," *Song Hits.* n236 (October 1985) 22–23. il.

Sutton, Rich. "Bon Jovi: Another Rocker Puts New Jersey on the Map," *Song Hits.* n267 (February 1989) 8–10. il.

Thompson, Dave, with Lorne Murdoch. "Bon Jovi," *Record Collector*. n93 (May 1987) 13–16. il., disc.

Walser, Robert. "Bon Jovi's Alloy: Discursive Fusion in Top 40 Pop Music," *OneTwoThreeFour: A Rock 'N' Roll Quarterly*. n7 (Winter 1989) 7–19. il., bio.

Bonham

Capozzoli, Michael A., Jr. "Bonham," *Song Hits*. n275 (July 1990) 8–10. il.

Considine, J.D. "Jason Bonham Grows Up," *Musician*. n140 (June 1990) 76–82, 113. il., bio., int.

Brilliant

Shaw, M. "Judas Kiss," *Melody Maker*. 61 (October 18, 1986) 38. il., int.

Britny Fox

Halbersberg, Elianne. "Britny Fox: Exclusive Interview with 'Dizzy' Dean Davidson," *Song Hits*. n274 (May 1990) 34–36. il.

Halbersberg, Elianne. "Britny Fox: Only the Beginning," *Song Hits*. n268 (April 1989) 48–50. il.

Cardenas, Luis

Dobrin, Gregory. "Cardenas Follows His Animal Instincts for a Solo Debut," *Cash Box*. (September 13, 1986) 11, 31. il., int.

Chastain, David T.

Nager, Larry. "David T. Chastain: Heavy Metal Workaholic," *Musician.* n105 (July 1987) 48–52, 133. il., int.

Cherry Bombz

The Unreal McCoy," *Melody Maker.* 61 (February 1, 1986) 34. il., int.

Cinderella

Halbersberg, Elianne. "Cinderella," *Song Hits.* n257 (July 1987) 16–17. il.

Halbersberg, Elianne. "Cinderella: Exclusive Interview with Eric Brittingham," *Song Hits.* n267 (February 1989) 40–42. il., int.

"New Faces to Watch: Cinderella," *Cash Box.* (August 9, 1986) 10. il., int. w/singer-songwriter Tom Keifer.

Tortora, Ralph. "Exclusive Interview With Cinderella's Tom Keifer and Bon Jovi's Richie Sambora and Dave Bryan," *Song Hits.* n260 (December 1987) 8–10. il., int.

Cult/Southern Death Cult

Elliott, Paul. "Taming the American Hordes," *Sounds.* (February 24, 1990) 30–35. il., disc., int.

Farber, J. "Peace, Love & the Cult," *Creem.* 17 (May 1986) 14–15. il.

"Flashback: The Cult," *Melody Maker.* 61 (April 12, 1986) 23–26. il.

McIlheney, B. "Resurrection Rockers," *Melody Maker.* 60 (January 12, 1985) 24. il., int.

Padgett, Stephen. "The Cult Creates a Following," *Cash Box.* XLIX:46 (May 3, 1986) 15. il., int. w/lead guitarist Billy Duffy.

"Shrink Rap," *Melody Maker.* 60 (May 18, 1985) 13. il., int. w/Ian Astbury.

"Shrink Rap," *Melody Maker.* 66:4 (January 27, 1990) 15. il., int. w/Astbury and Duffy.

Snow, Mat. "In My Tribe," *Spin.* 5:6 (September 1989) 62–67. il., int. w/Astbury and Duffy.

Sutherland, Sam. "This Ain't the Summer of Love," *Melody Maker.* 60 (October 26, 1985) 28–29. il., int.

Damn Yankees (See also: Night Ranger; Ted Nugent; Styx)

Santelli, Robert. "New Faces: Damn Yankees," *Rolling Stone.* n582/583 (July 12/26, 1990) 34. il., int.

Deep Purple (See also: Whitesnake)

Charlesworth, Chris. *Deep Purple: The Illustrated Biography.* London: Omnibus, 1983. il., disc. pap.

Marshall, Wolf. "Music Appreciation: Deep Purple," *Guitar.* (December 1990) 145–150. il.
Analysis of the band's musical technique.

Simmons, S. "Deep Purple Returns!," *Creem.* 16 (March 1985) 24–26ff. il.

Vare, E.A. "Deep Purple: 'Surprise of the Year'," *Billboard.* 97 (May 18, 1985) 41–42.

Def Leppard

"Def Leppard's Rick to Carry On," *Melody Maker.* 60 (January 19, 1985) 4.
Drummer Rick Allen decides to play despite the loss of an arm in an auto mishap.

Eddy, Chuck. "Music: Whitesnake Can Eat Puke," *Village Voice.* 32 (October 27, 1987) 83ff. il.

"Rick Loses Arm," *Melody Maker.* 60 (January 12, 1985) 3.

Tannenbaum, Rob. "Def Leppard Unleashes 'Hysteria'," *Rolling Stone.* n508 (September 10, 1987) 16, 93. il., int.

Van Horn, R. "Update," *Modern Drummer.* 9 (June 1985) 122.
Looks at Rick Allen's progress in the months following the amputation of his arm.

Des Barres, Michael (See also: Power Station)

Lounges, Tom. "Michael Des Barres," *Song Hits.* n253 (March 1987) 22–23. il.

Vare, E.A. "Michael Des Barres Gets Powered into the Spotlight," *Billboard.* 97 (August 10, 1985) 35. int.

Dio(, Ronnie James) (See also: Riverdogs)

Di Perna, A. "Profile: Claude Schnell of Dio Forges Heavy Metal on the Anvil of Classical Piano," *Keyboard Magazine.* 11 (August 1985) 16. il., int.

"Dio Sues ICM Agency, Reiterating Feyline Case Re. Alleged Threats," *Variety.* 321 (November 20, 1985) 103.

Gett, S. "Metal Artists: Let's Cut Out Fan Violence," *Billboard.* 98 (August 2, 1986) 1ff.

"News," *Melody Maker.* 61 (April 12, 1986) 4. Guitarist Craig Goldie replaces Vivian Campbell.

Obrecht, Jas. "Vivian Campbell: Dio's Fire and Brimstone," *Guitar Player.* 19 (February 1985) 14ff. il., int.

Rosen, Steven. "New Kid in Town," *Guitar World.* 11:8 (September 1990) 21–22, 101–104. il., int. re. his new guitarist Rowan Robertson.

Vare, E.A. "Dio Hits the Road in Grand Style," *Billboard.* 97 (August 24, 1985) 40ff. int. w/Dio.

Dokken (See also: Mob Rules)

Halbersberg, Elianne. "Dokken: Exclusive Interview With George Lynch," *Song Hits.* n266 (December 1988) 34–36. il., int.

Holdship. Bill. "Dokken," *Creem.* 16 (March 1985) 28–30ff. il., int.

Vare, E.A. "Dokken Exits Europe, Leaves Trouble Behind," *Billboard.* 98 (May 31, 1986) 21.

Enuff Z' Nuff

Lounges, Tom. "Enuff Z' Nuff," *Song Hits.* n276 (September 1990) 34–36. il.

Neely, Kim. "New Faces: Enuff Z' Nuff," *Rolling Stone.* n563 (October 19, 1989) 17. il., int. w/vocalist Donnie Vie.

Extreme

Stix, John. "Taking Matters into His Own Hands: Nuno Bettencourt; Extreme," *Guitar.* (December 1990) 74–84. il., int.

Ford, Lita (See also: Runaways)

Kay, Victor. "Lita Ford: Un-Effected," *Guitar.* (December 1990) 21–31. il., int.

Girlschool

Forte, Dan. "Intro: Kathy Valentine & Kelly Johnson—Girl Group Renegades," *Guitar Player.* 23 (January 1989) 16. int.

Giuffria

Burger, J. "Profile: Inside Gregg Giuffria's Powerhouse Synth Sounds," *Keyboard Magazine.* 12 (September 1986) 25. il.

Kordosh, J. "Another Look at Giuffria!," *Creem.* 17 (September 1985) 32–33ff. il.

Vare, E.A. "Timing is Right for Giuffria," *Billboard.* 97 (January 19, 1985) 35.

Great White

Halbersberg, Elianne. "Great White: Exclusive Interview With Jack Russell," *Song Hits.* n264 (August 1988) 16–18. il., int.

Halbersberg, Elianne. "Great White: Exclusive Interview With Mark Kendall," *Song Hits.* n271 (October 1989) 8–10. il., int.

Liveten, S. "Great White is Back in the Swim," *Billboard.* 98 (September 27, 1986) 22.

Guns N' Roses

Aledort, Andy. "Guitar in the '90's: Slash," *Guitar.* (December 1990) 35–39. il., music.
Analysis of the lead guitarist via notational illustrations.

Benjamin, Sandy Stert. "Talking With Slash of Guns N' Roses," *Goldmine.* n230 (May 19, 1989) 7–8. il., int.

Bernstein, Nils. "Guns N' Roses: Welcome to the Jungle," *Goldmine.* n230 (May 19, 1989) 5–8. il., disc.

Best, David. "Flash: Axl & Me," *Spin.* 6:4 (July 1970) 20. il.

"Guns N' Roses Shoot Way to 8-Mil Cert.," *Variety.* 336 (August 9, 1989) 63.

Halbersberg, Elianne. "Guns N' Roses: Exclusive Interview With Slash," *Song Hits.* n267 (February 1989) 16–18. il., int.

James, D. "The Rolling Stone Interview: Axl Rose," *Rolling Stone.* n558 (August 10, 1989) 42–44ff. il., int.

Le Ban, Linda. "Guns N' Roses," *Record Collector.* n118 (June 1989) 15–18. il., disc.

Moleski, L. "Controversial Hard Rock Act Must Make It on the Road," *Billboard.* (December 1987) 22.

Ressner, Jeffrey. "Slash: So What's the Big Deal?," *Rolling Stone.* n573 (March 8, 1990) 57. il., int. w/Slash.

Rowland, Mark. "If Guns N' Roses are Outlawed, Only Outlaws Will Have Guns N' Roses," *Musician.* n122 (December 1988) 62–72, 113. il., int.

Hanoi Rocks (See also: Michael Monroe)

"Chimes Change," *Melody Maker.* 60 (January 19, 1985) 4. Terry Chimes replaces Razzle; Yaffa leaves.

"Rocks Off," *Melody Maker.* 60 (June 8, 1985) 4. Change in the group's lineup.

Hunter and Ronson (r.n.: Ian Hunter and Mick Ronson; See also: David Bowie; Mott the Hoople)

Bent, Grahame. "The Artful Codgers," *Sounds.* (March 3, 1990) 16. il., int. w/Hunter.

Iron Maiden

"First Reports: Maiden: A Split in the Ranks; Adrian Smith Quits to Pursue Solo Project. Rumours That Bruce is Next Denied," *Sounds.* (February 24, 1990) 3. il.

Gett, Steve. "Maiden's Voyage Continue: New Album, Tour," *Billboard.* 98 (November 8, 1986) 20.

Hedges, D. "Iron Maiden's Powerslavin' Gear," *Creem.* 17 (May 1986) 66–69. il.

Schlossberg, K. "Iron Maiden: What's It all About, Eddie?," *Creem.* 17 (July 1985) 24–25ff. il., int. w/Bruce Dickinson and Steve Harris.

Stud Brothers. "Bruce Dickinson: The Filth Dimension," *Melody Maker.* 24:66 (June 16, 1990) 45. il., int.

Wall, M., and I. Blair. "Iron Maiden: World Slavery Special," *Billboard.* 97 (August 3, 1985) IM1ff. il., disc.

Jesters of Destiny

Iorio, Paul. "New Faces to Watch: The Jesters of Destiny," *Cash Box.* (January 30, 1987) 10. il., int. w/vocalist Bruce Duff.

Judas Priest

"Charge Judas Priest With Inciting Death of Nevada Youth," *Variety.* 325 (December 31, 1986) 55.

"Did Judas Priest Album Cause Teen Suicide Pact?," *Variety.* 332 (October 19, 1988) 500.

"News: Judas Priest 'Suicide' Trial," *Melody Maker.* (July 28, 1990) 4. il., int. w/guitarist Glenn Tipton.

Simmons, S. "Leathered, Studded Dudes or...Judas Priest?," *Creem.* 18 (September 1986) 6–9. il.

Karr, Tim

Sharp, Keith. "Sound Check: Tim Karr; Heir Apparent," *Me Music Express Magazine.* 14:145 (March 1990) 48. il., int.

Keel

Moleski, L. "Keel's Deal is Shipshape," *Billboard.* 98 (April 12, 1986) 26.

"New on the Charts," *Billboard.* 97 (March 30, 1985) 48. Re. *The Right to Rock.*

Kingdom Come

Capozzoli, Michael A., Jr. "Kingdom Come: Exclusive Interview With Lenny Wolf and Danny Stag," *Song Hits.* n266 (December 1988) 40–42. il., int.

Capozzoli, Michael A., Jr. "Kingdom Come," *Song Hits.* n270 (August 1989) 48–50. il.

Kings of the Sun

Doole, Kerry. "Sound Check: Kings of the Sun; Road Warriors," *Me Music Express Magazine.* 14:148 (June 1990) 22. il., int. w/lead vocalist-guitarist Jeffrey Hoad.

Henderson, Alex. "Heavy Metal," *Cash Box.* LIII:49 (June 30, 1990) 10. il., int. w/Hoad.

Levy, Joe. "Kings of the Sun," *Cash Box.* (July 23, 1988) 13. il., int. w/Hoad.

King's X

Kuipers, Dean. "Flash: Out of a Silent Plant," *Spin.* 6:6 (September 1990) 14. il., int.

Neely, Kim. "King's X," *Rolling Stone.* n566 (November 30, 1989) 43. il.

Kix

Halbersberg, Elianne. "Kix: Exclusive Interview with Steve Whiteman," *Song Hits.* n269 (June 1989) 33–35. il., int.

Krokus

Knapp, K. "Kalamazoo—and Krokus, Too!," *Creem.* 16 (March 1985) 31–33ff. il., int. w/Marc Storace.

Vare, E.A. "Krokus: Spring in Their Step," *Billboard.* 98 (April 5, 1986) 20ff.

Led Zeppelin (See also: Yardbirds)

Considine, J.D. "Led Zeppelin Box Due This Fall," *Rolling Stone.* n586 (September 6, 1990) 29. il., int. w/Jimmy Page.

Mylett, Howard. *Led Zeppelin.* Rev. ed. St. Albans, U.K.: Panther, 1981. il. pap. Previous eds.: 1976; 1978.

Pond, Steve. "Led Zeppelin Discography," *Rolling Stone.* n522 (March 24, 1988) 71. disc.

Pond, Steve. "The Song Remains the Same," *Rolling Stone.* n522 (March 24, 1988) 68–69. il.

Stambler, Irwin. "Led Zeppelin," In: *The Encyclopedia of Pop, Rock and Soul.* pp. 394–395.

PAGE, JIMMY

Welch, Chris. "Page Onstage '85," *Creem.* 16 (April 1985) 32–33ff. il., int.

PLANT, ROBERT

Altman, B. "Robert Plant: Moods 'n' Moments," *Creem.* 17 (September 1985) 28–31ff. il.

Bosso, Joe. "Danger Man," *Guitar World.* 11:12 (December 1990) 23–24, 93–98. il., int. w/his guitarist Doug Boyle.

Doole, Kerry. "Percy's Progress," *Me Music Express Magazine.* 14:148 (June 1990) 28–31. il., int.

Fricke, David. "Robert Plant," *Rolling Stone.* n522 (March 24, 1988) 54–64, 170–171. il., int.

Lord Tracy

Neely, Kim. "New Faces: Lord Tracy," *Rolling Stone.* n576 (April 19, 1990) 29. il., int. w/vocalist Terrence Lee Glaze.

Loud (See also: New Model Army)

Simpson, Dave. "Sidelines: Loud," *Melody Maker.* (October 13, 1990) 12. il., int. w/Chris McLaughlin.

Loudness

"New on the Charts," *Billboard.* 97 (March 16, 1985) 44.
Re. *Thunder in the East.*

Vare, E.A. "Japanese Rockers *Thunder* Westward," *Billboard.*
97 (April 6, 1985) 42A.

Magnum

Heatley, Michael. "Magnum," *Record Collector.* n130 (June
1990) 96–98. il., disc.

Heatley, Michael. "Magnum: The Long Road to Success,"
Goldmine. n230 (May 19, 1989) 27. il.

Malmsteen, Yngwie

Iorio, Paul. "Yngwie Malmsteen: Bach 'N' Roll Guitar Hero,"
Cash Box. (October 11, 1986) 11. il., int.

Mission (U.K.)

Hussey, Wayne, and C. Adams. "Around the World in an
Eighties Daze," *Melody Maker.* 65 (January 7, 1989) 8–10.
il.

Jackson, Richard. "The Mission," *Record Collector.* n95 (July
1987) 8–10. il., disc.

"Mercy Mission," *Melody Maker.* 61 (March 22, 1986) 5.
Another band claims names used by ex-Sisters of Mercy.

Scanlon, Ann. "Shootin' Their Mouths Off," *Sounds.* (March 3,
1990) 24–26. il., int. w/Wayne Hussey and Miles Hunt.

"Sisters are Doing It for Themselves," *Melody Maker.* 61 (March 8, 1986) 4.
Band abandons claim to name of The Sisterhood.

Smith, M. "Blood Brothers," *Melody Maker.* 61 (October 25, 1986) 24–25. il., int.

Smith, M. "Snake Charmers," *Melody Maker.* 61 (May 10, 1986) 14. il., int. w/Hussey.

Sutherland, Alastair. "Sound Check: The Mission; Sand Sculpture," *Me Music Express Magazine.* 14:145 (March 1960) 54. il., int. w/Hussey.

Williams, Simon. "Sons of a Beach," *New Musical Express.* (February 3, 1990) 28–29, 49. il., int. w/Hussey and Mick Brown.

Mob Rules (See also: Dokken)

Stix, John. "George Lynch: Mob Rules," *Guitar.* (May 1990) 88–100. il., int.

Monroe, Michael (See also: Hanoi Rocks)

Stud Brothers. "Michael Monroe: That's Entertainment," *Melody Maker.* 66:8 (February 24, 1990) 36–37. il., int.

Motley Crue

"Crue's Neil Sentenced in Drunk Driving Death," *Variety.* 320 (September 25, 1985) 138.

Goodwin, S. "Drum Tech Clyde Duncan on Tommy's Setup," *Modern Drummer.* 10 (September 1986) 21ff. il.

Goodwin, S. "Tommy Lee," *Modern Drummer.* 10 (September 1986) 16–21ff. il., int.

Handelman, David. "Money for Nothing and the Chicks for Free: On the Road With Motley Crue," *Rolling Stone.* n506 (August 13, 1987) 34–41, 59. il., int.

Johnson, Rick. "Ratt vs. Motley Crue!," *Creem.* 16 (February 1985) 26–29ff. il.

Kordosh, J. "Psychic Cruel and Motley Crue," *Creem.* 17 (April 1986) 42–46. il.

Kuipers, Dean. "Beyond the Valley of the Ultra Glam Boys," *Spin.* 5:10 (January 1990) 48–53, 85. il., int.

"Shrink Rap," *Melody Maker.* 61 (March 1, 1986) 41. il., int.

Stambler, Irwin. "Motley Crue," In: *The Encyclopedia of Pop, Rock and Soul.* pp. 478–479. il.

Motorhead

Burridge, Alan. *Motorhead: Born to Lose, Live to Win.* Manchester, U.K.: Babylon, 1980. il., bio., disc. pap.

Cohen, Scott. "Motorhead is the Loudest Band on Earth," *Spin.* n10 (February 1986) 36–37. il.

Gett, Steve. "Motorhead Runs Smoothly," *Billboard.* 98 (October 18, 1986) 22ff.

Kunkel, Rich. "The Great Lost Motorhead Album," *R.P.M.* n6 (July 1984) 44–48. il., disc.

Riegel, R. "Motorhead: Loving Them Like Reptiles," *Creem.* 17 (June 1985) 30–31ff. il.

Smith, Marcus. "Pumping Iron," *Melody Maker.* 61 (July 12, 1986) 29. il., int. w/Lemmy.

Wilde, Jon. "Rock of Ages," *Melody Maker.* 63 (September 12, 1987) 36–37. il., int. w/Lemmy.

Nugent, Ted (See also: Damn Yankees)

Moleski, L. "Nugent Contends No 'Danger' in Career Diversification," *Billboard.* 93 (January 25, 1986) 38. int.

Stambler, Irwin. "Nugent, Ted," In: *The Encyclopedia of Pop, Rock and Soul.* pp. 492–494.

O.A.O.

Goodman, Fred. "New Faces: O.A.O.," *Rolling Stone.* n561 (September 21, 1989) 25. il., int. w/singer Jesper Binzer.

Osbourne, Ozzy (See also: Black Sabbath)

"Animal Crackers," *Melody Maker.* 61 (August 30, 1986) 9. il., int.

"CBS, Osbourne Sued in Youth's Suicide," *Variety.* 321 (October 30, 1985) 2ff.

"Father Sues Ozzy, CBS Over His Son's Suicide," *Variety.* 321 (November 6, 1985) 2ff.

Iorio, Paul. "Osbourne Outgrows Outrageousness, Returns to Rock 'N Roll Basics," *Cash Box.* XLIX:44 (April 19, 1986) 11. il., int.

Jeske, Lee. "Ozzy Osbourne Tips His Hat to a Friend," *Cash Box.* (May 23, 1987) 13, 15. il., int.

"Osbourne Cleared on Charge His Song Prompted Suicide," *Variety.* 324 (August 13, 1986) 109.

"Ozzy Barks at Polygram," *Melody Maker.* 61 (May 10, 1986) 4. il.
Re. release of the video, *Bark at the Moon.*

Stambler, Irwin. "Osbourne, John "Ozzy"," In: *The Encyclopedia of Pop, Rock and Soul.* pp. 502–503.

Vare, E.A. "For Once, Osbourne Shuns Publicity," *Billboard.* 98 (February 8, 1986) 36ff. int.

Poison

Cassata, Mary Anne. "Exclusive Interview With Bret Michaels and Rikki Rockett of Poison," *Song Hits.* n259 (October 1987) 16–17. il., int.

Clerk, Carol. "Poison: Sex, Thighs & Videotape," *Melody Maker.* (July 21, 1990) 40–41. il., int. w/Michaels.

Halbersberg, Elianne. "Poison: Exclusive Interview With Bret Michaels," *Song Hits.* n264 (August 1988) 8–10. il., int.

La Ban, Linda. "Poison," *Record Collector.* n125 (January 1990) 36–38. il., disc.

Levy, Joe. "Poison," *Cash Box.* LI:45 (May 14, 1988) 10. int. w/drummer Rockett and lead singer Michaels.

"New Faces to Watch: Poison," *Cash Box.* (June 7, 1986) 10. il., int. w/Michaels.

Precious Metal

"New Faces to Watch: Precious Metal," *Cash Box.* XLIX:23 (November 16, 1985) 10. il., int. w/Leslie Knauer-Wasser.

Queen

Berk, Peter. "Queen Strengthens Its Film Music Connection With *Highlander*," *Cash Box.* XLIX:39 (March 15, 1986) 24. int. w/Bryn Bridenthal, PR rep. for the band.

Robertshaw, N. "Queen Plays for 80,000 Rock Fans in Budapest," *Billboard.* 98 (August 16, 1986) 62A.

Queensryche

Capozzoli, Michael A., Jr. "Queensryche," *Song Hits.* n270 (August 1989) 40–42. il.

Moleski, L. "Queensryche Breaks Heavy Metal Mold," *Billboard.* 98 (August 16, 1986) 27ff.

Quireboys/London Quireboys

Gleason, Holly. "Sound Check: London Quireboys; What's in a Name?," *Me Music Express Magazine.* 14:145 (March 1990) 44. il., int. w/Nigel Mogg.

Ratt (See also: Motley Crue)

Byrd, Jay. *Ratt.* Wauwatosa, WI: Robus, 1984. il., bio.

Connelly, Christopher. "Ratt: Lap Dogs of the Devil?," *Rolling Stone.* n436 (December 6, 1984) 50. il.

Des Cordobes, Dominique. *Ratt.* New York: Ballantine, 1986. il., bio.

Gaines, Robin. "Exclusive Interview With Ratt's Robbin Crosby," *Song Hits.* n226 (December 1984) 30–31. il., int.

Gett, Steve. *Ratt: Renegade Angels.* Port Chester, NY: Cherry Lane, 1985. il., bio.

Melanson, J. "Atlantic Records into Homevid With Ratt Vidclip Compilation," *Variety.* 319 (May 22, 1985) 85.

"Ratt Confident About Latest 'Invasion'," *Billboard.* 97 (May 25, 1985) 46ff.

Stix, John. "Warren DeMartini: Ratt: Getting Vibed," *Guitar.* (December 1990) 96–108, 152. il., int.

Sutton, Rich. "Ratt," *Super Song Hits.* n44 (Summer 1985) 20–21. il.

Razor

"Guelph Metal Band Released in UK," *Canadian Composer.* n204 (October 1985) 40–41. il.

Riverdogs (See also: Dio; Whitesnake)

Kleidermacher, Mordechai. "Pluck of the Irish," *Guitar World.* 11:8 (September 1990) 32–39, 99. il., int. w/Vivian Campbell.

Shotgun

Neely, Kim. "New Faces: Shotgun Messiah," *Rolling Stone.* n571 (February 8, 1990) 21. il., int. w/Harry K. Cody.

Skid Row

Black, Lee. "Born to be Wild," *Spin.* 5:9 (December 1989) 45–47. il., int.

Halbersberg, Elianne. "Skid Row: Exclusive Interview With Dave Sabo," *Song Hits.* n270 (August 1989) 8–10. il., int.

Smile

"New Faces to Watch: Smile," *Cash Box.* XLIX:36 (February 22, 1986) 10. il., int. w/bassist David Blade.

Sound Barrier

"New Faces to Watch: Sound Barrier," *Cash Box.* (May 31, 1986) 10. il., int. w/lead guitarist Spacey T.

Soundgarden

Corcoran, Michael. "Northwest of Hell," *Spin.* 5:9 (December 1989) 41–43. il., int.

MacNie, Jim. "Soundgarden's Full Punk Power Slide," *Musician.* n136 (February 1990) 32–40, 56–57. il.

Stud Brothers. "Soundgarden: Ambition Impossible," *Melody Maker.* (July 28, 1990) 17. il., int.

Spinal Tap

Del Rey, Teisco. "Spinal Rap," *Guitar World.* 11:8 (September 1990) 25–26, 104–105. il., int. w/Niger Tufnel.

Graham, Samuel. "Spinal Tap," *Musician.* n66 (April 1984) 12, 14, 34. il.

Spread Eagle

Henderson, Alex. "New Faces: Spread Eagle," *Cash Box.* (June 16, 1990) 5. il., int. w/axeman Paul DiBartolo.

Stryper

Capozzoli, Michael A., Jr. "Stryper: Exclusive Interview With Michael Sweet," *Song Hits.* n268 (April 1989) 34–36. il., int.

Jones, Elizabeth Leighton. "Stryper Keeps Going Strong," *The Magazine for Christian Youth!* 4:3 (November 1988) 8–9. il.

Surgin'

"New Faces to Watch: Surgin'," *Cash Box.* XLIX:22 (November 9, 1985) 12. il., int. w/guitarist-songwriter Jack Ponti.

Sweet F.A.

Henderson, Alex. "New Faces: Sweet F.A.," *Cash Box.* (August 18, 1990) 6. il., int. w/lead vocalist Steven David De-Long.

Taxxi

"Taxxi," *Super Song Hits.* n40 (Summer 1984) 48–49. il.

Tesla

Halbersberg, Elianne. "Tesla: Exclusive Interview With Brian Wheat," *Song Hits.* n269 (June 1989) 40–42. il., int.

Testament

Darzin, Daina. "Thy Will be Done," *Spin.* 5:10 (January 1990) 20. il., int. w/guitarist Alex Skolnick.

Triumph

Gaines, Robin. "Exclusive Interview With Triumph's Gil Moore," *Song Hits.* n227 (January 1985) 8–10. il., int.

Gross, J. "Canadian Musicians and Their Money," *Canadian Musician.* 8:4 (1986) 49. il.

Halbersberg, Elianne. "Triumph," *Song Hits.* n252 (February 1987) 16–17. il.

LaPointe. K. "Success of *Stages* Caps Triumph's Triumphant Year," *Billboard.* 98 (January 25, 1986) 60.

LaPointe, K. "Triumphant Wins With Album," *Billboard.* 98 (September 20, 1986) 23.

Lounges, Tom. "Triumph: A Decade of Canadian Thunder!," *Song Hits.* n244 (June 1986) 22–23. il.

Obrecht, Jas. "Rik Emmett of Triumph," *Guitar Player.* 19 (January 1985) 58–65ff. il., int.

Stern, P. "Triumph Make the Record from Hell," *Canadian Musician.* 8:5 (1986) 36–38ff. il., int.

Vare, E.A. "Canada's Triumph Triumphs by Acting; Veteran Hard-Rock Trio Insists on Going First Class," *Billboard.* 97 (April 13, 1985) 52. int. w/Rick Emmett.

Twisted Sister

Dobrin, Gregory. "Twisted Sister 'Does It Again'," *Cash Box.* XLIX:30 (January 11, 1986) 11. il., int. w/Dee Snider.

Miller, Debby. "The Angriest Band in the World," *Rolling Stone.* n435 (November 22, 1984) 64.

Snider, Dee, and Philip Bashe. *Dee Snider's Teenage Survival Guide, or How to be a Legend in Your Own Lunchtime.* Garden City, NY: Doubleday, 1987. il.

Sontana, Van. "Assisted Twister," *Spin.* 1 (August 1985) 64–65. il.

Stambler, Irwin. "Twisted Sister," In: *The Encyclopedia of Pop, Rock and Soul.* pp. 696–697.

Sutton, Rich. "Twisted Sister," *Song Hits.* n232 (June 1985) 16–17. il.

UFO

Hill, Tony. "UFO—End of the Trail," *Hit Parader.* (September 1983) 59.

"Rock 'n' Roll News," *Creem.* 19 (December 1987) 5.
  Band disbands.

Stambler, Irwin. "UFO," In: *The Encyclopedia of Pop, Rock and Soul.* pp. 704–706.

Uriah Heep

(Obituary), *Melody Maker.* 60 (March 9, 1985) 3.

Van Halen

DiMartino, Dave. "Give Us Van Halen," *Creem.* 17 (March 1986) 18–22ff. il.

Fish, S.K., and B. Cioffi. "Creem Showcase," *Creem.* 17 (February 1986) 65.

Fricke, David. "Can This be Love?," *Rolling Stone.* n477 (July 3, 1986) 28–30ff. il.

Gett, Steve. "Van Halen Cruises With Hagar at the Helm," *Billboard.* 98 (May 3, 1986) 22ff.

Iorio, Paul. "Van Hagar Floats Like a Butterfly, Stings Like a Bee," *Cash Box.* (May 31, 1986) 11. il., int. w/Sammy Hagar.

" 'Now What am I Supposed to Do?'," *Creem.* 16 (January 1985) 25–27. il.

Obrecht, Jas. "Eddie Van Halen and Sammy Hagar," *Guitar Player.* 21 (October 1987) 84–86ff. il., bio., disc., int.

Stambler, Irwin. "Van Halen," In: *The Encyclopedia of Pop, Rock and Soul.* pp. 710–712. il.

HAGAR, SAMMY

Yardumian, Rob. "Sammy Hagar: In Overdrive," *Cash Box.* (July 4, 1987) 12–13. il., int.

ROTH, DAVID LEE

Padgett, Stephen. "David Lee Roth and the Technicolor Dreamcoat," *Cash Box.* (July 12, 1986) 11, 32. il., int.

Sherman, L. "Profile: Brett Tuggle: High Wire Act in the David Lee Roth Circus," *Keyboard Magazine.* 13 (April 1987) 18.

Vare, E.A. "Van Halen's Roth: Maybe It's Over?," *Billboard.* 97 (January 12, 1985) 36.

Vixen

Buchsbaum, Brad. "Vixen: The Girls are Back in Town," *Cash Box.* (September 17, 1988) 11. il., int. w/vocalist Janet Gardner and bassist Share Pedersen.

Price, Deborah Evans. "Vixen," *Song Hits.* n271 (October 1989) 16–18. il.

W.A.S.P.

Capozzoli, Michael A., Jr. "W.A.S.P.: Exclusive Interview With Blackie Lawless," *Song Hits.* n272 (December 1989) 40–42. il., int.

La Ban, Linda. "W.A.S.P.," *Record Collector.* n120 (August 1989) 61–63. il., disc.

Warrant

Liveten, Sharon. "Flash: Down Boys," *Spin.* 5:8 (November 1989) 24. il.

White Lion

Black, Lee. "Flash: When Concern Wears Boots and Tight Trousers," *Spin.* 5:7 (October 1989) 16. il., int. w/ frontman Mike Tramp.

Halbersberg, Elianne. "White Lion: Exclusive Interview With Vito Bratta," *Song Hits.* n266 (December 1988) 16–18. il., int.

Halbersberg, Elianne. "White Lion: Exclusive Interview With Vito Bratta," *Song Hits.* n272 (December 1989) 8–10. il., int.

Whitesnake (See also: Deep Purple; Riverdogs)

"Shrink Rap," *Melody Maker.* 60 (February 23, 1985) 13. il., int. w/David Coverdale.

"Whitesnake: Absence of the Lord," *Creem.* 16 (March 1985) 26–27ff. il., int. w/Coverdale.

Winger

Capozzoli, Michael A., Jr. "Winger: Exclusive Interview With Kip Winger and Reb Beach," *Song Hits.* n269 (June 1989) 16–18. il., int.

Wolfsbane

Stud Brothers. "Wolfsbane," *Melody Maker.* 66:9 (March 30, 1990) 8–9. il.

L. SPEED METAL

General Sources

Fricke, David. "Heavy Metal Justice," *Rolling Stone.* n543 (January 12, 1989) 44–46ff.

Anthrax

Halbersberg, Elianne. "Anthrax: Exclusive Interview With Scott Ian," *Song Hits.* n269 (June 1989) 48–50. il., int.

Leland, John and Alexandria. "My Son the Headbanger," *Spin.* 3 (July 1987) 50–53. il.

Rabbit, Linda. "Anthrax," *Record Collector.* n101 (January 1988) 32–34. il., disc.

Reynolds, Simon. "Whoops Apocalypse," *Melody Maker.* 63 (September 5, 1987) 42–43. il., int.

DRI

Gittins, Ian. "Double Trouble," *Melody Maker.* 64 (December 17, 1988) 30–31. il., int.

"News," *Melody Maker.* 65 (January 21, 1989) 5. Josh leaves the band.

Damen, Das

True, E. "The Damenbusters," *Melody Maker.* 65 (January 7, 1989) 30–31. il., int.

Fields of the Nephilim

DeSavia, Tom. "New Faces to Watch: Fields of the Nephilim," *Cash Box.* (March 5, 1988) 11. il., int. w/lead vocalist Carl McCoy.

Stubbs, D. "Shoot It Up," *Melody Maker.* 61 (September 13, 1986) 12. il., int.

Flotsam and Jetsam

Buchsbaum, Brad. "Flotsam and Jetsam," *Cash Box.* (July 23, 1988) 13. il., int. w/lead vocalist Eric A.K.

Meat Puppets

Arnold, Gina. "The Meat Puppets Grind Minds," *Musician.* n111 (January 1988) 70–74, 98.

Fricke, David. "State of the Union: Sunny Side," *Melody Maker.* 60 (May 18, 1985) 32ff. il., int.

Grabel, R. "The Meat Puppets be Hep!," *Creem.* 18 (November 1986) 46–47ff. il.

"Reformed Punkers Play White House!," *Musician.* n78 (April 1985) 12. il.

Megadeth

Hobbs, Mary Anne. "In Their Own Words: Dave Mustaine," *Sounds.* (February 3, 1990) 19. il., int.

La Ban, Linda. "Megadeth," *Record Collector.* n121 (September 1989) 72–74. il., disc.

Metallica

Drozdowski, Ted. "Full Metal Justice: Metallica Rises Above the Crowd," *Musician.* n123 (January 1989) 44–52, 82.

Gett, S. "Metallica Thrashes Its Way to Top," *Billboard.* 98 (September 13, 1986) 6ff.

Halbersberg, Elianne. "Metallica: Exclusive Interview With Lars Ulrich," *Song Hits.* n268 (April 1989) 16–18.

(Jason Newsted Replaces Deceased Burton), *Melody Maker.* 61 (December 6, 1986) 4.

Pike, Jon R. "Metallica: Masters of Puppets," *Goldmine.* n207 (July 1, 1988) 24. 74.

Rabbitt, Linda. "Metallica," *Record Collector.* n112 (December 1988) 26–29. il., disc.

Simmons, S. "I Confronted Metallica on Their Own Terms!," *Creem.* 18 (October 1986) 32–35. il.

Slayer

McNeil, L. "Somewhere the Devil is Laughing," *Spin.* 4 (October 1988) 38–39. il., int.

M. JAZZ-ROCK FUSION (1970–)

Seventh Avenue South (club)

"Breakers Close Nitery," *Variety.* 321 (January 15, 1986) 223.

Albright, Gerald

Jeske, Lee. "New Faces to Watch: Gerald Albright," *Cash Box.* (December 26, 1987) 17. il., int.

Azymuth

Stewart, Jan. "Azymuth's Crazy Samba," *Down Beat.* (March 1986) 17–19. il., disc., int.

Beck, Jeff (See: Cream; Yardbirds)

Benson, George

"Appeals Court Orders New Trial for Lawsuit of Diskery vs. Warner," *Variety.* 318 (February 13, 1985) 141.

"Benson, Other Acts Pledge Funds for Anti-Piracy Drive," *Variety.* 319 (July 17, 1985) 105–106.

"CTI Presses Suit Against WB After Losing Benson Bid," *Variety.* 322 (February 5, 1986) 145–146.

Grein, Paul. "George Benson's $$ Pledge Spurs IFPI Piracy Fight," *Billboard.* 98 (June 29, 1985) 1ff.

Sippel, J. "CTI Sues Warner Bros. Over George Benson's '75 Signing," *Billboard.* 98 (February 1, 1986) 86.

Stambler, Irwin. "George Benson," In: *The Encyclopedia of Pop, Rock and Soul.* pp. 47–50.

Brecker, Michael

Brodowski, P. "Michael Brecker a Spirit of Discovery," *Jazz Forum.* n115 (1988) 30–35. il., disc., int.

Kynaston, T. "Pro Session: An Analysis of Michael Brecker's Harmonic Style," *Down Beat.* 52 (May 1985) 54–55.

Brecker, Randy

Ancrum, D., and S. Gunzy. "Randy Brecker: A Short Talk," *Cadence.* 12 (October 1986) 12–14. il.

Clarke, Stanley

Chamblis, Scott. "Stanley Clarke," *Cash Box.* (July 30, 1988) 19. il., int.

Jeske, Lee. "Stanley Clarke: Return to Fusion," *Cash Box.* (November 22, 1986) 10, 26.

Corea, Chick

Adams, S. "Chick's Career," *Jazz Journal International.* 39 (January 1986) 6–8. il., bio., disc.

Darter, T., and Bob Doerschuk. "Chick Corea: State of the Artist," *Keyboard Magazine.* 11 (October 1985) 52–54ff. il., disc., int., soundsheet.

Keepnews, P. "Chick Corea: 'Music Has No Boundaries,'" *Billboard.* 97 (May 25, 1985) 50. int.

Sutherland, Sam. "Jazz Super-Tour Motivated by Economic Necessity," *Billboard.* 98 (June 14, 1986) 29–30.

Zuegal, O. "Chick Corea Electric Band," *Jazz Podium.* 35 (July 1986) 32–33. il., int.

Davis, Miles

Dery, Mark, and Bob Doerschuk. "Miles Davis: His Keyboardists Present: Bobby Irving & Adam Holzman," *Keyboard.* (October 1987) 82, 85–88. il., int., music.

Doerschuk, Bob. "Jason Miles: Programming and Sessions With Miles Davis," *Keyboard.* (October 1987) 84. il., int.

Doerschuk, Bob. "Miles Davis: The Picasso of Invisible Art," *Keyboard.* (October 1987) 64–80. il., disc., int.

Keepnews, Orrin. "Miles Davis: His Keyboardists Past: Evans, Corea, Silver, Zawinul, Monk, Jarrett, Garland, Kelly . . . ," *Keyboard.* (October 1987) 50–103. il., bibl.
Includes sidebars, "Horace Silver: Miles Perspectives" and "Keith Jarrett: Miles Perspectives."

Santoro, G. "Miles Davis, Part 1: The Enabler," *Down Beat.* 55 (October 1988) 22–24. il.

Egan, Mark (See also: Arcadia; David Sanborn)

Santoro, Gene. "Mark Egan: The Face of the Bass," *Down Beat.* (March 1986) 23–25. il., disc., int.

Everything But the Girl

Collins, Andrew. "Thorn in the USA: Watt? Not in Hull,"
   New Musical Express. (February 17, 1990) 55–57. il., int.

Downer, S. "Star Struck," *Melody Maker.* 61 (August 30, 1986)
   22–23. il., int.

Kassan, Brian. "Everything But the Girl: Pop Chameleons
   With Style," *Cash Box.* (February 7, 1987)

Stern, Perry. "Sound Check: Everything But the Girl; Back to
   Basics," *Me Music Express Magazine.* 14:145 (March 1990)
   45. il., int. w/Ben Watt.
   Cited as part of the New Jazz movement along with Sade,
   the Style Council, etc.

Frank, David

Milano, Dominic. "David Frank: New York's Triple-Threat
   Hitmaker," *Keyboard.* (May 1986) 46–52, 140. il., disc., int.

Full Circle

Jeske, Lee. "New Faces to Watch: Full Circle," *Cash Box.* LI:48
   (June 4, 1988) 7.

Gottlieb, Danny

O'Donnell, Bob. "Danny Gottlieb: Sound Impressionist,"
   Down Beat. (September 1985) 17–19. il., disc., int.

Grisman, David

Cain, Linda. "David Grisman and His Dawg Music," *Goldmine.*
   n119 (February 15, 1985) 20–22. il., disc.

Hammer, Jan

Berk, Peter. "Jan Hammer: Helping Shape the New Rock and Role of Television Music," *Cash Box.* XL:19 (October 19, 1985) 30. il., int.

Chin, B. "Jan Hammer Scores *Miami Vice* Hit," *Billboard.* 97 (November 9, 1985) 61.

Milano, D. "Jan Hammer Scores Big With *Miami Vice*," *Keyboard Magazine.* 11 (September 1985) 38–4off. il., disc., int.

Milano, D. "*Miami Vice* Music: The Hot New Pulse of Prime Time TV," *Keyboard Magazine.* 11 (September 1985) 42. il., soundsheet.

"WKOX Chicago Recruits Jan Hammer; High-Tech Musical Identity Created for TV Spots," *Billboard.* 97 (May 11, 1985) 15.

Hancock, Herbie

Doerschuk, Bob. "Frenzy and Finesse Backstage at the Grammys With Wonder, Hancock, Dolby & Jones," *Keyboard Magazine.* 11 (June 1985) 10ff. il.

"France Honors Jazz Musicians," *BMI.* n3 (1985) 13.

"Hancock Expands into Film Composing, Acting," *Variety.* 317 (January 2, 1985) 129ff.

"Honored, I'm Sure," *Down Beat.* 53 (August 1986) 11. il. Hancock awarded honorary Doctor of Music degree at the Berklee College of Music.

Mandel, H. "Herbie Hancock: Of Films, Fairlights, Funk . . . and All That Other Jazz," *Down Beat.* 53 (July 1986) 16–19. il., bio., disc., int.

Woodard, Josef. "Herbie & Quincy: Talkin' Bout the Music of These Times," *Down Beat.* (January 1990) 16–21, 56–57. il., int.

Jobson, Eddie

Freff. "Eddie Jobson Does It Himself," *Musician.* n63 (January 1984) 80–82. il.

Johnson, Henry

Jeske, Lee. "New Faces to Watch: Henry Johnson," *Cash Box.* (March 21, 1987) 10. il., int.

Jordan, Stanley

Jeske, Lee. "Stanley Jordan: Making the Guitar Sing and Dance," *Cash Box.* (March 14, 1987) 10, 33. il., int.

Khan, Steve (r.n.: Steve Cahn)

Ferguson, J. "The Double Life of Steve Khan: Session Ace-Fusion Artist," *Guitar Player.* 19 (November 1985) 14ff. il., bio., disc., int.

"Jem Jazz Label Inks Khan as First Artist," *Variety.* 318 (April 10, 1985) 89.

Pye, Ian. "Sheer Khan," *Melody Maker.* 60 (February 9, 1985) 14–15.

Lavitz, T.

"New Faces to Watch: T. Lavitz," *Cash Box.* (August 23, 1986) 12. il., int.

Level 42

Cordry, M. "King's Gambit," *Melody Maker.* 60 (October 19, 1985) 51. il., int. w/Mark King.

DeMuir, H. "Newbeats: The Level Made Me Do It!," *Creem.* 18 (December 1986) 68. il.

Harvey, Rose. "Level 42," *Record Collector.* n109 (September 1988) 10–14. il., disc.

Padgett, Stephen. "America Finally Reaches Level 42," *Cash Box.* (June 21, 1986) 13.

Manhattan Transfer

Bourne, Michael. "Manhattan Transfer: From Doo-Wop to Bebop," *Down Beat.* (November 1985) 22–24. il., int.

Mantler, Karen

Futterman, Steve. "New Faces: Karen Mantler and Her Cat Arnold," *Rolling Stone.* n270 (January 25, 1990) 18. il.

McLaughlin, John

Ferguson, J. "John McLaughlin: From the Symphonic Stage to the Frontiers of Technology," *Guitar Player.* 19 (September 1985) 82–84ff. il., disc., int.

Ferguson, J. "Synclavier," *Guitar Player.* 20 (June 1986) 122ff. il.

Mandel, H. "John McLaughlin: Spirit of the Sine Wave," *Down Beat.* 52 (March 1985) 16–19. il., bio., int.

Najee

"New Faces to Watch: Najee," *Cash Box.* (February 7, 1987) 10. il., int.

Naked City

Stern, Chip. "New Faces: Naked City," *Rolling Stone.* n578 (May 17, 1990) 20. il.

Ponty, Jean Luc

Doerschuk, Bob. "Jean Luc Ponty, No Strings Attached: A Violinist Turns to Synthesizers," *Keyboard Magazine.* 12 (April 1986) 38–39ff. il., disc., int.

Ribot, Marc

Handelman, David. "Leapin' Lizard," *Rolling Stone.* n560 (September 7, 1989) 25. il., int.

Ritenour, Lee

"Lee Ritenour," *Song Hits.* n188 (October 1981) 18–19. il.

Rosen, Steven. "Lee Ritenour," *Musician.* n99 (January 1987) 38–43, 52. il.

Sade (r.n.: Helen Folasade Adu)

DeSavia, Tom. "Sade," *Cash Box.* LI:44 (May 7, 1988) 6.

Sanborn, David

Milkowski, B. "David Sanborn's Changes of Heart," *Down Beat.* 55 (August 1988) 4, 16–19. il., disc., int.

Sutton, Rich. "David Sanborn: Blows a Rock and Roll Horn," *Super Song Hits.* n40 (Summer 1984) 42–43. il.

Stern, Leni

Jeske, Lee. "New Faces to Watch: Leni Stern," *Cash Box.* (November 15, 1986) 10. il., int.

Sting (r.n.: Gordon Matthew Sumner; See also: Police)

Fricke, David. "The Rolling Stone Interview: Sting," *Rolling Stone.* n519 (February 11, 1988) 50–53, 115–117. il., int.

Fricke, David. "Sting," *Rolling Stone.* n512 (November 5, 1987) 297–298. il., int.

Gett, Steve. "Sting: Nothing Like Total Control Over Solo Career," *Billboard.* 99 (December 5, 1987) 19.

Milano, Dominic, and others. "Kenny Kirkland/Delmar Brown: Jazz Blasting With Sting," *Keyboard Magazine.* 14 (September 1988) 90–92ff. il., disc.

MARSALIS, BRANFORD

Fricke, David. "The Two Worlds of Branford Marsalis," *Rolling Stone.* n520 (February 25, 1988) 16–17. il., int.

Lange, A. "Sting & Band: Blue Turtles and Blue Notes," *Down Beat.* 52 (December 1985) 16–18ff. il., disc., int.

McGuigan, Cathleen. "Branford's Two Worlds: A Jazzman Gets Out of His Brother's Shadow," *Newsweek.* (January 4, 1988) 54. il., int.

Whitehead, Kevin. "The Many Sides of Branford Marsalis," *Down Beat.* (March 1987) 16–19. il., disc., int.

Weather Report

Bernarde, Scott, and Tom Moon. "Bassist Jaco Pastorius Dead at Thirty-Five," *Rolling Stone.* n513 (November 19, 1987) 29–30. il.

Henschen, R. "Jazz-Rock," *Musician Player & Listener.* 1:8 (1977) 12ff.

Rozek, M. "Alex Acuna: Transcending All Influences," *Modern Drummer.* 6 (May 1982) 12–15ff. il., int.

Sutherland, Sam. "Weather Report," *Billboard.* 97 (April 6, 1985) 42ff.

ZAWINUL, JOSEF

Keepnews, O. "Miles Davis: His Keyboards Past," *Keyboard Magazine.* 13 (October 1987) 90–91ff.

N. EURO-POP/EURO-ROCK (1973–)

Austria

FALCO (r.n.: JOHANNES HOELZEL; See also: Censorship)

"Falco to Make U.S. Visit; More Video also Planned," *Billboard.* 98 (April 12, 1986) 65.

"Falco Wins Top Honors in New Austrian Awards," *Billboard.* 98 (July 19, 1986) 71.
Re. Austrian Record Prize.

"Teldec: Falco is No Fluke," *Billboard.* 98 (June 28, 1986) 72.

"WEA, Sire Sign Falco," *Billboard.* 98 (August 2, 1986) 63.

OPUS

"New Faces to Watch: Opus," *Cash Box.* XLIX:41 (March 29, 1986) 12. il., int. w/Kurt Rene Plisnier.

Belgium

Stud Brothers. "New Beat: The Belgian Invasion," *Melody Maker.* 65 (January 28, 1989) 26–27. il.

France

GIPSY KINGS

Agudelo, C. "Will Gipsy Kings' Reign Reach U.S.?," *Billboard.* 101 (January 14, 1989) 18.

Dibbell, Julian. "Flash: The Wanderers," *Spin.* 5:11 (February 1990) 12. il., int. w/Jahloal Bouchikhi.

Goodman, Fred. "The Conquering Kings," *Rolling Stone.* n575 (April 5, 1990) 23–24. il., int.

LES NEGRESSES VERTES

Zwerin, Mike. "Flash: What's in a Name," *Spin.* 5:10 (January 1990) 16–17. il.

MANO NEGRA

Azerrad, Michael. "New Faces: Mano Negra," *Rolling Stone.* n579 (May 31, 1990) 34. il., int. w/leader Manu Chao.

Myers, Caren. "Sidelines: Mano Negra," *Melody Maker.* 66:8 (February 24, 1990) 12. il.

Germany

BELFEGORE

Mico, T. "It's Only Reich 'n' Roll," *Melody Maker.* 60 (March 2, 1985) 26. il., int.

BONEY M

Shearlaw, John, and David Brown. *Boney M.* London: Hamlyn, 1979. il., bio.

BUCKS FIZZ

Iorio, Paul. "New Faces to Watch: Bucks Fizz," *Cash Box.* (October 18, 1986) 10. il., int. w/Mike Nolan.

SCHILLING, PETER

Sutton, Rich. "Peter Schilling: No Error in the System," *Song Hits.* n217 (March 1984) 18–19.

Holland

FOCUS

Hoos, W. "Hocus Pocus: Focus is Back; Dutch Pop Group Re-Forms," *Billboard.* 97 (March 30, 1985) 47.

SHOCKING BLUE

Hill, Randal C. "Shocking Blue," *Goldmine.* n220 (December 30, 1988) 74. il.

SLEEZE BEEZ

Henderson, Alex. "New Faces: Sleeze Beez," *Cash Box.* (June 9, 1990) 6. il., int.

Norway

A-HA

"A-ha Wins Six Vid Awards," *Billboard.* 97 (November 30, 1985) 1ff.

Coverage of *Billboard*'s 7th annual Video Music Conference.

Armstrong, Mike. "A-ha," *Record Collector*. n116 (April 1989) 11–14. il., disc.

Clarkin, G. "On Record: A-ha: Why Not?," *Record*. 5 (January–February 1986) 8. il.

DiHauro, P. "Two Vidclips, One Production Firm Sweep MTV Video Music Awards," *Variety*. 324 (September–October 1986) 91.
Re. clip, "Take on Me".

Haugstad, Borre. "A-ha," *Record Collector*. n80 (April 1986) 10–12. il., disc.

Jeske, Lee. "For A-ha, The Sun Always Shines on TV—And How!," *Cash Box*. XLIX:24 (November 23, 1985) 13. il., int.

Vare, E.A. "Norway's A-ha 'Takes On' the Charts," *Billboard*. 97 (September 28, 1985) 47.

Sweden

ABBA (See also: Sampling)

Abba. *Abba in Their Own Words,* comp. by Rosemary York. London: W.H. Allen, 1982. il. Orig. pub.: London: Omnibus, 1981.

Borg, Christer. *Abba by Abba.* Knutsford, Cheshire, U.K.: Stafford Pemberton, 1977. il.

Edgington, Harry, and Peter Himmelstrand. *Abba.* Rev. ed. London: Magnum, 1978. il. Orig. pub.: London: Magnum, 1977.

(The Justified Ancients of MU MU: Trouble Over Their 1987 LP), *Melody Maker.* 63 (September 12, 1987) 3. "Dancing Queen" allegedly plagiarized.

Lindvall, Marianne. *Abba: The Ultimate Pop Group.* London: Pop Universal/Souvenir, 1977. il., disc. Also pub.: Edmonton, Alberta, Canada: Hurtig, 1977; New York: Visual Library, 1977.

"Silly Old Mu Mus," *Melody Maker.* 63 (September 19, 1987) 3. "Dancing Queen," sampled on *1987,* now to be credited; the outcome could threaten the future of record sampling.

Tobler, John. *Abba for the Record.* Knutsford, Cheshire, U.K.: Stafford Pemberton, 1980. il.

Ulvaeus, Bjorn, and Berry Andersson. *Abba: A Lyrical Collection 1972–1982.* Iver, Buckinghamshire, U.K.: Century 21 Merchandising, 1982. il.

T'Pau

Maxwell, Bill. "T'Pau," *Record Collector.* n104 (April 1988) 21–23. il., disc.

Switzerland

YOUNG GODS

Myers, Caren. "The Young Gods: Fear of Music," *Melody Maker.* 66:20 (May 19, 1990) 11. il., int. w/Franz Treichler.

Communist Block Countries
—Poland

BASIA

Myers, Caren. "Basia," *Melody Maker.* 66:5 (February 3, 1990) 14. il.

LADY PANK

Migaldi, R. "No Panks to You," *Creem.* 17 (August 1985) 20. il.

"Polish Lady Pank, Pronounced Punk, Prep Media Blitz," *Variety.* 318 (March 6, 1985) 371.

"Polish Rock Group Joins MCA Fold," *Billboard.* 97 (February 16, 1985) 86.

Swenson, John. "Iron Curtain Rock," *Saturday Review.* 11 (May–June 1985) 19.

—Romania

Sirrs, Ed. "Romania Mania," *Sounds.* (March 10, 1990) 14–15. il.
Survey of top acts set in the context of the recent overthrow of Ceausescu.

Staunton, Terry. "Rockin' in the Free World," *New Musical Express.* (March 10, 1990) 14–15, 54. il.

—U.S.S.R.

Yurchenkov, Vadim. "New Russian Revolution: Pop Charts," *Billboard.* 99:27 (July 4, 1987) 1, 75.

AUTOGRAPH

Trakin, R. "Autograph: The Writing's on the Wall," *Creem.* 17 (August 1985) 26–27ff. il.

GREBENSHIKOV, BORIS

Kissinger, David. "Is Boris Good Enough?," *Rolling Stone.* n560 (September 7, 1989) 16. il., int.

11. NOSTALGIA

A. ROCK AND ROLL REVIVAL

General Sources

Bell, Celina. "The Rock Revivalists," *Maclean's.* (March 2, 1987) 35. il., int. w/Paul James.

Steacy, Anne. "Rocking-Chair Rollers," *Maclean's.* (March 21, 1988) 52. il.

Edmunds, Dave

Stambler, Irwin. "Edmunds, Dave," In: *The Encyclopedia of Pop, Rock and Soul.* pp. 210–212.

Sha Na Na

Stambler, Irwin. "Sha Na Na," In: *The Encyclopedia of Pop, Rock and Soul.* pp. 610–611.

B. BLUES REVIVAL

General Sources

Darzin, Daina. "The Real Thing," *Spin.* 6:4 (July 1990) 16. il.

Forte, Dan. "Blues Who's Who," *Guitar World.* 11:8 (September 1990) 89–96. il., bio.

Pack, H. "The Blues Had a Baby: A Partial List of Blues Songs Copied by Rock, Soul, and Pop Artists," *Living Blues.* n76 (1987) 34–37.

Brooks, Lonnie

Freedman, S.G. "Blues Breaker: For Ten Years, Lonnie Brooks Has Taken the Chicago Blues to the College Towns of the Midwest," *Rolling Stone.* n509 (September 24, 1987) 91–92ff. il.

Bruce, Jack (See also: Cream)

Aledort, Andy. "Jack Bruce Opens Up," *Guitar.* (May 1990) 66–76. il., int.

Mack, Bob. "Skimming Off the Cream; Bassist Jack Bruce Teams With Drummer Ginger Baker for American Tour," *Rolling Stone.* n570 (January 25, 1990) 17. il.

Mulhern, T. "Cream's Bassist on Clapton's Influence," *Guitar Player.* 19 (July 1985) 43ff. il., int.

Woodard, Josef. "Jack Bruce: All Basses Covered," *Down Beat.* (March 1990) 19–20. il., int.

Buchanan, Roy

Kahn, A. "In Session: Roy Buchanan Gets the Blues," *Guitar Player.* 19 (August 1985) 50–53. il., bio., disc., int.

Milkowski, Bill. "The Lonesome Death of Roy Buchanan,"
  Guitar World. 11:8 (September 1990) 58–72. il.
  An investigation into the suspicious circumstances sur-
  rounding his alleged suicide.

(Obituary), *Rolling Stone.* n541–542 (December 15/29, 1988)
  135. il.

Butterfield, Paul

Moffitt, Phillip. "An Explorer's Journal: Living the Blues,"
  Esquire. (October 1987) 35–36. il.

(Obituary), *Notes.* 44:4 (1988) 697.

Collins, Albert

Birnbaum, L. "Albert Collins: The Iceman Strumeth," *Down
  Beat.* 51 (July 1984) 24–26. il., bio., disc., int.

Hollis, L., and E. Ferguson. "Albert Collins: Interview,"
  Cadence. 12 (May 1986) 20ff. il., bio., int.

Milkowski, Bill. "Mr. Freeze," *Guitar World.* 11:8 (September
  1990) 74–80, 99. il., bio.

Cooder, Ry

Santoro, G. "Ry Cooder: Blues & Roots," *Down Beat.* 53
  (August 1986) 26–28. il., disc., int.

Cray, Robert

Alden, Grant. "Rhythm & Bluesman," *Guitar.* 11:12 (December 1990) 27–30, 98–99. il., int.

Case, B. "Black and Blue," *Melody Maker.* 60 (August 3, 1985) 20. il., int.

Clayton, R. "Cray Wins Big at Blues Awards," *Billboard.* 98 (December 6, 1986) 25ff.
Re. National Blues Awards.

Cordery, M. "Smooth Operator," *Melody Maker.* 61 (November 1, 1986) 11. il., int.

Frith, Simon. "Britbeat," *Village Voice.* 30 (September 3, 1985) 71.

Hunt, K. "Peter Boe Brings Jazz to Robert Cray's Blues," *Keyboard Magazine.* 13 (October 1987) 26.

Jeske, Lee. "Robert Cray: Putting the Rhythm and Blues Back into Rhythm and Blues," *Cash Box.* (April 4, 1987) 11, 24. il., int.

Kaihatsu, T. "Robert Cray: Keeper of the Blue Flame," *Guitar Player.* 20 (February 1986) 32–33ff. il., bio., disc., int.

Moss, P. "Cray Named Year's Top Blues Wailer," *Variety.* 325 (November 26, 1986) 136. Re. seventh Blues Awards.

Porter, B. "Brief Encounters," *Jazz Times.* (December 1985) 25. il.

(Portrait), *Rolling Stone.* n515/516 (December 17/31, 1987) 114.

"Robert Cray," *Esquire.* (December 1986) 121. il., int.

Roberts, Jim. "Robert Cray: The Blues . . . and a Little Bit More," *Down Beat.* (March 1987) 23–25. il., disc., int. w/Cray and producer Dennis Walker.

Sutherland, Sam. "For Cray, Blues is Alive and Well," *Billboard.* 97 (November 30, 1985) 36.

Tolleson, Robin. "Robert Cray's Heart Full of Soul," *Down Beat.* (May 1988) 16–18. il., disc., int.

Creach, Papa John (See also: Jefferson Starship)

Adelson, David. "Palfi's Video Seeks to Set the Record Straight on Creach," *Cash Box.* XLIX:24 (November 23, 1985) 35.

Delaney and Bonnie

Browne, David. "Where are They Now? Delaney and Bonnie," *Rolling Stone.* n508 (September 10, 1987) 52. il., int.

Fabulous Thunderbirds (See also: Dave Edmunds; Mason Ruffner; Stevie Ray Vaughan)

Barol, Bill. "T-Birds in the Fast Lane," *Newsweek.* (May 5, 1986) 77. il.

Berk, Peter. "The Fabulous Thunderbirds Driven by the Blues," *Cash Box.* XLIX:47 (May 10, 1986) 13. il., int. w/lead singer Kim Wilson.

Birnbaum, Larry. "Red Hot Rhythm & Blues: The Fabulous Thunderbirds," *Down Beat.* 53 (February 1986) 23–25. il., int.

Jeske, Lee. "The Fabulous Thunderbirds Just Keep Thundering Along. Thunder, Thunder, Thunder," *Cash Box.* (December 19, 1987) 5, 6, 31. int. w/Wilson and lead guitarist Jimmie Vaughan.

(Portrait), *Creem.* 18 (December 1986) 36–37.

Schlossberg, K. "Fab T-Birds: *Tuff Enuff*, Were They Actual Meat," *Creem.* 17 (August 1986) 3, 38–40. il.

Trakin, R. "Can Rich Men Sing the Blues? The Fabulous T-Birds Find Out," *Creem.* 19 (December 1987) 9–11. il.

Vare, E.A. "Thunderbirds *Tuff* It Out," *Billboard.* 98 (May 10, 1986) 23ff.

Front

Smith, Mat. "The Front: Back to (Con)front," *Melody Maker.* 66:21 (May 26, 1990) 44. il., int. w/Michael Franano.

Healey, Jeff

Bosso, Joe. "Ed Stasium: Crunch Crunch," *Guitar World.* 11:8 (September 1990) 47. int. w/producer of Healey's *Hell to Pay* sessions.

Ginsburg, M. "Canadian Scene," *International Musician.* 87 (January 1989) 15ff. il.

O'Connor, T. "Talent, Blindness, Youth and Style Distinguish Guitarist," *Canadian Musician.* 8:3 (1986) 14. il.

Steinblatt, Harold. "Out of the Blues," *Guitar World.* 11:8 (September 1990) 42–55. il., int.

King, B.B.

"B.B. Gets Kingly Treatment; Veteran Bluesman Profiled on MTV," *Billboard.* 97 (March 2, 1985) 37.

Clerk, Carol. "BB King: When the Blues Comes to Town," *Melody Maker.* 66:4 (January 27, 1990) 11. il., int.

Ferri, B., and others. "Blues Archive Interview; B.B. King," *Living Blues.* n68 (1986) 12–14.

"15 Elected to Hall of Fame," *Billboard.* 98 (October 18, 1986) 101.

Ginsberg, J. "Three B.B. King *Into Night* Videos, Docu Feature Members of Cast," *Variety.* 318 (February 20, 1985) 77.

Langille, D. "B.B. King," *Coda.* n203 (August 1, 1985) 2–3. il., bio., int.

Migaldi, R. "Newbeats: Return of the King," *Creem.* 17 (February 1986) 77. il.

"Rock Hall of Fame to Induct 15 Acts," *Variety.* 324 (October 8, 1986) 147.

Russell, T. "That Old Blue Magic," *Jazz Journal International.* 38 (July 1985) 12–13. il., bio.

Schruers, Fred. "Mississippi Homecoming," *Rolling Stone.* n566 (November 30, 1989) 87–92, 118. il.

Mayall, John (See also: Eric Clapton; Fleetwood Mac; Yardbirds)

Frankel, David. "Where are They Now? John Mayall," *Rolling Stone.* n508 (September 10, 1987) 62. il., int.

Numbers Band

Howland, Don. "Flash: The Glamorous Life," *Spin.* 5:12 (March 1990) 12. il.

Raitt, Bonnie

Christman, Ed, and Edward Morris. "Grammys Give Big Boost to Raitt at Retail," *Billboard.* 102:10 (March 10, 1990) 1, 85.

Henke, James. "Bonnie Raitt: The Rolling Stone Interview," *Rolling Stone.* n577 (May 3, 1990) 38–42, 90, 92. il., int.

Rogers, Sheila. "It's Bonnie Raitt's 'Time'," *Rolling Stone.* n563 (October 19, 1989) 19. il., int.

Thomas, Chris

Harvey, Scott. "New Faces: Chris Thomas," *Cash Box.* (May 12, 1990) 7. il.

Thorogood, George(, and the Destroyers)

Freeman, K. "Thorogood Sliding into Country; New Direction for Blues/Rocker," *Billboard.* 97 (April 20, 1985) 42ff. int.

Treat Her Right

Walker, Cecilia. "New Faces to Watch: Treat Her Right,"
Cash Box. (April 23, 1988) 11. il., int.

Trower, Robin (See also: Procol Harum)

Arnold, T.K. "Robin Trower Checks out the Road Again;
Guitarist Playing Small Clubs After Five-Year Layoff,"
Billboard. 97 (March 16, 1985) 46. int.

Vaughan, Stevie Ray (See also: Jeff Beck)

Aledort, Andy. "So Real: Jimmie Lee & Stevie Ray Vaughan,"
Guitar. (December 1990) 89–94, 154–155. il., int.

"A Helluva Bluesman," *Guitar World.* 11:12 (December 1990)
73–74, 90.
Peers such as Nile Rodgers, Jesse Johnson, Gregg Allman
and Jeff Healey remember Vaughan.

"In Words & Pictures: Stevie Ray, Through the Years—
Selections from *Guitar World* Interviews, and a Gallery of
Rare Photos," *Guitar World.* 11:12 (December 1990)
56–67, 89. il., int.

Milkowski, Bill. "The Good Texan," *Guitar World.* 11:12
(December 1990) 38–54. il., bio.
A tribute encapsulating his career.

Milkowski, Bill. "Song Sung Blue," *Guitar World.* 11:12
(December 1990) 69–71, 76–80, 92–93. il.
Coverage of Vaughan's funeral.

Walker, Joe Louis

Goldberg, Michael. "New Faces: Joe Louis Walker," *Rolling Stone*. n572 (February 22, 1990) 30. il., int.

Williams, Lucinda

Rogers, Sheila. "New Faces: Lucinda Williams," *Rolling Stone*. n564 (November 2, 1989) 30. il., int.

ZZ Top

Graham, S., and others. "ZZ Top: Texas to the Universe," *Billboard*. 99 (October 3, 1987) ZZ1–4ff.

Obrecht, Jas. "ZZ Top: Billy Gibbons," *Guitar Player*. 20 (March 1986) 56–58ff. il., disc.

Padgett, Stephen. "That Lil' Ol' Band From Texas Turns on the Afterburner," *Cash Box*. XLIX:21 (November 2, 1985) 15. il.

Simmons, S. "Q & A With Z & Z," *Creem*. 17 (March 1986) 37–39. il., int.

"ZZ Top Teleconference," *Melody Maker*. 60 (August 3, 1985) 6. il., int.

C. RHYTHM & BLUES REVIVAL

Blues Brothers

McCullaugh, J. "Belushi's Boom Benefits from Book, Disk Ties," *Billboard*. 98 (February 15, 1986) 35.

Clemons, Clarence (See also: Bruce Springsteen)

Carnegie, J. "A Little from the Big Man," *Creem*. 17 (April 1986) 34–35. il., int.

Tabor, L. "Clarence Clemons Finds His Own Voice," *International Musician*. 84 (March 1986) 8ff. il.

Creedence Clearwater Revival

"Creedence Revival Sales Pace Otherwise Dull February Awards," *Variety*. 322 (March 5, 1986) 95–96ff.

FOGERTY, JOHN (SEE ALSO: SAUL ZAENTZ)

Christie, Leo. "Singapore, Bans Fogerty LP: 'Zombie' Track 'Glorifies Violence'," *Billboard*. (December 27, 1986) 87.

Forte, Dan. "Return of the Swamp Thing," *Record*. 4 (May 1985) 15ff.

Forte, Dan. "Woodsheds: Four Guitarists' Home Studios," *Guitar Player*. 19 (December 1985) 97ff. il., int.

Forte, Dan, and S. Soest. "John Fogerty Returns," *Guitar Player*. 19 (April 1985) 54–56ff. il., bio., int.

Gans, D. "Paper Bullets: Fogerty vs. Fantasy Rages On," *Record*. 4 (May 1985) 20. il.

Goldberg, M. "Fogerty Wins Unusual Self-Plagiarism Suit," *Rolling Stone*. n543 (January 12, 1989) 15.

McCullaugh, J. "Claymation Creator Molds Fogerty Clip," *Billboard.* 97 (July 13, 1985) 42. Re. "Vance Kant Dance".

"News," *Melody Maker.* 64 (December 3, 1988) 4. Found not guilty of plagiarism.

"Saul Zaentz Files Suit; Charges Fogerty Tunes, Interviews Libeled Him," *Variety.* 320 (July 31, 1985) 71.

Settle, K. "John Fogerty Returns," *Creem.* 17 (June 1985) 26–28ff. il., int.

Sippel, J. "Zaentz Sues John Fogerty," *Billboard.* 97 (August 10, 1985) 77.

Sutherland, Sam. "Rock Recluse Fogerty Returns," *Billboard.* 97 (February 2, 1985) 66ff. il., int.

Foghat

"*Foghat* Sues WB, Bearsville Over Royalties & Rent," *Variety.* 322 (February 19, 1986) 429.

Geils, J., Band (See also: Peter Wolf)

Hehler, M. "Keeping the Feeling and the Faith," *Record.* 4 (March 1985) 12ff.

NRBQ

Freedman, Samuel G. "NRBQ: RSVP," *Rolling Stone.* n569 (January 11, 1990) 51–53, 68. il., int.

Wilder, W. "The Spampinato Stomp: 20 Years on Bass With NRBQ," *Guitar Player.* 23 (August 1989) 82–84ff. il., int. w/Joey Spampinato.

Omar and the Howlers (See: Mason Ruffner)

Wolf, Peter (See also: J. Geils Band)

Goodman, Fred. "Peter Wolf: Back in the Groove," *Rolling Stone.* n582/583 (July 12/26, 1990) 35. il., int.

Perry, Steve. "Lone Wolf: Peter Wolf Blasts Out the Past," *Musician.* n106 (August 1987) 88–98. il., int.

Vare, E.A. "Wolf at the Door of Success," *Billboard.* 97 (December 7, 1985) 53. int.

D. ENGLISH RHYTHM AND BLUES REVIVAL

Bell, Maggie

"Maggie Bell," *Song Hits of the Super 70's.* (Fall 1975) 40–41. il.

Cocker, Joe

Gett, Steve. "Cocker Returns to Rock No Longer a *Civilized Man*," *Billboard.* 98 (May 17, 1986) 20ff.

Jeske, Lee. "Joe Cocker: With the Mad Dogs in the Past, the Englishman Rolls On," *Cash Box.* XLIX:48 (May 17, 1986) 15. il., int. w/Cocker and Capitol A&R VP Don Grierson.

Stambler, Irwin. "Cocker, Joe," In: *The Encyclopedia of Pop, Rock and Soul.* pp. 136–138.

E. NEO-ROCKABILLY

Cramps

Gibson, Robin, and Cathi Unsworth. "Shakin' the Disease," *Sounds.* (February 17, 1990) 16–19. il., int. w/Lux Interior and Poison Ivy.
Includes sidebars, "What's Behind the Mask" and "Discography."

Kiley, P. "The King and I," *Melody Maker.* 61 (March 29, 1986) 26–27. il., int. w/Lux and Ivy.

Myers, Caren. "The Cramps; Love It to Death," *Melody Maker.* (March 3, 1990) 16–17. il.

Phantom Chords (See also: Damned)

Clerk, Carol. "Sidelines: Dave Vanian," *Melody Maker.* (July 7, 1990) 12. il., int. w/Vanian.

Setzer, Brian

Williams, Joe. "The Timeliness of Brian Setzer," *Cash Box.* LI:49 (June 11, 1988) 6–7. int.

Stray Cats (See: Brian Setzer)

12. BUBBLEGUM (1967–)

Bay City Rollers

Allen, Ellis. *The Bay City Rollers.* St. Albans, U.K.: Panther, 1975. il. pap.

Patom, Tom, With Michael Wale. *The Bay City Rollers.* London: Everest. 1975. il. pap.

"Pop! The Glory Years: The Teenybop Years," *Melody Maker.* 63 (October 31, 1987) 11. suppl. il.

Bros.

"Bros.," *Record Collector.* n109 (September 1988) 30–32. il., disc.

Buchsbaum, Brad. "Bros.: 'When Will I Be Famous?'," *Cash Box.* (September 24, 1988) 9. il., int.

Bubble Puppy

Vorda, Allan, and Jack Ortman. "Bubble Puppy," *DISCoveries.* 3 (May 1990) 126–128.

Cassidy, David (See also: Partridge Family)

Cassidy, David. *David in Europe: Exclusive! David's Own Story in David's Own Words . . .* London: Daily Mirror, 1973. il. pap. Work employs a fanzine approach.

Farber, Celia. "David: We Think We Love You," *Spin.* 6:6 (September 1990) 69. il. Tribute.

Gregory, James. *The David Cassidy Story.* Manchester: World Distributors, 1973. il. pap.

Dino, Desi and Billy

Bleiel, Jeff. "Dino, Desi and Billy: Silver–Spoon Rebels," *Goldmine.* n140 (December 6, 1985) 18–20, 24. il., disc.

Donovan, Jason (See: Kylie Minogue)

Gibson, Debbie (See also: Tiffany)

Gibson, Debbie, with Mark Bego. *Between the Lines.* Austin, TX: Diamond, 1989. il., bio.
An unimaginative collection of personal black-and-white photos by the singer.

Gleason, Holly. "Debbie Gibson: Just a Matter of Proving Herself," *Song Hits.* n264 (August 1988) 24–25. il.

Jeske, Lee. "New Faces to Watch: Debbie Gibson," *Cash Box.* (August 29, 1987) 11. il., int.

McNichol, Kristy and Jimmy

"Kristy & Jimmy 45 Breaking Without Help of Radio Airplay," *Cash Box.* (July 30, 1988) 13.

Menudo

Cruz, N. "Viva Puerto Rico!: Menudo: The Very Best That Latin Youth Has to Offer," *Billboard.* 98 (May 24, 1986) P29.

Minogue, Kylie

Jackson, Richard. "Kylie and Jason," *Record Collector*. n123 (November 1989) 24–27. il., disc.

Monkees

DiMauro, P. "Sixties Reborn on New Disks, Second Coming of the Monkees," *Variety*. 324 (August 20, 1986) 77ff.

Holdship. Bill. "I Like the Monkees," *Creem*. 18 (December 1986) 38–41ff. il.

"Mad Maccs," *Melody Maker*. 61 (November 15, 1986) 3.
    The single, "Eh Up! We're the Macc Lads," alleged to be an unlicensed cover of "Hey Hey We're the Monkees."

"Monkees Reform!," *Melody Maker*. 61 (March 1, 1986) 7. il.

Morris, Chris. "Monkeemania Reaps $$ For Rhino," *Billboard*. 98 (July 12, 1986) 46.

Shalett, M. "On Target: 51% of Monkees' Audiences are Under 18," *Billboard*. 98 (August 30, 1986) 49.

Tamarkin, Jeff. "Monkees Dolenz, Tork, and Jones Regroup," *Billboard*. 98 (June 7, 1986) 24.

New Kids on the Block

Catalano, Grace. *New Kids on the Black*. New York: Bantam, 1989. il., bio.

Fletcher, Tony. "Fandemonium," *Spin*. 6:3 (June 1990) 57–61. il., int.

"New Kids on the Block," *Record Collector.* n128 (April 1990) 66–68. il., disc.

"New Kids on the Block," *Song Hits.* n276 (September 1990) 8–10. il.

New Kids on the Block. New York: Modern, 1989. il. pap.

Official New Kids on the Block—On Tour. New York: 1990. il. pap.

Rogers, Ray. "News: New Kids vs. Revolutionary Comics," *Spin.* 6:6 (September 1990) 24. il., int. w/New Kids' lawyer Philip Heller and Revolutionary's Todd Loren.

Wild, David. "Puberty to Platinum," *Rolling Stone.* n564 (November 2, 1989) 15–17. il., int.
Includes sidebar entitled, "Real–Life Fun Facts About the Kids."

Osmond, Donny (See also: Osmonds)

Church, John T. *Donny & Marie.* New York: Bonomo, 1979. il., bio.

Gregory, James. *At Last . . . Donny!* Manchester: World Distributors, 1973. il. pap.

Gregory, James, ed. *Donny.* New York: Curtis, 1973. il., bio.

Gregory, James, ed. *Donny and the Osmonds Backstage.* New York: Curtis, 1974. il.

Grove, Martin A. *The Real Donny and Marie.* New York: Zebra, 1977. il.

"Osmond Selling Stock," *Variety.* 317 (January 9, 1985) 176.

Roeder, Lynn and Lisa. *On Tour With Donny and Marie.* New York: Tempa, 1977. il.

Osmond, Marie (See also: Donny Osmond)

Osmond, Marie, with Julie Davis. *Marie Osmond's Guide to Beauty, Health and Style.* New York: Simon and Schuster, 1980. il.

Osmonds/Osmond Brothers (See also: Donny Osmond)

The Fantastic Osmonds! London: Daily Mirror, 1972. il. pap.

Hudson, James A. *The Osmond Brothers.* New York: Scholastic Book Services, 1972. il., bio.

Hudson, James A. *With the Osmonds.* New York: Scholastic Book Services, 1972. il.

Stambler, Irwin. "The Osmonds," In: *The Encyclopedia of Pop, Rock and Soul.* pp. 503–505.

Partridge Family (See also: David Cassidy)

Blackwell, Mark. "Moving Images: The Partridge Family Tree," *Spin.* 6:6 (September 1990) 67–68. il., int.

Columbia Pictures. *The Partridge Family Annual 1974.* Manchester, U.K.: World Distributors, 1973. il.

Meulenberg, Will. *The Partridge Family.* Amsterdam: Amsterdam, 1972.

Poppy Family

Yorke, Ritchie. "The Poppy Family," In: *Axes.* pp. 102–108. il.

Tiffany

DeSavia, Tom. "The Kids are Alright," *Cash Box.* (February 13, 1988) 7, 35. il., int.

Goodman, Fred, and Jeffrey Ressner. "Tiffany Embroiled in Legal Battle: Teen Singer Asks Court for Control of Her Own Career," *Rolling Stone.* n526 (May 19, 1988) 15, 18. il.

Morris, Chris. "Judge Puts Off Tiffany's Action For Adult Status," *Billboard.* 100:24 (June 11, 1988) 6, 92.

Orlean, Susan. "The Selling of Tiffany," *Rolling Stone.* n524 (April 21, 1988) 69–73. il.

Robinson, Julius. "Tiffany," *Cash Box.* (January 30, 1988) 8. il.

Wham! (See also: George Michael)

"China Takes Wham! in Stride; Attendees Sit Quietly in Seats," *Variety.* 318 (April 10, 1985) 89.

DeCurtis, Anthony. "Wham! Splits; Michael Goes Solo," *Rolling Stone.* n471 (April 10, 1986) 18.

Doerschuk, Bob. "Rock Veteran Tommy Eyre Finds Satisfaction and a Suntan With Wham!," *Keyboard Magazine.* 11 (October 1985) 14.

Grein, Paul. "Video Called Crucial to Wham!'s Stadium Success," *Billboard.* 97 (September 28, 1985) 86.

Grein, Paul. "Wham! Concerts in China to be Documented on Film," *Billboard.* 97 (April 20, 1985) 42ff.

Holden, S. "Wham! An Interview With George Michael," *ASCAP.* (Fall 1985) 24–27. il., int.

Jones, P. "Top-Level China Talks Make It Big; Lengthy IFPI Negotiations Led to Wham! Releases," *Billboard.* 97 (May 4, 1985) 9.

"Michael Says He's Leaving Nomis Mgmt.," *Billboard.* 98 (March 8, 1986) 9.

"News," *Melody Maker.* 61 (May 31, 1986) 3. The final single by the band is released.

Stambler, Irwin. "Wham!," In: *The Encyclopedia of Pop, Rock and Soul.* pp. 735–736.

Thomas, D. "Wham!," *Rolling Stone.* n444 (March 28, 1985) 17–18. il.

Weinger, H. "CBS/Fox Releasing Wham! Compilation; Cross Promotions Planned for Group's First Long-Form," *Billboard.* 97 (March 2, 1985) 34.

"Wham! in the Red After China Gigs," *Rolling Stone.* n448 (May 23, 1985) 14. il.

"Wham! Innocent," *Melody Maker.* 60 (November 16, 1985) 3. "Last Christmas" infringement claim on Manilow withdrawn.

"Wham! LP in China," *Variety.* 318 (April 24, 1985) 191. First Western musical group to have recording manufactured and released in People's Republic on full royalty basis.

"Wham! Pop Act Splits; South Africa Connection Moved Up the Decision," *Variety.* 322 (March 5, 1986) 1ff.

"Wham! Rap," *Melody Maker.* 61 (March 8, 1986) 3. Group break-up confirmed.

"Wham! Slam Club," *Melody Maker.* 60 (May 18, 1985) 3. Fan club terminated; money refunded.

"Wham! to Concertize in China; First Rock Band to Play There," *Variety.* 318 (March 13, 1985) 109–110.

"Wham! to Perform in China; a Rock Music First," *Billboard.* 97 (March 16, 1985) 3.

"Wham! Under Fire," *Melody Maker.* 60 (February 16, 1985) 3. Alleged copyright infringement of Manilow song, "Can't Smile Without You."

"Wham! Wrap Up," *Melody Maker.* 61 (March 1, 1986) 3. Rumors of split intensify.

"Wham!'s Visit to China Proves Costly," *Billboard.* 97 (April 20, 1985) 3ff.

RIDGELEY, ANDREW

Dickie, Mary. "Rock Notes: Racing Notes," *Me Music Express Magazine.* 14:148 (June 1990) 12. il., int.

13. THE COUNTRY CONNECTION

General Sources

Corcoran, Michael. "Nineties in Effect; Are You Ready for the Country?," *Spin.* 5:11 (February 1990) 62. il.

Marsh, Dave. "Music: Good Old Boys Gettin' Tough," *Village Voice.* (June 7, 1988) 71–72.

Simmons, D. "Music: Back to the Country," *Village Voice.* 31 (February 11, 1986) 65–67.

A. COUNTRY ROCK (1968–)

General Sources

Fish, S.K. "The History of Rock Drumming: The Country Influence," *Modern Drummer.* 6 (July 1982) 16–19ff. il.

Patoski, Joe Nick. "Why Lubbock? How the Home of the Flatlanders Became the Spiritual Center of Country Rock," *Texas Monthly.* (October 1988) 119. il.

Daniels, Charlie (See also: Volunteer Jam)

Bone, Michael. "Charlie Daniels: In Celebration of the Things We'd All Like to Believe In," *Quarter Notes.* (June 1982) 100–102. il., int.

Kirby, Kip. "Charlie Daniels' Career Shifting into High Gear," *Billboard.* 98 (January 18, 1986) 34ff. int.

Kirby, Kip. "Charlie Daniels Jams Again; Volunteer Surprises in the Works," *Billboard.* 97 (February 2, 1985) 40–41.

Kirby, Kip. "Sullivan Accents 'Personal' in Management," *Billboard.* 98 (March 29, 1986) 31–32.

Eagles

Stambler, Irwin. "The Eagles," In: *The Encyclopedia of Pop, Rock and Soul.* pp. 202–204.

Earle, Steve

Gleason, H. "Steve Earle: A Bad Boy Settles Down," *Rolling Stone.* n544 (January 26, 1989) 13. il.

McIlheney, B. "Honky Tonk Hero," *Melody Maker.* 61 (October 4, 1986) 18. il., int.

Morris, C. "Steve Earle Straddles Rock, Country," *Billboard.* 98 (August 23, 1986) 43.

Morthland, John. "The Good, The Bad, and the Country," *Texas Monthly.* (October 1988) 110–113, 156–157. il., int. w/Earle and George Strait.

Nash, Alannah. "Steve Earle," *Stereo Review.* 51 (November 1986) 158. il.

Ely, Joe

McCormick, Moira. "Newbeats: Ely for You to Say," *Creem.* 18 (June 1987) 66. il.

Face to Face

Robinson, Julius. "Face to Face," *Cash Box*. LII:1 (July 2, 1988) 11. il., int. w/vocalist Laurie Sargent.

Friedman, Kinky

Gaines, David. "Long Live the Kink," *Texas Monthly*. (August 1988) 114–118. il., int.

Gregson, Clive (See also: Any Trouble; Richard Thompson)

Robbins, Ira. "New Faces: Clive Gregson & Christine Collister," *Rolling Stone*. n575 (April 5, 1990) 28. il., int. w/ Gregson.

Jason and the Scorchers

Bessman, Jim. "Scorchers Find Modern Sound on *Lost,* Moving Beyond Country Punk," *Billboard*. 97 (March 16, 1985) 42ff.

Hill, C. "The 'Fervor' of Rural Mystics: Jason & the Scorchers Take It to the Limit," *Record*. 4 (June 1985) 3, 30ff. il.

Young, J. "Jason & the Scorchers: Hot Crackers to Go!," *Creem*. 17 (August 1985) 24–25ff. il., int.

Kristofferson, Kris

Lomax, John, III. "Kris Kristofferson," *BMI*. (1985) 24–25. il.

Schruers, Fred. "Kristofferson Meets the Cowboy Junkies: Country Music on the Morning After," *Musician*. n140 (June 1990) 26–34, 66.

Stambler, Irwin. "Kristofferson, Kris," In: *The Encyclopedia of Pop, Rock and Soul.* pp. 388–390.

Mason Proffit

Hopkins, Jack. "Mason Proffit: Come and Gone," *Goldmine.* n251 (March 9, 1990) 52, 108. il., disc.

Messina, Jim

Kirby, Kip. "Nashville Scene: Jim Messina Senses a 'New Movement'," *Billboard.* 97 (June 15, 1985) 40.

Murphey, Michael Martin

Delaney, Kelly. "Michael Martin Murphey," *Song Hits.* n237 (November 1985) 46–47. il.

Murray, Anne

Adilman, S. "Anne Murray Fronts Offer to Buy Maple Leaf Gardens in Toronto," *Variety.* 317 (January 23, 1985) 106.

Berk, Peter. "Anne Murray: Reaching Out Beyond Her Country Borders," *Cash Box.* XLIX:38 (March 8, 1986) 11. il., int.

Grein, Paul. "New Producers Bring Much to *Talk About*; Anne Murray Going Pop Again After Six Years," *Billboard.* 98 (February 15, 1986) 46. int.

Kirby, Kip. "Murray Re-Signs; Veteran Singer Retains Ties With Capitol," *Billboard.* (March 9, 1985) 63–64. int.

Nesmith, Mike (See also: Monkees)

"Pacific Arts' *Companion* to Test Effect of Trying in TV, Homevid," *Variety.* 319 (July 3, 1985) 32.

Stambler, Irwin, "Nesmith, Mike," In: *The Encyclopedia of Pop, Rock and Soul.* p. 482.

Nitty Gritty Dirt Band

Hochmann, S. "Hanna, McEuen and Ibbotson: The Multi-String Arsenal of the Nitty Gritty Dirt Band," *Guitar Player.* 19 (November 1985) 38–40ff. il., disc., int.

Kirby, Kip. "Dirt Band Push Targets Non-Commercial Radio, TV," *Billboard.* 97 (September 27, 1985) 42.

Kirby, Kip. "Nashville Scene: After 20 Years, Business as Usual for the Dirt Band," *Billboard.* 98 (March 1, 1986) 45.

Morris, E. "Dirt Band is Cleaning Up," *Billboard.* (April 20, 1985) 45ff.

Morris, E. "Partners, Brothers and Friends: The Dirt Band After 20 Years," *International Musician.* 84 (May 1986) 8. il.

Wood, G. "Nashville Scene: A Gala Concert Marks 20 Years of Nitty Gritty," *Billboard.* 98 (June 28, 1986) 26.

Notting Hillbillies (See also: Dire Straits)

Tannenbaum, Rob. "Mark Knopfler Heads for the Hills," *Rolling Stone.* n575 (April 5, 1990) 26. il., int.

Onionhead

Goldberg, Adrian. "Names for 1990: Nice Work," *Sounds.* (February 24, 1990) 56. il., int. w/singer Jules.

Parsons, Gram (See also: Byrds)

Stambler, Irwin. "Parsons, Gram," In: *The Encyclopedia of Pop, Rock and Soul.* pp. 510–512.

Walkabouts

True, Everett. "Sidelines: The Walkabouts," *Melody Maker.* 66:24 (June 16, 1990) 13. il., int.

Wilder, Webb, and the Beatnecks

Forte, Dan. "Webb Wilder and the Beatnecks," *Guitar Player.* 21 (December 1987) 42–44ff. il.

Iorio, Paul. "East Coastings," *Cash Box.* (March 7, 1987) 11. int. w/Wilder.

B. COUNTRY CROSSOVERS

General Sources

Armbruster, G. "Nashville Sessions: Deep Roots in America's Heartland," *Keyboard Magazine.* 12 (October 1986) 48ff.

Cash, Johnny

Conn, Charles. *The New Johnny Cash.* London: Hodder & Stoughton, 1973. il. pap.

Overly dramatic recounting of Cash's problems in coping with stardom and drugs.

Kirby, Kip. "Johnny Cash Charged With Breach of Contract, Fraud," *Billboard.* 97 (July 6, 1985) 79.

Kordosh, J. "Johnny Cash: A Little Farther Down the Line," *Creem.* 19 (June 1988) 3, 32–35. il., bio., int.

Morris, E. "Cash Seeks Label Deal," *Billboard.* 98 (August 2, 1986) 74.

Morris, E. "Cash Song Catalogs on Sale Block," *Billboard.* 98 (February 8, 1986) 6.

Shaw, R. "Whole Lotta Promotion for Rock Veterans' New Album," *Billboard.* 98 (June 7, 1986) 24ff.
Re. *Class of '55.*

Crowell, Rodney

Bessman, Jim. "Rodney Crowell Focuses on Performing," *Billboard.* 98 (November 1, 1986) 24.

Sandmel, B. "Progressive Country's Leading Light is Ready to Rock," *Musician.* n97 (November 1986) 27–28ff. il., int.

Exile

Delaney, Kelly. "Exile," *Song Hits.* n230 (April 1985) 40–41. il.

"Exile," *Song Hits.* n156 (February 1979) 8–9. il.

Kirby, Kip. "Ex-rockers Exile Make Smooth Musical Transition," *Billboard.* 97 (October 19, 1985) 64ff.

Morris, E. "Buddy Killen Likes to Keep His Artist Stretching," *Billboard.* 98 (February 8, 1986) 39ff.

Nash, Alanna. "Exile," *Stereo Review.* 49 (October 1984) 69–70, 121. il.

Roblin, A. "Exile Greatest-Hits Medley Meets Resistance at Radio," *Billboard.* 98 (September 27, 1986) 3ff.

"Tree International Honors Exile's Lemaire," *Billboard.* 97 (December 14, 1985) 47.

Woods, Brenda and Bill. "Exile: Hot 'New' Group or '70s Rock Band?," *Goldmine.* n136 (October 11, 1985) 24–25. il.

Harris, Emmylou

Nash, Alannah. "Emmylou Harris," *Stereo Review.* 50 (May 1985) 49–52. il.

Lang, K.D. (r.n.: Katherine Dawn Lang)

Atherley, Ruth. "Seeking Pop's Promised Land: K.D. Lang," *Maclean's.* (July 6, 1987) 36. il.

Dobrin, Gregory. "New Faces to Watch: K.D. Lang," *Cash Box.* (April 18, 1987) 10. il., int.

Lee, Johnny

Blaine, Montgomery. "Johnny Lee: Still Workin' for a Livin'," *Song Hits.* n229 (March 1985) 40–41. il.

"Johnny Lee," *Song Hits.* n183 (May 1981) 42–43. il.

"Johnny Lee," *Song Hits.* n215 (January 1984) 48–49. il.

Miller, Roger

Millard, Bob. "Roger Miller: The View from Nashville," *BMI.* (1985) 22–23. il.

Nelson, Willie

"American Music Award to Give Nelson the Nod," *Variety.* 333 (January 18, 1989) 157.
Re. Award of Merit.

Hilburn, Robert. "Willie Nelson: The Landmark Career of the Red-Headed Stranger," *Billboard.* (October 11, 1986) W-2, W-18, W-19. il., int.

Trio (See also: Emmylou Harris; Linda Ronstadt)

Holland, B. " 'Supertrio' Cutting for Autumn Release," *Billboard.* 98 (March 8, 1986) 56.

Padgett, Stephen. "Trio Takes Traditional Music to the Top," *Cash Box.* (May 16, 1987) 11, 31. il., int.

14. SINGER/SONGWRITER TRADITION (1970–)

Baerwald, David

Gilmore, Mikal. "Tales from the Dark Side: There's Nothing Soothing About David Baerwald's *Bedtime Stories*," *Rolling Stone*. n586 (September 6, 1990) 67–71, 96. il., int.

Bragg, Billy

"Christmas Joy," *Melody Maker*. 61 (December 13, 1986) 3. Bragg donates money to Nicaragua solidarity campaign to buy PA equipment.

Fricke, David. "Billy Bragg: Of Labour & Love," *Rolling Stone*. n543 (January 12, 1989) 18. il.
Re. *Workers Playtime*.

Irwin, C. "The Day the World Turned Upside Down," *Melody Maker*. 60 (March 23, 1985) 24–26. il., int.

Judge, Mark G. "Unafraid of the S-Word," *The Progressive*. (1988) 11.

Levy, Joe. "Billy Bragg: The Folkie, Punky, Political Soul Singer," *Cash Box*. (December 12, 1987) 10–11, 31. il., int.

Mehler, M. "What's New: The New Billy Bragg," *Record*. 4 (August 1985) 44. il.

Mico, Ted. "Close to the Wedge," *Melody Maker*. 61 (January 4, 1986) 10–11ff. il., int.

Migaldi, R. "Bragging With Billy!," *Creem*. 17 (July 1985) 18. il., int.

"New Acts," *Variety*. 318 (February 20, 1985) 81.

Rockmaker, Deirdre. "Billy Bragg: Greeting to the New Bayonet," *Goldmine*. n192 (December 4, 1987) 32, 35. il.

Schindelette, Susan. "A Simple Punk-Folk-Rock Protester, British Billy Bragg Makes Waves Onstage, Not Off," *People Weekly*. (July 29, 1985)

"Shrink Rap," *Melody Maker*. 60 (March 9, 1985) 10. il., int.

Browne, Jackson

"Browne Asks for Airings of 45, Clip Against U.S. Policy," *Variety*. 325 (December 10, 1986) 92.
Re. "Lives in the Balance."

DeCurtis, Anthony. "As Jackson Browne's 'World' Turns," *Rolling Stone*. n562 (October 5, 1989) 24–25. il., int.

DiMartino, Dave. "Browne Funds Video on Central America," *Billboard*. 98 (December 20, 1986) 72.

Richardson, D. "Rock On: Jackson Browne & the Nicaraguan New Song Movement," *Record*. 4 (August 1985) 7–9. il., int.

Stambler, Irwin. "Browne, Jackson," In: *The Encyclopedia of Pop, Rock and Soul*. pp. 83–84. il.

Bush, Kate

Bush, Kate. *Leaving My Tracks.* London: Sidgwick & Jackson, 1982. il. cased and pap. eds.

Diliberto, J. "Kate Bush: From Piano to Fairlight With Britain's Exotic Chanteuse," *Keyboard Magazine.* 11 (July 1985) 56–58ff. il., bio, disc., int.

Gillis, K. "Kate Bush Ascends U.S. Hill," *Billboard.* 97 (December 14, 1985) 42. int.

Mico, Ted. "Fairy Tales & Nursery Rhymes," *Melody Maker.* 60 (August 25, 1985) 18–19ff. il., int.

Rogers, Sheila. "The Sensual Woman," *Rolling Stone.* n571 (February 8, 1990) 16, 118. il., int.

Vermorel, Fred and Judy. *Kate Bush.* Rev. ed. London: Omnibus, 1982, 1982. il. Orig. pub.: London: Target 1980.

Carson, Lori

Harvey, Scott. "New Faces: Lori Carson," *Cash Box.* LIII:43 (May 19, 1990) 7. il., int.

Case, Peter

Hochman, Steve. "Peter Case," *Musician.* n96 (October 1986) 9–12, 22. il., int.

Champlin, Tamara

Robinson, Julius. "Tamara Champlin's Heart of Glass," *Cash Box.* (October 1, 1988) 11. il., int.

Chapin, Harry

Robbins, J. "Music and Politics Join Up in Tribute to Harry Chapin," *Variety.* 329 (December 9, 1987) 2ff.

"Stars Turn Out for Benefit Tribute to Harry Chapin," *Billboard.* 99 (December 19, 1987) 76.

Chapman, Tracy

DeCurtis, Anthony. "Tracy Chapman's Black and White World," *Rolling Stone.* n529 (June 30, 1988) 44–46. il., bio.

Mapp, Ben. "The 10 Most Interesting Musicians of the Last 5 Years: Tracy Chapman," *Spin.* 6:1 (April 1990) 40. il.

McGuigan, Cathleen. "The Oddball Divas of Pop," *Newsweek.* (June 20, 1988) 65. il.

Childs, Toni

Meyer, M. " 'Wild Weed' Toni Childs Takes Root," *Rolling Stone.* n544 (January 26, 1989) 16. il., bio.

Morris, Chris. "Childs Puts Her Dreams to Work," *Billboard.* 100 (June 25, 1988) 33.

Cockburn, Bruce

"Bruce Cockburn: In His Own Words," *Music Scene.* n352 (November–December 1986) 8–10. il., bio.

"Canada's True North Drops Out of Action Except for Cockburn," *Variety.* 323 (May 21, 1986) 91.

"Canadian TV Interview Retaped by Cockburn After Description Seen," *Variety.* 320 (October 9, 1985) 118.

Onellette, Dan. "Riffs: Bruce Cockburn," *Down Beat.* (May 1988) 14. il., int.

Cohen, Leonard

Collie, A. "Leonard Cohen: Old Skin for the New Ceremony," *Canadian Musician.* 7:4 (1985) 44ff. il., bio, int.

DiMartino, Dave. "Cohen Has New Disk, Same Ol' Sense of Humor," *Billboard.* 100:21 (May 21, 1988) 31, 35. int.

Cole, Jude

Dickie, Mary. "Sound Check: Jude Cole; A View from a Songwriter," *Me Music Express Magazine.* 14:148 (June 1990) 22. il., int.

Cole, Lloyd

Brown, James. "Do the No-Commitions," *New Musical Express.* (January 27, 1990) 26–27. il., int.

Reynolds, Simon. "Lloyd Cole: Stubble Trouble," *Melody Maker.* 66:7 (February 17, 1990) 14–15. il., int.

Ward, Ed. "Lost in the Atlantic With Lloyd Cole," *Musician.* n117 (July 1988) 88–92, 120. il., int.

Colvin, Shawn

Matthews, Janie. "New Faces: Shawn Colvin," *Rolling Stone.* n565 (November 16, 1989) 32. il., int.

Davis, Martha (See also: Motels)

Robinson, Julius. "Martha Davis on Her Own," *Cash Box.* (January 16, 1988) 10–11, 34. il., int.

Drake, Nick

Cresser, Wayne. "Nick Drake: We Know He's Here Now That He's Gone," *Goldmine.* n169 (January 16, 1987) 73. il.

Etheridge, Melissa

Schoemer, Karen. "Fast Car," *Spin.* 5:7 (October 1989) 76–79. il., int.

Scott, Benarde. "Melissa Etheridge," *Musician.* n128 (June 1989) 24–30. il., int.

Fogelberg, Dan

Ellis, C.A. "Dan Fogelberg," *Bluegrass.* 20 (June 1986) 40–43. il., int.

Gartner, R. "Dan Fogelberg," *Frets.* 7 (October 1985) 28–30ff. il., bio, disc., int.

Gartner, R. "Dan Fogelberg's Acoustic Style: Clear Touch-Hard Attack," *Frets.* 7 (October 1985) 31. il., int.

Foley, Ellen

"New Acts," *Variety.* 319 (July 3, 1985) 72.

Stuart, Jan. "Bright Lights, Big Season," *Saturday Review.* 11 (September–October 1985) 32–33. il.

Stuart, Jan. "Ellen Foley," *Saturday Review.* 11 (September–October 1985) 33. int.

Forbert, Steve

Wild, David. "Folk Rocker Steve Forbert Revived on Second Arrival," *Rolling Stone.* n537 (October 20, 1988) 20.

Fordham, Julie

Sprague, David. "Sound Check: Julie Fordham; Honeydripper," *Me Music Express Magazine.* 14:145 (March 1990) 50. il., int.

Gilder, Nick

Laursen, Byron. "Nick Gilder: Sex Meets Success," *Rolling Stone.* n280 (December 14, 1978) 20–23. il.

Gilkyson, Eliza

DeSavia, Tom. "New Faces to Watch: Eliza Gilkyson," *Cash Box.* (December 12, 1987) 11. int.

Goffin, Louise

DeSavia, Tom. "Louise Goffin: In Control," *Cash Box.* LI:50 (June 18, 1988) 10. il., int.

Harding, John Wesley

Goldberg, Michael. "New Faces: John Wesley Harding," *Rolling Stone.* n574 (March 22, 1990) 26–27. il., int.

Harris, Hugh

Ressner, Jeffrey. "New Faces: Hugh Harris," *Rolling Stone.* n570 (January 25, 1990) 18. il., int.

Harrison, Kodac

Iorio, Paul. "New Faces to Watch: Kodac Harrison," *Cash Box.*
(December 6, 1986) 10. il., int.

Hiatt, John

Hochman, S. "On the Charts: Family Man," *Rolling Stone.* n508
(September 10, 1987) 25. il.

Trowbridge, Susanne. "Family Man," *Buzz.* 3:1 (November
1987) 21–24. il., int.

Wild, D. "Clean & Sober," *Rolling Stone.* n543 (January 12,
1989) 56–57ff. il., bio, int.

Hickman, Sara

Woods, Karen. "Sara Hickman Would Like to Teach the
World to Sing Loudly," *Cash Box.* LIII:39 (April 21,
1990) 7. il., int.

Himmelman, Peter

Iorio, Paul. "New Faces to Watch: Peter Himmelman," *Cash
Box.* (October 11, 1986) 10. il., int.

Huxley, Parthenon

Williams, Joe. "New Faces to Watch: Parthenon Huxley,"
Cash Box. LII:1 (July 2, 1988) 12.

Isaak, Chris

Kassan, Brian. "Chris Isaak: A Man With a Mission," *Cash Box.*
L (May 2, 1987) 10, 24, 31. il., int.

Whiteside, Jonny. "Moody Blue," *Spin.* 3 (June 1987) 24–25. il.

Jandek

Coley, Byron. "The 10 Most Interesting Musicians of the Last 5 Years: Jandek," *Spin.* 6:1 (April 1990) 48. il.

Joel, Billy (See also: USA for Africa; "We are the World")

Benson, M.R. "Billy Joel's Russian Roadshow," *Rolling Stone.* n509 (September 24, 1987) 16. il.

Bessman, Jim. "Billy Joel Long-Form Will be a 'First'; Animated Story Line Connects 'Marking Time' Clips," *Billboard.* 97 (July 20, 1985) 32.

Bessman, Jim. "Schlock Values Telling a Good Story," *Billboard.* 98 (May 31, 1986) 45.

Clarke, Tina. "An Ordinary Joel?," *Me Music Express Magazine.* 14:145 (March 1990) 20–22. il., int.

Goodman, Fred. ". . . [Billy Joel] Sparks a Legal Battle," *Rolling Stone.* n565 (November 16, 1989) 29.

Iorio, Paul. "Billy Joel Comes of Age With a New Album That's Younger Than Yesterday," *Cash Box.* (August 16, 1986) 11. il., int.

"On Record: Billy Joel: Choose Life," *Record.* 4 (October 1985) 10. il.
Joel donates royalties from "You're Only Human" to the National Committee for Youth Suicide.

Rogers, Sheila. "Billy Joel Starts a Fire . . . ," *Rolling Stone.* n565 (November 16, 1989) 29. il., int.

Stambler, Irwin. "Joel, Billy," In: *The Encyclopedia of Pop, Rock and Soul.* pp. 336–339. il.

Wild, David. "The Rolling Stone Interview: Billy Joel," *Rolling Stone.* n570 (January 25, 1990) 34–39. il., int.

Yurchenkov, V. "Joel's Soviet Tour a Hit," *Billboard.* 99 (September 12, 1987) 76.

Jones, Rickie Lee

Pond, Steve. "Bellying Up to the Bar," *Rolling Stone.* n577 (May 3, 1990) 23–24. il.

Stambler, Irwin. "Jones, Rickie Lee," In: *The Encyclopedia of Pop, Rock and Soul.* pp. 347–348.

White, Timothy. "Sweetheart of the Rodeo," *Spin.* 5:8 (November 1989) 72–78, 114. il., int.

Jungklas, Rob

Bessman, Jim. "Label Gives Jungklas a High Profile," *Billboard.* 98 (September 27, 1986) 34.

"New Faces to Watch: Rob Jungklas," *Cash Box.* XLIX:46 (May 3, 1986) 14. il., int.

Kelly, Paul

Flanagan, Bill. "Paul Kelly: The Man Who Could Not Make Himself Go Away," *Musician.* n134 (December 1989) 56–68. il., int.

Kershaw, Nik

Jackson, Richard. "Nik Kershaw," *Record Collector*. n68 (April 1985) 15–18. il., disc.

Kilzer, John

DeSavia, Tom. "New Faces to Watch: John Kilzer," *Cash Box*. LII:1 (July 2, 1988) 11–12. il., int.

King, Carole (See also: Gerry Goffin)

"King Sues Biz Manager Re. Video, Use of Funds," *Variety*. 322 (March 5, 1986) 95.

Lach

Ahearn, Charlie. "Flash: Anti-Hero," *Spin*. 6:6 (September 1990) 16. il., int.

Lennon, Julian

Bessman, Jim. "Julian Lennon Long-Form: MCA to Release *Stand by Me*," *Billboard*. 97 (August 24, 1985) 26.

DeCurtis, Anthony. "Julian Lennon Forges His Independence," *Record*. 4 (April 1985) 19–20. il.

Derringer, L. "Julian Lennon Comes of Age," *Creem*. 17 (June 1985) 22ff. il.

McCullaugh, J. "Julian Lennon Explains *Stand by Me*," *Billboard*. 97 (December 28, 1985) 62. il., int.

Simmons, S. "Julian's Treatment," *Creem.* 17 (August 1986) 3, 41–43ff. il., int.

"*Stand by Me* Producer/Director Martin Lewis: Long-Forms Should 'Edify'," *Billboard.* 97 (November 30, 1985) 30–31.

Lofgren, Nils (See also: Bruce Springsteen)

Baker, Glenn A. "Nils Lofgren Down Under," *Goldmine.* n130 (July 19, 1985) 10–12. il.

Croft, S. "Control Zone: Little Big Man," *Melody Maker.* 61 (March 15, 1986) 34–35. il., int.

Flanagan, Bill. "Nils Lofgren: Second That Emotion," *Musician.* n71 (September 1984) 68, 98. il.

Obrecht, Jas, and J. Gay. "Nils Lofgren: A Cult Favorite Reaches Millions With Bruce Springsteen," *Guitar Player.* 19 (December 1985) 22–24ff. il., bio., disc.

"Shrink Rap," *Melody Maker.* 60 (July 6, 1985) 16. il., int.

Skidmore, Mick. "Nils Lofgren: Behind the Grin," *Goldmine.* n130 (July 19, 1985) 10–14. il., disc.

MacColl, Kirsty

Stern, Perry. "Sound Check: Kirsty MacColl," *Me Music Express Magazine.* 14:148 (June 1990) 18. il., int.

Martika

"Sidelines: Martika," *Melody Maker.* 65 (August 5, 1989) 15. il.

Mitchell, Joni (r.n.: Roberta Joan Anderson)

Barol, Bill, with Michael Reese. "Grown-Up James, Adult Joni," *Newsweek.* (November 4, 1985) 79–81. il.

Nash, Alanna. "Joni Mitchell," *Stereo Review.* (March 1986) 69–71. il., int.

Pond, Steve. "Mitchell 'Storms' Back," *Rolling Stone.* n521 (March 10, 1988) 20. il., int.

Stambler, Irwin. "Mitchell, Joni," In: *The Encyclopedia of Pop, Rock and Soul.* pp. 466–468.

Stern, P. "Joni Mitchell: The Benign Dictator," *Canadian Musician.* 8:1 (1986) 32–33ff. il., disc., int.

Sweeting, Adam. "*Dog* Day Afternoon," *Melody Maker.* 61 (January 4, 1986) 22. il., int.

Tabor, L. "Rock On," *International Musician.* 84 (December 1985) 8ff. il.

Morrison, Van

DeCurtis, Anthony. "On Record," *Record.* 4 (October 1985) 7ff. il., int.

DeCurtis, Anthony. "Van, Chieftains Unite," *Rolling Stone.* n523 (April 7, 1988) 23.

Jones, A. "Trouble in Paradise," *Melody Maker.* 61 (July 26, 1986) 36. il., int.

Stambler, Irwin. "Morrison, Van," In: *The Encyclopedia of Pop, Rock and Soul.* pp. 472–473.

Nelson, Lory (r.n.: Lois Norquist)

Kim, Jae-Ha. "New Faces: Lory Nelson," *Rolling Stone.* n581 (June 28, 1990) 22. il., int.

Newman, Randy

Philips, Chuck. "Randy Newman Matters," *Cash Box.* (October 29, 1988) 12–13. il., int.

O'Hara, Mary Margaret

Meyer, Marianne. "New Faces: Mary Margaret O'Hara," *Rolling Stone.* n570 (January 25, 1990) 18. il., int.

Patsy

"New Faces to Watch: Patsy," *Cash Box.* XLIX:18 (October 12, 1985) 12. il., int.

Penn, Michael

Wild, David. "Michael Penn's Music is No Myth," *Rolling Stone.* n572 (February 22, 1990) 24. il., int.

Phillips, Sam

Considine, J.D. "Sam Phillips," *Musician.* n121 (November 1988) 15–16. il.

DeSavia, Tom. "Who is Sam Phillips?," *Cash Box.* (October 1, 1988) 10. il., int.

Previn, Dory

Previn, Dory. *"Bog-Trotter: An Autobiography With Lyrics.* Garden City, NY: Doubleday, 1980.

Previn, Dory. *Midnight Baby.* New York: Macmillan, 1976.

Prine, John

"Folk-Oriented Artists Finding Mail Order is Key to Success," *Variety.* 319 (June 26, 1985) 89–90.

Reed, Lou (See also: John Cale; Velvet Underground)

Fricke, David. "Lou Reed," *Rolling Stone.* n512 (November 5, 1987) 292–295. il., int.

Fricke, David. "Lou Reed: Out of the Darkness," *Rolling Stone.* n483 (September 25, 1986) 64–66ff.

Fricke, David. "News," *Melody Maker.* 65 (January 21, 1989) 3. il.
Tribute to Andy Warhol, *Songs for Drella*, released.

Gett, Steve. "Reed Walks on the High-Profile Side," *Billboard.* 98 (June 7, 1986) 22. int.

Levy, Maury Z. "Lou: In the Age of Video Violence, Rock 'n' Roll's Premier Adult is Anything But a Pacifist," *Video Review.* 64–66, 150. il., int.

Morris, Chris. "Lou Reed Covers *New York* on Sire debut disk," *Billboard.* 101 (January 21, 1989) 38ff.

"The New York Music Awards," *BMI.* n1 (1986) 35–37. il.

Stambler, Irwin. "Reed, Lou," In: *The Encyclopedia of Pop, Rock and Soul.* pp. 561–562.

Robertson, Robbie (See also: Band)

Goldberg, Michael. "Robbie Robertson," *Rolling Stone.* n512 (November 5, 1987) 187–189. il., int.

Goldberg, Michael. "The Second Coming of Robbie Robertson," *Rolling Stone.* n513 (November 19, 1987) 65–74. il., int.

"A Man's Place: In the Workshop of Robbie Robertson," *Esquire.* (August 1988) 96–97. il., int.

Shear, Jules (See also: Reckless Sleepers)

Bessman, Jim. "Songwriter Shear Making Name Self," *Billboard.* 100 (October 8, 1988) 32–33.

Shocked, Michelle

Farber, C. "Shockingly Simple," *Spin.* 4 (October 1988) 20. il., bio.

Gleason, H. "Focus: 'The Way You Say It'," *Frets.* 10 (October 1988) 16–17. il., int.

Schoemer, Karen. "Swing Shift," *Spin.* 5:9 (December 1989) 62–66, 105. il., int.

"Shrink Rap," *Melody Maker.* 63 (September 26, 1987) 12. il., int.

Snow, Phoebe

Shewey, Don. "The Blues of Snow," *Esquire.* (May 1982) 74–81. il., bio., int.

Sobule, Jill

"Jill Sobule," *Cash Box.* LIII:41 (May 5, 1990) 3. il.

Stewart, Scott

Robinson, Julius. "Scott Stewart and the Other Side," *Cash Box.* LII:2 (July 9, 1988) 11. int.

Sutliff, Bobby

Iorio, Paul. "New Faces to Watch: Bobby Sutliff," *Cash Box.* (August 22, 1987) 11. il., int.

Sylvian, David

Prendergast, Mark. "David Sylvian," *Record Collector.* n129 (May 1990) 88–92. il., disc.

Taylor, James

Barol, Bill, with Michael Reese. "Grown-Up James, Adult Joni," *Newsweek.* (November 4, 1985) 79–81. il.

Taylor, Livingston

Browne, David. "Where are They Now? Alex, Kate and Livingston Taylor," *Rolling Stone.* n508 (September 10, 1987) 56. il., int.

Tikaram, Tanita

Wilde, Jon. "Tanita Tikaram: Inarticulate Speech of the Heart," *Melody Maker.* 66:4 (January 27, 1990) 24–25. il., int.

Vega, Suzanne

Costello, Elizabeth. "Suzanne Vega," *Stereo Review.* (November 1987) 127–129. il., int.

FitzGerald, H. "Bedsit Images," *Melody Maker.* 61 (May 10, 1986) 23. il., int.

Iorio, Paul. "Suzanne Vega Poised for Chart Success With 'Solitude Standing'," *Cash Box.* (April 25, 1987) 10, 31. il., int.

McGuigan, Cathleen, with Todd Barrett. "Suzanne Vega, Ethereal Girl," *Newsweek.* (August 3, 1987) 69. il., int.

Tabor, L. "Rock On," *International Musician.* 83 (May 1985) 8. il.

Wainwright, Loudon, III

Rogers, Sheila. "Random Notes," *Rolling Stone.* n585 (August 23, 1990) 15. il., int.
Re. his new song, "Jesse Don't Like It," which comments on Jesse Helm's assault on the First Amendment.

Wild, David. "Loudon Clear; Loudon Wainwright Discusses His 'Therapy'," *Rolling Stone.* n562 (October 5, 1989) 18. il., int.

Waits, Tom

Bull, Bart. "Boho Blues," *Spin.* 3 (September 1987) 56–61. il.

Flanagan, Bill. "Tom Waits," In: *Written in My Soul.* pp. 346–355. il.

Forman, Bill. "Night Visions," *Buzz.* 3:2 (December 1987) 38–40. il., int.

Graham, Samuel. "Tom Waits," *Musician.* n62 (December 1983) 16–22ff. il.

O'Brien, Glenn. "Tom Waits for No Man," *Spin.* n7 (November 1985) 67–71. il.

Petzke, Ken. "Tom Waits: Quiet Knights and the Nighthawk," *Goldmine.* n156 (July 18, 1986) 58–59. il., disc.

Rowland, Mark. "Tom Waits is Flying Upside Down (On Purpose)," *Musician.* (October 1987) 82–94. il., int.

Schoemer, Karen. "The 10 Most Interesting Musicians of the Last 5 Years: Tom Waits," *Spin.* 6:1 (April 1990) 42. il.

Stambler, Irwin. "Waits, Tom," In: *The Encyclopedia of Pop, Rock and Soul.* pp. 722–724.

Williams, Victoria

Wilde, Jon. "Victoria Williams: Animal Crackers," *Melody Maker.* (July 7, 1990) 41. il., int.

Winchester, Jesse

Druckman, Howard. "Jesse Winchester: Quiet Comeback of the Invisible Man," *Musician.* n129 (July 1989) 23–27, 118. il.

Y Kant Tori Read

Buchsbaum, Brad. "Y Kant Tori Read," *Cash Box.* (August 27, 1988) 10. il., int.

Young, Neil (See also: Crosby, Stills and Nash)

Bessman, Jim. "Neil Young Readies Self-Financed Tape," *Billboard.* 98 (August 30, 1986) 67.

Goldberg, Michael. "Neil Young Bows Blues Band," *Rolling Stone.* n517 (January 14, 1988) 18. il., int.

Guterman, Jimmy. "Neil Young Pulls Plug on Jeans Ad," *Rolling Stone.* n569 (January 11, 1990) 25.

Henke, James. "Neil Young: The Rolling Stone Interview," *Rolling Stone.* n527 (June 2, 1988) 42–49, 74. il., int.

"An Invidious Video?," *Newsweek.* (July 18, 1988) 60. il., int. Re. video to "This Note's for You," which criticizes Madison Avenue ad pitches.

Rogers, Sheila. "Neil Young Finds His Freedom," *Rolling Stone.* n563 (October 19, 1989) 20. il., int.

Stambler, Irwin. "Young, Neil," In: *The Encyclopedia of Pop, Rock and Soul.* pp. 758–759. il.

Sweeting, Adam. "Legend of a Loner," *Melody Maker.* 60 (September 7, 1985) 28–30. il., int.

Sweeting, Adam. "Legend of a Loner," *Melody Maker.* 60 (September 14, 1985) 38–39. il., int.

Zevon, Warren

Iorio, Paul. "Reconsidering Warren Zevon," *Cash Box.* (July 18, 1987) 11, 53. int.

Stambler, Irwin. "Zevon, Warren," In: *The Encyclopedia of Pop, Rock and Soul.* pp. 764–766.

15. SOFT ROCK

General Sources

Cioe, C. "Soft Rock: Pop Confections That Snap and Crackle as They Melt in Your Ears," *Musician Player & Listener.* n23 (March 1980) 12ff.

Association

Stambler, Irwin. "The Association," In: *The Encyclopedia of Pop, Rock and Soul.* pp. 20–21.

Bishop, Stephen

Vare, E.A. "Stephen Bishop: 'Always a Hustler'," *Billboard.* 97 (December 21, 1985) 46. int.

Bread (See also: Black Tie)

Puterbaugh, Parke, and others. "Where are They Now? Bread," *Rolling Stone.* n558 (August 10, 1989) 55–56. il.

Stambler, Irwin. "Bread," In: *The Encyclopedia of Pop, Rock and Soul.* pp. 80–81.

Carpenters (See also: Television)

Grein, Paul. "Carpenters' Hits Resurfacing," *Billboard.* 97 (May 18, 1985) 42.

Stambler, Irwin. "The Carpenters," In: *The Encyclopedia of Pop, Rock and Soul*. pp. 100–102.

Crosby, Stills and Nash/Crosby, Stills, Nash and Young (See also: Buffalo Springfield; Byrds; Hollies; Neil Young)

Goldberg, Michael. "CSNY Release *American Dream*," *Rolling Stone*. n540 (December 1, 1988) 15.

MacCambridge, M. "Springsteen, CSN&Y 'Reunion', Lots More Top Acoustic Benefit," *Variety*. 325 (October 29, 1986) 176.

Stambler, Irwin. "Crosby, Stills, Nash and Young," In: *The Encyclopedia of Pop, Rock and Soul*. pp. 153–155. il.

CROSBY, DAVID

"Parole for Crosby Just Around Corner," *Variety*. 324 (August 6, 1986) 81.

5th Dimension

Stambler, Irwin. "5th Dimension," In: *The Encyclopedia of Pop, Rock and Soul*. pp. 225–227.

Garfunkel, Art (See also: Simon and Garfunkel)

Givens, Ron. "Art Garfunkel," *Stereo Review*. (April 1988) 68–69. il., int.

Keith (r.n.: Barry Keefer)

Tamarkin, Jeff. "Keith: His Further Adventures," *Goldmine*. n155 (July 4, 1986) 10–12. il., int.

Loggins, Dave

Kirby, Kip. "Nashville Scene: Loggins Sans Deal—But Not for Long?," *Billboard.* 97 (November 9, 1985) 51.

Seals and Crofts (r.n.: Jim Seals and Dash Crofts)

Stambler, Irwin. "Seals and Crofts," In: *The Encyclopedia of Pop, Rock and Soul.* pp. 602–604.

Three Dog Night

Stambler, Irwin. "Three Dog Night," In: *The Encyclopedia of Pop, Rock and Soul.* pp. 687–688.

Welch, Bob

"Bob Welch," *Super Song Hits.* n21 (Fall 1979) 32–33. il.

A. MIDDLE-OF-THE-ROAD

Coolidge, Rita

Stambler, Irwin. "Coolidge, Rita," In: *The Encyclopedia of Pop, Rock and Soul.* pp. 143–144.

Denver, John (r.n.: Henry John Deutschendorf; See also: Parents Music Resource Center)

"Briefings," *Saturday Review.* 11 (July/August 1985) 22. il. Re. musical tour of the Soviet Union.

"Denver Concert in China is Approved, But No Time Set," *Variety.* 320 (August 7, 1985) 71.

"Denver Plans Live Broadcast from Peking," *Billboard.* 97 (August 3, 1985) 4.

Fleischer, Leonore. *John Denver.* New York/London: Flash, 1976. il., disc. pap.

Grein, Paul. "John Denver Takes Charge of His Career," *Billboard.* 97 (June 8, 1985) 48ff. int.

Holland, Bill. "A Gentle War of Words: Music Makers Confront Lawmakers," *Billboard.* 97 (September 28, 1985) 82.

Larson, Bob. "Antihero," *Spin.* 6:3 (June 1990) 72–73, 97. il., int.

Martin, James. *John Denver: Rocky Mountain Wonderboy.* London: Everest, 1977. il. pap.

"Private Firm Should Arrange U.S.-Soviet Exchanges: Denver," *Variety.* 320 (October 16, 1985) 4ff.

Schipper, H. "Denver Trip to Russia Signals U.S.-Soviet Cultural Thawing," *Variety.* 319 (June 26, 1985) 2ff.

Stambler, Irwin. "Denver, John," In: *The Encyclopedia of Pop, Rock and Soul.* pp. 168–171.

Steinbach, Alice. "Country Roads and Crossroads: John Denver's Journey; Getting Here from There," *Saturday Review.* (September–October 1985) 54–59, 82. il., bio, int.

Dinner Ladies

DJ. "The Dinner Ladies," *Melody Maker.* 66:5 (February 3, 1990) 14. il.

Easton, Sheena

Stambler, Irwin. "Easton, Sheena," In: *The Encyclopedia of Pop, Rock and Soul.* pp. 206–207.

Whatley, S. "Rock on: Sheena's Prince Connection," *Record.* 4 (June 1985) 8. il.

Hartman, Lisa

DeSavia, Tom. "Lisa Hartman," *Cash Box.* (February 20, 1988) 9–10, 23. il., int.

Manilow, Barry

Barry Manilow. London: Grandreams, 1982. il., bio.

Clarke, Alan. *The Magic of Barry Manilow.* London: Prize, 1981. il., disc. pap.

Fernandez, E. "Notas: Manilow, Roth Release Spanish-Language Albums," *Billboard.* 98 (October 11, 1986) 73.

Grein, Paul. "RCA Maps International Push for Manilow," *Billboard.* 97 (October 26, 1985) 6ff.

Holland, Bill. "Manilow: Bill Would Spell Disaster; Star Reacts to Source Licensing Moves," *Billboard.* 98 (October 11, 1986) 10ff.

Jasper, Tony. *Barry Manilow.* London: W.H. Allen, 1982. il., disc. Orig. pub.: Star, 1981.

"Manilow Contributes $25,000 to Flood Aid; Other Performers Wooed," *Variety.* 321 (November 20, 1985) 103.

Peter, Richard. *The Barry Manilow Scrapbook: His Magical World in Works and Pictures.* London: Pop Universal/Souvenir, 1982. il., disc.

Stambler, Irwin. "Manilow, Barry," In: *The Encyclopedia of Pop, Rock and Soul.* pp. 438–440.

Tabor, L. "Manilow Aids Red Cross," *International Musician.* 84 (December 1985) 1ff. il.

Weir, Simon. *Barry Manilow for the Record.* Alan Murray, art ed. Knutsford, Cheshire, U.K.: Stafford Pemberton, 1982. il. pap.

Mauriat, Paul

Fink, Stu. "Paul Mauriat," *Goldmine.* n244 (December 1, 1989) 32. il.

Newton-John, Olivia

Stambler, Irwin. "Olivia Newton-John," In: *The Encyclopedia of Pop, Rock and Soul.* pp. 485–486.

Reddy, Helen

Stambler, Irwin. "Reddy, Helen," In: *The Encyclopedia of Pop, Rock and Soul.* pp. 560–561.

B. POP STYLISTS

Davis, Sammy, Jr.

Jones, Quincy. "Tribute: Sammy Davis, Jr.," *Rolling Stone.* n581 (June 28, 1990) 35. il.

Humperdinck, Engelbert

Short, Don. *Engelbert Humperdinck: The Authorized Biography.* London: New English Library, 1972. il., disc. pap.

Jones, Tom

Stambler, Irwin. "Jones, Tom," In: *The Encyclopedia of Pop, Rock and Soul.* pp. 348–350.

Midler, Bette

Musto, M. "La Dolce Musto," *Village Voice.* 31 (February 4, 1986) 39. il.

Stambler, Irwin. "Midler, Bette," In: *The Encyclopedia of Pop, Rock and Soul.* pp. 463–465.

Streisand, Barbra

Berk, Peter. "Barbra Streisand: Taking Time to Look Back, Ready to Move Forward," *Cash Box.* XLIX:25 (November 30, 1985) 13, 42. il., int. w/associate Peter Matz.

C. POP-ROCK

Air Supply

Coupe, S. "Graham Russell & Air Supply," *APRA Journal.* 2:10 (1982) 2–5.

Grein, Paul. "Arden Lauds VH-1's Air Supply Deal," *Billboard.* 97 (June 8, 1985) 48.

Nite, Norm N., with Charles Crespo. "Air Supply," In: *Rock On . . . (Volume 3)*. pp. 4–5. il., disc.

Ambrosia

"Ambrosia," *Song Hits.* n157 (March 1979) 18–19. il.

"Ambrosia," *Song Hits.* n175 (September 1980) 8–9. il.

Nite, Norm N., with Charles Crespo. "Ambrosia," In: *Rock On . . . (Volume 3)*. p. 9. disc.

Ana

"Rock Notes: Closetful of Cuteness," *Me Music Express Magazine.* 14:145 (March 1990) 14. il., int.

Astley, Rick

"Rick Astley," *Record Collector.* n115 (March 1989) 39–41. il., disc.

Bad English (See also: Journey)

Edwards, Gavin. "Flash: Walk on the Wild Side," *Spin.* 5:12 (March 1990) 18. il.

Halbersberg, Elianne. "Bad English: Exclusive Interview With Jonathan Cain," *Song Hits.* n272 (December 1989) 34–35. il., int.

Balin, Marty

"Pop! The Glory Years: Boys Keep Swinging," *Melody Maker.* 63 (October 24, 1987) 24. supplement. il.

Bananarama *(See also: Shakespear's Sister)*

Iorio, Paul. "Bananarama: Sisters are Doing It for Themselves," *Cash Box.* (August 9, 1986) 11. il., int. w/Siobhan Fahey and associate Harry Anger.

Sullivan, Caroline. "Bananarama: Girls Together Outrageously," *Melody Maker.* (July 28, 1990) 42–43. il., int.

Branigan, Laura

"Branigan Sues Mgr., Claims Failure to Fulfill Pic Promise," *Variety.* 321 (December 18, 1985) 83–84.

Dobrin, Gregory. "Laura Branigan Shatters a Hiatus from Recording With 'Touch'," *Cash Box.* (July 18, 1987) 12–13. il., int.

"Joseph Responds to Laura Branigan's Suit," *Variety.* 321 (December 25, 1985) 53ff.

Kirby, Fred. "Branigan Loses Suit Versus Ex-Manager," *Variety.* 329 (December 2, 1987) 2ff.

Kirby, Fred. "Branigan Wins Infringement Case, Based on Lack of Access to Song," *Variety.* 324 (August 20, 1986) 83.
Re. "How Am I Supposed to Live Without?"

"Laura Branigan," *Cash Box.* LIII:39 (April 21, 1990) 3. il.

Terry, Ken. "Branigan Loses Lawsuit," *Billboard.* 99 (December 12, 1987) 6ff.

Captain and Tennille (r.n.: Darryl Dragon and Toni Tennille)

Browne, David. "Where are They Now? Captain and Tennille," *Rolling Stone.* n508 (September 10, 1987) 61. il., int.

Stambler, Irwin. "Captain and Tennille," In: *The Encyclopedia of Pop, Rock and Soul.* pp. 95–96.

TENNILLE, TONI

"New Acts," *Variety.* 324 (October 1, 1986) 112.

Carey, Mariah

Roberts, Chris. "Sidelines: Mariah Carey," *Melody Maker.* (August 25, 1990) 8. il., int.

Tannenbaum, Rob. "Building the Perfect Diva," *Rolling Stone.* n585 (August 23, 1990) 33. il., int. w/Carey and label associates.

Carnes, Kim

Robinson, Julius. "Kim Carnes," *Cash Box.* (August 20, 1988) 11. il., int.

Stambler, Irwin. "Carnes, Kim," In: *The Encyclopedia of Pop, Rock and Soul.* pp. 99–100.

Cashman, Pistilli and West/Cashman and West

Woodard, Rex. "Cashman, Pistilli and West," *Goldmine.* n67 (December 1981) 159–162. il., disc.

Cetera, Peter (See also: Chicago)

Gett, Steve. "Cetera Savors Solo Success of *Solitude/Solitaire*," *Billboard.* 98 (August 30, 1986) 25ff.

Iorio, Paul. "Peter Cetera, Rock's Mr. Clean, Scales the Charts," *Cash Box.* (August 16, 1986) 10, 25. il., int.

"Peter Cetera Exits Chicago: Wrote Hits for Veteran Combo," *Variety.* 319 (July 3, 1985) 63.

"Peter Cetera Leaving Chicago," *Billboard.* 97 (July 6, 1985) 86.

Wosahla, Steve. "Exclusive Interview With Peter Cetera," *Song Hits.* n257 (July 1987) 22–24. il.

Champaign

Pruter, Robert. "Champaign: How About Us?," *Goldmine.* n175 (April 10, 1987) 92.

Cher

Jeske, Lee. "Cher," *Cash Box.* (April 2, 1988) 10. il., int.

City

Kassan, Brian. "New Faces to Watch: The City," *Cash Box.* (October 25, 1986) 10. il., int. w/Peter McIan.

Clarke, Tony (See also: Hollies)

Pruter, Robert. "Tony Clarke: The Entertainer," *Goldmine.* n170 (January 30, 1987) 22. il., disc.

Dayne, Taylor

Wright, Christian Logan. "Great Dayne," *Spin.* 5:8 (November 1989) 52–54. il., int.

Diamond, Neil

Wild, David. "The Rolling Stone Interview: 'Am I a Rock Person, or What the Hell Am I?," *Rolling Stone.* n522 (March 24, 1988) 101–109. il., int.

Dr. Hook and the Medicine Show

Browne, David. "Where are They Now? Dr. Hook and the Medicine Show," *Rolling Stone.* n508 (September 10, 1987) 53. il., int. w/Dennis Locorriere.

Ferry, Bryan (See also: Roxy Music)

Sweeting, Adam. "The Art of Poise," *Melody Maker.* 60 (June 1, 1985) 24–26. il., int.

Gibb, Andy

[Obituary], *Rolling Stone.* n541/542 (December 15/29, 1988) 135. il.

[Obituary], *Spin.* 4 (December 1988) 70.

Ressner, Jeffrey. "Andy Gibb: 1958–1988," *Rolling Stone.* n524 (April 21, 1988) 23. il.

Stambler, Irwin. "Gibb, Andy," In: *The Encyclopedia of Pop, Rock and Soul.* pp. 256–258.

Hornsby, Bruce(, and the Range)

Barol, Bill. "Skipping the Chart Fodder," *Newsweek.* (November 3, 1986) 77. il., int.

Doerschuk, Bob. "Bruce Hornsby: The Elusive Ingredients of Pop Success," *Keyboard.* (July 1987) 62–76. il., int.

Pond, Steve. "Bruce Hornsby: The 'Other Bruce' Tires of His Trademark Sound and Moves Out of the Middle of the Road," *Rolling Stone.* n582/583 (July 12/26, 1990) 93–95. il., int.

Tabor, L. "Rock On," *International Musician.* 85 (November 1986) 9ff. il.

Isle of Man

"New Faces to Watch: Isle of Man," *Cash Box.* (July 12, 1986) 10. il., int. w/band producer Spencer Proffer.

Martin, Marilyn

"New Faces to Watch: Marilyn Martin," *Cash Box.* XLIX:38 (March 8, 1986) 10. il., int.

Marx, Richard

Dobrin, Gregory. "Richard Marx Steps into the Limelight," *Cash Box.* (August 1, 1987) 10–11. il., int.

Leland, John. "Flash: The Invisible Man," *Spin.* 5:9 (December 1989) 12–13. il.

Michael, George (r.n.: Georgios Pancyiotou; See also: Wham!)

Fricke, David. "The Second Coming of George Michael," *Rolling Stone.* n487 (November 20, 1986) 84–85ff. il.

"George Michael Honored; Named Top '84 U.K. Songwriter," *Billboard.* 97 (March 30, 1985) 9.
Re. 1984 Ivor Novello Awards.

Levy, Joe. "George Michael," *Cash Box.* (April 23, 1988) 10. int.

"Michael Says He's Leaving Nomis Mgmt.," *Billboard.* 98 (March 8, 1986) 9.

Nevil, Robbie

Dobrin, Gregory. "New Faces to Watch: Robbie Nevil," *Cash Box.* (November 22, 1986) 10. il., int.

New Monkees

Dupler, Steven. "Hey, Hey, It's the New Monkees," *Billboard.* 99 (September 19, 1987) 68.

Paper Lace

Tamarkin, Jeff. "Paper Lace," *Goldmine.* n220 (December 30, 1988) 24.

Parr, John

Halbersberg, Elianne. "John Parr," *Song Hits.* n245 (July 1986) 22–23. il.

Poindexter, Buster (aka David Johansen; See also: New York Dolls)

Murphy, Elliott. "Buster Poindexter: A Personality Crisis Resolved," *Rolling Stone.* n519 (February 11, 1988) il., int.

Rea, Chris

Thompson, Dave. "Chris Rea," *Record Collector.* n88 (December 1986) 36–39. il., disc.

Soul, David

Marshall, Steve. "Starsky and Hutch Rarities," *Record Collector.* n23 (August 1981) 41–43. il., disc.

Tepper, Robert

"New on the Charts," *Billboard.* 98 (March 8, 1986) 47.

Ullman, Tracey

McGuigan, Cathleen. "They Don't Know Tracey," *Newsweek.* (October 14, 1985) 98.

Vels

"Writer Sues Polygram Over Release by Vels," *Variety.* 322 (March 5, 1986) 95.

Vera, Billy

Dobrin, Gregory. "Billy Vera Beats a Path to Success With the Music He Believes In," *Cash Box.* (January 31, 1987) 11, 22. il., int.

Kordosh, J. "The Somewhat Singular Tales of Billy Vera," *Creem.* 18 (June 1987) 38–39ff. il., int.

Waldman, Wendy

Orloff, Katherine. "Wendy Waldman," In: *Rock 'n' Roll Women.* pp. 179–195. il.

Warnes, Jennifer (See also: Leonard Cohen)

Dobrin, Gregory. "Jennifer Warnes Awakens Listeners With the Songs of Leonard Cohen," *Cash Box.* (April 11, 1987) 11, 24. il., int.

Wilde, Kim

Clerk, Carol. "A Woman of the World," *Melody Maker.* 60 (June 1, 1985) 12–13. il., int.

Wilson Phillips

Benjamin, Sandy Stert. "Wilson Phillips: California Girls," *Goldmine.* n257 (June 1, 1990) 98. il.

Wild, David. "Wilson Phillips's California Dream," *Rolling Dream.* n578 (May 17, 1990) 46–49. il.

16. AOR

Animotion

R.G. "Going for the Platinum: Animotion Rocks Explosively," *Newsweek on Campus.* (March 1986) 54–55. il.

Bachman-Turner Overdrive (See also: Guess Who)

Corradetti, G. "BTO Look Out for No. 1," *Billboard.* 98 (August 30, 1986) 26.

"Propourri," *Music Scene.* n346 (November–December 1985) 22.

Bad Company (See also: Firm)

Liveten, S. "Bad Company is Back With Album, Tour," *Billboard.* 98 (December 27, 1986) 35.

Beaver Brown Band

Himes, G. "The Heart of Blue-Collar Rock," *Musician Player & Listener.* n35 (August 1981) 12ff. il.

Benatar, Pat

Grein, Paul. "Benatar's Music, Image in Transition," *Billboard.* 98 (January 11, 1986) 48ff.

Lovece, F. "Director Turns De-generation into 'Effective' Advantage," *Billboard.* 98 (February 8, 1986) 51. il.

Mendelssohn, John. "Pat Benatar: *Tropico* Dancer," *Creem.* 16 (March 1985) 22–23ff. il.

Black Tie (See also: Bread; Eagles)

"New Faces to Watch: Black Tie," *Cash Box.* XLIX:9 (August 17, 1985) 12. il., int. w/Randy Meisner.

Bloodrock

Puterbaugh, Parke, and others. "Where are They Now? Bloodrock," *Rolling Stone.* n558 (August 10, 1989) 56. il.

Boston

"Attorney Takes on CBS Records Over Charges Filed in Boston Suit," *Variety.* 321 (November 20, 1985) 105.

"CBS Loses Bid to Stop Boston from Going to MCA Records," *Variety.* 318 (April 24, 1985) 191.

"CBS Still Fighting to Retain Boston," *Variety.* 318 (February 27, 1985) 75–76.

Goodman, Fred. "Boston Back Strong After 8 Years," *Billboard.* 98 (September 27, 1986) 3ff.

"Judge Okays Payment of Boston's Royalties," *Variety.* 331 (June 8, 1988) 69.

"Summary Motions on Boston Albums Awaiting Decisions," *Variety.* 329 (December 9, 1987) 30ff.

Boys Don't Cry

"New Faces to Watch: Boys Don't Cry," *Cash Box.* (June 28, 1986) 10. il., int. w/keyboardist-vocalist Brian Chatton.

Branigan, Billy

Iorio, Paul. "New Faces to Watch: Billy Branigan," *Cash Box.* (February 28, 1987) 10. il., int.

Burtnick, Glen

"New Faces to Watch: Glen Burtnick," *Cash Box.* XLIX:48 (May 17, 1986) 14. il., int.

Yardumian, Rob. "New Faces to Watch: Glen Burtnick," *Cash Box.* (October 17, 1987) 11. il., int.

Caufield, Tom

Levy, Joe. "New Faces to Watch: Tom Caufield," *Cash Box.* (February 6, 1988) 13. il., int.

Cock Robin

Yardumian, Rob. "Cock Robin," *Cash Box.* (September 19, 1987) 10. il., int. w/Peter Kingsbery.

Collins, Phil (See also: Genesis; Marilyn Martin)

"Academy Causes Flap by Not Asking Collins to Sing," *Variety.* 318 (March 31, 1985) 109.

"Collins Awarded Honorary Degree," *Modern Drummer.* 11 (October 1987) 130.
Re. Fairleigh Dickinson University.

Cummins, Kevin. "Ugly Bald Bastard Speaks," *New Musical Express.* (March 30, 1990) 16, 51. il.

Fish, S.K., and B. Cioffi. "Creem Showcase," *Creem.* 17 (February 1986) 67. il.

Gett, Steve. "Collins Courts Multimedia Success," *Billboard.* 101 (January 7, 1989) 20. int.

Grein, Paul. "Phil Collins' Tour Keeping ITG Busy," *Billboard.* 97 (May 18, 1985) 41–42.

Lake, S. "Face the Press," *Melody Maker.* 60 (March 30, 1985) 14–15. il., int.

Milkowski, B. "Phil Collins: Genesis of a Drummer," *Down Beat.* 51 (July 1984) 20–22. il., bio, disc.

"Phil Collins Honored by ASCAP," *Billboard.* 100 (October 15, 1988) 67.

"Phil Collins Reigns Over British Awards," *Billboard.* 98 (February 22, 1986) 77.
Re. BPI.

"Phil Collins Sweeps ASCAP Awards," *Billboard.* 99 (October 17, 1987) 75.

Device

"New Faces to Watch: Device," *Cash Box.* (July 19, 1986) 10. il., int. w/Holly Knight.

Essex, David

Essex, David, Productions, Ltd. *David Essex Annual 1976.* Great Britain: World, 1975. il.

Tremlett, George. *The David Essex Story.* Great Britain: Futura, 1974. il., bio.

Firm (See also: Bad Company)

DeMuir, H. "Standing Firm, Kinda," *Creem.* 17 (July 1986) 12–15. il.

Foreigner

Gett, Steve. "Lou Gramm Inks Solo Deal With Atlantic," *Billboard.* 98 (April 19, 1986) 26.

Grein, Paul. "Foreigner Still Loyal to Records," *Billboard.* 97 (January 26, 1985) 41ff. il., int. w/Mick Jones.

Mercer, M. "Foreign Agents," *Melody Maker.* 60 (February 2, 1985) 18–19. il., int. w/Jones and Lou Gramm.

Rogers, Sheila. "A Foreigner Takes His Solo Sojourn," *Rolling Stone.* n561 (September 21, 1989) 32. il., int.

Simmons, S. "Foreigner: Feels Like the Fifth Time!," *Creem.* 17 (June 1985) 40–41ff. il., int.

Stambler, Irwin. "Foreigner," In: *The Encyclopedia of Pop, Rock and Soul.* pp. 234–236.

Frampton, Peter

Grein, Paul. "Frampton Regards His Modest Success a Good Promonition," *Billboard.* 98 (March 29, 1986) 23ff. int.

Tabor, L. "Rock On," *International Musician.* 84 (March 1986) 11. il.

Heart

Agnelli, L.E. "Heart's in the Right Place; or, If Anybody Had a Heart," *Creem.* 17 (February 1986) 3, 38–39ff. il.

Blair, Gwenda. "Rock Stars Ann and Nancy Wilson: Healing a Broken Heart," *Mademoiselle.* (June 1982) 39–44, 58. il., int.

Simmons, S. "Heart," *Creem.* 19 (September 1987) 38–40ff. il.

Stambler, Irwin. "Heart," In: *The Encyclopedia of Pop, Rock and Soul.* pp. 286–288. il.

Henley, Don (See also: Eagles)

Armbruster, G. "Profile: Touring With Their Eyes Closed: Jai Winding & Scott Plunkett on the Road With Don Henley," *Keyboard Magazine.* 11 (August 1985) 12. il.

Dupler, Steven. "Henley Wins Big at MTV Awards," *Billboard.* 97 (September 28, 1985) 40–41.

Gilmore, Mikal. "Don Henley," *Rolling Stone.* n512 (November 5, 1987) 287–291. il., int.

"Henley Sweeps MTV Awards; Geldof Gets Special Recognition," *Variety.* 320 (September 18, 1985) 74.

Jackson, A. "Quiet Flows the Don," *Melody Maker.* 60 (February 16, 1985) 26ff. il., int.

Scoppa, Bud. "The *Record* Interview: Don Henley's Deliverance," *Record.* 5 (December 1986) 22–25ff. il., int.

Stambler, Irwin. "Henley, Don," In: *The Encyclopedia of Pop, Rock and Soul.* pp. 291–292.

Insiders

Yardumian, Rob. "New Faces to Watch: The Insiders," *Cash Box.* (September 26, 1987) 11. il., int. w/guitarist Jay O'Rourke.

Johnson, Don

Gett, Steve. "*Vice* is Nice, but Johnson Wants Pop Stardom," *Billboard.* 98 (October 18, 1986) 22.

Iorio, Paul. "Don Johnson: A 'Heartbeat' Away from Musical Superstardom," *Cash Box.* (August 23, 1986) 13, 28. il., int.

Journey (See also: Bad English; Santana)

Dupler, Steven. "Studio Dilemma: Pro, or No Place Like Home?," *Billboard.* 99 (October 24, 1987) 80. il.

Gett, Steve. "Herbert and Schon Ink Journey Co. Buyout," *Billboard.* 98 (August 30, 1986) 92.

Gett, Steve. "Journey Glad to be on Long & Winding Tour Road," *Billboard.* 98 (October 25, 1986) 26ff.

Gett, Steve. "Smith Steps Ahead After Leaving Journey," *Billboard.* 98 (November 22, 1986) 35.

Stambler, Irwin. "Journey," In: *The Encyclopedia of Pop, Rock and Soul.* pp. 351–353.

CAIN, JONATHAN

Greenwald, T. "Jonathan Cain," *Keyboard Magazine*. 12 (November 1986) 98–99ff. il.

Kansas

Liveten, S. "Kansas Struggles to Get Back on Map," *Billboard*. 98 (December 13, 1986) 20.

Kassan, Brian. "Kansas 'Powers' Back With the Old and the New," *Cash Box*. (December 20, 1986) 11, 22. il., int. w/Steve Walsh and Steve Morse.

Stambler, Irwin. "Kansas," In: *The Encyclopedia of Pop, Rock and Soul*. pp. 355–357.

MORSE, STEVE

Baird, Jock. "Steve Morse," *Musician*. n74 (December 1984) 68–74, 96.

Le Roux

"Le Roux," *Super Song Hits*. n33 (Fall 1982) 46–47. il.

Lewis, Huey, and the News

Barol, Bill. "Lewis Sings the News," *Newsweek*. (November 3, 1986) 77, 81. il., int. w/Lewis.

FitzGerald, H. "The Late Late News," *Melody Maker*. 60 (October 5, 1985) 14. int.

Grein, Paul. "Huey Lewis Takes It One Song at a Time,"
    Billboard. 97 (February 9, 1985) 6ff.
    Sports is nominated for record of the year.

"Huey Lewis & News Win Five Awards in Bammie Contest,"
    Variety. 318 (March 27, 1985) 82.

"Huey Lewis Tops Bammies' Entrants, Gaining 8 Awards,"
    Variety. 322 (March 19, 1986) 76.

Irwin, C. "Yankee Dollar Dandy," *Melody Maker.* 61 (October
    18, 1986) 39. il., int.

"Lewis & the News Top Bammies," *Billboard.* 98 (March 29,
    1986) 23.

Stambler, Irwin. "Lewis, Huey," In: *The Encyclopedia of Pop,
    Rock and Soul.* pp. 501–503.

Martin, Marilyn (See also: Phil Collins)

Moleski, L. "Martin is 'on Her Own Feet': Album Won't
    Include Phil Collins," *Billboard.* 98 (February 15, 1986)
    46.

Meat Loaf (r.n.: Marvin Lee Aday)

Mercer, Mick. "Using Your Loaf," *Melody Maker.* 60 (January
    19, 1985) 12–13. il., int.

Mellencamp, John Cougar

Freeman, K. "Cougar Concert-Goers Get Unusual Refund
    Offer," *Billboard.* 97 (December 21, 1985) 70.

Guccione, Bob, Jr. "Man of Fire," *Spin.* 3 (September 1987) 32–36ff. il., int.

Holdship, Bill. "John Cougar Mellencamp: Working Class Hero in the Rumbleseat," *Creem.* 17 (February 1986) 12–16. il., int.

Iorio, Paul. "John Cougar Mellencamp: Voice of the American Heartland," *Cash Box.* XLIX:26 (December 7, 1985) 11. il., int. w/associates of the artist.

"Mellencamp Joining Long-Form Fray; *Ain't That America* Clip Compilation," *Billboard.* 97 (March 9, 1985) 38–39.

"Mellencamp Sues Goff's Pubberies," *Variety.* 328 (September 9, 1987) 68.

Moleski, Linda. "Mellencamp Sets Own Course," *Billboard.* 99 (September 5, 1987) 20.

Stambler, Irwin. "Mellencamp, John Cougar," In: *The Encyclopedia of Pop, Rock and Soul.* pp. 458–460.

Tabor, L. "Rock On," *International Musician.* 84 (October 1985) 7ff. il.
The release of *Scarecrow* is noted.

Mike and the Mechanics (See also: Genesis; Nick Lowe; Paul Young)

"New Faces to Watch: Mike and the Mechanics," *Cash Box.* XLIX:29 (December 28, 1985) 10. il., int.

Valentine, Marie. "Mike and the Mechanics," *Song Hits.* n248 (October 1986) 16–17.

Mr. Big

Capozzoli, Michael A., Jr. "Mr. Big: Exclusive Interview With Billy Sheehan," *Song Hits.* n273 (March 1990) 40–42. il., int.

Mr. Mister

Gaines, Robin. "Exclusive Interview With Steve George of Mr. Mister," *Song Hits.* n244 (June 1986) 16–17. il.

Iorio, Paul. "Mr. Mister: Enjoying the View from the Top of the Charts," *Cash Box.* XLIX:28 (December 21, 1985) 11. il., int. w/vocalist Richard Page.

Myles, Alannah

Sullivan, Caroline. "Sidelines: Alannah Myles," *Melody Maker.* 66:24 (June 16, 1990) 14. il., int.

Night Ranger

Armbruster, G. "Alan 'Fitz'gerald: Hard Rocking With Night Ranger," *Keyboard Magazine.* 11 (October 1985) 72ff. il., disc.

Halbersberg, Elianne. "Exclusive Interview With Jeff Watson of Night Ranger," *Song Hits.* n259 (October 1987) 8–9. il.

Lounges, Tom. "7 Wishes Keeps Night Ranger Rocking America!," *Song Hits.* n238 (December 1985) 8–10. il.

"Night Ranger," *Song Hits.* n223 (September 1984) 8–10. il.

Stambler, Irwin. "Night Ranger," In: *The Encyclopedia of Pop, Rock and Soul.* pp. 487–489.

Orleans

"Orleans," *Song Hits of the Super 70's.* n6 (March 1976) 40–41. il.

Petty, Tom (, and the Heartbreakers)

Clerk, Carol. "Tom Petty: Strange Days," *Melody Maker.* 65 (August 12, 1989) 8–9. il., int.

Corcoran, M. "Raised on Promises," *Spin.* 5 (August 1989) 42–44ff. il.

George, Nelson. The Rhythm & the Blues: Tom Petty Gets Flagged for *Plantation* Mentality," *Billboard.* 98 (May 10, 1986) 28.

Graff, G. "Tom Petty's New Tales of the Old South," *Creem.* 17 (October 1985) 24–25ff. il., int.

"The Heat is On," *Cash Box.* (May 30, 1987) 10. il. His Encino home is destroyed; arson is the suspected cause.

Petty, Tom, and Steve Hochman. "If It's Monday, This Must be Miami," *Rolling Stone.* n562 (October 5, 1989) 74–83. il.

Scoppa, Bud. "Year (or Two) of Living Dangerously," *Record.* 4 (August 1985) 16–18ff.

Stambler, Irwin. "Petty, Tom, and the Heartbreakers," In: *The Encyclopedia of Pop, Rock and Soul.* pp. 517–520. il.

Sutherland, Steve. "Southern Comfort," *Melody Maker.* 60 (May 11, 1985) 24–25ff. il., int.

Quarterflash

"Quarterflash," *Song Hits.* n195 (May 1982) 8–9. il.

REO Speedwagon

Alexander, S. "REO's Alan Gratzer," *Modern Drummer.* 5 (July 1981) 14–17ff.

Baruck, J. "Pay-Per-View Pull Could Dilute Impact of Rockers on Tour," *Variety.* 321 (January 8, 1986) 5ff.

Freeman, K. "REO Comes Back, Crosses Over," *Billboard.* 97 (March 16, 1985) 42.

Halbersberg, Elianne. "Exclusive Interview With Kevin Cronin," *Song Hits.* n257 (July 1987) 8–9. il., int.

Iorio, Paul. "REO Speedwagon's Kevin Cronin Talks About 'Life as We Know It'," *Cash Box.* (May 9, 1987) 11, 31. il., int.

Kirby, Fred. "Cronin Settles With Camerica on Publishing Rights to 2 Songs," *Variety.* 321 (January 1, 1986) 129.

Knapp, K. "REO Speedwagon: 'Do' Wanna' B'wanas!," *Creem.* 17 (July 1985) 22–23ff. int.

Stambler, Irwin. "REO Speedwagon" In: *The Encyclopedia of Pop, Rock and Soul.* pp. 562–565.

Springsteen, Bruce(, and the E Street Band) (See also: Nils Lofgren)

[Bruce Springsteen is in Trouble], *Melody Maker.* 63 (December 19/26, 1987) 3.
"I Ain't Got You" alleged to have copied Nagle/Mathews' "No Big Deal."

Castro, Janice, Scott Brown and Jeanne McDowell. "The Boss's Thunder Road to Riches," *Time.* (December 15, 1986) 60. il.

Ford, Richard. "The Boss," *Esquire.* (December 1985) 326–329. il.

Gilmore, Mikal. "Bruce Springsteen," *Rolling Stone.* n512 (November 5, 1987) 22–26. il., int.

Goodman, Fred. *"Forbes*: Springsteen is Rock's Top Earner," *Rolling Stone.* n511 (October 22, 1987) 21.

Goodman, Fred. "Low-Key Start for 'Tunnel of Love'," *Rolling Stone.* n513 (November 19, 1987) 15. il.

Handelman, David. "Is Bruce a Good Boss?," *Rolling Stone.* n508 (September 10, 1987) 17.
Paraphrases David McGee's article, "Blinded by the Hype," which was published in the *New Musical Express* the prior month.

Iorio, Paul. "Bruce Springsteen's Hometown: The Story of a Place," *Cash Box.* (December 27, 1986) 15, 35, 44. il., int.

Iorio, Paul. "New York is Mad About 'The Box'," *Cash Box.* (November 22, 1986) 6, 26.
Re. *Bruce Springsteen and the E Street Band Live/1975–1985.*

Iorio, Paul. "Springsteen Bio Tops Best-Seller Lists," *Cash Box.* (May 30, 1987) 10, 27.
  Re. Dave Marsh's *Glory Days.*

Johnson, Brian D., with Ann Walmsley and Ruth Atherley. "The Boss," *Maclean's.* (September 2, 1985) 24–29. il.

Kassan, Brian. "Springsteen Sales Create Retail Flurry," *Cash Box.* (November 22, 1986) 6, 26. il.
  Re. *Bruce Springsteen and the E Street Band Live/1975–1985.*

Levy, Joe. "Bruce Springsteen," *Cash Box.* (December 26, 1987) 16. il.

Loder, Kurt. *"Tunnel of Love* LP Due from Springsteen," *Rolling Stone.* (September 24, 1987) 15.

Stambler, Irwin. "Springsteen, Bruce," In: *The Encyclopedia of Pop, Rock and Soul.* pp. 634–638. il.

Tannenbaum, Rob. "Springsteen Goes It Alone," *Rolling Stone.* n569 (January 11, 1990) 15, 66. il., int.

BRITTEN, ROY

Doerschuk, Bob. "Roy Brittan: Rocking America With the Boss," *Keyboard.* (December 1986) 66–89. il., disc., int.

Summer, Henry Lee

DeSavia, Tom. "Henry Lee Summer," *Cash Box.* (April 16, 1988) 10. il., int.

Survivor

Lounges, Tom. "Survivor: From Chicago to the World!," *Song Hits.* n256 (June 1987) 22–24. il.

Nite, Norm N. , with Charles Crespo. "Survivor," In: *Rock On . . . (Volume 3).* p. 344. disc.

"Survivor," *Super Song Hits.* n49 (Fall 1986) 52–53. il.

Sutton, Rich. "Survivor," *Song Hits.* n235 (September 1985) 22–23. il.

Toto

Kassan, Brian. "Toto Holds the Line," *Cash Box.* (October 25, 1986) 11, 28. il., int. w/Jeff Porcaro and Steve Lukather.

Nite, Norm N., with Charles Crespo. "Toto," In: *Rock On . . . (Volume 3).* pp. 362–364. il., disc.

Robinson, Julius. "Toto," *Cash Box.* (March 19, 1988) 10, 35. il., int. w/David Paich.

Stambler, Irwin. "Toto," In: *The Encyclopedia of Pop, Rock and Soul.* pp. 691–693.

Woodard, J. "Toto: The Riddle of L.A.'s Top Popsters," *Musician.* n76 (February 1985) 82–84ff. il.

The Unforgiven

Adelson, David. "Tales of the Spaghetti West," *Cash Box.* (May 24, 1986) 12. il.

Vaughn, Robert

Yardumian, Rob. "New Faces to Watch: Robert Vaughn," *Cash Box.* (October 10, 1987) 9. il., int.

What Is This

"New Faces to Watch: What Is This," *Cash Box.* (August 31, 1985) 10. il., int. w/vocalist-guitarist Alex Johannes.

17. FUNK

Cameo

Stubbs, D. "Macho Man," *Melody Maker.* 64 (October 22, 1988) 10–11. il., int. w/L. Blackman.

Cinema

Levy, Joe. "New Faces to Watch: Cinema," *Cash Box.* LI:46 (May 21, 1988) 11. int. w/Craig Holliman.

Clinton, George (See also: Funkadelic)

George, Nelson. "Dr. Funkenstein Heads Multiple Operations," *Billboard.* 98 (May 24, 1986) 28ff. int.

George, Nelson. "The Rhythm and the Blues: As Usual, George Clinton Has a Lot of Topics Covered," *Billboard.* 98 (May 24, 1986) 28.

Lababedi, I. "The George Clinton Interview: 'Think, It Ain't Illegal, Yet," *Creem.* 18 (November 1986) 30–31ff. il., int.

McCann, Ian. "The Mame Man," *New Musical Express.* (February 19, 1990) 54. il., int.

Owen, F. "4th World Funk," *Melody Maker.* 61 (April 19, 1986) 18–19. il., int.

Puterbaugh, Parke. "George Clinton's Theory of Funk," *Rolling Stone.* n562 (October 5, 1989) 16. il., int.

Stambler, Irwin. "Clinton, George," In: *The Encyclopedia of Pop, Rock and Soul.* pp. 131–133.

Sullivan, C. "The Nut and the Nerd," *Melody Maker.* 60 (July 20, 1985) 12–13. il., int.

Commodores (See also: Lionel Ritchie)

Ivory, S. "Commodores' Hiatus Over; *Nightshift* Ends Long Chart Slump," *Billboard.* 97 (February 9, 1985) 50ff.

Jackson, A. "Back on the 'Nightshift'," *Melody Maker.* 60 (March 2, 1985) 13. il., int.

Dazz Band

Stubbs, D. "Clean Cut," *Melody Maker.* 61 (August 30, 1986) 31. il., int. w/B. Harris.

Earth, Wind and Fire (See also: Philip Bailey)

"After 4-Year Break, EW&F Reunites," *Billboard.* 99 (October 31, 1987) 26.
The LP, *Touch the World*, released.

Flans, R. "Triumvirate: Earth, Wind & Fire's Ralph Johnson, Freddie White, and Philip Bailey," *Modern Drummer.* 6 (February 1982) 22–24ff. il., int.

Levy, Joe. "Earth, Wind & Fire," *Cash Box.* (November 28, 1987) 8. il., int. w/Bailey and Maurice White.

Roberts, J. "Verdine White: Back in the Spotlight With Earth, Wind & Fire," *Guitar Player.* 22 (October 1988) 4, 60–62ff. il., bio, int.

Rogers, S. "Random Notes: Earth, Wind and Fire's New Chemistry," *Rolling Stone.* n514 (December 3, 1987) 13. il.

Stambler, Irwin. "Earth, Wind & Fire," In: *The Encyclopedia of Pop, Rock and Soul.* pp. 204–206. il.

WHITE, MAURICE

Dobrin, Gregory. "Maurice White Finds a New Romance With His Solo Career," *Cash Box.* XLIX:19 (October 19, 1985) 11. il., int.

Funkadelic (See also: George Clinton)

"Leber-Krebs Again Seeking Funkadelic $$," *Billboard.* 98 (January 11, 1986) 6ff.

Gap Band

Summers, G. "Gap Band Doing 'All Right Now' After Hit Gap," *Billboard.* 97 (February 16, 1985) 60ff.

Johnson, Jesse (See also: Time)

Bull, D. "Jesse Johnson: The Time's Guitarist Goes Solo After Leaving Prince's Camp," *Rolling Stone.* n446 (April 25, 1985) 21.

George, Nelson. "Does Johnson Have Time for Time?,"
   Billboard. 98 (November 1, 1986) 26.

Ivory, S. "Big Push for Jesse Johnson; A&M Boosting Ex-Time
   Guitarist," *Billboard.* 97 (February 23, 1985) 50ff. int.

McCormick, M. "Ta Mara, Johnson Link Produces Debut LP,"
   Billboard. 98 (February 15, 1986) 46.

Robinson, Julius. "Jesse Johnson," *Cash Box.* (April 9, 1988)
   10. int.

Kane Gang

"New Faces to Watch: The Kane Gang," *Cash Box.* XLIX:26
   (December 7, 1985) 10. il., int. w/vocalist and lyricist
   Martin Brammer.

Kemp, Johnny

"New Faces to Watch: Johnny Kemp," *Cash Box.* (June 14,
   1986) 10. il., int.

Khan, Chaka (r.n.: Yvette Marie Stevens)

Bessman, Jim. "Chaka Khan's New Album is a Mix," *Billboard.* 98 (September 27, 1986) 61–62.
   Re. *Destiny.*

Kirk, K. "Militant Diva," *Melody Maker.* 61 (August 9, 1986)
   30. il., int.

Kid Creole and the Coconuts (See also: Dr. Buzzard's Original Savannah Band)

Quill, G. "Promoters Battle Over Copa's Use; Kid Creole Shifts
   to Fresh Site," *Variety.* 318 (March 27, 1985) 95.

Klymaxx

Cassata, Mary Anne. "Klymaxx," *Song Hits.* n240 (February 1986) 32–33. il.

Ivory, S. "For Klymaxx, *Meeting* is Still in Session," *Billboard.* 98 (March 22, 1986) 61.

Lounges, Tom. "The Men All Pause for the Ladies of Klymaxx," *Song Hits.* n246 (August 1986) 36–37. il.

Kool and the Gang

"Ampex Bestows Golden Reel," *Billboard.* 98 (March 1, 1986) 40.

Chin, B. "Kool & the Gang Aim Higher," *Billboard.* 98 (December 6, 1986) 22ff.

George, Nelson. "The Rhythm and the Blues: Robert 'Kool' Bell Sticks to Bass-ics," *Billboard.* 97 (August 10, 1985) 43.

Greenberg, E. "Kool & the Gang," *BMI.* n2 (1985) 20–21. il., bio.

"Kool & Gang Takes Top Honor in BMI Popular Music Awards," *Variety.* 319 (June 19, 1985) 89.

"Kool & Gang Tops Tokyo Music Fest; Menudo Wins Gold," *Variety.* 318 (April 3, 1985) 70.

Long, Bob. "Kool & the Gang: The Rebirth of Kool," *Cash Box.* (September 23, 1989) 6–7. il., int. w/Robert "Kool" Bell.

Stambler, Irwin. "Kool & the Gang," In: *The Encyclopedia of Pop, Rock and Soul.* pp. 380–382.

Weinger, H. "Kool & the Gang Rock Out," *Billboard.* 97 (January 12, 1985) 47ff.
Re. *Emergency.*

Maze (featuring Frankie Beverly)

Ivory, S. "Crossover Not That Important to Maze," *Billboard.* 97 (October 26, 1985) 53.

Jackson, A. "Amazing Grace," *Melody Maker.* 60 (May 11, 1985) 29. il., int. w/Frankie Beverly.

Stambler, Irwin. "Maze Featuring Frankie Beverly," In: *The Encyclopedia of Pop, Rock and Soul.* pp. 450–452.

Ohio Players

"Ohio Players: Back and Hotter Than Ever," *Cash Box.* LII:1 (July 2, 1988) 17–18. il., int.

Preston, Billy

Tabor, L. "Preston and Hudson Helm Late Night Banks," *International Musician.* 85 (December 1986) 7ff. il.

S.O.S. Band

Berk, Peter. "The S.O.S. Band: Right on Course and Sailing to the Top," *Cash Box.* (June 14, 1986) 11, 48. il., int. w/lead vocalist Mary Davis.

Sly and the Family Stone/Sly Stone

George, Nelson. "Sly Stone to Rock Again, Now on A&M," *Billboard.* 98 (March 15, 1986) 63.

Stambler, Irwin. "Sly and the Family Stone," In: *The Encyclopedia of Pop, Rock and Soul.* pp. 620–621.

Technotronic

MacNie, Jim. "Technotronic's Philosophy of Phunk," *Musician.* n140 (June 1990) 18–20. il.

Wild Cherry

Hill, Randal C. "Wild Cherry," *Goldmine.* n220 (December 30, 1988) 80. il.

Womack, Bobby

Woodbridge, J. "Poetic License," *Melody Maker.* 60 (October 26, 1985) 10. il., int.

Zapp

Owen, F. "4th World Funk: Zapp," *Melody Maker.* 61 (May 24, 1986) 12. il., int. w/Robert Troutman.

A. FUNK-PUNK

D'Arby, Terence Trent

Dupler, Steven. "The Eye," *Billboard.* 99 (October 3, 1987) 49.

Gilmore, Mikal. "Can Terence Trent D'Arby be as Good as He Thinks He Is?," *Rolling Stone.* n528 (June 16, 1988) 52–57ff. il., bio.

Gilmore, Mikal. "Terence Trent D'Arby Makes American Debut," *Rolling Stone.* n513 (November 19, 1987) 17, 30. il.

Leland, John. "Son of a Preacher Man," *Spin.* 5:7 (October 1989) 54–62, 113. il., int.

Stambler, Irwin. "D'Arby, Terence Trent," In: *The Encyclopedia of Pop, Rock and Soul.* p. 161.

Yardumian, Rob. "Terence Trent D'Arby," *Cash Box.* (October 24, 1987) 10. il.

James, Rick (r.n.: James Ambrose Johnson)

Bell, P. "Music: Burn Your Moola," *Village Voice.* 31 (July 15, 1986) 68. il.

George, Nelson. " '85 'Not a Bad Year' for Rick," *Billboard.* 98 (February 22, 1986) 52.

Grein, Paul. "Rick James Taking Care of Business," *Billboard.* 97 (August 10, 1985) 35. int.

Levy, Joe. "Rick James," *Cash Box.* LI:51 (June 25, 1988) 6, 34. il., int.

Stambler, Irwin. "James, Rick," In: *The Encyclopedia of Pop, Rock and Soul.* pp. 323–325.

Kravitz, Lenny

Coleman, Mark. "If 9 Was 6 Lenny Kravitz Would Be Right at Home," *Musician.* n138 (April 1990) 48–50, 113. il.

Gittins, Ian. "Lenny Kravitz: All You Need is Love," *Melody Maker.* 66:20 (May 19, 1990) 10–11. il., int.

Mayer, Dana. "Sound Check: Lenny Kravitz; Incense and Dreadlocks," *Me Music Express Magazine.* 14:145 (March 1990) 52. il., int.

Wright, Christian. "Let Lenny Rule," *Spin.* 6:4 (July 1990) 62–64. il., int.

Prince (r.n.: Prince Rogers Nelson; See also: Wendy and Lisa)

Berk, Peter. "Radio Responds to Prince's Continuing Purple Reign," *Cash Box.* XLIX:42 (April 5, 1986) 13, 32. il.

Bessman, Jim. "A Prince of a Teenager; Early Recordings Surface," *Billboard.* 97 (October 5, 1985) 4.
Re. *Minneapolis Genius: Featuring the Band 94 East.*

DeCurtis, Anthony. "Prince's 'Lovesexy' Album Due in May," *Rolling Stone.* n524 (April 21, 1988) 16. il.

Freeman, K. "Radio is Mixed on Prince Album," *Billboard.* 97 (May 4, 1985) 1ff.
Re. *Around the World in a Day.*

George, Nelson. "Prince Anoints Retinue of New Business Handlers," *Billboard.* 101 (January 21, 1989) 96.

George, Nelson. "The Rhythm & the Blues: Prince Makes News Without Even Doing Anything," *Billboard.* 97 (November 2, 1985) 57.

Goodman, Fred. "Prince Ignores Industry Marketing Wisdom; *Parade*: Third Album in Less Than Two Years," *Billboard.* 98 (March 22, 1986) 50.

Grein, Paul. "Prince, Jackson Top NARM List; 'Gift of Music' Sales Award Nominees," *Billboard.* 97 (February 16, 1985) 6ff.

Grein, Paul. "Prince, Wonder Honored by Motion Picture Academy," *Billboard.* 97 (April 6, 1985) 6.
Purple Rain awarded best original song score.

Holdship, Bill. "The Wit & Wisdom of Prince Rogers Nelson," *Creem.* 17 (July 1985) 28–33ff.

Kordosh, J. "See, Me and Prince Had a Deal . . . ," *Creem.* 77 (July 1986) 18–19ff. il.

Kordosh, J. "Thinking of Babylon, Dreaming of Prince," *Creem.* 17 (July 1986) 16–18ff. il.

McCormick, Moira. "Prince Reigns Supreme at Minnesota Music Awards," *Billboard.* 97 (June 1, 1985) 46.

Morris, Chris, and Geoff Mayfield. " 'Lovesexy' Too Sexy For Some: Prince's Album Art Meets Resistance," *Billboard.* 100:21 (May 21, 1988) 1, 77.

"NARM Pays Homage to Prince's Reign," *Variety.* 318 (April 3, 1985) 69.

"News: Under the Black Cape," *Spin.* 5:8 (November 1989) 28. il.

Paige, E., and Fred Goodman. "*Around the World* Starts Fast at Retail; Single Due," *Billboard.* 97 (May 11, 1985) 1ff.

Paige, E., and Fred Goodman. "Prince Merchandising: Do-It-Yourself," *Billboard.* 97 (May 18, 1985) 20.

Perry, Steve. "The 10 Most Interesting Musicians of the Last 5 Years: Prince," *Spin.* 6:1 (April 1990) 36–37. il.

"Revolution Blues," *Melody Maker.* 61 (November 8, 1986) 3. il. Prince splits from his backing band.

Stambler, Irwin. "Prince," In: *The Encyclopedia of Pop, Rock and Soul.* pp. 538–541.

Tate, G. "And He Was Baa-aad," *Record.* 4 (January 1985) 22–27. il.

"Warner Bros. Held Back Promo of Prince LP Until They Had It," *Variety.* 322 (February 19, 1986) 427.
Re. *Parade.*

Whatley, S. "Rock on: Sheena's Prince Connection," *Record.* 4 (June 1985) 8.

Wilde, Jon. "Prince: Royal Flush," *Melody Maker.* 66:23 (June 9, 1990) 16. il.

SEACER, LEVI

Stubbs, David. "Sideline: Court Jester to Prince," *Melody Maker.* (July 7, 1990) 11. il., int. w/his "Nude" revue bassist Levi Seacer.

Sheila E.

Bloom, Pamela. "Sheila E. in Romancing the Throne," *High Fidelity.* (January 1986) 64–65, 79. il., int.

Time (See also: Jimmy "Jam" Harris and Terry Lewis)

George, Nelson. "Music: The Time Has Come," *Village Voice.* 31 (April 1, 1986) 75. il.
Re. production work.

Goodman, Fred. "The Time Has Come—Again," *Rolling Stone.* n586 (September 6, 1990) 20. il., int.

Nite, Norm N., with Charles Crespo. *Rock On . . . (Volume 3).* pp. 359–360. disc.

DAY, MORRIS

Berk, Peter. "Morris Day: Creating the Color of Solo Success," *Cash Box.* XLIX:18 (October 12, 1985) 13. il., int.

George, Nelson. "Morris Day's Solo Career Takes Root," *Billboard.* 97 (October 5, 1985) 45. int.

Wendy and Lisa (r.n.: Wendy Melvoin and Lisa Coleman; See also: Prince)

Frost, Deborah. "On Their Own," *Buzz.* 3:2 (December 1987) 50–54. il., int.

Sullivan, C. "Wendy & Lisa: Satisfy Yourself," *Melody Maker.* 65 (August 5, 1989) 8–9. il., int.

B. FUNK METAL

Defunkt

Gore, J. "Defunkt: Avant-Funk With a Metal Edge," *Guitar Player.* 22 (December 1988) 56–62ff. il., music score.

Electric Boys

Henderson, Alex. "New Faces: The Electric Boys," *Cash Box.* LIII:49 (June 30, 1990) 5. il., int. w/lead vocalist Conny Bloom.

Faith No More

Kassan, Brian. "New Faces to Watch: Faith No More," *Cash Box.* (May 30, 1987) 10. il., int. w/singer Chuck Mosley and drummer Mike Bordin.

Migaldi, R. "Newbeats: Losin' the Faith," *Creem.* 19 (December 1987) 67. il.

Neely, Kim. "Faith No More," *Rolling Stone.* n586 (September 6, 1990) 53–54, 96. il., int.

Stud Brothers. "Faith No More: The Bad News Tour," *Melody Maker.* 66:7 (February 17, 1990) 16–17. il., int.

Wells, Steven. "Jerkin' for a Living," *New Musical Express.* (February 17, 1990) 15–16. il., int.

Wilkinson, Roy. "Divide and Conquer," *Sounds.* (February 3, 1990) 24–26. il., int.

Living Colour

Fricke, David. "Black Rock: A Group of Musicians Unites to Reclaim the Right to Rock," *Rolling Stone.* n509 (September 24, 1987) 64ff. il.

Fricke, David. "New Shades of Living Colour," *Rolling Stone.* n585 (August 23, 1990) 39. il., int. w/Vernon Reid.

Jeske, Lee. "Living Colour: Good Day for Black Rock," *Cash Box.* (February 18, 1989) 10. il., int.

Santoro, G. "Blindfold Test," *Down Beat.* 54 (December 1987) 51. il.

Williams, Joe. "New Faces to Watch: Living Colour," *Cash Box.* LI:51 (June 25, 1988) 7, 34. il., int. w/guitarist Vernon Reid.

Reed, Dan, Network

Levy, Joe. "New Faces to Watch: Dan Reed Network," *Cash Box.* (March 19, 1988) 11. il., int.

Sutherland, Steve. "Sidelines: Dan Reed Network," *Melody Maker.* (July 21, 1990) 10. il., int. w/Reed.

18. DISCO (1974–)

General Sources

Blackford, Andy. *Disco Dancing Tonight.* London: Octopus, 1979. il.
    Despite a short historical sketch, the work is primarily concerned with revealing the excitement of discos. Illustrations consist of models dressed in hip, uptown costumes.

Fox-Cumming, Ray. *Disco Fever.* London: Mandabrook, 1978. il.

Goodman, Fred. "PolyGram Reissues Disco," *Billboard.* 97 (November 23, 1985) 6ff.

Lovisone, Carter. *The Disco Hustler.* London: Ward Lock, 1979. il. Orig. pub.: New York: Sterling, 1979.
    Short history followed by description of four of the most popular disco-dances accompanied by many frozen-frame ilustrations.

Brown, Peter

Fearon, Mike. "Pete Brown," *Record Collector.* n114 (February 1989) 78–81. il., disc.

Chic

George, Nelson. "Nile Rodgers," In: *The Year in Rock, 1981–82*. pp. 78–79. il.

Jancik, Wayne. "Nile Rodgers: Chic's Mister Good Times," *Goldmine*. n180 (June 19, 1987) 22, 66. il.

Clifford, Linda

McCormick, Moira. "Linda Clifford Dancing Back into the Chart Limelight," *Billboard*. 97 (November 30, 1985) 35–36.

Dr. Buzzard's Original Savannah Band (See also: Kid Creole and the Coconuts)

Grossweiner, Bob. "Cory Daye: Co-Co is Me," *Goldmine*. n197 (February 12, 1988) 26, 32. il.

Jones, Grace

"Grace Jones Gets Dual Support: Manhattan, Island Team for *Slave*," *Billboard*. 97 (October 26, 1985) 6.

Lipps, Inc.

Hill, Randal C. "Lipps, Inc.," *Goldmine*. n220 (December 30, 1988) 73.

McCoy, Van

Gari, Brian. "Van McCoy," *Goldmine*. n244 (December 1, 1989) 33. il.

Moroder, Giorgio

LaPoint, K. "Much Music Told: A Movie Isn't a Video; CRTC Says Music Channel Can't Air *Metropolis,*" *Billboard.* 97 (May 4, 1985) 63.

McCullaugh, J. "Moroder Forms Soundtrack House," *Billboard.* 98 (September 27, 1986) 6.

Pandy, Daryl

Smith, Andrew. "Stonefree: Daryl Pandy," *Melody Maker.* 66:24 (June 16, 1990) 11. il., int.

Summer, Donna

Stambler, Irwin. "Summer, Donna," In: *The Encyclopedia of Pop, Rock and Soul.* pp. 658–660.

Yardumian, Rob. "Donna Summer," *Cash Box.* (October 3, 1987) 10. il., int.

Sylvester (r.n.: James Sylvester or Sylvester James)

Coleman, B. "Sylvester Dead at 40," *Billboard.* 101 (January 7, 1989) 6ff.

[Obituary], *Melody Maker.* 65 (January 14, 1989) 5.

[Obituary], *Rock & Roll Confidential.* n64 (January 1989) 3.

Ressner, J. [Obituary], *Rolling Stone.* n544 (January 26, 1989) 16.

"Sylvester," *Song Hits.* n156 (February 1979) 34–35. il.

White, Barry

McBride, Murdoch. "Barry White," *Cash Box.* (September 26, 1987) 10. il., int.

A. DANCE-ORIENTED ROCK

General Sources

Daly, Steven. "Conscious Party," *Spin.* 6:4 (July 1990) 24–25. il.
     Family tree of the genre's leading practitioners.

Breakdancing

Kopytko, T. "Breakdance as an Identity Marker in New Zealand," *Yearbook for Traditional Music.* 18 (1986) 21–28. bibl.

Abdul, Paula

Robinson, Julius. "The 'Straight Up' Story: Paula Abdul Hits the Top," *Cash Box.* 52 (March 3, 1989) 8–9. il., int.

Stud Brothers. "Paula Abdul: Footloose," *Melody Maker.* 65 (March 25, 1989) 29. il., int.

Wilde, David. "All the Right Moves," *Rolling Stone.* n566 (November 30, 1989) 96–103. il.

Allen, Donna

Jeske, Lee. "New Faces to Watch: Donna Allen," *Cash Box.* (March 28, 1987) 10. il., int.

Amazulu

Sullivan, C. "The Exciters," *Melody Maker.* 60 (August 24, 1985) 14. il., int. w/C. Kenny and Nardo.

Ana

Henderson, Alex. "New Faces: Ana," *Cash Box.* 50 (July 7, 1990) 5. il.

Anthony and the Camp

"New Faces to Watch: Anthony and the Camp," *Cash Box.* (July 5, 1986) 12. il., int. w/singer Anthony Malloy.

Ashford and Simpson (r.n.: Nick A. and Valerie S.)

Bessman, Jim. "At Last, the Secret is Out," *Billboard.* 98 (September 20, 1986) 24.

"It's a Family Affair," *Melody Maker.* 60 (June 8, 1985) 20. il., int.

Stambler, Irwin. "Ashford and Simpson," In: *The Encyclopedia of Pop, Rock and Soul.* pp. 18–20.

Chimes

Lester, Paul. "The Chimes: Ringing in the Changes," *Melody Maker.* 66:21 (May 26, 1990) 16. il., int.

Deee-Lite

Daly, Steve. "Flash: Multi-Cultural Delight," *Spin.* 6:3 (June 1990) 11–12. il., int.

Downing, Will

Jeske, Lee. "Will Downing," *Cash Box.* (August 6, 1988) 10. il., int.

4 of Us

Mulkerns, Helena. "Sound Check: The 4 of Us; Irish Temptation," *Me Music Express Magazine.* 14: 148 (June 1990) 18. il., int. w/Brendan Murphy.

Fox, Samantha

Jeske, Lee. "New Faces to Watch: Samantha Fox," *Cash Box.* (November 29, 1986) 10. il., int.

Good Question

"The Douglas Brothers Go Paisley," *Cash Box.* (July 30, 1988) 18.

Jackson, Janet

DeCurtis, Anthony. "Free at Last," *Rolling Stone.* n572 (February 22, 1990) 40–44, 70. il., int.

George, Nelson. "The Rhythm and the Blues: Janet Jackson Takes Control on New Release," *Billboard.* 98 (February 22, 1986) 52ff.

"News: Janet Jackson's 1814 Mystery," *Spin.* 5:12 (March 1990) 19. il.

Wolcott, J. "The Jackson Family's Material Girl," *Vanity Fair.* 39 (July 1986) 28ff.

Kamen, Nick

Iorio, Paul. "New Faces to Watch: Nick Kamen," *Cash Box.* (June 6, 1987) 12. il., int.

King (r.n.: Paul King)

FitzGerald, H. "The Emperor's New Clothes," *Melody Maker.* 60 (January 17, 1985) 16–17. il., int.

Kaye, A. "Newbeats: Eight Things I Know About Paul King That You May or May Not Know," *Creem.* 18 (November 1986) 67. il.

Mico, T. "King for a Day," *Melody Maker.* (December 7, 1985) 28–29, il., int.

"Shrink Rap," *Melody Maker.* 60 (February 16, 1985) 11. il., int.

Last Few Days!

Stubbs, David. "Sidelines: Last Few Days!," *Melody Maker.* (July 7, 1990) 12. il., int. w/vocalist Keir.

M (r.n.: Robin Scott)

Bernstein, Nils. "M," *Goldmine.* n220 (December 30, 1988) 14.

Lamb, Joe. "M." *Record Collector.* n121 (September 1989) 63.
il., disc.

White, Chris. "Great Scott," *Music Week.* (June 10, 1989) 16.
il., int.
Robin Scott reissues his 1979 classic, "Pop Muzik."

Madonna (See also: Dire Straits)

Armbruster, G., and Bob Doerschuk. "Madonna's Keyboardists Bring the Spirit of Rock to the Material Whirl,"
Keyboard Magazine. 11 (June 1985) 12ff. il.

Bessman, Jim. "Madonna's *Sacrifice* Hits Home Market,"
Billboard. 97 (August 3, 1985) 30.

Christgau, Georgia. "Medley: Madonna Phenomena," *Hi Fi/
Musical America.* 35 (September 1985) 51.

Cohen, Scott. "The 10 Most Interesting Musicians of the Last
5 Years: Madonna," *Spin.* 6:1 (April 1990) 38. il.

Comer, B.S., and Bob Doerschuk. "Steve Bray & Pat Leonard
are into the Groove with Madonna on *True Blue,*" *Keyboard
Magazine.* 12 (July 1986) 16ff.

Duffy, Thom. "HBO to Telecast Madonna 'Ambition' Tour
From France," *Billboard.* (July 7, 1990) 78.

Edelstein, D. "Cheerfully Grilling Susan," *Village Voice.* 30
(April 2, 1985) 47ff.

Fissinger, Laura. "Maybe She's Good: Ten Theories on How
Madonna Got 'It'," *Record.* 4 (March 1985) 30–31ff. il., bio.

Gold, R. "Sophisticated Auds Seeks *Susan*; Yuppies going for *Lost* as Well," *Variety.* 318 (April 17, 1985) 6.

Grein, Paul. "Hot Madonna: July Fills Her Coffers With RIAA Metal," *Billboard.* (August 10, 1985) 1ff.

Gross, M. "Classic Madonna," *Vanity Fair.* 49 (December 1986) 102–107ff. il.

Iorio, Paul. "Madonna: From Superstar to 'True Blue' Pop Icon," *Cash Box.* (July 5, 1986) 13, 48. il.

Johnson, Rick. "How Green Was My Sex Goddess?," *Creem.* 17 (August 1985) 3, 30–33ff.

"Madonna Leaps Up on RIAA Metal Heep," *Variety.* 324 (October 8, 1986) 147–148.

Maslin, Janet. "Making Movies—the Long Jump from MTV," *Record.* 4 (September 1985) 3, 21–24. il.

McGuigan, Cathleen. "The New True Blue Madonna," *Newsweek.* (July 14, 1986) 71. il.

Mico, T. "The Immaculate Misconception," *Melody Maker.* 60 (September 28, 1985) 28–30. il., bio, int.

Newman, Melinda. "Banned Madonna Clip to be Issued as Video Single," *Billboard.* 102:49 (December 8, 1990) 1, 92.
Re. video, "Justify My Love."

Stambler, Irwin. "Madonna," In: *The Encyclopedia of Pop, Rock and Soul.* pp. 427–429. il.

"WSAM Keys to Madonna," *Billboard.* 97 (August 3, 1985) 19.

Wolcott, J. "Let the Mascara Run," *Vanity Fair.* 48 (August 1985) 70–71. il.

"A World Safe for Madonna," *Saturday Review.* 12 (March/ April 1986) 7.

Mercy Seat

Yardumian, Rob. "New Faces to Watch: The Mercy Seat," *Cash Box.* (November 7, 1989) 9. il., int. w/Zena Van Heppinstall.

Milli Vanilli

Giles, Jeff. "Pop's Hair Apparent," *Rolling Stone.* n566 (November 30, 1989) 25–36. il.

Pretty Poison

Jaske, Lee. "New Faces to Watch: Pretty Poison," *Cash Box.* LI:50 (June 18, 1988) 7, 22. il., int. w/lead singer Jade Starling and co-writer Whey Cooler.

St. Etienne

Mathur, Paul. "Stonefree: St. Etienne," *Melody Maker.* 66:24 (June 16, 1990) 11. il., int. w/Bob.

Shakespear's Sister (See also: Bananarama)

Agerrad, Michael. "Shakespear's Sister," *Rolling Stone.* n566 (November 30, 1989) 43. il.

Soul II Soul

Bloom, Steve. "From Soul II Gold," *Rolling Stone.* n560 (September 7, 1989) 15. il., int. w/Jazzie B.

Push. "Soul II Soul: Voice of the B Jive," *Melody Maker.* 66:24 (June 16, 1990) 28–29. il., int. w/Jazzie B.

Sandall, Robert. "Soul II Soul: Two London Club DJs Redefine Classic Soul With a New Approach to Making Music," *Rolling Stone.* n582/583 (July 12/26, 1990) 105–106. il., int.

Swing Out Sister

Iorio, Paul. "New Faces to Watch: Swing Out Sister," *Cash Box.* (July 4, 1987) 10–11. il., int. w/Andy Connell.

Times Two

Robinson, Julius. "New Faces to Watch: Times Two," *Cash Box.* LI:45 (May 14, 1988) 11. int. w/Shanti Jones and Johnny Dollar.

B. ALTERNATIVE DANCE MUSIC

Adamski (r.n.: Adam Tinley)

Hardy, Ernest. "New Faces: Adamski," *Cash Box.* LIII:49 (June 30, 1990) 5. il., int.

King, Sam. "Reel to Wheel," *Sounds.* (February 3, 1990) 18. il., int. w/Adamski and Baby Ford.

Age of Chance

Mercer, M. "Escape from *Motor City,*" *Melody Maker.* 60 (August 17, 1985) 17. int.

Reynolds, S. "The Big Kiss Off," *Melody Maker.* 61 (November 29, 1986) 22–23. int.

Walsh, Peter. "Who's Afraid of the Big Boss Groove," *New Musical Express.* (March 30, 1990) 20. il.

Baltimora (r.n.: Jimmy McShane)

"New Faces to Watch: Baltimora," *Cash Box.* XLIX:28 (December 21, 1985) 10. il., int.

Bang the Party

"Blow Up," *Melody Maker.* 64 (December 10, 1988) 12. il.

"Sidelines," *Melody Maker.* 65 (August 26, 1989) 13. il.

Beats International (See also: Housemartins)

Azerrad, Michael. "New Faces: Beats International," *Rolling Stone.* n582/583 (July 12/26, 1990) 34. il., int. w/ Norman Cook.

Hardy, Ernest. "New Faces: Beats International," *Cash Box.* LIII:43 (May 19, 1990) 7. il., int. w/Cook.

Lamacq, Steve. "Brighten New Beat," *New Musical Express.* (February 3, 1990) 42–43. il., int. w/Norman Cook.

Beloved

Barron, Jack. "They Wanna be Loved," *New Musical Express.* (January 27, 1990) 15. il., int.

Bronski Beat (See also: Communards)

Bessman, Jim. "Bronski Beat 'Dance Remix' Clip Beats Single into the Market," *Billboard.* 98 (April 5, 1986) 54. Re. "Hit That Perfect Beat."

"Bronski Sing," *Melody Maker.* 60 (October 19, 1985) 3. il. Report on the addition of a new vocalist, John Foster.

Chalmer, Lindsay. "Bromski Beat," *Record Collector.* n72 (August 1985) 11–14. il., disc.

Frith, Simon. "Britbeat: All Together New," *Village Voice.* 30 (February 12, 1985) 78.

Hoskyns, Barney. "What is Bronski Beat?," *Spin.* n1 (May 1985) 40–41. il.

"Jimi Bronski Beats It," *Melody Maker.* 60 (April 27, 1985) 3. il.

McIlheney, B. "Last of the Somerville Whines," *Melody Maker.* 60 (September 21, 1985) 28–30. il.

Cherry, Neneh

Pond, Steve. "Neneh Cherry's Popular Stance," *Rolling Stone.* n558 (August 10, 1989) 76–78ff. il., bio.

Communards (See also: Bronski Beat)

Gett, Steve. "The Communards Reject Rock Stereotypes," *Billboard.* 98:50 (December 20, 1986) 22.

Owen, Robert. "The Communards," *Record Collector.* n102 (February 1988) 15–17. il., disc.

Cool Down Zone

Lester, Paul. "Stonefree: Cool Down Zone," *Melody Maker.* (July 21, 1990) 13. il., int.

Dead or Alive

Iorio, Paul. "Dead or Alive: Recluses Ready for a Break-through," *Cash Box.* (January 17, 1987) il., int. w/ associates Jerry Jaffe and Anne Roseberry.

Sutherland, Steve. "Dead or Alive: Past Imperfect," *Melody Maker.* 65 (August 12, 1989) 26–27. il., int. w/Pete Burns.

Deee-Lite

Smith, Andrew. "Deee-Lite: Slipped Discodelia," *Melody Maker.* (August 25, 1990) 44–45. il., int.

Five Thirty

Price, Simon. "Sidelines: Five Thirty," *Melody Maker.* (August 25, 1990) 10. il., int.

Frankie Goes to Hollywood

" 'Bang' Goes Frankie," *Melody Maker.* 60 (March 30, 1985) 4. il.
  Re. the book, *And Suddenly There Came a Bang.*

Blair, Count Iain. *Frankie Goes to Hollywood.* Chicago: Contemporary, 1985.

Brown, Mick, and Howard Rosenberg. "Days of Whine and Poses," *Spin.* n1 (May 1985) 58–61, 73.
  Focuses on the hype surrounding the band.

Doggett, Peter. "Frankie Goes to Hollywood," *Record Collector.* n64 (December 1984) 28–30. il., disc.

"Frankie Say Obscene!," *Melody Maker.* 60 (February 9, 1985) 3. il.
  Re. the book, *And Suddenly There Came a Bang.*

"Frankie Split Denied," *Melody Maker.* 61 (February 1, 1986) 3.

Frith, Simon. "Frankie Says Buy Me: Taking Pop Seriously," *OneTwoThreeFour.* n2 (1985) 55–58. il.

Hizer, Brund. *Give It Loads! The Story of Frankie Goes to Hollywood.* New York: Proteus, 1984.

Hunter, N. "London Judge Sets Frankie Free," *Billboard.* 101 (August 12, 1989) 69.

Jackson, Danny. *Frankie Say: The Rise of Frankie Goes to Hollywood.* London: Virgin, 1985. Also pub.: New York: Fireside, 1985.

Mico. T. "Rage of Chance," *Melody Maker.* 61 (August 9, 1986) 24–26. il., int.

Pepe, B. "Frankie Say: Yoo-Hoo!," *Creem.* 16 (January 1985) 17. il.

Sullivan, J. "Frankie Say Buzz Off," *Record.* 4 (February 1985) 17–19. il.

Sutton, Rich. "Frankie Goes to Hollywood," *Super Song Hits.* n44 (Summer 1985) 28–29. il.

Thomas, David. "England's Crazy About Frankie Goes to Hollywood," *Rolling Stone.* n432 (October 11, 1984) 36, 44. il.

Frazier Chorus

Smith, Andrew. "Stonefree: Frazier Chorus," *Melody Maker.* 66:23 (June 9, 1990) 11. il., int. w/singer Tim Freeman.

Go West

FitzGerald, H., and T. Sheehan. "Judgement Day," *Melody Maker.* 60 (March 30, 1985) 10. il.

"New on the Charts." *Billboard.* 97 (March 9, 1985) 50. Re. the single, "We Close Our Eyes."

Hardcastle, Paul

Bessman, Jim. "Anti-War Clip Provokes Network Wrath; Hardcastle's '19' Recut Following ABC, NBC Objections," *Billboard.* 97 (June 1, 1985) 38–39.

"Chrysalis Shoots New '19' Videoclip, Sans Web Footage," *Variety.* 319 (June 5, 1985) 71ff.

"It Shouldn't Happen to a Vet," *Melody Maker.* 60 (May 18, 1985) 12–13. il., int.

Weinger, H. "Hardcastle Hip-Hops Across the Atlantic," *Billboard.* 97 (February 16, 1985) 60ff.

Haza, Ofra

Stubbs, D. "Strange Fruit," *Melody Maker.* 61 (October 18, 1986) 37. il., int.

Honeychild

Smith, Andrew. "Sidelines: Honeychild," *Melody Maker.* (July 28, 1990) 10. il., int. w/keyboardist Iggy and singer Eeon.

INXS

Agnelli, L.E. "INXS . . . in Hell?," *Creem.* 17 (April 1986) 38–39ff. il.

Baker, Glenn A. "INXS: Top of the Heap Down Under," *Billboard.* 97 (August 24, 1985) 40.

DeCurtis, Anthony. "New Sensation," *Rolling Stone.* n538 (June 16, 1988) 3, 76–77ff. il.

"INXS Again Sweeps Aussie Disk Awards," *Variety.* 323 (June 11, 1986) 74.
Re. annual Countdown Music and Video Awards.

"INXS Sweeps Aussie Awards," *Variety.* 319 (May 22, 1985) 87.
   Re. Countdown Music and Video Awards.

Levy, Joe. "20th Century Fox," *Spin.* 5:8 (November 1989) 64–70, 116. il., int. w/Michael Hutchence.

"Oz's Hoyts & Ronin Jointly to Handle *Dogs* Rock Film," *Variety.* 325 (October 29, 1986) 55.

St. John, E. "INXS," *APRA Journal.* 3:3 (1984) 12–14. il.

St. John, E. "INXS Update," *APRA Journal.* 4:2 (1986) 50.

Sullivan, S. "*Thieves* Like Us," *Melody Maker.* 61 (February 1, 1986) 29. il., int.

Tannenbaum, Rob. "The Sweet Success of INXS," *Rolling Stone.* n517 (January 14, 1988) 48–50. il., int. w/ Hutchence and Andrew Farris.

Vare, E.A. "INXS Eyes U.S. Breakthrough," *Billboard.* 97 (December 21, 1985) 45–46.

Idol, Billy

Fricke, David. "Raging Bill," *Melody Maker.* 60 (June 29, 1985) 20–21. il., int.

McNeil, Legs. "The Devil Finds Work for Idol Hands to Do," *Spin.* 6:6 (June 1990) 28–32, 88–89, il., int.

Nazam, Mo. "Control Zone: Guitar Idol," *Melody Maker.* (August 25, 1990) 41. il., int.

Needs, K. "Billy Idol: Nice Day for a New Album," *Creem.* 17 (August 1986) 28–31. il., int.

Ressner, Jeffrey. "Billy Idol Hobbles Back to Action," *Rolling Stone.* n582/583 (July 12/26, 1990) 32. il., int.

Sutherland, Steve. "Cracked Actor," *Melody Maker.* 61 (November 8, 1986) 24–26. il., int.

Law, Linda

Smith, Andrew. "Stone Free: Linda Law," *Melody Maker.* (October 13, 1990) 14. il., int.

Little Caesar

Gittins, Ian. "Stonefree: Little Caesar," *Melody Maker.* 66:23 (June 9, 1990) 11. il., int. w/Johnny Lovemuscle.

M/A/R/R/S

"MARRS Probe," *Melody Maker.* 63 (September 26, 1987) 3. il. Single, "Pump Up the Volume," alleged to infringe "Road Block" copyright.

Mind, Body & Soul

Push. "Stonefree: Mind, Body & Soul," *Melody Maker.* 66:24 (June 16, 1990) 11. il., int.

Papa Brittle

Push. "Stonefree: Papa Brittle," *Melody Maker.* 66:21 (May 26, 1990) 10. il., int.

Pet Shop Boys

Armstrong, Mike. "Pet Shop Boys," *Record Collector.* n89 (January 1987) 8–11. il., disc.

Armstrong, Mike. "Pet Shop Boys," *Record Collector.* n110 (October 1988) 28–32. il., disc.

DeMuir, H. "Pet Shop Boys: Out of the Doghouse," *Creem.* 18 (September 1986) 38–39ff. il.

Frith, Simon. "Britbeat: Kiss Kiss Bang Bang," *Village Voice.* 31 (February 11, 1986) 65.

Gett, Steve. "Pet Shop Boys: How Opportunity Came Knocking," *Billboard.* 98 (July 19, 1986) 1ff.

Jeske, Lee. "Pet Shop Boys: Looks, Brains and on Their Way to Lots of Money," *Cash Box.* (April 12, 1985) 15, 36. il., int.

Mathur, Paul. "Four-Legged Friends," *Melody Maker.* 61 (February 22, 1986) 10–11. il., int.

Needham, Graham. "Pet Shop Boys Rarities," *Record Collector.* n126 (February 1990) 34–38. il., disc.

"Pet Shop Boys," *Super Song Hits.* n49 (Winter 1987) 52–53. il.

Tamarkin, Jeff. "Duo Dazzles Dancers With *West End Girls,*" *Billboard.* 98 (March 29, 1986) 26.

Rebel MC

Lambert, Stu. "Control Zone: Rebel Talk," *Melody Maker.* (June 23, 1990) 60. il., int.

Renegade Soundware

Lamacq, Steve. "Dine of Thieves," *New Musical Express.* (February 3, 1990) 15. il., int.

Wilde, Jon. "Renegade Soundwave," *Melody Maker.* (March 3, 1990) 18. il.

Scritti Politti

Padgett, Stephen. "Scritti Politti: The Heart and Mind of Pop Music," *Cash Box.* XLIX:9 (August 17, 1985) 12. il.

Soup Dragons

Mercer, M. "Love & Hate," *Melody Maker.* 63 (September 26, 1987) 10–11. il., int. w/Sean and Ross.

Push. "The Soup Dragons: The Men Couldn't Hang," *Melody Maker.* (July 21, 1990) 42–43. il., int.

Style Council (See also: Jam)

"'New Music Whiplash—Part 2: Style Council—The Gospel According to Paul Weller," *Musician.* n66 (April 1984) 36–40. il., int.

Sunsonic

Ruddell, James. "Sidelines: Sunsonic," *Melody Maker.* 66:24 (June 16, 1990) 13. il., int.

Thrill Kill Kult

Stud Brothers. "My Life With the Three Kill Kult. Tabooed Love Boys," *Melody Maker.* (October 13, 1990) 46. il., int.

Tom Tom Club (See also: Talking Heads)

Givens, Ron. "Tom Tom Club," *Stereo Review.* 54 (December 1989) 100–101. il.

Wang Chung

Iorio, Paul. "Wang-Chunging Up the Charts With 'Mosaic'," *Cash Box.* (November 15, 1986) 11. il., int. w/Nick Feldman and Jack Hues.

Was (Not Was)

Sutherland, Steve. "Don Was: In Search of the Golden Touch," *Melody Maker.* (July 21, 1990) 44–45. il., int.
Re. his work as a producer with other artists.

C. ACID HOUSE

General Sources

Eddy, Chuck. "They Shoot Horses, Don't They?," *Spin.* 2 (October 1986) 23–28. il.

"First Reports: Acid House Bill Threatens Glastonbury," *Sounds.* (February 24, 1990) 2.

"News: Police Storm Acid Rave," *Melody Maker.* (July 28, 1990) 5. il.

O'Hagan, S. "Acid House," *Spin.* 4 (January 1989) 64–65. il.

Seaman, D. "Dance Trax: Acid House: U.K. Rage in '88," *Billboard.* 101 (January 14, 1989) 27.

Carter the Unstoppable Sex Machine

"News: Inspirals and Carter in Tee-Shirt Row," *Melody Maker.* (July 21, 1990) 3. il.

Push. "Carter the Unstoppable Sex Machine: More Songs About F***ing People Up," *Melody Maker.* 66:4 (January 27, 1990) 33. il., int.

Robb, John. "Names for 1990: Dame the Begrudgers," *Sounds.* (February 24, 1990) 54. il.

Electribe 101

Gittins, Ian. "Electribe 101: House to House Enquiries," *Melody Maker.* 66:7 (February 17, 1990) 18–19. il., int.

McCann, Ian. "Take It to the Fridge," *New Musical Express.* (February 24, 1990) 16. il., int. w/vocalist Billie Ray Martin.

Inspiral Carpets (See: Manchester Sound)

Psychic TV

Balmer, M. "Stoned Love," *Melody Maker.* 61 (May 3, 1986) 41. il., int. w/Genesis P. Orridge.

Gittins, Ian. "Sidelines: Psychic TV," *Melody Maker.* 66:4 (January 27, 1990) 15. il., int. w/Orridge.

D. HOUSE MUSIC

General Sources

George, Nelson. "House Music: Will It Join Rap and Go-Go?," *Billboard.* 98 (June 21, 1986) 27.

Johnson, Kevin. "First Came Hip House," *Serious Hip Hop.* 1:4 (May–June 1990) 15. il.

Owen, Frank. "Last Night a DJ Saved My Life: Chicago," *Melody Maker.* 61 (August 16, 1986) 32–33. il., int. w/D. Pandy and Candi.

Hip House

Owen, Frank. "Flash: Hip House," *Spin.* 5:9 (December 1989) 26. il.
Delineates the blend of hip hop and house.

Adeva

Owen, Frank. "This is a Warning," *Spin.* 5:7 (October 1989) 32–33. il., int.

Big Sound Authority

Irwin, C. "Waking Up With the House on Fire," *Melody Maker.* 60 (February 23, 1985) 12–13. il., int. w/Tony Burke and Julie Hadwen.

Blue Pearl

Deacon, Rob. "Stone Free: Blue Pearl," *Melody Maker.* (July 7, 1990) 15. il., int. w/vocalist Durga McBroom.

Ford, Baby (r.n.: Peter Ford; See also: Adamski)

"Ford Escorts," *Melody Maker.* 64 (December 3, 1988) 16. il.

"Porn-Again House," *Melody Maker.* 64 (June 11, 1988) 11. il.

"Shrink Rap," *Melody Maker.* 65 (January 28, 1989) 13. il.

Stud Brothers. "Baby Ford: Kid's Stuff," *Melody Maker.* 66:4 (January 27, 1990) 30–31. il., int.

Foremost Poets

Reynolds, Simon. "Stone Free: The Foremost Poets," *Melody Maker.* 66:21 (May 26, 1990) 10. il., int.

Jomanda

Hardy, Ernest. "Jomanda: House is Home," *Cash Box.* (March 3, 1990) 23. il., int.

Krush

"Sidelines: Homeland House," *Melody Maker.* 63 (December 12, 1987) 17. il., int.
Re. recording, *House Arrest.*

Lil Louis

Stern, Chip. "New Faces: Lil Louis," *Rolling Stone.* n578 (May 17, 1990) 20. il.

Meat Beat Manifesto

Lester, Paul. "Sidelines: Meat Beat Manifesto," *Melody Maker.* 66:24 (June 16, 1990) 14. il., int.

Musto and Bones (r.n.: Tommy M. and Frankie B.)

Smith, Andrew. "Stone Free: Musto and Bones," *Melody Maker.* (July 21, 1990) 13. il., int. w/Frankie.

Owens, Robert

Hardy, Ernest. "New Faces: Robert Owens," *Cash Box.* LIII:50 (July 7, 1990) 5. il.

Shamen

Gittins, Ian. "Sidelines: Synergy," *Melody Maker.* 66:4 (January 27, 1990) 14. il., int.

Technotronic

Owen, Frank. "Belgium in the House," *Spin.* 5:12 (March 1990) 20–21. il.

Thunderpussy

Sullivan, Caroline. "Sidelines: Thunderpussy," *Melody Maker.* 66:8 (February 24, 1990) 12. il.

Titiyo

Sullivan, Caroline. "Sidelines: Titiyo," *Melody Maker.* 66:4 (January 27, 1990) 14. il., int.

Torres, Liz, and Jesse Jone

Push. "Stone Free: Liz Torres & Jesse Jone," *Melody Maker.* (July 7, 1990) 15. il., int.

Ultrasonic

Push. "Stone Free: Ultrasonic," *Melody Maker.* (July 28, 1990) 13. il., int. w/Rik Levay.

Williams, Jay

Hardy, Ernest. "Jay Williams and the House of 'Sweat'," *Cash Box.* LIII:40 (April 28, 1990) 6–7. il.

Yargo

Gittins, Ian. "Yargo: Network Communication," *Melody Maker.* 66:8 (February 24, 1990) 16–17. il., int. w/ vocalist Basil Clarke.

Young Disciples

Push. "Stone Free: The Young Disciples," *Melody Maker.* (October 13, 1990) 14. il., int. w/Femir.

E. AMBIENT HOUSE

General Sources

Mack, Bob. "Flash: New Age Soul Boys," *Spin.* 5:12 (March 1990) 18. il., int. w/Martin Price.

Morton, Roger. "Gigglers With Attitude," *New Musical Express.* (February 24, 1990) 14–15. il., int.

Brown, Tim (aka KGB)

"Tim Brown," *Melody Maker.* 66:21 (May 26, 1990) 13. il., int.

808 State

Grant, Keith. "State Secrets," *Melody Maker.* 66:5 (February 3, 1990) 53. il., int.

" 'Hang All Indie Bands!'—Says Martin of 808 State," *Melody Maker.* (July 7, 1990) 17. il., int.

"Sidelines: 808 State," *Melody Maker.* 65 (August 5, 1989) 14. il.

Fingers Inc. (r.n.: Larry Heard)

Hewitt, Paolo."Happy as Larry," *New Musical Express.* (February 17, 1990) 36. il., int.

Grid

Reynolds, Simon. "The Grid: Mad About the Buoy," *Melody Maker.* (July 7, 1990) 42–43. il., int. w/Richard Norris.

History Featuring Q-Tie (r.n.: Tatsyana Mais)

Reynolds, Simon. "Sidelines: History Featuring Q-Tie," *Melody Maker.* 66:23 (June 9, 1990) 12. il., int.

KLF

Robb, John. "Accidental Anarchists," *Sounds.* (February 24, 1990) 17. il., int.

19. NEW WAVE (1975–   )

A. PUNK (1975–1978)

General Sources

Bisharat, T. "Punk: Nihilistic Narcissism," *Musician Player & Listener.* 1:10 (1977–1978) 22–23ff. il.

Burchill, Julie, and Tony Parsons. *The Boy Looked at Johnny: The Obituary of Rock and Roll.* London: Pluto, 1978. il.

Case, Brian, and Ted Mico. "Love Kills," *Melody Maker.* 61 (July 19, 1986) 22–23. int. w/Alex Cox.

Davis, Julie, ed. *Punk.* London: Millington, 1977. il. A collection of features, interviews and reviews concerned with leading punk artists and attitudes culled from fanzines.

Hennessy, Val. *In the Gutter.* London: Quartet, 1978. il.

Buzzcocks

Robbins, Ira. "Buzzcocks: Everybody's Happy Nowadays," *Rolling Stone.* n571 (February 8, 1990) 17. il., int.

Clash (See also: Big Audio Dynamite)

"Clash Deny Split," *Melody Maker.* 60 (November 23, 1985) 3.

"The Clash: Strummer Speaks Out," *Melody Maker.* 60 (November 30, 1985) 3.
Sheppard, White and Howard depart; future of the band is uncertain.

Lababedi, I. "Eleganza: Good Socialist Lads," *Creem.* 19 (June 1988) 12. il.

Miles. *Clash.* Art direction, Perry Neville; design, Andy Morton. London: Omnibus, 1981. il. pap.

Smith, Pennie. *The Clash: Before & After.* London: Eel Pie, 1980. il. pap.
Tour photos punctuated by comments from group members.

Stambler, Irwin. "The Clash," In: *The Encyclopedia of Pop, Rock and Soul.* pp. 126–129. il.

HEADON, NICK "TOPPER"

Mercer, M. "Headon and Hell," *Melody Maker.* 60 (January 5, 1985) 23ff. il., int.

Smith, W. "Wide Awake," *Melody Maker.* 61 (January 4, 1986) 14. il., int.

STRUMMER, JOE

Tannenbaum, Rob. "Career Opportunities," *Buzz.* 3:3 (February (1988) 15–17. il., int.

County, Jayne (Formerly: Wayne County)

Kirk, K. "Transformer," *Melody Maker.* 61 (June 7, 1986) 14. il., int.

"Shrink Rap," *Melody Maker.* 60 (September 21, 1985) 27. il., int.

Damned

Clerk, Carol. "Escape to New York," *Melody Maker.* 60 (December 21/28, 1985) 26–27. il., int.

Clerk, Carol. "Flashback: The Damned," *Melody Maker.* 61 (April 19, 1986) 27–30. il., int. w/Rat Scabies and D. Vanian.

Paytress, Mark. "The Damned," *Record Collector.* n81 (May 1986) 29–33. il., disc.

Paytress, Mark. "The Damned," *Record Collector.* n82 (June 1986) 36–41. il., disc.

Smith, M. "Tales from the Crypt," *Melody Maker.* 60 (August 10, 1985) 24 25. il., int. w/Scabies.

Fleshtones

Iorio, Paul. "East Coastings," *Cash Box.* (June 13, 1987) 11. il., int. w/vocalist Peter Zaremba.

Go-Go's (See also: Belinda Carlisle)

Pond, Steve. "Go-Go's Get Going Again," *Rolling Stone.* n578 (May 17, 1990) 18. il.

Stambler, Irwin. "The Go-Go's," In: *The Encyclopedia of Pop, Rock and Soul.* pp. 259–260.

Vare, E.A. "Go-Go's Gone; Lawsuit Looming?," *Billboard.* 97 (June 8, 1985) 48ff.

CARLISLE, BELINDA

Hochman, S. "Belinda Carlisle Go-Goes Solo—Sort of," *Billboard.* 98 (May 17, 1986) 20.

Kordosh, J. "Be Lovely, be Lucky, Belinda," *Creem.* 18 (October 1986) 42–43. il.

Mueller, Andrew. "Belinda Carlisle: Ready Steady Go-Go," *Melody Maker.* 66:4 (January 27, 1990) 31. il., int.

Sullivan, C. "Opportunities Knocked," *Melody Maker.* 61 (October 4, 1986) 45. il., int.

Van Meter, Jonathan. "Lucky Star," *Spin.* 5:10 (January 1990) 42–45, 86. il., int.

VALENTINE, KATHY

Forte, Dan. "Kathy Valentine of the Go-Go's," *Guitar Player.* 19 (January 1985) 12ff.

Jam

Doggett, Peter. "The Jam," *Record Collector.* n47 (July 1983) 3–7. il., disc.

Hewitt, Paolo. *The Jam: A Beat Concerto*. New York: Omnibus, 1983. il.

Honeyford, Paul. *The Jam: The Modern World By Numbers*. London: Eel Pie, 1980. il., disc. pap. Also Pub.: London: Star, 1982.

Miles, Barry. *The Jam: An Illustrated Biography*. New York: Omnibus, 1981. il., bio.

Nicholls, Mike. *About the Young Idea: The Story of the Jam, 1972–1982*. New York: Proteus, 1984. il., bio, disc. pap.

Rockmaker, Deirdre. "The Jam: Ace Face in the Crowd," *Goldmine*. n187 (September 25, 1987) 8–14. il.

Tucker, Rick. "Collecting the Jam," *Record Collector*. n20 (April 1981) 43–48. il., disc.

Williams, Ian. "The Jam," *Record Collector*. n90 (February 1987) 30–34. il., disc.

Jett, Joan, and the Blackhearts (See also: Runaways)

Bessman, Jim. "Jet Propelled by Hit CBS Album," *Billboard*. 101 (January 21, 1989)

King, W. "Life in the Jettstream," *Record*. 4 (January 1985) 32–34. il.

"Sidelines: Joan Jett," *Melody Maker*. 63 (September 12, 1987) 27. il., int.

Lunch, Lydia

Myers, Caren. "Lydia Lunch: Preminstrel Tension," *Melody Maker.* 66:23 (June 9, 1990) 39. il., int. w/former leader of Teenage Jesus and the Jerks.

Manitoba's Wild Kingdom

Woods, Karen. "Shock of the New," *Cash Box.* (June 2, 1990) 9.
New band includes seminal glitter band, The Dictators, within its ancestral tree.

Nash the Slash (r.n.: Jeff Plewman)

Collie, A. "Notes: Nash Sues Pepsi," *Canadian Musician.* 7:4 (1985) 13–14.

Pop, Iggy (See also: David Bowie; Stooges)

Morris, C. "David Bowie Pops Up on Another Iggy Album," *Billboard.* 98 (September 27, 1986) 20.

West, Mike. *The Lives and Crimes of Iggy Pop.* Manchester, U.K.: Babylon, 1983. il. pap.

Ramones

Bessman, Jim. "Ramones Have 'Something to Believe In'," *Billboard.* 98 (August 23, 1986) 58ff.
Re. video clip.

FitzGerald, H. "Da Brudders," *Melody Maker.* 60 (February 2, 1985) 12–13. il., int.

Forte, Dan. "Johnny & Dee Dee Ramone: Two Punks With an Axe to Grind," *Guitar Player.* 19 (April 1985 8–10ff. il., bio, int.

Ramone, Dee Dee. "My Life as a Ramone," *Spin.* 6:1 (April 1990) 88–92, 141. il., int.

"Shrink Rap," *Melody Maker.* 61 (April 26, 1986) 37. il., int. w/Dee Dee.

"Shrink Rap," *Melody Maker.* 61 (April 26, 1986) 37. il., int. w/Joey Ramone.

"Sidelines," *Melody Maker.* 63 (September 26, 1987) 12. il., int.

Stambler, Irwin. "The Ramones," In: *The Enclyclopedia of Pop, Rock and Soul.* pp. 551–552.

Williams, Joe. "The Ramones," *Cash Box.* LII:3 (July 16, 1988) 3, 13. il., int. w/Joey Ramone.

Sex Pistols (See also: Public Image Ltd.)

"Pistols Win a Million," *Melody Maker.* 61 (January 25, 1986) 3. il.
Re. lawsuit filed against Malcolm McLaren.

Stambler, Irwin. "The Sex Pistols," In: *The Encyclopedia of Pop, Rock and Soul.* pp. 608–609. il.

Smith, Patti

Muir, A. John, ed. *Patti Smith—High on Rebellion.* London: Babylon, 1979. il.

Roach, Dusty. *Patti Smith: Rock and Roll Madonna.* South Bend, IN: And, 1979. il., disc.

Simels, Steve. "Patti Smith," *Stereo Review.* 41 (August 1978) 78–81. il.

Smith, Patti. *Babel.* New York: Berkley, 1979.

Smith, Patti. *Seventh Heaven.* New York: Telegraph, 1971.

Stambler, Irwin. "Smith, Patti," In: *The Encyclopedia of Pop, Rock and Soul.* pp. 621–623.

Urian, Lynne Francek. "Patti Smith: The Return of the Dreamer," *Goldmine.* n212 (September 9, 1988) 8–10, il., disc.

Wolff, Carlo. "Patti Smith: 'Dream of Life'—The Album," *Goldmine.* n212 (September 9, 1988) 10, 67. il.

Squeeze/U.K. Squeeze

Bordowitz, Hank. "Squeezin' Out Sparks," *Buzz.* 3:1 (November 1987) 14–16. il., int.

Coleman, Mark. "Squeeze Finally Gets Its Hit," *Rolling Stone.* n514 (December 3, 1987) 26–29. il., int. w/Chris Difford and Glenn Tilbrook.

DiMartino, Dave. "Squeeze LP Could be Pivotal in Career," *Billboard.* 99 (September 26, 1987) 27.

Farrar, Ann. "Squeeze Together Again," *Stereo Review.* (January 1986) 58–60. il., int. w/keyboardist Julian "Jools" Holland.

Lababedi, I. "Squeeze: Access All Areas (Don't Pull That Trigger)," *Creem.* 19 (September 1987) 44–46ff. il.

Stambler, Irwin. "Squeeze," In: *The Encyclopedia of Pop, Rock and Soul.* pp. 638–640.

DIFFORD, CHRIS, AND GLENN TILBROOK

"Shrink Rap," *Melody Maker.* 60 (October 25, 1985) 16. il., int.

Stranglers

Gittins, Ian. "The Stranglers," Sob Stories," *Melody Maker.* 66:8 (February 24, 1990) 39. il., int. w/Hugh Cornwell.

Hook, Andrew. "Stranglers Rarities," *Record Collector.* n111 (November 1988) 31–34. il., disc.

Murdoch, Lorne. "The Stranglers," *Record Collectors.* n75 (November 1985) 28–34. il., disc.

Rockmaker, Deirdre. "The Stranglers: From Heroes to Eternity," *Goldmine.* n179 (June 5, 1987) 12, 14. il., disc.

Wells, Steve. "Silence is Golden," *New Musical Express.* (February 24, 1990) 20–21. il., int.

Sweet, Rachel

Himmelsbach, Erik. "Rachel Sweet: The Sweet Voice From Akron," *Goldmine.* n207 (July 1, 1988) 23, 71, 80. il., disc.

Wire

Grabel, R. "Wire of the Tastiest Kind," *Creem.* 19 (September 1987) 31ff. il.

Paytress, Mark. "Wire," *Record Collector.* n100 (December 1987) 48–51. il., disc.

Pike, Jon R. "Wire: Totally Wired," *Goldmine.* n206 (June 17, 1988) 24, 72. il., disc.

Williams, Joe. "Wire," *Cash Box.* LII:3 (July 16, 1988) 12–13. il., int. w/singer Colin Newman.

X

Bessman, Jim. "Elektra Takes a Chance on New X Clip," *Billboard.* 97 (September 21, 1985) 35–36.
Re. "Burning House of Love."

Bull, Bart. "X Marks the Spot," *Spin.* n7 (November 1985) 39–41. il.

Heiney, Conrad. "Are You X-perienced? Expansion or Exodus?," *Creem.* 19 (December 1987) 38ff.

Morris, Chris. F Stop Fitzgerald, ed. *Beyond and Back: The Story of X.* San Francisco: Last Gasp, 1983. il., disc.

Pond, Steve. "X Movie Finally Hits the Theaters," *Rolling Stone.* n477 (July 3, 1986) 17. il.
Re. *The Unseen Movie.*

Simmons, Doug. "X: In Sickness and in Health, Through

Hipness and Through Wealth," *Musician.* n64 (February 1984) 44–50. il.

Smith, M. "Altered States," *Melody Maker.* 63 (September 19, 1987) 42, 43. il., int.

Stambler, Irwin. "X," In: *The Encyclopedia of Pop, Rock and Soul.* pp. 751–754.

Williams, Joe. "X: All Grown Up and Just as Angry," *Cash Box.* LI:50 (June 18, 1988) 6–7. il., int. w/Exene Cervenka.

X-Ray Spex

Paytress, Mark. "X-Ray Spex," *Record Collector.* n123 (November 1989) 70–73. il., disc.

B. HARDCORE

General Sources

Ngaire. "What? Noise," *Melody Maker.* 66:5 (February 3, 1990) 13 il.

Zimmerman, K. "Tainted by Fascist Image, Hardcore Bands Defend Controversial Music Style," *Variety.* 333 (December 28, 1988/January 3, 1989) 35–36.

Alien Sex Fiend

Mercer, M. "Brigade," *Melody Maker.* 61 (May 31, 1986) 34–35. il., int.

Stud Brothers. "Infantile, Scatalogical and Musically Inept,"
Melody Maker. 61 (November 22, 1986) 20. il., int.

Bunchofuckingoofs

Colapinto, John. "Flash: Goofing Off," Spin. 6:3 (June 1990)
14. il., int. w/lead singer Steve Johnston.

Butthole Surfers

Heller, Phyllis. "This Butt's For You," Spin. 2 (June 1986) 82.

Kuipers, Dean. "Texas Crude," Spin. 6:4 (July 1990) 58–61,
94. il.

Paytress, Mark. "The Butthole Surfers," Record Collector. n114
(February 1989) 46–48. il., disc.

"Under-paid, Over-sexed & Over Here," Melody Maker. 61
(May 10, 1986) 10. il., int. w/G. Haynes and K. Coffee.

Christian Death

Mercer, M. "Godspell," Melody Maker. 61 (April 26, 1986)
36–37. il., int.

"News," Melody Maker. 64 (December 3, 1988) 4. il.
The band censored due to the release of a poster and
album cover depicting Christ using drugs.

Circle Jerks

Leland, J. "A Chip off the Old Punk," Musician. n90 (April
1986) 31. il.

Segal, D. "Newbeats: To Slam and Dive in L.A.," *Creem.* 18 (September 1986) 67. il.

Dead Kennedys (See also: Censorship)

Biafra, Jello. "Commentary: Don't Take Censorship Lying Down," *Billboard.* 99 (October 10, 1987) 9. il.

"Charges Against Jello Biafra Dismissed," *Cash Box.* (September 12, 1987) 5, 32.

"Dead Kennedys Poster: Harmful to Minors?," *Rolling Stone.* n478/479 (July 17/31, 1986) 27.

[Dead Kennedys Sued Over Shriner Photo], *Melody Maker.* 61 (October 18, 1986) 4.
Re. *Frankenchrist* album cover.

"Death Row," *Melody Maker.* 61 (December 20/27, 1986) 4.
HMV stores pull newspaper from albums, the Dead Kennedys pull albums from HMV.

Iorio, Paul. "Rock 'n' Roll on Trial: Jello Biafra Goes to Court," *Cash Box.* (August 15, 1987) 6, 33. int. w/L.A. deputy city attorney Michael Guarino.

Morris, Chris. "Porn Charges Leveled at Punkers' LP Poster," *Billboard.* 98 (June 14, 1986) 1, 85.
Re. *Frankenchrist.*

"News," *Melody Maker.* 63 (October 3, 1987) 4.
Jello Biafra acquitted in L.A. obscenity trial over Giger poster.

Ressner, J. "Biafra Trial Ends in Hung Jury," *Rolling Stone.* n510 (October 8, 1987) 22. il.

Simons, D. "Music: The First Porn Rock Case," *Village Voice.* 31 (July 1, 1986) 91. il.

Young, C.M. "Kennedys Bust," *Musician.* n94 (August 1986) 26. il.

Flipper

Ressner, Jeffrey. "Flipper Vocalist Dies: Will Shatter, 31, Spearheaded Bay Area Punk Scene," *Rolling Stone.* n519 (February 11, 1988) 25.

Germs

Adelson, David. "A Bit of Los Angeles History," *Cash Box.* XLIX:42 (April 5, 1986) 12. il.

Turkington, Gregg. "The Germs: Germicide," *Goldmine.* n205 (June 3, 1988) 26, 80. il.

Gwar

Gould, Lance. "Flash: Guerilla Gwarfield," *Spin.* 6:3 (June 1990) 19. il., int. w/leader Oderous Urungor.

Moho Pack

[Moho Pack Have Split], *Melody Maker.* 63 (September 26, 1987) 4.
Drummer Roberts rejoins UK Subs.

New Model Army

Lester, Paul. "New Model Army: Rolling Thunder," *Melody Maker.* 65 (August 26, 1989) 10. il., int.

"Old Model Army," *Melody Maker.* 60 (June 1, 1985) 4. il. Bassist Stuart Morrow leaves the band.

Prong

Darzin, Daina. "Attack Velocity," *Spin.* 5:12 (March 1990) 14. il., int.

Neely, Kim. "New Faces: Prong," *Rolling Stone.* n574 (March 22, 1990) 26. il., int. w/vocalist-guitarist Tommy Victor.

Stud Brothers. "Prong: Trial and Error," *Melody Maker.* 65 (January 28, 1989) 8. il., int.

UK Subs (See: Moho Pack)

Unforgiven

Cunha, Shelly da. "The Unforgiven," *Spin.* n7 (November 1985) 54–56. il.

C. THRASH

Gaye Bykers on Acid

"Bykers Ride Again; New Label Project and Album in the Pipeline," *Sounds.* (March 3, 1990) 9. il., int.

Clerk, Carol. "Dopeheads on Mopeds," *Melody Maker.* 63 (October 17, 1987) 34–36. il., int.
Re. release of new single, album, and video as well as a forthcoming feature film.

Sink

Ngaire. "Sidelines: Sink," *Melody Maker.* 66:5 (February 3, 1990) 12. il.

Spencer, Mr. "The Unholy Trinity," *Sounds.* (February 3, 1990) 17. il., int. w/Ed Shred.

Suicidal Tendencies

Myers, Caren. "Sidelines: Suicidal Tendencies," *Melody Maker.* (August 25, 1990) 9. il., int. w/singer Mike Muir.

D. OI

General Sources

Johnson, Gary. *The Story of Oi: A View from the Dead-End of the Street.* Manchester, U.K.: Babylon, 1981. il.
Survey of a genre that has come to include such practitioners as the 4 Skins, Rose Tattoo and the JJ All Stars.

Knight, Nick. *Skinhead.* London: Omnibus, 1982. il.
Photos of movement in London's East End accompanied by brief notes.

A Certain Ratio

Strange, P. "Trading Places," *Melody Maker.* 61 (March 1, 1986) 15. il., int. w/D. Johnson.

Revolting Cocks

Stud Brothers. "Revolting Cocks: Private Dicks," *Melody Maker.* 66:23 (June 9, 1990) 36–37. il., int.

E. POST-PUNK

General Sources

Carson, T. "Rock & Roll Quarterly: What We Do is Secret: Your Guide to Post-Whatever," *Village Voice.* 33 (October 18, 1988) RR21ff. il.

Gittins, Ian. "Suburban Relapse," *Melody Maker.* 63 (September 19, 1987) 48. il.

A.C. Marias

Reynolds, Simon. "A.C. Marias: Roll Up for the Magical Mystery Tourniquet," *Melody Maker.* 66:7 (February 17, 1990) 8–9. il., int. w/singer Angela Conway.

Black Flag

Chon, R. "Newbeats: Black Flag Day," *Creem.* 17 (March 1986) 76. il.

Rollins, Henry. "On the Road With Black Flag," *Spin.* 2 (April 1986) 90–95. il.

Creatures (See also: Siouxsie and the Banshees)

Rom, Ron. "Animal Magnetism," *Sounds.* (March 10, 1990) 41. il.

Sprague, David. "Sound Check: The Creatures; Travelling Light," *Me Music Express Magazine.* 14:145 (March 1990) 52. il., int.

Stud Brothers. "The Creatures: The Battle of the Sexes," *Melody Maker.* 66:8 (February 24, 1990) 14–15. il.

Currie, Cherie (See also: Runaways)

Carpenter, David. "Flash: Sobriety," *Spin.* 5:9 (December 1989) 18. il., int.

Divinyls

Altman, B. "It's Delightful, It's Delicious, It's Divinyls," *Creem.* 17 (May 1986) 38–39ff.

Bessman, Jim. "Divinyls Tone Down Their Attack," *Billboard.* 97 (December 28, 1985) 46.

Considine, J.D. "Divinyls," *Musician.* n90 (April 1986) 23–28. il.

Fall

Gittins, Ian. "The Fall; Funfair for the Common Man," *Melody Maker.* (March 3, 1990) 14–15. il.

Grant, Keith. "Control Zone: Fall Guys," *Melody Maker.* 66:7 (February 17, 1990) 46. il., int. w/Matt Black and Jonathan More.

Migaldi, R. "Newbeats: Falling into Place," *Creem.* 17 (August 1986) 69.

Paytress, Mark. "The Fall," *Record Collector.* n79 (March 1986) 26–29. il., disc.

Robb, John. "Cutting Loose," *Sounds.* (February 3, 1990) 12–13. il., int. w/Mark E. Smith.

Farm

Odell, Mike. "The Farm: It's the Rail Thing," *Melody Maker.* (August 25, 1990) 40. il., int. w/lead singer Peter Hooton.

Felt

"Independents Day," *Melody Maker.* 65 (January 7, 1989) 36. il., int. w/Lawrence.

A Flux of Pink Indians

"News," *Melody Maker.* 63 (September 26, 1987) 4.
    A three-year-old album is removed from stores for alleged obscene title.

Gang Green

Bent, Grahame. "Bud Brothers," *Sounds.* (February 24, 1990) 18. il., int.

Gittins, Ian. "Double Trouble," *Melody Maker.* 64 (December 17, 1988) 31. il., int.

Push. "Gang Green," *Melody Maker.* (March 3, 1990) 13. il.

Green on Red

DeMuir, H. "Green on Red: Out to Lunch in America," *Creem.* 18 (October 1986) 69. il.

Fricke, David. "The Underground Empire," *Rolling Stone.* n489/490 (December 18, 1986/January 1, 1987) 115–122. il.

Hogg, Brian. "Green on Red," *Record Collector.* n83 (July 1986) 50–51. il., disc.

Smith, M. "American Stars and Bars," *Melody Maker.* 60 (November 9, 1985) 16–17ff. il., int. w/Dan Stuart.

Sullivan, C. "State of the Union: Tangled Up in Green," *Melody Maker.* 60 (May 4, 1985) 14ff. il., int. w/Stuart.

Gun Club

Gittins, Ian. "Sons of the Gun," *Melody Maker.* 63 (October 10, 1987) 38. il., int. w/J.L. Pierce.
Re. *Mother Juneo.*

Morris, Chris. "Gun Club," *Musician.* n73 (November 1984) 13–14, 28. il.

Young, J. "The Gun Club Loads Up," *Creem.* 16 (April 1985) 19.

Hula

Mathur, Paul. "Life in a Northern Town," *Melody Maker.* 61 (February 8, 1986) 14. il., int.

Husker Du

Christgau, Georgia. "Music to Our Ears," *High Fidelity.* (April 1986) 62.

Dery, Mark. "Husker Du, in Their Own Way," *Creem.* 18 (June 1987) 28–30ff. il.

Fricke, David. "State of the Union: the Time Lords," *Melody Maker.* 60 (May 11, 1985) 12–13. il., int. w/Mould.

Iorio, Paul. "East Coasting," *Cash Box.* (January 31, 1987) 11. il., int.

Leland, J. "Due They Do," *Record.* 4 (February 1985) 40. il.

Mathur, Paul. "3 Angry Men," *Melody Maker.* 61 (March 22, 1986) 10–11. il., int.

Morris, Chris. "Husker Du," *Musician.* n80 (June 1985) 17–20. il.

Sullivan, C. "Husker, Guerves," *Melody Maker.* 60 (September 28, 1985) 14–15. il., int.

Tamarkin, Jeff. "Husker Du: Another New Day Rising," *Goldmine.* n172 (February 27, 1987) 81, 83.

Ward, Ed. "Down the Blue Highway With Husker Du," *Musician.* n106 (August 1987) 75–86. il.

Wheeler, Drew, and Mike Welch. "Garage Sale," *Spin.* n8 (December 1985) 22–25. il., int. w/Bob Mould.

MOULD, BOB

MacNie, Jim. "Husker Who? Bob Mould Buries His Band and Comes Up for Air," *Musician.* n128 (June 1989) 48–56. il., int.

Jesus and Mary Chain

Clerk, Carol. "Bible Bashes," *Melody Maker.* 60 (March 16, 1985) 12–13. il., int.

Cummings, Sue. "Jesus and Mary Chain," *Spin.* n7 (November 1985) 21–22. il.

Grout, Mark. "The Jesus and Mary Chain," *Record Collector.* n116 (april 1989) 72–75. il., disc.

Holdship, Bill. "The Jesus and Mary Chain: Immaculate Conception?," *Creem.* 17 (May 1986) 44–47ff. il.

Mico, Ted. "Flash: Power Discord," *Spin.* 5:9 (December 1989) 16. il., int.

Stud Brothers. "Let There be Light," *Melody Maker.* 63 (September 19, 1987) 28–30. il., int.
Re. album, *Darklands.*

Stud Brothers. "School's Out Forever," *Melody Maker.* 61 (December 13, 1986) 24–26. il., int.

Sutherland, Steve. "In Search of the Holy Grail," *Melody Maker.* 60 (November 23, 1985) 28–29. il., int. w/W. and J. Reid.

Killing Joke

Mercer, M. "Under the Volcano," *Melody Maker.* 60 (February 16, 1985) 10–11. il., int. w/Raven and Paul.

Smith, M. "Atomic Responses," *Melody Maker.* 61 (August 16, 1986) 24–25. il., int.

Leaving Trains

Morris, Chris. "Brash Promo is Based on 4-Letter Word; SST Label Sponsors Contest for Leaving Trains," *Billboard.* 99 (September 5, 1987) 38.

Lemonheads

Myers, Caren. "Lemonheads: Citrus Roots," *Melody Maker.* 66:23 (June 9, 1990) 45. il., int.

Lords of the New Church

"Lords all Change," *Melody Maker.* 61 (January 4, 1986) 3. Re. lineup shift and relocation to the U.S.

BATORS, STIV

Clerk, Carol. "The Glimmer Twins," *Melody Maker.* 60 (August 10, 1985) 16–17. il., int.

"Shrink Rap," *Melody Maker.* 60 (May 4, 1985) 16. il., int.

"Stiv Bators Dies in Paris," *Melody Maker.* 66:24 (June 16, 1990) 3. il.

Membranes

Gittins, Ian. "Suburban Relapse," *Melody Maker.* 63 (September 19, 1987) 48. il., int. w/J. Robb.

Midnight Oil

Bailie, Stuart. "Oily Green Giant," *New Musical Express.* (March 10, 1990) 10–11. il.

Fricke, David. "Rock & Roll," *Rolling Stone.* n581 (June 28, 1990) 48–57, 88. il., int.

"Midnight Oil," *Cash Box.* LI:48 (June 4, 1988) 6. il.

"News: Midnight Oil in Exxon Protest," *Melody Maker.* 66:23 (June 9, 1990) 3. il.

O'Donnell, John. "Oil Burns in the Outback," *Spin.* 6:1 (April 1990) 27–28, 145. il., int. w/lead singer Oeter Gerrett.

Strauss, D. "No More Mister Nice Guy," *Record.* 4 (July 1985) 19–21. il.

Minor Threat

Smith, K.J. "Faces: Hardcore Happiness," *Musician.* 61 (November 1983) 30ff. il.

Minutemen

McCormick, Moira. "Minutemen Short on Frills, Fuss; Method Paying Off," *Billboard.* 97 (November 2, 1985) 48ff.

Scoppa, Bud. "Wait a Minute, Men!," *Record.* 4 (February 1985) 40. il.

Primal Scream

Aston, M. "Primal Therapy," *Melody Maker.* 60 (August 17, 1985) 31. il., int. w/Bobby Gillespie.

Barron, Jack. "Bob's Full House," *New Musical Express.* (February 17, 1990) 22. il., int.

Bent, Grahame. "The Kick Inside," *Sounds.* (February 17, 1990) 14. il., int. w/Gillespie.

Downer, S. "Who Wants to be a Millionaire?," *Melody Maker.* 61 (May 31, 1986) 14. il., int.

Red Hot Chili Peppers

Cohen, Scott. "Flash: Magic Johnsons," *Spin.* 5:7 (October 1989) 14–15. il., int.

Coogan, Kevin. "The Red Hot Chili Peppers," *Cash Box.* (March 5, 1988) 10–11, 26. il., int. w/singer Anthony Kiedis.

Fantina, R. "Earthquake in Chili," *Creem.* 17 (June 1985) 18. il.

Kuipers, Dean. "Physical Graffiti," *Spin.* 5:11 (February 1990) 36–40, 84–85. il., int.

La Ban, Linda. "Red Hot Chili Peppers," *Record Collector.* n132 (August 1990) 64–66. il., disc.

Levy, Joe. "Hillel Slovak, Red Hot Chili Peppers Guitarist, Dead at 25," *Cash Box.* LII:2 (July 9, 1988) 5.

Morris, Chris. "Yogurt, Cottage Cheese, Wool Socks," *Musician.* n75 (January 1985) 16. il.

Myers, Caren. "Red Hot Chili Peppers: The Spice is Right," *Melody Maker.* 66:7 (February 17, 1990) 35. il., int.

"New Faces to Watch: Red Hot Chili Peppers," *Cash Box.* XLIX:15 (September 28, 1985) 12. il., int. w/Flea (aka Michael Balzary).

Ressner, Jeffrey. "Spice Cadets," *Rolling Stone.* n578 (May 17, 1990) 15–16. il.

Ross, Andy. "Onward and Upward," *Sounds.* (February 24, 1990) 16. il., int.

Strauss, D. "Chile [sic] Today, Hot Tamale," *Record.* 4 (December 1984) 44. il.

Trakin, Roy. "The Red Hot Chili Peppers Eat It Raw," *Musician.* n134 (December 1989) 16–18, 127. il.

Red Letters Day

Matzerath, O. "Punk Lives!," *Melody Maker.* 61 (October 25, 1986) 12. il., int.

Red Lorry Yellow Lorry

Gittins, Ian. "The Angry Brigade," *Melody Maker.* 61 (October 25, 1986) 32. il.

Weilson, J. "Newbeats: Keep on Lorrying!," *Creem.* 17 (March 1986) 76. il.

Replacements

"Aesthetic Trash," *Melody Maker.* 61 (March 8, 1986) 16. il., int. w/Paul Westerberg.

Holdship, Bill. "Drinking (and Drinking Lots More!) With the Replacements," *Creem.* 18 (September 1986) 46–49ff. il.

Holdship, Bill. "The Replacements: The Pleasure is All Yours," *Creem.* 19 (September 1987) 6–10. il.

Smith, R.J. "Swing Shift: Goin' the Church," *Village Voice.* 31 (February 18, 1986) 86.

Salem 66

Sprague, D. "Newbeats: By the Banks of the River Charles," *Creem.* 19 (October 1988) 69. il.

See No Evil

Robbins, Ira. "New Faces: See No Evil," *Rolling Stone.* n565 (November 16, 1989) 32. il., int. w/singer, songwriter and guitarist Robin Salmon.

Siouxie and the Banshees (See also: Creatures)

Goldstein, Toby. "A Match, a Flame, a Banshee Howls," *Creem.* 18 (October 1986) 40–41ff.

"Gotcher!," *Melody Maker.* 61 (November 29, 1986) 3. They become the first British band to play in post-Falklands Argentina.

"Heroes," *Melody Maker.* 64 (October 1, 1988) 36. il.

Sutherland, Sam. "Disturbing the Dust," *Melody Maker.* 60 (November 2, 1985) 14–15. il., int.

Sutherland, Sam. "Siouxie Flashback," *Melody Maker.* 61 (March 8, 1986) 27–30. il.

Sisters of Mercy (See also: Sigue Sigue Sputnik)

Denman, Paul. "The Sisters of Mercy," *Record Collector.* n99 (November 1987) 42–44. il., disc.

"Spiggy Spiggy Sputnik," *Sounds.* (February 3, 1990) 3. il.

Sutherland, Steve. "His Master's Voice," *Melody Maker.* 63 (September 5, 1987) 14–16. il., int. w/A. Eldritch.

Social Distortion

Ressner, Jeffrey. "New Faces: Social Distortion," *Rolling Stone.* n579 (May 31, 1990) 34. il., int. w/singer-songwriter-guitarist Mike Ness.

Soul Asylum

Levy, Joe. "Soul Asylum: Having Fun the Loud Way," *Cash Box.* LII:3 (July 16, 1988) 12. il., int. w/guitarist Dan Murphy.

We are Going to Eat You

Fletcher, Tony. "Flash: Appetite for Consumption," *Spin.* 5:12 (March 1990) 10–11. il.

Rockford. "Appetite for Consumption," *Sounds.* (March 3, 1990) 20. il., int.

F. INDUSTRIAL/MATERIAL MUSIC

Click Click

Seltzer, Jonathan. "Sidelines: Click Click," *Melody Maker.* 66:7 (February 17, 1990) 12. il., int. w/vocalist Adrian Smith.

Coil

Dery, Mark. "Profile: Coil: The Darker Side of Sampling," *Keyboard Magazine.* 13 (July 1987) 26. il.

Reed, T. "Muck and Brass," *Melody Maker.* 64 (June 11, 1988) 43. il., int.

Foetus, Jim/Foetus Interruptus/Scraping Foetus Off the Wheel (r.n.: Jim Thirlwell)

Arkun, Suzan. "Scraping Foetus off the Page," *Spin.* n10 (February 1986) 20–21. il.

Mico, Ted. "A Womb With a View," *Melody Maker.* 60 (September 14, 1985) 36–37. il., int.

Wilde, John. "Foetal Attraction," *Melody Maker.* 64 (October 1, 1988) 52–53.

Nine Inch Nails (r.n.: Trent Reznor)

Azerrad, Michael. "New Faces: Nine Inch Nails," *Rolling Stone.* n572 (February 22, 1990) 30. il., int. w/Trent Reznor.

Coleman, Mark. "Soul of a Pretty Hate Machine," *Musician.* n140 (June 1990) 22–24.

Reinhardt, Robin. "Flash: Black Celebration," *Spin.* 5:11 (February 1990) 11. il., int.

Nitzer Ebb

Mathur, Paul. "Body Talk," *Melody Maker.* 61 (August 9, 1986) 36. il.

Myers, Caren. "Nitzer Ebb: Style Wars," *Melody Maker.* 65 (January 28, 1989) 36. il., int.

Pink Industry

Mathur, Paul. "Pink Re-Think," *Melody Maker.* 60 (July 20, 1985) 24. il., int.

Psyche

Psyche," *Melody Maker.* 66:21 (May 26, 1990) 13. il., int. w/Carl Craig.

G. WHITE NOISE/CYBER-PUNK/POST-INDUSTRIAL
(See also: PRODUCERS)

Boo Radleys

Stanley, Bob. "The Boo Radleys: Have Mercy!," *Melody Maker.* (July 21, 1990) 36. il., int.

Dinosaur Jr.

"Dinosaur Jr. Split Again," *Melody Maker.* 66:24 (June 16, 1990) 3. il.

Reynolds, Simon. "Shock Treatment," *Melody Maker.* 63 (December 12,1987) 8. il., int.

Stubbs, D. "Apathy & Ecstasy," *Melody Maker.* 63 (October 24, 1987) 9. il.

True, Everett. "Dinosaur Jr.," *Melody Maker.* 66:21 (May 26, 1990) 14–15. il., int.

Godflesh (See: Loop)

Laibach

Bonner, S. "Righting History," *Spin.* 4 (January 1989) 14. il.

Gittins, Ian. "Laibach; Slavs Master the Scottish Play," *Melody Maker.* 66:5 (February 3, 1990) 48. il., int.

"Laibach in Anger," *Melody Maker.* 61 (July 19, 1986) 30–31. il., int.

Sonic Youth

Browne, David. "Sonic Youth," *Musician.* n125 (March 1989) 15–16, 50. il.

Davis, E. "Bring the White Noise," *Spin.* 4 (January 1989) 48–50. il., int.

DeMuir, Harold. "Sonic Youth: Go Forth and Multiply," *Melody Maker.* 66:24 (June 16, 1990) 42–43. il., int.

di Perna, Alan. "Looney Tunings: 'We're into Guitars That are Useful as Tools, Kind of Like a Hammer and Nail,' " *Guitar World.* 11:12 (December 1990) 37. il., int. w/Lee Ranaldo re. guitars used by band members.

di Perna, Alan. "Sonic Boom," *Guitar World.* 11:12 (December 1990) 31–35, 99–101. il., int. w/Ranaldo and Thurston Moore.

Eberwein, Eric. "Sonic Youth: Cranium-Cracking Noise," *Goldmine.* n185 (August 28, 1987) 77, 79. il.

Gordon, K. "Rock & Roll Quarterly: Boys are Smelly," *Village Voice.* 33 (October 18, 1988) RR20–22. il.

Greer, Jim. "Kool Things," *Spin.* 6:6 (September 1990) 41–43,
    65, 90. il.

Greer, Jim. "The Most Most Interesting Musicians of the Last
    5 Years: Sonic Youth," *Spin.* 6:1 (April 1990) 39. il.

Marnie, Jim. "Riffs: Sonic Youth," *Down Beat.* (March 1987)
    14ff. il., int. w/guitarist-vocalist Thurston Moore.

Paytress, Mark. "Sonic Youth," *Record Collector.* n115 (March
    1989) 14–18. il., disc.

Voivod

Davis, Erik. "Nineties in Effect; Long Live the New Flesh,"
    Spin. 5:11 (February 1990) 58–59. il.

H. INDUSTRIAL DANCE

Hilt (See also: Skinny Puppy)

Woods, Karen. "Shock of the New," *Cash Box.* LIII:50 (July 7,
    1990) 10. il., int. w/Cevin Key.

LeBlanc, Keith

Horkins, Tony. "Control Zone: Blanc Looks," *Melody Maker.*
    66:8 (February 24, 1990) 45. il., int.

Ministry

McCormick, Moira. "Joins the Ministry," *Creem.* 16 (May
    1985) 20. il.

Skinny Puppy (See also: Hilt)

Stubbs, D. "Slaughter and the Dogs," *Melody Maker.* 64 (October 29, 1988) 35–36. il., int. w/N. Ogre.

I. THE NEW WAVE PROPER

General Sources

International New Wave Discography, Vol. II, ed. by B. George and Martha Defoe, with Henry Beck, Nancy Breslaw and Jim Linderman. Graphics by Pam Meyer. London: Omnibus, 1982. il. Orig. pub.: *Volume: International Discography of the New Wave.* London: One Ten, 1980.

Shalett, M. "On Target: 'A Loyal Audience Takes a Ride on the New Wave'," *Billboard.* 98 (May 24, 1986) 44.

Alarm

Clerk, Carol. "Independence Day," *Melody Maker.* 60 (November 16, 1985) 13ff. il., int. w/Mike Peters.

Karr, Rick G. "The Alarm," *Stereo Review.* 55 (May 1990) 80–82. il.

McCormick, Moira. "Alarm's Sound Awakens Rebuilt IRS Wing," *Billboard.* 98 (April 5, 1986) 54.

Reinhardt, Robin. "Flash: Historic Preservation," *Spin.* 5:9 (December 1989) il., int. w/singer-songwriter Peters.

Schlosberg, K. "Nothing in Here But Alarm Clocks," *Creem.*
17 (April 1986) 10–11ff. il.

Sweeting, Adam. "Hollywood Heroes," *Melody Maker.* 61 (May
10, 1986) 33. il., int.

Sweeting, Adam. "Living in the Real World," *Melody Maker.*
60 (March 9, 1985) 10–11ff. il., int. w/Peters.

Vare, E.A. "No Shortcut to Success for the Alarm," *Billboard.*
97 (December 28, 1985) 4ff.

Big Country

"Big Country's Mark Brzezicki: No Stick in the Mud," *Creem.*
18 (December 1986) 53. il.

DeCurtis, Anthony. "Stay Alive, Stuart: Big Country Ain't
Gonna War No More," *Record.* 4 (December 1985) 12–15.
il.

Gittins, Ian. "Talk About the Passion," *Melody Maker.* 65
(January 21, 1989) 8–9. il., int. w/Stuart Adamson.

Hall, S. "Big Country Beat," *Modern Drummer.* 9 (February
1985) 14–17ff. il., int. w/Brzezicki.

Horkins, Tony. "Big Country: Songs of Innocence and Experience," *Melody Maker.* 66:21 (May 26, 1990) 40–41. il.,
int. w/Adamson.

Sutherland, Steve. "Labour of Love," *Melody Maker.* 61 (April
12, 1986) 12–13. il., int. w/Adamson.

Blancmange

"Blancmange Wobble Off (Split)," *Melody Maker.* 61 (June 14,
1986) 4.

Blondie

Blondie. Manchester, U.K.: Babylon, 1979. il. pap.
Fanzine format includes information not available else-
where.

Blondie. London: Omnibus, 1980. il. pap.

Boomtown Rats (See also: Charity; Bob Geldof)

Stone, Peter. *The Boomtown Rats: Having Their Picture Taken.*
London: Star, 1980. il. pp.
Consists primarily of photos of the band on tour.

Cars

"Cars Call It Quits," *Rolling Stone.* n521 (March 10, 1988) 19.

Iorio, Paul. "Ric Ocasek: Rock Imagist With a Fuel-Injected
Kick," *Cash Box.* (October 4, 1986) 11. il., int.

Stambler, Irwin. "The Cars," In: *The Encyclopedia of Pop, Rock
and Soul.* pp. 102–104.

"Syncro Sound Shuts Doors; Studio Owned, Operated by the
Cars," *Billboard.* 98 (December 27, 1986) 71.

EASTON, ELLIOT

"New Acts," *Variety.* 319 (May 15, 1985) 94.

Obrecht, Jas. "The Greatest Hits of Elliot Easton," *Guitar
Player.* 20 (February 1986) 14–17ff. il., bio, disc., int.

Vare, E.A. "Elliot Easton Gets into the Driver's Seat," *Billboard.* 97 (March 23, 1985) 37. int.

ORR, BENJAMIN

Tannenbaum, Rob. "Benjamin Orr," *Musician.* n101 (March 1987) 23–26, 114. il., int.

Costello, Elvis

Fricke, David. "The 'King' in America," *Melody Maker.* 61 (November 22, 1986) 9. il.
Re. his Spinning Songbook Spectacular Revue.

Jones, A. "Crown Time is Over," *Melody Maker.* 61 (March 1, 1986) 16–18. il., int.
Costello's name legally reverts to Declan MacManus.

Law, M. "Two of a Kind," *Melody Maker.* 60 (July 27, 1985) 16–17. il., int.

Morris, Chris. "Elvis is Main Attraction on U.S. Tour," *Billboard.* 98 (October 18, 1986) 23.

Stambler, Irwin. "Costello, Elvis," In: *The Encyclopedia of Pop, Rock and Soul.* pp. 146–149.

Traxler, L. "Elvis Costello's 'Cruel World' Blues," *Creem.* 16 (February 1985) 36–39ff. il., int.

Devo

Velazquez, J. "In the Beginning Was the End," *Spin.* 4 (October 1988) 41–43, il., int.

Dire Straits

"Bruce, Madonna, Straits Picked by Servicemen," *Variety.* 322 (February 26, 1986) 101.

Derringer, Liz. "Strait Talk With Mark Knopfler," *Creem.* 17 (February 1986) 3, 18–20ff. il., int.

"Dire Straits' Aussie/N.Z. Tour to be Biggest Ever 'Down Under'," *Variety.* 321 (October 30, 1985) 91.

Doershuck, Bob. "Keeping Their Cool in Dire Straits; Guy Fletcher & Alan Clark," *Keyboard Magazine.* 11 (December 1985) 46–48ff. il., int.

Lyons, Gene. "Brothers in Arms," *Newsweek.* (November 4, 1985) 81.

Robertshaw, N. "Philips CD Arm Backing Dire Straits; Multi-Million-Dollar Sponsorship for Year-Long Tour," *Billboard.* 97 (March 23, 1985) 3ff.

Dury, Ian (, and the Blockheads)

"Dury Service," *Melody Maker.* 61 (January 25, 1986) 5. Dury begins his stage and film career.

Fixx

Fissinger, L. "Phantom Squeezing With the Fixx," *Creem.* 16 (February 1985) 20–21ff. il., int. w/Jamie West-Oram.

Gett, S. "The Fixx Hopes New Album Will Break," *Billboard.* 98 (June 14, 1986) 29.

Mendelssohn, John. "Can You Fixx It, Doc?," *Record.* 4 (January 1985) 20–21.

General Public (See also: Beat; Ranking Roger)

Richardson, D.R. "The Beat Goes On: General Public in Search of Something New," *Record.* 4 (February 1985) 20–21.

Spurrier, Jeff. "A Private Conversation With General Public," *Spin.* n3 (July 1985) 26–28. il.

Haircut 100

Haircut 100: Not a Trace of Brylcreem. London: Mendura, 1982. il. pap.
A brief, slapdash account of the band's rise to stardom.

Payne, Sally. *The Haircut One Hundred Catalogue.* London: Omnibus, 1982. il. pap.
Culled from interviews conducted by the PR arm of Stiff Records.

Icicle Works

Kiley, P. "In the Deep End," *Melody Maker.* 61 (January 18, 1986) 32–33. il., int.

"Mersey Mouth," *Melody Maker.* 61 (August 9, 1986) 12. il., int. w/Ian McNabb.

Smith, M. "Bring on the Empty Horses," *Melody Maker.* 60 (June 15, 1985) 38–39ff. il., int.

Individuals

Trakin, R. "Fourth Wave Pop From Hoboken: dB's, Bongos, Individuals," *Musician.* n49 (November 1982) 42–45. il.

Japan

[Japan Founder Members Karn, Jansen and Barbieri are Working Together], *Melody Maker.* 61 (December 20/27, 1986) 4.

Pitt, Arthur A. *A Tourist's Guide to Japan.* London/New York: Proteus, 1981. il., disc. pap.

Lovich, Lene

Bergeron, Michael. "Lene Lovich, The 'Lucky Number', to Roll Through Town in Concert," *Public News.* n426 (June 27, 1990) 8. il., int.

Missing Persons (See also: Frank Zappa)

Miller, Debby. "Missing Persons Sizzle With Sex and Synthesizers," *Rolling Stone.* n393 (April 14, 1983) 55, 58–59. il.

Obrecht, Jas. "Warren Cuccurullo of Missing Persons," *Guitar Player.* 19 (February 1985) 26ff.

Sutton, Rich. "Exclusive Interview With Terry Bozzio of Missing Persons," *Song Hits.* n208 (June 1983) 18–21. il., int.

Sutton, Rich. "Missing Persons—'The Drive to '85'," *Song Hits.* n224 (October 1984) 30–32. il.

Oingo Boingo

Doerschuk, Bob, and Jeff Burger. "Danny Elfman—Plotting More High-Tech Mischief With Oingo Boingo," *Keyboard.* (Septemer 1987) 30–40. il., disc., int.

Robinson, Julius. *"Boingo Alive* Celebrates a Decade," *Cash Box.* (October 8, 1988) 10. il., int. w/Elfman.

Robinson, Julius. "Danny Elfman—Profile," *BMI.* (Fall 1988) 34–39. il.

Stambler, Irwin. "Oingo Boingo," In: *The Encyclopedia of Pop, Rock and Soul.* pp. 495–497.

Vare, E.A. "Oingo Boingo Aims for the Center," *Billboard.* 97 (August 10, 1985) 36. int. w/Elfman.

Payolas

Harrison, T. "Notes: The Payolas are Dead; Long Live the Payolas," *Canadian Musician.* 8:1 (1986) 10ff. il.

"Hot 10 Profiles: New Generation of Canadian Talent Bubbling Behind Long-Time Successes," *Billboard.* 97 (February 2, 1985) C3ff.

"Propourri," *Music Scene.* n346 (November–December 1985) 20–21.

Police (See also: Sting)

Goldsmith, Lynn. *The Police.* London: Vermillion, 1983. il. A collection of photos, many of them concert shots.

"Police Split Official," *Melody Maker.* 60 (March 30, 1985) 3.

"Police to Record New Album; Never Broke Up, Sez Copeland," *Variety.* 323 (July 16, 1986) 115–116.

Stambler, Irwin. "The Police," In: *The Encyclopedia of Pop, Rock and Soul.* pp. 530–532. il.

Pretenders

Coupe, Stuart. "The Pretenders: Packing Heat," *Melody Maker.* 66:21 (May 26, 1990) 42–43. il., int. w/Chrissie Hynde.

Flans, R. "Martin Chambers: High Energy Showman," *Modern Drummer.* 6 (July 1982) 24–27ff. il., bio, int.

Hochman, Steve. "Johnny Marr to Join Pretenders," *Rolling Stone.* n514 (December 3, 1987) 29.

"Hynde Quarters," *Melody Maker.* 61 (March 8, 1986) 4. il. Firing denied; session players to be featured on the band's forthcoming album.

Roger, S. "McDonald's Makes Hynde Eat Her Words," *Rolling Stone.* n558 (August 10, 1989) 25.

Stambler, Irwin. "Hynde, Chrissie, and the Pretenders," In: *The Encyclopedia of Pop, Rock and Soul.* pp. 303–306. il.

Shriekback

Dery, Mark. "Profile: Shriekback's Barry Andrews: Painting Landscapes, Abusing Pianos," *Keyboard Magazine.* 13 (June 1987) 18ff.

Segal, D. "Shriekback: The World's Second Best Pop Group With a Bald Singer," *Creem.* 18 (June 1987) 44–45ff. il.

Simple Minds

Barclay, Ben. "Simple Minds," *Record Collector.* n128 (April 1990) 56–59. il., disc.

Greene, Jo-Ann. "Simple Minds,"*Record Collector.* n60 (August 1984) 8–10. il., disc.

Hogg, Brian. "Simple Minds: The Early Years," *Record Collector.* n96 (August 1987) 13–16. il., disc.

Schruers, Fred. "Simple Minds: Jim Kerr Ghostdances Through a Stormy Landscape," *Musician.* n86 (December 1985) 42–48. il., int.

"Simple Minds," *Record Collector.* n83 (July 1986) pp. 19–23. il., disc.

Stambler, Irwin. "Simple Minds," In: *The Encyclopedia of Pop, Rock and Soul.* pp. 616–618.

Truman, James. "Local Heroes," *Spin.* 3:5 (August 1987) 36–41. il.

Talking Heads (See also: Tom Tom Club)

Cocks, Jay. "The Heads are Rolling," *Time.* (September 2, 1985) 64. il.

Iorio, Paul. "Talking Heads: The World's Greatest Rock Band?," *Cash Box.* (September 20, 1986) 11. il.

Moses, Mark. "Popular Music: Talking Heads '88," *New Yorker.* (June 20, 1988) 65–68.

Stambler, Irwin. "Talking Heads," In: *The Encyclopedia of Pop, Rock and Soul.* pp. 664–666. il.

"Stopped Making Cents," *Melody Maker.* 61 (November 8, 1986) 4. il.
Reports on the presence of brand-name items in the video, "Love for Sale," which has been criticized by the IBA.

BYRNE, DAVID

Bromberg, Craig. "David Byrne Puts Talking Heads on Hold for a Foray into Latin Music," *Rolling Stone.* n569 (January 11, 1990) 48–49, 66. il., int.

Cocks, Jay, and others. "Rock's Renaissance Man," *Time.* (October 27, 1986) 78–87. il.
Includes sidebar, "Divine Comedy for the '80s," about the film, *True Stories.*

Cohen, Scott. "Living Poets Society: David Byrne," *Spin.* 5:10 (January 1990) 60–61. il., int.

DeCurtis, Anthony. "The *Record* Interview: Catching Up With David Byrne," *Record.* 4 (June 1985) 12–14ff. il.

Kaplan, James. "Who is David Byrne? What is David Byrne? Does David Byrne Matter? Yes," *Esquire.* (January 1986) 80–87. il., int.

Milkowski, B. "David Byrne: Not Just Another Head Talking," *Down Beat.* 52 (October 1985) 19–21. il., bio, disc., int.

Thompson, Robert Farrio. "David Byrne: The Rolling Stone Interview," *Rolling Stone.* n524 (April 21, 1988) 42–52, 116. il., int.

FRANTZ, CHRIS

"Shrink Rap," *Melody Maker.* 60 (July 20, 1985) 39. il., int.

HARRISON, JERRY

Wilde, Jon. "Sidelines: Jerry Harrison," *Melody Maker.* 66:24 (June 16, 1990) 14. il., int.

Tears for Fears

Armbruster, G. "Tears for Fears Makes Room in *The Big Chair* for Ian Stanley's Keyboards," *Keyboard Magazine.* 11 (November 1985) 16. il.

DiMartino, Dave. "Tears for Fears," *Creem.* 16 (May 1985) 22–23ff.

FitzGerald, H. "On the Beach," *Melody Maker.* 60 (March 9, 1985) 20–21ff. il., int. w/Curt Smith.

McIlheney, B. "Songs from the Big Country," *Melody Maker.* 60 (October 19, 1985) 34–36. il., int.

Mehler, M. "No More Fears," *Record.* 4 (September 1985) 42–45. il., int.

Robbins, Ira. "Fear of Finishing," *Rolling Stone.* n565 (November 16, 1989) 21. il., int. w/Roland Orzabal.

Robbins, Ira. "Tears for Fears' American Soul Mate," *Rolling Stone.* n565 (November 16, 1989) 22. il., int. w/Oleta Adams.

"Tears for Fears to Tour," *Billboard.* 97 (March 9, 1985) 48ff.

"Tears for Sport," *Melody Maker.* 61 (May 17, 1986) 3. "Everybody Wants to Rule the World" remade and retitled "Everybody Wants to Run the World."

Wolfe, B. "Manny Elias," *Modern Drummer.* 10 (March 1986) 34–37ff. il.

Television (See also: Tom Verlaine)

Bernstein, Nils. "Television: The Blow-Up," *Goldmine.* n216 (November 4, 1988) 74–79. il.

Textones

Strauss, D. "Is It Rolling, Bob?," *Record.* 4 (January 1985) 35. il.

The The (r.n.: Matt Johnson)

Jefferson, S. "Emotional Rescue," *Melody Maker.* 61 (September 6, 1986) 22–23. il., int.

Mathur, Paul. "The Sights for Sick Souls," *Melody Maker.* 61 (December 13, 1986) 23. il., int. w/Johnson.

"Matt Attack," *Melody Maker.* 61 (May 3, 1986) 3. il. Johnson forces the release of "Sweet Bird of Truth."

Tonio K. (r.n.: Steve Krikorian)

DeSavia, Tom. "Tonio K.," *Cash Box*. (April 9, 1988) 7, 10–11. il., int. w/Krikorian.

Translator

Vare, Ethlie Ann. "Translater," *Goldmine*. n91 (December 1983) 123. il.

U2

Breskin, David. "Bono," *Rolling Stone*. n512 (November 5, 1987) 282–284. il., int.

Breskin, David. "The Rolling Stone Interview: Bono," *Rolling Stone*. n510 (October 8, 1987) 42–45ff. il., bio.

Creswell, Toby. "U2 Kicks Off Tour Down Under," *Rolling Stone*. n565 (November 16, 1989) 26. il.

Fisher, C. "Larry Mullen, Jr.," *Modern Drummer*. 9 (August 1985) 8–13ff. il., bio, int.

Gett, Steve. "One to One: Bob Catania, Island VP, Pop Promotion, Talks About U2's Big Breakthrough," *Billboard*. 99 (September 19, 1987) 24. int.

Henke, James. "The Edge: The Rolling Stone Interview," *Rolling Stone*. n521 (March 10, 1988) 50–53, 100. il., int.

King, W. "The Fire Within: An Interview With U2's Bono," *Record*. 4 (March 1985) 23–24ff. il.

Lhotsky, Tina. "The 10 Most Interesting Musicians of the Last 5 Years: U2," *Spin.* 6:1 (April 1990) 44–45. il.

"A Life in the Year of Bono," *Melody Maker.* 60 (December 21/28, 1985) 3. il., int.

Masterson, Eugene. "The Cutting Edge," *New Musical Express.* (January 27, 1990) 8. il., int. w/the Edge.

Mico, Ted. "Hating U2," *Spin.* 4 (January 1989) 34–37ff. il., int.

Neely, Kim. "In Brief: U2 Manager Slams McCartney, Who," *Rolling Stone.* n582/583 (July 12/26, 1990) 39.

Ressner, J. "Bono Less Than Boffo at Box Office," *Rolling Stone.* n543 (January 12, 1989) 16.
Re. film, *Rattle and Hum.*

Stambler, Irwin. "U2," In: *The Encyclopedia of Pop, Rock and Soul.* pp. 708–709. il.

"U2; On Location," *Rolling Stone.* n519 (February 11, 1988) 89–91. il., int. w/Bono and associates.

Verlaine, Tom (See also: Television)

Kamal, Azzar. "Control Zone: Wonderful Life," *Melody Maker.* 66:23 (June 9, 1990) 46. il., int.

Wilde, Jon. "Tom Verlaine: The Wonder Years," *Melody Maker.* 66:20 (May 19, 1990) 36–37. il., int.

Wall of Voodoo

Considine, J.D. "Wall of Voodoo: Oddballs Amok in the Melting Pot," *Musician.* n57 (July 1983) 12ff. il., int. w/Stan Ridgway.

McCormick, Moira. "Wall of Voodoo Casts a New Spell," *Billboard.* 97 (November 30, 1985) 35.

McIlheney, B. "Ghosts in the Machine," *Melody Maker.* 61 (March 29, 1986) 12. il., int.

Waterboys (See also: World Party)

DeMuir, H. "Great Scott!," *Creem.* 16 (May 1985) 18.

DiMartino, Dave. "Something About the Waterboys," *Creem.* 17 (April 1986) 8–9. il.

Henke, J. "Another Great Scott," *Rolling Stone.* n441 (February 14, 1985) 15ff. il., int. w/Mike Scott.

Jones, A. "The Incredible String Band," *Melody Maker.* 65 (January 7, 1989) 16. il., int.

"Rainbow Warriors," *Melody Maker.* 61 (June 21, 1986) 24–26. il., int. w/Scott.

Smith, M. "The Water Margin," *Melody Maker.* 60 (October 5, 1985) 26. il., int. w/Scott.

Sullivan, J. "Honesty as the Best Policy," *Record.* 4 (March 1985) 42

XTC

Stambler, Irwin. "XTC," In: *The Encyclopedia of Pop, Rock and Soul.* pp. 754–755.

Trakin, R. "The New English Art Rock," *Musician Player & Listener.* n30 (February 1981) 20ff. il.

J. ATHENS SOUND

B-52's

Azerrad, Michael. "Mission Accomplished," *Rolling Stone.* n574 (March 22, 1990) 42–49. il., int.

"Deja Vu With B-52's," *Billboard.* 101 (August 26, 1989) 38.

Dobrin, Gregory. "The B-52's: Back in Orbit and Sticking Together With 'Bouncing off the Satellites'," *Cash Box.* (November 15, 1986) 10, 22. int. w/Kate Pierson.

Puterbaugh, Parke. "B-52's' Cosmic Homecoming," *Rolling Stone.* n566 (November 30, 1989) 27. il.

Schoemer, Karen. "Beehives & Ballyhoo," *Spin.* 5:12 (March 1990) 40–44, 86–87. il., int.

Stambler, Irwin. "The B-52's," In: *The Encyclopedia of Pop, Rock and Soul.* pp. 23–25.

Stanley, B. "B-52's: Georgia on My Mind," *Melody Maker.* 65 (August 5, 1989) 38. il., int. w/Fred Schneider.

Flat Duo Jets

Schoemer, Karen. "Flash: Hellfire," *Spin.* 6:1 (April 1990) 12–13. il., int. w/leader Dexter Romweber.

Stenger, Wif. "New Focus: Flat Duo Jets," *Rolling Stone.* n574 (March 22, 1990) 27. il., int. w/drummer Crow.

Guadalcanal Diary

Aston, M. "Rage in Heaven." *Melody Maker.* 60 (October 5, 1985) 37. int.

DeCurtis, Anthony. "Back to Bataan," *Record.* 4 (May 1985) 35. il.

Fricke, David. "Big Man's Diary," *Melody Maker.* 60 (June 1, 1985) 10ff. il., int.

Let's Active

Forte, Dan. "The South Rises Again," *Guitar Player.* 19 (June 1985) 30ff. il., int. w/Mitch Easter.

Schlosberg, K. "Let's Active's Easter Parade," *Creem.* 17 (August 1985) 22–23ff. il., int. w/Easter.

Tannenbaum, Rob. "Eastern Rebellion," *Musician.* n94 (August 1986) 56–60, 89. il., int. w/Easter.

Love Tractor

Kassan, Brian. "Love Tractor Gets Serious," *Cash Box.* (March 21, 1987) 10, 24. il., int. w/guitarist Cline.

R.E.M.

Anderson, Thomas, and Peter Buck. " On the Road With Roky & Pete," *Creem.* 17 (March 1986) 46.

Arnold, Gina. "Lonely at the Top," *Buzz.* 3:3 (February 1988) 12–14. il., int. w/Peter Buck and Mike Mills.

"Critics' 1985 Choice," *Record.* 5 (January–February 1986) 32–35. il.
Re. Group of the Year.

DeCurtis, Anthony. "The Price of Victory: Confident But Confused, R.E.M. Comes all the Way Home," *Record.* 4 (July 1985) 10–12ff. il.

DeCurtis, Anthony. "The Reckonings of a Critics' Choice: Peter Buck," *Record.* 5 (January–February 1986) 36–39. il., int.

DiMartino, Dave. "R.E.M.: Into the Mainstream," *Billboard.* 99 (September 26, 1987) 25.

FitzGerald, H. "State of the Union: Tales from the Black Mountain," *Melody Maker.* 60 (April 27, 1985) 14–15. il., int. w/Michael Stipe.

Forte, Dan. "Peter Buck of R.E.M.," *Guitar Player.* 19 (January 1985) 32ff. il.

Holdship, Bill. "R.E.M.'s Rock *Reconstruction*: Getting There from Here," *Creem.* 17 (September 1985) 24–26ff. il., int.

Jones, A. "In the Heat of the Night," *Melody Maker.* 60 (June 15, 1985) 16–18ff. il., int.

Kordosh, J. "R.E.M.: Notes from Near Normaltown," *Creem.* 18 (November 1986) 6–10. il.

McCormick, Moira. "R.E.M. Clearly Has Fun on Latest I.R.S. Album," *Billboard.* 98 (August 2, 1986) 23.

McCormick, Moira. "R.E.M. Surprised by Its Success," *Billboard.* 97 (July 13, 1985) 46.

Morton, T. "Southern Accents," *Melody Maker.* 61 (September 6, 1986) 24–25. il., int. w/Stipe and Mills.

Pond, Steve. "R.E.M.: In the Real World," *Rolling Stone.* n514 (December 3, 1987) 46–55. il., int.

Smith, M. "Welcome to the Occupation," *Melody Maker.* 63 (September 12, 1987) 14–16. il., int.

Yardumian, Rob. "R.E.M. 'Documents' a New Sound," *Cash Box.* (September 12, 1987) 10–11, 32. int. w/Buck.

STIPE, MICHAEL

Bessman, Jim. "R.E.M.'s Stipe Makes Interview Clip," *Billboard.* 99 (September 19, 1987) 67.

"News: I am a Camera," *Spin.* 5:10 (January 1990) 28. il., int. w/Stipe and C-00 Film Corp. partner, Jim McKay.

"News: Stipe's Human Touch," *Melody Maker.* (July 31, 1990) 3. il., int.
Re. work on a "pro-humanity" LP.

K. GOTH ROCK

Caterwaul

Rogers, Raymond. "Sidelines: Caterwaul—Animal Crackers," *Melody Maker.* 66:20 (May 19, 1990) 14. il.

Cope, Julian (See also: Teardrop Explodes)

Bessman, Jim. "Island's Julian Cope: He's an Acquired Taste," *Billboard.* 101 (January 14, 1989) 18.

Heatley, Michael. "Julian Cope: The Exploding Saint," *Goldmine.* n177 (May 8, 1987) 18, 20. il.

Robbins, Ira. "Julian Cope," *Spin.* 3 (May 1987) 20–22. il.

Stanley, Bob. "Julian Cope: Skellingtons in the Cupboard," *Melody Maker.* 66:8 (February 24, 1990) 8–9. il., int.

Cranes

Stubbs, David. "Cranes: Welcome to the Traumadome," *Melody Maker.* (July 28, 1990) 28–29. il., int.

Crazy House

Jeske, Lee. "New Faces to Watch: Crazy House," *Cash Box.* (April 30, 1988) 7. int. w/David Luckhurst.

Cure

Azerrad, Michael. "Searching for the Cure," *Rolling Stone.* n560 (September 7, 1989) 47–50. il., int.

Bessman, Jim. "Elektra Launches New Line With Cure Clip Compilation," *Billboard.* 98 (June 7, 1986) 72.

Dery, Mark. "Lol Tolhurst: A Dose of Keyboard Fever for the Cure," *Keyboard Magazine.* 13 (August 1987) 26–27ff. il., disc.

DiMartino, Dave. "Group Says Cure Song Defames Arabs in U.S.," *Billboard*. 98 (December 13, 1986) 74. Re. "Killing an Arab."

DiMartino, Dave. "The Head on the Cure," *Creem*. 18 (December 1986) 6–10. il.

Frost, D. "Taking the Cure With Robert Smith," *Creem*. 19 (October 1987) 32–35ff. il.

Gett, Steve. "Compromise is No Cure for Quirky British Band," *Billboard*. 98 (June 28, 1986) 18.

Iorio, Paul. "Cure Song Pulled from Radio, Stickered at Retail After Arab Protest," *Cash Box*. (January 31, 1987) 5, 22.

Padgett, Stephen. "The Cure for America," *Cash Box*. (July 26, 1986) 10. il., int. w/Smith.

[Portrait], *Creem*. 19 (December 1987) 36–37.

Roberts, C. "Kissing to be Clever," *Melody Maker*. 63 (December 5, 1987) 24–26. il., int. w/Smith.

Simmons, S. "There is No Easy Cure," *Creem*. 17 (March 1986) 8–10. il.

Sutherland, Steve. "Flashback: The Cure, Those in Between Days," *Melody Maker*. 61 (February 22, 1986) 23–26. il., bio.

Sutherland, Steve. "A Suitable Case for Treatment," *Melody Maker*. 60 (August 17, 1985) 24–25ff. il., int. w/Smith.

Sutherland, Steve. "Under the Cheri Moon," *Melody Maker.* 61 (August 30, 1986) 24–26. il., int.

Dax, Danielle (, and the Lemon Kittens)

"Desperate Danielle," *Melody Maker.* 60 (November 23, 1985) 40. il., int.

Paytress, Mark. "Danielle Dax and the Lemon Kittens," *Record Collector.* n123 (November 1989) 14–18. il., disc.

Gene Loves Jezebel

Dobrin, Gregory. "New Faces to Watch: Gene Loves Jezebel," *Cash Box.* (September 27, 1986) 10. il., int.

FitzGerald, H. "Brothers in Charms," *Melody Maker.* 61 (July 5, 1986) 11. il., int.

"James Stevenson (Has Joined Full-Time)," *Melody Maker.* 60 (December 21/28, 1985) 4.

"News," *Melody Maker.* 61 (August 9, 1986) 3. Drummer Marcus Gilvear replaced by Chris Bell.

"Obscure Objects of Desire," *Melody Maker.* 61 (January 18, 1986) 30–31. il., int.

Sutherland, Steve. "Band of Gypsies," *Melody Maker.* 63 (September 19, 1987) 18–19. il., int.

"Talk Talk," *Melody Maker.* 60 (November 9, 1985) Guitarist Ian Hudson replaced by James Stevenson.

Helter Skelter

Gittins, Ian. "Sidelines: Helter Skelter," *Melody Maker*. (July 28, 1990) 12. il., int. w/singer Paul Smith.

House of Love

Collins, Andrew. "E.T., Beaty, Big and Bouncy," *New Musical Express*. (February 3, 1990) 12–14. il., int. w/Guy Chadwick.

"Guy Chadwick Regrets Squabbles," *Sounds*. (January 27, 1990) 8. il., int.

Moore, Robb. "Mansion of Glory: The House of Love Keeps the Home Fires Burning," *Cash Box*. LIII:39 (April 21, 1990) 6, 9. il., int. w/Chadwick.

Mundy, Chris. "New Faces: House of Love," *Rolling Stone*. n581 (June 28, 1990) 22. il., int. w/singer-guitarist Guy Chadwick.

James

Georgis, Z. "Salad Days," *Melody Maker*. 60 (August 3, 1985) 14–15. il., int.

Reynolds, S. "The Gentle Touch," *Melody Maker*. 61 (June 21, 1986) 10. il., int.

Jane's Addiction

Roberts, C. "Jane's Addiction," *Melody Maker*. 65 (January 21, 1989) 24. il., int. w/Perry Farrell.

Joy Division (See also: New Order)

Keeps, David. "Joy Division," In: *The British Invasion,* by Nicholar Schaffner. p. 235. il.

Love and Rockets

FitzGerald, H. "Love Will Tear Us Apart," *Melody Maker.* 61 (July 19, 1986) 32. il., int.

McIlheney, B. "From Bauhaus to Our House," *Melody Maker.* 60 (October 5, 1985) 11. il., int.

Perna, Alan di. "Love and Rockets Take Off," *Musician.* n132 (October 1989) 46–50, 92. il.

Ressner, Jeffrey. "From Bauhaus to Our House: Love and Rockets Conquer America's Pop Charts," *Rolling Stone.* n561 (September 21, 1989) 23. il., int.

Wright, C.L. "The Second Coming," *Spin.* 5 (August 1989) 30–31. il.

Monochrome Set

Aston, M. "Snakes and Ladders," *Melody Maker.* 60 (March 2, 1985) 10. int.

Morrissey (See also: Smiths)

Wright, Christian L. "The 10 Most Interesting Musicians of the Last 5 Years: Morrissey," *Spin.* 6:1 (April 1990) 50. il.

Motels

Wosahla, Steve. "Exclusive Interview With the Motels' Martha Davis," *Song Hits.* n220 (June 1984) 12–14. il.

Murphy, Peter (See also: Bauhaus)

Gittins, Ian. "Peter Murphy: The Cheek (Bones) of the Devil," *Melody Maker.* 66:20 (May 19, 1990) 35. il., int.

Kassan, Brian. "Peter Murphy: Form Still Follows Function," *Cash Box.* (April 11, 1987) 10, 25. il., int.

McCormick, Moira. "New Faces: Peter Murphy; the Former Bauhaus Frontman Builds His Solo Career With 'Deep'," *Rolling Stone.* n577 (May 3, 1990) 30. il.

Williams, Joe. "Peter Murphy: From Bauhaus to Our House," *Cash Box.* LI:48 (June 4, 1988) 6–7, 16. il., int.

Prefab Sprout

Pye, Ian. "Run Silent Run Deep," *Melody Maker.* 60 (June 1, 1985) 14–15. il., int. w/P. McAloon.

Simmons, S. "Newbeats: Prefab Sprouting All Over," *Creem.* 17 (February 1986) 75. il.

Rosetta Stone

Smith, Mat. "Sidelines: Rosetta Stone," *Melody Maker.* (July 21, 1990) 12. il., int. w/singer-guitarist Parl.

Teenage Fan Club

True, Everett. "Sidelines: Teenage Fan Club," *Melody Maker.* (October 13, 1990) 12. il., int. w/singer Norman.

That Petrol Emotion

Camerson, Keith. "Out of the Blue (into the Black)," *Sounds.* (March 10, 1990) 24–25, 31. il.

FitzGerald, H. "Pump It Up," *Melody Maker.* 60 (July 13, 1985) 31. il., int.

Frost, Deborah. "Putting Out Fire With Gasoline," *Buzz.* 3:1 (November 1987) 19. il., int. w/Sean O'Neil and Raemonn O'Gormainn.

Iorio, Paul. "New Faces to Watch: That Petrol Emotion," *Cash Box.* (August 1, 1987) 10–11. il., int. w/O'Gormainn and Damien O'Neill.

McIlheney, B. "Burning Issues," *Melody Maker.* 61 (May 10, 1986) 30–31. il., int.

Savage, J. "Emotional Rescue," *Spin.* 3 (September 1987) 19–20. 3. il., int. w/S. Mack.

Theatre of Hate

Snow, Mat. "In My Tribe," *Spin.* 5:6 (September 1989) 62–67. il., int. w/Ina Astbury and Billy Duffy.

Ultra Vivid Scene (r.n.: Kurt Ralske)

McDonnell, Evelyn. "New Faces: Ultra Vivid Scene," *Rolling Stone.* n586 (September 6, 1990) 25. il., int. w/Kurt Ralske.

"My Favorite Year," *Melody Maker.* 65 (January 7, 1989) 26. il.

Rogers, Raymond. "Flash: Ultra Glowing Groovy," *Spin.* 6:6 (September 1990) 20. il., int. w/Ralske.

Wood, Karen. "Ultra Vivid Scene: A Man, a Plan and Someday a Band," *Cash Box.* (February 18, 1989) il., int.

X-Mal Deutschland

Migaldi, R. "Merry Xmal," *Creem.* 16 (March 1985) 19. il., int.

Sullivan, C. "The Band That Came in from the Cold," *Melody Maker.* 61 (October 11, 1986) 32. il., int.

Xymox/Clan of Xymox

Balmer, M. "Hollandaise Sauce," *Melody Maker.* 60 (July 20, 1985) 18. int.

L. NEO-PSYCHEDELIA

Bessman, Jim. "S.F. Light Show Borrows Clip Technology; No Joshing, Psychedelia Returns to '80s-Era Fillmore," *Billboard.* 98 (January 25, 1986) 33–34.

Gosse, V. "Psychedelia—England's Next Big Thing?," *Musician Player & Listener.* n31 (March 1981) 38ff. il.

Passantino, R. "Riffs & Licke: When Bad Music Happens to Good People," *Village Voice.* 30 (March 5, 1985) 65–66ff.

Bangles (See also: Susanna Hoffs)

Adelson, David. "The Bangles Want to be Seen in a 'Different Light'," *Cash Box.* XLIX:34 (February 8, 1986) 11. il., int. w/Susanna Hoffs and Vicky Peterson.

"The Bangles," *Stereo Review.* (January 1987) 85–87. il., int.

Cocks, Jay, and B. Russell Leavitt. "Come On, Let's Get Banglesized!," *Time.* (April 14, 1986) 88. il., int.

Corcoran, M. "L.A. Women," *Spin.* 4 (December 1988) 5, 50–53ff. il., int.

Stambler, Irwin. "The Bangles," In: *The Encyclopedia of Pop, Rock and Soul.* pp. 32–34.

Beat Farmers

Leland, John. "The Beat Farmers: A Field Study," *Spin.* 1 (August 1985) 20, 23.

Bridewell Taxis

Lester, Paul. "Sidelines: The Bridewell Taxis," *Melody Maker.* (August 25, 1990) 9. il., int.

Chameleons (U.K.) (See also: Sun and the Moon)

Aston, M. "The Meaning of Life," *Melody Maker.* 60 (June 1, 1985) 16–17. il., int.

Gittins, Ian. "Strange Days," *Melody Maker.* 61 (October 25, 1986) 36. il., int. w/M. Burgess.

Smith, M. "The Strangers," *Melody Maker.* 61 (July 19, 1986) 11. il., int.

Chills

Aston, M. "Cool Jerks," *Melody Maker.* 61 (February 15, 1986) 26. il., int. w/M. Phillipps.

Cavanagh, David. "For Whom the Bells Toll," *Sounds.* (March 10, 1990) 20–21. il.

Reynolds, Simon. "Frost at Midnight," *Melody Maker.* 63 (October 3, 1987) 41. il., int. w/M. Phillipps.

True, E. "The Chills Have Eyes," *Melody Maker.* 64 (December 3, 1988) 44. il., int. w/Martin Phillipps.

Church

Coleman, Mark. "Keeping Faith With the Church: Australia's neo-Psychedelic Band Comes of Age," *Rolling Stone.* n526 (May 19, 1988) 16. il., int.

DiMartino, Dave. "You Must Like the Church," *Creem.* 16 (March 1985) 20–21ff. il., int.

Grule, Richard J. "Profile: Solid Gold," *Guitar World.* 11:8 (September 1990) 29–30, 106–107. il., int. w/Peter Koppes and Marty Willson-Piper.

Heatley, Michael. "The Church: Remote Luxury," *Goldmine.* n211 (August 26, 1988) 74, 78. il., disc.

Holdship, Bill. "Psychedelic Confessions and the Church," *Creem.* 17 (August 1986) 46–48ff. il.

Lake, S. "Miles of Aisles," *Melody Maker.* 60 (April 6, 1985) 10–11. il., int. w/Willson-Piper.

Myers, Caren. "The Church: Whinge of Change," *Melody Maker.* 66:20 (May 19, 1990) 45. il., int.

Perry, Steve. "The Church," *Musician.* n120 (October 1988) 18–27. il., int.

Peters, S. "Let Us Pray for the Church," *Creem.* 19 (June 1988) 14–16. il.

Smith, M. "Forever Down Underlings?," *Melody Maker.* 61 (May 31, 1986) 26. il., int.

KILBEY, STEVE

Iorio, Paul. "The Sadness That Comes After Making Love," *Cash Box.* XLIX:44 (April 19, 1986) 11. il., int. w/lead singer and songwriter Kilbey.

Mueller, Andrew. "Sidelines: Steve Kilbey," *Melody Maker.* 66:8 (February 24, 1990) 10. il.

WILLSON-PIPER, MARTY

"News," *Melody Maker.* 61 (June 21, 1986) 4. Willson-Piper departs the Church.

Woods, Karen. "You Met Him in Church: Marty Willson-Piper's Reason to the 'Rhyme'," *Cash Box.* (February 24, 1990) 7. il., int.

Doctor and the Medics

FitzGerald, H. "Christmas Crackers," *Melody Maker.* 61 (December 6, 1986) 21. il., int.

FitzGerald, H. "Medics Heads," *Melody Maker.* 60 (November 23, 1985) 37. il., int.

Needs, K. "Newbeats: The Doctor is in," *Creem.* 18 (November 1986) 68. il.

"Psychic Vacation," *Melody Maker.* 61 (July 12, 1986) 22–23. il.

Smith, M. "Operation Paisley," *Melody Maker.* 61 (May 17, 1986) 30–31. il., int. w/Doctor.

Dream Syndicate

Pond, Steve. "L.A.'s Garage Psychotics Tighten Up," *Musician.* n71 (September 1984) 32–36, 60. il., int.

Sweeting, Adam. "Reanimators," *Melody Maker.* 61 (June 14, 1986) 42–43. il., int. w/Steve Wynn.

WYNN, STEVE

Ngaire. "Sidelines: Steve Wynn," *Melody Maker.* 66:23 (June 9, 1990) 14. il., int.

Echo and the Bunnymen (See also: Teardrop Explodes)

"Bunny Rabbit," *Melody Maker.* 61 (March 15, 1986) 3. Pete de Freitas replaced by Blair Cunningham.

"Bunnymen Sleep Tonight," *Spin.* 4 (January 1989) 18. il. Spotlight on the career moves of Ian McCulloch.

Goldberg, Michael. "On the Charts: Echo and the Bunnymen," *Rolling Stone.* n514 (December 3, 1987) 20. il., int. w/McCulloch.

McCulloch, Ian. "Mac Snaps," *Melody Maker.* 61 (March 22, 1986) 4.

Mico, Ted. "Lost in America," *Melody Maker.* 63 (October 10, 1987) 30–32. il.
Tour coverage.

Mico, Ted. "Still Lost in America," *Melody Maker.* 63 (October 17, 1987) 16–17. il., int. re. tour.

Stambler, Irwin. "Echo and the Bunnymen," In: *The Encyclopedia of Pop, Rock and Soul.* pp. 207–209.

Sweeting, Adam. "Electric Horsemen," *Melody Maker.* 60 (December 14, 1985) 24–26. il., int.

Far Voyagers

McDonnell, Evelyn. "Flash: Far Voyagers," *Spin.* 5:6 (September 1989) 14. il., int.

Fuzztones

"Crutches and Crotchets," *Melody Maker.* 64 (June 18, 1988) 13. il.

Smith, M. [Interview With R. Protrudi], *Melody Maker.* 61 (November 8, 1986) 3.

Williams, Joe. "The Fuzztones vs. the World," *Cash Box.* (September 17, 1988) 26. il., int. w/singer Rudi Protrudi.

Hitchcock, Robyn (, and the Egyptians)

Cresser, Wayne. "Robyn Hitchcock: Listening to the Hitchcocks," *Goldmine.* n174 (March 27, 1987) 24, 87.

Pareles, Jon. "Robyn Hitchcock," *Musician.* n114 (April 1988) 60–67, 98. il., int.

Juncosa, Sylvia

Bent, Grahame. "No Thing Compares to Ju," *Sounds.* (February 24, 1990) 22. il.

Kaiser, Henry

Forte, Dan. "Going Against the Current . . . and Making a Living at It," *Guitar Player.* 21 (September 1987) 42–48ff. il., bio, disc., int.

Milkowski, B. "Profile," *Down Beat.* 52 (May 1985) 48–50. il., int.

Mazzy Star

McDonnell, Evelyn. "New Faces: Mazzy Star," *Rolling Stone.* n585 (August 23, 1990) 36. il., int. w/songwriter-guitarist David Loback.

True, Everett. "Mazzy Star: Ghost Riders in the Sky," *Melody Maker.* 66:23 (June 9, 1990) 10. il., int.

Mindwarp, Zodiac, and the Love Reaction

"Heroes," *Melody Maker.* 61 (October 11, 1986) 24. il
Re. Zodiac's influences.

"It's Zodiac Blindwarp," *Melody Maker.* 61 (November 29, 1986) 3. il.

"News: Records," *Melody Maker.* 65 (January 28, 1989) 4. Zodiac Mindwarp's video, "Sleazegrinder," ordered edited.

"Shrink Rap," *Melody Maker.* 61 (June 7, 1986) 16. il., int.

Smith, M. "Notes of a Young Man," *Melody Maker.* 61 (August 2, 1986) 18–19. il., int. w/Zodiac Mindwarp.

Smith, M. "The Wild Bunch," *Melody Maker.* 61 (April 26, 1986) 14–15. il., int. w/Zodiac Mindwarp.

My Bloody Valentine

Paytress, Mark. "My Bloody Valentine," *Record Collector.* n128 (April 1990) 14–17. il., disc.

Psychedelic Furs

Cavanagh, David. "Retro: All the Fun of the Furs," *Sounds.* (January 27, 1990) 14–15. il., disc.

Stambler, Irwin. "The Psychedelic Furs," In: *The Encyclopedia of Pop, Rock and Soul.* pp. 543–544.

Sutherland, Steve. "Atom Heart Brothers," *Melody Maker.* 61 (June 21, 1986) 12–13. il., int.

Sweeting, Adam. "Castles in Spain," *Melody Maker.* 61 (March 15, 1986) 9. il., int. w/Richard Butler.

Rain Parade

Aston, M. "State of the Union: Soft Parade," *Melody Maker.* 60 (May 18, 1985) 32–33. il., int.

Fricke, David. "Faces: Psychedelic Power," *Musician.* n65 (March 1984) 34. il.

Johnson, Jon. "Dropping in on the Raid Parade," *R.P.M.* n6 (July 1984) 54–55. il., disc.

Redd Kross

Fox, Randy. "Redd Kross: Psych-Glam-Metal-Pop-Trash Lives!," *Goldmine.* n218 (December 2, 1988) 32, 85. il.

Sonic Boom (See also: Loop; Spacemen 3)

Cavanagh, David. "Strange Daze," *Sounds.* (March 3, 1990) 18–19. il., int. w/Pete Kember.

"My Favorite Year," *Melody Maker.* 65 (January 7, 1989) 26. il.

Spacemen 3 (See also: Loop; Sonic Boom)

"News: Spacemen 3 Split," *Melody Maker.* 66:23 (June 9, 1990) 3.

Reynolds, Simon. "Spiritualized: Lost in Space," *Melody Maker.* 66:24 (June 16, 1990) 10. il., int.

Sun and the Moon (See also: Chameleons U.K.)

"The Sun and the Moon: It's a Partial Eclipse," *Sounds.* (February 24, 1990) 8. il.

Teardrop Explodes (See also: Julian Cope)

Cooper, Mark. *Liverpool Explodes: The Teardrop Explodes, Echo and the Bunnymen.* London: Sidgwick & Jackson, 1982. il., disc. pap.

Panter, Steven. "The Teardrop Explodes," *Record Collector.* n87 (November 1986) 42–46. il., disc.

Three O'Clock

Doerschuk, Bob. "Profile: Bringing Echoes of the '60s into the '80s With Synthesizers—Mike Mariano of the Three O'Clock," *Keyboard Magazine.* 11 (July 1985) 16ff.

Kendall, D. "The Time Lords," *Melody Maker.* 60 (August 17, 1985) 32–33. il., int.

Liveten, S. "Three O'Clock: Tocking Heads?," *Creem.* 17 (March 1986) 44. il.

Williams, Joe. "Three O'Clock and All is Well," *Cash Box.* (October 1, 1988) 11. il., int. w/singer-guitarist Michael Quercio.

Warrior Soul

Darzin, Daina. "Soul Soldiers," *Spin.* 6:1 (April 1990) 16. il., int. w/frontman Kory Clarke.

Wonder Stuff

"News: Wonder Stuff in 'Day of Conscience' Bust Up," *Melody Maker.* (June 23, 1990) 3. il., int. w/singer Miles Hunt.

M. NEW ROMANTICS/BLITZ

ABC

Baird, Jock. "ABC: Cancel Our Subscription to the Club Tropicana," *Musician.* n65 (March 1984) 42–48. il.

Farber, J. "The Agony & the ABC," *Creem.* 17 (February 1986) 37ff.

"Shrink Rap," *Melody Maker.* 61 (January 4, 1986) 11. il., int. w/Martin Fry.

Vare, E.A. " 'Masochistic' ABC 'Chasing Perfection'," *Billboard.* 97 (October 12, 1985) 52ff.

Adam and the Ants/Adam Ant (r.n.: Stuart Goddard; See also: Bow Wow Wow)

Adam and the Ants Annual. Knutsford, Cheshire, U.K.: Stafford Pemberton, 1982. il.

Ant, Adam, and Marco Pirroni, words and music. Stephen Lavers, text. *Adam and the Ants "king": The Official Adam and the Ants Song Book.* n.p., n.d. il.

Maw, James. *The Official Adam Ant Story.* London/Sydney: Futura MacDonald, 1981. il., disc.

Stambler, Irwin. "Ant, Adam," In: *The Encyclopedia of Pop, Rock and Soul.* pp. 12–15. il.

Staunton, Terry. "Not Over the Anthill Yet," *New Musical Express.* (March 30, 1990) 47. il.

Vare, E.A. "Adam Ant Makes Some Changes," *Billboard.* 97 (September 28, 1985) 47ff. int.

Vermoral, Fred. *Adam and the Ants.* London: Omnibus, 1981. il.

Welch, Chris. *Adam and the Ants.* London: Star, 1981. il., disc.

West, Mike. *Adam and the Ants.* Manchester, U.K.: Babylon, 1981. il., disc.

Arcadia (See also: Duran Duran)

Derringer, L. "And Then Came Arcadia," *Creem.* 17 (March 1986) 11–13. il.

Doerschuk, Bob. "Idylls in Arcadia: Nick Rhodes," *Keyboard Magazine.* 12 (February 1986) 70–71ff.

Gillis, K. "Arcadia: The Rest of Duran Duran," *Billboard.* 97 (October 12, 1985) 51–52.

Bow Wow Wow (See also: Adam and the Ants)

Irwin, C. "Play to Livin," *Melody Maker.* 60 (October 26, 1985) 15. il., int. w/Annabella Lu Win.

Culture Club (See also: Duran Duran)

"CBS Makes Apology to Jewish Groups for Album Cover," *Variety.* 318 (February 27, 1985) 75.

"Club Shutdown," *Melody Maker.* 61 (December 13, 1986) 4. il.
All members involved in solo projects but they deny an imminent split.

"Duran, Culture Club Worldwide Concert Gets Ax on Coast," *Variety.* 321 (November 20, 1985) 103–104.

Stambler, Irwin. "Culture Club," In: *The Encyclopedia of Pop, Rock and Soul.* pp. 158–160.

BOY GEORGE (r.n.: GEORGE O'DOWD)

"Blitzed Kids," *Melody Maker.* 61 (August 9, 1986) 3. il.
Boy George fined 250 pounds for possession of heroin.

"The Boy Can't Help It," *Melody Maker.* 61 (July 19, 1986) 3. il.
Boy George arrested for possession of heroin and enrolled in a treatment program.

"Boy George is Fined $375," *Billboard.* 98 (August 9, 1986) 86. Re. penalty for heroin possession.

"Boy George Suit Dismissed in U.S.," *Variety.* 328 (October 14, 1987) 217.

"A Comeback—by George!," *Melody Maker.* 61 (February 22, 1986) 3.

"Culture Shock," *Melody Maker.* 61 (October 18, 1986) 4. Inquest into Michael Rudetsky's overdose.

Denberg, J. "The Boy, Straight Up," *Record.* 4 (February 1985) 22–24ff. il.

"Do You Really Want to Sue Me," *Melody Maker.* 61 (November 15, 1986) 3. il.
Boy George allegedly sued by parents of the late Michael Rudetsky.

"George and the Dragon," *Melody Maker.* 61 (September 13, 1986) 3. il.
He breaks alleged promise to participate in an anti-heroin campaign.

"George Cleared," *Melody Maker.* 63 (October 10, 1987) 3.
Boy George cleared of killing Rudetsky; lawsuit dismissed by New York Supreme Court.

"George Fined, Released," *Variety.* 324 (August 6, 1986) 77.

Goldberg, M. "Mr. Clean: Boy George Straightens Up His Act," *Rolling Stone.* n510 (October 8, 1987) 87–88ff. il.

"How to Win Friends and Influence People: The George O'Dowd Way," *Melody Maker.* 60 (May 18, 1985) 6. il.

Simmons, S. "Hey There, Georgie Boy," *Creem.* 16 (April 1985) 25–27ff. il.

Duran Duran (See also: Arcadia; Culture Club; Power Station)

"Duran Mild Boy Splits," *Melody Maker.* 61 (April 26, 1986) 3. il.
Roger Taylor temporarily replaced by Steve Ferrone.

"Duran Pirate Wars," *Melody Maker.* 61 (January 4, 1986) 3. il.

"Duran to Split?," *Melody Maker.* 61 (May 17, 1986) 3.

"Duran: We're Still Here," *Melody Maker.* 60 (November 30, 1985) 4.

Hedges, D. "Wild Boys Cooling Out: Duran Duran Come Apart to Come Together," *Record.* 4 (April 1985) 15ff. il.

Iorio, Paul "Duran Duran is 'Notorious' for Going Platinum," *Cash Box.* (November 22, 1986) 11. il., int. w/Nick Rhodes.

Iorio, Paul "Duran Spin-Off Makes the Charts for Abstract Pop," *Cash Box.* XLIX:31 (January 8, 1986) 11. il., int.

Stambler, Irwin. "Duran Duran," In: *The Encyclopedia of Pop, Rock and Soul.* pp. 193–196. il.

Sullivan, Caroline. "Sidelines: Duran Duran," *Melody Maker.* (August 25, 1990) 9. il., int. w/Rhodes and John Taylor.

TAYLOR, ANDY

"Andy Taylor Quits Duran Duran to Pursue Solo Plans," *Variety.* 324 (October 8, 1986) 145ff.

Last Few Days

Reynolds, Simon. "Last Few Days: Glitterbest,' *Melody Maker.* 66:4 (January 27, 1990) 36. il., int.

Power Station (See also: Michael Des Barres; Duran Duran)

Cassata, Mary Anne. "The Power Station," *Song Hits.* n235 (September 1985) 16–17. il.

Fissinger, L. "Power Station Soars! Is There Life Beyond Duran?," *Creem.* 16 (May 1985) 24–26ff. il.

Freeman, K. "Duran Duo in Power Project," *Billboard.* 97 (February 2, 1985) 66.

Sutherland, Steve. "Reflex Action," *Melody Maker.* 60 (March 30, 1985) 30–31. il., int. w/John Taylor and Robert Palmer.

Vare, E.A. "Robert Palmer Turns off the Power," *Billboard.* 97 (November 30, 1985) 35–36.

THOMPSON, TOBY

Stern, C. "Toby Thompson," *Modern Drummer.* 9 (December 1985) 8–13ff. il., bio, int.

Woodbridge, J. "Human Beatbox," *Melody Maker.* 60 (November 2, 1985) 36–37ff. il., int.

Sigue Sigue Sputnik

Clerk, Carol, and others. "The Trial of Tony James," *Melody Maker.* 61 (July 26, 1986) 3. il., int.
Re. the cancellation of the band's British tour.

"Shrink Rap," *Melody Maker.* 60 (November 23, 1985) 17. il., int. w/Tony James.

"Sputniks: The Final Decision?," *Melody Maker.* 61 (July 19, 1986) 3.
Concerned with the question of whether or not the band is splitting.

Sutherland, Steve. "The State of Pop," *Melody Maker.* 60 (November 2, 1985) 12. il., int. w/James.

N. POWER POP

Badfinger

Puterbaugh, Parke, and others. "Where are They Now? Badfinger," *Rolling Stone.* n558 (August 10, 1989) 52. il.

Bongos (See also: Individuals)

Trakin, R. "The Beat Goes On: Bongos in the U.S.A.," *Creem.* 17 (September 1985) 18. il.

Crenshaw, Marshall

Beuttler, Bill. "Marshall Crenshaw: Rock & Roll Craftsman," *Down Beat.* (March 1986) 20–22. il., disc., int.

[Portrait], *Village Voice.* 30 (December 31, 1985) 58ff.

Crowded House (See also: Split Enz)

Isler, Scott. "The Anti-Man Cometh: Neil Finn's Crowded House Does the Australian Crawl to Stardom," *Musician.* n120 (October 1988) 56–64. il., int.

Kassan, Brian. "Crowded House: Building Pop Foundations," *Cash Box.* (April 25, 1987) 11, 31. il., int. w/Neil Finn.

Lounges, Tom. "Crowded House: The Dream is Just Beginning," *Song Hits.* n258 (August 1987) 22–24. il.

Padgett, Stephen. "New Faces to Watch: Crowded House," *Cash Box.* (September 6, 1986) 8. il., int. w/Neil Finn.

Sprague, D. "Crowded House: With Three You Get Egg Roll,"
  Creem. 19 (October 1988) 18–21. il.

dB's (See also: Individuals)

DeMuir, H. "dBunking History," *Creem.* 19 (December 1987)
  64–65ff. il.

McCormick, Moira. "The dB's Try Again" *Rolling Stone.* n514
  (December 3, 1987) 23. il.

Robbins, Ira. "dB's," *Musician.* n74 (December 1984) 21, 24,
  114. il.

Trowbridge, Susanne. "From a Rambler Six," *Buzz.* 3:2 (December 1987) 56–60. il., int. w/Peter Holsapple.

Wheeler, D. "dB or Not dB: What was the Question?," *Creem.*
  16 (January 1985) 22–23ff. il., int.

Dancing Hoods

"New Faces to Watch: The Dancing Hoods," *Cash Box.*
  XLIX:35 (February 15, 1986) 10. il., int. w/vocalist-
  guitarist Bob Bortnick.

Feelies

Wright, C. "The Feelies: The Band With the Blue Guitars,"
  Spin. 4 (January 1989) 58–59. il.

Keene, Tommy

"New Faces to Watch: Tommy Keene," *Cash Box.* XLIX:37
  (March 1, 1986) 12. il., int.

Wheeler, D. "Keene is Keen!," *Creem.* 17 (June 1985) 20. il.

Lowe, Nick

Dancis, Bruce. "Nick Lowe's Pure Pop Odyssey," *Record.* n7 (May 1982) 8–9. il., int.

Stambler, Irwin. "Lowe, Nick," In: *The Encyclopedia of Pop, Rock and Soul.* pp. 423–425.

Tamarkin, Jeff. "The Nick Lowe Interview," *Goldmine.* n73 (June 1982) 28–29. 188.

Tomashoff, Craig. "Nick Lowe: Fighting the Good Fight," *Rock Magazine.* 2 (August 1983) 30–31. il.

Merry-Go-Round

Himmelsbach, Erik. "The Merry-Go-Round: They Missed the Brass Ring," *Goldmine.* n197 (February 12, 1988) 24, 32. il.

Outfield

Bessman, Jim. "How the Outfield Became Sluggers," *Billboard.* 98 (July 26, 1986) 3ff.

Gett, Steve. "Starship Boosted by Outfield on Summer Tour," *Billboard.* 98 (October 11, 1986) 26.

Halbersberg, Elianne. "The Outfield," *Song Hits.* n251 (January 1987) 16–17. il.

"New Faces to Watch: The Outfield," *Cash Box.* XLIX:42 (April 5, 1986) 12. il., int.

"The Outfield Aim for the Chart—Tops With 'Bangin'," *Cash Box.* (July 11, 1987) 10–11. il., int. w/guitarist John Spinks and drummer Alan Jackman.

Padgett, Stephen. "The Outfield: Playing Deep, Scoring Big," *Cash Box.* (July 26, 1986) 11. il., int. w/John Spinks.

Revillos

"Fast Forward," *Melody Maker.* 60 (July 13, 1985) 4. Rocky Rhythm quits.

Rubinoos

Beeson, Frank. "The Rubinoos," *Goldmine.* n126 (May 24, 1985) 66. il., disc.

O. SKA/BLUEBEAT REVIVAL

General Sources

Miles. *The 2-Tone Book.* Perry Neville and Jimmy Egerton, book design. London: Omnibus, 1981. il.

And Why Not?

Sullivan, Caroline. "And Why Not?: Look Alive," *Melody Maker.* 66:4 (January 27, 1990) 30. il.

Beat/English Beat (See also: General Public; Ranking Roger)

Halasha, Malu. *The Beat: Twist and Crawl.* London: Eel Pie, 1981. il., disc.

Stambler, Irwin. "The English Beat," In: *The Encyclopedia of Pop, Rock and Soul.* pp. 215–216.

Campbell, Stan

Yardumian, Rob. "New Faces to Watch: Stan Campbell," *Cash Box.* (July 18, 1987) 12–13. il.

Fun Boy Three

Shand, Mary. "Fun Boy Three," *Record Collector.* n38 (October 1982) 20–25. il., disc.

Madness

Goertzel, Khaaryn. "Madness," *Goldmine.* n90 (November 1983) 58. il.

"Loony Tunes," *Melody Maker.* 61 (December 13, 1986) 3. il. Ex-members Smith, Foreman, Thompson and McPherson to form a new edition of the band.

McIlheney, Barry. "Flashback: Madness!," *Melody Maker.* 61 (March 1, 1986) 27–30. il.

McIlheney, Barry, "The Nutty Boys and the Black Stuff," *Melody Maker.* 60 (November 9, 1985) 12–13. il., int.

"News," *Melody Maker.* 61 (September 13, 1986) 3. il. Band splits.

Smith, W. "Clown Time is Over," *Melody Maker.* 61 (December 20/27, 1986) 10–11. il.
Suggs, Carl and Chris reminisce over their recordings.

Tucker, Rick. "Madness," *Record Collector.* n31 (March 1982) 48–52. il., disc.

Williams, Mark. *A Brief Case of Madness.* London: Proteus, 1982. il.

Maroon Town

Buttenweiser, Susan. "Flash: The International State of Ska; Maroon Town," *Spin.* 5:6 (September 1989) 16. il., int. w/guitarist Deaun German.

Ranking Roger (See also: English Beat; General Public)

Williams Joe. "Ranking Roger," *Cash Box.* (July 23, 1988) 11. il., int.

Toasters

Houlton, Jennifer. "Flash: The Internationa State of Ska; The Toasters," *Spin.* 5:6 (September 1989) 16. il., int.

P. TECHNO-POP/SYNTH-POP

Almond, Marc

"Blacked Marc," *Melody Maker.* 61 (November 1, 1986) 4. il. Almond protests alleged BBC1 play ban of "Ruby Red."

"A Life in the Year of Marc Almond," *Melody Maker.* 60 (December 21/28, 1985) 20. il., int.

Mico, Ted. "Flashback: Marc Almond, From Gutterheart to Willing Sinner," *Melody Maker.* 61 (February 15, 1986) 27–30. il., bio.

Mico, Ted. "Stories from the Gutter," *Melody Maker.* 60 (September 14, 1985) 16–18. il.

Berlin

Hill, Randal C. "Berlin," *Goldmine.* n244 (December 1, 1989) 12, 14. il.

Depeche Mode (See also: Erasure; Yaz)

Doerschuk, Bob. "The Wilder Side of Depeche Mode," *Keyboard Magazine.* 12 (October 1986) 66–67ff. il., int.

Fox, Marisa. "Pop a la Mode," *Spin.* 6:4 (July 1990) 52–56. il.

Giles, Jeff. "The Band Wants Your Respect. Depeche Mode May Sell Millions of Albums and Play to Capacity Crowds in Huge Football Stadiums, But These Technopop Idols Still Aren't Happy," *Rolling Stone.* n582/583 (July 12/26, 1990) 60–65. il., int.

Keeps, D. "Depeche Mode's Kinky Moods," *Creem.* 17 (July 1986) 42–43. il.

Maconie, Stuart. "Sin Machine," *New Musical Express.* (February 17, 1990) 34–35. il., int. w/Martin Gore and Alan Wilder.

Ressner, Jeffrey. "Depeche Mode," *Rolling Stone.* n577 (May 3, 1990) 25. il.

Devo

Stambler, Irwin. "Devo," In: *The Encyclopedia of Pop, Rock and Soul.* pp. 175–176.

MOTHERSBAUGH, MARK

Doerschuk, Bob, and others. "MIDI: The Human Connection," *Keyboard Magazine*. 12 (January 1986) 56ff. il., int.

Dolby, Thomas

Anderton, Craig. "Thomas Dolby," *Electronic Musician*. 2 (June 1986) 56–58ff. il., int.

Burger, J. "Profile: *Howard the Duck* Soars to the Sounds of Thomas Dolby," *Keyboard Magazine*. 12 (August 1986) 14.

DeSavia, Tom. "Thomas Dolby," *Cash Box*. (April 30, 1988) 6–7, 18. il., int.

Doerschuk, Bob. "Frenzy and Finesse Backstage at the Grammys With Wonder, Hancock, Dolby & Jones," *Keyboard Magazine*. 11 (June 1985) 10ff. il.

Doerschuk, Bob. "Thomas Dolby: Buick Eaten by Aliens—Film at Eleven," *Keyboard Magazine*. 14 (May 1988) 82–86ff. il., disc., int.

Dupler, Steve. "Thomas Dolby Keeps Diverse Company," *Billboard*. 97 (May 25, 1985) 51. int.

Peel, Mark. "Thomas Dolby," *Stereo Review*. (September 1988) 76–78. il., int.

Sullivan, C. "The Nut & the Nerd," *Melody Maker*. 60 (July 20, 1985) 12–13. il., int.

Sutherland, Sam. "Dolby Moves into Movies," *Billboard.* 98 (May 31, 1986) 20ff. int.

Vare, E.A. "Dolby in Director's Chair," *Billboard.* 98 (July 19, 1986) 61–62.
Re. *Howard the Duck.*

Dolby's Cube (See: George Clinton; Thomas Dolby)

Erasure (See also: Depeche Mode; Yaz)

Kirk, K. "Who Wants to be a Millionaire?," *Melody Maker.* 61 (May 31, 1986) 14. int.

Lester, Paul. "Sidelines: Erasure," *Melody Maker.* (July 28, 1990) 11. il.

Levy, Joe. "Erasure," *Cash Box.* (August 20, 1988) 11. il., int. w/Vince Clarke.

Leytze, D., and M. Davis. "Vince Clarke: Snyth-Pop Stalwart," *Keyboard Magazine.* 14 (April 1988) 31. il.

Neely, Kim. "Just a Little Respect," *Rolling Stone.* n576 (April 19, 1990) 28. il., int.

"New Faces to Watch: Erasure," *Cash Box.* (May 24, 1986) 12. il., int.

Reed, John. "Erasure," *Record Collector.* n125 (January 1990) 44–49. il., int.

Strange, P. "Erasureheads," *Melody Maker.* 60 (October 26, 1985) 14. il., int. w/Clarke.

Eurythmics

Irwin, D. "Thorn of Crowns," *Melody Maker.* 61 (November 22, 1986) 24–25. il., int.

"The Ministry of Truth," *Melody Maker.* 60 (May 4, 1985) 27–30. il., int.

Pepe, B. "Eurythmics: This is 1985, OK?," *Creem.* 17 (August 1985) 37–39ff. il., int.

Stambler, Irwin. "Eurythmics," In: *The Encyclopedia of Pop, Rock and Soul.* pp. 218–220.

Stojanovic, S. "On Record," *Record.* 4 (September 1985) 6–7. il., int.

Fast, Larry (aka Synergy)

Milano, D. "Preview the Upcoming Album by Larry [Synergy] Fast," *Keyboard Magazine.* 12 (August 1986) 58ff. il., soundsheet.

Foxx, John

Jenkins, M. "Control Zone: Keyboards," *Melody Maker.* 60 (October 26, 1985) 41. il., int.

Heaven 17 (See also: Human League)

Hill, Dave. "Heaven 17: Definitive Synthpop," *Musician.* n75 (January 1985) 63–64, 86, 98. il., int.

Reynolds, Simon. "H17: Paradise Postponed," *Melody Maker.* 61 (October 11, 1986) 10–11. il., int.

Horse

Mueller, Andrew. "Sidelines: Horse," *Melody Maker.* (July 21, 1990) 12. il., int. w/Horse MacDonald.

Human League (See also: Heaven 17)

Doerschuk, Bob. "Human League Takes a Crash Course in Making Hits from Jam & Lewis," *Keyboard.* (May 1985) 81, 85–89. il., int. w/Phil Oakey.

Nash, Peter. *The Human League.* London: Star, 1982. il., disc. pap.

Sutherland, Steve. "The Human Touch," *Melody Maker.* 61 (October 11, 1986) 22–23ff. il., int.

Jones, Howard (See also: Thomas Dolby)

Anderton, Craig. "Keeping Up With Howard Jones," *Electronic Musician.* 2 (March 1986) 28–32. il., int.

Bessman, Jim. "Howard Jones Single Hinges on Unusual Clip," *Billboard.* 98 (November 1, 1986) 51.
Re. "You Know I Love You . . . Don't You."

Doerschuk, Bob. "Howard Jones: Techno-Rock's Top Solo Synthesist," *Keyboard Magazine.* 11 (May 1985) 46–48ff. il.

Gett, Steve. "Jones: Things Can Only be Better on 3rd Album," *Billboard.* 98 (November 1, 1986) 22ff.

"Howard Jones," *Super Song Hits.* n49 (Winter 1987) 28–29. il.

Jackson, Richard. "Howard Jones," *Record Collector.* n69 (May 1985) 11–14. il., disc.

Kordosh, J. "Howard Jones: Words of Wisdom, Moos of Peace," *Creem.* 17 (October 1985) 28–29ff. il., int.

Young, Jon. "Howard Jones' Cock-Eyed Optimism," *Musician.* n82 (August 1985) 69–70, 106. il.

Loop (See also: Sonic Boom; Spacemen 3)

Collins, Andrew. "Spacemen-Free," *New Musical Express.* (January 27, 1990) 11–12. il., int.

King, Sam. "Extreme Noise Terrorists," *Sounds.* (February 24, 1990) 24–25. il., int.

New Order (See also: Joy Division)

Mico, Ted. "One Nation Under a Groove," *Melody Maker.* 61 (October 4, 1986) 26–27ff. il., int.

"News: Brand New Order," *Spin.* 5:12 (March 1990) 19. il.

Sweeting, Adam. "Shaming the Nation," *Melody Maker.* 61 (January 11, 1986) 24–26. il., int.

Vare, E.A. "New U.S. Deal for U.K.'s New Order," *Billboard.* 97 (June 29, 1985) 39ff.

Numan, Gary (r.n.: Gary Webb)

Coleman, Ray. *Gary Numan: An Unauthorised Biography.* London: Sidgwick & Jackson, 1982. il., disc. pap.

Jenkins, M. "Control Zone: Control Zone at Frankfurt: Two Minds Crack," *Melody Maker.* 60 (February 9, 1985) 44–45. il., int.

Trakin, R. "The New English Art Rock," *Musician Player and Listener.* n30 (February 1981) 20ff. il.

Vermorel, Fred and Judy. *Numan by Computer.* London: Omnibus, 1981. il. pap.

Octave One

"Octave One," *Melody Maker.* 66:21 (May 26, 1990) 13. il., int.

Orchestral Manoeuvres in the Dark/OMD

Dobrin, Gregory. "Orchestral Manoeuvres in the Dark: U.S. Cult Status No Longer," *Cash Box.* XLIX:17 (October 5, 1985) 13. il., int. w/co-founder Andy McCluskey.

Doerschuk, Bob. "Orchestral Manoeuvres in the Dark," *Keyboard Magazine.* 12 (March 1986) 72–74ff. il.

Keeps, D. "Odd Musical Duo," *Creem.* 17 (July 1985) 19. il., int. w/Andy McCluskey and Paul Humphreys.

McIlheney, Barry. "A Song for Europe," *Melody Maker.* 60 (June 29, 1985) 34–35.
The band's name is shortened to OMD.

Moleski, L. "OMD in the Spotlight," *Billboard.* 98 (October 11, 1986) 26.

Padgett, Stephen. "OMD Manoeuvres for U.S. Push," *Cash Box.* (August 31, 1985) 10, 38.

West, Mike. *Orchestral Manoeuvres in the Dark.* London: Omnibus, 1982. il., disc. pap.

Pritchard, Bill

Webb, Selina. "French Dressing," *Music Week.* (June 10, 1989) 16. il., int.

Solar Enemy

Oldfield, Paul. "Stone Free: Solar Enemy," *Melody Maker.* (August 25, 1990) 11. il., int. w/Ian Sharp.

Stabilizers

Dobrin, Gregory. "New Faces to Watch: The Stabilizers," *Cash Box.* (December 20, 1986) 10. il., int. w/Dave Christenson.

Thompson Twins

Dauphin, E. "Thompson Twins: Can You Spot the Replicant?," *Creem.* 17 (February 1986) 42–44ff. il.

DeCurtis, Anthony. "The Thompson Twins Aim for the Fine Line Between Art and Commerce," *Record.* 4 (October 1985) 3, 42–44. il., int.

"News," *Melody Maker.* 61 (May 3, 1986) 3. Joe Leeway has left the band.

Stambler, Irwin. "The Thompson Twins," In: *The Encyclopedia of Pop, Rock and Soul.* pp. 682–683.

"Twins No Go," *Melody Maker.* 60 (October 19, 1985) 3. Poor tickets sales kill tour.

Times

Robb, John. "Names for 1990: Sign of the Times," *Sounds.* (February 24, 1990) 54. il., int. w/Ed Ball.

Ultravox

Charlesworth, Chris. *Ultravox: In Their Own Words.* Port Chester, New York: Cherry Lane, 1984. il., int. Also pub.: London: Omnibus, 1984.

Jackson, Richard. "Ultravox," *Record Collector.* n39 (November 1982) 43–48. il., disc.

Nite, Norm N., with Charles Crespo. "Ultravox," In: *Rock On . . . (Volume 3).* pp. 376–377. disc.

Vega, Alan

Coleman, M. "Suicide Tendencies," *Melody Maker.* 60 (December 7, 1985) 25. il., int.

Myers, Caren. "Alan Vega: Forget-Me-Knots," *Melody Maker.* (July 7, 1990) 45. il., int.

Yaz

Nite, Norm N., with Charles Crespo. "Yaz," In: *Rock On . . . (Volume 3).* p. 405. disc.

MOYET, ALISON

Chin, B. "Moyet Content With 'Alf's' Notice on European Charts," *Billboard.* 97 (November 2, 1985) 48.

DeCurtis, Anthony. "What's New: The Smart Combination," *Record.* 4 (July 1985) 37. il., int.

"A Life in the Year of Alison Moyet," *Melody Maker.* 60 (December 21/28, 1985) 22. il., int.

"New on the Charts," *Billboard.* 97 (April 6, 1985) 44. Re. chart single, "Invisible."

Pead, Debbie. "Alison Moyet," *Record Collector.* n67 (March 1985) 10–13. il., disc.

Simmons, S. "Alison Moyet: Yaz, Alf & Other Three-Letter Words," *Creem.* 17 (September 1985) 37ff. il., bio, int.

Young, Jon. "Alison Moyet," *Musician.* n79 (May 1985) 17–20.

Yello

Lake, S. "Mellow Yello," *Melody Maker.* 60 (March 16, 1985) 32. int. w/D. Meier.Shelley, J. "Dream of Everything," *Melody Maker.* 61 (August 9, 1986) 22–23. il., int. w/Meier.

Yellow Magic Orchestra/Y.M.O.

Doerschuk, Bob. "The Techno-Rock Legacy of Yellow Magic Orchestra: Ryuichi Sakamoto & Haruomi Hosono," *Keyboard Magazine.* 11 (August 1985) 32–36ff. il.

Nite, Norm N., with Charles Crespo. "Yellow Magic Orchestra," In: *Rock On . . . (Volume 3).* p. 406. disc.

20. AVANT-GARDE

Anderson, Laurie

Diliberto, J., and K. Haas. "The Laurie Anderson Interview," *Electronic Musician.* 1:2 (1985) 18–19ff. il., disc.

Goodman, Fred. "A Double Dose of Laurie Anderson," *Rolling Stone.* n566 (November 30, 1989) 37. il.

Groome, C.V. "Laurie Anderson," *Ear.* 13:6 (1988) 16–19. il., int.

Passantino, Rosemary. "User Friendly," *High Fidelity.* (June 1986) 74–75, 88. il., disc.

Beefheart, Captain (r.n.: Don Van Vliet; See also: Frank Zappa)

The Lives and Times of Captain Beefheart. Manchester, U.K.: Babylon, 1979. il., disc. pap.
Fanzine-format bio comprised of press cuttings, writings, illustrations and lyrics.

Stambler, Irwin. "Captain Beefheart and the Magic Band," In: *The Encyclopedia of Pop, Rock and Soul.* pp. 96–98.

Cale, John (See also: Lou Reed; Velvet Underground)

Cohen, Scott. "Velvet Madman," *Spin.* 6:2 (May 1990) 23–30. il., bio, int.
Focuses on his collaboration with Lou Reed, *Songs for 'Drella—A Fiction.*

"Shrink Rap," *Melody Maker.* 60 (May 11, 1985) 13. il., int.

Thompson, D. "Tales of the Unexpected," *Melody Maker.* 60 (September 21, 1985) 16ff. il., int.

Domino, Ana (See also: Anne Taylor)

Mathur, Paul. "A Song for Europe," *Melody Maker.* 61 (May 31, 1986) 26. int.

Fast, Larry (aka Synergy)

Diliberto, J. "Profile," *Down Beat.* 54 (September 1987) 50ff. il.

Greenwald, T. "Think Fast," *Keyboard Magazine.* 13 (March 1987) 50–51ff. il., disc., int.

Fripp, Robert (See also: King Crimson)

Mulhern, Tom. "Frippertronics *Easter Sunday*: Fripp's Equipment," *Guitar Player.* 20 (January 1986) 90–91. il., int.

Mulhern, Tom. "On the Discipline of Craft & Art: Robert Fripp," *Guitar Player.* 20 (January 1986) 88–91ff. il., disc., int.

Obrecht, Jas. "Roland GR," *Guitar Player.* 20 (June 1986) 113ff. il., int.

Frith, Fred

Dery, M. "Notes from the Underground," *Keyboard Magazine.* 14 (July 1988) 28. il., int.

Giorno, John

Anderson, T. "Newbeats: Death Rattle 'n' Roll," *Creem.* 18 (June 1987) 67. il.

Mothers of Invention/Mothers (See also: Frank Zappa)

"Former Mothers Sue Zappa in L.A.; Charge Breach of Contract," *Variety.* 317 (January 30, 1985) 77.

Ono, Yoko (See also: John Lennon)

Bessman, Jim. "Ono Documentary Posed Audio Challenges; Sound Mixer Porath Describes Re-Tracking Adventure," *Billboard.* 97 (February 2, 1985) 39.
Re. *Yoko Ono Then and Now.*

Dauphin, E. "Yoko Ono: In & Out of the Danger Box," *Creem.* 16 (January 1985) 32–33. il., int.

Flanagan, Bill. "The Price You Pay: An Interview With Yoko Ono," *Record.* 4 (December 1984) 28–30ff. il.

Fricke, David. "Yoko Ono," *Rolling Stone.* n512 (November 5, 1987) 53–54. il., int.

Moleski, L. "Ono to Tour for First Time in 12 Years," *Billboard.* 98 (February 22, 1986) 44. il.

Penguin Cafe Orchestra

Jeske, Lee. "Penguin Cafe Orchestra Waddles Through *Malcolm*," *Cash Box.* (September 6, 1986) 34. int. w/film's writer (David Parker) and director (Nadia Tass). Relates how music from the group's first two albums came to be used in the film.

Young, Jon. "Penguin Served Here," *Creem.* 17 (July 1985) 17. il., int. w/Simon Jeffes.

Renaldo and the Loaf

"Sidelines," *Melody Maker.* 63 (September 26, 1987) 14. il., int.

Residents

Bordowitz, H. "Digital but Residential," *Hi Fi/Musical America.* 38 (August 1988) 49.

Mathur, Paul. "Eyeball [to] Eyeball," *Melody Maker.* 61 (October 25, 1986) 11. il., bio, int.

"Rock Notes: The Eyes Have It," *Me Music Express Magazine.* 14:145 (March 1990) 14. il.

Riley, Terry

La Barabara, Joan. "Terry Riley: After a Quiet Decade, a New Style Emerges," *Musical America.* (March 1986) 12–13. il.

Siberry, Jane

"New Faces to Watch: Jane Siberry," *Cash Box.* XLIX:47 (May 10, 1986) 12. il., int.

Switzer, J. "Stages and Studio: Defining the Difference," *Canadian Musician.* 10:4 (1988) 24.

Wilde, J. "Flowing Muses," *Melody Maker.* 64 (August 6, 1988) 8–9. il., int.

Woodward, Josef. "Jane Siberry's Post-Pop Populism," *Musician.* n117 (July 1988) 51–54, 128.

Velvet Underground (See also: John Cale; Lou Reed)

Goodman, Fred. "Velvet Underground Surfaces Again; Previously Unreleased Tracks Due Out This Month," *Billboard.* 97 (February 9, 1985) 6.

Stambler, Irwin. "The Velvet Underground," In: *The Encyclopedia of Pop, Rock and Soul.* p. 716.

Zappa, Frank (See also: Mothers of Invention; Censorship)

Aikin, Jim, and Bob Doerschuk. "Frank Zappa: Sample This!," *Keyboard Magazine.* 13 (February 1987) 58–74. il., disc., bibl., disc.

Alvarez, Rafael. "Frank Zappa: The Maryland Years," *Sun Magazine; The Baltimore Sun.* (October 12, 1986) 9–12. il., int.

Ash, Jennifer. "The Zappa Zoo," *Life.* 11:9 (August 1988) 73–76. il., int.
Photo scrapbook of Zappa and his immediate family.

Bamford, John. "Tinseltown Rebellion: Continuing the Story of Francis V. Zappa—Plus an Exclusive Interview; Part 2," *Hi-Fi Answers.* (November 1986) 75–79. il., disc.

Bamford, John. "Tinseltown Rebellion: The Life and Times of Francis Vincent Zappa; Part 1," *Hi-Fi Answers.* (October 1986) 73–76. il.

Bessman, Jim. "Sony's Stickering Plans Come Unglued; Zappa Calls a Halt to Warning Tags on His Release," *Billboard.* 98 (March 22, 1986) 46.
Re. *Does Humor Belong in Music?*

Forte, Dan. "Faces," *Musician Player & Listener.* n25 (June/July 1980) 30. il.

Forte, Dan. "Synclavier," *Guitar Player.* 20 (June 1986) 122ff. il.

Forte, Dan. "Zappa Zappa," *Musician Player & Listener.* n19 (July/August 1979) 34–43. il., bio, int.

Fricke, David. "Q & A: Frank Talk," *Rolling Stone.* n486 (November 6, 1986) 26. il., int.

Goodman, Fred. "Griffey, Zappa Begin Seminar on Political Note," *Billboard.* 97 (October 5, 1985) 1ff.
Re. New Music Seminar.

Iorio, Paul. "Frank Talk from Zappa on Politics and Music, Yesterday and Today," *Cash Box.* XLIX:24 (November 23, 1985) 36. il., int.

Kassan, Brian. "Frank Zappa: Still Doing It His Way," *Cash Box*. (January 24, 1987) 7, 24. il., int.

Marsh, Dave. "Sympathy for the Devil; Has the Record Industry Sold Its Soul to the Devil?," *Village Voice*. 30 (October 8, 1985) 13–19. il.

"RIAA Rep Picks Zappa to Fight Porno Bill, but It's News to Assn.," *Billboard*. 98 (March 22, 1986) 4ff.

Riordan, J. "Frank Zappa: A Study in Survival," *Musician Player & Listener*. 1:9 (1977) 30–31. il., int.

Smolen, Michael. "Zappa," *Stereo Review*. (June 1987) 93–95. il., int.

Stambler, Irwin. "Zappa, Frank," In: *The Encyclopedia of Pop, Rock and Soul*. pp. 762–764. il.

Zimmerman, K. "Rykodisc Sees to It That Zappa Isn't a Stranger to the Shelves," *Variety*. 331 (June 22, 1988) 64.

Zucchino, D. "Big Brother Meets Twisted Sister," *Rolling Stone*. n460 (November 7, 1985) 9–10ff. il.

A. ELECTRONIC MUSIC

Brucken, Claudia

Lester, Paul. "Sidelines: Claudia Brucken," *Melody Maker*. (July 21, 1990) 11. il., int.

Dali's Car

Mercer, M. "Back Seat Drivers," *Melody Maker*. 60 (January 5, 1985) 8–9. il., int.

Jarre, Jean-Michel

Aiken, Jim, and John Diliberto. "Jean-Michel Jarre: Electronic Jongleur for the Global Village," *Keyboard Magazine.* 12 (March 1986) 52–54ff. il., bio, disc., soundsheet.

Jenkins, M. "French Tickler," *Melody Maker.* 60 (January 19, 1985) 32. il., int.

Jones, Peter. "Creditors Jilted by Jarre's London Show," *Billboard.* 101 (January 28, 1989) 69.

Woodard, Josef. "Jean-Michel Jarre: Mega-Synthesist," *Musician.* n97 (November 1986) 58–62, 110–112.

Zwerin, M., and P. Crocq. "Jarre Extravaganza Planned; Houston to Get Texas-Sized Show," *Billboard.* 98 (April–May 1986) 35. Re. Rendezvous Houston.

Kraftwerk

Henschen, B. "Jazz-Rock: The Electronic Future," *Musician Player & Listener.* n13 (July–August 1978) 10–11. il.

Neon Judgement

Roberts, Chris. "Sidelines: The Neon Judgement," *Melody Maker.* (July 28, 1990) 10. il., int.

"Sidelines," *Melody Maker.* 63 (September 5, 1987) 25. il., int.

Sanity Plexus

Simpson, Dave. "Sanity Plexus," *Melody Maker.* 66:5 (February 3, 1990) 12. il.

Tangerine Dream

Diliberto, John. "Tangerine Dream: The Electronic Trinity of Space," *Down Beat*. (October 1986) 16–18, 59. il., disc., int.

DiMartino, Dave. "Tangerine Dream Label Deal Bears Fruit," *Billboard*. 100 (October 15, 1988) 23.

Roberts, Steve. "Tangerine Dream," *Record Collector*. n117 (May 1989) 71–76. il., disc.

Vangelis

Schaefer, John. "New Sounds," *Spin*. n2 (June 1985) 49.

B. EXPERIMENTAL

Cabaret Voltaire

Pye, Ian. "Alternating Cabaret," *Melody Maker*. 60 (January 12, 1985) 34–36. il., int.

Reynolds, Simon. "For Cab & Country," *Melody Maker*. 61 (July 26, 1986) 30–31. il., int.

Young, J. "Newbeat: Come to Ze Cabaret!," *Creem*. 17 (February 1986) 76.

Copeland, Stewart (See also: Police)

"Copelands Launch Anti-Cancer 'War'," *Variety*. 321 (November 13, 1985) 118.
    Re. "Guerrilla War Against Cancer" fund-raising drive.

Flans, R. "Stewart Copeland: Landing on It," *Musician*. n84 (October 1985) 84ff. il., int.

Flans, R. "Update," *Modern Drummer*. 9 (December 1985) 116.

Mieses, S. "Keynotes: Beating Around the Bush," *Record*. 4 (September 1985) 15ff. il., int.
Re. the video, *The Rhythmatist*.

"News: Hello Cleveland," *Spin*. 5:7 (October 1989) 29. il., int.

"Police Drummer," *Melody Maker*. 60 (August 17, 1985) 3.
He expands his solo career by composing soundtrack music.

Vare, E.A. "Stewart Copeland Drums Up New Genre," *Billboard*. 97 (August 10, 1985) 30. int.
Re. videocassette, *The Rhythmatist*.

Einstuerzende Weubauten

Owen, Frank. "Metal Guru," *Melody Maker*. 60 (September 14, 1985) 36–37. int. w/Blixa and Mufti.

Godley and Creme (r.n.: Kevin G. and Lol C.; See also: Charity)

Moleski, L. "Godley & Creme 'Play With Pictures'," *Billboard*. 97 (July 27, 1985) 22ff.

Sweeting, Adam. "A Tale of Two Heads," *Melody Maker*. 60 (April 27, 1985) 35. il., int.

Hugo Largo

Iorio, Paul. "New Faces to Watch: Hugo Largo," *Cash Box.* (May 2, 1987) 10. il., int. w/Tim Sommer.

Jackson, Joe

Dupler, Steve. "Album Shows Another Way to Record," *Billboard.* 98 (February 15, 1986) 42Aff. il., int. Re. album, *Big World.*

Dupler, Steve. "Joe Jackson Cuts *Big World* Direct to Two-Track Digital," *Billboard.* 98 (February 15, 1986) 42ff. il.

Iorio, Paul. "And Now For Something Completely Different from Joe Jackson," *Cash Box.* (March 28, 1987) 10, 24. int.

"Jackson's Digital Transfer Method Breaks New Ground in Pop Field," *Variety.* 322 (February 19, 1986) 429.

Milkowski, B. "Joe Jackson: Live and in the Studio," *Down Beat.* 53 (May 1986) 54–55. il., int. w/D. Kershenbaum.

Milkowski, B. "Joe Jackson's Sophisticated Pop," *Down Beat.* 53 (May 1986) 20–22. il., disc., int.

Public Image, Ltd./PiL (See also: Sex Pistols)

Bessman, Jim. "Generic Campaign Supports Lydon's Latest," *Billboard.* 98 (April 5, 1986) 20ff.

Considine, J.D. "One Man's Poison," *Buzz.* 3:3 (February 1988) 20–21. il., int.

Frith, Simon. "Britbeat: Maybe I'm Amazed," *Village Voice.* 31 (March 11, 1986) 67.

Frith, Simon. "Britbeat: Walls Came Tumbling Down," *Village Voice.* 30 (July 30, 1985) 75.

Goldstein, Toby. "A Private Hour With John Lydon's Public Image," *Creem.* 17 (August 1986) 3, 32–34ff. il., int.

Paytress, Mark. "Public Image, Ltd.," *Record Collector.* n127 (March 1990) 48–53. il., disc.

"The Primal Gown," *Melody Maker.* 61 (February 8, 1986) 11. il., int.

Thomas, David

Mico, Ted. "Unscrambling the Egg Man," *Melody Maker.* 60 (March 30, 1985) 16. il., int.

"Shrink Rap," *Melody Maker.* 61 (January 18, 1986) 11. il., int.

21. BLACK CONTEMPORARY (See also: RADIO)

General Sources

George, Nelson. "The Rhythm and the Blues: The Ballad Sound is Crossing Over Impressively," *Billboard.* 98 (April 12, 1986) 28.

Gordy, R.C. "Commentary: Black Music Gets Its Top 40 Reward," *Billboard.* (June 11, 1988) 9.

Nathan, D., and others. "The World of Black Music," *Billboard.* 100 (June 18, 1988) B1ff.

Shalett, M. "On Target: Black/Urban Crossover to AC Gains Momentum," *Billboard.* 98 (October 11, 1986) 42.

Abbott, Gregory

"Gregary Abbott," *Cash Box.* LI:47 (May 28, 1988) 6. il., int.

Jeske, Lee. "Gregory Abbott: All Dressed Up and Ready to Shake You Down," *Cash Box.* (December 13, 1986) 11, 28. il., int.

Answered Questions

Hardy, Ernest. "Answered Questions," *Cash Box.* (August 11, 1990) 6. il., int.

Atlantic Starr

McAdams, J. "Bryant Shines Without Starr," *Billboard.* 101 (August 5, 1989) 27.

"Sidelines," *Melody Maker.* 63 (August 15, 1987) 13. il., int. w/J. Lewis.

Austin, Patti

Patrick, D. "Patti Austin," *Jazz Times.* (December 1988) 23. il., int.

Bailey, Philip (See also: Earth, Wind and Fire)

George, Nelson. "The Rhythm and the Blues: A Few Words on Crossover from Someone Who Knows," *Billboard.* 98 (September 6, 1986) 23.

Baker, Anita

Chin, B. "*Rapture* Turns to Top 20 Pleasure for Anita Baker," *Billboard.* 98 (May 10, 1986) 52ff. int.

Kirk, K. "Songstress," *Melody Maker.* 61 (August 9, 1986) 10. il., bio, int.

Bell Biv DeVoe (See also: New Edition)

Henderson, Alex. "Bell Biv DeVoe: Newer Than New Edition," *Cash Box.* LIII:38 (April 14, 1990) 7. il.

Rogers, Sheila. "New Edition's New Division," *Rolling Stone.* n581 (June 28, 1990) 25. il.

Wetherbee, Peter. "Rough and Silky," *Me Music Express Magazine.* 14:148 (June 1990) 8–9. il., int.

Belle, Regina

Bloom, Steve. "The Belle of New Jersey," *Rolling Stone.* n575 (April 5, 1990) 24. il., int.

Jeske, Lee. "Regina Belle: Making It Big All by Herself," *Cash Box.* (June 13, 1987) 11. il., int.

Blu, Peggi

Jeske, Lee. "New Faces to Watch: Peggi Blu," *Cash Box.* (July 11, 1987) 10–11. il., int.

Bobby Z (See also: Prince)

Neely, Kim. "New Faces: Bobby Z," *Rolling Stone.* n571 (February 8, 1990) 21. il., int.

Brown, Bobby (See also: New Edition)

Cooper, B.M. "Paid in Fall," *Spin.* 4 (December 1988) 41–42. il.

Tannenbaum, Rob. "Bobby Brown's Uneasy Passage: Will the Jack of Swing be the Next King of Soul?," *Rolling Stone.* n560 (September 7, 1989) 68–72. il., int.

Brown, Jocelyn

"Jocelyn Brown Sues Prelude as She Exits to Warner Bros.," *Variety.* 320 (October 23, 1985) 80.

Bryant, Sharon (See: Atlantic Starr)

Bryson, Peabo

Grein, Paul. "Peabo Bryson Reaffirms His Roots," *Billboard.* 97 (July 6, 1985) 38. int.

Nite, Norm N., with Charles Crespo. "Peabo Bryson," In: *Rock On . . . (Volume 3).* pp. 46–47. disc.

Robinson, Julius. "Peabo Bryson," *Cash Box.* (April 30, 1988) 6. int.

Cameo

Bessman, Jim. "Cameo: Black Rock in the Footsteps of Hendrix," *Billboard.* 98 (November 15, 1986) 22.

Bessman, Jim. "Rybczynski's Cameo Clip Makes HDTV History," *Billboard.* (December 6, 1986) 53–54.

Grein, Paul. "Cameo Wants More Than a Token White Audience," *Billboard.* 98 (February 22, 1986) 44–45.

Cara, Irene

"Cara Slaps Coury With $12 Mil. Suit," *Variety.* 318 (March 6, 1985) 373.

"Cara Takes Legal Action Against Coury, Network," *Billboard.* 97 (June 1, 1985) 76.

"New Acts," *Variety.* 318 (April 3, 1985) 76.

Cherrelle (r.n. Cheryl Norton)

Dobrin, Gregory. "For Cherrelle, Success as a Singer Has Been a 'High Priority'," *Cash Box.* XLIX:41 (March 29, 1986) 13. il., int.

Woodbridge, J. "Cocktails for 2," *Melody Maker.* 61 (February 1, 1986) 13. il., int.

Chimes

"New Faces: The Chimes; Britain's Unlikely New Soul Trio," *Rolling Stone.* n577 (May 3, 1990) 30. il.

"Sidelines: Chimes," *Melody Maker.* 65 (August 12, 1989) 15. il.

Club Nouveau (See also: Timex Social Club)

Iorio, Paul. "Club Nouveau: Gunning for Double Platinum and Beyond," *Cash Box.* (March 14, 1987) 11. int. w/Jay King.

Kassan, Brian. "New Faces to Watch: Club Nouveau," *Cash Box.* (November 8, 1986) 10. il., int. w/Jay King.

Debarge

Chin, B. "The Heart of the *Rhythm*: Debarge's New High-Gloss Burn," *Record.* 4 (July 1985) 3, 15–17. il., int. w/El Debarge.

Croom, Troy. "Debarge: Four 'Bad Boys' Feelin' *Very* Good," *Cash Box.* (August 15, 1987) 10. int. w/manager Joe Tanous.

Doerschuk, Bob. "Keyboard Heavyweights Collaborate on Debarge's *Rhythm of the Night*," *Keyboard Magazine.* 11 (September 1985) 12.

Jackson, A. "A Plague of Stars," *Melody Maker.* 60 (June 1, 1985) 32. il., int.

Kirk, K. "Rhythm," *Melody Maker.* 61 (August 2, 1986) 9. il., int. w/El Debarge.

Weinger, H. "Debarge Gets Hit *Rhythm*; Family Act Cracks the Pop Top 10," *Billboard.* 97 (April 27, 1985) 55.

Deele

Sutton, Rich. "Exclusive Interview With the Deele," *Song Hits.* n222 (August 1984) 36–37. il.

Double Destiny

Prince, Dinah. "Street Inspirations," *New York.* (August 17, 1987) 33–37. il., int.

Family Stand

Light, Alan. "New Faces: The Family Stand," *Rolling Stone.* n585 (August 23, 1990) 36. il., int.

Fit

Robinson, Julius. "New Faces to Watch: The Fit—Nice and Tight," *Cash Box.* (April 2, 1988) 11. il., int. w/Chuck Gentry.

Force M.D.'s

Levy, Joe. "The Force M.D.'s," *Cash Box.* (March 12, 1988) 8,
    30. il., int.

Gill, Johnny (See also: New Edition)

Henderson, Alex. "Johnny Gill," *Cash Box.* LIII:40 (April 28,
    1990) 3.

Guthrie, Gwen

George, Nelson. "Club Play Opens Gwen Guthrie's *Padlock,*"
    Billboard. 97 (August 17, 1985) 58.

(Portrait), *Village Voice.* 31 (September 2, 1986) 65.

"Shrink Rap," *Melody Maker.* 61 (November 22, 1986) 31. il.,
    int.

Stubb, D. "Money Matters," *Melody Maker.* 61 (August 16,
    1986) 10–11. il., int.

Hendryx, Nona (See: Melba Moore)

Jeske, Lee. "Nona Hendryx: Still Applying 'The Heat'," *Cash
    Box.* (November 23, 1985) 12.

Holliday, Jennifer

Kirk, K. "Dreamgirl," *Melody Maker.* 60 (September 21, 1985)
    14. il., int.

Houston, Whitney

Anderson, T. "Houston's Mass Appeal is No Sin," *Billboard.* 100 (June 25, 1988) 9.

Corliss, Richard, with Elizabeth L. Bland and Elaine Dutka. "The Prom Queen of Soul," *Time.* (July 13, 1987) 58–62. il., int.

Freeman, K. "Whitney Houston's Success is Global," *Billboard.* 97 (June 8, 1985) 58.

George, Nelson. "The Rhythm and the Blues: Defenders of Whitney Come Out in Force," *Billboard.* 100 (June 11, 1988) 26.

Grein, Paul. "Chart Recap: Whitney is Top Artist," *Billboard.* 98 (December 26, 1986) 3ff.

Grein, Paul. "Jackson and Houston Achieve Rare Chart Feats," *Billboard.* 99 (September 26, 1987) 3ff.

Holden, Peter. "Houston Saves Her Talent for Debut," *Cash Box.* XLIX:27 (December 14, 1985) 11. il., int.

"Houston May Pass Lauper," *Billboard.* 98 (July 19, 1986) 71. Re. best-selling album ever in Canada by a female artist.

"New Acts," *Variety.* 318 (February 20, 1985) 81.

Robertshaw, N. "Houston Attains Global Stardom," *Billboard.* 98 (August 9, 1986) 67.

"The Young Meteors," *Saturday Review.* 11 (May–June 1985) 43. il.

Jackson, Freddie

Cutchin, Rusty. "Freddie Jackson: Quick Success is His Lady Now," *Cash Box.* XLIX:9 (August 17, 1985) 13. il., int.

Ivory, S. "Freddie Jackson Rocks the Pop Charts," *Billboard.* 97 (November 2, 1985) 47ff. int.

McGee, D. "What's New: Out of Gridlock," *Record.* 4 (August 1985) 44. il.

Vare, E.A. "Freddie's 'Naive'—But Ready for Stardom," *Billboard.* 98 (January 25, 1986) 38ff.

Woodbridge, J. "I for My Baby," *Melody Maker.* 61 (February 8, 1986) 36. il., int.

Jackson, Millie

Pye, Ian. "Sexual Healing," *Melody Maker.* 60 (April 6, 1985) 16–17. il., int.

Jamaica Boys (See also: Miles Davis; Luther Vandross)

Henderson, Alex. "New Faces: The Jamaica Boys," *Cash Box.* (May 12, 1990) 7. il., int. w/bassist-producer Marcus Miller.

Jet Set (See: Timex Social Club)

Jets

Halbersberg, Elianne. "The Jets," *Song Hits.* n251 (January 1987) 36–37. il.

Hill, Randal C. "The Jets: They've Got It All," *Goldmine.* n201 (April 8, 1988) 22, 25. il.

Jones, Oran "Juice"

Malone, Bonz. "Flash: Radio Grafitti," *Spin.* 5:12 (March 1990) 14.

Jones, Quincy

Goodman, Fred. "The Word from Friesen, Quincy Jones; Label Presidents Offer Upbeat Speeches at NARM," *Billboard.* 97 (April 13, 1985) 3ff.

Grein, Paul. "Nominated in Producer and Music Categories— Quincy Jones Up for Three Oscars," *Billboard.* 98 (February 15, 1986) 6ff.

Hewitt, Paolo. "The Mighty Quince," *New Musical Express.* (February 17, 1990) 18–19. il., int.

"Jones Tops Oscar Music Bids," *International Musician.* 84 (March 1986) 1.

"Quincy Jones Tells Record Sellers Meet to be 'Color Blind'," *Variety.* 318 (April 3, 1985) 1ff.

Stewart, Z. "The Quincy Jones Interview," *Down Beat.* 52 (April 1985) 16–19ff. il., bio, disc.

Sutherland, Sam. "Quincy Expands His Qwest," *Billboard.* 98 (May 3, 1986) 4ff.

Joneses

Drozdowski, Ted. "The Joneses," *Musician.* n136 (February 1990) 62, 66–67. il.

Junior

Levy, Joe. "Junior: Just Being Himself," *Cash Box.* LI:51 (June 25, 1988) 6–7. il., int.

Kashif (See also: Meli'sa Morgan)

Lindsey, Darryl. "Kashif's 'Positive' Career," *Cash Box.* XLIX:36 (February 22, 1986) 10. int.

Snowden, D. "Kashif: A Noted R & B Producer Goes Solo," *Keyboard Magazine.* 11 (May 1985) 29–33. il., bio, disc., int.

Knight, Gladys

Bloom, Steve. "Gladys Knight in No Man's Land; Why Can't the Veteran Singer Score With a Mainstream Audience?," *Rolling Stone.* n529 (June 30, 1988) 23.

Grein, Paul. "Knight & the Pips 'Diversify' Carefully," *Billboard.* 97 (May 18, 1985) 53ff. int.

Jeske, Lee. "Gladys Knight and the Pips: Still Hot After 35 Years," *Cash Box.* (February 13, 1988) 7, 18. il., int. w/Knight.

LaBelle, Patti (r.n. Patricia Louise Holt)

Charles, P. "Patti LaBelle: She's No R & B Singer," *Village Voice.* (February 19, 1985) 91–93.

Dobrin, Gregory. "Patti LaBelle: On a Winning Streak With 'Winner in You'," *Cash Box.* (May 24, 1986) 13. il., int.

Gooch, B. "LaBelle Appeal," *Vanity Fair.* 48 (November 1985) 114–115. il.

Hoffman, J. "Music: Backing Up is Hard to Do," *Village Voice.* 31 (March 18, 1986) 70ff.

Levert

George, Nelson. "New Sounds from a Philly Veteran," *Billboard.* 97 (March 23, 1985) 51.

Loose Ends

Holden, Peter. "Loose Ends: Tying Up the United States Market," *Cash Box.* XLIX:8 (August 10, 1985) 11. il., int.

Love, Joeski

George, Nelson. " 'Pee Wee' Record is Superduper Success," *Billboard.* 98 (May 31, 1986) 23ff.

Trebay, G. "Voice Centerfold: 'I Meant to do That," *Village Voice.* 31 (March 25, 1986) 71. il.

Marie, Teena (r.n.: Tina Marie Brockert or Mary Christine Brockner)

Fissinger, L. "Teena Marie: *Lovergirl* on Parade!," *Creem.* 17 (September 1985) 38ff. il.

Hill, Randal C. "Teena Marie: Star Light, Star Bright," *Goldmine.* n181 (July 3, 1987) 84–85. il.

Hoerburger, R. "Teena Marie Makes Chart Breakthrough; Her Legal Woes Over, Singer Clicks With *Lovergirl*," *Billboard.* 97 (March 9, 1985) 48ff.

Kirk, K. "Teena Returns," *Melody Maker.* 61 (September 6, 1986) 38. il., int.

Mehler, M. "Ike and Teena?," *Record.* 4 (May 1985) 6. il.

Mary Jane Girls (See also: Rick James)

Lounges, Tom. "The Mary Jane Girls are Funkin' Four You!," *Song Hits.* n238 (December 1985) 32–33. il.

"Mary Jane Girls Sued by Motown," *Variety.* 324 (September 17, 1986) 104.

McAlley, J. "Rock On: Mary Jane Girls Beg to Differ," *Record.* 4 (August 1985) 7. il.

Trakin, R. "The Beat Goes On: Mary Jane Girls Can't Help It," *Creem.* 17 (October 1985) 20. il., int.

McFadden and Whitehead

"McFadden and Whitehead," *Song Hits.* n165 (November 1979) 34–35. il.

McFerrin, Bobby

Jeske, Lee. "Bobby McFerrin Wants to be Alone," *Cash Box.* (September 27, 1986) 10, 32. int.

Midnight Star

Ivory, S. "Midnight Star Plans Pop Invasion," *Billboard*. 97 (January 5, 1985) 52. int. w/Reggie Calloway.

Ivory, S. "Midnight Star Shoots for Supergroup Constellation," *Billboard*. 98 (November 22, 1986) 24.

Milli Vanilli

Duffy, Tom, and Carey Fleck. "Milli Vanilli Didn't Start the Fire: Vocal Substitution Has Long History," *Billboard*. 102:49 (December 8, 1990) 4, 89.

Giles, Jeff. "Milli Vanilli: Sprechen Sie Pop?," *Rolling Stone*. n574 (March 22, 1990) 32. il.

Mills, Stephanie

Dobrin, Gregory. "Stephanie Mills Lets the Music Shine Through With 'If I Were Your Woman'," *Cash Box*. (June 6, 1987) 13, 25. il., int.

Moore, Melba

Chin, B. "Melba Takes on More Projects," *Billboard*. 98 (October 11, 1986) 30ff.

George, Nelson. "Surprise Nominations for Hendryx & Moore; Tapped for Grammys as Female Rock Vocalists," *Billboard*. 98 (February 1, 1986) 53ff. int.

Moore, M. "Commentary: Performers Should Speak Out Against Drugs," *Billboard*. 98 (September 20, 1986) 9.

Morgan, Meli'sa (See also: Kashif; Chaka Khan)

Berk, Peter, and Darryl Lindsey. "Meli'sa Morgan: Out of the Shadows and Into the Limelight," *Cash Box*. XLIX:35 (February 15, 1986) 11. il., int.

Murphy, Eddie

Berk, Peter. "For Eddie Murphy, a Singing Career is No Laughing Matter," *Cash Box*. XLIX:32 (February 15, 1986) 9, 36. il.

New Edition (See also: Bell Biv DeVoe; Bobby Brown; Johnny Gill)

Chin, B. "New Edition Hits Big Time With Little Notice," *Billboard*. 98 (May 3, 1986) 22ff.

DeCurtis, Anthony. "The New Edition of What?," *Record*. 4 (March 1985) 38–39. il.

George, Nelson. "The Rhythm and the Blues," *Billboard*. 97 (April 20, 1985) 52.

George, Nelson. "The Rhythm and the Blues: Is Age Catching Up With New Edition?," *Billboard*. 97 (November 16, 1985) 45.

Goodman, Fred. "New Edition Loses Name," *Billboard*. 97 (June 1, 1985) 53.

Goodman, Fred. "New Edition Wins Suit," *Billboard*. 98 (July 19, 1986) 88.

Ivory, S. *"Cool* New Creative Team," *Billboard.* 97 (August 17, 1985) 58ff.

"New Edition Fights Again for Name Via New Court Case," *Variety.* 319 (June 12, 1985) 75.

"New Edition Name Doesn't Belong to MCA, Rules Court," *Variety.* 319 (May 22, 1985) 87–88.

"Street Crime Erupts After New Edition Concert at Garden," *Variety.* 323 (June 11, 1986) 73–74.

Ocean, Billy

Chin, B. "Producers' Aim: Singles, Longevity," *Billboard.* 98 (May 31, 1986) 20.

"Ocean's Reign," *Melody Maker.* 60 (February 23, 1985) 5. il., int.

Woodbridge, J. "Soul Survivor," *Melody Maker.* 61 (June 7, 1986) 22. il., int.

O'Neal, Alexander

Iorio, Paul. "Alexander O'Neal's High-Flying Debut," *Cash Box.* (August 22, 1987) 10. il., int.

Parker, Ray, Jr.

FitzGerald, H. *"Sex & the Single Man,"* *Melody Maker.* 61 (January 18, 1986) 32–33. il., int.

Pebbles

Halbersberg, Elianne. "Exclusive Interview With Pebbles," *Song Hits.* n265 (October 1988) 40–41. il.

Robinson, Julius. "Pebbles," *Cash Box.* LI:49 (June 11, 1988) 6. int.

Pendergrass, Teddy (See also: Harold Melvin and the Blue Notes)

Doerschuk, Bob. "Disabilities Diminish With MIDI," *Keyboard Magazine.* 14 (July 1988) 32–33. il.

Pointer Sisters/Pointers

Hoerburger, R. "Pointers in Platinum Territory," *Billboard.* 97 (March 2, 1985) 48ff. int.

Morris, E. "Chevrolet Sets $15 Million Tour Promotion," *Billboard.* 98 (February 15, 1986) 1ff.

Ray, Goodman and Brown

Iorio, Paul. "Ray, Goodman & Brown Take It to the Limit," *Cash Box.* (December 6, 1986) 11. il., int. w/the trio.

Ready for the World

Jeske, Lee. "Ready for the World are Ready for the World," *Cash Box.* XLIX:20 (October 26, 1985) 13. il., int. w/Melvin Riley.

Richie, Lionel (See also: Commodores)

Schipper, H. "Richie Silence on Minority Hiring Causing Flap Over NAACP Honor," *Variety.* 329 (December 9, 1987) 71ff.

Royal Crescent Mob

Corcoran, Michael. "The Ohio Players," *Spin.* 5:9 (December 1989) 26. il., int. w/singer David Ellison.

Rushen, Patrice

Hill, Randal C. "Patrice Rushen: Forget Her Not," *Goldmine.* n248 (January 26, 1990) 85.

Wosahla, Steve. "Patrice Rushen," *Song Hits.* n230 (April 1985) 38–39. il.

Russell, Brenda

Robinson, Julius. "Brenda Russell," *Cash Box.* (February 13, 1988) 3, 35. il., int.

Shannon

Wosahla, Steve. "Shannon," *Song Hits.* n225 (November 1984) 60–61. il.

Slave

"Slave," *Song Hits.* n192 (February 1982) 34–35. il.

Soul II Soul

Fab Five Freddie. "Soul to Sell," *Spin.* 6:2 (May 1990) 38–42. il., int. w/Jazzie B. Introduction by Frank Owen.

Rowland, Mark. "Soul II Soul: Jazzie B Keeps on Movin'," *Musician.* n140 (June 1990) 36–42. il.

Stacey Q

Lounges, Tom. "Stacey Q Connects at Last," *Song Hits.* n259 (October 1987) 22–23. il.

Surface

Iorio, Paul. "Surface Surfaces With a Crossover Hit," *Cash Box.* (May 30, 1987) 11. il., int. w/Dave Conley.

Ivory, S. "Surface Emerges as Winning Act," *Billboard.* 99 (September 19, 1987) 29.

Terry, Tony

Jeske, Lee. "New Faces to Watch: Tony Terry," *Cash Box.* (December 5, 1987) 9. il., int.

Timex Social Club (See also: Club Nouveau)

Chin, B. "Rumors Surround Timex Social Club; Splinter Group—Jet Set—Forms," *Billboard.* 98 (July 12, 1986) 24.

Goodman, Fred. "A Hit Single on a Shoestring; Jay King Produced Timex's 'Rumors'," *Billboard.* 98 (August 23, 1986) 79ff.

Turner, Tina

Albertson, Chris. "*Stereo Review* Salutes Tina Turner," *Stereo Review.* 50 (October 1985) 59–61. il.

Cohen, Scott. "The Legacy of Tina Turner," *Spin.* 5:10 (January 1990) 56–59. il., int.

Coleman, M. "Random Notes: Tina Returns; With New LP, She's on Her Own But Not Alone," *Rolling Stone.* n480 (August 14, 1986) 6. il.

Collins, N. "The Rolling Stone Interview: Tina Turner," *Rolling Stone.* n485 (October 23, 1986) 46–47ff.

Dobrin, Gregory. "A Rocker With Black Music Roots, Tina Turner Rides High With a New 'Earthiness'," *Cash Box.* (February 28, 1987) 11, 34. il., bio.

Freeman, K. "Southern Black Outlets Boycott Tina," *Billboard.* 97 (November 30, 1985) 12ff.

Grein, Paul. "Pepsi Backing Tina's Tour," *Billboard.* 97 (May 18, 1985) 41.

Jeske, Lee. "Tina Turner," *BMI.* n1 (1985) 20–21. il.

Mehler, M. "I'm Naughty, I'm Raunchy, I'm Rough," *Record.* 4 (December 1984) 17–18ff. il., bio.

Mehler, M. "On Record: 'I Stand Here Alone'," *Record.* 4 (October 1985) 14. il.

Norment, Lynn. "Tina Turner: Simple, Sassy and Going Strong," *Ebony.* (June 1982) 66–70. il., int.

Vandross, Luther

Dobrin, Gregory. "A Broadening Audience Discovers the Luther Vandross Platinum Touch," *Cash Box.* (November 29, 1986) 11, 22. il., int.

Dobrin, Gregory. "Luther Vandross and Gregory Hines: A Winning Combination," *Cash Box.* (March 21, 1987) 11, 27. il., int.

George, Nelson. "The Rhythm and the Blues: Vandross Deserves 'Superstar' Status," *Billboard.* 100 (October 22, 1988) 27.

Himes, G. "Luther Vandross: a R & B Reconciliation of Disco-Tech and Soul-Era Emotion," *Musician.* n50 (December 1982) 28ff. il., bio, int.

Jackson, A. "Big Baaad Boy," *Melody Maker.* 60 (May 18, 1985) 16. il., int.

Kirk, K. "Ladies' Man," *Melody Maker.* 61 (November 1, 1986) 10. il., int.

"News," *Melody Maker.* 61 (January 25, 1986) 4. He is involved in a fatal auto accident.

Ritz, David. "State of Luxe," *Rolling Stone.* (September 6, 1990) 74–81. il., int.

Vanity

"Starspot: Carl Weathers and Vanity," *Video Review.* (August 1988) 15. il., int.

Warwick, Dionne

"Suit Seeking Ouster of Warwick on *Gold*," *Variety.* 320 (August 14, 1985) 48.

Watley, Jody

Padgett, Stephen. "Jody Watley is for Real!," *Cash Box.* (June 20, 1987) 7. il., int.

White, Karyn

Johnson, Belma. "Karyn White: What Warner Bros. Must Do to Make Her a Superstar," *Cash Box.* (November 12, 1988) 8–9. il.

Wilson, Shanice

DeSavia, Tom. "Shanice Wilson," *Cash Box.* (September 5, 1987) 10, 32. il., int. w/Wilson and A & M VP John McClain.

A. GO-GO

General Sources

George, Nelson. "Go-Go Music Ready to go Global," *Billboard.* 97 (March 9, 1985) 65.

George, Nelson. "The Rhythm and the Blues: Washington Industryites Say Go-Go's Hot," *Billboard.* 99 (October 17, 1987) 25.

Brown, Chuck

Pye, Ian. "Pavement and Penitentiary," *Melody Maker.* 60 (June 29, 1985) 36–37. il., int.

Trouble Funk

George, Nelson. "D.C. Go-Go Fizzles, But Trouble Funk Survives," *Billboard.* 99 (October 3, 1987) 30.

"How Far Can Go-Go-Go?," *Musician.* n94 (August 1986) 26. il.Reynolds, Simon. "Crucial Brew," *Melody Maker.* 61 (August 2, 1986) 10–11. il., int.

"Two Go-Go Acts Honored in D.C.," *Billboard.* 97 (October 26, 1985) 53ff.
Re. Washington Area Music Awards.

B. RAP/HIP HOP

General Sources

Adler, Jerry, with Jennifer Foote and Ray Sawhill. "The Rap Attitude," *Newsweek.* (May 19, 1990) 56–59. il.
Includes lyric quotes and the sidebar, "Rating Rap's Top 10."

Allen, H. "Electromag: Invisible Band," *Village Voice.* 33 (October 25, 1988) E10–11.
Re. hip-hop and electronics.

"Anti-Midas Thrust," *Melody Maker.* 65 (January 14, 1989) 16.

Birnbaum, L. "Hip Hop—a Schoolboy's Primer," *Ear, Magazine of New Music.* 13:2 (1988) 6–7. il.

Bruno, V. "Commentary: Rap: A Positive Force for Social Change," *Billboard.* 98 (November 8, 1986) 9.

Cohen, D.S., and J. Eilertsen. "Folklore and Folklife in a Juvenile Corrections Institution," *Western Folklore.* 44:1 (1985) 16–19.

Coleman, Bill. "Female Rappers Give Males Run for the Money," *Billboard.* 100:21 (May 21, 1988) 1, 29.

"Draggin' the Line," *Rock & Roll Confidential.* n63 (December 1988) 7–8.
Rap blamed for crime.

Ford, Glen. "Guest Commentary: Rap Demographics: Not as Young as You Think," *Cash Box.* (July 23, 1988) 19.

Frith, Simon. "Britbeat: Police & Thieves," *Village Voice.* 33 (June 14, 1988) 81.
Hip-hop culture blamed for U.K. crime.

Gates, David, and others. "Decoding Rap Music," *Newsweek.* (March 19, 1990) 60–63. il.
Includes quotes drawn from rap lyrics.

George, Nelson. "The Rhythm and the Blues: Corporate Black Music Has Its Raw Edges Rubbed Off," *Billboard.* 98 (July 26, 1986) 23.

George, Nelson. "The Rhythm and the Blues: Hip-Hop Keeps Hopping Via Records, Concerts, Film," *Billboard.* 97 (September 7, 1985) 46.

George, Nelson. "The Rhythm and the Blues: News Show Notes Rap's Role in Shaping Black Attitude," *Billboard.* 98 (February 8, 1986) 56.

George, Nelson. "The Rhythm and the Blues: Stop the Violence to Repair Rap's Bad Rep," *Billboard.* 100 (October 29, 1988) 26.

George, Nelson, and B. Haring. "Insurer Cancels Coverage for Promoter of Rap Show," *Billboard.* 100 (December 24, 1988) 6ff.

George, Nelson, and others. *Fresh: Hip Hop Don't Stop.* New York: Random House, 1985. il. pap.

Hager, S. "Herculords at the Hevalo," *Record.* 4 (February 1985) 32–37.
Excerpt from the book, *Hip Hop: The Illustrated History of Break Dancing, Rap Music, and Graffiti,* by Hager.

Hager, S. *Hip Hop: The Illustrated History of Break Dancing, Rap Music, and Graffiti.* New York: St. Martin's, 1984. il. pap.

Horne, E. "Commentary: Rap Talk: Here Today, Gone Tomorrow," *Billboard.* 99 (September 5, 1987) 9.
A street lexicon.

Iorio, Paul. "The State of Rap 1987," *Cash Box.* (February 28, 1987) 30. il.

Levy, Joe, and Tom DeSavia. "Rap: A Major Topic," *Cash Box.* LI:47 (May 28, 1988) 14.

Long, Bob, and Joe Williams. "Rap: The Executives Speak," *Cash Box.* LI:47 (May 28, 1988) 14, 16, 20–21. int.

Lorrell, Elyse. "Why Parents Don't Like Rap," *Serious Hip Hop.* 1:4 (May–June 1990) 15. il.

Mack, Bob. "Hip-Hop Map of *America,*" *Spin.* 6:3 (June 1990) 36–37. map w/labels.

Nathan, D., and others. "Spotlight: Rap," *Billboard.* 100 (December 24, 1988) R1ff. il.

Nelson, H. "Label's Rap Commitment is No Jive," *Billboard.* 100 (June 25, 1988) 24.

Olson, Y. "As Rap Goes Pop, Some Say Black Radio is Missing Out," *Billboard.* 100 (June 18, 1988) 1ff.

Owen, Frank. "Freshers' Ball," *Melody Maker.* 61 (July 19, 1986) 24–25. il. An analysis of the genre.

Owen, Frank. "Hip Hop Bebop," *Spin.* 4 (October 1988) 60–61ff.

Peaslee, D. "Rappers Spur James Brown Revival," *Billboard.* 99 (September 12, 1987) 29.

Rahsaan, Anthony. "Rap Music and Stereotypes," *Cash Box.* LII:1 (July 2, 1988) 18.

"Rap: A Glossary," *Cash Box.* LI:47 (May 28, 1988) 3.

Reynolds, Simon. "Nasty Day," *Melody Maker.* 61 (July 19, 1986) 26. il. An analysis of the inner meanings of hip-hop.

Robinson, Julius. "Rap in Film," *Cash Box.* LI:47 (May 28, 1988) 16.

Rubin, R. "Music: Authorities Puzzled," *Village Voice.* 31 (August 19, 1986) 70. il. Report on the violence at rap concerts.

Sartwell, C. "On Record: Hip Hop to Heavy Hop," *Record*. 4 (September 1985) 8ff.

Schipper, H. "Long Beach Center to Curtail Concerts Following Rap Riots." *Variety*. 324 (August 20, 1986) 78.

Slovenz, M. "Rock the House: The Aesthetic Dimensions of Rap Music in New York City," *New York Folklore*. 14:3/4 (1988) 151ff. il., disc., bibl.

Stud Brothers. "Rap," *Melody Maker*. 64 (December 24/31, 1988) 45. il.

Toop, David. *Rap Rap Attack: African Jive to New York Hip Hop*. Boston, London: Pluto, 1984. pap.

"Wizards of a Word," *Spin*. 4 (October 1988) 58.

Wood, T. "More Top 40 Jocks Rock to the Rhyme With Rap," *Billboard*. 101 (January 28, 1989) 10. il.

Christian Rap

Mills, David. "Flash: Rappers With Beatitude," *Spin*. 6:4 (July 1990) 14. il.

Surf Rap

SURF MC'S

Croom, Troy. "New Faces to Watch: Surf MC's," *Cash Box*. (September 19, 1987) 11. int. w/Paul "Sidewalk" Rodriguez.

Above the Law

Blackwell, Mark. "Flash: Ruthless People," *Spin.* 6:3 (June 1990) 21. il., int.

Audio Two/MC Lyte

"Atlantic Faces Heat From Gays Over Rap Lyrics," *Billboard.* 102:28 (July 14, 1990) 78.

Levy, Joe. "New Faces to Watch: Audio Two/MC Lyte," *Cash Box.* (May 28, 1988) 7, 24. il., int.

Beastie Boys

"Beastie Boys," *Song Hits.* n256 (June 1987) 8–9. il.

"Beastie Boys Continue to Fight Against Jacksonville Tix 'Warning'," *Variety.* 328 (August 12, 1987) 89ff.

"Beastie Boys Suit Settled in Florida," *Variety.* 331 (June 29, 1988) 58.

"Beasties, Rubin Accused of Stealing '77 Record," *Variety.* 328 (September 9, 1987) 65.
Re. "Hold It Now, Hit It."

Braun, M. "Licensed to Act," *Rolling Stone.* n529 (June 30, 1988) 37. il.

Bruce, Caryn. "Def Jam Cites Capitol Offense in Suit Over Beastie Boys," *Billboard.* 101 (August 5, 1989) 92.

"Centerstage," *Creem.* 18 (June 1987) 53ff. il.

Cohen, Scott. "Beastie Boys are the Bigfoot of Rap," *Spin.* n3 (July 1985) 60–61. il.

Cohen, Scott. "Crude Stories," *Spin.* 2 (March 1987) 40–46. il.

"Def Jam Sues Capitol for Beastie Boys Label Switch," *Variety.* 333 (January 4, 1989) 77.

Hill, Randal C. "The Beastie Boys: Playing It Loud (and Smart)," *Goldmine.* n179 (June 5, 1987) 34. il.

"Jacksonville Willing to Drop Ordinance," *Variety.* 328 (September 2, 1987) 73.

Leland, John. "Beastie Boys: An Ugly Cinderella Story," *Musician.* n83 (September 1985) 36. il.

Mico, Ted. "The Beastie Boys: Animal Crackers," *Melody Maker.* 65 (August 5, 1989) 28–30. il., int.

Newman, N. "Def Jam Sues Over Beasties," *Billboard.* 101 (January 21, 1989) 10ff.

Owen, Frank. "Escape from New York," *Melody Maker.* 61 (February 8, 1986) 12. il.

Owen, Frank. "Paid in Full," *Spin.* 5:7 (October 1989) 35–36. il., int.

Sutherland, Sam. "The Brat Pack," *Melody Maker.* 61 (September 13, 1986) 24–25. il., int.

Walters, B. "The King of Rap: Rick Rubin Makes the Music Industry Walk His Way," *Village Voice.* 31 (November 4, 1986) 19–25. il.

Big Mouth

Levy, Joe. "Big Mouth," *Cash Box.* (September 17, 1988) 11. il., int. w/Bob Sullivan and Johnny Milian.

Blow, Kurtis (r.n.: Kurt Walker)

George, Nelson. " 'King of Rap' to Wear More Caps," *Billboard.* 97 (November 9, 1985) 64.

George, Nelson. "Rappin' With Russell," *Village Voice.* 30 (April 30, 1985) 42–43ff. il.

Owen, Frank. "A Blow-by-Blow Guide to Rapping," *Melody Maker.* 61 (April 5, 1986) 10. il., int.

Boo, Betty (r.n.: Alison Clarkson)

Lester, Paul. "Betty Boo: Sextreme Prejudice," *Melody Maker.* (July 28, 1990) 8. il.

Smith, Andrew. "Sidelines: Betty Boo," *Melody Maker.* 66:23 (June 9, 1990) 14. il., int.

Boo-Yaa T.R.I.B.E.

Weinger, Harry. "New Faces: Boo-Yaa T.R.I.B.E.," *Rolling Stone.* n578 (May 17, 1990) 20. il.

Boogie Boys

"Boogie Boys 'Fly' on Capitol," *Billboard.* 97 (September 28, 1985) 63.

Cold Chillin'

Nelson, Havelock. "Cold Chillin' a Rap Powerhouse," *Billboard.* 100 (January 28, 1989) 22ff.

D-Mob

Hewitt, Paolo. "Married to D-Mob," *New Musical Express.* (January 27, 1990) 32–33. il., int. w/Danny D.

DJ Jazzy Jeff and the Fresh Prince

Levy, Joe A. "Hip Hop for Beginners: DJ Jazzy Jeff and the Fresh Prince Get Stupid," *Spin.* 4 (October 1988) 44–46.

Sutherland, Steve. "Sidelines: Iron Mike," *Melody Maker.* 66:7 (February 17, 1990) 11. il.

D.O.C.

Ressner, Jeffrey. "New Faces: The D.O.C.," *Rolling Stone.* n564 (November 2, 1989) 30. il., int.

Dane, Dana

Levy, Joe. "New Faces to Watch: Dana Dane," *Cash Box.* (January 23, 1988) 9. il., int.

De La Soul (See also: Turtles)

Huhn, M. "Rock & Roll Quarterly: Fresh as a Daisy," *Village Voice.* 33 (December 27, 1988) RR14–15. il.

"News: Soul Controversy," *Melody Maker.* 65 (August 19, 1989) 3. il.
The group is sued by the Turtles.

Digital Underground

"Digital Underground," *Cash Box*. LIII:42 (May 12, 1990) 3. il.

Owen, Frank. "Rock the Art House," *Spin*. 5:8 (November 1989) 32–33. il., int.

Tannenbaum, Rob. "Up from the Underground: Digital Underground's Rappers Hawk Their New 'Sex Packets'," *Rolling Stone*. n576 (April 19, 1990) 27. il., int. w/Shock-G.

Dream Warriors (See: Krush and Skad)

Expose (See also: Girl Groups)

Owen, Frank. "The Secret Life of Girls," *Spin*. 5:6 (September 1989) 28–29. il., int. w/Ann Curless.

Fat Boys

"Fat Boys Sue Piscopo, Miller Over TV Brew Ad," *Variety*. 331 (June 22, 1988) 63.

FitzGerald, H. "Eat to the Beat," *Melody Maker*. 60 (May 4, 1985) 17ff. il., int.

George, Nelson. "Fat Boys Returning to Big Screen," *Billboard*. 97 (December 7, 1985) 62–63.

Gross, J. "Who Gets the Tab?," *Record*. 4 (May 1985) 34. il.

Holden, Peter. "The Fat Boys: Eating Up the Charts," *Cash Box*. XLIX:22 (November 9, 1985) 13. il., int. w/Sutra president Art Kass.

Force M.D.'s

George, Nelson. "Tommy Boy—Warners Deal Bears First Fruit," *Billboard.* 98 (April 5, 1986) 23.

Iorio, Paul. "The Force M.D.'s Chill-Out the Hip-Hop Doo-Wop Way," *Cash Box.* XLIX:37 (March 1, 1986) 13. il., int. w/T.C.D.

Full Force (See also: Lisa Lisa)

Levy, Joe. "Full Force," *Cash Box.* (December 5, 1987) 8. il., int. w/Bowlegged Lou.

Grandmaster Dee

"Great Escape," *Melody Maker.* 61 (September 27, 1986) 29. il., int.

Grandmaster Flash

Owen, Frank. "4th World Funk: The Return of Grandmaster Flash," *Melody Maker.* 61 (May 24, 1986) 12. il., int.

Reynolds, Simon. "UK Fresh '86," *Melody Maker.* 61 (July 19, 1986) 26. il., int.

Groove B Chill

Hardy, Ernest. "New Faces: Groove B Chill," *Cash Box.* (May 12, 1990) 7. il., int.

Guy (group)

Goldberg, M. "Tour Rivalry Ends in Murder," *Rolling Stone.* n559 (August 24, 1989) 28.

Hammer, M.C. (r.n.: Stanley Kirk Burrell)

Blackwell, Mark. "Murder Rap," *Spin.* 6:2 (May 1990) 22. il., int.
Delineates the alleged feud between Hammer and 3rd Bass.

Hochman, Steve. "Hammerin' Out the Hits," *Rolling Stone.* n582/583 (July 12/26, 1990) 29. il., int.

Ressner, Jeffrey. "Hammer Time," *Rolling Stone.* n586 (September 6, 1990) 46–50, 96. il., int. w/Hammer and associates.

Heavy Shift

Push. "Stone Free: Heavy Shift," *Melody Maker.* (August 25, 1990) 11. il., int.

Ice-T

"The Censorship Zone," *Rock & Roll Confidential.* (August 1989) 3–4.

McCann, Ian. "Ire and Ice," *New Musical Express.* (February 19, 1990) 37. il., int.

Stud Brothers. "Ice-T; Fear and Loathing in LA," *Melody Maker.* 66:5 (February 3, 1990) 46–47. il., int.

KMC

Henderson, Alex. "New Faces: KMC," *Cash Box.* (September 15, 1990) 4. il., int. w/Travis "Tee" Lane.

Kane, Big Daddy

Coleman, Mark. "Big Daddy Kane's Climb to Fame," *Rolling Stone.* n573 (March 8, 1990) 65. il., int.

Kid Flash (r.n.: Sean Collins)

Robinson, Julius. "Kid Flash—A Positive Rap," *Cash Box.* LI:47 (May 28, 1988) 16, 18. il., int.

Kid 'N Play

Wild, David. "Kid 'N Play Throw a Party for Two," *Rolling Stone.* n578 (May 17, 1990) 105–108. il.

Kool Rock Jay

Push. "Stone Free: Kool Rock Jay," *Melody Maker.* 66:21 (May 26, 1990) 10. il.

Krush and Skad

Push. "Flair Canada," *Melody Maker.* (July 28, 1990) 36–37. il., int.

LL Cool J (r.n.: James Todd Smith)

Coleman, M. "On the Charts: The Cool Life," *Rolling Stone.* n510 (October 8, 1987) 16–17. il.

"Cool Sued," *Melody Maker.* 63 (October 10, 1987) 3. il. Radio plagiarism suit dismissed.

Dobrin, Gregory. "LL Cool J Emerges as the King of Rap," *Cash Box.* (July 25, 1987) 10–11. il., int.

Gordon, Kim. "Meaty Beaty Big and Bouncy," *Spin.* 5:6 (September 1989) 50–52, 102–103. il., int.

"The Harder They Come," *Melody Maker.* 61 (September 27, 1986) 28–29. il., int.

"LL Cool J Accused of Stealing Name, Songs, Recordings of Old 'Friend'," *Variety.* 324 (September 17, 1986) 104.

Lichtman, Irv. "Lawsuit Charges Theft LL Cool J Name, Songs," *Billboard.* 98 (September 20, 1986) 86.

"New Faces to Watch: LL Cool J," *Cash Box.* XLIX:33 (February 1, 1986) 12. il., int.

"News," *Melody Maker.* 63 (October 3, 1987) 3. Plagiarism alleged on "I Need Love."

Owen, Frank. "Escape from New York," *Melody Maker.* 61 (February 8, 1986) 13. il., int.

[Portrait], *Rolling Stone.* n515/516 (December 17/31, 1987) 118.

"Suit vs. LL Cool J Dismissed by Judge," *Variety.* 328 (October 7, 1987) 100.

Trakin, R. "Newbeats: Float Like a Butterfly, Sting Like a Beat Box," *Creem.* 17 (August 1986) 68. il.

Walters, B. "The King of Rap; Rick Rubin Makes the Music Industry Walk His Way," *Village Voice.* 31 (November 4, 1986) 19–25. il.

Young, J. "LL Cool J Takes the Rap," *Creem.* 19 (October 1987) 3, 38–39. il.

Lisa Lisa and the Cult Jam (With Full Force) (See also: Full Force)

Goldstein, T. "Newbeats: Lisa and the Cult: So Nice You Wanna Rap It Twice," *Creem.* 18 (October 1986) 68. il.

Hill, Randal C. "Lisa Lisa and Cult Jam: Lisa Squared But Not Square," *Goldmine.* n205 (June 3, 1988) 27, 79. il.

Holden, Peter. "Lisa Lisa and the Cult Jam: Breaking Open the Dance Charts," *Cash Box.* (August 31, 1985) 11. il., int.

Nelson, H. "Lisa Lisa & Cult Jam Aim *Sky* High," *Billboard.* 101 (August 19, 1989) 20ff.

London Posse

McCann, Ian. "Posse Footing," *New Musical Express.* (March 30, 1990) 32. il.

Push. "Sidelines: London Posse," *Melody Maker.* 66:8 (February 24, 1990) 12. il.

Love, Monie

Daly, Steven. "Flash: One Love: Monie Love Arrives in This Country With a Rep as the Only British Rapper Who Matters," *Spin.* 6:6 (September 1990) 12–13. il.

MC 900 Ft. Jesus (r.n.: Mark Griffin)

Mack, Bob. "Flash: 900 Feet High and Rising," *Spin.* 6:3 (June 1990) 19. il., int.

Stud Brothers. "Sidelines: MC 900 Foot Jesus," *Melody Maker.* (July 7, 1990) 10. il., int.

Mantronix (r.n.: Curtis Mantronik)

Chin, B. "Mantronix Makes Inroads in British Pop, But Black Duo Still Waiting for a U.S. Hit," *Billboard.* 98 (June 14, 1986) 24.

Lester, Paul. "Mantronix: The Sweet Smell of Success," *Melody Maker.* 66:4 (January 27, 1990) 8–9. il., int.

Levy, Joe. "Mantronix," *Cash Box.* LI:47 (May 28, 1988) 14, 18. il., int. w/Mantronix and McTee.

Owen, Frank. "The Hardcore Life," *Melody Maker.* 61 (March 22, 1986) 12–13. il., int.

Owen, Frank. "Sonic Assassins," *Melody Maker.* 61 (December 6, 1986) 24–25. il., int.

"Shrink Rap," *Melody Maker.* 61 (May 24, 1986) 15. il., int.

Smith, Andrew. "Mantronix: Cashing In or Selling Out?," *Melody Maker.* 66:21 (May 26, 1990) 38. il., int. w/ Mantronix.

Markie, Biz

Levy, Joe. "New Faces to Watch: Biz Markie," *Cash Box.* LI:49 (June 11, 1988) 7. int.

Mel, Grandmaster Melle (r.n.: Melvin Glover)

"Grandmaster Melle Mel, 'Trying to Get Respect'," *Billboard.* 97 (July 6, 1985) 60ff. int.

Smith, R.J. "Swing Shift: Don't Do It," *Village Voice.* 31 (August 26, 1986) 73.

Miami Bass

Coleman, Bill, and Bruce Haring. "Miami Party Scene Set Rappers' Sound," *Billboard.* 102:10 (March 10, 1990) 99.

Mtume (, James)

Iorio, Paul. "James Mtume Scores With the *Native Son* Soundtrack," *Cash Box.* (January 24, 1987) 7, 22. int.

N.W.A. (See also: Censorship)

Henderson, Alex. "Compton's Most Wanted," *Cash Box.* (August 11, 1990) 6. il., int.

Leland, John. "Flash: Kicking the Ballistics," *Spin.* 5:6 (September 1989) 12.

"News: NWA: Banned in Brum," *Melody Maker.* 66:23 (June 9, 1990) 3. il.

Odell, Michael. "Niggers With Attitude," *Melody Maker.* 66:20 (May 19, 1990) 28–29. il., int. w/Dr. Dre.

Owen, Frank. "Hanging Tough," *Spin.* 6:1 (April 1990) 32–34. il., int. w/band and associates.

Push. "Niggers With Attitude: Street Hassle," *Melody Maker.* 65 (August 5, 1989) 42–43. il., int. w/Ice Cube.

Ressner, Jeffrey. "Congressman Chides FBI Over N.W.A. Letter," *Rolling Stone.* n565 (November 16, 1989) 31.

Papa Dee

Barron, Jack. "Dee Light," *New Musical Express.* (March 30, 1990) 33. il.

Pop Will Eat Itself

Reinhardt, Robin. "Wise Up, Suckers," *Spin.* 5:6 (September 1989) 19. il., int. w/singer Clint Mansell.

Professor Griff (See also: Public Enemy; 2 Live Crew)

Pearlman, Jill. "Repentant Professor," *Spin.* 6:1 (April 1990) 94–96. il., int.

Public Enemy (See also: Professor Griff)

Cole, Lewis. "Def or Dumb? Public Enemy Blasted Its Way to Success With the Pulse of Black Power," Only to Lose Control of Its Message—and Maybe Its Destiny," *Rolling Stone.* n563 (October 19, 1989) 47–55, 95–97. il., int.

Cole, Lewis. "Loose Cannon Guns Down Public Enemy," *Rolling Stone.* n558 (August 10, 1989) 24. il.

Leland, John. "Do the Right Thing," *Spin.* 5:6 (September 1989) 68–74, 100. il., int. w/Chuck D.

Light, Alan. "Public Enemy's Tour de Force," *Rolling Stone.* n585 (August 23, 1990) 29–32. il., int. w/Chuck D.

Malone, Bonz. "The 10 Most Interesting Musicians of the Last 5 Years: Public Enemy," *Spin.* 6:1 (April 1990) 46. il.

Morris, Chris, and Janine McAdams. "Racism Tract Invites New Heat for Public Enemy," *Billboard.* 102:18 (May 5, 1990) 5, 88.

"News: Beyond the Terrordome," *Spin.* 5:11 (February 1990) 18. il., int. w/Chuck D.

Owen, Frank. "Public Service," *Spin.* 5:12 (March 1990) 56–61, 86. il., int. w/Chuck D.

"Public Enemy Fight the Power; Birmingham Show Goes Ahead Despite Council Bid to Halt It," *Sounds.* (February 17, 1990) 3. il.

Reynolds, Simon. "Public Enemy: Strength to Strength," *Melody Maker.* 63 (October 17, 1987) 14–15. il., int. w/Chuck D.

"Shrink Rap," *Melody Maker.* 64 (October 8, 1988) 17. il.

Queen Latifah

Light, Alan. "New Faces: Queen Latifah," *Rolling Stone.* n572 (February 22, 1990) 30. il., int.

"Rap It Up," *Rolling Stone.* n582/583 (July 12/26, 1990) 109–111. il., bio & fashion spread.

Red Alert

Mapp, Ben. "Zulu Son," *Spin.* 6:1 (April 1990) 24–25. il., int.

Riley, Teddy

Cooper, B.M. "Rock & Roll Quarterly: Teddy Riley's New Jack Swing," *Village Voice.* 33 (October 18, 1988) RR9–10ff.

Roxanne (rap motif)

George, Nelson. "*Roxanne, Roxanne* Rocks On," *Billboard.* 97 (February 9, 1985) 50.

Morris, E. "Compleat's *Roxanne* Album Racks Up Sales Rapidly," *Billboard.* 97 (July 13, 1985) 77. Re. *The Complete Story of Roxanne—The Album.*

Ruff Jusdis

Sullivan, Caroline. "Sidelines: Ruff Jusdis," *Melody Maker.* (July 28, 1990) 12. il., int.

Run-D.M.C.

Jeske, Lee. "Run-D.M.C.: Raising Hell and Rapping Up Sales," *Cash Box.* (July 19, 1986) 11, 32. il., int. w/Run.

"News," *Melody Maker.* 63 (December 12, 1987) 3. Confirmation of the sound engineer's minor head wound.

Ruthless Rap Assassins

Push. "Ruthless Rap Assassins: Marc Warfare," *Melody Maker.* (July 21, 1990) 38–39. il., int.

Salt 'n' Pepa (r.n.: Cheryl James and Sandy Denton)

"All Rapped Up," *Melody Maker.* 65 (January 28, 1989) 14. il.

"Salt 'n' Pepa Suit to Halt Spinderella Use," *Variety.* 332 (August 10, 1988) 50.

She Rockers 18

James, Mandi. "Jam On: Pump Up the Jam," *New Musical Express.* (January 27, 1990) 10. il.

Silk Tymes Leather

Hardy, Ernest. "New Faces: Silk Tymes Leather," *Cash Box.* (June 9, 1990) 6. il., int.

Silver Bullet (r.n.: Rapper Richard)

Smith, Andrew. "Sidelines: Silver Bullet," *Melody Maker.* 66:4 (January 27, 1990) 14. il., int.

Sindecut

Smith, Andrew. "Stonefree: Sindecut," *Melody Maker.* (July 21, 1990) 13. il., int. w/MC Crazy Noddy.

Stetsasonic

Levy, Joe. "Stetsasonic," *Cash Box.* LI:50 (June 18, 1988) 6, 22. il., int. w/Daddy O.

Sugar Hill House Band

Leland, John. "The Sugar Hill House Band," *Musician.* n81 (July 1985) 77–85, 112.

Tairrie B.

Henderson, Alex. "New Faces: Tairrie B.," *Cash Box.* (June 2, 1990) 5. il., int.

Technotronic

Farber, Jim. "Technotronic: Who's That Girl?," *Rolling Stone.* n581 (June 28, 1990) 20. il., int. w/lead rapper Ya Kid K.

3rd Bass (See also: MC Hammer)

Barrett, A.J. "Prickly Pair," *New Musical Express.* (March 30, 1990) 14. il.

Push. "3rd Bass; Rap's Next Step Forward," *Melody Maker.* 66:5 (February 3, 1990) 47. il., int.

Winthorpe, Otis. "Sound Check: 3rd Bass; Black and White in Color," *Me Music Express Magazine.* 14:145 (March 1990) 44. il., int.

Thunder, Shelly

Mapp, Ben. "Flash: Rolling Thunder," *Spin.* 5:8 (November 1989) 27. il.

Tragedy

Hardy, Ernest. "New Faces: Tragedy," *Cash Box.* (June 16, 1990) 5. il., int.

A Tribe Called Quest

Odell, Michael. "A Tribe Called Quest: The New Rap Manifesto," *Melody Maker.* (August 25, 1990) 19. il., int. w/Q-Tip.

2 Live Crew (See also: Censorship)

Benarde, Scott. "Much More Than Nasty," *Rolling Stone.* n573 (March 8, 1990) 62. il., int. w/Luke Skyywalker.

Haring, Bruce, Melinda Newman, and Chris Morris. " 'Nasty' Ruling, Arrests Galvanize Industry," *Billboard.* (June 23, 1990) 1, 5.

Newman, Melinda, Bruce Haring, and Craig Rosen. " 'Banned in U.S.A.' Rockets on Radio. Controversy Fuels Campbell's Solo Effort," *Billboard.* 102:28 (July 14, 1990) 4, 78.

Owen, Frank. "Fear of a Black Penis," *Spin.* 6:6 (September 1990) 35–37. il., int. w/Luther Campbell and lawyer Jack Thompson.

Owen, Frank. "Pump the Bass," *Spin.* 5:11 (February 1990) 22–24. il., int. w/Skyywalker.

Rosen, Craig. "Lucasfilm Says Luke in Contempt," *Billboard.* (July 14, 1990) 78.

"2 Live Crew: A Sampler; A Taste of 'Nasty' Lyrics," *Billboard.* 102:10 (March 10, 1990) 99.

"2 Live Crew Album Ruled Obscene in Florida," *Billboard.* (June 16, 1990) 5ff.

Urban Dance Squad

Hardy, Ernest. "New Faces: Urban Dance Squad," *Cash Box.* (May 26, 1990) 6. il.

Williams, Wendell, and the Criminal Element Orchestra

Lester, Paul. "Sidelines: Wendell Williams and the Criminal Element Orchestra," *Melody Maker.* (October 13, 1990) 10. il., int. w/Williams and producer Arthur Baker.

X-Clan

Owen, Frank. "Bust a Groove," *Spin.* 5:10 (January 1990) 32–33. il., int.

Pearlman, Jill. "Flash: Funky Pharaohs," *Spin.* 6:2 (May 1990) 11. il., int.

Young MC (See also: Tone-Loc)

Ressner, Jeffrey. "The Stone-Cold Success of Young MC," *Rolling Stone.* n572 (February 22, 1990) 33. il., int.

22. NEW AGE

General Sources

Bessman, Jim. "New Age Product Enters the Mainstream," *Billboard.* 98 (March 1, 1986) 23ff.

DiMauro, P. "Instrumental Music Gathers Steam on Records, Radio; Perceived as Alternative for Baby Boomers," *Variety.* 323 (July 2, 1986) 57ff.

Freeman, K. "Christening a New Format; Is It New Age or . . . ," *Billboard.* 99 (September 5, 1987) 14.

Jenkins, Mark. "How the Music Came of Age," *Music Week.* (June 10, 1989) 28–29.

Jenkins, Mark. "There's Variety in the Newness!," *Music Week.* (June 10, 1989) 30–31. il.

LaPointe, K. "New Age Music Finds a Niche in Toronto," *Billboard.* 98 (September 20, 1986) 66.

McGowan, C., and others. "New Age Music," *Billboard.* 98 (October 25, 1986) N1ff.

"On Other Side of Atlantic New Age in Toddler Stage," *Variety.* 322 (February 5, 1986) 143–144.

Owen, Frank. "Feed Your Head," *Melody Maker.* 61 (March 22, 1986) 32.

Robertshaw, N. "U.K. to Meet the 'New Age'," *Billboard.* 98 (January 25, 1986) 9.

Terry, Ken. "Major Labels Joining New Age Parade; Instrumental LPs Starting to Click," *Variety.* 324 (August 20, 1986) 77ff.

Ackerman, William

Forte, Dan. "New Directions in Acoustic Steel-String," *Guitar Player.* 19 (February 1985) 64ff. il.

Owen, Frank. "Feed Your Head," *Melody Maker.* 61 (March 22, 1986) 32. int.

Alomar, Carlos (See also: David Bowie)

Mulhern, Tom. "Carlos Alomar: Bowie's Right-Hand Man Makes His Solo Debut," *Guitar Player.* 21 (August 1987) 24–26ff. il., bio, disc., int.

Santoro, Gene. "Carlos Alomar: Generating Electric Dreams," *Down Beat.* (November 1987) 20–22. il., disc., int.

Ciani, Suzanne

Doerschuk, Bob. "Suzanne Ciani & Her Ace Apprentices Set the Pace of Commercial Synthesis," *Keyboard Magazine.* 11 (April 1985) 16–17ff. il., int.

Dupler, Steve. "New York Composer Debuts State-of-the-Art Facility," *Billboard.* 98 (June 28, 1986) 61. il.

Milano, Dominic. "The Fine Art of Programming Synthesizers: Top Studio Programmers," *Keyboard Magazine.* 11 (June 1985) 38–40ff. il., int.

Enya (r.n.: Enya Brennan)

"Career Opportunities," *Melody Maker.* 65 (January 28, 1989) 16. il.

Hedges, Michael

Forte, Dan. "New Directions in Acoustic Steel-String: Michael Hedges," *Guitar Player.* 19 (February 1985) 65–69. il., bio, int.

Hanson, M. "Plugging in With Room to Move," *Frets.* 8 (November 1986) 36. il.

Hanson, M., and P. Hood. "Michael Hedges," *Frets.* 8 (November 1986) 34–40ff. il., int.

Isham, Mark

Carlberg, R. "Mark Isham Interview," *Electric Musician.* 2 (February 1986) 43ff. il.

"New Acts," *Variety.* 324 (August 20, 1986) 86.

Kitaro (r.n.: Masanori Takahashi)

Freff. "Kitaro," *Keyboard Magazine.* 13 (May 1987) 26–37. il., bio, disc., int.

Strickland, E. "New Age Profile: Kitaro," *Fanfare.* 9:1 (1985) 308–311.

Sutherland, Sam. "Geffen Maps Massive Push for Kitaro," *Billboard.* 97 (August 17, 1985) 6.

Kottke, Leo

Dupler, Steven. "Kottke's Acoustic Music is Again in Vogue," *Billboard.* 98 (February 22, 1986) 45.

"Leo's Private Vocals," *Billboard.* 101 (August 19, 1989) 29.

Movement 98

Oldfield, Paul. "Stone Free: Movement 98," *Melody Maker.* 66:21 (May 26, 1990) 10. il.

O'Hearn, Patrick (See also: Missing Persons)

Hedges, D. "Patrick O'Hearn: Sounds for a New Age," *Creem.* 17 (April 1986) 68–69ff. il., int.

Milano, Dominic, and Bob Doerschuk. "Patrick O'Hearn's Mom Thinks He's a Lousy Keyboard Player," *Keyboard Magazine.* 14 (September 1988) 66–67ff. il., soundsheet, int.

Souther, Richard

"New Faces to Watch: Richard Souther," *Cash Box.* (January 17, 1987) 10. il., int.

Sylvian, David

Gett, Steve. "David Sylvian Talks *Secrets of the Beehive*," *Billboard.* 99 (December 12, 1987) 17.

Tuck and Patti

Weinger, Harry. "New Faces: Tuck and Patti," *Rolling Stone.*
n562 (October 5, 1989) 28–29. il., int.

Vangelis

"Vangelis, Choreographer Compose Score on Phone," *Variety.*
325 (December 3, 1986) 2.
Re. *Beauty and the Beast.*

A. SPACE MUSIC

Diliberto, John. "Is Space the Place?," *Down Beat.* (September
1985) 61, 63. il.

B. AMBIENT (See also: AMBIENT HOUSE)

Bel Canto

Woods, Karen. "Shock of the New," *Cash Box.* (August 11,
1990) 11. il., int. w/Anneli Drecker.

Cocteau Twins

"Cocteau Twins and the Glorious Nothing," *Cash Box.* (October 8, 1988) 10–11. il., int. w/singer Elizabeth Fraser.

Mico, Ted. "Working Dreamers," *Melody Maker.* 61 (May 3,
1986) 11–12. il., int.

Sutherland, Steve. "Cocteau Twins: Bringing Up Baby," *Melody Maker.* (August 25, 1990) 16–18. il., int.

Sutherland, Steve. "Worlds Apart," *Melody Maker*. 60 (November 16, 1985) 24–25ff. il.

Cruise, Julee

Reynolds, Simon. "Julee Cruise," *Melody Maker*. 66:8 (February 24, 1990) 42–43. il., int.

Wise, Damon. "Angel of the Night," *Sounds*. (January 27, 1990) 40–41. il., int. Includes a David Lynch film retrospective.

Eno (See also: Roxy Music; Talking Heads)

Aikin, Jim. "Brian Eno: Calm in the Eye of the Storm," *Keyboard*. (January 1987) 72–79. il., int.

Lush

Robb. "Lush for Life," *Sounds*. (March 3, 1990) 21. il., int.

Sutherland, Steve. "Lush: Lust for Life," *Melody Maker*. 66:7 (February 17, 1990) 42–43. il., int.

Propaganda

"The Duellists," *Melody Maker*. 60 (May 18, 1985) 24–25. il., int.

"Fast Forward," *Melody Maker*. 60 (December 7, 1985) 4. The band denies that Ralf Dorper has quit.

Morley, P. "The Sculpture of Dreams," *Melody Maker*. 60 (November 9, 1985) 28–30. il., int.

"Propaganda: We're Back!," *Melody Maker.* 61 (August 30, 1986) 3. il.
    The band leaves the ZTT label, but doesn't split. Bracken remains with ZTT.

This Mortal Coil

Reynolds, Simon. "Shadow Play," *Melody Maker.* 61 (October 4, 1986) 39. il., int. w/Ivo.

23. ALTERNATIVE ROCK

General Sources

Reynolds, Simon. "Younger Than Yesterday," *Melody Maker.* 61 (June 28, 1986) 32–33.
Delineates the alternative/"indie" pop vs. mainstream pop scene in the U.K.

Zimmerman, K. "Schizoid College Rock: Hip Radio, Safe Acts," *Variety.* 336 (August 16, 1989) 67.

Bears (See also: Adrian Belew; King Crimson; Frank Zappa)

Nager, L. "What's Adrian Belew Doing on the Club Circuit With a Band of Bears?," *Musician.* n90 (April 1986) 64–66ff. il.

Yardumian, Rob. "New Faces to Watch: The Bears," *Cash Box.* (September 5, 1987) 11. il., int. w/Adrian Belew.

Beat Farmers

Gans, D. "What's New: Country Dick as Blue Plate Special," *Record.* 4 (July 1985) 37. il.

Jones, A. "Beats Go Wild," *Melody Maker.* 61 (July 19, 1986) 36–37. il., int.

Jones, A. "The Wild Bunch," *Melody Maker.* 60 (July 20, 1985)
    16–17ff. il., int.

Morris, C. "Serious Lunacy at the Bar," *Musician.* n82 (August
    1985) 26.

Big Audio Dynamite (See also: Clash)

"BAD: The Show Goes On; Don Letts Splits, But Mick Jones
    Soldiers On," *Sounds.* (February 3, 1990) 2. il.

Clerk, Carol. "Midnight Cowboys," *Melody Maker.* 64 (June 11,
    1988) 8–9. il., int. w/Mick Jones.

Isler, Scott. "Big Audio Dynamite," *Musician.* n89 (March
    1986) 11–14, 22–23. il.

Salewicz, Chris. "The Clash Goes B.A.D.: Joe Strummer and
    Mick Jones Bury the Hatchet," *Musician.* n98 (December
    1986) 84– 90. il.

JONES, MICK

Clerk, Carol. "Beatboxing Lever," *Melody Maker.* 61 (October
    18, 1986) 26–27. il., int.

Big Country

Morton, Tom. "Native Country," *Melody Maker.* 60 (February
    16, 1985) 12–13. il., int.

Sutherland, Steve. "Flashback: Big Country," *Melody Maker.* 61
    (April 26, 1986) 27–30. il., int.

Sutherland, Steve. "Labour of Love," *Melody Maker.* 61 (April 12, 1986) 12–13. il., int. w/S. Anderson.

Young, J. "Big Country: Hoedown in Steeltown," *Creem.* 16 (April 1985) 20–21ff. il.

Big Dipper

Gittins, Ian. "Backwood Ways," *Melody Maker.* 64 (December 10, 1988) 39. il., int.

Gittins, Ian. "Heavens Above," *Melody Maker.* 64 (June 4, 1988) 10. il., int.

Wheeler, D. "Newbeats: Are the Stars Out Tonight?," *Creem.* 19 (June 1988) 66. il.

Big Dish

FitzGerald, H. "New Beginnings," *Melody Maker.* 60 (August 3, 1985) 19. il., int.

Iorio, Paul. "New Faces to Watch: The Big Dish," *Cash Box.* (February 14, 1987) 12. il., int. w/Steve Lindsay and Brian McPhie.

Blue Aeroplanes

Cavanagh, David. "Acrodynamics," *Sounds.* (January 27, 1990) 24–25. il., int. w/Gerard Langley.

Langley, Gerard. "Blue Aeroplanes; The Attraction of Opposites," *Melody Maker.* 66:5 (February 3, 1990) 10–11. il., int. w/Jon Wilde.

Roberts, Chris. "The Blue Aeroplanes: Preparing for Take Off," *Melody Maker.* 66:20 (May 19, 1990) 8–9. il.

Roberts, Chris. "Miracle Lesion," *Melody Maker.* 63 (October 31, 1987) 36. il., int. w/Langley.

Staunton, Terry. "Life in the Fast Plane," *New Musical Express.* (February 3, 1990) 7. il., int.

Tannenbaum, Rob. "New Faces: Blue Aeroplanes," *Rolling Stone.* n579 (May 31, 1990) 34. il., int. w/vocalist Langley.

BoDeans

Cullman, Brian. "The Sound and the Power," *Spin.* 2 (September 1986) 21–22. il.

Iorio, Paul. "The BoDeans are from Waukesha, Wisc.," *Cash Box.* XLIX:47 (May 10, 1986) 13. il., int. w/Beau and Sammy BoDean.

"New Acts," *Variety.* 328 (October 21, 1987) 541.

Bolshoi

FitzGerald, Helen. "Don't Stop the Dance," *Melody Maker.* 60 (September 28, 1985) 36. il., int. w/Trevor Tanner.

"Clever Trevors," *Melody Maker.* 61 (April 19, 1986) 12. il., int. w/Tanner.

Brandos

Browne, David. "New Faces: The Brandos: Real Contenders," *Rolling Stone.* n513 (November 19, 1987) 20. il., int.

Cactus World News

Fricke, David, and Anthony DeCurtis. "In the Shadow of U2; Two Young Irish Bands Struggle to Maintain Their Own Identities," *Rolling Stone.* n483 (September 25, 1986) 29–30. il.

Liveten, S. "Cactus World News—Out of U2's Shadow," *Billboard.* 98 (October 18, 1986) 25.

McIlheney, B. "The New Frontier," *Melody Maker.* 61 (January 18, 1986) 12–13. il., int. w/E. McEvoy.

McIlheney, B. "On the 'Beach'," *Melody Maker.* 61 (April 19, 1986) 36–37. il., int.

Call

Himes, G. "The Call: Love & Politics for Tense Times," *Musician.* n58 (August 1983) 12ff. il., int.

Mendelssohn, John. "The Call: This Headline Contains No Puns," *Creem.* 17 (August 1986) 10–11ff. il.

Cave, Nick

"Heroes," *Melody Maker.* 64 (October 22, 1988) 37. il.

McKenna, Kristine. "The Caveman Cometh," *Spin.* n3 (July 1985) 24–25. il.

Reynolds, Simon. "Knight of the Living Dead," *Melody Maker.* 64 (June 18, 1988) 32–34. il., int.

"Shrink Rap," *Melody Maker.* 60 (August 3, 1985) 16. il., int.

"Solitary Confinement," *Melody Maker.* 61 (August 23, 1986) 30–31. il., int.

Chamberlains (See also: Lucy Show)

Woods, Karen. "Shock of the New," *Cash Box.* (April 28, 1990) 7. il.

Concrete Blonde

Linden, Amy. "Concrete Blonde's Ambition," *Spin.* 6:6 (September 1990) 56. il., int. w/Johnette Napolitano.

Cowboy Junkies

Arnold, Gina. "Sister Ray," *Spin.* 6:2 (May 1990) 24–25. il., int. w/Margo Timmins.

Roberts, Chris. "Cowboy Junkies: Horse Latitudes," *Melody Maker.* 66:8 (February 24, 1990) 28–30. il., int. w/ Michael and Margo Timmins.

Dead Milkmen

Kuipers, Dean. "Spilled Milkmen," *Spin.* 6:3 (June 1990) 38–40. il., int.

Fine Young Cannibals (See also: English Beat)

"New Faces to Watch: Fine Young Cannibals," *Cash Box.* XLIX:43 (April 12, 1986) 14. il., int. w/David Steele.

Pond, Steve. "Looking a Gift Horse in the Mouth," *Rolling Stone.* n562 (October 5, 1989) 44–52. il., int.

Fire Town

Iorio, Paul. "New Faces to Watch: Fire Town," *Cash Box.* (June 20, 1987) 10–11. il., int. w/Phil Davis and Doug Erickson.

Peter, S. "Newbeats: There is a Fire in the Town . . . ," *Creem.* 19 (December 1987) 69. il.

Fisher, Climie

Meyer, Stuart. "New on the Charts," *Billboard.* 100:21 (May 21, 1988) 32. il.

Robinson, Julius. "Climie Fisher," *Cash Box.* (August 13, 1988) 10–11. il., int.

Flesh for Lulu

Clerk, Carol. "Flesh Eaters," *Melody Maker.* 61 (January 11, 1986) 14. il., int.

Kassan, Brian. "New Faces to Watch: Flesh for Lulu," *Cash Box.* (March 14, 1987) 10. il., int.

Fugazi

Mercer, M. "Bash the Fash," *Melody Maker.* 64 (December 10, 1988) 36–37. il., int.

Galaxie 500

Blashill, Pat. "Flash: Satellite of Love," *Spin.* 5:9 (December 1989) 14. il., int.

King, Sam. "Standing on Ceremony," *Sounds.* (February 24, 1990) 23. il., int.

Reynolds, Simon. "Galaxie 500: Final Curtain," *Melody Maker.* 65 (August 19, 1989) 11. il., int.

True, Everett. "Galaxie 500: Planet Rock," *Melody Maker.* 66:7 (February 17, 1990) 39. il., int.

Hitchcock, Robyn (, and the Egyptians)

Holdship, Bill. "Robyn Hitchcock: God Walks Among Us," *Creem.* 17 (March 1986) 48–49ff.

"New Acts," *Variety.* 320 (August 7, 1985) 77.

Rosenbluth, J. "Hitchcock: Cult Status is for the Birds," *Billboard.* 98 (November 29, 1986) 23.

"Shrink Rap," *Melody Maker.* 60 (April 6, 1985) 17. il., int.

Smith, M. "Strangers on a Train," *Melody Maker.* 60 (November 16, 1985) 9. il., int.

Hoodoo Gurus

Brunetti, Frank. "Hoodoo Gurus: Hoodoo You Love," In: *Next Thing,* ed. by Walker. pp. 47–51. il.

FitzGerald, H. "Hoodoo Voodoo," *Melody Maker.* 60 (December 14, 1985) 12–13. il., int.

Neilson, J. "Chasing Out Some Hoodoo There!," *Creem.* 16 (May 1985) 18. il.

Ruhlmann, William. "The Hoodoo Gurus: Coming Up Down Under," *Goldmine.* n245 (December 15, 1989) 20. il.

St. John, E. "The Hoodoo Gurus," *APRA Journal.* 4:2 (1986) 12–13. il.

Hothouse Flowers

Clarke, Tina. "Sound Check: Hothouse Flowers; In Full Bloom," *Me Music Express Magazine.* 14:148 (June 1990) 24. il., int. w/Liam O'Maonlai.

Kelly, N. "Flower Power," *Melody Maker.* 61 (May 10, 1986) 10. il., int.

House of Freaks

Corcoran, Michael. "Flash: Bomb the Bass," *Spin.* 5:6 (September 1989) 22. il., int.

It's Immaterial

Crant, Keith. "Control Zone: Material World," *Melody Maker.* (July 28, 1990) 45. il., int.
Discussion centered around the making of the band's second l.p.

McIlheney, B. "Out to Lunch," *Melody Maker.* 60 (October 19, 1985) 12–13. il., int.

Smith, M. "Screwy Drivers," *Melody Maker.* 61 (April 19, 1986) 6. il., int.

James

Wilde, J. "Fountains of Youth," *Melody Maker.* 63 (September 19, 1987) 31. il., int.

Wilkinson, Roy. "On the Buses," *Sounds.* (March 10, 1990) 22–23. il.

Jane's Addiction (See also: Censorship)

Kuipers, Dean. "Gonna Kick Tomorrow," *Spin.* 6:6 (September 1990) 58–62. il., int.

Jones, Jesus

"New Faces: Jesus Jones," *Cash Box.* (September 15, 1990) 4. il.

"Resurrection Shuffle," *Melody Maker.* 65 (January 21, 1989) 13. il.

Williams, Simon. "Nineties in Effect; You've Gotta Walk and Don't Look Back," *Spin.* 5:11 (February 1990) 57. il.

Latin Quarter

"Christmas Joy," *Melody Maker.* 61 (December 13, 1986) il. Re. a donation to the Nicaragua Solidarity Campaign to buy PA equipment.

Irwin, C. "Give 'em Enough Rope," *Melody Maker.* 60 (October 19, 1985) 15. il., int. w/Steve Skaith.

Kirk, K. "Radio Free Europe," *Melody Maker.* 61 (March 15, 1986) 10. il., int.

Lightning Seeds (See also: Echo and the Bunnymen)

Garcia, Jane. "New Faces: Lightning Seeds," *Rolling Stones.* n586 (September 6, 1990) 25. il., int. w/Ian Broudie.

Jennings, D. "The Lightning Seeds: Quiet Revolution," *Melody Maker.* 65 (August 5, 1989) 10. il., int. w/Broudie.

"New Faces: The Lightning Seeds," *Cash Box.* LIII:41 (May 5, 1990) 7. il., int. w/Broudie.

Reacock, Tim. "In Their Own Words: Ian Broudie," *Sounds.* (January 27, 1990) 22. il., int.

Williams, Simon. "Poppy Seeds," *New Musical Express.* (January 27, 1990) 20–21. il., int. w/Ian Broudie.

Loop

Stubbs, David. "Loop: Lost in Space," *Melody Maker.* 66:4 (January 27, 1990) 10–11. il., int.

Lucy Show (See also: Chamberlains)

FitzGerald, H. "Juicy Lucy," *Melody Maker.* 60 (September 21, 1985) 39ff. int.

Gittins, Ian. "Cloud Bursting," *Melody Maker.* 61 (May 10, 1986) 37. il., int. w/W. Heggie.

Kassan, Brian. "New Faces to Watch: The Lucy Show," *Cash Box.* (January 24, 1987) 10. il., int.

Luxuria (See also: Buzzcocks)

Grant, Keith. "Control Zone: Howard's Way," *Melody Maker.*
66:21 (May 26, 1990) 46. il., int. w/Howard Devoto and
Noko.

"Stumped!," *Melody Maker.* 63 (December 12, 1987) 4.

Williams, Joe. "Luxuria," *Cash Box.* LII:2 (July 9, 1988) 11,
13. il., int. w/Devoto.

Lyres

Cresser, Wayne. "The Lyres: Back to Monoman," *Goldmine.*
n212 (September 9, 1988) 22, 26.

Johnson, D. "Keepers of the Flame," *Record.* 4 (November
1984) 12. il.

Mekons

Georgis, Z. "*Whiskey* Galore," *Melody Maker.* 60 (August 24,
1985) 20. il., int.

Reynolds, Simon. "Edge of Darkness," *Melody Maker.* 61
(August 2, 1986) 12. il., int.

Microdisney

Aston, M. "Micro Waves," *Melody Maker.* 60 (January 12,
1985) 29. il., int.

"Disney Tunes," *Melody Maker.* 60 (December 7, 1985) 12–13.
il., int.

Georgis, Z. "Disney's World," *Melody Maker.* 60 (July 27, 1985) 31ff. il., int.

Pixies (See also: Breeders)

Macnie, Jim. "The Pixies: Feedback and Applesauce," *Musician.* n132 (October 1989) 16–18, 26.

Poi Dog Pondering

Blashill, Pat. "Flash: Dogs in Space," *Spin.* 5:8 (November 1989) 20. il., int. w/singer, guitarist and conductor Frank Orrall.

Pop Will Eat Itself

Birrell, I. "Hairy Monsters," *Melody Maker.* 61 (January 28, 1986) 31. int.

Revenge (See also: Joy Division; New Order)

Greer, Jim. "Everything's Gone Black," *Spin.* 6:4 (July 1990) 29, 91–92. il., int. w/Peter Hook.

Rhythm Corps

Buchsbaum, Brad. "Rhythm Corps," *Cash Box.* (August 6, 1988) 11. il., int. w/lead singer Michael Persh.

Scruffy the Cat

Iorio, Paul. "New Faces to Watch: Scruffy the Cat," *Cash Box.* (October 4, 1986) 10. il., int. w/Stona Fitch.

Silencers

Jeske, Lee. "New Faces to Watch: The Silencers," *Cash Box.* (October 24, 1987) 11. il., int. w/Jimmie O'Neil.

Silos

Gates, David. "Something Old, Something New; The Silos: Rock Purist," *Newsweek.* (April 9, 1990) 72. il., int. w/Walter Salas-Humara and Bob Rupe.

Sprague, David. "Sound Check: The Silos; Keep on Chooglin'," *Me Music Express Magazine.* 14:145 (March 1990) 54. il., int. w/Walter Salas-Hamara.

Smithereens

DeYoung, Bill. "The Smithereens," *Backstage Magazine.* 1 (August 17–30, 1988) 10–11. il.

Holdship, Bill. "Arsenio Hall," *Spin.* 6:2 (May 1990) 16. il. A look behind the scenes as the band appears on *The Arsenio Hall Show.*

Schulps, Dave. "The Smithereens Get Non-Technical," *Musician.* n118 (August 1988) 45–46, 57–59. il., int.

Simels, Steve. "The Smithereens," *Stereo Review.* 53 (November 1988) 98–100. il.

Tamarkin, Jeff. "The Smithereens: Jersey Sure," *Goldmine.* n245 (December 15, 1989) 8–14, 28. il. Appended with "Smithereens Complete U.S./U.K. Discography," compiled by Jeff Tamarkin and Dennis Diken.

Smiths

DiMartino, Dave. "We'll Meet Again: Doing it Smiths-Style," *Creem.* 17 (February 1986) 8–10ff. il., int. w/Morrissey.

Marr, Johnny, with Scott Isler. "Heaven Knows Johnny Marr's Not Miserable Now," *Musician.* n131 (September 1989) 52–60. il., int.

"Marr in Car Crash," *Melody Maker.* 61 (November 22, 1986) 3. il.

McIlheney, Barry. "The Thoughts of Chairman Marr," *Melody Maker.* 60 (August 3, 1985) 32–33. il., int.

Middles, Mick. *The Smiths.* London: Omnibus, 1985. il., bio.

Murdoch, Lorne. "The Smiths," *Record Collector.* n73 (September 1985) 11–14. il., int.

Murdoch, Lorne. "The Smiths," *Record Collector.* n96 (August 1987) 40–42. il., disc.

"News," *Melody Maker.* 63 (September 5, 1987) 4. il. Replacement for Johnny Marr sought.

Reynolds, Simon. "How Soon is Now?," *Melody Maker.* 63 (September 26, 1987) 28. il.
Post-split analysis of The Smiths.

Savage, Jon. "The Smiths," *Spin.* n2 (June 1985) 68–69. il.

"Smiths Split!," *Melody Maker.* (September 12, 1987) 3. il.

Tarkin, Roy. "The Smiths," *Musician.* n68 (June 1984) 13–14. il.

Thompson, Mark. "Smiths Rarities," *Record Collector.* n104 (April 1988) 12–16. il. Includes sidebar, "Collectable Smiths Rarities."

"What a Marr-velous Recovery," *Melody Maker.* 61 (November 29, 1986) 3. il.
Marr now wearing a neck brace.

MORRISSEY (r.n.: STEVEN PATRICK MORRISSEY)

"Bigmouth Struck Again," *Melody Maker.* 61 (November 8, 1986) 3. il.
Morrissey hit by objects thrown at concerts.

Jones, A., and others. "Trial by Jury," *Melody Maker.* 60 (March 16, 1985) 23–26. il., int.

Leboff, G. "Goodbye Cruel World," *Melody Maker.* 63 (September 26, 1987) 26–27. il., int.

Owen, Frank. "Home Thoughts from Abroad," *Melody Maker.* 61 (September 27, 1986) 14–16. il., int.

Spear of Destiny (See also: Theatre of Hate)

Kassan, Brian. "New Faces to Watch: Spear of Destiny," *Cash Box.* (May 23, 1987) 12. il., int. w/singer-songwriter Kirk Brandon.

Stamey, Chris (See also: dB's; Golden Palominos)

DeSavia, Tom. "New Faces to Watch: Chris Stamey," *Cash Box.* (January 30, 1988) 9. il., int.

Sugarcubes

Linden, Amy. "The Sugarcubes," *Musician.* n120 (October 1988) 15–16. il.

"My Favorite Year," *Melody Maker.* 65 (January 7, 1989) 5. il.

Press, J. "Newbeats: 500 Micrograms of Love," *Creem.* 19 (October 1988) 67–68. il.

Roberts, Chris. "One Lump or Two," *Melody Maker.* 63 (September 5, 1987) 10–11. il., int.

The The

"News," *Melody Maker.* 65 (January 7, 1989) 4. The band features a new lineup.

They Might Be Giants

Doole, Kerry. "Sound Check: They Might Be Giants; One Giant Step," *Me Music Express Magazine.* 14:145 (March 1990) 43. il., int. w/John Linnell and John Flansburgh.

Iorio, Paul. "New Faces to Watch: They Might Be Giants," *Cash Box.* (December 13, 1986) 10. il., int.

Jennings, Dave. "They Might Be Giants; Before and After the Flood," *Melody Maker.* 66:7 (February 17, 1990) 37. il., int.

Robbins, Ira. "They Might Be Giants; Rock's Absurdist Duo Stake Their Claim With *Lincoln,*" *Rolling Stone.* n543 (January 12, 1989) 26.

Woods, Karen. "They Might Be Giants: Then Again, Maybe Not," *Cash Box.* (March 3, 1990) 22. il., int.

Thrashing Doves

Liveten, S. "Newbeats: Out of the Rubble," *Creem.* 19 (September 1987) 69. il.

Mico, Ted. "On the Wings of Love," *Melody Maker.* 61 (June 21, 1986) 32–33. il., int.

Walters, Barry. "When Doves Whine," *Spin.* 3:5 (August 1987) 68–69. il.

Throwing Muses (See also: Breeders)

Hampton, H. "Music: Femme Fatalism," *Village Voice.* 31 (October 28, 1986) 73–74. il.

Macnie, Jim. "Throwing Muses," *Musician.* n127 (May 1989) 15–16, 97. il.

Roberts, Chris. "Cents & $ensibility," *Melody Maker.* 63 (September 19, 1987) 12–13. il., int.

Stubbs, D. "Throwing Muses: Daughters of the Fatherland," *Melody Maker.* 65 (January 28, 1989) 28–30. il., int.

Timbuk 3

Bessman, Jim. "Timbuk 3 Videos Come to the Fore," *Billboard.* 100 (June 4, 1988) 55.

McCormick, Moira. "New Faces: The Bright Future of Timbuk 3," *Rolling Stone.* n486 (November 6, 1986) 31. il.

[Portrait], *Creem.* 18 (June 1987) 36–37. il.

"Street Life," *Melody Maker.* 61 (September 13, 1986) 12. il., int.

Triffids

Barber, L. "Kangaroo Courting," *Melody Maker.* 60 (May 18, 1985) 31. il., int.

Senior, J., and S. Lawrence. "Roads to Freedom," *Melody Maker.* 61 (June 7, 1986) 13. il., int.

Sweeting, Adam. "Desert Songs," *Melody Maker.* 61 (August 2, 1986) 14–15. il., int. w/D. McComb.

Velvet Elvis

Williams, Joe. "Velvet Elvis," *Cash Box.* (July 23, 1988) 11. il., int. w/singer-guitarist Dan Trisko.

Violent Femmes

Lake, S. "State of the Union: Spanish Inquisition," *Melody Maker.* 60 (May 4, 1985) 15ff. il., int.

Murphy, E. "On Record: Heads' Harrison Producing Femmes," *Record.* 5 (January/February 1986) 13. il.

Sutherland, Steve. "Trinity Rockers," *Melody Maker.* 61 (March 1, 1986) 40–41. int.

Wild Seeds

Tamarkin, Jeff. "Wild Seeds: Why They Won't Rock You All Night Long," *Goldmine.* n202 (April 22, 1988) 20, 75, 79, 89. il.

Woodentops

Mico, Ted. "The Hills are Alive," *Melody Maker.* 60 (November 30, 1985) 22–23. il., int. w/Rolo McGinty.

Reynolds, Simon. "The Happy Few," *Melody Maker.* 61 (July 12, 1986) 24–25. il., int. w/McGinty.

Tamarkin, Jeff. "Columbia Bows Woodentops' Debut Album," *Billboard.* 98 (August 30, 1986) 26.

A. POSTMODERN

General Sources

Owen, Frank. "Flash: Post Modern," *Spin.* 5:7 (October 1989) 20.

APB

Morton, T. "Escape from 'Granite City'," *Melody Maker.* 60 (April 27, 1985) 31. il., int.

Morton, T. "Sharp Shooters," *Melody Maker.* 61 (May 24, 1986) 10. il., int. w/I. Slater.

Act Fuseli

Downer, S. "Sweet Drummer," *Melody Maker.* 61 (August 16, 1986) 14. int. w/D. Lenten.

Adult Net

Mico, Ted. "Just Like Edie," *Melody Maker.* 60 (November 30, 1985) 31. il., int.

Adventures

McIlheney, Bruce. "Deep in the Heart of Texas," *Melody Maker.* 60 (October 5, 1985) 16–17. il., int.

McIlheney, Bruce. "Heart in Motion," *Melody Maker.* 60 (February 2, 1985) 10–11. il., int. w/Terry Sharpe.

Age of Chance

Robb, John. "The Harder They Come The Higher They Fall," *Sounds.* (March 3, 1990) 21. il., int.

All About Eve

Mercer, M. "Dawn Chorus," *Melody Maker.* 61 (June 14, 1986) 14. int.

Alone Again Or

Morton, T. "Escape from 'Granite City'," *Melody Maker.* 60 (April 27, 1985) 31. il., int.

Alternative TV

"Clowntime is Over," *Melody Maker.* 61 (March 22, 1986) 32. int. w/Mark Perry.

Animal Nightlife

Sullivan, C. "Animal Rights," *Melody Maker.* 60 (July 27, 1985) 22.

Sullivan, C. "Nocturnal Admissions," *Melody Maker.* 60 (August 31, 1985) 11. il., int. w/Andy Polaris.

Animotion

Vare, E.A. "Animotion Not Obsessed With Success," *Billboard.* 97 (May 4, 1985) 40A.

Any Trouble

"Pictures of 1984," *Melody Maker.* 60 (January 5, 1985) 31. il.

Apple Mosaic

Oldfield, Paul. "Bitter Fruit," *Melody Maker.* 63 (August 8, 1987) 10–11. il., int. w/Lawrence and Shane.

Arsenal

"Gunning for Glory," *Melody Maker.* 64 (December 10, 1988) 10. il.

Asphalt Ribbons

Spencer, Mr. "Names for 1990: Wined Up," *Sounds.* (February 24, 1990) 56. il., int. w/singer Stuart Staples.

Assassins

Smith, Jerry. "Jam On: Looking for a Hit," *New Musical Express.* (January 27, 1990) 10. il., int.

Aztec Camera

Sutherland, Steve. "Aztec Camera: Street Hassle," *Melody Maker.* 66:23 (June 9, 1990) 28–29. il., int. w/Roddy Frame.

Sutherland, Steve. "Dream Topping," *Melody Maker.* 64 (June 18, 1988) 30–31. il., int. w/Frame.

Badlands

Halbersberg, Elianne. "Badlands: Exclusive Interview With Ray Gillen," *Song Hits.* n273 (March 1990) 34–36. il.

Balaam and the Angel

FitzGerald, H. "Angels With Dirty Faces," *Melody Maker.* 61 (March 29, 1986) 14. il., int.

Sutherland, Steve. "The Greatest Story Ever Told," *Melody Maker.* 60 (September 7, 1985) 10–11. il., int.

Bananarama

Lababedi, I. "Bananarama: These Charming Girls," *Creem.* 18 (December 1986) 42–44ff. il.

Nite, Norm N., with Charles Crespo. "Bananarama," In: *Rock On: . . . (Volume 3).* pp. 20–21. il., disc.

Sullivan, C. "The Blues Sisters," *Melody Maker.* 61 (June 21, 1986) 14. il., int.

Tamarkin, Jeff. "Bananarama: U.K. Trio Gets Down to Business," *Billboard.* 98 (August 2, 1986) 25. il.

Band of Holy Joy

Stud Brothers. "Band of Holy Joy: Summer Holiday," *Melody Maker.* 65 (August 19, 1989) 16. il., int.

Band of Susans

Stubbs, D. "Susie Q's & Answers," *Melody Maker.* 63 (October 17, 1987) 26. il., int.

Bang Bang

"New Faces to Watch: Bang Bang," *Cash Box.* XLIX:8 (August 10, 1985) 10. il., int. w/lead vocalist and songwriter Julian Raymond.

Bang Tango

Halbersberg, Elianne. "Bang Tango—Exclusive Interview With Joe LeSte," *Song Hits.* n275 (July 1990) 16–18. il.

Bardots

Williams, Simon. "Take It to the Bridget," *New Musical Express.* (February 17, 1990) 10. il.

Bastro

Robb, John. "Names for 1990: The Gripe Stuff," *Sounds.* (February 24, 1990) 57. il., int. w/frontman Dave Grubbs.

Batfish Boys

Denbigh, S. "The Winged Loony," *Melody Maker.* 61 (October 4, 1986) 46. il., int.

Beat Rodeo

Agnelli, L.E. "The Beat Goes On: Cowboys aus New York?," *Creem.* 17 (August 1985) 18. il.

Kirby, Kip. "Beat Rodeo: Hybrid Rockers," *Billboard.* 97 (December 21, 1985) 46.

Young, J. "Not Weird, Only Different," *Musician.* n84 (October 1985) 36. il.

Beautiful South (See also: Housemartins)

Hardy, Ernest. "New Faces: The Beautiful South," *Cash Box.* (May 12, 1990) 7. il.

Beloved

"New on the Charts," *Billboard.* 101 (August 5, 1989) 29. il.

Stud Brothers. "The Beloved; Listomania," *Melody Maker.* 66:4 (January 27, 1990) 12–13. il., int. w/Steven Waddington and Jon Marsh.

Beltane Fire

FitzGerald, H. "Sword in the Stone," *Melody Maker.* 61 (March 1, 1986) 35. il., int.

Voss, M. "Men of Good Fortune," *Melody Maker.* 60 (October 5, 1985) 38. il.

Bible

Irwin, C.L. "God Squad," *Melody Maker.* 61 (May 3, 1986) 41. il., int. w/Tom Sheperd and Bob Hewerdine.

Biff Bang Pow!

Stanley, Bob. "Sidelines: Biff Bang Pow!," *Melody Maker.* 66:8 (February 24, 1990) 12. il.

Big Stick

Mercer, M. "Beat It!," *Melody Maker.* 61 (June 14, 1986) 42. il., int.

Big Wheel

FitzGerald, H. "This Wheel's on Fire," *Melody Maker.* 60 (July 27, 1985) 18ff. il., int. w/Jake Burns.

Big Youth (r.n.: Manley Muchanan)

"New Acts," *Variety.* 320 (August 7, 1985) 77.

Birdland

Rom, Ron. "The Eve of Destruction," *Sounds.* (January 27, 1990) 17. il., int. w/vocalist Rob.

Black (r.n.: Colin Vearncombe; See also: Darling Buds)

Kiley, P. "After Dark," *Melody Maker.* 61 (November 8, 1986) 9. il., int. C. Vearncombe.

Robinson, Julius. "Black Fights Back," *Cash Box.* (March 12, 1988) 9, 30. il., int.

Black Box

Horkins, Tony. "Control Zone: Boxing Clever," *Melody Maker.* 66:20 (May 19, 1990) 46. il., int. w/Mirko Limoni.

Black Britain

Mathur, Paul. "Grooving Guerillas," *Melody Maker.* 61 (April 12, 1986) 10–11. il., int.

Blake Babies

McCormick, Moira. "New Faces: Blake Babies," *Rolling Stone.* n576 (April 19, 1990) 29. il., int. w/John Strohm.

Bliss

"Sidelines: The Bliss," *Melody Maker.* 63 (December 12, 1987) 13. il., int. w/R. Morrison.

Blow Monkeys

Aston, Martin. "Theories and Evolution," *Melody Maker.* 61 (March 8, 1986) 36. int. w/"Dr." Robert Howard.

"New Faces to Watch: Blow Monkeys," *Cash Box.* XLIX:31 (January 8, 1986) 10. il., int. w/lead singer Howard.

Reynolds, Simon. "The Perfect Primate," *Melody Maker.* 61 (April 26, 1986) 34–35. il., int. w/Howard.

Blue Aeroplanes

Aston, Martin. "Aces High," *Melody Maker.* 60 (September 28, 1985) 27. il., int. w/Gerard Langley.

Doole, Kerry. "Sound Check: Blue Aeroplanes; Bohemian Rockers," *Me Music Express Magazine.* 14:145 (March 1990) 48. il., int. w/singer-lyricist Gerard Langley.

FitzGerald, Helen. "Flights of Fancy," *Melody Maker.* 61 (May 10, 1986) 15. il., int. w/Gerard Langley.

Blue in Heaven

FitzGerald, Helen. "Blue Murder," *Melody Maker.* 61 (July 19, 1986) 11. il., int. w/S. O'Neill.

Blue Murder

Capozzoli, Michael A., Jr. "Blue Murder: Exclusive Interview With John Sykes and Carmine Appice," *Song Hits.* n272 (December 1989) 16–18. il.

Blue Nile

"New Faces to Watch: The Blue Nile," *Cash Box.* (September 7, 1985) 10. il., int.

Bogmen

Granthan, B. "Irish Trio The Bogmen Mutilate Classic Rock to Cult Status; Shlock Sells," *Variety.* 321 (December 4, 1985) 1ff.

Bomb Party

McIlheney, B. "Bombs Away," *Melody Maker.* 60 (September 14, 1985) 40–41. il., int.

Book of Love

Mathur, Paul. "Chapter Verse," *Melody Maker.* 61 (July 5, 1986) 10. il., int.

Boom Boom Boom

Strange, P. "The Big Bang," *Melody Maker.* 61 (April 12, 1986) 15. il., int.

Boss

"Sidelines: The Boss," *Melody Maker.* 63 (October 31, 1987) 21. il., int.

Boss Hog

Robb, John. "Mutant Moments," *Sounds.* (February 3, 1990) 12. il., int.

Bourgeois Tagg

Doole, Kerry. "Sound Check: Brent Bourgeois; No Tagg-Team," *Me Music Express Magazine.* 14:148 (June 1990) 21. il., int.

Boy Meets Girl

Vare, E.A. "Boy Meets Girl: Right Group, Right Time," *Billboard.* 97 (June 1, 1985) 46. int.

Breeders (See also: Pixies; Throwing Muses)

Mico, Ted. "The Breeders: Let It Breed," *Melody Maker.* 66:21 (May 26, 1990) 28–30. il., int.

Woods, Karen. "Shock of the New," *Cash Box.* LIII:49 (June 30, 1990) 10. il., int. w/Kim Deal.

Brickell, Edie, and the New Bohemians

Roberts, Chris. "Star Gazing," *Melody Maker.* 65 (January 21, 1989) 10. il., int.

Brighter Side of Darkness

Pruter, Robert. "Brighter Side of Darkness: Addicted to Love," *Goldmine.* n179 (June 5, 1987) 32, 36. il.

Brilliant

Smith, M. "World in Action," *Melody Maker.* 60 (November 2, 1985) 36–37. il., int.

Broken Homes

DeSavia, Tom. "The Broken Homes: Built to Last," *Cash Box.* (October 29, 1988) 14. il., int. w/lead vocalist Michael Doman.

Brother Beyond

Mathur, Paul. "Big Brothers," *Melody Maker.* 61 (October 18, 1986) 36. il., int.

CBI

Clerk, Carol. "Bad Magic," *Melody Maker.* 61 (August 2, 1986) 12–13. il., int.

Camper Van Beethoven (See also: Touring)

Boyko, Ron. "Camper Van Beethoven," *Backstage Magazine.* 1 (July 20–August 2, 1988) 10–11. il.

Fricke, David. "Camper Van Beethoven's Notes from the Underground," *Rolling Stone.* n526 (May 19, 1988) 47–52. il., int.

Tamarkin, Jeff. "Camper Van Beethoven," *Goldmine.* n216 (November 4, 1988) 76, 78, 80. il., disc.

Candy

"New Faces to Watch: Candy," *Cash Box.* XLIX:14 (September 14, 1985) 12. il., int. w/Jonathan Daniel and Gilby Clarke.

Captain Sensible (r.n.: Ray Burns)

Clerk, Carol. "Game$ People Play," *Melody Maker.* 60 (November 23, 1985) 10. il., int.

Captains of Industry

Thomas, D. " 'Monkey' Music," *Melody Maker.* 60 (July 20, 1985) 36. il.

Cardiacs

Push. "Sheer Heart Attack," *Melody Maker.* 63 (October 17, 1987) 47. il., int.

Carey, Tony

Nite, Norm N., with Charles Crespo. "Tony Carey," In: *Rock On: . . . (Volume 3).* pp. 54–55. il., disc.
Brief career sketch of artist who also has recorded under the name "Planet P."

Case, Peter

Hochman, S. "Former Plimsoul Goes Back to Basics," *Billboard.* 98 (August 16, 1986) 27.

Jones, A. "Horizons West," *Melody Maker.* 61 (August 16, 1986) 30–31. il., int.

Kordosh, J. "Newbeat: Do You Want a Man of Steel?," *Creem.* 18 (December 1986) 66. il.

"Sidelines: Peter Case," *Melody Maker.* 65 (August 26, 1989) 16. il.

Sutherland, Sam. "Manager Draws on Past; Performer Handles Peter Case," *Billboard.* 98 (August 16, 1986) 27.

Cast of 1000s

McIlheney, B. "Passion by Numbers," *Melody Maker.* 61 (August 9, 1986) 14. il., int. w/D. Hervey.

Chakk

Pye, Ian. "Pleasures of the Flesh," *Melody Maker.* 60 (May 11, 1985) 14–15. il., int.

Reynolds, Simon. "Chakk Attack!," *Melody Maker.* 61 (March 8, 1986) 14–15. il., int. w/J. Harries and J. Stuart.

Chandra, Sheila

Seltzer, Jonathan. "Sidelines: Sheila Chandra," *Melody Maker.* 66:8 (February 24, 1990) 11. il.

Chequered Past

Trakin, P. "From a Chequered Past to a Spotted Future," *Creem.* 16 (March 1985) 18. il.

Christians

Horkins, Tony. "Control Zone: The Second Coming," *Melody Maker.* 66:4 (January 27, 1990) 37. il., int. w/Henry Priestman.

Push. "Harvest Festival," *Melody Maker.* 64 (October 15, 1988) 44. il., int.

Circus Circus Circus

Mercer, M. "Cracking the Whip!," *Melody Maker.* 61 (April 26, 1986) 13. il., int.

Circus X3

"Three-Ringed Circus," *Melody Maker.* 64 (June 25, 1988) 10. il.

Claytown Troupe

Collins, Andrew. "Revenge of the Vegetarian Lager Louts," *New Musical Express.* (February 24, 1990) 13. il.

Clean

Davis, Erik. "Shephard Rock," *Spin.* 6:2 (May 1990) 14. il., int.

Clocks

Nite, Norm N., with Charles Crespo. "Clocks," In: *Rock On:
. . . (Volume 3).* p. 73. disc.

Cock Robin

Jones, P. "Who Billed Cock Robin? U.S. Band Clicks Overseas, Not at Home," *Billboard.* 98 (June 14, 1986) 62.

"New on the Charts," *Billboard.* 97 (July 20, 1985) 40.

Cole, Lloyd

Holdship, Bill. "The Beat Goes On," *Creem.* 17 (October 1985) 20. il., int.

Mehler, M. "What's New: Pride in Pretension," *Record.* 4 (July 1985) 38. il., int.

Colour Field (See also: Fun Boy Three)

DeMuir, H. "Newbeats: Playing the Field," *Creem.* 17 (April 1986) 76. il.

"New Faces to Watch: The Colour Field," *Cash Box.* XLIX:30 (January 11, 1986) 10. il., int. w/Terry Hall.

Smith, M. "No More 'Mr. Misery'," *Melody Maker.* 61 (January 25, 1986) 14–15. il., int. w/Hall.

Sutherland, Sam. "I'm a Miserable Bastard," *Melody Maker.* 60 (May 14, 1985) 10–11. il., int. w/Hall.

Cowboy Junkies

Stern, Perry. "Back in the Saddle," *Me Music Express Magazine.* 14:145 (March 1990) 56–58. il., int.

Crazyhead

Clerk, Carol. "Heads Will Roll," *Melody Maker.* 64 (June 25, 1988) 30. il., int.

Clerk, Carol. "Sons of the Desert," *Melody Maker.* 64 (October 22, 1988) 59. il., int.

Creaming Jesus

"Whipped Cream," *Melody Maker.* 65 (January 14, 1989) 16. il.

Creepers

Downer, S. "Creeping Up," *Melody Maker*. 61 (July 26, 1986) 9. il., int. w/M. Riley.

Crime and the City Solution

Reynolds, Simon. "Breaking and Entering," *Melody Maker*. 61 (June 21, 1986) 11. il., int.

Smith, M. "Pennies from Heaven," *Melody Maker*. 60 (October 19, 1985) 45. il., int. w/Mick Havvey and R.S. Howard.

Cucumbers

Smith, K.J. "Swing Shift: Pearls Before Brine," *Village Voice*. 32 (December 1, 1987) 106. il.

Curiosity Killed the Cat

Sullivan, C. "Glamour Pussies," *Melody Maker*. 61 (August 9, 1986) 14. il., int.

Yardumian, Rob. "New Faces to Watch: Curiosity Killed the Cat," *Cash Box*. (July 25, 1987) 10–11. il., int. w/vocalist Ben Volpebere-Pierrot.

Cutting Crew

Kassan, Brian. "Cutting Crew Sets Sail in America," *Cash Box*. (March 28, 1987) 11, 23. il., int. w/guitarist Kevin MacMichael.

Sullivan, C. "Slush Yuppies," *Melody Maker*. 61 (September 13, 1986) 23. int.

Cycle Sluts

"New Sexation," *Melody Maker.* 65 (January 21, 1989) 13. il.

Daffodils

Birrell, I. "Petal Power," *Melody Maker.* 61 (August 9, 1986) 33. il., int.

Daintees

Jones, A. "Moving Pictures," *Melody Maker.* 61 (September 13, 1986) 30–31. il., int. w/M. Stephenson.

Mathur, Paul. "Bolivian Busking Power," *Melody Maker.* 61 (May 17, 1986) 31. il., int. w/Stephenson.

Danny Wilson

Holland, Duncan. "Be Bop a-Lula," *Music Week.* (June 10, 1989) 16. il., int. w/Jed Grimes.

Darling Buds (See also: Black)

Mathur, Paul. "Bouquet of Barbed Wire," *Melody Maker.* 64 (June 25, 1988) 14–15. il., int.

True, Everett. "The Darling Buds: Petal Machine Music," *Melody Maker.* 66:21 (May 26, 1990) 36–37. il., int.

Deacon Blue

Ireland, David. "Deacon Blue," *Record Collector.* n130 (June 1990) 16–19. il., disc.

Wild, David. "New Faces: Deacon Blue," *Rolling Stone.* n565 (November 16, 1989) 32. il., int. w/leader Ricky Ross.

DeBurgh, Chris

Sutton, Rich. "Exclusive Interview With Chris DeBurgh," *Super Song Hits.* n39 (Spring 1984) 36–37. il.

Sutton, Rich. "Exclusive Interview With Chris DeBurgh," *Song Hits.* n227 (January 1985) 6–7. il.

Thompson, Dave. "Chris DeBurgh," *Record Collector.* n86 (October 1986) 23–26. il., disc.

Thompson, Dave. *'From a Spark to a Flame': The Chris DeBurgh Story.* London: Omnibus, 1987. il.

Del Amitri

Jennings, Dave. "Del Amitri: Waking Up With the Charts on Fire," *Melody Maker.* 66:8 (February 24, 1990) 44. il., int. w/Justin Currie.

Smith, Jerry. "Treasure Highland," *New Musical Express.* (February 3, 1990) 18–19. il.

Del Conte, Andrea

Farber, Jerry. "Andrea Del Conte," *Cash Box.* (January 6, 1988) 11. int.

Deltones

"Skatellettes," *Melody Maker.* 61 (July 5, 1986) 9. il., int. w/Penny Leyton.

Diesel Park West

"Way Out West," *Melody Maker.* 64 (October 15, 1988) 14. il.

Dig

Kassan, Brian. "New Faces to Watch: The Dig," *Cash Box.* (May 9, 1987) 10. il., int.

Easterhouse (See also: Censorship)

"Easter EP Ban," *Melody Maker.* 61 (May 31, 1986) 3. il. Re. the banning of *Inspiration* from England's Radio One.

Iorio, Paul. "New Faces to Watch: Easterhouse," *Cash Box.* (September 20, 1986) 10. il., int. w/Andy Perry.

McIlheney, Bruce. "Working Class Heroes," *Melody Maker.* 61 (June 14, 1986) 12–13. il., int. w/Perry.

Morton, T. "Easter Rising," *Melody Maker.* 60 (June 8, 1985) 36–37. il., int.

Smith, W. "The Easter Rebellion," *Melody Maker.* 61 (January 25, 1986) 12–13. il., int. w/Andy Perry.

Eddie, John

Bessman, Jim. "John Eddie: I Wasn't Born to Clone," *Billboard.* 98 (September 6, 1986) 22. il., int.

"New Acts," *Variety.* 324 (October 1, 1986) 112.

Eddie and the Tide

"New Faces to Watch: Eddie and the Tide," *Cash Box.* XLIX:17 (October 5, 1985) 12. il., int. w/lead singer Eddie Rice.

Ege Bam Yasi

Morton, T. "Eggheads," *Melody Maker.* 61 (June 21, 1986) 9. il., int. w/K. Smyth.

Eighth Wonder

Henry, J. "Absolute Beginners," *Melody Maker.* 60 (September 28, 1985) 36. il., int. w/Patsy Kensit.

Mico, Ted. "Patsy Through the Looking Glass," *Melody Maker.* 60 (November 30, 1985) 24–25. il., int. w/Kensit.

Electric Morning

Kiley, P. "The 'Liverbyrds'," *Melody Maker.* 61 (June 21, 1986) 11. int.

Kiley, P. "Operation Daybreak," *Melody Maker.* 60 (April 27, 1985) 32. int.

An Emotional Fish

Myers, Caren. "Sidelines: An Emotional Fish," *Melody Maker.* 66:20 (May 19, 1990) 13. il.

Smith, Mat. "An Emotional Fish: Another Time, Another Place," *Melody Maker.* (July 7, 1990) 8–9. il., int. w/ Gerard Whelan.

Energy Orchard

Bailie, Stuart. "Louder Than Bombs," *New Musical Express.* (January 27, 1990) 16, 39. il., int.

Clerk, Carol. "Energy Orchard; Belfast Children Strike Back," *Melody Maker.* 66:5 (February 3, 1990) 43. il., int.

Kane, Peter. "Personality Crisis," *Sounds.* (February 17, 1990) 20. il., int. w/Joby Fox and Paul Toner.

Escape Club

McIlheney, Bruce. "International Rescue," *Melody Maker.* 60 (November 23, 1985) 15. il., int. w/Trevor and Dave.

Eurogliders

"New Acts," *Variety.* 318 (March 20, 1985) 140.

FM

Clerk, Carol. "Radio Ga! Ga!," *Melody Maker.* 61 (August 2, 1986) 29. il., int.

Face to Face

Nite, Norm N., with Charles Crespo. "Face to Face," In: *Rock On: . . . (Volume 3).* pp. 109–110. il.

Fairground Attraction

Houlton, J. "All's Fair in Love," *Spin.* 4 (January 1989) 20. il.

Faith Brothers

Mico, Ted. "Eyesight to the Blind," *Melody Maker.* 60 (November 2, 1985) 10ff. int. w/B. Frank and L. Hirons.

Faster Pussycat

Capozzoli, Michael A., Jr. "Faster Pussycat," *Song Hits.* n276 (September 1990) 16–18. il.

Fatal Charm

Thomas, D. "Charm School," *Melody Maker.* 60 (August 10, 1985) 30. il., int.

Faze One

Owen, F. "A Political Party," *Melody Maker.* 61 (November 1, 1986) 12. il., int.

Felt

Mathur, Paul. "Lost & Found," *Melody Maker.* 61 (October 18, 1986) 44. il., int. w/Lawrence.

"Seven Types of Ambiguity," *Melody Maker.* 60 (November 23, 1985) 36. int. w/Lawrence.

Sinker, M. "In Search of Space," *Melody Maker.* 64 (December 10, 1988) 37. il., int.

Fire

Kiley, P. "Burning Ambition," *Melody Maker.* 61 (June 7, 1986) 31. il., int. w/D. Wibberly.

Fire Next Time

Henry, J. "Hothothot," *Melody Maker.* 61 (June 7, 1986) 23. il., int. w/J. Maddocks and L. Humler.

McCoid, B. "Playing With Fire," *Melody Maker.* 61 (September 6, 1986) 38. int.

Fish (r.n.: Derek William Dick; See also: Marillion)

Clerk, Carol. "That Riviera Touch," *Melody Maker.* 60 (June 29, 1985) 18–19. il., int.

Elliott, Paul. "Through the Glass Darkly," *Sounds.* (February 3, 1990) 16–17. il., int.

"Shrink Rap," *Melody Maker.* 60 (June 1, 1985) 13. il., int.

Fishbone

Gore, J. "The Groove According to Fishbone," *Guitar Player.* 23 (August 1989) 24–28ff. il., disc., music score, int. w/Norwood Fisher and Kendall Jones.

Hochman, S. "Fishbone LP is Doing Swimmingly," *Billboard.* 98 (December 27, 1986) 26.

McCormick, M. "A Wild Band Stays Wild," *Billboard.* 97 (September 28, 1985) 54.

Perry, S. "The Revolution Will Not be Sanitized," *Musician.* n123 (January 1989) 14ff. il., int.

[Portrait], *Village Voice.* 30 (July 23, 1985) 62–63.

"Salmon Chanted Evening," *Melody Maker.* 65 (January 7, 1989) 11. il.

Scoppa, Bud. "The Bus Was No Greyhound," *Record.* 4 (May 1985) 34. il.

Five Star

Jackson, Richard. "Five Star," *Record Collector.* n98 (October 1987) 17–20. il., disc.

Kirk, K. "Family Fortunes: Five Star," *Melody Maker.* 61 (June 14, 1986) 38–39. int.

McIlheney, Bruce. "Chocs Away," *Melody Maker.* 61 (October 18, 1986) 16–17. il., bio, int.

5TA

Cordery, M. "Heat Treatment," *Melody Maker.* 61 (January 18, 1986) 14–15. il., int.

Downer, S. "Lads Ahoy!," *Melody Maker.* 61 (August 23, 1986) 12.

Flaming Mussolinis

FitzGerald, Helen. "The Great Dictators," *Melody Maker.* 60 (September 28, 1985) 12. il., int.

Flesh

Morton, T. "Off the Bone," *Melody Maker.* 61 (April 26, 1986) 13. int.

Floy Joy

Mico, Ted. "Come Floy With Me," *Melody Maker.* 61 (January 18, 1986) 10–11. il.

Fountainhead

FitzGerald, Helen. " 'Rhythm' Methodists," *Melody Maker.* 61 (June 7, 1986) 13. il., int.

400 Blows

Smith, M. "Blowing Up a Storm," *Melody Maker.* 60 (July 13, 1985) 10. il., int.

4,000,000 Telephones

McIlheney, Bruce. "Subscriber Trunk Dialing," *Melody Maker.* 61 (March 15, 1986) 29. il., int.

Fra Lippo Lippi

Downer, S. "Alpine Echoes," *Melody Maker.* 61 (June 21, 1986) 33. il., int.

Frank Chickens

Kiley, P. "Educating Frank," *Melody Maker.* 61 (September 6, 1986) 30. il., int.

Morton, T. "Frank Confessions," *Melody Maker.* 60 (August 31, 1985) 33. il., int.

"Shrink Rap," *Melody Maker.* 63 (October 10, 1987) 21. il., int.

Freeez

Murray, A. "Control Zone: Ice Squad," *Melody Maker.* 60 (November 9, 1985) 44. il., int. re. *Idle Vices.*

Friction Groove

FitzGerald, Helen. "Creative Friction," *Melody Maker.* 60 (August 10, 1985) 30–31. il., int.

Friday, Gavin, and the Man Seezer (r.n.: Fionan Hanvey and Maurice Roycroft; See also: Virgin Prunes)

Woods, Karen. "Gavin Friday and the Man Seezer: Having a Weill Weekend," *Cash Box.* (September 23, 1989) 8–9. il., int. w/Friday.

Fruits of Passion

Sullivan, C. "State of Fop," *Melody Maker.* 61 (March 1, 1986) 13. il., int. w/D. Fullerton and F. Donleavy.

Furniture

Aston, M. "Suite Harmony," *Melody Maker.* 60 (February 2, 1985) 25. il., int.

Downer, S. "Our 'Brilliant' Career," *Melody Maker.* 61 (November 22, 1986) 10. int. w/J. Irvin.

Fury

"New Faces to Watch: Fury," *Cash Box.* XLIX:21 (November 2, 1985) 14. il., int. w/Brian LaBlanc.

Fuzzbox

O'Brien, Glenn. "Girls Just Wanna Have Fuzz," *Spin.* 3:5 (August 1987) 60–61. il.

[Portrait], *Creem.* 19 (September 1987) 36–37.

Roberts, Chris. "Fuzzbox: Bang on Target," *Melody Maker.* 65 (August 26, 1989) 40–41. il., int.

Geldof, Bob (See also: Band Aid; Boomtown Rats; Charity)

"Band Aid Bob is Back!," *Melody Maker.* 61 (January 18, 1986) 3. il.
Re. famine in Sudan.

"Bob Geldof Snub Riles the British," *Variety.* 321 (January 22, 1986) 79.
Re. New Year's royal honours list.

"Geldof is Knighted Alongside Ex-Actor Brian Rix, Others," *Variety.* 323 (June 18, 1986) 2ff.

"Geldoff Knighted," *Billboard.* 98 (June 21, 1986) 80.

"Geldoff: No More Band Aid," *Melody Maker.* 61 (January 4, 1966) 3. il.
He returns to his own career.

"The Gentile Touch!," *Melody Maker.* 60 (February 23, 1985) 3. il.
He denies belittling the Nazi holocaust.

Gett, Steve. "Geldoff Takes Time Out for Himself," *Billboard*. 98 (December 20, 1986) 6.

"Give Me Your Votes!," *Melody Maker*. 61 (May 10, 1986) 3. He endorses proportional parliamentary representation.

"An Irish Stew," *Melody Maker*. 61 (January 11, 1986) 5. il. He is denounced as a profiteer.

Jones, Allan. "Geldof: Still Ranting After All These Years," *Melody Maker*. 66:24 (June 16, 1990) 8–9. il., int.

Jones, P. "Geldof Among the Missing on Queen's Honor List," *Billboard*. 98 (January 11, 1986) 80.

McIlheney, Bruce. "The Year of the Saint," *Melody Maker*. 60 (December 21/28, 1985) 28–29. il.

Mehler, M. "Rock On: Calling Mr. Band Aid," *Record*. 4 (August 1985) 6.

"No Bells for Bob," *Melody Maker*. 61 (July 5, 1986) 3. The SDP denies reports he's a candidate for the next election.

"Oh, What a Knight!," *Melody Maker*. 61 (June 21, 1986) 3. Because he is not a British citizen, he will be referred to as Bob Geldof KBE (rather than "Sir").

General Public (See also: English Beat; Ranking Roger)

Gittins, Ian. "Men of the People," *Melody Maker*. 61 (October 18, 1986) 14. int. w/David Wakeling.

Grabel, R. "Being of General Public Interest," *Creem.* 17 (July 1985) 26–27ff. il., int.

Richardson, D. "The Beat Goes on: General Public in Search of Something New," *Record.* 4 (February 1985) 20–21.

Getting the Fear

"Fast Forward," *Melody Maker.* 60 (July 13, 1985) 4.
Report on the group's split.

Giant Sand (formerly: Giant Sandworms; See also: Dream Sandworms; Green on Red)

Cavanagh, David. "Cactus World Views," *Sounds.* (February 24, 1990) 19. il., int. w/Howe Gelb.

"Desert Brats," *Melody Maker.* 64 (December 3, 1988) 16. il.

Smith, M. "Sidelines: Giant Sand," *Melody Maker.* 66:7 (February 17, 1990) 11. il., int. w/guitarist Howe Gelb.

Smith, M. "Strangers on the Shore," *Melody Maker.* 61 (May 3, 1986) 12. int.

Gibbons, Shannon

Jeske, Lee. "New Faces to Watch: Shannon Gibbons," *Cash Box.* (April 16, 1988) 11. il.

Glover, Crispin

Ressner, Jeffrey. "New Faces: Crispin Glover," *Rolling Stone.* n571 (February 8, 1990) 21. il., int.

Go-Betweens

DiMartino, Dave. "Go-Betweens Aim to Strike Public Chord," *Billboard.* 101 (January 14, 1989) 18.

FitzGerald, Helen. "From Here to Eternity," *Melody Maker.* 61 (February 22, 1986) 12. int. w/R. Forster and G. McLennan.

Go Fundamental

"Fundamentally Yours," *Melody Maker.* 60 (July 20, 1985) 36. il., int.

Godfathers

Clerk, Carol. "The Cosa Nostra," *Melody Maker.* 60 (December 14, 1985) 23. il., int. w/C. and P. Coyne.

Clerk, Carol. "Godfathers; Valentine's Day Massacre," *Melody Maker.* 66:7 (February 17, 1990) 40–41. il., int.

Downer, S. "Family Business," *Melody Maker.* 61 (May 3, 1986) 13. il., int.

McCormick, Moira. "On the Charts: The Godfathers Make a Hit," *Rolling Stone.* n527 (June 2, 1988) 28. il.

Mercer, M. "Four Steps to Heaven," *Melody Maker.* 63 (October 17, 1987) 46. il., int. Re. "Birth School Work Death."

Stud Brothers. "Rebel Yell," *Melody Maker.* 61 (October 11, 1986) 32–33. il.

Golden Horde

FitzGerald, Helen. "Fun Fun Fun," *Melody Maker.* 61 (June 14, 1986) 42–43. il., int. w/S. Carmody.

Malik, J. "Band of Gold," *Melody Maker.* 60 (February 23, 1985) 22. il., int. w/Carmody.

Gone

Oldfield, Paul. "Soldiers of Fortune," *Melody Maker.* 64 (October 17, 1988) 10–11. il., int.

Goodbye Mister MacKenzie

Morton, T. "Parting Ways," *Melody Maker.* 61 (October 4, 1986) 17. il., int.

Great Divide

"Great Divide Wins Starmaker Quest," *Apra Journal.* 3:4 (1985) 46–47.

"Talk Talk," *Melody Maker.* 60 (June 8, 1985) 10.
   The group splits.

Greenhouse of Terror

Smith, M. "Avant Gardeners," *Melody Maker.* 61 (June 7, 1986) 15. il., int.

Half Man Half Biscuit

"Biscuits to Crumble?," *Melody Maker.* 61 (October 25, 1986) 4. il.
   Split rumored.

Kiley, P. "TV and Biscuits," *Melody Maker*. 61 (January 4, 1986) 16. il., int.

McIlheney, Bruce. "Square-Eyed and Legless," *Melody Maker*. 61 (March 1, 1986) 10–11. il., int.

Hard Corps

"Sidelines: Hard Corps," *Melody Maker*. 63 (October 24, 1987) 18. il., int.

Hard Rock Soul Movement

Owen, Frank. "A Political Party," *Melody Maker*. 61 (November 1, 1986) 12. il., int.

Head of David

Matzerath, O. "Urban Goliaths," *Melody Maker*. 61 (October 25, 1986) 33. il., int.

Heart Throbs

Lester, Paul. "The Heart Throbs: Gripping Yarns," *Melody Maker*. (October 27, 1990) 52–53. il., int.

Reynolds, Simon. "The Heart Throbs: In Every Dreamtime A Heartache," *Melody Maker*. (July 7, 1990) 32–33. il., int. w/Rossa Carlotti and Stephen Ward.

Spencer, Mr. "Ever Fallen in Love?," *Sounds*. (March 3, 1990) 18. il., int.

"Throbbing Bristle," *Melody Maker*. 64 (June 18, 1988) 13. il.

Hearts and Minds

"Sidelines: The Hearts and Minds," *Melody Maker.* 63 (October 10, 1987) 19. il., int. w/David Scott.

Hearts on Fire

Smith, M. Heart Breaking," *Melody Maker.* 60 (December 7, 1985) 17. il., int.

Heyman, Richard X

Henderson, Alex. "New Faces: Richard X. Heyman," *Cash Box.* (June 9, 1990) 6. il., int.

Heyward, Nick

"Shrink Rap," *Melody Maker.* 61 (May 3, 1986) 41. il., int.

Hipsway

Iorio, Paul. "Hipsway: Hit-Bound Funk from Scotland," *Cash Box.* (March 7, 1987) 11, 13. il., int. w/Grahame Skinner.

Mico, Ted. "Sanctify Yourself," *Melody Maker.* 61 (March 8, 1986) 10–11. il., int. w/S. Skinner.

Sutherland, Steve. "Broken Years," *Melody Maker.* 60 (September 21, 1985) 26–27. il., int.

Hoffs, Susanna (See also: Bangles)

Dickie, Mary. "Rock Notes: Solo Shot," *Me Music Express Magazine.* 14:148 (June 1990) 12. il., int.

Hollow Sunday

Lester, Paul. "Sidelines: Hollow Sunday," *Melody Maker.* 66:20 (May 19, 1990) 13. il.

Hollywood Beyond

Owen, Frank. "Hollywood Babble On," *Melody Maker.* 61 (June 28, 1986) 1, 10. il., int.

Honey Smugglers

Mueller, Andrew. "The Honey Smugglers," *Melody Maker.* (October 13, 1990) 7. il., int.

Honeydrippers

Hutchinson, J. "The *Record* Interview: Robert Plant," *Creem.* 4 (August 1985) 22–24ff.

Hook 'N' Pull Gang

Morton, T. "Hook Line," *Melody Maker.* 61 (August 9, 1986) 33. il., int.

Hooters

Gaines, Robin. "The Hooters," *Song Hits.* n243 (May 1986) 16–17. il.

"Hooters," *Super Song Hits.* n48 (Summer 1986) 20–21. il.

"New on the Charts," *Billboard.* 97 (June 8, 1985) 50.

Wheeler, D. "Hooters, Moi!," *Creem.* 17 (August 1985) 18. il.

Housemartins

"Housemartins Hit Back," *Melody Maker.* 61 (October 25, 1986) 3. The band's reaction to charges of obscenity.

Irwin, C. "Clown Time is Over," *Melody Maker.* 61 (July 5, 1986) 22–23. il., int.

Lababedi, I. "Eleganza: Good Socialist Lads," *Creem.* 19 (June 1988) 12.

"The Mouthmartins!," *Melody Maker.* 61 (October 18, 1986) 3. il. Alleged obscenities provoke call for radio tape-delay on use of only pre-recorded pop concerts.

"Shrink Rap," *Melody Maker.* 63 (December 5, 1987) 13. il., int. w/Paul and Norman.

Smith, W. *"Sheep* & Cheerful," *Melody Maker.* 61 (March 8, 1986) 34–35ff. il., int.

Strange, P. "Fly the Flag," *Melody Maker.* 60 (December 14, 1985) 10. il., int. w/Paul Heaton.

Hue and Cry

Morton, T. "Righteous Brothers," *Melody Maker.* 61 (April 12, 1986) 32–33. il., int.

Hypnotics, Thee

Oldfield, Paul. "Thee Hypnotics: Song from the Middle of Nowhere," *Melody Maker.* 66:24 (June 16, 1990) 41. il., int.

I Start Counting

Mathur, Paul. [Interview], *Melody Maker*. 61 (December 6, 1986) 23. il.

Thomas, D. "Countdown to Solvency," *Melody Maker*. 60 (May 11, 1985) 18. il., int.

Immaculate Fools

Yardumian, Rob. "New Faces to Watch: Immaculate Fools," *Cash Box*. (June 27, 1987) 10–11. il., int. w/lead singer, guitarist and songwriter Kevin Weatherill and drummer Peter Ross.

Impossibles

Lester, Paul. "Sidelines: The Impossibles," *Melody Maker*. (July 28, 1990) 12. il., int.

Innes, Neil

Kenton, G. "The Return of Neil Innes," *Creem*. 17 (October 1985) 18. il.

Innocence Mission

Meyer, Marianne. "Innocence Mission," *Rolling Stone*. n566 (November 30, 1989) 43. il.

Smith, Mat. "Sidelines: The Innocence Mission," *Melody Maker*. 66:8 (February 24, 1990) 10. il.

Into Paradise (See also: Blue in Heaven)

Cavanagh, David. "Names for 1990: Blue in Heaven," *Sounds.* (February 24, 1990) 55. il., int. w/singer-guitarist-songwriter Dave Long.

It Bites

Roberts, Steve. "It Bites," *Record Collector.* n129 (May 1990) 82–84. il., disc.

Jack Rubies

McCoid, B. "The Death Squad," *Melody Maker.* 61 (September 13, 1986) 32. il., int.

Jamie Wednesday

Smith, W. "Election Day," *Melody Maker.* 60 (December 7, 1985) 9. il., int.

Jazz Butcher

Roberts, Chris. "Sidelines: The Jazz Butcher," *Melody Maker.* (July 7, 1990) 13. il., int. w/Pat Fish.

Jimmy Jimmy

Thompson, D. "Busking It," *Melody Maker.* 60 (December 14, 1985) 22. il., int. w/J. O'Neill.

Jo Jo and the Real People

"Sidelines: Jo Jo and the Real People," *Melody Maker.* 63 (September 19, 1987) 14. int. w/Tony Griffin.

Joboxers

"Joboxers Split Up," *Melody Maker.* 61 (February 15, 1986) 5.

John, Lee

Isaacs, A. "Solid Gold Concepts," *Melody Maker.* 60 (January 5, 1985) 9. il., int.

"Shrink Rap," *Melody Maker.* 60 (September 7, 1985) 11. il., int.

Johnson, Eric

"New Faces to Watch: Eric Johnson," *Cash Box.* (August 30, 1986) 10. il., int.

Jones, Marti

DeSavia, Tom. "Marti Jones," *Cash Box.* LII:3 (July 16, 1988) 11. il., int.

Kajagoogoo/Kaja

"Kaja—Formerly Kajagoogoo—Have Officially Split," *Melody Maker.* 60 (December 7, 1985) 3.

Kalahari Surfers

"Sidelines: The Kalahari Surfers," *Melody Maker.* 63 (September 5, 1987) 25. il., int. w/Warric Sony.

Kane Gang

"Sidelines: The Kane Gang," *Melody Maker.* 63 (September 26, 1987) 15. il., int. w/M. Brammer.

Katrina and the Waves

Ferrar, Ann. "Katrina and the Waves," *Stereo Review.* 50 (November 1985) 78–80. il.

Lababedi, I. "Katrina and the Waves: Songs for the Common Man (and Woman)," *Creem.* 17 (August 1986) 44–45ff. il.

Leland, J. "Low Tide," *Record.* 4 (August 1985) 32–33. il.

Sutton, Rich. "Katrina and the Waves—'Walking on New-found Success'," *Song Hits.* n239 (January 1986) 28–29. il.

Vare, E.A. "Katrina's Waves Finally Find the *Sunshine*," *Billboard.* 97 (July 20, 1985) 40ff.

Kennedy, Brian

Morton, Gavin. "Emotional Rescue," *New Musical Express.* (February 17, 1990) 10. il., int.

Kihn, Greg (, Band)

Nite, Norm N., with Charles Crespo. "Greg Kihn Band," In: *Rock On . . . (Volume 3).* p. 173. disc.

Kill Ugly Pop

"Sidelines: The Kill Ugly Pop," *Melody Maker.* 63 (September 19, 1987) 17. il., int.

Killdozer

Eddy, C. "Music: Howls from the Heartland," *Village Voice.* 31 (July 29, 1986) 66.

King, James

Morton, T. "The Fun & the Fury," *Melody Maker.* 61 (July 12, 1986) 22. il.

"Shrink Rap," *Melody Maker.* 61 (August 9, 1986) 22–23. il.

Sutherland, Steve. "Walking With the King," *Melody Maker.* 60 (January 26, 1985) 10–11. il., int.

Kinney, Kevin (See also: Drivin' n' Cryin'; R.E.M.)

Woods, Karen. "Two for the Road: Kevin Kinney and Peter Buck Take a Holiday," *Cash Box.* (March 24, 1990) 7. il., int.

Kiss That

Thompson, D. "Lip Service," *Melody Maker.* 61 (April 19, 1986) 12. il., int.

Kissing Bandits

Morton, T. "The Outlaw Tribe," *Melody Maker.* 61 (January 1, 1986) 14. il., int. w/R. Costley.

Kitchens of Distinction

Reynolds, Simon. "Kitchens of Distinction: Somewhere Over the Rainbow," *Melody Maker.* 66:23 (June 9, 1990) 38–39. il., int.

Williams, Simon. "Nothing Compares 2 Utensils," *New Musical Express.* (March 10, 1990) 18–19, 53. il.

L.A.'s

Stanley, Bob. "The L.A.'s Scouse Honour," *Melody Maker.* (October 13, 1990) 8–9. il., int. w/Lee Mavers and John Powers.

Laughing Academy

Morton, T. "Breaking the Cattle Market," *Melody Maker.* 60 (May 11, 1985) 31. il., int. w/Paul Blyth.

Lauper, Cyndi

Beck, Peter. "Cyndi Lauper Adds 'True Colors' to Her Best Musical Canvas," *Cash Box.* (September 6, 1986) 9, 34. il., int.

Bessman, Jim. "How Clips Helped Break Cyndi, Walz Recalls Smooth Segue from 'Girls' to 'Time'," *Billboard.* 97 (March 9, 1985) 38–39.

Bischoff, D. "You've Really Got a Hold on Me: The Wrestling Sensation Rocks the Nation," *Village Voice.* 30 (March 19, 1985) 1ff. il.

Cassata, Mary Anne. "Cyndi Lauper," *Song Hits.* n233 (July 1985) 13, 17. il.

"Cyndi Lauper," *Song Hits.* n254 (April 1987) 8–10. il.

"Cyndi Lauper Wins Six Video Awards at 3d AVA Show," *Variety.* 318 (April 10, 1985) 89.

DiMauro, P. "Cyndi Lauper," *BMI.* n1 (1985) 22–23. il.

Dupler, Steven. "Cyndi Lauper Pulls no Emotional Punches," *Billboard.* 97 (February 16, 1985) 6ff.
"Girls Just Want to Have Fun" receives the nomination for the record of the year.

Feczo, Mary Anna. "Cyndi Lauper Bops," *Musician.* n72 (October 1984) 25ff.

Hill, Randal C. "Cyndi Lauper: She Bops!," *Goldmine.* n200 (March 25, 1988) 20, 37. il.

Kamin, Philip, and Peter Goodard. *Cyndi Lauper.* New York: McGraw-Hill, 1986. il., bio. pap.

"Lauper Made Sales History, CRIA Certifications Reveal," *Billboard.* 97 (March 23, 1985) 65.
Re. *She's So Unusual.*

Mercer, M. "The Dolly Bites Back," *Melody Maker.* 61 (November 8, 1986) 34. il., int.

Morreale, Marie, and Susan Mittelkauf. *The Cyndi Lauper Scrapbook.* New York: Bantam, 1985. il. pap.

Leather Nun

"The Nuns' Story," *Melody Maker.* 61 (August 2, 1986) 28–29. il., int. w/singer Jonas.

Mathur, Paul. "Twisted Sisters," *Melody Maker.* 63 (September 12, 1987) 12. il., int. w/Jonas.

Lilac Time

Woods, Karen. "Now is the Lilac Time," *Cash Box.* LIII:40 (April 28, 1990) 6, 18. il., int. w/Duffy.

Lost Loved Ones

Thomas, D. "Raising the Flag," *Melody Maker.* 60 (March 30, 1985) 16. il.

Love and Money

Mico, Ted. "Sweet Conspiracy," *Melody Maker.* 61 (April 19, 1986) 10. il., int. w/J. Grant.

Sullivan, C. "The Colour of Money?," *Melody Maker.* 61 (July 26, 1986) 10–11. il.

Mad Professor (r.n.: Neil Frazer)

Owen, Frank. "The Wild Bunch," *Melody Maker.* 61 (March 15, 1986) 22–23. il., int.

Madame X

Clerk, Carol. "Call Me Madame X," *Melody Maker.* 60 (May 4, 1985) 18. il., int.

Mainframe

Mico, Ted. "Binary Vision," *Melody Maker.* 60 (July 27, 1985) 18. il., int.

Makin' Time

Georgia, Z. "Time Out," *Melody Maker.* 60 (September 21, 1985) 14. il., int.

Malo-Tones

Kiley, P. "Loony Tones," *Melody Maker.* 60 (June 29, 1985) 39.
il., int.

March Violets

"Fast Forward," *Melody Maker.* 60 (February 16, 1985) 4.
Simon D and Travis leave group.

"Fast Forward," *Melody Maker.* 60 (November 16, 1985) 3.
Drummer Travis quits.

Mary My Hope

Hobbs, Mary Anne. "Hope and Glory," *Sounds.* (February 3,
1990) 21. il., int. w/singer James Hall and guitarist
Clinton Steele.

Masquerade

Downer, S. "Funk for Thought," *Melody Maker.* 61 (June 28,
1986) 22–23. il., int.

Max Q (See also: INXS)

Scanlon, Ann. "Maximum Overload," *Sounds.* (February 24,
1990) 13. il., int. w/Ollie Olsen.

McKay, Kris (See also: Wild Seeds)

Stern, Perry. "Sound Check: Kris McKay; Endurance Test," *Me
Music Express Magazine.* 14:148 (June 1990) 27. il., int.

Membranes

Mercer, M. "Class Warfare," *Melody Maker.* 60 (July 13, 1985) 32–33. il., int.

Men They Couldn't Hang

[Bassist Shanne Hasler is Leaving], *Melody Maker.* 61 (December 6, 1986) 3.

McIlheney, Barry. "Gold-Diggers of '86," *Melody Maker.* 61 (June 21, 1986) 22–23. il., int. w/P. Simmonds.

Smith, W. "Dead Men's Tales," *Melody Maker.* 60 (January 26, 1985) 27. il., int.

Metros

"Minn.'s Metros Join MTM—Nashville Label's First Rock Signing," *Billboard.* 97 (October 12, 1985) 52.

Mighty Lemon Drops

Downer, S. "The Lemondrop Kids," *Melody Maker.* 61 (April 26, 1986) 38–39. il., int.

Reinhardt, Robin. "Flash: Rock Candy," *Spin.* 5:10 (January 1990) 18. il., int.

Reynolds, Simon. "Sweet Dreams," *Melody Maker.* 61 (October 4, 1986) 34–35. il., int.

Mighty Mighty

"Jaynie and Sara," *Melody Maker.* 61 (November 8, 1986) 33. il., int.

Mind Over Four

Bilbrey, Scott. "Minds for Motivation," *Village Noize.* n9 (Spring 1990) 8. il., int. w/singer Spike Xavier and guitarist Mike Jensen.

Miracle Legion

Aston, M. "Range Rovers," *Melody Maker.* 61 (April 26, 1986) 12. il., int.

Liveten, S. "Newbeats: Miracle in the Works," *Creem.* 17 (July 1986) 74. il.

Miro

Brown, Len. "Miro, Miro, Off the Wall," *New Musical Express.* (March 10, 1990) 19.

Mofungo

Smith, R.J. "Mofungo in a Landslide!," *Village Voice.* 31 (April 8, 1986) 82.
Re. the New York Music Awards.

Moho Pack

Voss, M. "Running With the Pack," *Melody Maker.* 60 (October 26, 1985) 14. il., int. w/Wolf and Icen.

Mojos

Doggett, Peter. "The Mojos," *Record Collector.* n29 (January 1982) 54–59. il., disc.

Moodists

Migaldi, R. "Moody Blue," *Creem.* 16 (April 1985) 18. il.

Moore, Gary (See also: Thin Lizzy)

Murdoch, Lorne, with Graham Gulliver. "Gary Moore," *Record Collector.* n109 (September 1988) 68–72. il., disc.

Welch, Chris. *Gary Moore.* London: Bobcat, 1986. il., bio.

Motels

Grein, Paul. "Motels Make Room for Business Savvy," *Billboard.* 98 (January 11, 1986) 48ff.

Whatley, S. "The *Shock* of Recognition," *Record.* 5 (January/February 1986) 41ff. il.

Mothers

Myers, Caren. "The Mothers: King Tut," *Melody Maker.* (October 27, 1990) 49. il., int.

Mumbles

Selzer, Jonathan. "Mumbles," *Melody Maker.* 66:5 (February 3, 1990) 16. il.

Mute Drivers

Unsworth, Cathi. "Driving the Point Home," *Sounds.* (February 24, 1990) 20. il., int.

Ned's Atomic Dustbin

Wilde, Jon. "Ned's Atomic Dustbin: Too Much Monkey Business," *Melody Maker*. 66:20 (May 19, 1990) 38–39. il., int.

Neurotics

Dixon, T. "Dole Age Diehards," *Melody Maker*. 61 (May 17, 1986) 32. il., int.

Nina and the UFO's

Bull, Bart. "Nina and the UFO's," *Spin*. n10 (February 1986) 23–25, 70. il.

No Sweat

Clerk, Carol. "Sidelines: No Sweat," *Melody Maker*. 66:24 (June 16, 1990) 13. il., int.

Nomads

Smith, M. "Duelling Swedes," *Melody Maker*. 60 (November 16, 1985) 12. il., int. w/N. Vahlberg and J. Tarnstorm.

Nomeansno

"The Independent Class of '86," *Music Scene*. n350 (July/August 1986) 13. il.

Northern Girls

Owen, Frank. "Boulevard Beauties," *Melody Maker*. 61 (April 19, 1986) 19. il., int.

Nuns

Turner, G. "Newbeats: Life-Affirming Nuns," *Creem.* 17 (March 1986) 75. il.

O'Connor, Sinead

Christmas, Ed. "Nothing Compares 2 O'Connor," *Billboard.* 102:17 (April 28, 1990) 8.

FitzGerald, Helen. "Girl Talk," *Melody Maker.* 61 (March 15, 1986) 23. il., int.

Lambert, Pam. "Sinead O'Connor: An Irish Lioness Roars," *Rolling Stone.* n524 (April 21, 1988) 24. il.

Masterson, Eugene. "Under New Management," *New Musical Express.* (February 17, 1990) 6, 50. il.

McNeil, Legs. "Sinead," *Spin.* 6:1 (April 1990) 52–58, 142–144. il., int.

"My Favorite Year," *Melody Maker.* 65 (January 7, 1989) 4. il.

Yardumian, Rob. "New Faces to Watch: Sinead O'Connor," *Cash Box.* (November 28, 1987) 9. il., int.

Orange Juice

"Orange Juice: The Last Show," *Melody Maker.* 60 (February 2, 1985) 3. il.

Rose, C. "Freshly Squeezed Orange Juice," *Creem.* 16 (January 1985) 18. il.

Pastels

Aston, M. "Leather and Anoraks," *Melody Maker.* 61 (February 1, 1986) 11. il., int. w/Stephen.

Petted Lips

Morton, T. "South Side Shuffle," *Melody Maker.* 60 (July 27, 1985) 32. il., int.

Phranc

"Phrankie Says," *Melody Maker.* 60 (December 7, 1985) 7. il.

"Shrink Rap," *Melody Maker.* 61 (August 2, 1986) 15. il., int.

Sullivan, C. "Phrancie Comes from Hollywood!," *Melody Maker.* 61 (April 5, 1986) 12–13. il., bio, int.

Pink Peg Slax

Gittins, Ian. [Your Dad and Mum May Like It], *Melody Maker.* 61 (November 8, 1986) 35. il., int.

Play Dead

Smith, M. "Alive & Kicking," *Melody Maker.* 60 (November 30, 1985) 31. int.

Playground

Mercer, M. "Play for Today," *Melody Maker.* 61 (October 18, 1986) 36. il., int.

Playn Jayn

Strange, R. "Evil Thoughts," *Melody Maker.* 60 (September 7, 1985) 14. il., int.

Poison Girls

Kirk, K. "Violent Femme," *Melody Maker.* 60 (December 14, 1985) 11. il., int. w/V. Subversa.

Power

Sullivan, C. "Soul Mining," *Melody Maker.* 61 (May 10, 1986) 26. il.

Primevals

Morton, T. "Prime Evil," *Melody Maker.* 61 (September 6, 1986) 12. il., int. w/M. Rooney and R. Burnett.

Morton, T. "South Side Shuffle," *Melody Maker.* 60 (July 27, 1985) 32. il., int. w/Rooney.

Primitives

Downer, S. "Flower Children," *Melody Maker.* 61 (July 26, 1986) 12. il., int.

Jaynie and Sara. "Wild Things," *Melody Maker.* 61 (November 8, 1986) 10. il., int.

Williams, Joe. "The Primitives," *Cash Box.* (August 6, 1988) 10. il., int. w/lead singer Tracey.

Pritchard, Bill

Lester, Paul. "Bill Pritchard," *Melody Maker.* 66:5 (February 3, 1990) 13. il.

Prunes

Selzer, Jonathan. "Sidelines: The Prunes," *Melody Maker.* (July 7, 1990) 14. il., int. w/vocalist Mary.

Psych-Oh Rangers, Das

Downer, S. "Knutters: Daft Loo-Knee," *Melody Maker.* 61 (November 8, 1986) 11. il., int. w/B. Decart.

Psycho Surgeons

Smith, B. "Have Scalpel Will Travel," *Melody Maker.* (December 13, 1986) 14. il., int.

Pursuit of Happiness

Wood, T. "Happiness is . . . a Hit!," *Billboard.* 101 (January 28, 1989) 33ff.

Railway Children

Collins, Andrew. "Wigan Aesthetic," *New Musical Express.* (March 30, 1990) 46. il.

Robinson, Julius. "The Railway Children—On the Move," *Cash Box.* LII:3 (July 16, 1988) 12. int. w/Gary Newby.

Raindogs

Meyer, Marianne. "New Faces: The Raindogs," *Rolling Stone.* n575 (April 5, 1990) 28. il., int.

White, Timothy. "The Raindogs," *Nusician.* n136 (February 1990) 60–61. il.

Rainmakers

Levy, Joe. "The Rainmakers: Cynicism vs. Rock 'N' Roll Salvation," *Cash Box.* (December 26, 1987) 16–17, 121. il., int. w/frontman and songwriter Bob Walkenhorst.

Rosenbluth, J. "Rainmakers Make Waves With Debut LP," *Billboard.* 98 (September 27, 1986) 22.

Rave-Ups

Robbins, Ira. "New Faces: The Rave-Ups; The Los Angeles Quartet Makes Its Escape from the Mail Room," *Rolling Stone.* n577 (May 3, 1990) 30. il.

Woods, Karen. "Taking a 'Chance' With the Rave-Ups," *Cash Box.* LIII:38 (April 14, 1990) 9. il., int. w/lyricist-guitarist Jimmer Podrasky and drummer Tim Jimenez.

Raymonde

Mathur, Paul. "These Charming Men," *Melody Maker.* 61 (January 18, 1986) 24–25. il., int. w/J. Maker and P. Huish.

Razorcuts

Gittins, Ian. [Interview With Angus], *Melody Maker.* 61 (December 6, 1986) 22. il.

Reckless Sleepers

Levy, Joe. "The Reckless Sleepers," *Cash Box*. (August 13, 1988) 11. il., int. w/Jules Shear.

Young, Jon. "Reckless Sleepers," *Musician*. n121 (November 1988) 18–22, 30. il., bio.

Red Box

Iorio, Paul. "New Faces to Watch: Red Box," *Cash Box*. (April 4, 1987) 10. il., int. w/Julian Close.

Mathur, Paul. "Box of Ricks," *Melody Maker*. 60 (August 31, 1985) 18. il., int.

Red Guitars

Gittins, Ian. "Every Day I Write the Book," *Melody Maker*. 61 (May 31, 1986) 16. il., int.

Mercer, M. "Better Red Than Dead!," *Melody Maker*. 60 (March 23, 1985) 14–15. il., int.

Red Harvest

"Harvest Home," *Melody Maker*. 61 (June 21, 1986) 32–33. il., int.

Redskins

"Dean Smartin'," *Melody Maker*. 61 (December 20/27, 1986) 3. The band splits.

[Drummer King Quits], *Melody Maker.* 60 (May 18, 1985) 4.

FitzGerald, Helen. "Redskins: The Insanity Clause," *Melody Maker.* 60 (June 29, 1985) 28–29. il., int. w/Chris Dean.

McIlheney, Barry. "Heroes & Villains," *Melody Maker.* 60 (November 30, 1985) 11. il., int. w/Chris Dean.

"Redskins Win Single Battle," *Melody Maker.* 60 (November 16, 1985) 3.

"Skins Peel Off," *Melody Maker.* 61 (December 13, 1986) 3. Farewell tour, benefits cancelled.

Smith, W. "The Positive Punch," *Melody Maker.* 61 (May 17, 1986) 10–11. il., int.

Reverb Brothers

Kiley, P. "Brothers-in-Arms," *Melody Maker.* 60 (November 16, 1985) 16. int.

Sullivan, C. "Jukebox Jive," *Melody Maker.* 61 (August 9, 1986) 36. il., int.

Richman, Jonathan, and the Modern Lovers

Cohen, Scott. "Funny How Love Is," *Spin.* 2 (June 1986) 25–28. il.

Romeo's Daughter

Woods, Karen. "Romeo's Daughter Romances the Airwaves," *Cash Box.* (October 28, 1988) 15. il., int.

Royal Court of China

Jeske, Lee. "New Faces to Watch: The Royal Court of China," *Cash Box.* (November 14, 1987) 9. il., int. w/bassist-mandolinist Robert Logue.

Salvation Sunday

Mercer, M. "A Winters Tale," *Melody Maker.* 63 (September 19, 1987) 45. il., int. w/S. and J. Winterbottom.

Satriani, Joe

Goodman, Fred. "Joe Satriani's Alien Surfing Safari," *Rolling Stone.* n524 (April 21, 1988) 25. il., int.

Scandal (featuring Patty Smyth)

Gaines, Robin. "Exclusive Interview With Patty Smyth of Scandal," *Song Hits.* n231 (May 1985) 8–10. il., int.

Greenleaf, Vicki, and Stan Hyman. "Exclusive Interview With Scandal," *Super Song Hits.* n38 (Winter 1984) 28–29. il., int.

Nite, Norm N., with Charles Crespo. "Scandal," In: *Rock On . . . (Volume 3).* pp. 298–300. il., disc.

Sutton, Rich. "Patty Smyth of Scandal," *Super Song Hits.* n47 (Spring 1986) 46–47. il.

Scarlet Fantastic

Sutherland, Steve. "Glamnesiacs," *Melody Maker.* 63 (September 26, 1987) 34–35. il., int.

Scruffy the Cat

McCormick, Moira. "Newbeats: The Litter of the Pack," *Creem.*
19 (September 1987) 67. il.

Sharkey, Feargal

Scott, Steve. "Feargal Sharkey," *Record Collector.* n77 (January
1986) 10–14. il., disc.

Shinehead

Mapp, B. "Who the Cap Fits," *Spin.* 4 (January 1989) 54–55.
il., int.

Shrubs

Oldfield, Paul. "Branching Out," *Melody Maker.* 63 (September 5, 1987) 43. il., int. w/N. Hobbs.

Simple Minds

de Lisle, T. "Jim Kerr: Simply Speaking," *Creem.* 17 (April
1986) 12–15. il., int.

"Jim and the Coat of Many Colours," *Melody Maker.* 61 (April
12, 1986) 9. il. Kerr to star in Lloyd Webber musical
Joseph and the Amazing Technicolour Dreamcoat.

Mehler, M. "Rock On: Of One Mind," *Record.* 4 (June 1985)
11. il.

Sinister Cleaners

"Sidelines," *Melody Maker.* 63 (September 12, 1987) 26. int.

Skin Games

"Flesh for Fantasy," *Melody Maker.* 64 (October 22, 1988) 16. il.

Sleeping Dogs Wake

"Grim Fairy Tales," *Melody Maker.* 64 (October 15, 1988) 16. il.

Smash Palace

"New Faces to Watch: Smash Palace," *Cash Box.* XLIX:34 (February 8, 1986) 10. il., int. w/lead guitarist and composer Stephen Butler.

Snapdragons

"Bare Necessities," *Melody Maker.* 65 (January 7, 1989) 12. il.

So Good So Far

Robinson, Julius. "New Faces to Watch: So Good So Far," *Cash Box.* LII:2 (July 9, 1988) 11. il., int. w/Marcus Bell.

Something Happens

Schlosberg, Karen. "New Faces: Something Happens," *Rolling Stone.* n582/583 (July 12/26, 1990) 34. il., int. w/singer-lyricist Tom Dunne.

Spear of Destiny

Hendry, Shaun. "Spear of Destiny," *Record Collector.* n102 (February 1988) 59–65. il., disc.

"News," *Melody Maker.* 63 (September 5, 1987) 3.
Band cancels Reading Festival appearance; K. Brandon in
the hospital.

"News," *Melody Maker.* 63 (September 26, 1987) 4.
Group split is denied; Brandon returns to the hospital.

Stewart, Mark

Stubbs, David. "Mark Stewart: Capitalist Punishment," *Melody
Maker.* 66:20 (May 19, 1990) 17. il., int.

Sundays

Giles, Jeff. "New Faces: The Sundays," *Rolling Stone.* n581
(June 28, 1990) 22. il., int. w/guitarist David Gavurin.

Harvey, Scott. "New Faces: The Sundays," *Cash Box.* (June 2,
1990) 5. il.

Roberts, Chris. "Sundays Best," *Melody Maker.* 65 (January 14,
1989) 24–26. il., int.

Stern, Perry. "Sound Check: The Sundays; Lush, Lilting and
Laid-Back," *Me Music Express Magazine.* 14:148 (June
1990) 16. il., int.

10,000 Maniacs

Chon, R. "Newbeats: How Many Maniacs Can You Cram in a
Phone Booth?," *Creem.* 17 (May 1986) 74.

Flanagan, Bill. "More Songs About Toxic Defoliants," *Musician.* n77 (March 1985) 14. il.

Flanagan, Bill. "10,000 Maniacs," *Musician.* n87 (January 1986) 11–15, 30. il.

Fricke, David. "Wishing and Hoping," *Melody Maker.* 60 (December 14, 1985) 22. il., int.

Irwin, C. "Just One Maniac," *Folk Roots.* 9 (December 1987) 15ff. il., int. w/Natalie Merchant.

Milano, B. "*Saturday Review* Talks to 10,000 Maniacs," *Saturday Review.* 12 (January–February 1986) 91. il.

Pareles, Jon. "The Journey of 10,000 Maniacs Begins With a Single," *Musician.* n130 (August 1989) 44–54, 114. il., bio.

Van Meter, Jonathan. "She Sells Sanctuary," *Spin.* 5:6 (September 1989) 44–48. il., int. w/Natalie Merchant.

Wilde, J. "Loonytoons," *Melody Maker.* 63 (September 12, 1987) 34–35. il., int.

Wing, E. "Small-Time Rockers on a Roll," *Rolling Stone.* n457 (September 26, 1985) 86. il.

Texas

Schoemer, Karen. "And the Skies are Not Cloudy All Day," *Spin.* 5:9 (December 1989) 32–33. il., int. w/singer Sharleen.

Thee Hypnotics (See: Hypnotics, Thee)

This Poison!

Roberts, Chris. "Strange Brew," *Melody Maker.* 63 (December 5, 1987) 31. il., int.

Three Johns

Kendall, D. "Newbeats: The Johns' Royal Flush," *Creem.* 17 (May 1986) 77. il.

McIlheney, B. "A Change is Gonna Come," *Melody Maker.* 60 (July 13, 1985) 12. il., int.

Reynolds, Simon. "Social Surrealists," *Melody Maker.* 61 (May 17, 1986) 14. il., int.

'Til Tuesday

Armbruster, G., and J. Aiken. "Joey Pesce's Keyboards Carry With 'Til Tuesday," *Keyboard Magazine.* 11 (October 1985) 16. il.

Fissinger, Laura. "The Beat Goes On: Tuesday's Children," *Creem.* 17 (October 1985) 18. il.

Fricke, David. "Blueprint for Success," *Rolling Stone.* n457 (September 26, 1985) 15–17. il.

Iorio, Paul. "'Til Tuesday Gambles and Wins on 'Welcome Home'," *Cash Box.* (November 1, 1986) 11. il., int. w/guitarist Robert Holmes and vocalist Aimee Mann.

Wexler, Erica Bettina. "Tuesday's Child," *Spin.* 1:9 (January 1986) 22–25. il., int. w/Aimee Mann.

Toad the Wet Sprocket

Ressner, Jeffrey. "New Faces: Toad the Wet Sprocket," *Rolling Stone.* n562 (October 5, 1989) 28. il., int.

Toy Matinee

Hardy, Ernest. "New Faces: Toy Matinee," *Cash Box.* (August 18, 1990) 6. il., int.

Trident Mist

"Sidelines," *Melody Maker.* 63 (September 19, 1987) 14. il., int.

True West

Aston, M. "State of the Union: Western Promise," *Melody Maker.* 60 (May 11, 1985) 12ff. il., int.

Fricke, David. "Hearts of the West," *Melody Maker.* 60 (January 26, 1985) 19. il., int.

Lloyd, R. "How Brown Was My Rawhide," *Creem.* 17 (July 1985) 17. il.

Strauss, D. "Holding Out Promise," *Record.* 4 (November 1984) 12.

Turncoats

FitzGerald, Helen. [Interview], *Melody Maker.* 61 (November 29, 1986) 14. il.

Two Nations

"Sidelines," *Melody Maker.* 63 (September 12, 1987) 26. il., int. w/D. Wright.

Ulrich, Peter

Gittins, Ian. "Sidelines: Peter Ulrich," *Melody Maker.* 66:24 (June 16, 1990) 12. il., int.

Venetians

Dobrin, Gregory. "New Faces to Watch: The Venetians," *Cash Box.* (March 7, 1987) 10. il., int. w/lead vocalist Rik Swinn.

Venus in Furs

Mercer, M. "Agony Uncle," *Melody Maker.* 61 (December 13, 1986) 14. il., int. w/songwriter Times.

Violence

"The Crimes They are A-Changin'," *Melody Maker.* 64 (August 20, 1988)

Voivid

McCormick, Moira. "New Faces: Voivid," *Rolling Stone.* n573 (March 8, 1990) 63. il., int. w/drummer Michel Langevin (aka Away).

Wang Chung

Halbersberg, Elianne. "Wang Chung," *Song Hits.* n256 (June 1987) 16–18. il.

Sutton, Rich. "What's in a Name? An Exclusive Interview With Wang Chung," *Song Hits.* n226 (December 1984) 6–7. il., int.

We've Got a Fuzzbox and We're Gonna Use It

Frith, Simon. "Britbeat: Revenge of the Nerds," *Village Voice.* 31 (August 19, 1986) 63.

Irwin, Chris. "Educating Fuzzbox!," *Melody Maker.* 61 (November 15, 1986) 22–23. il., int.

Sharpe, L. "Ghost in the Machine," *Melody Maker.* 61 (March 8, 1986) 13. int.

Sutherland, Steve. "Good Time Girls," *Melody Maker.* 61 (May 10, 1986) 12–13. il., int.

Weather Prophets

Downer, S. "Truth Tellers," *Melody Maker.* 61 (June 14, 1986) 16. il., int. w/Pete Astor.

FitzGerald, Helen. "Prophet Motive," *Melody Maker.* 61 (October 25, 1986) 10. il., int. w/Astor.

Wednesday Week

Iorio, Paul. "New Faces to Watch: Wednesday Week," *Cash Box.* (April 11, 1987) 10. il., int. w/Kristi Callan.

Weller, Paul

Frith, Simon. "Britbeat: Walls Come Tumbling Down," *Village Voice.* 30 (July 30, 1985) 75.

"The New Pop Aristocracy," *Melody Maker.* 60 (February 23, 1985) 23–25. il.

"No Respond," *Melody Maker.* 61 (February 22, 1986) 3. il.

"Weller Protest," *Melody Maker.* 60 (March 9, 1985) 4. il.
Re. the cutting out of welfare benefits for dropouts.

"Weller's School Report," *Melody Maker.* 60 (February 2, 1985)
4. il.
He opposes conditions on dropouts' welfare benefits.

Wet Wet Wet

Jackson, Richard. "Wet Wet Wet," *Record Collector.* n108
(August 1988) 34–36. il., disc.

Morton, T. "Hot Hot Hot," *Melody Maker.* 60 (February 23,
1985) 14. il., int.

Staunton, Terry. "Auf Wiedersehen, Wet," *New Musical Express.* (March 10, 1990) 16. il.

What is This

Simmons, S. "Who and What is This?," *Creem.* 16 (January
1985) 16. il.

White, Andy

Jennings, Dave. "Andy White; Tradition Impossible," *Melody
Maker.* (March 3, 1990) 17. il.

White Rope

Mico, Ted. "To Hell & Back," *Melody Maker.* 64 (October 8,
1988) 28–30. il., int. w/Guy Kyser and Roger Kunkel.

Wiedlin, Jane (See also: Go-Go's)

DeSavia, Tom. "Jane Wiedlin," *Cash Box.* LII:3 (July 16, 1988) 11. il., int.

Wigs

Mercer, M. [Interview], *Melody Maker.* 61 (November 29, 1986) 14. il.

Wild Choir

Iorio, Paul. "New Faces to Watch: Wild Choir," *Cash Box.* (April 25, 1987) 10. il., int. w/Gail Davies.

Wolfhounds

True, E. "The Wolfhounds: Voice of the People," *Melody Maker.* (January 28, 1989) 13. il., int.

Wood Children

King, Sam. "Names for 1990: Bitter Sweet," *Sounds.* (February 24, 1990) 57. il., int. w/singer Nick Stockman.

Working Week

Lake, S. "Jazzin' With New Genes," *Melody Maker.* 60 (January 19, 1985) 14–15. il., int. w/S. Booth.

Stubbs, D. "Fusion Fury," *Melody Maker.* 61 (September 13, 1986) 36. il., int.

World Party (See also: Waterboys)

Bessman, Jim. "Party Time for Chrysalis," *Billboard.* 98 (December 6, 1986) 24.

Buskin, Richard. "World Party," *Musician.* n99 (January 1987) 44–48. il.

FitzGerald, Helen. *"Private Revolution,"* *Melody Maker.* 61 (August 23, 1986) 15. int. w/Karl Wallinger.

Giles, Jeff. "Pure Pop for Party People," *Rolling Stone.* n581 (June 28, 1990) 71–73. il., int. w/Wallinger.

Iorio, Paul. "Karl Wallinger's 'Private Revolution' is Open to the Public," *Cash Box.* (November 1, 1986) 10, 31. il., int.

Pareles, Jon. "World Party—Karl Wallinger: The Man With the Band in His Head," *Musician.* n142 (August 1990) 62–67, 90. il.

Yeah Yeah Noh

Aston, M. "Noh Hiding Place," *Melody Maker.* 61 (February 8, 1986) 31. il., int.

"Joboxers Split Up," *Melody Maker.* 61 (February 15, 1986) 5.

Young Neal and the Vipers

Drozdowski, Ted. "Young Neal and the Vips," *Musician.* n136 (February 1990) 64, 68–69. il.

B. MANCHESTER (MANC) SOUND

General Sources

Pond, Steve. "Music, Drugs and . . . Twenty-Six-Inch Bell Bottoms?," *Rolling Stone.* n579 (May 31, 1990) 52–55, 72. il.

Berry, Andrew

Lester, Paul. "Sidelines: Andrew Berry," *Melody Maker.* (July 7, 1990) 11. il., int.

Candy Flip

Smith, Andrew. "Candy Flip: Sweet Surrender," *Melody Maker.* (July 21, 1990) 8. il., int. w/Ric Peet.

Charlatans (U.K.)

Brown, James, and Derek Rodgers. "Northwich Victorious," *New Musical Express.* (February 17, 1990) 14, 50. il., int.

Roberts, Chris. "The Charlatans: May the Force Be With You," *Melody Maker.* 66:23 (June 9, 1990) 8–9. il., int.

Stud Brothers. "The Charlatans," *Melody Maker.* (October 13, 1990) 36–38. il., int. w/Tim Burgess.

Distant Cousins

Giles, David. "Sidelines: Distant Cousins," *Melody Maker.* 66:4 (January 27, 1990) 14. il., int.

Flowered Up

Lester, Paul. "A Bloom With a View: Flowered Up," *Melody Maker*. (July 21, 1990) 48–59. il., int.

Stanley, Bob. "Flowered Up: The Revolution Will Be Pollenised," *Melody Maker*. 66:20 (May 19, 1990) 42–43. il., int.

Happy Mondays

Mathur, Paul. "Happy Hour!," *Melody Maker*. 61 (August 2, 1986) 16. il., int.

Reinhardt, R. "Manic Mondays," *Spin*. 5 (August 1989) 14. il.

Inspiral Carpets

Maconie, Stuart. "Rug Culture," *New Musical Express*. (March 30, 1990) 30–31, 53. il.

Reed, John. "Inspiral Carpets," *Record Collector*. n129 (May 1990) 46–51. il., disc.

Mock Turtles

Anderson, Penny. "Jam On: Terrapinheads," *New Musical Express*. (January 27, 1990) 10. il., int.

Jennings, Dave. "The Mock Turtles: A Very British Soup," *Melody Maker*. (October 27, 1990) 46–47. il., int.

Lester, Paul. "The Mock Turtles: Just for the Shell of It," *Melody Maker*. (July 28, 1990) 38–39. il., int. w/Martin Coogan.

Northside

Stanley, Bob. "Northside: The Manc of England," *Melody Maker.* 66:24 (June 16, 1990) 38–39. il., int.

Stanley, Bob. "Sidelines: Northside—Plum on Feel the Noise," *Melody Maker.* 66:20 (May 19, 1990) 14. il., int.

True, Everett. "Northside: Star You Experienced?," *Melody Maker.* (October 27, 1990) 54–55. il., int.

Stone Roses

Azerrad, Michael. "New Faces: The Stone Roses," *Rolling Stone.* n563 (October 19, 1989) 17. il., int. w/lead singer Ian Brown.

Blashill, Pat. "Flash: Would You Like Some Candy?," *Spin.* 5:7 (October 1989) 18. il., int.

Brown, James. "Fool's Gold," *Spin.* 6:2 (May 1990) 56–57. il., int.

Dickie, Mary. "Sound Check: The Stone Roses; Positive Vibrations," *Me Music Express Magazine.* 14:145 (March 1990) 47. il., int.

"News: War of the Roses," *Melody Maker.* 66:23 (June 9, 1990) 3. il.

Pond, Steve. "The Stone Roses: Ready to Bloom in the U.S.A.," *Rolling Stone.* n579 (May 31, 1990) 55. il., int.

Reed, John. "The Stone Roses," *Record Collector.* n126 (February 1990) 12–16. il., disc.

Stanley, Bob. "The Stone Roses; Where Angels Play," *Melody Maker*. 66:21 (May 26, 1990) 8–9. il.

What? Noise

Oldfield, Paul. "Sidelines: What? Noise," *Melody Maker*. 66:23 (June 9, 1990) 12. il., int.

24. ROOTS ROCK

Blasters (See also: X)

"News," *Melody Maker.* 61 (July 5, 1986) 5. Dave Alvin and Gene Taylor leave the band; Hollywood Fats joins.

Perry, Steve. "Romeo's Return," *Buzz.* 3:2 (December 1987) 42–47. il., int.

Broadcasters

Levy, Joe. "New Faces to Watch: The Broadcasters," *Cash Box,* (February 20, 1988) 10. il., int. w/Billy Roues and Blackie Pagano.

Cruzados (See also: Havalinas)

McCormick, Moira. "If at First You Don't Succeed . . . ," *Musician.* n87 (January 1986) 33. il.

"New Acts," *Variety.* 321 (November 13, 1985) 125.

"New Faces to Watch: The Cruzados," *Cash Box.* XLIX:19 (October 19, 1985) 10. il., int. w/lead vocalist-guitarist Tito Larricia.

"New on the Charts," *Billboard.* 97 (December 21, 1985) 45.

Del Fuegos

Fricke, David. "State of the Union: Backseat Drivers," *Melody Maker.* 60 (April 27, 1985) 14. il.

Johnson, D. "You Name It . . . the Del Fuegos Call It Rock 'n Roll," *Record.* 4 (November 1984) 10. il.

Panebianco, J. "The Del Fuegos: Edgy Guys With Hearts in Their Caved-In Bodies," *Musician.* n85 (February 1986) 23–24ff. il., int.

Riegel, R. "Del Fuegos: Banned in Boston," *Creem.* 17 (March 1986) 34–35. il.

Del-Lords

Fricke, David. "Lords of the New *Frontier*," *Melody Maker.* 60 (October 26, 1985) 40. il., int.

Leland, J. "In the Land of Opportunity," *Record.* 4 (February 1985) 41. il.

"Sidelines: Del-Lords," *Melody Maker.* 65 (August 5, 1989) 12. il.

Dreams So Real

Meyer, S. "New on the Charts," *Billboard.* 100 (December 10, 1988) 22. il.

Eat

Reinhardt, Robin. "New for a Feast," *Spin.* 6:1 (April 1990) 16. il., int.

Edmunds, Dave (See also: Fabulous Thunderbirds)

Gett, Steve. "Dave Edmunds Produces Success With *Tuff Enuff*," *Billboard.* 98 (July 19, 1986) 20ff.

Georgia Satellites

Paris, T. "Georgia Satellites," *Spin.* 4 (December 1988) 4ff. il., int. w/Dan Baird.

Smith, M. [Interview], *Melody Maker.* 61 (November 15, 1986) 33. il.

Havalinas (See also: Cruzados)

Clerk, Carol. "Sidelines: The Havalinas," *Melody Maker.* 66:8 (February 24, 1990) 11. il.

Ressner, Jeffrey. "New Faces: The Havalinas," *Rolling Stone.* n573 (March 8, 1990) 63. il., int.

Hewerdine, Boo, and Darden Smith

McCormick, Moira. "New Faces: Boo Hewerdine and Darden Smith," *Rolling Stone.* n564 (November 2, 1989) 30. il., int. w/Smith.

Johnson, Eric

Bissett, Deron. "Eric Johnson: Organic Guitar," *Goldmine.* n228 (April 21, 1989) 102–104, 118. il.

Milkowski, Bill. "Eric Johnson," *Guitar World.* 5 (May 1984) 44–46. il.

Obrecht, Jas. "Eric Johnson," *Texas Guitar.* 3 (Winter 1987) 40–45, 48–51. il.

Woodard, Josef. "Eric Johnson's Big Texas Honk," *Musician.* n95 (September 1986) 39–42, 98. il.

Lone Justice

FitzGerald, Helen. "Home Off the Range," *Melody Maker.* 61 (November 29, 1986) 30. il., int. w/Maria McKee.

Roblin, A. "Lone Justice's Rocky Road," *Billboard.* 97 (August 17, 1985) 53ff.
The group makes the country charts.

McKEE, MARIA

Schoemer, Karen. "Lonesome Dove," *Spin.* 5:10 (January 1990) 23. il., int.

Long Ryders

DeMuir, H. "Newbeats: Gone Rydin'," *Creem.* 17 (July 1986) 75. il.

FitzGerald, Helen. "Gallop Poll," *Melody Maker.* 60 (August 31, 1985) 16. il., int.

Fricke, David. "Ryders on the Storm," *Melody Maker.* 60 (January 12, 1985) 30–31. il., int.

Hogg, Brian. "The Long Ryders," *Record Collector.* n79 (March 1986) 36–37. il., disc.

Knapp, K. "Long Ryders Adopt the Missionary Position," *Creem.* 16 (May 1985) 19. il.

Mehler, M. "Look Goofy, Be Cool," *Record.* 4 (February 1985) 41. il.

Santoro, G. "Profile," *Down Beat.* 53 (April 1986) 46–47. il., int. w/Sid Griffin.

Tamarkin, Jeff. "Long Ryders: Don't Call Us Country-Rock," *Billboard.* 97 (January 5, 1985) 44. int. w/Stephen Mc-Carthy.

Tamarkin, Jeff. "The Long Ryders: Rockin' and Record Collectin'," *Goldmine.* n184 (August 14, 1987) 109, 112. il.

May, Raymond

Levy, Joe. "New Faces to Watch: Raymond May," *Cash Box.* LII:2 (July 9, 1988) 12. int.

Paladins

Iorio, Paul. "New Faces to Watch: The Paladins," *Cash Box.* (May 16, 1987) 10. il., int. w/vocalist and guitarist David Gonzalez.

Phantom, Rocker and Slick (See also: David Bowie; John Lennon; Stray Cats; John Waite)

"New Faces to Watch: Phantom, Rocker & Slick," *Cash Box.* XLIX:27 (December 14, 1985) 10. il., int.

Rank and File

Eden, Dawn. "Rank and File: From Buckskin to Leather," *Goldmine.* n188 (October 9, 1987) 90, 94. il.

Reivers

Robinson, Julius. "New Faces to Watch: The Reivers," *Cash Box.* (February 13, 1988) 17–18. il., int. w/singer and guitarist John Crosline.

Ruffner, Mason

Adelson, David. "Mason Ruffner Has Paid His Dues," *Cash Box.* (June 21, 1986) 12.

Considine, J.D. "Mason Ruffner," *Musician.* n105 (July 1987) 15–16. il.

Sexton, Charlie

Bull, Bart. "Go, Charlie, Go," *Spin.* 2 (May 1986) 44–48, 73. il., int.

Slide

Elliott, Paul. "The Long Riders," *Sounds.* (January 27, 1990) 22. il., int. w/drummer Richard Hynd and singer Grant Richardson.

Thomas, Chris

Guralnick, Peter. "The Shape of Blues to Come: Chris Thomas Wakes Up a Venerable Tradition," *Musician.* n133 (November 1989) 20–26, 121. il., int.

True Believers

Blashill, Pat. "On the Road to Nowhere," *Spin.* 3 (May 1987) 54–58. il.

Kalogerakis, George. "True Believers," *Rolling Stone.* n561 (September 21, 1989) 100–110. il.

Standish, P. "Small-Time Rocks on a Roll," *Rolling Stone.* n457 (September 26, 1985) 86.

Williams, Lucinda

Flanagan, Bill. "Lucinda Williams: A New Rocker Outgrows the Rules," *Musician.* n126 (April 1989) 15–18. il.

Wire Train

Arnold, Gina. "Wire Train," *Musician.* n88 (February 1986) 11–12, 113. il.

Woods, Karen. "New Music," *Cash Box.* (August 18, 1990) 11. il., int. w/singer-songwriter Kevin Hunter.

25. WORLD BEAT (See also: AFRO-ROCK; JUNKANOO; REGGAE)

Separate Genres

MERENGUE (DOMINICAN SOUND)

McLane, Daisann. "World Beat! Uptown Dominica," *Spin.* 6:2 (May 1990) 86. il.
Survey of a genre transplanted into a Manhattan setting.

SOUKOUS (See: LOKETO)

Badarou, Wally

Davis, Michael, and Bob Doerschuk. "Wally Badarou: Taking the World View on 'Echoes' and 'Kiss of the Spider Woman'," *Keyboard.* (May 1986) 66–69. il., disc., int.

Bonedaddys

McCormick, Moira. "New Faces: The Bonedaddys," *Rolling Stone.* n573 (March 8, 1990) 63. il., int. w/percussionist Mike Tempo.

Keita, Salif

Zwerin, Mike. "Flash: Africa Fete," *Spin.* 5:6 (September 1989) 18. il., int.

Kreutzmann, Bill, and Mickey Hart (See also: Grateful Dead)

Vaughan, Chris. "Bill Kreutzmann/Mickey Hart: Rhythm Devils," *Down Beat.* (November 1987) 23–25. il., disc., int.

Loketo

Gehr, Richard. "World Beat!," *Spin.* 6:6 (September 1990) 84. il. Column delineates genre called "soukous."

McLaren, Malcolm (See also: Sex Pistols)

Bromberg, Craig. *The Wicked Ways of Malcolm McLaren.* New York: Harper & Row/Perennial Library, 1989. il.

"Charisma—No Fans of McLaren," *Melody Maker.* 60 (March 2, 1985) 3. il.

Cohen, Scott. "Topical Verse: Malcolm McLaren," *Spin.* 5:8 (November 1989) 88–89. il., int.

Trakin, R. "Malcolm McLaren: Innovation or Exploitation?," *Musician Player & Listener.* n40 (February 1982) 12ff. il., bio, int.

Vare, E.A. "Reluctant Artist Malcolm McLaren Has His 'Fans'," *Billboard.* 97 (March 9, 1985) 50.

Shankar, Ravi

Jones, Steve. "Ravi Shankar: India's Sitar Master," *R.P.M.* n9 (March 1985) 8–11. il., disc.

26. RELATED TOPICS

Advertising (See also: Beatles)

Savan, L. "Music: Rock Rolls Over," *Village Voice.* 32 (August 11, 1987) 2ff.

Schwartz, John, with Harry Hurt III. "Wing-Tip Rock and Roll," *Newsweek.* (September 26, 1988) 48–49. il.

Vare, Ethlie Ann. "The Vail Group," *Billboard.* (October 11, 1986) W-19.

Archives

ARChive

Barol, Bill. "One of Each, Please: A Collection of Global Pop Music Grows in New York," *Newsweek.* (April 6, 1987) 55ff. il., int. w/David Wheeler and B. George.

"Devoted Discophiles," *Insight.* (August 10, 1987) 53. int. w/Wheeler.

ARCHIVE OF CONTEMPORARY MUSIC (NEW YORK)

Bessman, Jim. "Flash: Pop History," *Spin.* 6:4 (July 1990) 14. il.

MUSEUM OF BROADCAST COMMUNICATIONS (CHICAGO)

Jedeikin, Jenny, and Robert Love. "The Next Page: Tapeheads' Paradise," *Rolling Stone.* n585 (August 23, 1990) 17. il., int. w/director Michael Mertz.

ROCK HALL OF FAME (CLEVELAND)

Goldberg, M. "Cleveland Affirms Rock Hall of Fame Deal," *Rolling Stone.* n558 (August 10, 1989) 25.

STANFORD ARCHIVE OF RECORDED SOUND

"Stanford Spins Pre-LP Recordings; Copies Available for Steep Price," *Sound Choice.* n12 (Autumn Equinox, 1989) 6–7.

STRADER, DAVID (VANCOUVER; PRIVATE)

O'Hara, Jane. "A Collector's World," *Maclean's.* (March 21, 1988) 47. il., int. w/Strader.

Art (See also: Album Covers; Censorship; Posters)

Burns, Mal. *Visions of Rock.* London/New York: Proteus, 1981. il. pap.

Ocean, Humphrey. *The Ocean View.* Preface by Paul McCartney. London: Plexus, 1983. il.
Collection of paintings depicting Wings on their 1976 tour of the United States.

Peellaert, Guy, and Nik Cohn (text). *Rock Dreams.* Introduction by Michael Herr. London: Picador, 1982. il. Orig. pub.: London: Pan, 1974; New York: Popular Library, 1974. Peellaert's use of photomontage depicts the major stars of popular music from the 1940s up to the early 1970s. Considered by many to be a genre classic; it has unerringly captured the essence of each figure.

Sandison, David. *Oxtoby's Rockers.* Oxford: Phaidon, 1978. il. pap.

Awards

GRAMMYS

Jeske, Lee. "NARAS Adds Rap, Heavy Metal and Bluegrass Grammys," *Cash Box.* LI:48 (June 6, 1988) 4.

ROCK AND ROLL HALL OF FAME

"Rock & Roll Hall of Fame," *Rolling Stone.* n571 (February 8, 1990) 71–84. il., int.
Cites the year's inductees. Includes testimonials by luminous contemporaries and sections entitled "Nonperformers" (by Jeffrey Ressner) and "Forefathers" (by Lee Jeske).

ROLLING STONE ANNUAL MUSIC AWARDS

"1989 Music Awards," *Rolling Stone.* n573 (March 8, 1990) 35–50. il.
Includes picks by readers, artists and critics, respectively.

Censorship (See also: Marc Almond; Audio Two; Beastie Boys; Christian Death; Johnny Clegg; Cure; Dead Kennedys; A Flux of Pink Indians; John Fogerty; Heavy Metal; Zodiac Mindwarp; Pretenders; Prince; 2 Live Crew; Frank Zappa)

GENERAL SOURCES

Blackwell, Mark, and Nathaniel Wice. "X-Rated Music," *Spin.* 6:3 (June 1990) 32–34. il., int. w/various artists and music industry spokesmen.

Haring, Bruce, Melinda Newman and Chris Morris. "Trade Fears Nasty Consequences of Crew Ruling," *Billboard.* (June 23, 1990) 5.

Jones, A., and others. "'87 Review (July): The Big Ban," *Melody Man.* 63 (December 19/26, 1987) 42. il.

Marsh, Dave. "Sympathy for the Devil; Has the Record Industry Sold Its Soul to the Devil?," *Village Voice.* 30 (October 8, 1985) 13–19. il.

Morthland, John. "Backbeat: Rock 'n' Roll Feels the Fire," *Hi Fi/Musical America.* 35 (December 1985) 74–75ff. il.

Ostling, Richard N., Nina Burligh and Michael P. Harris. "No Sympathy for the Devil," *Time.* (March 19, 1990) 55–56. il.

O'Steen, K. "Censorship a Threat in U.S., Though Grimmer Overseas," *Variety.* 336 (August 23, 1989) 84.

Walls, R.C. "Prime Time: Spank Me Senator Faster, Faster," *Creem.* 17 (February 1986) 63. il.

Weiss, G.D. "Commentary: Porn-Rock: A Script for Censorship," *Billboard.* 97 (June 29, 1985) 10.

ALABAMA—RETAILING (TOMMY HAMMOND)

"Editorial: Hats Off to Tommy Hammond," *Billboard.* 102:10
(March 10, 1990) 13.

Haring, Bruce. "Hammond Wins Case, But He's Still Troub-
led By Lyrics," *Billboard.* (March 10, 1990) 1, 98.

Ryan, Shawn. "Ala. Retailer Cleared in Obscenity Case: Jury
Overrules Fine on 2 Live Crew Sale," *Billboard.* 102:10
(March 10, 1990) 1, 99.

ALBUM PACKAGING

"Kennedy Accused of Obscenity," *Melody Maker.* 61 (June 21,
1986) 4.
Re. *Frankenchrist* l.p., which contains the poster, *Penis
Landscape*, by H.R. Giger.

"News," *Melody Maker.* 64 (October 29, 1988) 4.
PolyGram refuses to distribute Violence's single owing to
vomit on sleeve.

ANTI-CENSORSHIP

"The Artists Speak: We're Not Gonna Take It . . . Never Did
and Never Will," *Musician.* n86 (December 1985) 54.

Bloom, Howard. "Commentary: It's Time to Campaign Against Censorship," *Billboard.* 101 (January 21, 1989) 13.
Re. Child Protection and Obscenity Enforcement Act.

Duffy, Thom. "KSHE Sets St. Louis Rally: Stars to Join Anti-Stickering Event," *Billboard.* 102:11 (March 17, 1990) 106.

Goldberg, D. "Commentary: Hitting Back at the Witch-Hunters," *Billboard.* 98 (June 14, 1986) 9.

Haring, Bruce, and others. "Industry Leaders Stand Up for Crew; Urge Action Against All Censorship Efforts," *Billboard.* 102:27 (July 7, 1990) 6.

Holland, Bill. "Songwriters Academy Back Sticker Fight," *Billboard.* 102:15 (April 14, 1990) 87.

Holland, Bill, and Sean Ross. "Poe Goes Jump on Free-Speech Stick," *Billboard.* 102:27 (July 7, 1990) 1, 12.

McCullough, Jim, and Earl Paige. "Camelot's Bonk Lashes Out Against Rating Stickers," *Billboard.* 97:41 (October 12, 1985) 1, 83.

Nanes, Susan. "Freedom of Speech," *Spin.* 6:4 (July 1990) 19. il.
An album dedicated to fighting the censor, *Soundbites from the Counterculture* (Atlantic), has been censored itself.

"New Citizens Body to Attack Efforts to Censor Records," *Variety.* 320 (September 25, 1985) 138.

Newcomb, Brian Q. "Anti-Stickering Rally Draws Thousands in St. Louis," *Billboard.* 102:17 (April 28, 1990) 8.

Schipper, H., and P. DiMauro. "Agents, Managers and Artists Form Group Versus Lyric Ratings; Industry Cross-Section Involved," *Variety.* 320 (September 18, 1985) 73ff.

Sutherland, Sam. "Eight Labels Take Anti-Ratings Stance," *Billboard.* 97:40 (October 5, 1985) 1, 68.
Re. the Musical Majority.

Tabor, L. "Music Community Fighting Drugs, Censorship," *International Musician.* 85 (October 1986) 9ff.

CANADA (See also: LYRICS; RATINGS; STICKERING)

"CRIA Meeting on Lyric Issue," *Billboard.* 97 (November 16, 1985) 60.

"Canadian Disk Biz to Sticker Albums With Risque Lyrics," *Variety.* 321 (January 1, 1986) 127.

"Industry Mulls Ratings; CRIA Watching U.S. Situation," *Billboard.* 97 (September 7, 1985) 62.

LaPointe, K. "Industry Follows U.S. Lead in Lyrics Controversy," *Billboard.* 97 (December 14, 1985) 58.

CHRISTIANITY

Bloom, H. "Commentary: Censorship Crusade Targets Rock," *Billboard.* 98 (September 13, 1986) 9.

Dean, R. "Commentary: Christianity Fundamentalism vs. Humanism," *Billboard.* 98 (October 25, 1986) 9.
Reaction to Bloom's "Commentary: Censorship Crusade Targets Rock."

COMMUNIST BLOC NATIONS

Terry, Ken. "Iron Curtain Still Stifles Rock Music," *Billboard.* 100 (June 4, 1988) 8ff.

FLORIDA

Duffy, Thom. "Fla. Judge Insists Sales of 2 Live Crew May Be Illegal," *Billboard.* 102:12 (March 24, 1990) 5, 77.

HEAVY METAL

Broyde, S. "Metal Ban at Catholic WSOU Still an Exception," *Billboard.* 100 (June 18, 1988) 10.

Ivany, J.S. "Commentary: Lowering the Boom on Heavy Metal," *Billboard.* 97 (July 6, 1985) 10.

LABELING (See: STICKERING)

LAWS AND LEGISLATION (See also: MARYLAND; STICKERING)

Holland, Bill. "Congress Stays Action on Child-Obscenity Bill," *Billboard.* 100 (October 29, 1988) 104.

Holland, Bill. "13 State Lawmakers Back Off Sticker Bills," *Billboard.* 102:15 (April 14, 1990) 1, 87.

Holland, Bill. "Trade Cries Foul on Porn Bills," *Billboard.* 100 (June 25, 1988) 1ff.

Holland, Bill. "Trade Fears Latest Kid-Porn-Bill Strategy," *Billboard.* 100 (October 15, 1988) 3.

"The Naked Gun," *Rock & Roll Confidential.* n64 (January 1989) 4–5.
Re. Child Protection and Obscenity Enforcement Act.

Neely, Kim. "Louisiana Law to Require LP Stickers," *Rolling Stone.* n585 (August 23, 1990) 35.

Neely, Kim. "States Withdrawing Labeling Bills," *Rolling Stone.* n578 (May 17, 1990) 23.

LOUISIANA (See also: STICKERING)

"Shock Trade Faces Louisiana Stickering Law," *Billboard.* (June 16, 1990) 5ff.

LYRICS (See also: PMRC; RATINGS)

"Commentary: Lyrics: Enough Ground Surrendered," *Billboard.* 97 (August 24, 1985) 10.

DePierro, T. "Commentary: Lyrics, Labels, AIDS—A Connection?," *Billboard.* 97 (November 16, 1985) 10.

Duffy, Thom. "A & R Execs Watchful of Artists' Lyrics," *Billboard.* (April 7, 1990) 4, 93.

George, Nelson. "At Philly BMA Meet Gamble Speaks on Lyric Controversy," *Billboard.* 97 (November 2, 1985) 60.

Goldberg, Danny. "How to Answer Warning Label Advocates: The Great Lyrics Debate Will Not Go Away," *Billboard.* 102:17 (April 28, 1990) 9, 70. il.

Haring, Bruce. "Lyrics Concerns Brighten Sales at Indie Stores," *Billboard.* 102:7 (April 28, 1980) 1, 82.

Neely, Kim. "Retailers, Labels Give in on Lyrics," *Rolling Stone.* n575 (April 5, 1990) 30.

Ross, Sean. "Racy Lyrics: Gettin' Busy in a Bathroom Has PDs Busy, Too," *Billboard.* (June 16, 1990) 1, 18.

"So Who Understands Rock Lyrics, Anyway?," *Newsweek.* (July 14, 1986) 71.
Summary of Lorraine Prinsky–Jill Rosenbaum study of secondary school students.

Wharton, D. "Porn Rock Foes Charge Labels Have Ignored Pact on Racy Lyrics," *Variety.* 325 (December 17, 1986) 85–86.

LYRICS—RAP

"Atlantic Faces Heat from Gays Over Rap Lyrics," *Billboard.* (July 14, 1990) 78.

Rosen, Craig. "Geffen Refuses to Distribute Geto Boys Album," *Billboard.* (August 25, 1990) 1, 95.

MAGAZINES, NEWSLETTERS, ETC.

Browne, David. "Newsletter Eyes Liberal Musicians," *Rolling Stone.* n566 (November 30, 1989) 29.
Report on the establishment of *TV, etc.*, an eight-page bimonthly newsletter concerned with monitoring the left-wing biases of the entertainment world.

"Rock Mag Folds as Distribs Fear Pressure Groups," *Variety.* 324 (August 20, 1986) 1ff.
Re. *Hard Rock.*

Schipper, H. "Second Retail Chain May Pull Rock Mags; RIAA Protests Trend," *Variety.* 324 (July 30, 1986) 69–70.

MARYLAND (See also: LAWS AND LEGISLATION; STICKERING)

Holland, Bill. "Defeat Seen for Maryland Obscenity Bill," *Billboard.* 98 (March 1, 1986) 4ff.

Holland, Bill. "Maryland Committee Kills Labeling Bill; W. Va. Measure Also Set Back; Others are Pending," *Billboard.* 102:12 (March 24, 1990) 5, 77.

"Maryland House Passes Ban on 'Obscene' Disks," *Variety.* 322 (February 19, 1986) 3ff.

"Record Obscenity Bill Rejected in Maryland," *International Musician.* 84 (May 1986) 11.

PARENT TEACHER ASSOCIATION (See also: PARENTS MUSIC RESOURCE CENTER; RATINGS)

Paige, E. "PTA Meet Looks at Ratings," *Billboard.* 97 (March 2, 1985) 27ff.

PARENTS MUSIC RESOURCE CENTER (PMRC)

Cocks, Jay, with Richard Stengel and Denise Worrell. "Rock is a Four-Letter Word," *Time.* (September 30, 1985) 70–71. il.

DiMauro, P. "PMRC Still Watching Industry; Indie Label Releases Draw Ire," *Variety.* 322 (April 23, 1986) 241.

Dolan, M. " 'Porn Rock' Hearing Hot Ticket in D.C.; Zappa Lashes PMRC," *Variety.* 320 (September 18, 1985) 73–74.

Dougherty, Steven. "Parents vs. Rock," *People Weekly.* (September 30, 1985) 46–53.

Dupler, S. "Lyrics: Video Outlets Seem Confident; National Programmers Don't See Problems With PMRC," *Billboard.* 97 (September 21, 1985) 3ff.

"Frank Zappa on the PMRC," *Newsletter on Intellectual Freedom.* (January 1986) 3, 23–25.
Full text of Zappa's September 19, 1985, statement before the Senate Commerce Committee.

Goodman, Fred. "Parents, RIAA in Lyrics Accord," *Billboard.* 97:45 (November 9, 1985) 1, 87.

Haring, Bruce. "The PMRC's Record-Stickering Campaign: A Five-Year History," *Billboard.* 102:15 (April 14, 1990) 87–88.

Harrington, Richard. "The Capitol Hill Rock War: Emotions Run High as Musicians Confront Parents' Group at Hearing," *Washington Post.* (September 20, 1985) B1, B6. il.

Holland, Bill. "A Gentle War of Words: Music Makers Confront Lawmakers," *Billboard.* 97 (September 28, 1985) 82.

Holland, Bill. "Lyric Row: New Developments: PMRC Says Beach Boys' Mike Love Gave Seed Money," *Billboard.* 97:37 (September 14, 1985) 1, 100.

Holland, Bill. "PMRC Back on Warpath Over Explicit Albums," *Billboard.* 100 (December 10, 1988) 1ff.

Holland, Bill. "PMRC Calls for Uniform Labeling: Cites Good Faith of Record Companies," *Billboard.* 98:50 (December 20, 1986) 3, 67.

Holland, Bill. "PMRC is on the Warpath Again," *Billboard.* 99:27 (July 4, 1987) 1, 78.

Holland, Bill. "PTA, PMRC Unite on Lyrics," *Billboard.* 97 (September 21, 1985) 1ff.

Holland, Bill. "Senators to Labels: Clean Up Your Act," *Billboard.* 97:38 (September 28, 1985) 1, 82.

"Lyrics Accord is Reached," *International Musician.* 84 (December 1985) 1ff.

Nevius, S., and others. "Commentary: PMRC: Censorship in Not the Goal," *Billboard.* 98 (October 11, 1986) 13.

"PMRC Targets 15 '86 Albums," *Billboard.* (December 20, 1986) 67.

The Record; a Newsletter from the Parents' Music Resource Center. Arlington, VA: PMRC, 1985– . Monthly.

Sandow, Gregory. "Doctors Deny PMRC Alliance," *Rolling Stone.* n572 (February 22, 1990) 34.

Schipper, H. "D.C. Wives Pull Political ʼAid in Music Face-Off," *Variety.* 324 (October 15, 1986) 3ff.

Schipper, H. "Washington Wives Ready to Discuss New Labeling Deal," *Variety.* 325 (November 12, 1986) 2ff.

" 'Settlement' Reached in Rock Lyric Dispute," *Newsletter on Intellectual Freedom.* (January 1986) 3–4.

Shalett, M. "On Target: The PMRC Isn't Taken Seriously— It's Too Unreal for Kids Now," *Billboard.* 98 (March 15, 1986) 26.

Sutherland, Sam. "Zappa on the Offensive in Lyric Battle," *Billboard.* 97:37 (September 14, 1985) 3, 100.

Sutherland, Sam, and S. Dupler. "RIAA, Parents Fail to Harmonize," *Billboard.* 97 (August 24, 1985) 1ff.

Tabor, L. "Lyrics Accord Expected," *International Musician.* 84 (November 1985) 1ff.

"Thanks for the Free Promotion," *Canadian Composer.* n205 (November 1985) 42.
Report on the recent attempt by a group of U.S. congressional wives to clean up rock lyrics.

Wharton, D. "RIAA, PMRC Reach Accord on Record Lyrics; Labels Agree to Use Stickers or Print Words," *Variety.* 321 (November 6, 1985) 85ff.

Zappa, Frank. " 'Extortion, Pure and Simple . . . ' An Open Letter to the Music Industry," *Cash Box.* XLIX:12 (August 31, 1985) 3. il.

"Zappa, Denver to Testify on Lyrics at Senate Hearing," *Variety.* 320 (September 11, 1985) 1ff.

RADIO (See also: LYRICS)

Freeman, K. "Radio Caught Up in New Controversy Over Lyrics," *Billboard.* 97 (June 8, 1985) 1ff.

Holland, Bill. "NAB's Fritts Urges Labels: Supply Radio With Lyrics," *Billboard.* 97 (June 15, 1985) 1ff.

Terry, Ken. "Record Labels, Programmers React Diversely to NAB Letter," *Variety.* 319 (June 12, 1985) 76.

Wharton, D. "B'casters Start Blast Against Violent Lyrics," *Variety.* 319 (June 5, 1985) 1ff.

RATINGS (See also: RETAILERS AND RETAILING; STICKERING)

"Editorial: Record Companies at a Crossroad," *Variety.* 320 (August 14, 1985) 68.
Re. lyrics warning on album packaging.

Goodman, Fred. "RIAA: Warning Yes, But Ratings No," *Billboard.* 97 (August 17, 1985) 1ff.

Holland, Bill. "Will Industry Rate Records?," *Billboard.* 97 (August 10, 1985) 1ff.

Lichtman, Irv. "NARM 'Unanimously' Against Ratings," *Billboard.* 97 (November 2, 1985) 3ff.

"Next: R-Rated Record Albums?," *Newsweek.* (August 26, 1985) 69.

"Ratings Drive Called 'Harassment' by Rosenblatt at Coast NARAS," *Variety.* 320 (October 2, 1985) 146.

Sutherland, Sam, and others. "Trade Reacts to Lyric Agreement," *Billboard.* 97 (November 16, 1985) 1ff.

RETAILERS AND RETAILING (See also: ALABAMA; LYRICS: STICKERING; TEXAS)

Bonk, J. "Commentary: Where Does the Responsibility Lie?," *Billboard.* 97 (October 19, 1985) 10.
Provides a retailer's view of the lyrics controversy.

Holland, Bill. "Malls Could Press Dealers on Lyrics if Faced With Community Protests," *Billboard.* 97 (December 7, 1985) 7.

McAdams, Janine, and Susan Nunziata. "Rap Labels Decry Retail Moves," *Billboard.* (March 3, 1990) 81.

Schipper, H. "Retailers Oppose Record Ratings, Fearing Buyer, Landlord Backlash," *Variety.* 320 (October 9, 1985) 118.

SOUTH AFRICA

"Anomaly Unearthed in Ban on Wonder's Music," *Variety.* 319 (June 19, 1985) 89.

"S. Africa May End Stevie Wonder Ban," *Variety.* 319 (July 17, 1985) 46.

STICKERING (See also: LOUISIANA; LYRICS; RATINGS; RETAILERS AND RETAILING)

Bessman, Jim. "Sony's Stickering Plans Come Unglued; Zappa Calls a Halt to Warning Tags on His Release," *Billboard.* 98 (March 22, 1986) 46.
Re. *Does Humor Belong in Music?*

Goldberg, Michael. "At a Loss for Words; Record-Industry Acceptance of Stickering is Already Having a Chilling Effect," *Rolling Stone.* n579 (May 31, 1990) 19–22. il.

Goldberg, Michael, and Jeffrey Ressner. "Retailers Take on Stickering," *Rolling Stone.* n576 (April 19, 1990) 26.

Goodman, Fred. "PolyGram Starts Stickering; Bar-Kays Album Carries Warning," *Billboard.* 97 (September 14, 1985) 102.

Grein, Paul. "Lyric Warning Stickers Blasted," *Billboard.* 97 (September 7, 1985) 3ff.

Haring, Bruce. "Indie Labels Begrudgingly Support Standard Stickering System," *Billboard.* 102:12 (March 24, 1990) 81.

Haring, Bruce. "NAIRD, Fearing a Split, Won't OK Stickering," *Billboard.* (June 16, 1990) 1, 98.

Holland, Bill. "Labeling Bills Hit Snags in Tenn., Md.," *Billboard.* 102:10 (March 10, 1990) 98.

Holland, Bill. "RIAA Strives to Finalize Lyrics Stickers; 4 State Lawmakers Await Industry's Next Move," *Billboard.* 102:6 (April 21, 1980) 7.

Holland, Bill. "Support for Stickering Bills Seems to Erode," *Billboard.* (April 7, 1990) 1, 93.

Morris, Chris, Edward Morris, Bruce Haring and Maurie Orodenker. "Northwest Dealer Lauches Six-State Sticker Policy," *Billboard.* 102:18 (May 5, 1990) 5, 81.

Nunziata, Susan. "Wax Works Drops All Stickered Albums," *Billboard.* (March 3, 1990) 1, 81, 83.

Rabey, S. "Can Rock Clean Up Its Act?," *Christianity Today.* 34 (May 14, 1990) 42–43ff. il.
Focuses on the use of warning stickers.

Rosen, Bradley C. "Labeling Laws Violate U.S. Constitution," *Billboard.* 102:10 (March 10, 1990) 13, 84.

Schipper, H. "MCA, A&M Reject Sticker Plan of RIAA; Fear Retailer Backlash," *Variety.* 320 (October 2, 1985) 141ff.

Terry, Ken. "Trade Unites on Self-Labeling," *Billboard.* 102:12 (March 24, 1990) 1, 81.

TELEVISION (See also: UNITED KINGDOM)

"ABC Censor Zaps Easton Tune; Can't do 'Sugar' on 'Bandstand'," *Variety.* 318 (April 3, 1985) 72.

Bessman, Jim. "Local Chip Outlets Don't Feel Pressure; Programmers Unfazed by Controversy Over Lyrics," *Billboard.* 97 (September 21, 1985) 35–36.

DiMauro, P. "Benjamin Predicts Attack on Vid Smut, Urges Labels to Vidclips," *Variety.* 320 (August 7, 1985) 69ff.

Grantham, B. "BBC's Control Over Risque Disks Has Lessened With Competition," *Variety.* 321 (November 13, 1985) 120.

Spahr, W. "Nation's Best-Selling Single Banned by German Stations," *Billboard.* 98 (February 1, 1986) 9.

TELEVISION—MTV

Hannusch, Jeff. "Town Fails to Unplug MTV," *Rolling Stone.* n566 (November 30, 1989) 28.

News coverage of how Cher's "If I Could Turn Back Time" spurred board of directors of Texarkana to attempt to remove MTV from their cable service.

Roblin, A. "Antichrist Cooled Down for MTV Debut," *Billboard.* 97 (May 4, 1985) 37.
Re. DeGarmo and Key's video of "Six, Six, Six."

TENNESSEE (See also: LYRICS; STICKERING)

Morris, Edward. "Tenn. D.A. Deems Rap Albums Obscene," *Billboard.* 102:15 (April 14, 1990) 87.

Morris, Edward. "Tennessee Joins Labeling List," *Billboard.* (March 3, 1990) 81.

Morris, Edward. "VSDA Fails to Hold Back Tenn. Obscenity Measure," *Billboard.* 102:16 (April 21, 1990) 7.

Morris, Edward, and Bruce Haring. "2 Live Crew, N.W.A. Called Obscene by Tenn. Judge," *Billboard.* (April 7, 1990) 4, 93.

TEXAS—RETAILING

Burr, Ramiro. "Texas Retailer Faces Charges for Selling 'Nasty'," *Billboard.* 102:28 (July 14, 1990) 1, 78.
Re. David Richer, owner of Hogwild Records and Tapes.

TEXAS—SAN ANTONIO CONCERTS

DiMauro, P. "ACLU, Promoter to Challenge Texas Law Re. 'Obscene' Shows," *Variety.* 321 (November 27, 1985) 142.

Sutherland, Sam. "One City Mulls Concert Control in Lyric Row," *Billboard.* 97 (September 21, 1985) 1ff.

UNITED KINGDOM (See also: TELEVISION)

"Controversy Greets New Brit Council to Police Airwaves," *Billboard.* 100 (June 4, 1988) 57.

Charity (See also: Record Companies—Executives)

GENERAL SOURCES

Dupler, Steven, and Paul Grein. "Charity Efforts Intensify," *Billboard.* 97 (July 6, 1985) 1ff.

Grein, Paul. "Charity Events Compete for Spotlight," *Billboard.* 98 (April 5, 1986) 1ff.

Miller, Jim, and others. "Brother, Can You Spare a Song? Charity Has Become Chic as Musicians Line Up Behind the Latest Worthy Cause," *Newsweek.* (October 28, 1985) 94–95. il.

AIDS

Neely, Kim. "Arista Sets AIDS Benefit," *Rolling Stone.* n564 (November 2, 1989) 23.

"Streisand Donates Coin for Peace, AIDS Work," *Variety.* 321 (November 27, 1985) 141.

Tannenbaum, Rob. "Arista AIDS Benefit Held," *Rolling Stone.* n577 (May 3, 1990) 26. il.

A.R.M.S.

"A.R.M.S. Project Off to Fast Start With Album, Video," *Variety.* 319 (May 22, 1985) 89.

"Lane is Defendent in a Civil Suit vs. ARMS of America," *Variety.* 323 (May 21, 1986) 92ff.

AMNESTY INTERNATIONAL

Gold, Todd. "Roll Over, Elvis—The Latest Jailhouse Rock Was an All-Star Benefit for Political Prisoners," *People Weekly.* (1986) 34–37. il.
    Re. the Conspiracy of Hope Concert (New Jersey).

Henke, J. "Chimes of Freedom; Amnesty International's Super-star Human Rights Now! Tour Hits the Road," *Rolling Stone.* n537 (October 20, 1988) 15–16.

McNamara, D. "Competitors in Truce for Amnesty; Stations to Share Concert Simulcast," *Billboard.* 98 (June 14, 1986) 10.

"U2 Concert Blackout," *Melody Maker.* 61 (June 28, 1986) 3.

ARTISTS UNITED AGAINST APARTHEID

"Artists Unite Against Apartheid," *Cash Box.* (August 31, 1985) 7.

"Pop! The Glory Years: Missing the Botha," *Melody Maker.* 63 (October 24, 1987) 23. supplement.

BAND AID

"Bob Geldof's Band Aid Grosses $84,326,000; Tops British Gift List," *Variety.* 324 (August 27, 1986) 1ff.

Goodman, Fred. "No U.S. Re-Release for Band Aid Charity Single," *Billboard.* 97 (December 14, 1985) 70. Re. "Do They Know It's Christmas."

Jones, P. "Geldof Blasts Indonesia on Bootlegging," *Billboard.* 97 (December 21, 1985) 3ff.

"Pop! The Glory Years: The Global Juke Box," *Melody Maker.* 63 (October 24, 1987) 23. supplement. il.

BLUES FOR SALVADOR

Goldberg, Michael. "Blues for Salvador; Benefit Raises $100,000," *Rolling Stone.* n521 (March 10, 1988) 21. il.

CHAIN TAPE

Ressner, Jeffrey. "Kevin Godley's 'Chain Tape'; World-Music Project Tied to Ecology Broadcast," *Rolling Stone.* n579 (May 31, 1990) 33. il.

CROSBY, STILLS, NASH AND YOUNG (CONCERT)

Ressner, Jeffrey. "CSNY Honors Its Former Drummer," *Rolling Stone.* n578 (May 17, 1990) 18. il.

DISCO AID

Kink, K. "Club Yopicana," *Melody Maker.* 61 (November 1, 1986) 30. int. w/S. Walsh re. recording "Give Give Give."

FARM AID (See also: WILLIE NELSON)

Fricke, David. "Farm Aid," *Melody Maker.* 60 (October 5, 1985) 36ff. il.

Grein, Paul. "TV Coverage of Farm Aid Will Reach 90% of U.S," *Billboard.* 97 (September 21, 1985) 74.

Grein, Paul, and Kip Kirby. "Farm Aid Concert Raises $10 Million in Sales, Pledges," *Billboard.* 97 (October 5, 1985) 1ff.

"Harvest Song: Willie Plans at Benefit," *Time.* (September 23, 1985) 32. il.

McBride, Murdoch. "Willie & Co. Take Farm Aid to Nebraska—Haggard, Mellencamp, Neil Young to Perform," *Cash Box.* (September 19, 1987) 10–11.

Millard, B. "Farm Aid Bandwagon Rolling, But Without Plan to Divvy Funds," *Variety.* 320 (September 11, 1985) 77.

Morris, E. "Morris Names Set to Perform at Farm Benefit," *Billboard.* 97 (September 7, 1985) 1ff.

Wood, G. "Nashville Scene: Willie Nelson Discusses His Work for Farm Aid," *Billboard.* 98 (July 12, 1986) 28.

FARM AID II

"Major Acts Agree to do Farm Aid II," *Variety.* 323 (May 7, 1986) 53ff.

"Nelson is Planning July 4th Sequel to Farm Aid in Austin," *Variety.* 322 (February 26, 1986) 97.

Wood, G. "Nashville Scene: Reflections on Farm Aid II and Predictions for a Sequel," *Billboard.* 98 (July 19, 1986) 30.

FARM AID III

"Farm Aid III Last for Nelson; Little Impact on Farmers," *Variety.* 328 (September 23, 1987) 1ff.

Millard, B. "Nebraska Guv Aids Nelson in Setting Up Farm Aid III," *Variety.* 324 (December 3, 1986) 111.

Nelson, Willie. "Commentary: Why the Farmer Needs Your Support," *Billboard.* 99 (September 17, 1987) 9.

Roth, M. "Farm Aid III Was Fine Concert, But Didn't Raise Much Money," *Variety.* 328 (September 23, 1987) 157.

FARM AID IV

Redmond, Mike. "Farming IV Aid," *Spin.* 6:4 (July 1990) 27. il.

FERRY AID

Cassata, Mary Anne. "Ferry Aid: Behind the Scenes," *Song Hits.* n260 (December 1987) 22–23. il.

GLASNOST ROCK CONCERT

Jones, Peter. "Glasnost Rock Concert to Benefit Quake Victims," *Billboard.* 101 (January 28, 1989) 5ff.

GREENPEACE (ALBUM AND TOUR)

"£50,000 Loss for Greenpeace," *Melody Maker.* 61 (May 3, 1986) 3.

Sutherland, Sam. "British Acts Team for Greenpeace Album," *Billboard.* 97 (August 17, 1985) 78.

HANDS ACROSS AMERICA (See also: KENNETH KRAGEN)

"Aid for America," *Rolling Stone.* n462 (December 5, 1985) 18.

Gett, Steve. "Charity Offers Breakdown on $33 Million; Hands Across America Spent $17 Million on Event," *Billboard.* 98 (September 6, 1986) 90.

Gett, Steve. "Kragen Hails Success of 'Hands'," *Billboard.* 98 (June 7, 1986) 3ff. il.

Holland, Bill. "Kragen Gets Together With Geldof," *Billboard.* 97 (September 21, 1985) 3.

"Kragen Bows Drive to Help U.S. Poor Via Human Chain," *Variety.* 320 (October 23, 1985) 81.

Moleski, L. "Kragen Readies Another Mega-Event; 'Hands Across America' to Reach Out to Hungry Here," *Billboard.* 97 (November 2, 1985) 4ff.

Sutherland, Sam. "Vidclip Key to 'Hands Across America',"
  Billboard. 98 (January 25, 1986) 74.

HEAR 'N' AID

Mayfield, G. "Rockers Urge Dealers to Give Heavy Push to
  'Aid'," *Billboard.* 98 (June 21, 1986) 40A. il.

Vare, E.A. "Sony Mines Precious Metal With *Hear 'N' Aid*
  Cassette," *Billboard.* 98 (May 17, 1986) 59.

KRAGEN, KENNETH (See also: HANDS ACROSS AMERICA; U.S.A. FOR AFRICA)

"Award to Kragen," *Variety.* 318 (March 27, 1985) 94.
  Re. U.S.A. for Africa famine relief.

"Boys Club to Honor Kragen in October," *Variety.* 320
  (October 2, 1985) 158.

LIVE AID (See also: COUNTERFEITING, BOOTLEGGING, ETC.)

"Brits Waive Sales Tax on Live Aid Receipts," *Variety.* 319
  (July 24, 1985) 131.

Clerk, Carol, and B. McIlheney. "Live Aid: Staging the
  Greatest Show on Earth," *Melody Maker.* 60 (July 13,
  1985) 16–18. il.

DiMauro, P. "Philly Live Aid Electrifies Rock Fans," *Variety.*
  319 (July 17, 1985) 105ff.

"Gallic Live Aid Flops," *Variety.* 320 (October 16, 1985) 443.

George, Nelson. "The Rhythm and the Blues: Grumblings About the Live Aid Talent Lineup," *Billboard.* 97 (July 6, 1985) 60.

Grein, Paul. "Broadcasters Team for 'Live Aid' Benefit," *Billboard.* 97 (June 22, 1985) 1ff.

Grein, Paul. "Live Aid Hailed as Pop Music's Triumph," *Billboard.* 97 (July 27, 1985) 1ff.

"Live Aid Cash," *Melody Maker.* 60 (July 27, 1985) 3.

"Live Aid Down Under!," *Melody Maker.* 60 (July 6, 1985) 3.

"Live Aid Expected to Raise $40-Mil for Famine Relief," *Variety.* 319 (July 17, 1985) 105.

"Live Aid Telecast Organizers Plan Five TV Events for Global B'cast," *Variety.* 322 (March 19, 1986) 60.

Marsh, Dave. "Riffs & Licks: We are Not the World," *Village Voice.* 30 (July 23, 1985) 83–84.

McIlhency, B., and others. "The Greatest Show on Earth: Live Aid," *Melody Maker.* 60 (July 20, 1985) 25–32. il.

Mieses, S. "Keynotes: Live Aid: Whose Benefit?," *Record.* 4 (October 1985) 48–49. il.

"Music That Moved the World," *People Weekly.* (1985) 26–36. il.

" 'Nyet' to Famine Relief? Say Russia Offers No Live Aid $$," *Billboard.* 97 (August 3, 1985) 85.

"Philly-to-London Rock Concert Includes TV Blurbs on Hunger," *Variety.* 319 (June 26, 1985) 48.

"Pirated Live Aid Tapes Rob $3-Mil from Famine Relief," *Variety.* 321 (December 4, 1985) 105.

Schipper, H. "Christian Network Withheld Its Phone Bank from Live Aid," *Variety.* 320 (August 7, 1985) 72.

Schipper, H. "Live Aid Donations Hampered by Insufficient Telephone Lines," *Variety.* 319 (July 24, 1985) 125.

"Talk Talk," *Melody Maker.* 60 (September 21, 1985) 8. Uses of Live Aid donations defended by Geldof.

NELSON MANDELA INTERNATIONAL TRIBUTE CONCERT

Fielder, Hugh. "Mandela U.K. Show Gets Big Turnout, But U.S. Tunes Out," *Billboard.* 102:17 (April 28, 1990) 8. April 16, 1990 production set in London's Wembley Stadium.

NORDOFF-ROBBINS MUSIC THERAPY CENTER (LONDON)

DeCurtis, Anthony. "Rock's Favorite Charity," *Rolling Stone.* 2582/583 (July 12/26, 1990) 23–25. il.
Covers benefit show in Knebworth. Includes sidebar "What the Musicians Say."

RHYTHM AND BLUES FOUNDATION

"News: God Save the Blues," *Spin.* 5:11 (February 1990) 18. il.

SELF-AID

"Self-Aid to Help Irish Unemployed," *Billboard.* 98 (May 10, 1986) 90.

"Self LP!," *Melody Maker.* 61 (May 31, 1986) 3. il.
   Re. *Rock for a Living.*

SPRINGSTEEN, BRUCE

Tabor, L. "Springsteen Aids Hunger Groups During U.S. Tour," *International Musician.* 83 (February 1985) 1ff.

SUN CITY

Barol, Bill. " 'I Ain't Gonna Play Sun City'," *Newsweek.* (October 28, 1985) 94–95. il., int. w/Steven Van Zandt.

Christgau, Georgia. "Sun City S.O.S.," *High Fidelity.* (January 1986) 51.

George, Nelson. "New Single Attacks Apartheid," *Billboard.* 97 (July 27, 1985) 48.
   Re. "I Ain't Gonna Play Sun City."

George, Nelson. "The Rhythm and the Blues: More Artists Have Lent Their Voices to *Sun City*," *Billboard.* 97 (August 24, 1985) 49.

McIlheney, B. "Apart-aid!," *Melody Maker.* 60 (August 31, 1985) 12–13. il., int. w/Van Zandt re. recording, "Sun City."

CHICAGO BEARS' SUPER BOWL SHUFFLE

McCormick, Moira. " 'Shuffle' Scores for Needy," *Billboard.* 98 (December 20, 1986) 72.

"TEARS ARE NOT ENOUGH" (CANADA)

LaPointe, K. "Rush Release for All-Star Charity Single," *Billboard.* 97 (March 9, 1985) 74.

LaPointe, K. " 'Tears are Not Enough' Set for U.S. Single Release," *Billboard.* 97 (May 18, 1985) 63.

" 'Tears' Documentary Opens Amid Black-Tie Fanfare," *Billboard.* 97 (November 2, 1985) 67.

"Top Canadian Stars Make a Single for Relief of Famine," *Variety.* 318 (February 13, 1985) 141.

USA FOR AFRICA (See also: "WE ARE THE WORLD")

Goodman, Fred. "USA for Africa Moves to Close Books," *Rolling Stone.* n510 (October 8, 1987) 23.

McGowan, C. "USA for Africa Tops Funds Goal: More Than $51 Million Raised," *Billboard.* 98 *(October 25, 1986) 6.*

"Paycable Review," *Variety.* 319 (May 15, 1985) 68.

"USA for Africa Audit Confirms $43-Mil Gross, Royalty Income Counts," *Variety.* 324 (September 17, 1986) 1ff.

"USA for Africa Distributes 20% of Its Funds in 8 Lands," *Variety.* 320 (August 14, 1985) 67.

"USA for Africa to Benefit from CBS-TV Special," *Variety.* 321 (November 13, 1985) 118.

"WE ARE THE WORLD" (See also: USA FOR AFRICA; COUNTERFEITING, BOOTLEGGING, ETC.)

"HBO Licenses Video of 'We are the World'; $2,000,000 Gift," *Variety.* 318 (March 20, 1985) 131ff.

Kirk, C. "Rock Artists' Famine Relief Group Mounting Many-Sided Campaign," *Variety.* 318 (February 6, 1985) 117ff.

"Many U.K. Retailers Won't Handle Famine Disk; Blame Terms," *Variety.* 318 (April 3, 1985) 69.

"Merchandise Bootleggers Plague 'We are the World' Famine Project," *Variety.* 318 (April 17, 1985) 4ff.

"Pirated Versions of 'We are the World' are Robbing Millions," *Variety.* 319 (July 24, 1985) 125.

"U.K. Stores Change Tune on 'We are World' 45," *Variety.* 318 (April 10, 1985) 89.

"*We are the World*: USA for Africa," *Billboard*. 97 (April 6, 1985) USA3ff. il., int. w/Harry Belafonte.

" 'We are the World' Vid Docu Issued at $14.95 for Africa Famine Aid," *Variety*. 319 (May 1, 1985) 491.

White, A. "CBS Makes $6.5 Million 'World' Payment," *Billboard*. 97 (May 25, 1985) 1ff.

Charts

"Hot 100 Radio Panel Changes With the Times," *Billboard*. 97 (November 9, 1985) 1ff.

"New Chart Track Music Videocassettes," *Billboard*. 97 (March 30, 1985) 3.

"New Chart Weighting Debuts in *Billboard*; System Will Better Reflect Sales and Airplay," *Billboard*. 98 (July 12, 1986) 3.

"On the Beam," *Billboard*. 97 (September 28, 1985) 22–23. Debut of Compact Disc charts covering both pop and classical titles.

"Radio Stations Sue *Cash Box* for Not Yielding Chart Information," *Variety*. 321 (January 22, 1986) 73ff.

"Sales Chart for 12-Inch Singles Debuts," *Billboard*. 97 (March 16, 1985) 3.

UNITED KINGDOM

"Phonogram U.K. Fined for Chart Hyping," *Billboard*. 97 (September 28, 1985) 9.

Rice, Jo, Paul Gambaccini and Mike Reed. *The Guinness Book of 500 Number One Hits.* Enfield, U.K.: Guinness Superlatives, 1982. il.
Chronological listing of the 500 recordings which reached the top of the British singles charts between 1952 and 1982. Includes discussions of each song; e.g., analysis of the reasons for this success.

Savile, Jimmy, and Tony Jasper. *Nostalgia Book of Hit Singles.* London: Frederick Muller, 1982. il.
Twenty recordings from each year between 1954 and 1982 are described. The only criterion for this subjective compilation is that the song appeared in the British top twenty charts and has, to some extent, retained its popularity.

"U.K. Chart Hyping Targeted," *Billboard.* 97 (August 3, 1985) 9.

WEST GERMANY

Spahr, W. "W. Germany Bows Top 100 Singles Chart," *Billboard.* 101 (August 26, 1989) 81–82.

Clubs and Concert Venues

Goldberg, Michael. "Studio 54 Co-Owner Steve Rubell Dead at 45," *Rolling Stone.* n560 (September 7, 1989) 24. il.

Iorio, Paul. "Hilly Kristal's CBGB's: The Site of a Revolution in Popular Music," *Cash Box.* XLIX:42 (April 5, 1986) 12.

Kuipers, Dean. "Chasing the Dragon," *Spin.* 6:2 (May 1990) 32–36, 93–97. il., int. Surveys the role of heroin in the Los Angeles rock scene.

Kuipers, Dean. "To Pay and Play in LA," *Spin.* 6:3 (June 1990) 22. il., int. w/band members of Gung Ho!, a spokesman for Rock Against Pay to Play, and John Egger of First Class Productions.

Webb, Selina. "Making Mountains from Moles' Bills," *Music Week.* (June 10, 1989) 9. il.
Re. Moles Club (Bath, U.K.).

DISC JOCKEYS

Bessman, Jim. "Club Jocks Bemoan Lack of Attention; Record Companies Taken to Task," *Billboard.* 97 (October 12, 1985) 39–40.

Bessman, Jim. "Club Jocks Tell How They Remix It Up; Clips Get Extended, Enhanced Via Technical Wizardry," *Billboard.* 97 (October 19, 1985) 59–60.

Concerts, Festivals, Touring

CONCERTS—GENERAL SOURCES

Handelman, David. "Is It Live or . . . ," *Rolling Stone.* (September 6, 1990) 15–16. il.

Kesterson, M. "Guest Editorial: Is Live Music Dying?," *Keyboard Magazine.* 14 (September 1988) 12.

CONCERTS—ADMISSION PRACTICES

"Fan's Anger at Queen Stabbing," *Melody Maker.* 61 (August 23, 1986) 3. il.
Overbooking figures disputed.

"Music Store Cited for Antitrust Action to Avoid 'Scalping'," *Variety.* 319 (July 10, 1985) 2ff.

"Queen Fan Dead," *Melody Maker.* 61 (August 16, 1986) 3. Tragedy blamed on overbooking and poor organization.

CONCERTS—BOOKING AGENTS AND BOOKING COMPANIES

Iorio, Paul. "Premier Talent's Frank Barsalona: A Total Booking Agent," *Cash Box.* XLIX:43 (April 12, 1986) 14.

Levy, Joe. "GTI on the Right Track," *Cash Box.* (April 30, 1988) 18.

MacCambridge, M. "Jam Prods. Spreads Over Pop Music Booking Scene," *Variety.* 325 (November 19, 1986) 76ff.

Roth, M. "Chi. Promoters Blame Springsteen for 'Festival' Seating Problem," *Variety.* 320 (July 31, 1985) 77.

FESTIVALS—GENERAL SOURCES

Sandford, Jeremy, and Ron Reid. *Tomorrow's People.* London: Jerome, 1974. il.
Historical background of the phenomena is covered with a special emphasis on those organized in Great Britain between 1967 and 1973.

FESTIVALS—ALTAMONT

Booth, Stanley. "Altamont Remembered," *Rolling Stone.* (September 13, 1984) 25ff. il.

FESTIVALS—CAMBRIDGE FOLK FESTIVAL

Von Schmidt, Eric. *Baby, Let Me Follow You Down: The Illustrated Story of the Cambridge Folk Years.* Garden City, NY: Anchor, 1979. il.

FESTIVALS—GLASTONBURY

Gittins, Ian, Steve Sutherland and Ben Stud. "Glastonbury: It's a Mud Mud Mud Mud World," *Melody Maker.* (July 7, 1990) 47–50. il.

"Glastonbury: The Wrong Arm of the Law," *Melody Maker.* (July 7, 1990) 3. il.

FESTIVALS—KNEBWORTH

Duffy, Thom. "P'Gram Plans Blitz for 'Knebworth' Album," *Billboard.* (July 14, 1990) 83.

FESTIVALS—MOSCOW MUSIC PEACE FESTIVAL

Duffy, Thom, and others. "Moscow Festival a Rock Success," *Billboard.* 101 (August 26, 1989) 6ff.

Gundersen, Edna. "Tell Tchaikovsky the News," *Rolling Stone.* n562 (October 5, 1989) 15–16. il.

FESTIVALS—NEW MUSIC FESTIVAL

Goodman, Fred. "New Music Fest Marks Tenth Year," *Rolling Stone.* n566 (November 30, 1989) 37.

FESTIVALS—READING '90

"Reading '90 12 Page Pull-Out," *Melody Maker.* (August 25, 1990) p1–12 (separately paged insert). il.

FESTIVALS—VOLUNTEER JAM

Millard, B. "Record Turnout at Volunteer Jam; Gov. Lamar Hosts 2-Hour Seg.," *Variety.* 323 (July 16, 1986) 116.

Millard, B. "Volunteer Jam Beats Weather; Showtime Shoots Cable Special," *Variety.* 318 (February 6, 1985) 118.

Morris, E. "14,000 Brave Heatwave for Volunteer Jam," *Billboard.* 98 (July 26, 1986) 32.

Morris, E. "Volunteer Jam Widens Its Reach; Live TV Audience for 11th Event," *Billboard.* 97 (February 23, 1985) 44ff.

"Vol Jam Set Attendance Record, Partly Due to Skynyrd Reunion," *Variety.* 328 (September 9, 1987) 65.

FESTIVALS—WOODSTOCK

Goodman, Fred. "No Encore for Woodstock," *Rolling Stone.* n558 (August 10, 1989) 26.

"Woodstock Remembered: The Artists," *Rolling Stone.* n559 (August 24, 1989) 87.

TOURING

Arnold, Gina. "First Flight," *Musician.* n118 (August 1988) 92–104.

A look at small group tours with a special emphasis upon Camper Van Beethoven, the Dead Milkmen and Dag Nasty.

Newberry, Scarlett. "Rock Tours: '87 was a Banner Year," *Rolling Stone.* n520 (February 25, 1988) 18–19.
Includes top ten listings of "Top-Grossing Rock Tours of 1987" and "Top-Grossing Rock Concerts of 1987."

Ressner, Jeffrey. "Touring: The Road to Ruin?," *Rolling Stone.* n515/516 (December 17/31, 1987) 81–82.

Copyright (See also: Counterfeiting, Bootlegging, etc.; Beastie Boys; Rap; Bruce Springsteen; Turtles)

GENERAL SOURCES

Goodman, Fred. "Jem Fighting Copyright Infringement Suit," *Billboard.* 97 (October 26, 1985) 3ff.

Goodman, Fred. "Major Labels Sue Tower Over Parallel Imports," *Billboard.* 98 (March 22, 1986) 1ff.

Holland, Bill. "Senators Argue Home-Tape Bill: No Answer Yet," *Billboard.* 97:45 (November 9, 1985) 1ff.

"New Copyright Bill to Reverse Court Goes to Congress," *Variety.* (August 14, 1985) 1ff.

"Plunder and Consolation; Canadian CD Sampler Causes More Heartaches for the Record Industry," *Sounds.* (February 17, 1990) 6. il.

" 'That'll Be the Day' Copyright Disputed," *Variety.* 318 (February 27, 1985) 77.

COPY CODE SYSTEM

Ramada, David. "Interrupted Melody: CBS's Copy Code System Cannot do What Its Proponents Claim, Will Cripple the Growth of DAT, and Will Hurt Both Creators and Consumers of Recorded Music," *High Fidelity.* (July 1987) 44–51. chart, music notation.

Riggs, Michael. "Sony, CBS, and Copy Code," *High Fidelity.* (February 1988) 6.

Counterfeiting, Bootlegging, etc. (See also: Copyright)

BOOTLEGGING

Holland, Bill. "Supreme Court: Bootlegging No Felony," *Billboard.* 97 (July 13, 1985) 3ff.

"Supreme Court Rules Elvis Bootlegger to be Tried Under C'right Act," *Variety.* 319 (July 3, 1985) 65.

COUNTERFEITING

Agudelo, Carlos. "Trade Group: More Than 1 Mil Illicit Cassettes Seized in '89," *Billboard.* 102:11 (March 17, 1990) 8, 104.

Fletcher, Tony. "Tape Rape," *Spin.* 6:4 (July 1990) 19. il.

"Malaco Targeting Counterfeiters (sic): Bogus Product Being Sold Openly," *Billboard.* (July 7, 1990) 78.

Terry, Ken, Ed Christman and Bruce Haring. "Labels Demand Action Against Pirates: Losses from Illicit Product Seen Deepening," *Billboard.* 102:27 (July 7, 1990) 1, 78.

COUNTERFEITING—AUSTRALIA

Baker, Glenn A. "Australian Government Acts to Combat Record and Video Piracy," *Billboard.* 98 (March 8, 1986) 9.

Baker, Glenn A. "Cassette Piracy Epidemic Hits Australia," *Billboard.* 97 (August 17, 1985) 9.

PLAGIARISM (See also: STEVIE WONDER)

Walsh, Michael. "Has Somebody Stolen Their Song?," *Time.* (October 19, 1987) 86. il.

"ROXANNE" RECORDINGS

"Suit Hits 'Roxanne' Spinoffs," *Billboard.* 97 (August 31, 1985) 91.

"U.T.F.O. Select Sue 30 Firms Over 'Roxanne' Answer Records," *Variety.* 320 (August 21, 1985) 126.

Drugs (See also: Boy George)

Berry, M. "Commentary: Drugs and Talent Don't Mix," *Billboard.* 98 (August 23, 1986) 9.

"Bill Graham Plan Anti-Crack Concert to Up Awareness," *Variety.* 324 (August 27, 1986) 93.

Dupler, Steven. "RAD Kicks Off Antidrug Campaign," *Billboard.* 98 (November 29, 1986) 6ff.

George, Nelson. "Concert to Highlight Anti-Crack Campaign," *Billboard.* 98 (August 2, 1986) 78.

George, Nelson. "The Rhythm and the Blues: The Music Industry Must Speak Out Against Crack," *Billboard.* 98 (July 12, 1986) 24.

Gett, Steve. "Pop, Latin Stars Join Crackdown on Crack," *Billboard.* 98 (October 25, 1986) 88.

Jones, P. "Popsters Sing vs. Drugs," *Billboard.* 98 (September 20, 1986) 64. Re. single, "Live-In World."

Levine, M. "Commentary: The Solution Begins at the Top," *Billboard.* 98 (August 23, 1986) 9.

Moore, M. "Commentary: Performers Should Speak Out Against Drugs," *Billboard.* 98 (September 20, 1986) 9.

"Rockers Add Voice to Battle vs. Drugs," *Variety.* 325 (November 26, 1986) 135.

Zwerin, Mike. "Straight, No Chaser," *Spin.* 5:8 (November 1989) 91–93. il.

Economics and Marketing (See also: Music Industry)

Foote, J. "Not-So-Square Squires: Britain's Rock Rebels Become Country Gents," *Newsweek.* 116 (July 2, 1990) 45. il.

Frith, Simon. "All Together Now," *Village Voice.* 30 (February 12, 1985) 78.
British music and marketing are deemed to be indistinguishable.

Silverman, Leigh. "Finding Fame Without Fortune," *Rolling Stone.* n561 (September 21, 1989) 33. il.

PRICING POLICIES

Terry, Ken. "More Labels Try $10.98-List Tape/LP," *Billboard.* (August 25, 1990) 1, 97.

TOYS

Pett, S. "The Barbie Trials," *Spin.* 3 (September 1987) 14. Talent search for human version of new doll, Rocker Barbie.

Education

Neely, Kim. "Do Recording Schools Have the Inside Track?," *Rolling Stone.* n562 (October 5, 1989) 112–116, 155. il.

Small, Christopher. "Music: A Resource for Survival: How Young People are Bypassing the Classical Tradition," *Musical America.* (November 1985) 6–10.

Vulliamy, Graham, and Ed Lee, eds. *Pop Music in School.* Cambridge: Cambridge University Press, 1980. il., bibl., disc. Orig. pub.: 1976.
8 essays arguing for the utilization of pop music in the classroom.

Vulliamy, Graham, and Ed Lee, eds. *Pop, Rock and Ethnic Music in School.* Rev. ed. Cambridge: Cambridge University Press, 1982. il., bibl., disc. Orig. pub.: 1980.

Includes the various forms of ethnic music associated with Great Britain's ethnic minorities.

Vulliamy, Graham, and Ed Lee. *Popular Music: A Teacher's Guide.* London: Routledge and Kegan Paul, 1982. bibl.

Fans, Audiences, etc.

Fried, S. "I'm With the Movie, Ally Sheedy Gets Set to Film Pamela Des Barre's Remembrance of Flings Past," *Rolling Stone.* n537 (October 20, 1988) 29ff. il.
Based on the book, *I'm With the Band.*

Mason, B.H. "Reaching the Stars: My Life as a Fifties Groupie," *New Yorker.* 62 (May 26, 1986) 30–38. il.

Shalett, M. "On Target: Many Over-30 Concert-Goers Consider Themselves Hard Rockers," *Billboard.* 97 (June 8, 1985) 22.

Fashion

Bendinger, Jessica, ed. Introduction by Christian L. Wright. "Street Smart," *Spin.* 5:7 (October 1989) 65–74. il.

Cragin, Sally. "Karma Chameleon: The History of Rock and Roll Wardrobe," *Village Voice.* 30 (January 15, 1985) 37. il.

Films

Dellar, Fred. *The NME Guide to Rock Cinema.* Foreword by Monty Smith. Feltham, Middlesex: Hamlyn, 1981. il.

Pielke, Robert G. "Film: A Creative Tension," In: *You Say You Want a Revolution.* Chicago: Nelson-Hall, 1986. pp. 96–100.

PRESLEY, ELVIS

"The Man Who Would be Elvis," *Texas Monthly.* (September 1988) 74. il.
Covers actor David Keith's forays as a musician on the heels of his film role as Presley in *Heartbreak Hotel.*

Travers, Peter. "An Elvis Ghost Ride," *Rolling Stone.* n566 (November 30, 1989) 47. il.
Details the influence of Presley on the new film, *Mystery Train.*

SOUNDTRACKS (See also: Danny Elfman; Prince)

Dove, Ian. "Soundtracks Score With Rock 'n' Roll," *ASCAP.* (Spring 1986) 34–35. il.

Jacobs, M. "Movies, Music Help Each Other; Soundtrack Boom Leads to Symbiosis," *Billboard.* 98 (September 13, 1986) 86.

Mabry, Marcus, and Rhonda Adams. "How to Sell a Soundtrack," *Newsweek.* (August 28, 1989) 47. il.

Schipper, H. "A&M Records Prez Sees Plunge in Use of Pop Music Soundtracks," *Variety.* 319 (July 3, 1985) 65.

Terry, Ken. "Music Pubberies Benefit from Pop TV-Movie Soundtracks; Small Firms Get Shots, Too," *Variety*. 321 (December 25, 1985) 53ff.

Terry, Ken. "Pics Leery of Pop Soundtracks," *Variety*. 322 (April 9, 1986) 1ff.

Formats

GENERAL SOURCES

"Same-Time Release of CD, LP & Tape Tried by Polygram," *Variety*. 318 (March 13, 1985) 109–110.

CASSETTES

ITA Looking to Improve Cassette Quality," *Cash Box*. (August 31, 1985) 7.

Nunziata, Susan. "Cassettes are Still Being Improved," *Billboard*. (June 23, 1990) 8, 81.

CASSETTES—CASSETTE SINGLES

Baker, Glenn A. "Festival Looks for 'Cassingles' Boom; Australian Indie Hopes Its 'Innovation' Will be Copied," *Billboard*. 97 (February 16, 1985) 9ff.

Terry, Ken, and G. Mayfield. "Cassette Singles Earn Fan Favor; CD-3, CDV Lag," *Billboard*. 101 (January 28, 1989) 1ff.

CASSETTES—MAXICASSETTES

Terry, Ken, and Thom Duffy. "Indies Give New Zip to Maxicassette; Tape Format Replacing 12-Inch Sales," *Billboard.* 102:18 (May 5, 1990) 1, 87.

COMPACT DISCS (See also: DIGITAL AUDIO TAPE)

Bessman, Jim. "CD Makers Hear a Warning," *Billboard.* 99 (December 19, 1987) 45–46.

Birchall, Steve. "The Magic of CD Manufacturing," *Stereo Review.* (October 1986) 67–70, 114. il.

Blonstein, M. "Commentary: There Must be Something Wrong With CD," *Billboard.* 98 (May 10, 1986) 9.

"CDs Could Self-Destruct," *Sound Choice.* n12 (Autumn Equinox, 1989) 5.

George, Nelson. "Slowly, Black Buyers Take to CDs," *Billboard.* 99 (December 5, 1987) 1ff.

"Giving a New Meaning to 'Solid Gold'," *Newsweek.* (March 19, 1990) 45. il.
Re. Mobile Fidelity Sound Lab's gold-plated CDs.

Hennessey, M. "CD Called Music Industry's 'Savior'," *Billboard.* 98 (February 8, 1986) 64.

Horowitz, Is, and others. "Compact Disk: Inside the Expanding Universe," *Billboard.* 99 (September 26, 1987) C1ff. il.

Joy, K. "CDs a Logical Crossover for Hi-Tech Consumer," *Billboard.* 98 (December 13, 1986) 43ff.

"On Target: A Portrait of the CD Buyer—Definitely a Different Breed," *Billboard.* 97 (August 3, 1985) 22.

Ranada, David. "Error-Correction Myths Exploded," *High Fidelity.* (October 1987) 45–50. il.
Includes sidebars, "Error-Correction Basics," and "It's the Pits: Detecting Defective CDs."

Robertshaw, N., and others. "Compact Discs, Digital Audio," *Billboard.* 97 (January 12, 1985) CD1–2ff. il.

Spahr, W. "Jung Warns of CD Euphoria, Affirms Multi-Format Future," *Billboard.* 98 (February 1, 1986) 73.

Sutherland, Sam. "1985: Year of Studio Digital; Manufacturers Cite Recording, Mastering Sales Boom," *Billboard.* 97 (January 26, 1985) 1ff.

COMPACT DISCS—CATALOG MATERIAL

"Atlantic's Vast Reissue Program Seems Related to Advent of CD," *Variety.* 325 (November 12, 1986) 79.

"CD Consumers Want Unavailable Titles, But Won't Buy LPs," *Variety.* 320 (October 9, 1985) 117–118.

Libbey, T. "Medley: Golden Oldies Coming to CD," *Hi Fi/Musical America*. 35 (July 1985) 50.

Lichtman, Irv. "Pop, Rock Favorites Return on CD," *Billboard*. 98 (November 1, 1986) 4ff.

Terry, Ken. "New Releases Become Focus on CD Biz But Catalog is Moving Steadily," *Variety*. 318 (April 24, 1985) 189–190.

COMPACT DISCS—COMPACT DISC GROUP (See also: SHORTAGES)

Horowitz, Is. "CD Shortages," *Billboard*. 97 (August 24, 1985) 1ff.

Sutherland, Sam. "CD Group Disbanding," *Billboard*. 97 (November 23, 1985) 1ff.

COMPACT DISCS—COMPACT DISC JUKEBOXES

"CD Jukeboxes can Bring Albums Where Singles Once Held Sway," *Variety*. 319 (July 3, 1985) 2ff.

COMPACT DISCS—ECONOMICS

Christman, Ed. "CDs Surpass Cassettes in $$ Volume," *Billboard*. 102:11 (March 17, 1990) 8, 107.

DiMartino, Dave, and Ed Christman. "CD Edges Up on Cassette as Top Format," *Billboard*. (June 23, 1990) 1, 81.

DiMauro, P. "Music Publishers Eye CD Payout as Future Source of Added Coin," *Variety*. 322 (March 5, 1986) 97.

Fujita, S., and C. Leo. "Japan Trends Follow World Market; CDs Phase Out LPs in Singapore," *Billboard*. 101 (August 5, 1989) 6ff. graph.

Gett, Steve. "Labels Push Low-Price Catalog CDs," *Billboard*. 99 (October 24, 1987) 4ff.

Goodman, Fred. "Labels Rethink CD Royalties," *Billboard*. 98 (August 9, 1986) 1ff.

Greenleaf, Christopher. "CD Boom! Compact Disc Pressing Plants are Spreading Across North America," *Stereo Review*. (June 1987) 89-92. il.

Horowitz, Is. "CDs Keep Business on Even $ Keel," *Billboard*. 98 (November 1, 1986) 1ff.

Hunter, N., and others. "CDs Gain on LPs in Australia," *Billboard*. 101 (August 12, 1989) 9ff. graph.

Lichtman, Irv, and G. Mayfield. "CD Sales Unharmed by Price Hikes," *Billboard*. 98 (March 29, 1986) 3ff.

Mayfield, G. "CDs are a Growth Business for In-Store Thieves, Too," *Billboard*. 98 (May 24, 1986) 1ff.

Morris, Chris. "CDs Sail Past LPs in $ Volume: RIAA/NARM Survey for '86," *Billboard*. 99:27 (July 4, 1987) 1. 84.

Morris, Chris, and G. Mayfield. "Dealers: Cut CD Prices on

Hits; NARMites See Growth Stymied," *Billboard.* 99
(October 10, 1987) 1ff.

Petrone, E. "Compact Disk Market Growing Along With
Consumer Awareness," *Variety.* 317 (January 16, 1985)
199.

Quinn, J. "Commentary: Help CDs Reach Their Market
Potential," *Billboard.* 99 (December 12, 1987) 9.

"Renting CDs & Selling Blank Tapes: A Retail Growth
Industry, or Blight?," *Variety.* 328 (September 2, 1987)
2ff.

Shulman, J. "Compact Discs Expected to Boost Overall Sales,"
Variety. 321 (January 8, 1986) 209ff.

Terry, Ken. "Compact Disk Biz Begins to Take Off; Dropping
Prices Motivate Consumers," *Variety.* 317 (January 2,
1985) 129ff.

COMPACT DISCS—EDUCATION

Roberts, D. "Compact Discs: An Exciting New Educational
Aid," *NASM.* n74 (1986) 81–84.

COMPACT DISCS—FINLAND

Helopaltio, K. "Finn Radio Prompts Promotional Pressing of
Local Hits on CD," *Billboard.* 101 (August 26, 1989) 82.

COMPACT DISCS—FORMAT SPINOFFS—CD-5

Christman, Ed. "CD-5 Picks Up Steam as Labels Boost Commitment," *Billboard.* (March 3, 1990) 6, 84.

COMPACT DISCS—FORMAT SPINOFFS—CD-3

DiMartino, Dave. "CD Pressers Hazy on CD-3 Future," *Billboard.* 100 (October 22, 1988) 3ff.

Dupler, Steven. "Sony's CD-3 Portable Player Gets Slow Start," *Billboard.* 101 (January 14, 1989) 74.

Goodman, Fred. "Labels Embrace Three-Inch CDs," *Rolling Stone.* n524 (April 21, 1988) 23.

Mayfield, G. "Dealers to Give 3-Inch CD a Try," *Billboard.* 99 (October 31, 1987) 1ff.

Terry, Ken. "Labels Divided Over How to Program, Market CD-3s," *Billboard.* 100 (October 29, 1988) 1ff.

COMPACT DISCS—FORMAT SPINOFFS—CD-V

"The 5-Inch CD-V: Are We Seeing and Hearing the Future? A Viewer's/Listener's Guide," *High Fidelity.* 39 (January 1989) 72ff. il.

Riggs, M. "The Future of CD-V," *High Fidelity.* 37 (October 1987) 5.

"Vidclip-Capable CDs Near," *Billboard.* 97 (July 13, 1985) 6.

COMPACT DISC—FORMAT SPINOFFS—
RECORDABLE CDs

Guterman, Jimmy. "Recordable CD Due," *Rolling Stone.* n527
(June 2, 1988) 23.

COMPACT DISCS—PACKAGING

Goldberg, Michael. "The Battle Over the Box; Ecological
Concerns Fuel Movement to Ban Cardboard Packaging
for CDs," *Rolling Stone.* n581 (June 28, 1990) 20.

Goodman, Fred. "More All-Board CDs Due," *Billboard.* 97
(July 27, 1985) 1ff.

Gout, H.G. "Commentary: The Package is the Product—CD
& the Jewel Box," *Billboard.* 97 (May 18, 1985) 10.

Horowitz, Is. "Clearer View Seen in Types of CD Boxes,"
Billboard. 97 (February 2, 1985) 1ff.

Horowitz, Is. "Jewel Box Dumped for New Prince CD,"
Billboard. 97 (April 6, 1985) 1ff.

Horowitz, Is. "No Board? Two Labels Seen Abandoning New
CD Packaging," *Billboard.* 97 (October 5, 1985) 1ff.

Horowitz, Is. "Test Results Give Boost to All-Board CD
Package," *Billboard.* 97:8 (February 23, 1985) 1, 72.

Jeske, Lee. "Some Retailers Finding Prince CD Package a
Purple Pain," *CD.* (May 18, 1985) 11, 43.

Kern, A. "Commentary: Packaging the Future to CD," *Billboard.* 97 (January 19, 1985) 10.

LaPointe, Kirk. "Canada Deep-Sixes 6-by-12 CD Box," *Billboard.* (March 3, 1990) 6.

Lichtman, Irv. "New CD Package to Face Pop Market Test," *Billboard.* 98 (January 25, 1986) 6ff.
Re. Digi-Pak design.

Mayfield, G. "Labels Praise New Antitheft Package," *Billboard.* 98 (December 6, 1986) 1ff.

Nowlin, Bill. "6-by-12 Package Inflates CD Prices," *Billboard.* (March 19, 1988) 9, 107.

Ressner, Jeffrey. "Will Box Boom Go Bust? Inferior Sound Quality and Packaging Mar Deluxe Reissues," *Rolling Stone.* n572 (February 22, 1990) 21–23. il.
Includes sidebar, "The Master of Remastering," which looks at Bill Inglot.

Sutherland, Sam. "A&M, Capitol Testing New CD Box," *Billboard.* 98 (February 22, 1986) 1ff.

COMPACT DISCS—RECORD COMPANIES

DiMauro, P. "Polygram to Debut Sub-$10 Pop CDs for an Industry First," *Variety.* 319 (June 26, 1985) 87ff.

Gett, Steve. "Labels Increasing Service of Promo-Only CDs," *Billboard.* 98 (November 15, 1986) 12.

Sutherland, Sam. "On the Beam," *Billboard.* 97 (November 30, 1985) 22–23.
CD payoff includes smaller specialty labels.

Terry, Ken. "Artists Balk at Low CD Royalty; Labels Say Small Profits Justify Payout Rate," *Variety.* 322 (March 5, 1986) 1ff.

COMPACT DISCS—RETAILING

Goodman, Fred. "Eight-Track Bins Reborn: Dealer Brings Fixtures in CD Age," *Billboard.* 97 (June 8, 1985) 27.

McCullaugh, J. "Waldenbooks Reads Profits in Compact Disk's Future," *Billboard.* 98 (June 7, 1986) 1ff.

Sippel, J. "CD Finds Warm Welcome at Video Outlets," *Billboard.* 98 (January 25, 1986) 3.

Sippel, J. "Rackers Testing CDs in Discount Stores," *Billboard.* 97 (May 25, 1985) 4ff.

Sutherland, Sam. "On the Beam," *Billboard.* 97 (September 14, 1985) 35–36. Re. CD-only stores.

COMPACT DISCS—RETAILING—CBS COMPACT DISC CLUB

"CBS Record Club Has CDs for $11," *Variety.* 325 (December 10, 1986) 90.

Lichtman, Irv. "CBS Unveils Compact Disc Club," *Billboard.* 98 (January 18, 1986) 6.

COMPACT DISCS—SHORTAGES IN SUPPLY
(See also: COMPACT DISC GROUP)

Angus, R. "Currents—CD Availability: The Line Forms to the Right," *Hi Fi/Musical America*. 35 (June 1985) 16.

Goodman, Fred. "Indie Labels Feel the CD Pinch," *Billboard*. 97 (May 11, 1985) 3.

Handelman, D. "Compact Discontent," *Rolling Stone*. n515/516 (December 17/31, 1987) 88.

Horowitz, Is. "CBS/Sony: No CD Custom Work; Domestic Pressing Crunch," *Billboard*. 97 (February 9, 1985) 1ff.

Horowitz, Is. "CD Shortages," *Billboard*. 97 (August 24, 1985) 1ff.

Horowitz, Is. "PolyGram's Glut: CD Catchup Near," *Billboard*. 97:8 (February 23, 1985) 3.

Horowitz, Is, and Fred Goodman. "CBS Institutes CD Allocation; Label Wipes Slate Clean in Pressing Crunch," *Billboard*. 97 (March 16, 1985) 1ff.

Iorio, Paul. "CD Crunch: Too Little of a Good Thing?," *Cash Box*. XLIX:17 (October 5, 1985) 30.

Robertshaw, N. "Japanese Firms Boosting CD Output; JVC, Nippon Columbia Move to Meet World Demand," *Billboard*. 97 (February 23, 1985) 3ff.

Schipper, H. "CD Sales Hit Wall of Price Resistance; Inventories Pass Retail Volume," *Variety*. 328 (October 7, 1987) 97ff.

Sippel, J. "CD Fill Still Slipping," *Billboard.* 97 (November 9, 1985) 24ff.

Terry, Ken. "CD Plants Face Uncertainty as Supply Exceeds Demand," *Billboard.* 99 (December 5, 1987) 1ff.

Terry, Ken. "CD Shortages Curtail U.S. Market by 20–30%, Per CBS' Shulman," *Variety.* 320 (September 11, 1985) 75ff.

COMPACT DISCS—UNITED KINGDOM

Jones, P. "CDs Gain Ground in U.K.," *Billboard.* 100 (June 18, 1988) 60.

Libbey, T. "Medley-British CD: From Bloom to Bloom," *Hi Fi/ Musical America.* 35 (November 1985) 51.

"Rise of CD Rental Libraries Worries British Industry," *Billboard.* 97 (April 13, 1985) 66.

DIGITAL AUDIO TAPE (DAT)

Birchall, Steve. "DAT: Digital Audio Tape; Issues and Answers," *Stereo Review.* (March 1987) 56–59. il.

"Commentary: Unity Provides Strength on DAT," *Billboard.* (March 19, 1988) 9.

"GRP to Launch DAT Line," *Rolling Stone.* n520 (February 25, 1988) 13.

McCormick, Moira. "DAT: One Step Closer?," *Rolling Stone.* n524 (April 21, 1988) 17.

Nunziata, Susan. "Japanese DAT Units Due in Summer," *Billboard.* (June 16, 1990) 1, 99.
Report notes that a publishing group is considering legal steps to stop their importation.

DIGITAL AUDIO TAPE—CONTROVERSY OVER ITS AVAILABILITY

Anderton, Craig. "Letters: DAT's What We Need! *Electronic Musician* Editor States Case LOUD and CLEAR," *Sound Choice.* n12 (Autumn Equinox, 1989) 11–12.

"DAT Legislation Moves Forward," *International Musician.* 86 (September 1987) 1ff.

DeCurtis, Anthony. "Artists Split on DAT," *Rolling Stone.* n517 (January 14, 1988) 22.

Duplcr, Steven. "Musicians' Pro-DAT Lobby Planned," *Billboard.* 99 (October 3, 1987) 5ff.

Goldberg, Michael. "Labels Back Down on DAT," *Rolling Stone.* n561 (September 21, 1989) 26.

Hardy, P. "Hardware Makers to Examine C'right Problem Posed by DAT," *Variety.* 329 (December 16, 1987) 79.

"Stevie Wonder to Congress: I Like My DAT," *Billboard.* 99:27 (July 4, 1987) 1, 79.

Terry, Ken, and Chris Morris. "Labels Will Not Support DAT Rollout," *Billboard.* (June 16, 1990) 1, 99.

Wilkinson, P. "What is DAT, and Why are the Record Companies Trying to Keep It Away from You?," *Rolling Stone.* n508 (September 10, 1987) 69–70ff. il.

DIGITAL AUDIO TAPE—COPY PROTECTION

"Congressional Action on DAT Expected," *Cash Box.* (September 12, 1987) 5, 32.
Re. whether or not to require that all DAT machines incorporate the CBS Technology Center's copy code scanner system.

McCullaugh, Jim. "Song Goes Public With DAT System," *Billboard.* 98:24 (June 14, 1986) 1, 84.

DIGITAL AUDIO TAPE—RELATIONSHIP TO COMPACT DISCS

"IFPI Sees Digital Audio Tape as Threat to CD Market Growth," *Variety.* 323 (April 30, 1986) 163ff.

McCormick, Moira. "R-DAT vs. CD Debated," *Billboard.* 98 (May 31, 1986) 46Aff.

FORTY-FIVE R.P.M. SINGLE

Meyer, Marianne. " . . . As the 45-RPM Single Fades," *Rolling Stone.* n563 (October 19, 1989) 24.

LONG-PLAYING RECORD ALBUM (LP)

Christman, Ed. "No Label Wants to be Seen as Pulling Plug on Vinyl," *Billboard.* (March 3, 1990) 73.

Goodman, Fred. "Record Industry Preparing to Bury the LP," *Rolling Stone.* n521 (March 10, 1988) 24. il.

Hoos, W. "Dutch Exec: Vinyl is Breathing Its Last," *Billboard.* 100 (October 22, 1988) 85.

LaPointe, Kirk. "Canada's Indies Tell Labels to Keep Vinyl Vital," *Billboard.* 100 (October 29, 1988) 1ff.

Lichtman, Irv. "CBS Vows to Stand by LP; Move is Counter to Japan Label Plans," *Billboard.* 100 (December 10, 1988) 5ff.

Morris, Chris, and Ken Terry. "WEA Cuts 40% of Its Catalog Titles on Vinyl," *Billboard.* (March 3, 1990) 1, 73.

Terry, Ken. "Dealers Decry Rapid LP Phase-Out," *Billboard.* 100 (October 1, 1988) 1ff.

MUSIC VIDEO—HOME VIDEOCASSETTES

Bessman, Jim. "Selectivity Breeds Success for Music Cassette Sales," *Billboard.* 99 (September 5, 1987) 51–52.

Fisher, B. "Commentary: Music's Home Video Opportunities," *Billboard.* 97 (August 3, 1985) 10. il.

Piccarella, John. "Guess Who's Coming to Dinner: Home Video Brings Punks Into Your Living Room. Enter

Alienated Youth; Exit Their Subculture," *High Fidelity.*
(November 1985) 67–68, 74–75.

Seideman, T. "Vidclip Compilations Seen Emerging as Strong
Sellers," *Billboard.* 97 (January 5, 1985) 1ff.

"Study Sez Music-Buyers Shell Out for Video Too, Merchan-
disers in Dark," *Variety.* 318 (April 3, 1985) 69.

MUSIC VIDEO—HOME VIDEOCASSETTES— DELILAH

"Delilah Expands Its Horizons to TV, Film in the Music
Genre," *Variety.* 322 (January 29, 1986) 78.

McCormick, Moira. "Delilah Stays in Docu-Rock," *Billboard.*
98 (January 25, 1986) 33.

MUSIC VIDEO—HOME VIDEOCASSETTES— POPE, TIM

Sutherland, Steve. "Under the Cheri Moon," *Melody Maker.* 61
(August 30, 1986) 24–26.
Re. Cure feature film.

MUSIC VIDEO—VIDEO CLIPS

Bessman, Jim. "Clip Makers at a Crossroads; Creativity Seen
Waning as Commercial Pressures Grow," *Billboard.* 97
(September 14, 1985) 42–43.

Bessman, Jim. "Vidclip Makers Ask: 'Where's the Recession?," *Billboard.* 98 (August 9, 1986) 54ff.

Dempsey, J. "More Indie TV Stations Use Vidclips as Staple; MTV Exclusivity Hurts," *Variety.* 318 (March 27, 1985) 88.

DiMauro, P. "Music Video: Cable's Baby Boomer," *Variety.* 319 (May 29, 1985) 129ff.

DiMauro, P. "Vidclips Pay Off in Record Promotion; But Budgets are Still Going Up," *Variety.* 318 (March 27, 1985) 83ff.

Farren, Mick. "Bringing Too Much Back Home," *Creem.* 16 (March 1985) 47. il.

Goldstein, Richard. "Tube Rock: How Music Video is Changing Music," *Village Voice.* 30 (September 17, 1985) 38ff. il.

Jung, W. "Commentary: Let's Kiss Music Videos Goodbye," *Billboard.* 97 (April 27, 1985) 10.

Mayfield, G. "Music Video: The Picture Brightens," *Billboard.* 100 (October 15, 1988) 1ff.

Straw, W. "Music Video in Its Contexts: Popular Music and Post-Modernism in the 1980s," *Popular Music.* 7:3 (1988) 247–266.

Sutherland, Sam. "Music Earnings Dance to TV's New Beat," *Billboard.* 97 (December 28, 1985) 3ff.

Walz, K. "Commentary: Why aren't Music Videos Better?," *Billboard.* 97 (March 9, 1985) 10.

MUSIC VIDEO—VIDEO CLIPS—DIRECTORS

Peisch, J. "Clip Producers, Director Faced With Creative, Budget Problems," *Variety.* 318 (April 3, 1985) 71.

MUSIC VIDEO—VIDEO CLIPS—DIRECTORS— MULCAHY, RUSSELL

Bessman, Jim. "Mulcahy Just Wants to Have Fun," *Billboard.* 101 (January 7, 1989) 48–49.

MUSIC VIDEO—VIDEO CLIPS—DIRECTORS— TEMPLE, JULIEN

Dobrin, Gregory. "From the Sex Pistols to 'The Valley' Julien Temple Remains Pop's Most Controversial Director," *Cash Box.* (May 23, 1987) 10, 39. il., int.

MUSIC VIDEO—VIDEO CLIPS—THE NETHERLANDS

Hoos, W. "Vidclips Face Slow Growth in the Netherlands," *Billboard.* 101 (January 28, 1989) 53.

MUSIC VIDEO—VIDEO CLIPS—ODYSSEY

Zuckerman, F. "Odyssey Surviving Without Advertising; New Music Video Service Claims Eight Million Viewers," *Billboard.* 97 (March 16, 1985) 6ff.

MUSIC VIDEO—VIDEO CLIPS—PAY-FOR-PLAY

Baker, Glenn A. "Pay-for-Play Turmoil Rocks Australian Industry," *Billboard.* 99 (September 5, 1987) 57ff.

Bessman, Jim. "Outlets Enraged by Chrysalis' Pay-for-Play Plan," *Billboard.* 100 (October 22, 1988) 79–80.

DiMauro, P. "WEA Postpones Deadline for Start of TV Vidclip Payments," *Variety.* 321 (November 13, 1985) 119–120.

Dobrin, Gregory. "PolyGram to Adopt Video Charges," *Cash Box.* XLIX:24 (November 23, 1985) 35.

"Pay-for-Play Principle in England Now Seems Firm for Music Vids," *Variety.* 324 (August 27, 1986) 95.

Robertshaw, N. "U.K. Industry Pushing for Vidclip Payment," *Billboard.* 97 (June 8, 1985) 9.

MUSIC VIDEO—VIDEO CLIPS—PROPAGANDA FILMS

Farber, Jim. "Clip Corporation: Propaganda Films Rule the Music-Video World," *Rolling Stone.* n585 (August 23, 1990) 137. il., int. w/founders Steve Golin and Joni Sighvatsson.

MUSIC VIDEO—VIDEO CLIPS—SWEDEN

Roe, Keith, and M. Loefgren. "Music Video Use and Educational Achievement: A Swedish Study," *Popular Music.* 7:3 (1988) 303–314.

MUSIC VIDEO—VIDEO CLIPS—UNITED KINGDOM
(See also: MUSIC VIDEO—VIDEO CLIPS—PAY-FOR-PLAY; VIDEO JUKEBOXES)

"Music in Britain Lively But Pigeonholed as Promo," *Variety.* 318 (March 27, 1985) 83ff.

MUSIC VIDEO—VIDEO CLIPS—VIDEO JUKEBOXES

"Clip Jukebox Firm Covers Europe; Britain's Diamond Time Enjoying Steady Growth," *Billboard.* 97 (April 27, 1985) 36.

"New Videodisk Jukebox Enters Market; Can Hold 1,000 Clips," *Variety.* 321 (November 13, 1985) 120.

Robbins, A. "New Ploys from Clip Jukebox Firms; Advertisements, Specialized Reels," *Billboard.* 98 (March 8, 1986) 44–45.

TWELVE-INCH SINGLES/EXTENDED PLAY DISCS

Aletti, Vince. "Declaration of Independents," *Hi Fi/Musical America.* 35 (April 1985) 83ff.

Aletti, Vince. "The 12-Inch Report," *High Fidelity.* 35 (January 1985) 74.

Horowitz, Is. "Polygram Puts Maxi-Single on Hold," *Billboard.* 97 (September 28, 1985) 86.

Health

Toufexis, Anastasia, with Mike Cannell and D. Blake Hallanan. "A Fire Hose Down the Ear Canal," *Time.* (September 26, 1988) 78. il.

History

Gilmore, Mikal. "The 60s," *Rolling Stone.* n585 (August 23, 1990) 61–65, 142–144. il.

Palmer, Robert. "The 50s," *Rolling Stone.* n576 (April 19, 1990) 44–48. il.

Piazza, T. "The Roots of Rock," *Scholastic Update (Teachers' Edition).* 122 (May 18, 1990) 6–7. il.

Silver, Caroline. *The Pop Mainstream.* New York: Scholastic Book Service, 1966. il.

Stubbs, D., and Simon Reynolds. "The Terminal Gears: 56! 66! 76! 86?," *Melody Maker.* 61 (December 20/27, 1986) 48–49. il.
Hypothesis set forth that decade years ending in "6" await new trends with respect to popular music.

Humor

NONSENSE HUMOR—BONZO DOG BAND

Thompson, Dave. "The Bonzo Dog Band," *Record Collector.* n100 (December 1987) 39–42. il., disc.

NONSENSE HUMOR—CHEECH AND CHONG

Dobrin, Gregory. "Cheech and Chong Smoke in a New Format," *Cash Box*. XLIX:23 (November 16, 1985) 11. il., int. w/Richard "Cheech" Marin.

McCullaugh, J. "Cheech & Chong Expand," *Billboard*. 97 (December 7, 1985) 39.
Focuses on the development and release of the video, *Get Out of My Room*.

SATIRE—BLACK, KAREN

Yablonsky, Linda. "Flash: The Band Next Door," *Spin*. 6:3 (June 1990) 16. il., int.

SATIRE—BROWN, JULIE

DeSavia, Tom. "New Faces to Watch: Julie Brown," *Cash Box*. (October 31, 1987) 11, 35. il.

Goodman, Fred. "Julie Brown Charts Laughs; Rock Satirist Making Progress," *Billboard*. 97 (February 9, 1985) 39ff.

Instruments

ACCORDIANS

Doerschuk, Bob. "Rock's New Main Squeeze: The Neglected Step-Child of the Keyboard Family Stages a Dramatic Comeback," *Keyboard Magazine*. 13 (December 1987) 66–68ff. il., disc.

Morthland, John. "What's Wrong With This Instrument? Nothing! The Rehabilitation of the Accordian: American

Pop's Got a Squeeze-Box," *High Fidelity*. (August 1987) 71–72. il.

DRUMS

Richardson, Ken. "Wanted: Snare Drums," *High Fidelity*. (June 1987) 54.
Apology for use of real drummers, rather than machines, on recordings.

DRUMS, ELECTRONIC

Reed, T. "Control Zone: Funky Drummer," *Melody Maker*. 65 (January 28, 1989) 42. il.

Thomas, Glyn. "Electronic Drums—Their Origins & Future," *Music Trades*. 134 (October 1986) 70.

ELECTRONIC EQUIPMENT

Bacon, Tony, ed. *Rock Hardware: The Instruments, Equipment and Technology of Rock*. Poole, Dorset: Blandford, 1981. il., disc.

Hammond, Ray. *The Musician and the Micro*. Poole, Dorset: Blandford, 1982. il.

Mackay, Andy. *Electronic Music*. Oxford: Phaidon, 1981. il.

GUITARS, ELECTRIC

Denyer, Ralph, with Isaac Guillory and Alastair M. Crawford. *The Guitar Handbook*. London: Dorling Kindersley, 1982. il.

Hannusch, Jeff. "U.S. Bids Sayonara to Vintage Guitars," *Rolling Stone.* n573 (March 8, 1990) 58.

Mulhern, T. "Trends & Innovations," *Guitar Player.* 21 (December 1987) 50–52ff. il.

Webster, B. "The Electric Guitar Means Rock 'n' Roll," *Canadian Musician.* 9:5 (1987) 55–57.

Wheeler, Tom. *The Guitar Book: A Handbook for Electric and Acoustic Guitarists.* Foreword by B.B. King. Rev. ed. London: Macdonald Futura, 1981. il.

GUITAR SYNTHESIZERS

Anderton, Craig. "Electronic Guitar: Careers in Musical Electronics," *Guitar Player.* 19 (May 1985) 92ff.

Mulhern, T. "British High-Tech: SynthAxe & Bond," *Guitar Player.* 19 (March 1985) 29–30ff.

Mulhern, T. "The Guitar Synthesizer: History & Development," *Guitar Player.* 20 (June 1986) 16–17ff. il.

PICCOLO TRUMPET

"World News: The P5800 Trumpet," *Brass Bulletin.* n60 (News Supplement 1987) 1.
Instrument that soloed in the Beatles' recording of "Penny Lane" sold.

SEQUENCERS

Milano, D., and others. "The Pros Tell How Sequencers Changed Their Lives (or Didn't)," *Keyboard Magazine.* 13 (June 1987) 58ff. il., soundsheet, int.

SYNTHESIZERS

Mann, E. "Percussion Sound Sources and Synthesis," *Modern Drummer.* 11 (December 1987) 67–68.

Lyrics, Song (See also: Censorship)

Damsher, Matt, ed. *Rock Voices: The Best Lyrics of an Era.* London: Arthur Barker, 1981. Orig. pub.: New York: St. Martin's, 1980.

Davis, S. "Beating the Drums for Lyric Literacy," *Billboard.* 98 (July 26, 1986) 9.

Jasper, Tony. *Sound Seventies.* Great Yarmouth, Norfolk, U.K.: Galliard, 1972. il.

Managers (See also: Drugs)

Goldberg, Michael. "Top Rock Manager Pleads Guilty to Drug Charges," *Rolling Stone.* n521 (March 10, 1988) 19.

Mass Media

COMIC BOOKS

"Metal Strips," *Rolling Stone.* n575 (April 5, 1990) 21. il.
Rock 'n' Roll Comics chronicles the unauthorized tales of rock bands in separate monthly issues.

FANZINES

The Bible. London: Big O Publications, 1978. il.
A collection of reproductions of the first ten issues of
Sniffin' Glue (1976–1977), the most influential of the
fanzines of the London punk movement during its heyday.

Jedeikin, Jenny, and Robert Love. "The Next Page: Cinderella's Family Affair," *Rolling Stone.* n585 (August 23,
1990) 17. il.
Re. the fan club newsletter, *Cinderella After Midnight.*

Ngaire. "Sidelines: Dead Eye Video," *Melody Maker.* (August
25, 1990) 10. il.

JOURNALISM

Bangs, Lester. Edited by Greil Marcus. *Psychotic Reactions and
Carburetor Dung.* New York: Knopf, 1987.

Mendelssohn, John. "Eleganza: On Rock Criticism," *Creem.* 17
(February 1986) 34ff.

MAGAZINES/PERIODICALS

Johnson, Rick. "Rock Magazines: All Washed Up!," *Creem.* 18
(June 1987) 40–43ff. il.

Mendelssohn, John. "Rock Magazines: Why They're So Good,"
Creem. 17 (July 1986) 20–22ff. il.

MAGAZINES/PERIODICALS—*ROLLING STONE*

Alter, Jonathan. "Just Like a Rolling Stone," *Newsweek.* (June
17, 1985) 63. il.

Focus on founder Jann Wenner's role in the journal's development.

Cooper, Ann. "Jann Wenner Grows from Gonzo to Gotham," *Advertising Age.* (January 28, 1985) 3ff.

Hafferkamp, Jack. "*Rolling Stone* Moves into Mainstream," *Advertising Age.* (October 18, 1984) 13ff.

Hafferkamp, Jack. "Summer Issue Leaves No Stone Unturned," *Advertising Age.* (October 18, 1984) 13.

Love, Barbara. "Henry W. Mark: 'We Have No Competitor But Ignorance', Contends Persuasive Sales Exec.," *Folio.* 13 (February 1984) 48ff. il.

Redmond, Tim. "Janny, We Hardly Know Ye," *Mother Jones.* (January 1986) 9. il.

Sherrid, Pamela. "An Out-of-Focus Image," *Forbes.* (September 23, 1985) 181. il.

MAGAZINES/PERIODICALS—*SPIN*

O'Brien, Glenn. "My Earliest Memories of *Spin*," *Spin.* 6:1 (April 1990) 146. il.

"*Spin* Sells—Out to Investor; Guccione Will Stay as Editor," *Sound Choice.* n12 (Autumn Equinox, 1989) 5.

MUSIC PUBLISHERS—ATV MUSIC CORP.
(See also: BEATLES; MICHAEL JACKSON)

Schipper, H. "CBS Songs to Administer ATV for Jackson; Beatles Tunes Prize," *Variety.* 320 (September 11, 1985) 75ff.

Schipper, H. "Jackson Acquires ATV Music, Including 260 Beatles Tunes; Pubbery Fetched $47.5-Million," *Variety.* 320 (August 21, 1985) 121ff.

PAYOLA (See also: RADIO; RECORDING INDUSTRY)

Clark, Rick. "Indie Promoter Convicted of Payola Charges," *Billboard.* 102:28 (July 14, 1990) 1, 83.
Re. Howard Goodman and the Memphis area company, Good Choice Productions Inc.

Freeman, K. "Payola Allegations Terms 'Witchhunt'," *Billboard.* 98 (March 8, 1986) 12.

Goldberg, Michael. "FCC Hears Payola Allegations," *Rolling Stone.* n522 (March 24, 1988) 25, 181.

Goldberg, Michael. "Inside the Payola Scandal," *Rolling Stone.* n517 (January 14, 1988) 13–15.

Goldberg, Michael. "Payola Investigation Widening Its Net," *Rolling Stone.* n520 (February 25, 1988) 13.

Goldberg, Michael. "Payola Probe Gets Hot," *Rolling Stone.* n569 (January 11, 1990) 16.

Goldberg, Michael. "Payola: The Record-Label Connection," *Rolling Stone.* n524 (April 21, 1988) 15, 114. il.

Goldberg, Michael. "Warners Sues Isgro," *Rolling Stone.* n522 (March 24, 1988) 32.

Holland, Bill. "A Federal Case: The Legal Side of Payola Probes," *Billboard.* 98:10 (March 8, 1986) 91.

Holland, Bill. "No New Payola Evidence, Says Committee," *Billboard.* 98 (March 15, 1986) 3.

Lichtman, Irv, and Sam Sutherland. "Capitol, MCA Drop Indies; RIAA Subpoenaed," *Billboard.* 98:10 (March 8, 1986) 1, 91.

Morris, Chris. "Judge Pulls Plug on Isgro Payola Trial," *Billboard.* (September 15, 1990) 1, 98.

"RIAA Response to NBC," *Billboard.* 98:10 (March 8, 1986) 91.
Re. statement issued in response to reports by NBC News of alleged wrongdoing in the recording industry.

Schipper, H. "NBC's 'New Payola' Statements Draw Isgro Retraction Demand," *Variety.* 322 (April 9, 1986) 115–116.

RADIO (See also: RAP)

Brauer, L. "Commentary: Why I Resigned from Rock Radio," *Billboard.* 98 (May 17, 1986) 9.

Holland, Bill. "DAB May Jolt Radio's Status Quo," *Billboard.* 102:27 (July 7, 1990) 5, 81.

Jacobs, M. "Commentary: Trudging Along the Same Old Paths," *Billboard.* 97 (November 30, 1985) 10.

Pielke, Robert G. "Radio: The Creation of a New Community," In: *You Say You Want a Revolution.* Chicago: Nelson-Hall, 1986. pp. 63–80.

Pond, Steve. "What's Wrong With Radio," *Rolling Stone.* n515/516 (December 17/31, 1987) 85–87. il.

"Radio Daze," *Life.* 13:8 (June 1990) 89–95. il.

RADIO—BLACK REPRESENTATION

Ford, Glen. "Guest Commentary: 'Black Radio: Who are You Fooling?'," *Cash Box.* LII:3 (July 16, 1988) 20.

Jack the Rapper. "Commentary: Let's Maintain the Difference," *Billboard.* 97 (November 30, 1985) 10. Re. black radio.

Long, Bob. Commentary: Black Radio: Stand and Be Counted," *Cash Box.* LII:2 (July 9, 1988) 19.

RADIO—DISC JOCKEYS (See also: CLUBS . . .)

Trelin, R. "Personality Formatting: The Wave of the Future?," *Billboard.* 98 (August 30, 1986) 14ff.

Williamson, Bill. *The Dee JAU Book.* London: Parnell, 1969. il. Includes a behind-the-scenes look at the work of the leading British disc jockeys from the 1960s.

RADIO—DISC JOCKEYS—BACK-ANNOUNCING

Holland, Bill. "Labels Hope Stats Spur DJs," *Billboard.* 100 (October 1, 1988) 6.

Evidence supports the practice of back-announcing tunes and artists.

Terry, Ken, and G. Mayfield. "Tough Talk on Back-Announcing: NARM-Goers Air Views on RIAA Study," *Billboard.* 100 (October 8, 1988) 4ff.

RADIO—DISC JOCKEYS—LEADING PERSONALITIES—COUSIN BRUCIE

Freeman, K. "Pro in Profile: Cousin Brucie: Let's Rehumanize the Airwaves," *Billboard.* 98 (October 11, 1986) 25.

RADIO—DISC JOCKEYS—LEADING PERSONALITIES—KASEM, CASEY

"Countdown to More Success, Kasem Embarks on New Top 40 Show," *Variety.* 334 (January 25, 1979) 51ff. il., int.

Ingram, B. "Ex-Top 40 Host Kasem Still Top Dog to Listeners—2–1 Over Shadoe," *Variety.* 333 (December 8, 1988/January 3, 1989) 34.

RADIO—DISC JOCKEYS—LEADING PERSONALITIES—MORALES, DAVID

Walters, B. "Last Night a DJ Saved My Life; David Morales Remakes Dance Music," *Village Voice.* 33 (June 7, 1988) 21–25ff. il.

RADIO—DISC JOCKEYS—LEADING
PERSONALITIES—MORROW, BRUCE
(See: COUSIN BRUCIE)

RADIO—DISC JOCKEYS—LEADING
PERSONALITIES—PEEL, JOHN
(r.n.: JOHN RAVENSCROFTS)

"Shrink Rap," *Melody Maker.* 60 (January 26, 1985) 12. il., int.

Stubbs, D. "Talking Heads: Sound of the Suburbs," *Melody Maker.* 61 (November 29, 1986) 31. il., bio.

RADIO—DISC JOCKEYS—LEADING
PERSONALITIES—SHANNON, SCOTT

Wall, G. "Inside Scott Shannon's 'Z Morning Zoo'," *Billboard.* 97 (September 14, 1985) 26–27. il.

RADIO—DISC JOCKEYS—TEXAS

Patoski, Joe Nick. "Turn It UP!," *Texas Monthly.* (March 1986) 133–137, 203–207. il.

RADIO—NETWORKS/STATIONS—ATLANTIC
252 (IRELAND)

Davis, Sarah. "Ad Revenue Fears as Atlantic Beams into UK," *Music Week.* (June 10, 1989) 14.

RADIO—NETWORKS/STATIONS— WESTWOOD ONE

Freeman, K. "Westwood One Reaches Agreement to Buy Mutual," *Billboard.* 97 (September 28, 1985) 1ff.

Grein, Paul. "Westwood One Steps Up Sponsorship," *Billboard.* 97 (December 14, 1985) 40.

Kamin, Morton. "The Entrepreneur: Making Waves in Radio," *Esquire.* (November 1985) 70. il.

Kamin, Morton, and others. *"Billboard* Salutes Westwood One," *Billboard.* 98 (September 13, 1986) WO1ff. il.

Pond, Steve. "The King of Rock Radio," *Rolling Stone.* n448 (September 25, 1986) 32.

"Westwood One Buys *Radio & Records,*" *Variety.* 325 (December 10, 1986) 91.

RADIO—PIRATE STATIONS (See also: PRINCE)

Tannenbaum, Rob. "FCC Shuts Hatch on Pirate Station," *Rolling Stone.* n509 (September 24, 1987) 32ff. il.

RADIO—PIRATE STATIONS (UNITED KINGDOM)

Alex, Peter. *Who's Who in Pop Radio.* London: New English Library, 1966. il.

Harris, Paul. *When Pirates Ruled the Waves.* London: Impulse, 1968. il.

RADIO—PROGRAMMERS—ABRAMS, LEE (See also: AOR)

Freeman, K. "Abrams Offers Information to Artists," *Billboard.* 97 (June 5, 1985) 47–48.

Marsh, Dave. "Beware Radio 1984," *Musician Player & Listener.* n24 (April/May 1980) 14ff.

McNamara, D. "Abrams Tells AORs: Let's Jazz It Up," *Billboard.* 98 (January 25, 1986) 1ff.

Terry, Ken. "Abrams' Market Reports Receive Mixed Reviews from Artists, Diskeries," *Variety.* 319 (June 5, 1985) 72.

RADIO—PROGRAMMERS—GAVIN, BILL

Bornstein, R. "*Gavin Report* Founder Bill Gavin Dies at 77," *Billboard.* 97 (February 9, 1985) 12ff.

[Obituary], *Variety.* 318 (February 6, 1985) 134.

RADIO—PROGRAMMING—ADULT CONTEMPORARY (AC)
(See also: BLACK ADULT CONTEMPORARY)

"Adult Contempo Again Leads Survey of Radio Formats," *Variety.* 322 (April 9, 1986) 116.

DiMauro, P. "Rockers Stir Up Placid Waters of Adult Contempo Outlets as They Vie With AOR for 21–45 Audience," *Variety.* 322 (April 2, 1986) 79ff.

Freeman, K. "AC Programmers See VH-1 as Partner," *Billboard.* 97 (June 15, 1985) 15–16.

Goldstein, Steven. "AC Stations Face New Challenges," *Billboard.* 97 (August 31, 1985) 19–20. il.

Holland, Bill. "P.D. to P.D.: Latest Research Finds AC Still on Top; NRBA Format Survey," *Billboard.* 98 (April 12, 1986) 18. il.

LaPointe, Kirk. "'87 Radio Fans Favored AC Format," *Billboard.* 101 (January 14, 1989) 60.
Re. Canada.

Ross, Sean. "AC Format is Still Tops in Winter Ratings," *Billboard.* (June 9, 1990) 1, 12, 15, 20–21. Pie charts.

RADIO—PROGRAMMING—AOR (See also: LEE ABRAMS; CONTEMPORARY HITS RADIO)

"Abrams Urges Deeper Playlists, Jazz & '60s–'70s Blocks for AOR," *Variety.* 322 (February 5, 1986) 146.

"Album Radio Under Attack for Ignoring New Music," *Variety.* 323 (July 23, 1986) 69.

Buckman, A. "AOR PDs Seek Support," *Billboard.* 97 (October 12, 1985) 18.

Freeman, K. " 'New' AOR Gets Mixed Reviews," *Billboard.* 97 (May 25, 1985) 3ff.

Vare, E.A. "Mr. Mister Living Proof AOR Can Still Break Pop Radio," *Billboard.* 97 (November 9, 1985) 61–62.

RADIO—PROGRAMMING—BLACK ADULT CONTEMPORARY (See also: ADULT CONTEMPORARY; BLACK REPRESENTATION)

Ingram, B. "Chi FMer Debuts New Format," *Variety.* 333 (October 26, 1988) 47.

RADIO—PROGRAMMING—CLASSIC ROCK

Denberg, Jody. "Around the Clock Rock," *Texas Monthly.* (October 1987) 142–145. il.

Freeman, K. "Classic Rock Thrives in 18 Months," *Billboard.* 98 (October 25, 1986) 10ff.

"Jacobs: 'Won't Get Fooled' Has Not Burned Out . . . Yet," *Billboard.* 102:16 (April 21, 1980) 14, 16.

McNamara, D. "Classic Cuts Squeeze Out Currents at AOR," *Billboard.* 98 (April 5, 1986) 10ff.

McNamara, D. " 'Classic Rock' Forces Defensive Strategy," *Billboard.* 98 (June 21, 1986) 10ff.

RADIO—PROGRAMMING—CONTEMPORARY HITS RADIO (CHR)

Christgau, Robert. "The Rise of the Corporate Single," *Village Voice.* 30 (February 19, 1985) 29–30ff. il.

Iorio, Paul. "Europe Targets CHR from an AOR/MTV Base," *Cash Box.* (February 7, 1987) 11. il., int. w/Diarmuid Quinn, an Epic product manager.

RADIO—PROGRAMMING—MIDDLE-OF-THE-ROAD (MOR)

"New MOR Format Aims at Older Set," *Variety.* 322 (April 23, 1986) 243.

RADIO—PROGRAMMING—OLDIES (See also: NOSTALGIA)

"Crockett's Oldies Has Emotional Appeal; 'Southern Gold' Mastermind," *Billboard.* 97 (January 26, 1985) 17ff.

Ross, Sean. "Gold Titles Withstand Test of Time," *Billboard.* 102:16 (April 21, 1980) 14, 20.

Sokolow, Brian Cary. "Radio Kills Music, Self," *High Fidelity.* (August 1987) 56.

RADIO—PROGRAMMING—TOP 40

Freeman, K. "Top 40's Pop Pipeline Lacks Power," *Billboard.* 98 (May 31, 1986) 10ff.

Gaudioso, A. "Top 40 Outlets Dancing to New Beat," *Billboard.* 97 (August 10, 1985) 12.

Hennessey, Mike. "Panel's Debate: Top 40 a Hit Maker or Hit Taker?," *Billboard.* (May 28, 1988) 73.

Set at the Third International Music and Media Conference, May 12–14, 1988, at Montreux, Switzerland.

RECORDING INDUSTRY

Dufour, Barry. Special consultant, Dave Laing. *The World of Pop and Rock.* London: Macdonald Educational, 1977. il., bibl., filmography.

Pielke, Robert G. "Records: The Newest Testament," In: *You Say You Want a Revolution.* Chicago: Nelson-Hall, 1986. pp. 81–95.

Pike, Jeff. *Rock World.* London: Marshall Cavendish Children's Books, 1979. il.
Survey of the industry geared to children and young adolescents.

Plimmer, Martin. *The Rock Factory.* London/New York: Proteus, 1982. il.

Powell, Peter. *Peter Powell's Book of Pop.* London: Armada, 1980. il.
Aimed at the young adolescent. Coverage includes life on the road, record companies, the role of charts, the radio studio, and bios of major stars.

"RIAA Revises Gold and Platinum Standards," *Cash Box.* LII:2 (July 9, 1988) 5.

RECORDING INDUSTRY—MINORITY REPRESENTATION, STATUS, ETC.

George, Nelson. "Artist 'Blacklist' Issue Causes Conflict at NAACP," *Billboard.* 97 (July 20, 1985) 3ff.

Morrison, R. "Commentary: For a Strong Black Music Association," *Billboard.* 98 (April 6, 1986) 9.

"NAACP Has 'Second Thoughts' About Stance Toward Disk Biz," *Variety.* 323 (June 18, 1986) 81ff.

Schipper, H. "NAACP Likely to Target Paucity of Blacks as Personal Managers," *Variety.* 323 (July 2, 1986) 64.

Schipper, H. "NAACP, Other Groups Petition Congress on Labels' Treatment of Blacks, Including Promoters," *Variety.* 322 (March 26, 1986) 89ff.

Schipper, H. "NAACP Probe of Record Biz Finds 'Limits' for Blacks," *Variety.* 325 (December 17, 1986) 1ff.

Ware, G. "Commentary: For a Strong Black Music Association," *Billboard.* 98 (March 22, 1986) 10.

RECORDING INDUSTRY—RECORD COMPANIES

DiMartino, Dave. "Growth Spurs Label Offshoots," *Billboard.* 101 (January 7, 1989) 4ff.

Gosse, V. "The New Independents," *Musician Player & Listener.* n33 (June 1981) 24ff. il.

RECORDING INDUSTRY—RECORD COMPANIES—A&M

Huttenhower, Bryan, and Alonzo Brown. "Where the Music Comes From . . . and is Going," *Billboard.* (June 30, 1990) W-5. il.

RECORDING INDUSTRY—RECORD COMPANIES—ALLIGATOR

"Alligator Grins as Top Blues Diskery," *Variety.* 325 (November 19, 1986) 79ff.

McCormick, Moira. " 'Guitar Heroes' Boost Alligator's Sales," *Billboard.* 97 (June 8, 1985) 82.

Poses, Jonathan W. "Our Blues," *High Fidelity.* (December 1987) 84–85. il.

RECORDING INDUSTRY—RECORD COMPANIES—ANTILLES

Moleski, L. "Antilles Sets New Label Distributed by WEA," *Billboard.* 99 (October 17, 1987) 6ff.

RECORDING INDUSTRY—RECORD COMPANIES—ARIOLA (See: RCA)

RECORDING INDUSTRY—RECORD COMPANIES—ARISTA

Davis, Clive. "Entering a New Stage of Growth," *Billboard.* (June 30, 1990) W-6. il.

Fox, T. "Clive Davis: Finding Songs for Singers," *Audio.* 69 (July 1985) 28–33.

RECORDING INDUSTRY—RECORD COMPANIES—ATLANTIC (See also: COMPACT DISCS)

Keepnews, P. "Blue Notes: Something Was Missing at Atlantic's Birthday Party," *Billboard.* 100 (June 4, 1988) 25.

Pond, Steve. "Atlantic's Birthday Bash," *Rolling Stone.* n529 (June 30, 1988) 48–50ff. il.

Santoro, G. "Atlantic at 40," *Down Beat.* 54 (August 1987) 63.

Zimmerman, K. "Atlantic Concert Eyes $6.12 Mil Net; Album, Homevideo Planned," *Variety.* 331 (June 1, 1988) 84.

RECORDING INDUSTRY—RECORD COMPANIES—BEARSVILLE (See: RHINO)

RECORDING INDUSTRY—RECORD COMPANIES—BLUE CHIP

Jeske, Lee. "Ron Rogers Revs Up Blue Chip," *Cash Box.* (October 4, 1986) 10. int. w/Rogers.

RECORDING INDUSTRY—RECORD COMPANIES—BON AMI

George, Nelson. "Sylvia Robinson Returns With Own Firm," *Billboard.* 99 (December 19, 1987) 25.

"Robinson Sets Up Bon Ami Records With Son at Side,"
Variety. 329 (December 9, 1987) 71.

RECORDING INDUSTRY—RECORD
COMPANIES—BRUNSWICK

British Brunswick Singles History: 1952 to 1967. Bromley, Kent,
U.K.: Record Information Services, 1978– .

RECORDING INDUSTRY—RECORD
COMPANIES—CBS

"Commentary: Sony Says 'Yes' to Record Business Future,"
Billboard. 99 (December 5, 1987) 9.

Freeman, K. "Reaction to CBS Vidclip Charge Cools," *Billboard.* 97 (June 22, 1985) 12ff.

George, Nelson. "Labels Seek Minority Policy; CBS Plan is
Prototype," *Billboard.* 99 (September 5, 1987) 82.

Goodman, Fred. "CBS Records Sold to Sony," *Rolling Stone.*
n517 (January 14, 1988) 17.

Jones, P. "CBS Records U.K. Revises Trading Terms," *Billboard.* 98 (October 18, 1986) 3ff.

Mattola, Tommy. "The '90s: Fasten Your Seatbelts," *Billboard.*
(June 30, 1990) W-10. il.

"Record Breakers," *Melody Maker.* 61 (August 9, 1986) 3.
    CBS abolishes the existing "sale or return" method of
    buying for British record shops and, in turn, lowers the
    dealer price of their pop and rock albums.

Rosenbluth, J. "CBS Pacts for New Acts Ire Pubs, Writers," *Billboard.* 99 (December 19, 1987) 1ff.

Schipper, H. "Japan, U.S. Govts. Give Thumbs Up to Sony Purchase of CBS Records," *Variety.* 329 (December 30, 1987) 35.

Seideman, T. "CBS Charge for Vidclip Use Nears," *Billboard.* 97 (May 25, 1985) 1ff.

Seideman, T. "Video Outlets in CBS Boycott; Clip Fee Plan Angers Programmer," *Billboard.* 97 (June 8, 1985) 1ff.

RECORDING INDUSTRY—RECORD COMPANIES—CTI (See: WARNER BROS.)

RECORDING INDUSTRY—RECORD COMPANIES—CAPITOL (See also: NETTWERK PRODUCTIONS)

DiMartino, Dave. "Capitol Sues Geffen re. Lennon CD," *Billboard.* 99 (October 31, 1987) 6ff.
Re. *The John Lennon Collection.*

Dobrin, Gregory. "Points West," *Cash Box.* (August 1, 1987) 10. il.
Re. restoration of the Capitol Tower.

Grein, Paul. "Capitol/EMI/Manhattan Raises Black Music Profile," *Billboard.* 97 (November 30, 1985) 58.

Milgrim, Hale. "The Promise of the '90s," *Billboard.* 102 (June 30, 1990) W-11, W-45. il.

RECORDING INDUSTRY—RECORD
COMPANIES—CAPITOL (U.K.)

British Capitol Singles & E.P.s, Part One: 1948–1955. London: Record Information Services, 1977.

Pelletier, Paul M. *British Capitol 45 R.P.M. Singles Catalogue: 1954–1981.* London: Record Information Services, 1982.

RECORDING INDUSTRY—RECORD
COMPANIES—CHRYSALIS

Hunter, N. "Chrysalis Group May be Target of Geffen Takeover," *Billboard.* 101 (January 14, 1989) 6.

Sykes, John. "Understanding the Ever-Changing Music Marketplace," *Billboard.* (June 30, 1990) W-13. il.

RECORDING INDUSTRY—RECORD
COMPANIES—COLD CHILLIN'

Coleman, B. "Cold Chillin' Gets Hot Under WB Distrib Deal," *Billboard.* (June 11, 1988) 94.

RECORDING INDUSTRY—RECORD
COMPANIES—COLUMBIA

Ienner, Don. "Taking the Big Step Forward," *Billboard.* 102 (June 30, 1990) W-14. il.

RECORDING INDUSTRY—RECORD COMPANIES—COMBAT

Moleski, L. "Important Records Rediscovers Relativity," *Billboard*. 97 (August 24, 1985) 70.

RECORDING INDUSTRY—RECORD COMPANIES—COYOTE

Iorio, Paul. "Coyote's Steve Fallon: Shaping a Sound With a Label and a Club," *Cash Box*. (May 31, 1986) 10.

RECORDING INDUSTRY—RECORD COMPANIES—CREATION

Aston, Martin. "New Industry," *Melody Maker*. 60 (April 27, 1985) 12. il.

RECORDING INDUSTRY—RECORD COMPANIES—CRITIQUE

"Boston's Critique Expands Its Horizons," *Cash Box*. (January 31, 1987) 22.

RECORDING INDUSTRY—RECORD COMPANIES—CYPRESS

Berk, Peter. "Cypress Records: Offering Its Artists the Personal Touch," *Cash Box*. (December 6, 1986) 10, 28.

RECORDING INDUSTRY—RECORD COMPANIES—DEF JAM

George, Nelson. "Rappin' With Russell," *Village Voice.* 30 (April 30, 1985) 42–43ff.

Mieses, S. "Keynotes: Pipe Dreams and 'Sweet Dreams'," *Record.* 4 (December 1985) 16–17ff.

RECORDING INDUSTRY—RECORD COMPANIES—DELICIOUS VINYL

Malone, Bonz. "Planet Janet Rock," *Spin.* 6:4 (July 1990) 31–32. il.

Turbov, Pamela, and Michael Ross. "More of a Funky Thing in the '90s," *Billboard.* (June 30, 1990) W-17. il.

RECORDING INDUSTRY—RECORD COMPANIES—DUNHILL

Sutherland, Sam. "Dunhill Records Reborn as CD Label," *Billboard.* 98 (April 5, 1986) 78.

RECORDING INDUSTRY—RECORD COMPANIES—EMI

Licata, Sal. "EMI Today, Tomorrow and Beyond," *Billboard.* 102 (June 30, 1990) W-19. il.

Rosenbluth, Jean. "Wolf, Easton Lead EMI-Manhattan Exodus," *Rolling Stone.* n519 (February 11, 1988) 31.

RECORDING INDUSTRY—RECORD COMPANIES—ENIGMA

Martone, Jim. "Are You Ready for the '90s?," *Billboard.* 102 (June 30, 1990) W-20. il.

RECORDING INDUSTRY—RECORD COMPANIES—EPIC

Glew, Dave. "Stepping into the '90s on a Bedrock of Talent," *Billboard.* 102 (June 30, 1990) W-21. il.

RECORDING INDUSTRY—RECORD COMPANIES—FLY

Mahlowe, Gerald. "Fly by Rights," *Music Week.* (June 10, 1989) 24. il.

RECORDING INDUSTRY—RECORD COMPANIES—FLYING NUN

Schoemer, Karen. "Nineties in Effect; The World Through a Whiskey Glass," *Spin.* 5:11 (February 1990) 60–61. il.

RECORDING INDUSTRY—RECORD COMPANIES—GRP (See: MCA)

RECORDING INDUSTRY—RECORD COMPANIES—GEFFEN (See also: CHRYSALIS; MCA)

Rosenblatt, Ed. "Spanning the Full Spectrum of Music," *Billboard.* 102 (June 30, 1990) W-23. il.

RECORDING INDUSTRY—RECORD COMPANIES—GIANT

Moleski, L. "Grass Route: New Giant Records Makes a Mark With Punk, Hardcore," *Billboard.* 99 (December 12, 1987) 32.

RECORDING INDUSTRY—RECORD COMPANIES—GLOBESTYLE

Gehr, Richard. "World Beat!," *Spin.* 6:4 (July 1990) 88. il.

RECORDING INDUSTRY—RECORD COMPANIES—GOLD CASTLE

Padgett, Stephen. "Goldberg Launches Gold Castle; Aims for the 'Boomers'," *Cash Box.* (January 24, 1987) 7, 22. il., int. w/president Danny Goldberg.

RECORDING INDUSTRY—RECORD COMPANIES—HIT-N-RUN

"New Companies," *Billboard.* 99 (December 19, 1987) 70.

RECORDING INDUSTRY—RECORD COMPANIES—HOLLAND GROUP

Robinson, Julius. "The Birth of a Record Company," *Cash Box.* (August 27, 1988) 11. il., int. w/Brian and Eddie Holland.

Re. the formation of three new labels: AB Records, HDH Records and Music Merchant Records.

RECORDING INDUSTRY—RECORD COMPANIES—ISLAND

Bone, Mike. "Bringing Fresh and Forward Music to the '90s," *Billboard.* 102 (June 30, 1990) W-25. il.

RECORDING INDUSTRY—RECORD COMPANIES—JEM

Goodman, Fred. "Jem Bows New Label," *Billboard.* 98 (May 24, 1986) 89.

"Jem Runs Up Loss," *Variety.* 321 (November 6, 1985) 88.

Lichtman, Irv. "Accord Reached on Import Mechanicals," *Billboard.* 99 (December 12, 1987) 3.

"Sales Increases are Registered in Jem Records' Year," *Variety.* 320 (August 28, 1985) 38.

RECORDING INDUSTRY—RECORD COMPANIES—JIVE

Calder, Clive. "What About the Music of the '90s?," *Billboard.* 102 (June 30, 1990) W-26. il.

RECORDING INDUSTRY—RECORD COMPANIES—K-TEL

"K-Tel Petition for Chap. 11 Revamp Approved by Court," *Variety.* 320 (October 23, 1985) 77.

"K-Tel Seems Financially Stable Nine Mos. After Chapter 11 Filing," *Variety*. 319 (June 12, 1985) 77.

"K-Tel Still Trying to Reorganize Debt as Red Ink Mounts," *Variety*. 318 (March 20, 1985) 131.

RECORDING INDUSTRY—RECORD COMPANIES—MCA

DiMartino, Dave. "Surprise! It's MCA Inc. That Gets Geffen," *Billboard*. 102:12 (March 24, 1990) 1, 71.

DiMartino, Dave. "Teller Eyes Baby Boomers in MCA's Purchase of GRP," *Billboard*. 102:11 (March 17, 1990) 8, 104.

George, Nelson. "The Rhythm and the Blues: Busby Puts MCA on the Black Music Map," *Billboard*. 100 (June 18, 1988) 24.

Goldberg, Michael. "Risky Business: How Did a Reputed Mobster Become a Deal Maker for MCA Records?," *Rolling Stone*. n527 (June 2, 1988) 17–21, 76. il.

"MCA Label Booms, Helped by Homevid, Motown Distribution," *Variety*. 318 (February 20, 1985) 73ff.

"MCA Streak Powers Expansion Planning," *Billboard*. 98 (April 19, 1986) 32–33.

"MCA to Buy Motown?," *Variety*. 325 (December 31, 1986) 55.

Morris, Chris. "Settlement Due for Sugar Hill v. MCA," *Billboard*. 101 (January 28, 1989) 84ff.

Sippel, J. "Former Executive Says MCS Fired Him Unfairly," *Billboard.* 97 (May 25, 1985) 86.

Sutherland, Sam. "MCA's Unicity is Duo's Idea of 'Dream Company'," *Billboard.* 98 (August 9, 1986) 6ff.

Sutherland, Sam. " 'New Blood' Transforms MCA Music," *Billboard.* 97 (June 8, 1985) 6ff.

Teller, Al. "Developing the Talent to Stay on Top," *Billboard.* (June 30, 1990) W-27. il.

Terry, Ken. "MCA on Firing Line Over Cutout Sales; N.J. Distributor Sues Label, Execs," *Variety.* 322 (March 26, 1986) 89–90.

RECORDING INDUSTRY—RECORD COMPANIES—MALACO

Mannush, Jeff. "Malaco's Down-Home Blues," *Rolling Stone.* n527 (June 2, 1988) 32. il., int.

RECORDING INDUSTRY—RECORD COMPANIES—MANHATTAN (See: EMI)

RECORDING INDUSTRY—RECORD COMPANIES—METAL BLADE

Henderson, Alex. "Indie Profile: Metal Blade," *Cash Box.* LIII:50 (July 7, 1990) 9. il.

RECORDING INDUSTRY—RECORD COMPANIES—MIDNIGHT

"New Companies," *Billboard.* 99 (September 5, 1987) 70.

RECORDING INDUSTRY—RECORD COMPANIES—MOTOWN (See also: MCA)

Dupler, Steven. "Hitsville Closes Up Shop and Goes on the Block," *Billboard.* 101 (January 7, 1989) 6.

McAdams, J.C. "Clips are Key to Motown Renewal," *Billboard.* 101 (January 21, 1989) 62.

Mayfield, G. "Motown Drops Midline LPs," *Billboard.* 98 (September 20, 1986) 86.

Morse, David. *Motown and the Arrival of Black Music.* London: Studio Vista, 1971. il. Orig. pub.: New York: Macmillan, 1971.

Schipper, H. "Motown Settles in Isgro Suit; Payment Estimated Near 100G," *Variety.* 328 (September 30, 1987) 127.

Sippel, J. "Motown Leaves RIAA," *Billboard.* 98 (March 8, 1986) 92.

RECORDING INDUSTRY—RECORD COMPANIES—MOTOWN (U.K.)

British Tamla Motown Complete Listing: Part One (1959 to 1970 Inclusive). New Malden, Surrey: Record Information Services, 1980. il. Reissue of 1976 ed.

RECORDING INDUSTRY—RECORD COMPANIES—NETTWERK PRODUCTIONS

"Propourri," *Music Scene.* n348 (March/April 1986) 16.

Stern, P. "Growing Indie Signs With Capitol," *Canadian Musician.* 8:4 (1986) 16.

RECORDING INDUSTRY—RECORD COMPANIES—ODE

Morris, Chris. "Ode Records Reactivated," *Billboard.* 101 (January 21, 1989) 10ff.

RECORDING INDUSTRY—RECORD COMPANIES—POLYGRAM

"The Continuity of Artistry," *Billboard.* (June 30, 1990) W-31, W-45. il.

Goodman, Fred. "Trim PolyGram is Sticking With Branches," *Billboard.* 97 (June 15, 1985) 1ff.

RECORDING INDUSTRY—RECORD COMPANIES—PORTRAIT

Jeske, Lee. "A Portrait of Portrait: 'Eclectic But Not Weird'," *Cash Box.* (August 27, 1988) 10. il., int. w/label executives Don Grierson and Bob Thiele.

RECORDING INDUSTRY—RECORD COMPANIES—PROFILE

Iorio, Paul. "Cory Robbins' Profile Records Branching From Its Rap Roots," *Cash Box.* XLIX:37 (March 1, 1986) 12.

Levy, Joe. "Tougher Than Vinyl: Profile Records," *Cash Box.* LI:47 (May 28, 1988) 25.

Robbins, Cory. "Striving for Balance in Diversity," *Billboard.* (June 30, 1990) W-33. il.

RECORDING INDUSTRY—RECORD COMPANIES—QWEST

Sutherland, Sam. "Childs Outlines Qwest's Expansion," *Billboard.* 97 (August 3, 1985) 6ff.

Sutherland, Sam. "WB Handling Qwest Functions," *Billboard.* 98 (February 22, 1986) 78.

RECORDING INDUSTRY—RECORD COMPANIES—RCA

Buziak, Bob. "Creativity and Consolidation in the '90s," *Billboard.* (June 30, 1990) W-34. il.

Hennessey, M. "RCA Deal Gives Bertelsmann Multinational Label Ranking," *Billboard.* 98 (September 20, 1986) 1ff.

"RCA, Bertelsmann Finish Merger of Record, Musvid Operations," *Variety.* 320 (August 14, 1985) 63.

"RCA Record Arm's Sales Soar, Due to Ariola Merger," *Variety.* 322 (March 19, 1986) 77.

RECORDING INDUSTRY—RECORD COMPANIES—ROIR

Push. "ROIR," *Melody Maker.* (June 23, 1990) 57. il., int. w/Neil Cooper.

RECORDING INDUSTRY—RECORD COMPANIES—RHINO

Barol, Bill, with Janet Huck. "B-Rated Rock and Roll," *Newsweek.* (October 7, 1985) 90. il.

"Bearsville Catalog Licensed to Rhino," *Cash Box.* (May 23, 1987) 15.

DiMartino, Dave. "One to One: Harold Bronson, Co-Founder of Rhino Records, Discusses the Label's Success," *Billboard.* 99 (December 12, 1987) 17. il., int.

Morris, Chris. "Rhino Records Thrives on the Unusual," *Billboard.* 98 (November 1, 1986) 45ff.

Stewart, Gary. "Growing Older and Kicking Tail in the '90s," *Billboard.* (June 30, 1990) W-35. il.

RECORDING INDUSTRY—RECORD COMPANIES—ROULETTE

"KB May Acquire Roulette Records," *Variety.* 332 (August 10, 1988) 53.

Lichtman, Irv. "Roulette Agrees to $4.5 Mil Sale to KB Communications," *Billboard.* 100 (August 20, 1988) 6ff.

RECORDING INDUSTRY—RECORD COMPANIES—ROUNDER

Barol, Bill. "Rounder's Real Deal," *Newsweek.* (July 18, 1988) 58. il., int. w/Rony Levy.

RECORDING INDUSTRY—RECORD COMPANIES—SBK

Koppelman, Charles. "Flexing Major Muscle for Real Music," *Billboard.* (June 30, 1990) W-38. il.

RECORDING INDUSTRY—RECORD COMPANIES—SST

Eddy, C. "Music: An Indie Rises Above," *Village Voice.* 32 (September 22, 1987) 83–84ff. il.

RECORDING INDUSTRY—RECORD COMPANIES—SAVOY

Darden, B. "Lectern: Black Gospel Album, Video Keeps Savoy Label Stomping," *Billboard.* 101 (January 28, 1989) 58.

RECORDING INDUSTRY—RECORD COMPANIES—SHIMMY DISC

True, Everett. "Shimmy Disc: Kramer v. Kramer," *Melody Maker.* 66:7 (February 17, 1990) 36–37. il., int.

RECORDING INDUSTRY—RECORD COMPANIES—SOLAR

Morris, Chris. "Solar, WCI Reach Accord After 2-Year Legal Dispute," *Billboard.* 101 (January 7, 1989) 4ff.

"Solar's Suit Against WCI May be Near Private Settlement," *Variety.* 328 (September 30, 1987) 127–128.

RECORDING INDUSTRY—RECORD COMPANIES—STAX

George, Nelson. "Al Bell, Stax Mover and Shaker, is Starting Over," *Billboard.* 98 (August 2, 1986) 26.

"Will Stax Studios Survive?," *Spin.* 5:12 (March 1990) 19. il.

RECORDING INDUSTRY—RECORD COMPANIES—SUE (U.K.)

British Sue Complete Singles, E.P.s & L.P.s Listing. London: Record Information Services, 1976.

RECORDING INDUSTRY—RECORD COMPANIES—SUGAR HILL (See also: MCA)

Schipper, H. "Pisello Case Drops Bombshells on MCA," *Variety.* 328 (September 23, 1987) 157–158.

RECORDING INDUSTRY—RECORD COMPANIES—SURVIVAL (U.K.)

Blows, Kirk. "Built on Solid Rock," *Music Week.* (June 10, 1989) 16.

RECORDING INDUSTRY—RECORD COMPANIES—TOMMY BOY

Lynch, Monica. "In Search of the Perfect Beat," *Billboard.* 102 (June 30, 1990) W-40, W-42. il.

RECORDING INDUSTRY—RECORD COMPANIES—TRUE NORTH

"Canada's True North Drops Out of Action Except for Cockburn," *Variety.* 323 (May 21, 1986) 91.

RECORDING INDUSTRY—RECORD COMPANIES—WARNER BROS. (WEA) (See also: COLD CHILLIN')

Goodman, Fred. "Warner Bros. Reactivates Reprise," *Rolling Stone.* n509 (September 24, 1987) 33.

Grein, Paul. "L.A. Stations End Boycott vs. Warner Bros.," *Billboard.* 97 (May 4, 1985) 1ff.

Schipper, H. "Boycott of Warner Bros. Disks Ended by Black Radio Stations; Label Pledges Policy Change," *Variety.* 319 (May 1, 1985) 4ff.

RECORDING INDUSTRY—RECORD COMPANY EXECUTIVES—ASCH, MOE

"Folkways' Asch Dies," *Billboard.* 98 (November 1, 1986) 6.

Kenton, G. "Moe Asch: 1905–1986," *Village Voice.* 31 (November 4, 1986) 83. il.

[Obituary], *Bluegrass.* 21 (December 1986) 13.

[Obituary], *Cadence.* 12 (December 1986) 92.

[Obituary], *Living Blues.* n72 (1986) 41.

[Obituary], *Variety.* 325 (November 5, 1986) 102.

RECORDING INDUSTRY—RECORD COMPANY EXECUTIVES—COPELAND, IAN

Iorio, Paul. "F.B.I.'s Ian Copeland Keeps Rock's Cutting Edge Sharp," *Cash Box.* XLIX:41 (March 29, 1986) 12.

RECORDING INDUSTRY—RECORD COMPANY EXECUTIVES—DAVIS, CLIVE

Davis, Clive. "Commentary: What Does 'New Artist' Really Mean?," *Billboard.* 98 (January 18, 1986) 8. il.

"Davis Raps Radio Programmers for Their 'Play it Safe' Mentality," *Variety.* 323 (May 7, 1986) 535–536.

DiMauro, P. "Davis Speech on Black Music Arouses Controversy in Industry Over Necessity of Crossover," *Variety.* 324 (July 30, 1986) 67ff.

Sutherland, Sam. "Clive Davis Blasts Radio 'Conservatism'," *Billboard.* 98 (May 17, 1986) 3ff. int.

RECORDING INDUSTRY—RECORD COMPANY EXECUTIVES—ERTEGUN, NESUHI

Blum, J. "Straight Talk from Atlantic's Nesuhi Ertegun," *Jazz Times.* (August 1987) 23.

RECORDING INDUSTRY—RECORD COMPANY EXECUTIVES—FRIESEN, GIL

Pond, Steve. "Behind the Scenes: Gil Friesen," *Rolling Stone.* n515/516 (December 17/31, 1987) 103–106. il., int.

RECORDING INDUSTRY—RECORD COMPANY EXECUTIVES—LEVY, MORRIS

Goodman, Fred. "Morris Levy Severing Music Industry Ties," *Billboard.* 98 (December 20, 1986) 1ff.

Rutledge, Jeffrey. "Morris Levy, Convicted Label Exec, Dead at 62," *Rolling Stone.* n581 (June 28, 1990) 16.

RECORDING INDUSTRY—RECORD COMPANY EXECUTIVES—MOSS, JERRY

Ressner, Jeffrey. "Ecologically Sound; A Record Executive and His Wife Come to the Aid of the Dolphins," *Rolling Stone.* n579 (May 31, 1990) 25. il.

RECORDING INDUSTRY—RECORD COMPANY EXECUTIVES—WEXLER, JERRY

Fox, T. "Jerry Wexler: Navigator of the Atlantic Sound," *Audio.* 69 (May 1985) 52–59. il.

Fox, T. "Jerry Wexler: Navigator of the Atlantic Sound," *Audio.* 69 (June 1985) 62–71. il.

RECORDING INDUSTRY—RECORD COMPANY EXECUTIVES—YETNIKOFF, WALTER

Goodman, Fred. "The Rolling Stone Interview: Walter Yetnikoff," *Rolling Stone.* m541/542 (December 15/29, 1988) 166–167ff. il., int.

Lombardi, John. "King of the Schmooze," *Esquire.* (November 1986) 118–128. il.

RECORDING INDUSTRY—RECORD COMPANY EXECUTIVES—ZAENTZ, SAUL (See also: JOHN FOGERTY)

"Saul Zaentz Files Suit; Charges Fogerty Tunes, Interviews Libeled Him," *Variety.* 320 (July 31, 1985) 71.

Sippel, J. "Zaentz Sucs John Fogerty," *Billboard.* 97 (August 10, 1985) 77.

RECORDING INDUSTRY—RECORD COMPANY EXECUTIVES—ZUTAUT, TOM

DiMartino, Dave. "One to One: Geffen Records' Tom Zutaut Talks About His Amazing String of Successes," *Billboard.* 101 (August 19, 1989) 28.

RECORDING INDUSTRY—RECORD
PROMOTERS

Gett, Steve, and Chris Morris. "Indie Promoters are Back in Town," *Billboard.* 100 (October 15, 1988) 1ff.

RECORDING INDUSTRY—STUDIOS

Dupler, Steven. "Digital Over Analog in Two Years," *Billboard.* 98 (August 9, 1986) 63.

Forte, Dan. "Woodsheds: Four Guitarists' Home Studios," *Guitar Player.* 19 (December 1985) 97ff. il., int.

RECORDING INDUSTRY—STUDIOS—A&M

DiMartino, Dave. "A&M Studios: State of the Art," *Billboard.* 100 (October 29, 1988) 40ff.

RECORDING INDUSTRY—STUDIOS—ABBEY
ROAD

Southall, Brian. *Abbey Road: The Story of the World's Most Famous Recording Studio.* Foreword by Paul McCartney; preface by George Martin; additional research and original idea by Peter Vince and Allan Rouse. Cambridge, U.K.: Patrick Stephens, 1982. il., disc.

RECORDING INDUSTRY—STUDIOS—SUNSET

DiMartino, Dave. "Synchavier Checks into the Sunset; L.A. Hotel Offers Guest a Digital Audio Studio," *Billboard.* 100 (October 22, 1988) 77.

RECORDING INDUSTRY—STUDIOS—ARTIST AND REPERTOIRE (A & R) MEN

George, Nelson. "The Rhythm and the Blues: Blacks are Moving Up The A&R Ranks," *Billboard.* 99 (August 15, 1987) 26.

Lamacq, Steve. "Nice Face, Shame About the Ligs," *New Musical Express.* (February 17, 1990) 12–13, 61. il., int. w/Ben Wardle and Tony Smith re. the U.K. scene.

RECORDING INDUSTRY—STUDIOS—A & R MEN—CHERTOFF, RICK

Iorio, Paul. "Columbia's Rick Chertoff: A & R With an Accent on Production," *Cash Box.* XLIX:30 (January 11, 1986) 10.

RECORDING INDUSTRY—STUDIOS—A & R MEN—SHULMAN, DEREK

Iorio, Paul. "PolyGram's Derek Shulman Talks About A & R," *Cash Box.* XLIX:27 (December 14, 1985) 39. il., int.

RECORDING INDUSTRY—STUDIOS—A & R MEN—SILAS, LOVIL, JR.

Iorio, Paul. "MCA's Silas: Moving R & B and A & R in New Directions," *Cash Box.* XLIX:32 (February 25, 1986) 8.

RECORDING INDUSTRY—STUDIOS— ENGINEERS—HODGE, STEVE

Doerschuk, Bob. "In Control With Jam & Lewis: Engineer Steve Hodge," *Keyboard Magazine.* 13 (May 1987) 76ff. il., int.

RECORDING INDUSTRY—STUDIOS— PRODUCERS

Chin, B. "Art of Dance-Track Remix Comes of Age," *Billboard.* 99 (September 5, 1987) 3ff.

Tobler, John, and Stuart Grandy. *The Record Producers.* London: British Broadcasting Corp., 1982. il., disc.

RECORDING INDUSTRY—STUDIOS— PRODUCERS—BAKER, ARTHUR

Cioe, C. "Arthur Baker's Makeovers," *High Fidelity.* 35 (April 1985) 81–82ff. il., int.

George, Nelson. "Arthur Baker, Producer of *Sun City*, Bows Label," *Billboard.* 98 (August 16, 1986) 28.

Shewey, Don. "Riffs: Arthur Baker's Baby Boom," *Village Voice.* 30 (January 1, 1985) 54. il.

"Sidelines," *Melody Maker.* 65 (August 5, 1989) 12.

RECORDING INDUSTRY—STUDIOS— PRODUCERS—BARRI, STEVE

Padgett, Stephen. "Barri Bows Starsong," *Cash Box.* (August 19, 1986) 10.

RECORDING INDUSTRY—STUDIOS— PRODUCERS—BENITEZ, "JELLYBEAN"

Vare, E.A. "Life is Sweet for 'Jellybean' Benitez," *Billboard.* 97 (November 16, 1985) 50–51. int.

RECORDING INDUSTRY—STUDIOS— PRODUCERS—CREWE, BOB

Tannenbaum, Rob. "Where are They Now? Bob Crewe," *Rolling Stone.* n508 (September 10, 1987) 60. il., int.

RECORDING INDUSTRY—STUDIOS— PRODUCERS—DEODATO, EUMIR

Doerschuk, Bob. "New York Producer Eumir Deodato," *Keyboard Magazine.* 14 (September 1988) 40. il.

RECORDING INDUSTRY—STUDIOS— PRODUCERS—DR. DRE (See also: N.W.A.)

Lambert, Stu. "Control Zone: Dr. Beat," *Melody Maker.* 66:24 (June 16, 1990) 46. il., int.

RECORDING INDUSTRY—STUDIOS— PRODUCERS—HACKFORD, TAYLOR, AND JOEL SILL

Berk, Peter. "Hackford and Sill Join Forces at New Visions," *Cash Box.* (September 6, 1986) 8, 32.

RECORDING INDUSTRY—STUDIOS— PRODUCERS—HARTMAN, DAN

Kelly, Linda. "Flash: License to Chill," *Spin.* 5:8 (November 1989) 26. il., int.

RECORDING INDUSTRY—STUDIOS—
PRODUCERS—HINE, RUPERT

Baird, Jock. "Rupert Hine," *Musician.* n73 (November 1984)
80–82, 96. il.

RECORDING INDUSTRY—STUDIOS—
PRODUCERS—HOLLAND-DOZIER-HOLLAND
(r.n.: EDDIE HOLLAND; LAMONT DOZIER;
BRIAN HOLLAND)

George, Nelson. "The Rhythm and the Blues: Awards for
Holland-Dozier-Holland Team," *Billboard.* 99 (December 5, 1987) 22.

RECORDING INDUSTRY—STUDIOS—
PRODUCERS—JAM, JIMMY, AND TERRY LEWIS
(r.n.: JAMES HARRIS III AND TERRY LEWIS; See
also: STEVE HODGE; HUMAN LEAGUE; JANET
JACKSON; TIME)

Chin, B. "Hitmaker Jimmy Jam: No Secret to Success,"
Billboard. 98 (December 20, 1986) 24.

Doerschuk, Bob. "Jam & Lewis: Grammy-Winning Keyboar-
dist/ Producers," *Keyboard Magazine.* 13 (May 1987)
74–75, 77–85. il., bibl., disc., int.

Ivory, S. "Harris & Lewis: Out Time Has Come; Prince
Proteges Find Fame as Hot Production Team," *Billboard.*
97 (February 2, 1985) 50ff.

Ivory, S. "Time Off from Time Brings Fame to Duo," *Billboard.* 98 (March 8, 1986) 62Aff.

Rowland, Mark. "Jimmy 'Jam' Harris and Terry Lewis," *Musician.* n95 (September 1986) 11–16, 114. il., int.

Walters, Barry. "Auteurs of Soul," *Hi Fi/Musical America.* 36 (September 1986) 73–74ff. il., disc.

Walters, Barry. "Backbeat: Producers Jimmy Jam and Terry Lewis: An Annotated Discography," *High Fidelity.* (September 1986) 73–74, 87. il., disc.

Walters, Barry. "The 10 Most Interesting Musicians of the Last 5 Years: Jimmy Jam & Terry Lewis," *Spin.* 6:1 (April 1990) 45. il.

RECORDING INDUSTRY—STUDIOS— PRODUCERS—KRAMER(, MARK) (See also: SHIMMY-DISC)

Fricke, David. "Kramer: Life at the Top of the Underground," *Rolling Stone.* n578 (May 17, 1990) 85–88. il.

Push. "Sidelines: Kramer," *Melody Maker.* (July 28, 1990) 9. il., int.

Wilkinson, Roy. "Retro: The Shimmy Shimmy Sheik," *Sounds.* (March 3, 1990) 14–15. il., disc., int.

RECORDING INDUSTRY—STUDIOS—
PRODUCERS—LANOIS, DANIEL

Goldberg, Michael. "Chairman of the Boards," *Rolling Stone.* n566 (November 30, 1989) 39. il.

Henke, James. "Behind the Scenes: Daniel Lanois," *Rolling Stone.* n515/516 (December 17/31, 1987) 93–98. il., int.

Henke, James. "Daniel Lanois; The Producer of U2, Peter Gabriel and Robbie Robertson Talks About the State of Record Making," *Rolling Stone.* n515/516 (December 17/31, 1987) 93–94ff.

Horkins, Tony. "Daniel Lanois," *Melody Maker.* 66:5 (February 3, 1990) 18–19. il., int.

Tannenbaum, Rob. "Daniel Lanois," *Musician.* n98 (December 1986) 47–50, 92.

RECORDING INDUSTRY—STUDIOS—
PRODUCERS—LLOYD, MICHAEL

Berk, Peter. "Producer Michael Lloyd Enjoys A Banner Year," *Cash Box.* (August 30, 1986) 10, 36. il., int.

RECORDING INDUSTRY—STUDIOS—
PRODUCERS—MILLAR, ROBIN

Robertshaw, N. "Sade's Producer is Trying to 'Star Hungry'," *Billboard.* 98 (March 15, 1986) 74Aff. int.

RECORDING INDUSTRY—STUDIOS—
PRODUCERS—OMERTIAN, MICHAEL

Doerschuk, Bob, and Greg Armbruster. "Michael Omertian," *Keyboard.* (September 1987) 90–109, 154. il., disc., int.

Woodard, Josef. "Michael Omertian," *Musician.* n73 (November 1984) 84–86. il.

RECORDING INDUSTRY—STUDIOS—
PRODUCERS—ONELLANA, RAUL

Hardy, Ernest. "New Faces: Raul Onellana," *Cash Box.* (September 15, 1990) 4. il.

RECORDING INDUSTRY—STUDIOS—
PRODUCERS—RAMONE, PHIL

Fox, T. "The Audio Interview: Phil Ramone—Years in the Limelight," *Audio.* 70 (July 1986) 38–45. il.

Grein, Paul. "Kamon, Ramone Enjoy Studio Marriage," *Billboard.* 97 (January 12, 1985) 36ff. int.

RECORDING INDUSTRY—STUDIOS—
PRODUCERS—RODGERS, NILE (See also: CHIC)

George, Nelson. "Nile Rodgers: Sophisticated Strut from a Master of the Groove," *Guitar World.* 4 (September 1983) 50–54. il.

RECORDING INDUSTRY—STUDIOS—
PRODUCERS—RUBIN, RICK

Nelson, Havelock. "Rick Rubin: Def Jam's Man With the Plan," *Musician.* n103 (May 1987) 34–39, 58. il., int.

RECORDING INDUSTRY—STUDIOS—
PRODUCERS—SLAY, FRANK

Natchez, Marty. "Frank Slay: Songwriter, Producer," *Goldmine.* n89 (October 1983) 170–171, 174, 177ff. il., disc.

RECORDING INDUSTRY—STUDIOS—
PRODUCERS—STASIUM, ED

DeCurtis, Anthony. "Ed Stasium," *Musician.* n73 (November 1984) 88–90. il.

RECORDING INDUSTRY—STUDIOS—
PRODUCERS—VERNON, MIKE

Brunning, Bob. "Mike Vernon," In: *Blues.* pp. 150–165. il.

RECORDING INDUSTRY—STUDIOS—
PRODUCERS—VISCONTI, TONY

Thompson, Dave. "Tony Visconti," *Record Collector.* n78 (February 1986) 29–36. il., disc.

RECORDING INDUSTRY—STUDIOS— SAMPLING (See also: COPYRIGHT)

Alvaro, S. "Guest Editorial: What is Musical Property? The Ethics of Sampling," *Keyboard Magazine.* 12 (October 1986) 10ff.

Anderton, Craig. "Sampling Takes Hold," *Record.* 4 (May 1985) 46.

Bernstein, B. "Commentary: Sampling Challenges Copyright Theories," *Billboard.* 99 (December 19, 1987) 9ff.

Dupler, Steven. "Digital Sampling: Is It Theft? Technology Raises Copyright Questions," *Billboard.* 98:31 (August 2, 1986) 1, 74.

Fryer, T. "Digital Sampling: The Legality of Sampling from Unauthorized Sources," *Keyboard Magazine.* 12 (December 1986) 120. il.

Holland, Bill, and Steven Dupler. "Experts Doubt Legality of Sampling," *Billboard.* 98 (August 9, 1986) 4ff.

Stewart, Dave. "Private Lesson—Rock Keyboards: Sampling, Splitting and Layering in the Real World," *Keyboard Magazine.* 12 (September 1986) 104. music.

Stewart, Dave. "Rock Keyboards: Factory Samples are a Disease; Originality is the Cure," *Keyboard Magazine.* 12 (August 1986) 97. music.

RECORDING INDUSTRY—STUDIOS—SESSION PLAYERS—APPICE, VINNY

Appice, Vinny. "Rock Drumming in the Studio," *Modern Drummer.* 10 (July 1986) 40. il.

Flans, R. "Vinny Appice: Playing for the Band," *Modern Drummer.* 9 (September 1985) 14–17ff. il., bio, int.

RECORDING INDUSTRY—STUDIOS—SESSION PLAYERS—ARONOFF, KENNY

Mattingly, R. "Kenny Aronoff," *Modern Drummer.* 10 (June 1986) 16–21ff. il.

RECORDING INDUSTRY—STUDIOS—SESSION PLAYERS—BECKETT, BARRY

Armbruster, G., and Bob Doerschuk. "Piano Meets Synthesizer," *Keyboard Magazine.* 12 (October 1986) 52–54ff. il., bio.

RECORDING INDUSTRY—STUDIOS—SESSION PLAYERS—BLAINE, HAL

Leiune, D. "Hal Blaine: The Fundamentals of Prolific Hitmaking," *Musician.* 49 (November 1982) 78ff. il., int.

Spagnardi, Ronald, comp. and ed. "Staying in Shape: Tips from the Pros," *Modern Drummer.* 10 (November 1986) 26. il.

RECORDING INDUSTRY—STUDIOS—SESSION PLAYERS—BURTON, JAMES

"Guitar Player Lifetime Achievement Awards," *Guitar Player.* 21 (December 1987) 110–11. il.

RECORDING INDUSTRY—STUDIOS—SESSION PLAYERS—CARLTON, LARRY

Farber, Celia, and Robert Condon. "Against All Odds," *Spin.* 5:10 (January 1990) 22. il.

RECORDING INDUSTRY—STUDIOS—SESSION PLAYERS—GADD, STEVE (See also: SIMON PHILLIPS)

Ferry, J. "Different View: Reflections of the New York Producer," *Modern Drummer.* 13 (August 1989) 76.

Santelli, R. "Steve Gadd," *Modern Drummer.* 10 (January 1986) 18–19ff. il., int.

RECORDING INDUSTRY—STUDIOS—SESSION PLAYERS—JORDAN, STEVE

Blair, Michael. "Steve Jordan: Drummer's Summit," *Musician.* n140 (June 1990) 68–75. il., int.

RECORDING INDUSTRY—STUDIOS—SESSION PLAYERS—KELTNER, JIM

Scherman, Tony. "Jim Keltner's Beatnik Beat," *Musician.* n128 (June 1989) 76–81, 103. il., int.

RECORDING INDUSTRY—STUDIOS—SESSION PLAYERS—LINDLEY, DAVID

Grant, Peter. "Solo Close-Up: David Lindley," *Frets.* 8 (October 1986) 46–47. score.

RECORDING INDUSTRY—STUDIOS—SESSION PLAYERS—MARTINEZ, EDDIE

McCormick, Moira. "Eddie Martinez," *Musician.* n103 (May 1987) 40–44, 105. il., int.

RECORDING INDUSTRY—STUDIOS—SESSION PLAYERS—VAI, STEVE

"Steve Vai: From Zappa to Alcatrazz," *Creem.* 17 (July 1985) 58–59. il., int.

TELEVISION (See also: MUSIC VIDEO)

Baruck, John. "Pay-Per-View Pall Could Dilute Impact of Rocker on Tour," *Variety.* 321 (January 8, 1986) 5ff.

Pielke, Robert G. "Television: Bringing It All Back Home," In: *You Say You Want a Revolution.* pp. 111–128.

Shalett, M. "On Target: Music and TV: Sophisticated Mix," *Billboard.* 98 (April 12, 1986) 42.

TELEVISION—CABLE

Shalett, M. "On Target: Cable is Seen as a Useful Tool for Plugging Concerts and Records," *Billboard.* 97 (September 14, 1985) 32.

TELEVISION—CABLE NETWORKS—BET

"BET Viewers Voice Concern Over Clips," *Billboard.* 97 (July 13, 1985) 55.

TELEVISION—CABLE NETWORKS—MTV

Bessman, Jim. "Martha Quinn: Japan Wants Its MTV," *Billboard.* 97 (April 13, 1985) 23–24.

DiMauro, Phil. "MTV Launches Ad Campaign With Network TV Time Buys," *Variety.* 321 (October 30, 1985) 91.

Dupler, Steven. "Europe Gets Its MTV," *Billboard.* 98 (November 29, 1986) 1ff.

Dupler, Steven. "MTV Turns to Demo Data from New Ratings Service," *Billboard.* 98 (August 9, 1986) 86.

Dupler, Steven. "MTV's Garland Speaks Out on Clips, Ratings," *Billboard.* 98 (May 24, 1986) 83. il., int.

Dupler, Steven. "MTV's Garland: Vidclip Future Remains Bright," *Billboard.* 98 (May 24, 1986) 1ff.

Dupler, Steven. "Now, Dance Hits are OK on MTV," *Billboard.* 99 (October 24, 1987) 1ff.

Gelman, Eric, and others. "MTV's Message," *Newsweek.* (December 30, 1985) 54–56. il.

Goldberg, Michael. "MTV's Sharper Picture," *Rolling Stone.* n571 (February 8, 1970) 60–64, 118. il.

Jeske, Lee. "MTV '88: Battling to Zap the Zappers, Eeking Out a Nice Little Business," *Cash Box.* (July 30, 1988) 10. il., int. w/Tom Freston, MTV network president and CEO.

"MTV: 1981–1986," *Billboard.* 98 (August 2, 1986) MTV1ff. il.

"MTV Reports Big Revenue and Profit Increases for 1984," *Variety.* 318 (April 17, 1985) 219–220.

"MTV's Prez Sez Video Business is Healthy, Growing," *Variety.* 323 (May 14, 1986) 89.

"News: MTV Goes Acoustic," *Spin.* 5:12 (March 1990) 19. il. Re. "MTV Unplugged."

Rosenbluth, Jean. "MTV Playlist Tightens Against Indies," *Billboard.* 100:24 (June 11, 1988) 72.

Schipper, H. "Survey Claims MTV Has Passed Radio as Disk Sales Stimulus," *Variety.* 321 (November 6, 1985) 87.

Vare, E.A. "MTV Retreat Threatens to Cast Metal Back into Dark Age—With Gold Lining," *Billboard.* 97 (April 27, 1985) MH4ff. il.

Waters, Harry F. "Down to the Sea in Shtik; MTV's Undry Humor," *Newsweek.* (March 19, 1990) 55. il.

Zoglin, Richard, with Elaine Dutka and William Tynan. "MTV Faces a Mid-Life Crisis," *Time.* (June 29, 1987) 67. il.

TELEVISION—CABLE NETWORKS—VIDEO HITS ONE (VH-1)

Bessman, Jim. "VH-1 Set to Unveil a New Look," *Billboard.* 99 (September 12, 1987) 68.

"MTV's New Service Offers an Integrated Musical Mix," *Billboard.* 97 (January 19, 1985) 51ff.

Shalett, M. "On Target: Viewers are Aware of VH-1—and It Appears to Sell Records," *Billboard.* 97 (August 17, 1985) 22.

TELEVISION—CHANNELS—HIT VIDEO

"Hit Video Channel May be Gone in Month, Unless It's Rescued," *Variety.* 328 (September 23, 1987) 159.

TELEVISION—CHANNELS—TV5

Dupler, Steven. "Houston Clips Channel Files Antitrust Suit vs. MTV," *Billboard.* 97 (October 26, 1985) 3ff.

"Houston's TV5 Has 'Community Touch'," *Billboard.* 97 (October 5, 1985) 33.

TELEVISION—CHANNELS—U68

Walter, B. "The Tube: Don't Tread on U68; Why Cable Won't Carry MTV's Competition," *Village Voice.* 31 (January 14, 1986) 39–40.

TELEVISION—PROGRAMS AND PROGAMMING

Dupler, Steven. "Local Vidclip Shows Playing Key Role in Label Promos," *Billboard.* 98 (December 13, 1986) 1ff.

TELEVISION—PROGRAMS AND PROGRAMMING—CLARK, DICK, PRODUCTIONS

Goodman, Fred. "Dick Clark Productions Makes IPO," *Billboard.* 98 (November 29, 1986) 59.

Schipper, Henry. "Dick Clark," *Rolling Stone.* n576 (April 19, 1990) 67–70, 126. il., int.

Seideman, T. "Vestron, Dick Clark Team for *Best of Bandstand*," *Billboard.* 97 (August 31, 1985) 38ff.

TELEVISION—PROGRAMS AND PROGRAMMING—LATE NIGHT WITH DAVID LETTERMAN

Milkowski, Bill. "Hiram Bullock: Late Night Vagabond," *Down Beat.* 51 (June 1984) 24–26. il., disc. Guitarist on the NBS show.

TELEVISION—PROGRAMS AND PROGRAMMING—NIGHT MUSIC

Light, Alan. "NBC's 'Night Music' Awaits Its Fate," *Rolling Stone.* n578 (May 17, 1990) 17.

TELEVISION—PROGRAMS AND PROGRAMMING—NIGHT TRACKS

McGowan, Chris. "The *Night Tracks* Story—from the Beginning," *Billboard.* (June 4, 1988) N-1, N-6, N-12, N-13, N-16. il.

TELEVISION—PROGRAMS AND PROGRAMMING—PUMP IT UP!

Love, Robert, and Jenny Jedeikin. "You! Denise Raps, Too," *Spin.* 6:1 (April 1990) 13. il.

TELEVISION—PROGRAMS AND PROGRAMMING—ROCK 'N' ROLL EVENING NEWS

Dupler, Steven. "Syndicated TV Rock New Program to Bow," *Billboard.* 98 (August 23, 1986) 94.

TELEVISION—PROGRAMS AND PROGRAMMING—ROCK MOMENTS

Bessman, Jim. " 'Rock Moments' Readying TV Debut," *Billboard.* 97 (May 5, 1985) 32.
Re. thirty-second insert series.

TELEVISION—PROGRAMS AND PROGRAMMING—ROCKPLACE

Bessman, Jim. "Houston's *Rockplace* Creates Own Niche," *Billboard.* 97 (February 9, 1985) 37–38.

TELEVISION—REVIEWS (See also: CARPENTERS)

"Editorial: TV Writers Faked Review," *Billboard.* 101 (January 28, 1989) 9.
  Re. *The Karen Carpenter Story.*

TELEVISION—SOUNDTRACKS (See also: FILM SOUNDTRACKS)

Berk, Peter. "*Ruthless People*: The Making of an Epic Soundtrack," *Cash Box.* (June 28, 1986) 11. il.

Dove, I. "Soundtracks Score With Rock 'n' Roll," *ASCAP.* (Spring 1986) 34–35.

Nostalgia (See also: Radio; Rock and Roll Revival)

Corelli, Rae, and others. "Nostalgia Trips," *Maclean's.* (March 21, 1988) 44–47. il.
  Article runs the gamut of 1950s and 1960s culture, with an emphasis on pop music.

DiMauro, Phil. "Sixties are Reborn on New Disks, Second Coming of the Monkees," *Variety.* 324 (August 20, 1986) 77ff.

Handelman, D. "The Same Old Songs: Bands and Radio Programmers Look to Remakes for Sure-Fire Hits," *Rolling Stone.* n544 (January 26, 1989) 11.

Jennings, Nicholas. "The Fight Over Golden Oldies," *Maclean's.* (March 2, 1987) 36–37. il.

Jennings, Nicholas, and others. "Rock Goes Gold," *Maclean's.* (March 2, 1987) 30–34. il.

Politics (See also: Billy Bragg; Jackson Browne; Paul Hardcastle; MC5; Bruce Springsteen; U2)

Harker, Dave. *One for the Money: Politics and Popular Song.* London: Hutchinson, 1980. bibl.

Hibbard, D.J., and C. Kaleialoha. *The Role of Rock: A Guide to the Social and Political Consequences of Rock Music.* Englewood Cliffs, NJ: Prentice-Hall, 1984. il.

Rodgers, S.D. "No Nukes: A Rhetorical Analysis of Music Messages," Ph.D thesis, 1986.

ATWATER, LEE (See also: BLUES REVIVAL)

"Mr. Lee," *Rock & Roll Confidential.* n70 (August 1989) 8. Profile of Atwater.

Owen, Frank. "Chairman of the Blues," *Spin.* 6:3 (June 1990) 29–30. il., int.

UNITED KINGDOM

Frith, Simon. "Britbeat: Soap Box/Soap Opera," *Village Voice.* (November 19, 1985) 67.

"Red Wedge: The Great Debate: The Great Debate," *Melody Maker.* 61 (January 25, 1986) 23–26. il.

Reyonds, Simon, and Frank Owen. "These Loafers Kill Tories,"
   Melody Maker. 61 (November 8, 1986) 20–21. il.
   Delineates the relationship between Socialist realism and
   pop music.

Posters (See also: Art; Record Album Covers)

Farren, Mick, ed. *Get on Down: A Decade of Rock and Roll Posters.*
   London: Big O Publishing Limited, 1977. il.

Grushkin, Paul D. *The Art of Rock: Posters from Presley to Punk.*
   Abbeville, n.p. 1987. il.

Mouse & Kelley. Limpfield, Surrey: Paper Tiger, 1979. il. A
   collection of the work of Mouse (aka Stanley Miller) and
   Alton Kelley.

Public Relations

Taylor, Derek, and George Harrison. *Fifty Years Adrift.* Guildford, U.K.: Genesis, 1985.
   Chronicles the U.S. and U.K. music industry experiences
   of Taylor, the former PR officer for the Beatles.

Record Album Covers (See also: Art; Posters)

Goldmann, Frank, and Klaus Hitscher, eds. *The Gimmix Book
   of Records.* London: Virgin, 1981. il.
   Covers a wide array of curiosities re. packaging and record
   format reaching back decades prior to the rock era.

Lester, Paul. "4AD Day," *Melody Maker.* 66:7 (February 17,
   1990) 10.
   Chronicles the ten-year retrospective exhibition of
   Vaughan Oliver's sleeve designs for the label as well as a

commemorative concert by three of its hottest acts: Lush, the Pale Saints and the Wolfgang Press.

Thorgerson, Storm, and George Hardie, compilers. *An ABC of the Work of Hipgnosis: "Walk Away Rene."* 2nd ed. Limpsfield, Surrey, U.K.: Paper Tiger, 1979. il. Orig. ed.: Limpsfield, Surrey: Dragon's World, 1978.

Religion

Lawhead, Steve. *Rock Reconsidered: A Christian Looks at Contemporary Music.* Downers Groves, IL: Inter-Varsity, 1981.

Riedel, Johannes. *Soul Music, Black and White: The Influence of Black Music on the Churches.* Minneapolis: Augsberg, 1975. disc.

Retailing (See also: Formats; Record Companies)

Goodman, Fred. "NARM Survey: Cassette Sales Outpace LPs Five to Four," *Billboard.* 97 (June 1, 1985) 1ff.

"Label Execs Assure One-Stops, Jobbers About Future of LPs," *Variety.* 321 (November 6, 1985) 87.

Mayfield, Geoff. "Sound Warehouse, Strawberries are Sold," *Billboard.* 101 (January 28, 1989) 1ff.

Mayfield, Geoff. "Stores Eager to Break New Artists," *Billboard.* 100 (October 15, 1988) 34ff.

Moleski, L. "NARM Confab: Rethink Use of Black Vinyl," *Billboard.* 98 (November 15, 1986) 6ff.

PERSONICS

DiMartino, Dave. "Goldman Joins Personics; Firm Readies Taping Test," *Billboard*. 99 (December 19, 1987) 4ff.

DiMartino, Dave, and E. Paige. "Personics to Bow L.A. Test of In-Store Taping System," *Billboard*. 100 (October 22, 1988) 1ff.

"Electronic Disc Jockeys: A New Hit," *Newsweek*. (August 28, 1989) 47. il.

Friedman, Ted. "News: Personic Youth," *Spin*. 6:6 (September 1990) 24. il.

Kassan, Brian. "Personics Custom Audio Cassette System to be Unveiled Soon," *Cash Box*. (May 16, 1987) 29, 31.

Ressner, Jeffrey. "Personics Steps to the Fore . . . ," *Rolling Stone*. n563 (October 19, 1989) 24. il.

Yardumian, Rob. "Enigma Inks With Personics," *Cash Box*. (September 5, 1987) 6, 32.

UNITED KINGDOM

One Stop Shop and Bop," *Rolling Stone*. n575 (April 5, 1990) 21. il.

Sociology

Darzin, Daina. "Multiracial Rock 'N' Roll," *Spin*. 6:1 (April 1990) 18. il.

Doney, Malcolm. *Summer in the City: Rock Music and Way of Life.* Berkhamsted, U.K.: Lion, 1978. il.

Johnson, Brian D., with Nicholas Jennings and Jane Mingay. "Rock 'n' Rebels With a Cause," *Maclean's.* (September 2, 1985) 30–31. il.

Owen, Frank. "The Greening of Planet Pop," *Spin.* 5:10 (January 1990) 38–40, 87. il.

Pielke, Robert G. *You Say You Want a Revolution: Rock Music in American Culture.* Chicago: Nelson-Hall, 1986.

Raeburn, S.D. "Occupation Stress and Coping in a Sample of Professional Rock Musicians: Part 2," *Medical Problems of Performing Artists.* 2:3 (1987) 77–82. bibl., table.

Rogers, Sheila. "The Women's Movement," *Rolling Stone.* n561 (September 21, 1989) 73–86. il.

Savary, Louis M., ed. *Popular Song & Youth Today.* New York: Association, 1971. il.

Silberger, Katherine. "Saturday Night Fervor; Across the American Prairie, Anti-Abortionists Use Rock 'n' Roll and Say-No-to-Sex Pizza Parties to Sell Their Message to Teens," *Spin.* 5:10 (January 1990) 35–37, 86. il.

UNITED KINGDOM

Brake, Mike. *The Sociology of Youth Culture and Youth Subcultures: Sex and Drugs and Rock 'n' Roll?* London: Routledge & Kegan Paul, 1980.

Originally a doctoral thesis, the main thrust is that youth subcultures, as reflected in their musical tastes (among other things), should be viewed as collectively adopted cultural solutions to the problems faced by contemporary youth. Emphasis upon the U.K.

Cohen, Stanley. *Folk Devils and Moral Panics: The Creation of Mods and Rockers.* London: MacGibbon and Kee, 1972. Also pub.: London: Paladin, 1973.

Willis, Paul E. *Profane Culture.* London: Routledge & Kegan Paul, 1978.
Academic approach concerned with British subcultures of the 1960s and early 1970s.

Songwriters

Robinson, Julius. "Demos of Hits Songs on Cypress LP," *Cash Box.* (August 13, 1988) 10.
Re. the compilation of demos from original songwriters.

BACHARACH, BURT, AND HAL DAVID (See: BRILL BUILDING ERA)

BARRY, JEFF, AND ELLIE GREENWICH (See: BRILL BUILDING ERA)

BERRY, RICHARD

Greene, Bob. "The Man Who Wrote 'Louie Louie'," *Esquire.* (September 1988) 63–67. il., int.

" 'Louie Louie' Goes Home," *Musician.* n81 (July 1985) 34.

Smith, R.J. "Swingshift: Mental Health," *Village Voice.* 33 (June 7, 1988) 78. il.
Re. the "Louie Louie" copyright.

BETTIS, JOHN

Robinson, Julius. "Songwriter's Spotlight: John Bettis," *Cash Box.* (July 30, 1988) 12. il., int.

BLACKWELL, BUMPS

[Obituary], *Billboard.* 97 (April 6, 1985) 70.

[Obituary], *Cadence.* 11 (May 1985) 77.

[Obituary], *Variety.* 318 (March 20, 1985) 150.

BLACKWELL, OTIS (See: DEVELOPMENT OF ROCK AND ROLL . . .)

GOFFIN, GERRY, AND CAROLE KING (See: BRILL BUILDING ERA)

JAY, MICHAEL

Robinson, Julius. "Songwriter's Spotlight: Michael Jay," *Cash Box.* (July 23, 1988) 12. il., int.

LEIBER, JERRY, AND MIKE STOLLER (See:
DEVELOPMENT OF ROCK AND ROLL . . .)

MANN, BARRY, AND CYNTHIA WEILL (See:
BRILL BUILDING ERA)

PERCETTO, JEFF

Robinson, Julius. "Songwriter's Spotlight—Jeff Percetto,"
Cash Box. LII:2 (July 9, 1988) 12. il., int.

PETTAWAY, BILL

Considine, J.D. "Bill Pettaway Pumps Out a Hit," *Rolling
Stone.* n574 (March 22, 1990) 33. il.
Profile of writer of Milli Vanilli's "Girl You Know It's
True."

PITCHFORD, DEAN

Mercer, Robert Pierce. "Dean Pitchford: BMI Songwriter of
the Year 1984," *BMI.* (1985) 24–25. il., int.

PREVITE, FRANKE

Robinson, Julius. "Songwriter's Spotlight—Franke Previte,"
Cash Box. LI:44 (May 7, 1988) 18. il., int.

SEDAKA, NEIL (See: BRILL BUILDING ERA)

VALLANCE, JIM (See also: BRYAN ADAMS)

Jennings, Nicholas. "At Work With a Wizard of Song," *Maclean's.* (July 6, 1987) 38. il., int.
A look at the tune crafting techniques employed by Vallance, who is best known as the songwriting partner of Canadian AOR star, Bryan Adams.

WARREN, DIANNE

Edwards, Gavin. "Flash: Solid Gold, Easy Action," *Spin.* 6:6 (September 1990) 18. il., int.

WEBB, JIM

Grein, Paul. "Chart Beat: *Highwayman* Returns Jim Webb to the Top of the Country List," *Billboard.* 97 (August 17, 1985) 6.

"Hall of Fame Inductees," *Variety.* 321 (November 27, 1985) 139.

"*Highwayman* Born Again; Stars Give New Life to Webb Song," *Billboard.* 97 (May 11, 1985) 48.

"Pop Music Academy Adds New Members," *Variety.* 322 (March 12, 1986) 151.

Violence (See also: Rap)

Gett, Steve. "Metal Artist: Let's Cut Out Fan Violence," *Billboard.* 98:31 (August 2, 1986) 1, 77.

Morris, E. "U.K. Promoter Calms Acts on European-Tour Safety," *Billboard.* 98 (May 24, 1986) 32ff.

Orodenker, M.H. "Study: Vidclip Violence Exaggerated," *Billboard.* 98 (September 13, 1986) 43.

Robin, A. "Study on Violence Endorsed; Programmers: There's Too Much," *Billboard.* 97 (January 12, 1985) 32.

Rubin, R. "Music: Authorities Puzzled," *Village Voice.* 31 (August 19, 1986) 70. il.

Schipper, H. "Long Beach Center to Curtail Concerts Following Rap Riots," *Variety.* 324 (August 20, 1986) 78.

Schipper, H. "Terrorism Threat Deters Some Artists from Touring O'Seas," *Variety.* 323 (April 30, 1986) 163ff.

"Violence Following N.Y. Rap Concert Prompts City Action," *Variety.* 323 (July 23, 1986) 70.

APPENDIX A: "REFERENCES" FOR THE LITERATURE OF ROCK III, 1984–1990

1. Albert, George, and Frank Hoffmann (comps.). *The Cashbox Black Contemporary Singles Charts, 1960–1984.* Metuchen, NJ: Scarecrow, 1986.

2. Allen, Doc (ed). *The Electric Anthology: Probes Into Mass Media And Popular Culture.* Dayton, OH: Pflaum, 1975.

3. Aquila, Richard. *That Old Time Rock And Roll: A Chronicle Of An Era, 1954–1963.* New York: Schirmer, 1989.

4. Attali, Jacques. *Noise: The Political Economy Of Music.* Manchester, U.K.: Manchester University Press, 1985.

5. Bacon, Tony (comp.). *Blues Hardware: The Instruments, Equipment, And Technology Of Rock.* New York: Harmony Books, 1981.

6. Baker, Jr., Houston A. *Blues, Ideology, And Afro-American Literature: A Vernacular Theory.* Chicago: University of Chicago Press, 1985.

7. Balfour, Victoria. *Rock Wives: The Hard Lives And Good Times Of The Wives, Girlfriends, And Groupies Of Rock And Roll.* New York: Beech Tree/William Morrow, 1986.

8. Bane, Michael. *White Boy Singin' The Blues: The Black Roots Of White Rock.* New York: Penguin Books, 1982.

9. Bangs, Lester (edited by Greil Marcus). *Psychotic Reactions And Carburetor Dung—The Work Of A Legendary Critic: Rock 'N' Roll As Literature And Literature As Rock 'N' Roll.* New York: Alfred A. Knopf, 1988.

10. Baraka, Amiri, and Amini Baraka. *The Music: Reflections On Jazz And Blues.* New York: William Morrow, 1987.

11. Barlow, William. *"Looking Up At Down": The Emergence Of The Blues Culture.* Philadelphia: Temple University Press, 1989.

12. Barnard, Stephen. *On The Radio: Music Radio In Britain.* Milton Keynes, U.K.: Open University Press, 1989.

13. ———. *Rock: An Illustrated History.* London: MacDonald Orbis, 1986.

14. Barry, Bob. *1990 Daily Celebrity Almanac.* Menomonee Falls, WI: Record Research, 1990.

15. Barson, Michael (comp.). *Rip It Up! Postcards From The Heyday Of Rock 'N' Roll.* New York: Pantheon Books, 1989.

16. Bashe, Philip. *Heavy Metal Thunder: The Music, Its History, Its Heroes.* Garden City, NY: Dolphin Books/Doubleday, 1985.

17. Baskerville, David. *Music Business Handbook And Career Guide* (3rd ed.). Denver, CO: Sherwood Company, 1982.

18. Bastin, Bruce. *Red River Blues: The Blues Tradition In The Southeast.* Urbana, IL: University Of Illinois Press, 1986.

19. Bego, Mark. *Aretha Franklin: The Queen Of Soul.* New York: St. Martin's Press, 1989.

20. ———. *TV Rock.* New York: PaperJacks, Ltd., 1988.

21. Belsito, Peter, and Bob Davis. *Hardcore California: A History Of Punk And New Wave.* Berkeley, CA: Last Gasp Press of San Francisco, 1983.

22. Belz, Carl. *The Story Of Rock* (2nd ed.). New York: Harper and Row, 1972.

23. Bennett, Tony, *et al.* (eds.). *Popular Culture And Social Relations.* Milton Keynes, U.K.: Open University Press, 1986.

24. Benson, Joe (comp.). *Uncle Joe's Record Guide–Volume Three: Eric Clapton, Jimi Hendrix, And The Who.* Glendale, CA: J. Benson Unlimited, 1987.

25. ———. *Uncle Joe's Record Guide–Volume Four: Hard Rock— The First Two Generations.* Glendale, CA: J. Benson Unlimited, 1988.

26. Bergman, Billy, and Richard Horn. *Recombinant Do Re Mi: Frontiers Of The Rock Era.* New York: William Morrow, 1985.

27. Bergman, Billy, Andy Schwartz, Isabelle Leymarie, Tony Sabournin, and Rob Baker. *Hot Sauces: Latin And Caribbean Pop.* New York: Quill Books, 1985.

28. Berlin, Edward A. *Reflections And Research On Ragtime.* Brooklyn, NY: Institute For Studies In American Music, 1987.

29. Betrock, Alan (Comp.). *Rock and Roll Movie Posters.* New York: Shake Books, 1979.

30. Bianco, David. *Heat Wave: The Motown Fact Book.* Ann Arbor, MI: Pierian Press, 1988.

31. ———— (comp.). *Who's New Wave In Music: An Illustrated Encyclopedia, 1976–1982* (The First Wave). Ann Arbor, MI: Pierian Press, 1985.

32. Bigsby, C.W.E. (ed.). *Approaches To Popular Culture.* Bowling Green, OH: Bowling Green State University Popular Press, 1976.

33. ————. *Superculture: American Popular Culture And Europe.* Bowling Green, OH: Bowling Green State University Popular Press, 1975.

34. Birosik, Patti Jean. *The New Age Music Guide: Profiles And Recordings Of 500 Top New Age Musicians.* New York: Collier Books, 1989.

35. Blackwell, Lois S. *The Wings Of The Dove: The Story Of Gospel Music In America.* Norfolk, VA: B. Donning Press. 1978.

36. Bohlman, Philip V. *The Study Of Folk Music In The Modern World.* Bloomington, IN: Indiana University Press, 1988.

37. Booth, Mark W. (comp.). *American Popular Music: A Reference Guide.* Westport, CT: Greenwood Press, 1983.

38. Brake, Robert J. (ed.). *Communication In Popular Culture.* Bowling Green, OH: Bowling Green State University Popular Press, 1975.

39. Breen, Marcus (ed.). *Missing In Action: Australian Popular Music In Perspective.* Kensington, Victoria, Australia: Verbal Graphics, 1987.

40. Brigerman, Chuck. *Record Collector's Fact Book—Volume One: 45 R.P.M., 1952–1965.* Westminster, MD: Disc Publishing, 1982.

41. Bronson, Fred. *The Billboard Book Of Number One Hits: The Inside Story Behind The Top Of The Charts.* New York: Billboard Publications, 1985.

42. ———. *The Billboard Book Of Number One Hits* (revised and enlarged edition). New York: Billboard Publications, 1988.

43. Broughton, Viv. *Black Gospel: An Illustrated History Of The Gospel Sound.* Poole, Dorset, U.K.: Blandford Press, 1985.

44. Broven, John. *South To Louisiana: The Music Of The Cajun Bayous.* Gretna, LA: Pelican Publishing, 1983.

45. Brown, Ashley, and Michael Heatley (eds.). *The Motown Story.* London: Bedford Press, 1985.

46. Brown, Charles T. *The Art of Rock And Roll* (second edition). Englewood Cliffs, NJ: Prentice-Hall, 1987.

47. ———. *Music U.S.A.: America's Country And Western Tradition.* Englewood Cliffs, NJ: Prentice-Hall, 1986.

48. ———. *The Rock And Roll Story: From The Sounds Of Rebellion To An American Art Form.* Englewood Cliffs, NJ: Prentice-Hall, 1983.

49. Browne, Ray B. *Against Academia: The History Of The Popular Culture Association/American Culture Association And The Popular Culture Movement, 1967–1988.* Bowling Green, OH: Bowling Green State University Popular Press, 1989.

50. Bruner, David, *et al. America Through The Looking Glass: A Historical Reader In Popular Culture.* Englewood Cliffs, NJ: Prentice-Hall, 1974.

51. Brunning, Bob. *Blues: The British Connection.* Poole, Dorset, U.K.: Blandford Press, 1986.

52. Buhle, Paul (ed.). *Popular Culture In America.* Minneapolis, MN: University of Minnesota Press, 1987.

53. Burns, Mal (comp.). *Visions Of Rock.* New York: Proteus Books, 1981.

54. Burt, Rob. *Surf City/Drag City.* New York: Sterling Publishing, 1986.

55. Busnar, Gene. *It's Rock 'N' Roll: A Musical History Of The Fabulous Fifties.* New York: Wanderer Books, 1979.

56. Butterfield, Arthur. *Encyclopedia Of Country Music.* New York: Gallery Books, 1985.

57. Canale, Larry (ed.). *Digital Audio's Guide To Compact Discs.* New York: Bantam Books, 1986.

58. Carlton, Joseph R. (comp.). *Carlton's Complete Reference Book Of Music.* Studio City, CA: Carlton Publications, 1980.

59. Carney, George O. (ed.). *The Sounds Of People And Places: Readings In The Geography Of American Folk And Popular Music.* Lanham, MD: University Press of America, 1987.

60. ———. *The Sounds Of People And Places: Readings In The Geography Of Music.* Washington, DC: University Press of America, 1979.

61. Carr, Ian, Digby Fairweather, and Brian Priestley. *Jazz: The Essential Companion.* London: Grafton Press, 1987.

62. Case, Brian, *et al. The Illustrated History Of Jazz* (revised edition). London: Salamander Press, 1986.

63. Castleman, Harry, and Walter J. Podrazik. *Watching TV: Four Decades Of American Television.* New York: McGraw-Hill, 1982.

64. *CD International/CD World Reference Guide: Popular Music Edition.* Milwaukie, OR: Compact Disc International Publishing, 1990.

65. Chantry, Art. *Instant Litter: Concert Posters From Seattle Punk Culture.* Seattle: Real Comet Press, 1985.

66. Chapple, Steve, and Reebee Garofalo. *Rock 'N' Roll Is Here To Pay: The History And Politics Of The Music Industry.* Chicago: Nelson-Hall, Inc., 1977.

67. Charlesworth, Chris. *A–Z Of Rock Guitarists.* New York: Proteus Press, 1982.

68. Chase, Gilbert. *America's Music: From The Pilgrims To The Present* (revised 3rd ed.). Urbana, IL: University of Illinois Press, 1987.

69. Christensen, Roger and Karen (comps.). *Christensen's Ultimate Movie, TV, And Rock 'N' Roll Directory* (3rd ed.). San Diego, CA: Cardiff-By-The-Sea Press, 1988.

70. Christgau, Robert. *Any Old Way You Choose It: Rock And Other Pop Music, 1967–1973.* Baltimore: Penguin Books, 1973.

71. ———— (comp.). *Christgau's Record Guide: Rock Albums Of The Seventies.* New York: Ticknor and Fields, 1981.

72. ————. *Rock Albums Of The '70s: A Critical Guide.* New York: Da Capo Press, Inc., 1990.

73. Clark, Al (comp.). *The Rock Yearbook 1982.* New York: St. Martin's Press, 1981.

74. ———— (ed.). *The Rock Yearbook 1983.* New York: St. Martin's Press, 1982.

75. ———— (ed.). *The Rock Yearbook 1984.* New York: St. Martin's Press, 1984.

76. Clark, Alan (comp.). *Legends Of Sun Records.* West Covina, CA: A. Clark Productions, 1986.

77. ————. *Rock And Roll Legends—Number One.* West Covina, CA: Leap Frog Productions, 1981.

78. ————. *Rock And Roll Legends—Number Two.* West Covina, CA: Leap Frog Productions, 1982.

79. ————. *Rock And Roll Legends—Number Three.* West Covina, CA: Leap Frog Productions, 1982.

80. ————. *Rock And Roll Legends—Number Four.* West Covina, CA: Leap Frog Productions, 1983.

81. ————. *Rock And Roll Legends—Number Five.* West Covina, CA: Leap Frog Productions, 1984.

82. ————. *Rock And Roll Memories—Number One.* West Covina, CA: Alan Lungstrum Productions, 1987.

83. ————. *Rock And Roll Memories—Number Two.* West Covina, CA: Alan Lungstrum Productions, 1987.

84. ————. *Rock And Roll In The Movies—Number Four.* West Covina, CA: Alan Lungstrum/National Rock 'N' Roll Archives, 1989.

85. ————. *Rock-A-Billy And Country Legends—Number One.* West Covina, CA: Alan Clark Productions, 1986.

86. ————. *Sun Photo Album.* West Covina, CA: National Rock 'N' Roll Archives, 1986.

87. Clark, Ed (ed.). *Rock Yearbook 1982*. London: Virgin Books, 1981.

88. Clarke, Donald (ed.). *The Penguin Encyclopedia Of Popular Music*. New York: Viking/Penguin, 1989.

89. Clayson, Alan. *Call Up The Groups! The Golden Age Of British Beat, 1962–1967*. Poole, Dorset, U.K.: Blandford Press, 1986.

90. Clayton, Peter, and Peter Gammond. *Jazz A–Z*. New York: Sterling Publishing, 1987.

91. Clee, Ken (comp.). *The Directory Of American 45 R.P.M. Records—3 Volumes*. Philadelphia: Stak-O-Wax, 1981.

92. ———. *The Directory Of American 45 R.P.M. Records—3 Volumes*. Philadelphia: Stak-O-Wax, 1981.

93. ———. *The Directory Of American 45 R.P.M. Records— Volume One*. Philadelphia: Stak-O-Wax, 1981.

94. ———. *The Directory Of American 45 R.P.M. Records— Volume Two* (revised edition). Philadelphia: Stak-O-Wax, 1985.

95. ———. *The Directory Of American 45 R.P.M. Records— Volume Two*. Philadelphia: Stak-O-Wax, 1981.

96. ———. *The Directory Of American 45 R.P.M. Records— Volume Three*. Philadelphia: Stak-O-Wax, 1981.

97. ———. *The Directory Of American 45 R.P.M. Records— Volume Three* (revised edition). Philadelphia: Stak-O-Wax, 1986.

98. ———. *The Directory Of American 45 R.P.M. Records—Volume Four.* Philadelphia: Stak-O-Wax, 1983.

99. ———. *The Directory Of American 45 R.P.M. Records: Reissue Directory.* Philadelphia: Stak-O-Wax, 1984.

100. ———. *A Discography Collection Of Artists And Labels* (2nd ed.). Philadelphia: Stak-O-Wax, 1979.

101. Clifford, Mike. *The Harmony Illustrated Encyclopedia Of Rock* (5th ed.). New York: Crown Publishers, 1986.

102. Cohen, Norm (with music edited by David Cohen). *Long Steel Rail: The Railroad In American Folksong.* Urbana, IL: University of Illinois Press, 1981.

103. Cohen-Stratyner, Barbara (editor). *Popular Music, 1900–1919: An Annotated Guide To American Popular Songs.* Detroit: Gale Research, 1988.

104. Cohn, Nik. *Ball The Wall: Nik Cohn In The Age Of Rock.* London: Picador Books, 1989.

105. Collins, John. *African Pop Roots: The Inside Rhythms Of Africa.* London: Foulsham Books, 1985.

106. Colman, Stuart. *They Kept On Rockin': The Giants Of Rock 'N' Roll.* Poole, Dorset, U.K.: Blandford Press, 1982.

107. Cooper, B. Lee, and Wayne S. Haney. *Response Recordings:An Answer Song Discography.* Metuchen, NJ: Scarecrow, 1990.

108. Cooper, Michael. *Blinds And Shutters: The Photographs Of Michael Cooper.* Atlanta: Christopher, Cabot, and Fuller, 1990.

109. Corenthal, Michael G. *The Iconography Of Recorded Sound 1886–1986: One Hundred Years Of Commercial Entertainment And Collecting Opportunity.* Milwaukee, WI: Yesterday's Memories, 1986.

110. Cott, Jonathan, and Christine Doudna (eds.). *The Ballad Of John And Yoko.* Garden City, NY: Doubleday, 1982.

111. Cotten, Lee. *Shake, Rattle, And Roll—The Golden Age Of American Rock 'N' Roll: Volume One, 1952–1955.* Ann Arbor, MI: Pierian Press, 1989.

112. Coupe, Stuart, and Glenn A. Baker. *The New Rock 'N' Roll: The A–Z Of Rock In The '80s.* New York: St. Martin's Press, 1983.

113. Cranna, Ian (ed.). *The Rock Yearbook 1986.* New York: St. Martin's Press, 1985.

114. ————. *The Rock Yearbook—Volume 8* New York: St. Martin's Press, 1988.

115. Cross, Colin, with Paul Kendall and Mick Farren (comps.). *Encyclopedia Of British Beat Groups And Solo Artists Of The Sixties.* London: Omnibus Press, 1980.

116. Crowther, Bruce, and Mike Pinfold. *The Jazz Singers: From Ragtime To The New Wave.* Poole, Dorset, U.K.: Blandford Press, 1986.

117. Curry, Jack. *Woodstock: The Summer Of Our Lives.* New York: Weidenfeld and Nicolson, 1989.

118. Curtis, James M. *Rock Eras: Interpretations Of Music And Society, 1954–1984.* Bowling Green, OH: Bowling Green State University Popular Press, 1987.

119. Cuscuna, Michael, an Michel Ruppli (comps.). *The Blue Note Label: A Discography.* Westport, CT: Greenwood Press, 1988.

120. Dahl, Linda. *Stormy Weather: The Music And Lives Of A Century Of Jazz Women.* New York: Pantheon, 1984.

121. Daniels, William R. (comp.). *The American 45 And 78 RPM Record Dating Guide, 1940–1959.* Westport, CT: Greenwood Press, 1985.

122. Darter, Tom (ed.). *The Whole Synthesizer Catalogue.* Milwaukee, WI: Hal Leonard Publishing, 1985.

123. Davis, Sharon. *Motown: The History.* Enfield, Middlesex, U.K.: Guinness Superlatives, Ltd., 1989.

124. Dearling, Robert, and Celia Dearling. *The Guinness Book Of Music* (3rd ed.). New York: Sterling Publishing, 1986.

125. Debenham, Warren (comp.). *Laughter On Record: A Comedy Discography.* Metuchen, NJ: Scarecrow, 1988.

126. Dellar, Fred. *Rock And Pop Crosswords.* London: Zomba Books, 1983.

127. ———. *Where Did You Go To, My Lovely? The Lost Sounds And Stars Of The Sixties.* London: Star Books, 1983.

128. Dellar Fred, and Alan Lackett. *The Harmony Illustrated Encyclopedia Of Country Music.* New York: Harmony Books, 1987 (c. 1986).

129. Dellar, Fred, and Richard Wootton (comps.). *The Country Music Book Of Lists.* New York: Times Books, 1984.

130. Denisoff, R. Serge. *Inside MTV.* New Brunswick, NJ: Transaction Books, 1988.

131. ————. *Sing A Song Of Social Significance* (3rd ed.). Bowling Green, OH: Bowling Green State University Popular Press, 1983.

132. ————. *Solid Gold: The Popular Record Industry.* New Brunswick, NJ: Transaction Books, 1975.

133. Denisoff, R. Serge, and Richard A. Peterson (eds.). *The Sounds Of Social Change: Studies In Popular Culture.* Chicago: Rand McNally, 1972.

134. Denisoff, R. Serge, with the assistance of William L. Schurk. *Tarnished Gold: The Record Industry Revisited.* New Brunswick, NJ: Transaction Books, 1986.

135. Des Barres, Pamela. *I'm With The Band: Confessions Of A Groupie.* New York: Beech Tree Books, 1987.

136. DeWitt, Howard A. *Chuck Berry: Rock 'N' Roll Music* (2nd ed.). Ann Arbor, MI: Pierian Press, 1985.

137. Dr. Licks. *Standing In The Shadows Of Motown: The Life And Music Of Legendary Bassist James Jamerson.* Milwaukee WI: Hal Leonard Publishing, 1989.

138. Doerschuk, Bob (ed.). *Rock Keyboard.* New York: Quill/ Keyboard Books, 1985.

139. Dorf, Michael, and Robert Appel (eds.). *Gigging: The Musician's Underground Touring Directory.* Cincinnati, OH: Writer's Digest, 1989.

140. Doyle, Mike. *A History Of Marshall Valve Guitar Amplifiers*. Shaftesbury, Dorset, U.K.: Musical New Services, 1982.

141. Duncan, Robert. *The Noise: Notes From A Rock 'N' Roll Era*. New York: Ticknor and Fields, 1984.

142. ———. *Only The Good Die Young: The Rock 'N' Roll Book Of The Dead*. New York: Harmony Books, 1986.

143. Durant, J.B. *A Student's Guide To American Jazz And Popular Music: Outlines, Recordings, And Historical Commentary*. Scottsdale, AZ: J.B. Durant, 1984.

144. Dutfoy, Serge, Dominique Farran, and Michael Sadler. *Rock Toons: A Cartoon History Of The First Thirty Years Of Rock 'N' Roll*. New York: Harmony Books, 1986.

145. Duxbury, Janell R. *Rockin' The Classics And Classicizin' The Rock: A Selectively Annotated Discography*. Westport, CT: Greenwood Press, 1985.

146. Eberling, Philip K. *Music In The Air: America's Changing Tastes In Popular Music, 1920–1980*. New York: Hastings House, 1982.

147. Edelstein, Andrew J. *The Pop Sixties: A Personal And Irreverent Guide*. New York: World Almanac Publications, 1985.

148. Editors of Guitar Player Magazine. *The Guitar Player Book* (revised and updated 3rd ed.). New York: Grove Press, 1983.

149. Edwards, Joseph (comp.). *Top 10's And Trivia Of Rock And Roll And Rhythm And Blues, 1950–1980.* St. Louis: Blueberry Hill Publishing, 1981.

150. Eisen, Jonathan (ed.). *The Age Of Rock: Sounds Of The American Cultural Revolution.* New York: Vintage Books, 1969.

151. ———. *The Age Of Rock/2: Sights And Sounds Of The American Cultural Revolution.* New York: Vintage Books, 1970.

152. ———. *Twenty-Minute Fandangos And Forever Changes: A Rock Bazaar.* New York: Vintage Books, 1971.

153. Eisenberg, Evan. *The Recording Angel: Explorations In Phonography.* New York: McGraw-Hill, 1987.

154. Eliot, Marc. *Rockonomics: The Time Behind The Music.* New York: Watts Press, 1989.

155. Ellison, Mary. *Lyrical Protest: Black Music's Struggle Against Discrimination.* New York: Praeger Books, 1989.

156. Elrod, Bruce C. (comp.). *Your Hit Parade And American Top Ten Hits, 1958–1984* (3rd ed.). White Rock, SC: B. Elrod, 1985.

157. Elson, Howard. *Early Rockers.* New York: Proteus Books, 1982.

158. Endres, Clifford. *Austin City Limits: The Story Behind Television's Most Popular Country Music Program.* Austin, TX: University of Texas Press, 1987.

159. Eremo, Judie (ed.). *Country Musicians: The Carter Family, Charlie Daniels, Waylon Jennings, Bill Monroe, Willie Nelson, Ricky Skaggs, Merle Travis, And 27 Other Great American Artists—Their Music And How They Make It.* New York: Grove Press, 1987.

160. Escott, Colin, and Martin Hawkins. *Sun Records: The Brief History Of The Legendary Record Label.* New York: Quick Fox, 1980.

161. ————. *Sun Records: The Discography.* Bremen, West Germany: Bear Family, 1987.

162. Evans, David. *Big Road Blues: Tradition And Creativity In The Folk Blues.* Jersey City, NJ: Da Capo Press, 1987.

163. Evans, Tom, and Mary Anne Evans. *Guitars: Music, History, Construction, And Players From Renaissance To Rock.* New York: Facts On File, 1977.

164. Ewen, David. *American Songwriters: 144 Biographies Of America's Greatest Popular Composers And Lyricists* (expanded edition). New York: Wilson Press, 1986.

165. Fantel, Hans, and Ivan Berger. *The New Sound Of Stereo: The Complete Buying Guide To Buying And Using The Latest Hi-Fi Equipment.* New York: New American Library, 1986.

166. Feather, Leonard. *The Jazz Years: Earwitness To An Era.* New York: Quartet Books, 1986.

167. Feigin, Leo (ed.). *Russian Jazz—New Identity.* New York: Quartet Books, 1985.

168. Ferguson, Charles, and Herb Johnson (comps.). *Mainstream Jazz Reference And Price Guide, 1949–65.* Phoenix: O'Sullivan Woodside and Company, 1984.

169. Ferlingere, Robert D. (comp.). *A Discography of Rhythm & Blues And Rock 'N' Roll Vocal Groups, 1945 to 1965.* Hayward, CA: California Trade School, 1976.

170. Ferris, William, and Mary L. Hart (eds.). *Folk Music And Modern Sound.* University, MS: University of Mississippi Center for the Study of Southern Culture, 1982.

171. Field, Shelly. *Career Opportunities In The Music Industry.* New York: Facts On File, 1986.

172. Fink, Michael. *Inside The Music Business: Music In Contemporary Life.* New York: Schirmer Books, 1989.

173. Finn, Julio. *The Bluesman: The Musical Heritage Of Black Men And Women In The Americas.* London: Quarter Books, 1986.

174. Fisher, Clive. *Music Industry Organizations: A Specially Commissioned Report.* London: Longman, 1987.

175. Flanagan, Bill. *Written In My Soul: Conversations With Rock's Great Songwriters.* Chicago: Contemporary Books, 1987.

176. Flans, Robyn. *Musicmania: From Rock To New Wave.* Cresskill, NJ: Starbook/Sharon Publications, 1983.

177. Floyd, Samuel A., Jr. *Black Music In The Harlem Renaissance.* Westport, CT: Greenwood Press, 1991.

178. Fornatale, Pete. *The Story Of Rock 'N' Roll.* New York: William Morrow, 1987.

179. Fowler, Gene, and Bill Crawford. *Border Radio.* Austin, TX: Texas Monthly Press, 1987.

180. Fox, Ted. *In The Groove: The Men Behind The Music.* New York: St. Martin's Press, 1986.

181. Frame, Pete. *The Complete Rock Family Trees—Books I and II.* London: Omnibus Press, 1983.

182. Frame, Pete, John Tobler, Ed Hanel, Roger St. Pierre, Chris Trengove, John Beecher, Clive Richardson, Gary Cooper, Marsha Hanlon, and Linda Sandahl. *The Harmony Illustrated Encyclopedia Of Rock* (6th ed.). New York: Harmony Books, 1989.

183. Frith, Simon (ed.). *Facing The Music.* New York: Pantheon Books, 1988.

184. Frith, Simon. *Music For Pleasure: Essays In The Sociology Of Pop.* New York: Routledge, Chapman, and Hall, 1988.

185. Frith, Simon. *Soul And Motown.* London: Routledge and Kegan Paul, 1988.

186. Frith, Simon. *Sound Effects: Youth, Leisure, And The Politics Of Rock 'N' Roll.* New York: Pantheon Books, 1981.

187. Frith, Simon (ed.). *World Music, Politics, And Social Change.* Manchester, U.K.: Manchester University Press, 1989.

188. Frith, Simon, and Andrew Goodwin (eds.). *On Record: Rock, Pop, And The Written Word.* New York: Pantheon Books, 1990.

189. Frith, Simon, and Howard Horne. *Art Into Pop.* New York: Methuen Books, 1987.

190. Funaro, Artie, and Artie Traum. *Chicago Blues Guitar.* New York: Oak Publications, 1983.

191. Gambaccini, Paul. *Masters Of Rock.* London: Omnibus Press, 1982.

192. Gambaccini, Paul. *The Top 100 Rock 'N' Roll Albums Of All Time.* New York: Harmony Books, 1987.

193. Gambaccini, Paul. *Track Records: Profiles Of 22 Rock Stars.* North Pomfret, VT: David and Charles, 1986.

194. Gammond, Peter. *The Oxford Companion To Popular Music.* New York: Oxford University Press, 1991.

195. Gans, David, and Peter Simon. *Playing In The Band.* New York: St. Martin's Press, 1985.

196. Ganzl, Kurt. *The Blackwell Guide To The Musical Theatre On Record.* Cambridge, MA: Basil Blackwell, 1990.

197. Garbutt, Bob. *Rockabilly Queens: The Careers And Recordings Of Wanda Jackson, Janis Martin, And Brenda Lee.* Toronto, Ontario, Canada: Ducktail Press, 1979.

198. Garfield, Simon. *Expensive Habits: The Dark Side Of The Music Industry.* London: Faber and Faber, 1986.

199. Garland, Phyl. *The Sound Of Soul: The History Of Black Music.* Chicago: Henry Regnery, 1969.

200. Gart, Galen (comp.). *ARLD: The American Record Label Directory And Dating Guide, 1940–1959.* Milford, NH: Big Nickel Publications, 1988.

201. ———— (comp.). *First Pressings—The History Of Rhythm And Blues: Volume Three, 1953.* Milford, NH: Big Nickel Publications, 1989.

202. ———— (comp.). *First Pressings—The History Of Rhythm And Blues: Volume Four, 1954.* Milford, NH: Big Nickel Publications, 1989.

203. Gart, Galen, and Roy C. Ames, with contributions from Ray Funk, Rob Bowman and David Booth. *Duke/Peacock Records: An Illustrated History With Discography.* Milford, NH: Big Nickel Publications, 1990.

204. Garvey, Mark (ed.). *1990 Song Writer's Market: Where And How To Market Your Songs.* Cincinnati, OH: Writer's Digest, 1989.

205. Geist, Christopher D., Ray B. Browne, Michael T. Marsden, and Carole Palmer (comps). *Directory Of Popular Culture Collections.* Phoenix: Oryx Press, 1989.

206. George, Nelson. *The Death Of Rhythm And Blues.* New York: Pantheon Books, 1988.

207. ————. *Top Of The Charts—The Most Complete Listing Ever: The Top 10 Records And Albums For Every Week Of Every Year From 1970.* Piscataway, NJ: New Century, 1983.

208. ———. *Where Did Our Love Go? The Rise And Fall Of The Motown Sound.* New York: St. Martin's Press, 1985.

209. *Giants In A Small World: Music Life Rock Photo Gallery.* New York: Chappell Music, 1975.

210. Gibson, James R. *How You Can Make $30,000 A Year As A Musician—Without A Record Contract.* Cincinnati, OH: Writer's Digest, 1986.

211. Giddins, Gary. *Rhythm-A-Ning: Jazz Tradition And Innovation In The '80s.* New York: Oxford University Press, 1985.

212. ———. *Riding On A Blue Note: Jazz And American Pop.* New York: Oxford University Press, 1981.

213. Gillett, Charlie. *Making Tracks: Atlantic Records And The Growth Of A Multi-Billion-Dollar Industry.* New York: E.P. Dutton, 1974.

214. ———. *The Sound Of The City: The Rise Of Rock And Roll* (rev. ed.). New York: Pantheon Books, 1983.

215. Godwin, Jeff. *The Devil's Disciples: The Truth About Rock.* Chino, CA: Chick Publications, 1985.

216. Goldman, Albert. *Freakshow.* New York: Atheneum Press, 1971.

217. Golson, G. Barry (ed.). *The Playboy Interview With John Lennon And Yoko Ono.* New York: Playboy Press, 1981.

218. Gordon, Mark, and Jack Nachbar (comps.). *Currents Of Warm Life: Popular Culture In American Higher Education.*

Bowling Green, OH: Bowling Green State University Popular Press, 1980.

219. Gordon, Robert. *Jazz West Coast: The Los Angeles Jazz Scene Of The 1950s.* New York: Quartet Books, 1986.

220. Gore, Tipper. *Raising PG Kids In An X-Rated Society.* Nashville, TN: Abingdon Press, 1987.

221. Goshen, Larry G. (edited by Stephen Sylvester). *Indy's Heart Of Rock 'N' Roll.* Los Angeles, CA: Metro Publications, 1986.

222. Govenar, Alan. *Living Texas Blues.* Dallas: Dallas Museum of Art, 1985.

223. ————. *Meeting The Blues: The Rise Of The Texas Sound.* Dallas: Taylor Publishing, 1988.

224. Gowans, Alan. *Learning To See: Historical Perspectives On Modern Popular/Commercial Arts.* Bowling Green, OH: Bowling Green State University Popular Press, 1981.

225. Gray, Michael H. (comp.). *Bibliography Of Discographies— Volume Three: Popular Music.* New York: R.R. Bowker, 1983.

226. Green, Jeff (comp.). *The 1987 Green Book: Songs Classified By Subject.* Altadena, CA: Professional Desk Reference, 1986.

227. Green, Lucy. *Music On Deaf Ears: Musical Meaning, Ideology, And Education.* Manchester, U.K.: University Press, 1988.

228. Greenberg, Keith Elliot. *RAP.* Minneapolis: Lerner Publications, 1988.

229. Greig, Charlotte. *Will You Still Love Me Tomorrow? Girl Groups From The 50s On . . .* London: Virago Press, 1989.

230. Grendysa, Peter A. *Catalog-Index Of Articles On Rhythm 'N' Blues, Blues, And Rock 'N' Roll, 1970–1983.* Caledonia, WI: Sorghum Switch Press, 1983

231. Gridley, Mark C. *Jazz Styles: History And Analysis* (2nd ed.). Englewood Cliffs, NJ: Prentice-Hall, 1985.

232. Gritter, Headley. *Rock 'N' Roll Asylum.* New York: Delilah Books, 1984.

233. Groia, Philip. *They All Sang On The Corner: A Second Look At New York City's Rhythm And Blues Vocal Groups* (rev. ed.). West Hempstead, NY: Phillie Dee Enterprises, 1984.

234. Grushkin, Paul D. *The Art Of Rock: Posters From Presley To Punk.* New York: Abbeville Press, 1987.

235. Guernsey, Otis (ed.). *Broadway Song And Story: Playwrights/Lyricists/Composers Discuss Their Hits.* New York: Dodd, Mead and Company, 1985.

236. Guralnick, Peter. *Feel Like Going Home: Portraits In Blues And Rock 'N' Roll.* New York: Outerbridge and Dienstfrey, 1971.

237. ———. *Listener's Guide To The Blues.* New York: Facts On File, 1982.

238. ———. *Lost Highway: Journeys And Arrivals Of American Musicians.* Boston: David R. Godine, 1979.

239. ———. *Sweet Soul Music: Rhythm And Blues And The Southern Dream Of Freedom.* New York: Harper and Row, 1986.

240. Hagensen, Rich (comp.). *Strictly Instrumental.* New Westminster, British Columbia, Canada: R. Hagensen, 1986.

241. Hall, Stuart, and Paddy Whannel. *The Popular Arts: A Critical Guide To The Mass Media.* New York: Pantheon Books, 1964.

242. Hamm, Charles. *Afro-American Music, South Africa, And Apartheid.* Brooklyn, NY: Institute for Studies in American Music, 1988.

243. Hamm, Charles. *Music In The New World.* New York: W.W. Norton and Company, 1983.

244. Hamm, Charles E., Brunno Nettl, and Ronald Byrnside. *Contemporary Music And Music Cultures.* Englewood Cliffs, NJ: Prentice-Hall, 1975.

245. Hammel, William M. (ed.). *The Popular Arts In America: A Reader.* New York: Harcourt Brace Jovanovich, 1972.

246. Hanel, Ed (comp.). *The Essential Guide To Rock Books.* London: Omnibus Books, 1983.

247. Haralambos, Michael. *Right On: From Blues To Soul In Black America.* New York: Drake Publishers, 1975.

248. Hardy, Phil, and Dave Laing, *The Faber Companion To 20th-Century Popular Music.* London: Faber and Faber, 1990.

249. Hardy, Phil, and Dave Laing, with additional material by Stephen Barnard and Don Perretta. *Encyclopedia Of Rock* (updated version). London: MacDonald Books, 1987.

250. Harker, Dave. *One For The Money: Politics And The Popular Song.* London: Hutchinson and Co., 1980.

251. Harper, Betty. *Suddenly And Gently: Visions Of Elvis Through The Art Of Betty Harper.* New York: St. Martin's Press, 1987.

252. Harris, Sheldon (comp.). *Blues Who's Who: A Biographical Dictionary Of Blues Singers.* New Rochelle, NY: Arlington House, 1979.

253. Harris, Steve. *Jazz On Compact Disc: A Critical Guide To The Best Recordings.* New York: Harmony Books, 1987.

254. Hasse, John Edward (ed.). *Ragtime: Its History, Composers, And Music.* New York: Schirmer Books, 1985.

255. Havlice, Patricia Pate (comp.). *Popular Song Index.* Metuchen, NJ: Scarecrow, 1975.

256. ——— (comp.). *Popular Song Index—First Supplement.* Metuchen, NJ: Scarecrow, 1978.

257. ——— (comp.). *Popular Song Index—Second Supplement.* Metuchen, NJ: Scarecrow, 1984.

258. ——— (comp.). *Popular Song Index—Third Supplement.* Metuchen, NJ: Scarecrow, 1989.

259. Heggeness, Fred (comp.). *Promo Record Price Guide.* Detroit Lakes, MN: F.H. Publishing, 1986.

260. ——— (comp.). *Rarest Of The Rare: Record Price Guide.* Detroit Lakes, MN: F.H. Publishing, 1986.

261. Heilbut, Anthony. *The Gospel Sound: Good News And Bad Times* (revised and updated). New York: Limelight Editions, 1985.

262. Heintze, James R. *American Music Studies: A Classified Bibliography Of Master's Theses.* Detroit: Information Coordinators, 1985.

263. Helander, Brock (comp.). *The Rock Who's Who: A Biographical Dictionary And Critical Discography—Including Rhythm-And-Blues, Soul, Rockabilly, Folk, Country, Easy Listening, Punk, And New Wave.* New York: Schirmer Books, 1982.

264. Hendler, Herb. *Year By Year In The Rock Era: Events And Conditions Shaping The Rock Generations That Reshaped America.* Westport, CT: Greenwood Press, 1983.

265. Herbst, Peter (ed.). *The Rolling Stone Interviews: Talking With The Legends Of Rock And Roll, 1967–1980.* New York: St. Martin's/Rolling Stone Press, 1981.

266. Herman, Gary. *Rock 'N' Roll Babylon.* London: Plexus Books, 1982.

267. Hibbard, Don J., and Carol Kaleialoha. *The Role Of Rock.* Englewood Cliffs, NJ: Prentice-Hall, 1983.

268. Hibbert, Tom (comp.). *The Perfect Collection.* London: Proteus Books, 1982.

269. ———— (comp.). *Rare Records: Wax Trash And Vinyl Treasures.* New York: Proteus Books, 1982.

270. ———— (ed.). *The Rock Yearbook 1987.* New York: St. Martin's Press, 1986.

271. Hill, Dave. *Designer Boys And Material Girls: Manufacturing The 80's Pop Dream.* New York: Sterling Publishing, 1986.

272. Hirsch, Paul, and James W. Carey (eds.). *Communication And Culture: Humanistic Models In Research.* Beverly Hills, CA: Sage Publications, 1978.

273. Hirshey, Gerri. *Nowhere To Run: The Story Of Soul Music.* New York: Penguin Books, 1984.

274. Hiscock, Melvyn. *Make Your Own Electric Guitar.* Poole, Dorset, U.K.: Blandford Press, 1986.

275. Hoare, Ian, Tony Cummings, Clive Anderson, and Simon Frith. *The Soul Book.* New York: Dell Publishing, 1976.

276. Hockinson, Michael J. *Nothing Is Beatle Proof: Advanced Beatles Trivia For Fab Four Fanciers.* Ann Arbor, MI: Popular Culture, Ink., 1990.

277. Hoffmann, Frank W. (comp.). *The Literature Of Rock, 1954–1978.* Metuchen, NJ: Scarecrow, 1981.

278. ———— (comp.). *Popular Culture And Libraries.* Hamden, CT: Library Professional Publications, Shoe String Press, 1984.

279. Hoffmann, Frank, and George Albert, with the assistance of Lee Ann Hoffmann (comps.). *The Cashbox Album Charts, 1955–1974.* Metuchen, NJ: Scarecrow, 1988.

280. ————. *The Cashbox Album Charts, 1975–1985.* Metuchen, NJ: Scarecrow, 1987.

281. ————. *The Cash Box Country Album Charts, 1964–1988.* Metuchen, NJ: Scarecrow, 1989.

282. Hoffmann, Frank W., and William G. Bailey. *Arts And Entertainment Fads.* Binghamton, NY: Haworth Press, 1990.

283. Holmes, Thomas B. *Electronic And Experimental Music.* New York: Charles Scribner's Sons, 1985.

284. Holt, Sid (ed.). *The Rolling Stone Interviews: The 1980s.* New York: St. Martin's/Rolling Stone Press, 1989.

285. Hood, Phil (ed.). *Artists Of American Folk Music: The Legends Of Traditional Folk, The Stars Of The Sixties, And Virtuosi Of New Acoustic Music.* New York: Quill/William Morrow, 1986.

286. Hoover, Cynthia A. *Music Machines—American Style: A Catalog Of The Exhibition.* Washington, DC: Published for the National Museum of History and Technology by the Smithsonian Institution Press, 1971.

287. Horn, David (comp.). *The Literature Of American Music In Books And Folk Music Collections: A Fully Annotated Bibliography.* Metuchen, NJ: Scarecrow, 1977.

288. Horn, David, with Richard Jackson (comps.). *The Literature Of American Music In Books And Folk Music Collections: A Fully Annotated Bibliography—Supplement I.* Metuchen, NJ: Scarecrow, 1988.

289. Horstman, Dorothy. *Sing Your Heart Out, Country Boy* (revised edition). Nashville, TN: Country Music Foundation, 1986.

290. Hoskyns, Barney. *Say It One Time For The Broken Hearted: The Country Side Of Southern Soul.* London: Fontana Books, 1987.

291. Hounsome, Terry (comp.). *New Rock Record.* New York: Facts On File, 1983.

292. ——— (comp.). *Rock Record: A Collectors' Directory Of Rock Albums And Musicians* (enlarged, revised, expanded edition). New York: Facts On File, 1987.

293. Hudgeons III, Thomas E. (ed.). *The Official 1983 Price Guide To Records* (fourth edition). Orlando, FL: House of Collectibles, 1983.

294. Huebel, Harry Russell (ed.). *Things In The Driver's Seat: Readings In Popular Culture.* Chicago: Rand McNally, 1972.

295. Hume, Martha. *You're So Cold I'm Turning Blue: Martha Hume's Guide To The Greatest In Country Music.* New York: Viking Books, 1982.

296. Inge, M. Thomas (ed.). *Concise Histories Of American Popular Culture.* Westport, CT: Greenwood Press, 1982.

297. ———— (ed.). *Handbook of American Culture* (2nd ed.). Westport, CT: Greenwood Press, 1989.

298. ———— (ed.). *Handbook Of American Popular Culture: Volume One.* Westport, CT: Greenwood Press, Inc., 1978.

299. ———— (ed.). *Handbook Of American Popular Culture: Volume Three.* Westport, CT: Greenwood Press, 1981.

300. Iwaschkin, Roman (comp.). *Popular Music: A Reference Guide.* New York: Garland Publishing, 1986.

301. Jacobs, Dick. *Who Wrote That Song?* Crozet, VA: Betterway Publications, 1988.

302. Jahn, Mike. *Rock: From Elvis Presley To The Rolling Stones.* New York: Quadrangle Books, 1973.

303. Jancik, Wayne. *The Billboard Book Of One-Hit Wonders.* New York: Billboard/Watson-Guptill, 1990.

304. Jasper, Tony. *Fab! The Sounds Of The Sixties—The Records, The Charts, The Stars, Radio And TV, Pop Films, The Festivals.* Poole, Dorset, U.K.: Blandford Press, 1984.

305. ————. *I Read The News Today: Great Rock And Pop Headlines.* London: Willow Books, 1986.

306. ————. *The 70s: A Book Of Records.* London: MacDonald Futura Publishers, 1980.

307. Jasper, Tony, Derek Oliver, Steve Hammond, and Dave Reynolds (comps.). *The International Encyclopedia Of Hard Rock And Heavy Metal.* New York: Facts On File, 1983.

308. Javna, John. *The TV Theme Song Sing-Along Song Book— Volume 2.* New York: Hal Leonard Publishing/St. Martin's Press, 1985.

309. Johnson, Howard, and Jim Pines. *Reggae: Deep Roots Music.* London: Proteus Books, 1982.

310. Jones, Allan. *The Rock Yearbook 1985.* New York: St. Martin's Press, 1985.

311. Jones, Hettie. *Big Star Fallin' Mama: Five Women In Black Music.* New York: Viking Press, 1974.

312. Jones, LeRoi. [Imamu Amiri Baraka] *Black Music.* New York: William Morrow, 1968.

313. ————. *Blues People.* New York: William Morrow, 1963.

314. Jones, Mablen. *Getting It On: The Clothing Of Rock 'N' Roll.* New York: Abbeville Press, 1987.

315. Jones, Wayne. *Rockin', Rollin', And Rappin'.* Fraser, MI.: Goldmine Press, 1980.

316. Jordan, Charles. *The Official Price Guide To Collectibles Of The '50s And '60s.* New York: Ballantine/House Of Collectibles, 1988.

317. Josefs, Jai. *Writing Music For Hit Songs.* Cincinnati, OH: Writer's Digest, 1989.

318. Joynson, Vernon (comp.). *The Acid Trip: A Complete Guide To Psychedelic Music.* Todmorden, U.K.: Babylon Books, 1984.

319. Kaiser, Charles. *1968 In America: Music, Politics, Chaos, Counterculture, And The Shaping Of A Generation.* New York: Weidenfeld and Nicolson, 1988.

320. Kaplan, E. Ann. *Rocking Around The Clock: Music Television, Postmodernism, And Consumer Culture.* New York: Methuen Press, 1987.

321. Keil, Charles. *Urban Blues.* Chicago: University of Chicago Press, 1966.

322. Kent, Jeff. *The Rise And Fall Of Rock.* Stoke-On-Trent, U.K.: Witan Books, 1983.

323. Kienzle, Rich. *Great Guitarists: The Most Influential Players In Blues, Country Music, Jazz And Rock.* New York: Facts On File, 1985.

324. Kienzle, Rich, *et al. Country Music Catalog, 1989–1990.* El Cerrito, CA: Down Home Music, 1989.

325. Kiersh, Edward. *Where Are You Now, Bo Diddley? The Artists Who Made Us Rock And Where They Are Now.* Garden City, NY: Dolphin/Doubleday Books, 1986.

326. Kinder, Bob. *The Best Of The First: The Early Days Of Rock And Roll.* Chicago: Adams Press, 1986.

327. Kingman, Daniel. *American Music: A Panorama* (2nd ed.). New York: Schirmer Books, 1990.

328. Kingsbury, Paul, and Alan Axelrod (eds.). *Country: The Music And The Musicians.* New York: Abbeville Press, 1988.

329. Klaase, Piet (text by Mark Gardner and J. Bernlef). *Jam Session: Portraits Of Jazz And Blues Musicians Drawn On The Scene.* Newton Abbot, Devon, U.K.: David and Charles, 1985.

330. Klavens, Kent J. *Protecting Your Songs And Yourself: The Songwriter's Legal Guide.* Cincinnati, OH: Writer's Digest, 1989.

331. Klitsch, Hans Jurgen, with assistance from Mike Korbik (comps.). *Great Bands/Small Labels.* Mulheim, West Germany: Gorilla Beat, 1979.

332. Kocandrle, Mirek (comp.). *The History Of Rock And Roll: A Selective Discography.* Boston: G.K. Hall, 1988.

333. Koskoff, Ellen (ed.). *Women and Music in Crass-Cultural Perspective.* Champaign-Urbana, IL: University of Illinois, 1989.

334. Kozinn, Allan, Pete Welding, Dan Forte, and Gene Santoro. *The Guitar: The History, The Music, The Players.* New York: Quill Books, 1984.

335. Kratochvil, Laurie (ed.). *Rolling Stone: The Photographs.* New York: Simon and Schuster, 1989.

336. Kris, Eric. *Beginning Blues Piano: Everything You Need To Know To Become An Accomplished Performer Of Blues Piano.* New York: Amsco Publications, 1984.

337. Krummel, D.W., Jean Geil, Doris J. Dyen, and Deane L. Root. *Resources Of American Music History: A Directory Of Source Materials From Colonial Times To World War II.* Urbana, IL: University of Illinois Press, 1981.

338. ———. *Bibliographical Handbook Of American Music.* Urbana, IL: University of Illinois Press, 1987.

339. LaBlanc, Michael L. *Contemporary Musicians—Volume One: Profiles Of The People In Music.* Detroit: Gale Research, 1989.

340. LaForse, Martin W., and James A. Drake. *Popular Culture And American Life: Selected Topics In The Study Of American Popular Culture.* Chicago: Nelson-Hall, Inc., 1981.

341. Laing, Dave. *One Chord Wonders: Power And Meaning In Punk Rock.* Milton Keynes, U.K.: Open University Press, 1985.

342. Landrum, Larry N. *American Popular Culture: A Guide To Information Sources.* Detroit: Gale Research, 1982.

343. Larson, Bob. *Your Kids And Rock.* Wheaton, IL: Tyndale House, 1988.

344. Law, Lisa. *Flashing On The Sixties.* New York: State Mutual Book and Publishing, 1988.

345. Lawhead, Steve. *Rock Of This Age: The Real And Imagined Dangers Of Rock Music.* Downers Grove, IL: Intervarsity Press, 1987.

346. Lax, Roger, and Frederick Smith (comps.). *The Great Song Thesaurus.* New York: Oxford University Press, 1984.

347. ———— (comps.). *The Great Song Thesaurus* (updated edition). New York: Oxford University Press, 1988.

348. Lazell, Barry, and Dafydd Rees (comps.). *The Illustrated Book Of Rock Records—Volume 2.* New York: Delilah Books, 1983.

349. Lazell, Barry, with Dafydd Rees and Luke Crampton (eds.). *Rock Movers And Shakers: An A To Z Of The People Who Made Rock Happen.* New York: Billboard Publications, 1989.

350. Leadbitter, Mike, and Neil Slaven. *Blues Records, 1943–70: A Selective Discography* (2nd ed.). London: Record Information Services, 1987.

351. LeMesurier, Robin, and Peggy Sue Honeyman-Scott. *Rock 'N' Roll Cuisine.* New York: Billboard Books, 1988.

352. Leonard, Neil. *Jazz And White Americans: The Acceptance Of A New Art Form.* Chicago: University of Chicago Press, 1962.

353. ————. *Jazz: Myth And Religion.* New York: Oxford University Press, 1987.

354. Leonard, Terry. *Goldmine's Jazz Price Guide.* Iola, WI: Krause Publications, 1990.

355. Leppert, Richard, and Susan McClary (eds.). *Music And Society: The Politics Of Composition, Performance, And Reception.* Cambridge, U.K.: Cambridge University Press, 1987.

356. Levine, Lawrence W. *Black Culture And Black Consciousness: Afro-American Folk Thought From Slavery To Freedom.* New York: Oxford University Press, 1977.

357. Lewis, George H. (ed.). *Side-Saddle On The Golden Calf: Social Structure And Popular Culture In America.* Pacific Palisades, CA: Goodyear Publishing Company, 1972.

358. Lewis, Peter M., and Jerry Booth. *The Invisible Medium: Public, Commercial, And Community Radio.* London: Macmillan Books, 1989.

359. Lieberman, Robbie. *My Song Is My Weapon: People's Songs, American Communism, And The Politics Of Culture, 1930–1950.* Urbana, IL: University of Illinois Press, 1989.

360. Lifton, Sarah. *The Listener's Guide To Folk Music.* New York: Facts On File, 1983.

361. Liggett, Mark, and Cathy Liggett. *The Complete Handbook Of Songwriting: An Insiders' Guide To Making It In The Music Industry.* New York: New American Library, 1985.

362. Lindsay, Joe (comp.). *The "Record Label" Guide For Domestic LPs: The Reference Manual For "Disc-Dating" Your 12-Inch Phono Albums.* Scottsdale, AZ: Biodisc, 1986.

363. Locantro, Tony. *Some Girls Do And Some Girls Don't: Sheet Music Covers.* New York: Quartet Books, 1985.

364. Logan, Nick, and Bob Woffinden. *The Illustrated Encyclopedia Of Rock.* (rev. ed.). London: Salamander Books, 1982.

365. Lohof, Bruce A. *American Commonplace: Essays On The Popular Culture Of The United States*. Bowling Green, OH: Bowling Green State University Popular Press, 1982.

366. Lomax III, John. *Nashville: Music City U.S.A.* New York: Harry N. Abrams, 1985.

367. London, Herbert I. *Closing The Circle: A Cultural History Of The Rock Revolution*. Chicago: Nelson-Hall, Inc., 1984.

368. Lowe, Jacques, Russell Miller, and Roger Boar. *The Incredible Music Machine: 100 Glorious Years*. London: Quartet/Visual Arts Books, 1982.

369. Lull, James (ed.). *Popular Music And Communication*. Newbury Park, CA: Sage Publications, 1987.

370. Lydon, Michael. *Rock Folk: Portraits From The Rock 'N' Roll Pantheon*. New York: Dial Press, 1971.

371. Lydon, Michael, and Ellen Mandel. *Boogie Lightning: How Music Became Electric* (2nd ed.). New York: Da Capo Press, 1980.

372. MacDonald, J. Fred. *Blacks And White TV: Afro-Americans In Television Since 1948*. Chicago: Nelson-Hall, Inc., 1983.

373. ———. *Don't Touch That Dial! Radio Programming In American Life From 1920 To 1960*. Chicago: Nelson-Hall, Inc., 1979.

374. ———. *Television And The Red Menace: The Video Road To Vietnam*. New York: Praeger Books, 1985.

375. Macken, Bob, Peter Fornatale, and Bill Ayres (comps.). *The Rock Music Source Book.* Garden City, NY: Doubleday, 1980.

376. Makower, Joel. *Woodstock: The Oral History.* Garden City, NY: Tilden Press/Doubleday, 1989.

377. Malone, Bill C., *Country Music U.S.A.* (rev. ed.). Austin, TX: University of Texas Press, 1985.

378. Maltby, Richard. *Dreams For Sale: Popular Culture In The 20th Century.* London: Harrap, 1989.

379. Marcus, Greil. *Lipstick Traces: A Secret History Of The Twentieth Century.* Cambridge, MA: Harvard University Press, 1989.

380. ———. *Mystery Train.* (rev. and exp. ed.). New York: E.P. Dutton, 1982.

381. ——— (ed.). *Stranded: Rock And Roll For A Desert Island.* New York: Alfred A. Knopf, 1979.

382. Mare, Jeremy, and Hannah Charlton. *Beats Of The Heart: Popular Music For The World.* New York: Pantheon Books, 1985.

383. Marschall, Rick [Richard]. *The Encyclopedia Of Country And Western Music.* New York: Exeter Books, 1985.

384. Marsh, Dave. *Fortunate Son.* New York: Random House, 1985.

385. ———. *The Heart Of Rock And Soul: The 1001 Greatest Singles Ever Made.* New York: New American Library, 1989.

386. ————. *Sun City, By Artists United Against Apartheid: The Struggle For Freedom In South Africa—The Making Of The Record.* New York: Penguin Books, unpaged.

387. Marsh, Dave, with Lee Ballinger, Sandra Choron, Wendy Smith, and Daniel Wolff. *The First Rock And Roll Confidential Report: Inside The Real World Of Rock And Roll.* New York: Pantheon Books, 1985.

388. Marsh, Dave, Sandra Choron, and Debbie Geller. *Rocktopicon: Unlikely Questions And Their Surprising Answers.* Chicago: Contemporary Books, 1984.

389. Marsh, Ritchie, and Sam Johnson. *Encyclopedia Of Rock/ Pop Stars.* New York: Gallery Books, 1985.

390. Martin, George (ed.). *Making Music: The Guide To Writing, Performing, And Recording.* London: Pan Books, 1983.

391. Martin, Linda, and Kerry Segrave. *Anti-Rock: The Opposition To Rock 'N' Roll.* Hamden, CT: Archon Books, 1988.

392. Marty, Daniel. *The Illustrated History Of Phonographs.* New York: VILO, Inc., 1979.

393. Mason, Michael (ed.). *The Country Music Book.* New York: Charles Scribner's Sons, 1985.

394. Mawhinney, Paul C. (comp.). *MusicMaster: The 45 RPM Record Directory, 1947–1982* (Volume I–Artist). Pittsburgh: Record-Rama, 1983.

395. ————. *MusicMaster: The 45 RPM Record Directory, 1947–1982* (Volume II–Title). Pittsburgh: Record-Rama, 1983.

396. ———. *MusicMaster—The 45 RPM Record Directory: 35 Years Of Recorded Music, 1947 To 1982.* (2 vols.). Allison Park, PA: Record-Rama, 1983.

397. Mayo, Edith (ed.). *American Material Culture: The Shape Of Things Around Us.* Bowling Green, OH: Bowling Green State University Popular Press, 1984.

398. McCutcheon, Lynn Ellis. *Rhythm And Blues.* Arlington, VA: Beatty Publications, 1971.

399. McDonough, Jack. *San Francisco Rock: The Illustrated History Of San Francisco Rock Music.* San Francisco: Chronicle Books, 1985.

400. McGuiness, Tom. *So You Want To Be A Rock 'N' Roll Star?* London: Javelin Books, 1986.

401. McKee, Margaret, and Fred Chisenhall. *Beale Black And Blue: Life And Music On Black America's Main Street.* Baton Rouge, LA: Louisiana State University Press, 1981.

402. McKenna, John, and Michael Moffitt. *The Complete Air Guitar Handbook.* New York: Pocket Books, 1983.

403. McNutt, Randy. *We Wanna Boogie: An Illustrated History Of The American Rockabilly Movement.* Fairfield, OH: Hamilton Hobby Press, 1988.

404. McRobbie, Angela (ed.). *Zoot Suits And Second-Hand Dresses: An Anthology Of Fashion And Music.* Winchester, MA: Unwin Hyman, 1989.

405. McWilliams, Jerry. *The Preservation And Restoration Of Sound Recordings.* Nashville, TN: American Association for State and Local History Press, 1979.

406. Meeth, L.R. and Dean S. Gregory (comps.). *Directory Of Teaching Innovations In History.* Arlington, VA: Studies in Higher Education, 1981.

407. Melhuish, Martin. *Heart Of Gold: 30 Years Of Canadian Pop Music.* Toronto, Ontario, Canada: Canadian Broadcasting Corporation, 1983.

408. Mellers, Wilfrid. *Angels Of The Night: Popular Female Singers Of Our Time.* New York: Basil Blackwell, 1986.

409. ————. *Angels Of The Night: Popular Female Singers Of Our Time.* Oxford: Basil Blackwell, 1986.

410. Meltzer, Richard. *The Aesthetics Of Rock.* Jersey City, NJ: Da Capo Press, 1987.

411. Middleton, Richard. *Studying Popular Music.* Milton Keynes, U.K.: Open University Press, 1989.

412. Middleton, Richard, and David Horn (eds.). *Popular Music 1: Folk Or Popular? Distinctions, Influences, Continuities.* Cambridge, U.K.: Cambridge University Press, 1981.

413. ———— (eds.). *Popular Music 2: Theory And Method.* Cambridge, U.K.: Cambridge University Press, 1982.

414. ———— (eds.). *Popular Music 3: Producers And Markets.* Cambridge, U.K.: Cambridge University Press, 1983.

415. ———— (eds.). *Popular Music 4: Performers And Audiences.* Cambridge, U.K.: Cambridge University Press, 1984.

416. Miles (ed.). *Sex, Drugs, And Rock 'N' Roll.* London: Gallo Books, 1984.

417. Miller, Jim (ed.). *The Rolling Stone Illustrated History Of Rock And Roll* (2nd ed.). New York: Random House/ Rolling Stone Press, 1980.

418. Miller, Terry E. *Folk Music In America: A Reference Guide.* New York: Garland Publishers, 1986.

419. Mollica, Gary (comp.). *Vintage Rock 'N' Roll Catalog, 1986.* El Cerrito, CA: Down Home Music, 1986.

420. Morley, Paul. *Ask: The Chatter Of Pop.* London: Faber and Faber, 1986.

421. Morris, Gina. *Happy Doin' What We're Doin': The Pub Rock Years, 1972–1975.* San Fancisco: Nightbird Books, 1984.

422. ————. *Off-Beat: Pub Rock For The '80s.* San Francisco: Nightbird Books, 1985.

423. Morrison, Joan, and Robert Morrison. *From Camelot To Kent State: The Sixties Experience In the Words Of Those Who Lived It.* New York: Quadrangle/Times Books, 1987.

424. Morse, David. *Motown And The Arrival Of Black Music.* New York: Collier Books, 1971.

425. Morthland, John. *The Best Of Country Music: A Critical And Historical Guide To The 750 Greatest Albums.* Garden City, NY: Dolphin/Doubleday, 1984.

426. Muirhead, Bert. *The Record Producers File: A Directory Of Rock Album Producers, 1962–1984.* Poole, Dorset, U.K.: Blandford Press, 1984.

427. Muirhead, Bert, and Mark Hagen. *The Hit Songwriter's File: A Directory Of Writers, Artists, And Their Chart Hits, 1955–1985.* Poole, Dorset, U.K.: Blandford Press, 1986.

428. Murrells, Joseph (comp.). *Million Selling Records From The 1900s To The 1980s: An Illustrated Directory.* New York: Arco, 1984.

429. Musto, Michael. *Downtown.* New York: Vintage Books, 1986.

430. Nachbar, Jack, Deborah Weiser, and John L. Wright (comps.). *The Popular Culture Reader.* Bowling Green, OH: Bowling Green State University Popular Press, 1978.

431. Naha, Ed (comp.). *Lillian Roxon's Rock Encyclopedia.* (revised edition). New York: Grosset and Dunlap, 1978.

432. Nash, Alanna. *Behind Closed Doors: Talking With The Legends Of Country Music.* New York: Alfred A. Knopf, 1988.

433. Nickerson, Marina, and Cynthia Farah. *Country Music: A Look At The Men Who've Made It.* El Paso, TX: C.M. Publishing, 1981.

434. Nightingale, Anne. *Chase To Fade: Music, Memories, And Memorabilia.* Poole, Dorset, U.K.: Blandford Press, 1981.

435. Nite, Norm N. (comp.). *Rock On—The Illustrated Encyclopedia Of Rock 'N' Roll: Volume 1—The Solid Gold Years* (updated edition). New York: Harper and Row, 1982.

436. ————. *Rock On Almanac: The First Four Decades Of Rock 'N' Roll—A Chronology.* New York: Harper and Row, 1989.

437. Nite, Norm N., with Charles Crespo (comps.). *Rock On—The Illustrated Encyclopedia Of Rock 'N' Roll: Volume 3—The Video Revolution, 1978–Present.* New York: Harper and Row, 1985.

438. Nite, Norm N., with Ralph M. Newman (comps.). *Rock On—The Illustrated Encyclopedia Of Rock 'N' Roll: Volume 2—The Years Of Change, 1964–1978* (updated edition). New York: Harper and Row, 1984.

439. Noble, Peter L. *Future Pop: Music For The Eighties.* New York: Delilah Books, 1983.

440. Norman, Philip. *The Road Goes On Forever: Portraits From A Journey Through Contemporary Music.* New York: Fireside Books, 1982.

441. Nye, Russel B. (ed.). *New Dimensions In Popular Culture.* Bowling Green, OH: Bowling Green State University Popular Press, 1972.

442. ———. *The Unembarrassed Muse: The Popular Arts In America.* New York: Dial Press, 1970.

443. Oakley, Giles. *The Devil's Music: A History Of The Blues* (rev. ed.). London: British Broadcasting Corporation, 1983.

444. Obrecht, Jas (ed.). *Masters Of Heavy Metal.* New York: Quill/Guitar Player Books, 1984.

445. ———. (ed.). *Texas Guitar.* Cupertino, CA: Guitar Player Books, 1987.

446. O'Brien, Geoffrey. *Dream Time: Chapters From The Sixties.* New York: Penguin Books, 1989.

447. O'Brien, Lucy. *Dusty.* London: Sidgwick & Jackson, 1989.

448. Obst, Lynda R. (ed.). *The Sixties: The Decade Remembered Now, By The People Who Lived It Then.* New York: Random House/Rolling Stone Press, 1977.

449. Oermann, Robert K., with Douglas B. Green. *The Listener's Guide To Country Music.* New York: Facts On File, 1983.

450. Oliver, Paul (ed.). *The Blackwell Guide To Blues Records.* Cambridge, MA: Basil Blackwell, 1989.

451. Oliver, Paul. *Blues Fell This Morning: Meaning In The Blues.* Cambridge, U.K.: Cambridge University Press, 1990 (c. 1960).

452. Oliver, Paul, Max Harrison, and William Bolcom. *The New Grove Gospel, Blues, and Jazz.* New York: W.W. Norton, 1988.

453. ———. *The New Grove Gospel, Blues, And Jazz, With Spirituals And Ragtime.* New York: W.W. Norton, 1986.

454. Orman, John. *The Politics Of Rock Music.* Chicago: Nelson-Hall, Inc., 1984.

455. Osborne, Jerry. *The Complete Library Of American Phonograph Recordings 1959.* Port Townsend, WA: Osborne Enterprises, 1987.

456. Osborne, Jerry (comp.). *Elvis: Like Any Other Soldier.* Port Townsend, WA: Osborne Enterprises, 1989.

457. ——— (comp.). *Our Best To You—From Record Digest.* Prescott, AZ: Record Digest, 1979.

458. ———. *Rockin' Records: 1989 Edition.* Port Townsend, WA: Osborne Enterprises, 1989.

459. ——— (comp.). *Rockin' Records: Buyers/Sellers Reference Book And Price Guide* (Tenth Anniversary Edition). Tempe, AZ: Osborne Enterprises, 1986.

460. Osborne, Jerry, and Bruce Hamilton (comps.). *Blues/ Rhythm And Blues/Soul: Original Record Collectors Price Guide* (first edition). Phoenix, AZ: O'Sullivan, Woodside and Company, 1980.

461. O'Shea, Shad. *Just For The Record.* Cincinnati, Ohio: Positive Feedback Communications, 1986.

462. Palmer, Robert. *Deep Blues.* New York: Viking Press, 1981.

463. Palmer, Roy. *The Sound Of History: Songs And Social Comment.* New York: Oxford University Press, 1988.

464. Pareles, Jon, and Patricia Romanowski (eds.). *The Rolling Stone Encyclopedia Of Rock And Roll.* New York: Rolling Stone/Summit Books, 1983.

465. Parents' Music Resource Center. *Let's Talk Rock: A Primer For Parents.* Arlington, VA: Parents' Music Resource Center, 1986.

466. Parker, Thomas, and Douglas Nelson. *Day By Day: The Sixties.* New York: Facts On File, 1983.

467. Pascall, Jeremy, and Bob Burt. *The Stars And Superstars Of Black Music.* Secaucus, NJ: Chartwell Books, 1977.

468. Pattillo, Craig W. *TV Theme Soundtrack Directory And Discography With Cover Versions.* Portland, OR: Braemer Books, 1990.

469. Pattison, Robert. *The Triumph Of Vulgarity: Rock Music In The Mirror Of Romanticism.* New York: Oxford University Press, 1987.

470. Pavletich, Aida. *Sirens Of Song: The Popular Female Vocalist In America.* New York: Da Capo Press, 1980.

471. Pavlow, Al. *Big Al Pavlow's The Rhythm 'N' Blues Book: A Disc-History Of Rhythm 'N' Blues.* Providence, RI: Music House Publishing, 1983.

472. Pawlowski, Gareth L. *How They Became The Beatles: A Definitive History of the Early Years, 1960–1964.* New York: Dutton, 1989.

473. Pearson, Barry Lee. *"Sounds So Good To Me": The Bluesman's Story.* Philadelphia: University of Pennsylvania Press, 1984.

474. Pearson, Jr., Nathan W. *Goin' To Kansas City.* Urbana, IL: University of Illinois Press, 1987.

475. Peck, Richard. *Rock: Making Musical Choices.* Greenville, SC: Bob Jones University Press, 1985.

476. Peters, Dan, *et al.* *What About Christian Rock?* Minneapolis: Bethany House, 1986.

477. Petrie, Gavin (ed.). *Black Music.* London: Hamlyn Publishing, 1974.

478. ———— (comp.). *Rock Life.* London: Hamlyn Publishing, 1974.

479. Petts, Leonard. *The Story Of "Nipper" And The "His Master's Voice" Picture Painted By Francis Barraud* (second revised edition). Bournemouth, U.K.: E. Bayly/Talking Machine Review International, 1983.

480. Philbin, Marianne (ed.). *Give Peace A Chance: Music And The Struggle For Peace.* Chicago: Chicago Review Press, 1983.

481. Pichaske, David R. *A Generation In Motion: Popular Music And Culture In The Sixties.* Granite Falls, MN: Ellis Press, 1989.

482. ————. *The Poetry Of Rock: The Golden Years.* Peoria, IL: Ellis Press, 1981.

483. Pielke, Robert G. *You Say You Want A Revolution: Rock Music In American Culture.* Chicago: Nelson-Hall, Inc., 1986.

484. Podell, Janet (ed.). *Rock Music In America.* New York: H.W. Wilson, 1987.

485. Pollock, Bruce (ed.). *Popular Music—An Annotated Index Of American Popular Songs: Volume 7—1970–1974.* Detroit: Gale Research, 1984.

486. —— (ed.). *Popular Music—An Annotated Index Of American Popular Songs: Volume 8—1975–1979.* Detroit: Gale Research, 1984.

487. —— (ed.). *Popular Music 1980–1984: Volume 9.* Detroit: Gale Research, 1986.

488. —— (ed.). *Popular Music 1985—Volume 10.* Detroit: Gale Research, 1986.

489. —— (ed.). *Popular Music 1986—Volume 11.* Detroit: Gale Research, 1987.

490. —— (ed.). *Popular Music 1987—Volume 12.* Detroit: Gale Research, 1988.

491. —— (ed.). *Popular Music 1988—Volume 13.* Detroit: Gale Research, 1989.

492. Pratt, Ray. *Rhythm And Resistance: Explorations In The Political Uses Of Popular Music.* New York: Praeger Books, 1990.

493. Priest, Daniel B. (comp.). *American Sheet Music With Prices: A Guide To Collecting Sheet Music From 1775 To 1975.* Des Moines, IA: Wallace-Homestead Book Company, 1979.

494. Quirin, Jim, and Barry Cohen. *Chartmasters' Rock 100: An Authoritative Ranking Of The 100 Most Popular Songs For Each Year, 1956 Through 1986* (4th ed.). Covington, LA: Chartmasters, 1986.

495. Rachlin, Harvey. *The Songwriter's And Musician's Guide To Demos.* Cincinnati, OH: Writer's Digest, 1988.

496. Ramsey, Frederic, Jr. *Been Here And Gone.* New Brunswick, NJ: Rutgers University Press, 1960.

497. Redd, Lawrence N. *Rock Is Rhythm And Blues: The Impact Of Mass Media.* East Lansing, MI: Michigan State University Press, 1974.

498. Rees, Tony. *Rare Rock: A Collectors' Guide.* Poole, Dorset, U.K.: Blandford Press, 1985.

499. ————. *Rare Rock: A Collectors' Guide.* New York: Sterling Books, 1986.

500. Reiff, Carole. *Nights In Birdland: Jazz Photographs, 1954–1960.* New York: Simon and Schuster, 1987.

501. Repsch, John. *The Legendary Joe Meek: The Telstar Man.* London: Woodford House, 1989.

502. Riese, Randall. *Nashville Babylon: The Uncensored Truth And Private Lives Of Country Music's Stars.* New York: Congdon and Weede, 1988.

503. Rimler, Walter. *Not Fade Away: A Comparison Of Jazz Age With Rock Era Pop Song Composers.* Ann Arbor, MI: Pierian Press, 1984.

504. Rimmer, Dave. *Like Punk Never Happened: Culture Club And The New Pop.* London: Faber and Faber, 1985.

505. Riordan, James. *Making It In The New Music Business.* Cincinnati, OH: Writer's Digest, 1988.

506. Rissover, Fredric, and David C. Birch (eds.). *Mass Media And The Popular Arts* (3rd ed.). New York: McGraw-Hill, 1983.

507. Riswick, Don (comp.). *Nothin' But Instrumentals: A Compendium Of Rock Instrumentals.* Virginia Beach, VA: D. Riswick, 1985.

508. Robbins, Ira A. (ed.). *The New Trouser Press Record Guide* (2nd ed.). New York: Charles Scribner's Sons, 1985.

509. ———— (ed.). *The Rolling Stone Review 1985: The Year In Rock Music.* New York: Charles Scribner's Sons/Rolling Stone Press, 1985.

510. ———— (ed.). *The Trouser Press Guide To New Wave Records.* New York: Charles Scribner's Sons, 1983.

511. Roberts, John Storm. *Black Music Of Two Worlds.* New York: William Morrow, 1974.

512. *Rock Guitarists.* Saratoga, NY: Guitar Player Productions, 1974.

513. *Rock Guitarists—Volume 2.* Saratoga, NY: Guitar Player Productions, 1978.

514. Rockwell, John. *All American Music: Composition In The Late Twentieth Century.* New York: A.A. Knopf, 1983.

515. Rogers, Alice. *Dance Bands And Big Bands: Reference Book And Price Guide.* Tempe, AZ: Jellyroll Productions, 1986.

516. Rogers, Dave. *Rock 'N' Roll.* London: Routledge and Kegan Paul, 1982.

517. Rogers, Don. *Dance Halls, Armories, And Teen Fairs: A History And Discography Of Pacific Northwest Rock And Pop*

Recording Artists Of The Fifties And Sixties—Volume One. Hollywood, CA: Music Archives Press, 1989.

518. Rogers, Jimmie N. *The Country Music Message: All About Lovin' and Livin'.* Englewood Cliffs, NJ: Prentice-Hall, 1983.

519. ————. *The Country Music Message: Revisited.* Fayetteville, AR: University of Arkansas Press, 1989.

520. Rollin, Roger (ed.). *The Americanization Of The Global Village: Essays In Comparative Popular Culture.* Bowling Green, OH: Bowling Green State University Popular Press, 1989.

521. Rooney, John F. Jr., Wilber Zelinsky, and Dean R. Louder (general editors). *This Remarkable Continent: An Atlas Of United States And Canadian Society And Cultures.* College Station, TX: For The Society For The North American Cultural Survey By Texas A&M University Press, 1982.

522. Root, Jr., Robert L. *The Rhetorics of Popular Culture: Advertising, Advocacy, And Entertainment.* Westport, CT: Greenwood Press, 1987.

523. Rose, Brian (ed.). *TV Genres: A Handbook And Reference Guide.* Westport, CT: Greenwood Press, 1985.

524. Rosenberg, Neil V. *Bluegrass: A History.* Urbana, IL: University of Illinois Press, 1985.

525. Roth, Arlen. *Rock Guitar For Future Stars.* New York: Ballantine Books, 1986.

526. Rowe, Mike. *Chicago Blues: The City And The Music.* New York: Da Capo Press, 1981.

527. Ruppli, Michel, with the assistance of Bill Daniels (comps.). *The King Labels: A Discography.* Westport, CT: Greenwood Press, 1985.

528. Ruppli, Michel, with assistance from Bob Porter (comps.). *The Clef/Verve Labels: A Discography (2 Volumes).* Westport, CT: Greenwood Press, 1986.

529. ————. *The Prestige Label: A Discography.* Westport, CT: Greenwood Press, 1980.

530. ————. *The Savoy Label: A Discography.* Westport, CT: Greenwood Press, 1980.

531. Russell, Ethan A. *Dear Mr. Fantasy: Ten Years In The Heart Of Rock And Roll.* Boston: Houghton Mifflin, 1985.

532. Russell, Tony (ed.). *The Encyclopedia Of Rock.* London: Crescent Books, 1983.

533. Ryan, Jack. *Recollections—The Detroit Years: The Motown Sound By The People Who Made It.* Detroit: J. Ryan (Data Graphics/Whitlaker Marketing), 1982.

534. Ryan, John. *The Production Of Culture In The Music Industry: The ASCAP—BMI Controversy.* Lanham, MD: University Press of America, 1985.

535. Rypens, Arnold. *The Originals: 'You Can't Judge A Song By The Cover'.* Brussels, Belgium: BRT Vitgrave, 1987.

536. Sallis, James. *The Guitar Players: One Instrument And Its Masters In American Music.* New York: William Morrow, 1982.

537. Sanjek, Russell. *American Popular Music And Its Business— The First Four Hundred Years: Volume One, The Beginning To 1790.* New York: Oxford University Press, 1988.

538. ————. *American Popular Music And Its Business—The First Four Hundred Years: Volume Two, 1790–1909.* New York: Oxford University Press, 1988.

539. ————. *American Popular Music And Its Business—The First Four Hundred Years: Volume Three, 1900–1984.* New York: Oxford University Press, 1988.

540. ————. *From Print To Plastic: Publishing And Promoting America's Popular Music, 1900–1980.* Brooklyn, NY: Institute for Studies in American Music in The Conservatory of Music at Brooklyn College, City University of New York, 1983.

541. Santelli, Robert. *Sixties Rock: A Listener's Guide.* Chicago: Contemporary Books, 1985.

542. Savage, William W., Jr. *Singing Cowboys And All That Jazz: A Short History Of Popular Music In Oklahoma.* Norman, OK: University of Oklahoma Press, 1983.

543. Savoy, Ann Allen. *Cajun Music: A Reflection Of A People— Volume One.* Eunice, LA: Bluebird Press, 1984.

544. Sayres, Sohnya, Anders Stephanson, Stanley Aronowitz, and Fredric Jameson (eds.). *The '60s Without Apology.* Minneapolis: University of Minnesota Press, 1985.

545. Schaefer, John. *New Sounds: A Listener's Guide To New Music.* New York: Harper and Row, 1987.

546. Scheer, David W. *PG: A Parental Guide To Rock.* Camp Hill, PA: Christian Publications, 1986.

547. Scheurer, Timothy E. (ed.). *American Popular Music— Volume One; The 19th Century And Tin Pan Alley.* Bowling Green, OH: Bowling Green State University Popular Press, 1989.

548. ——— (ed.). *American Popular Music—Volume Two: The Age Of Rock.* Bowling Green, OH: Bowling Green State University Popular Press, 1989.

549. Schmidt–Joos, Siegfried (ed.). *Let It Bleed: The Rolling Stones In Altamont.* Frankfurt, Germany: Ullstein Press, 1984.

550. Schrieber, Norman. *The Scouting Party Index Of Independent Record Labels.* Brooklyn, NY: Scouting Party Press, 1986.

551. Schroeder, Fred E.H. *Outlaw Aesthetics: Arts And The Public Mind.* Bowling Green, OH: Bowling Green State University Popular Press, 1977.

552. ——— (ed.). *Twentieth-Century Popular Culture In Museums And Libraries.* Bowling Green, OH: Bowling Green State University Popular Press, 1981.

553. Schuster, Arlene, and Patty Matranga (eds.). *Rock 'N' Roll Handbook.* New York: Delilah Books, 1984.

554. Schwartze, Klaus. *The Scouse Phenomenon: The Scrapbook Of The New Liverpool Rock Scene (Part One).* Dreleich, West Germany: Bitsch Books, 1987.

555. Scott, Frank, *et al.* (comps.). *The Blues Catalog–1982.* El Cerrito, CA: Down Home Music, 1982.

556. ———, *et al.* (comps.). *Blues And Gospel Catalog, 1987–1988.* El Cerrito, CA: Down Home Music, 1988.

557. Scott, Frank, Ray Funk, Scott Glasscoe, *et al.* (comps.). *1984/1985 Blues And Gospel Catalog.* El Cerrito, CA: Down Home Music, 1984.

558. Scott, John Anthony. *The Ballad Of America: The History Of The United States In Song And Story.* Carbondale, IL: Southern Illinois University Press, 1983.

559. ———. *The Ballad Of America: The History Of The United States In Song And Story.* New York: Bantam Books, 1966.

560. Sculatti, Gene, and Davin Seay. *San Francisco Nights: The Psychedelic Music Trip, 1965–1968.* New York: St. Martin's Press, 1985.

561. Sears, Richard S. (comp.). *V–Discs: First Supplement.* Westport, CT: Greenwood Press, 1987.

562. Seay, Davin, with Mary Neely. *Stairway To Heaven: The Spiritual Roots Of Rock 'N' Roll From The King And Little Richard To Prince And Amy Grant.* New York: Ballantine Books, 1986.

563. Seeger, Pete, and Bob Reiser. *Carry It On: A History In Song And Pictures Of The Working Men And Women Of America.* New York: Simon and Schuster, 1985.

564. Seltzer, George. *Music Matters: The Performer And The American Federation Of Musicians.* Metuchen, NJ: Scarecrow, 1989.

565. Sexton, Richard. *American Style.* San Francisco: Chronicle Books, 1987.

566. Shannon, Bob, and John Javna. *Behind The Hits: Inside Stories Of Classic Pop And Rock And Roll.* New York: Warner Books, 1986.

567. Shannon, Doug. *Off The Record: Everything Related To Playing Recorded Dance Music In The Nightclub Industry.* Cleveland, OH: Pacesetting Publishing, 1985.

568. Shapiro, Bill. *The CD Rock And Roll Library: Thirty Years Of Rock And Roll On Compact Disc.* Kansas City, MO: Andrews and McMeel, 1988.

569. Shapiro, Harry. *A–Z Of Rock Drummers.* New York: Proteus Books, 1982.

570. ———. *Waiting For The Man: The Story Of Drugs And Popular Music.* New York: William Morrow, 1989.

571. Shapiro, Nat, and Bruce Pollock (eds.). *Popular Music, 1920–1979—A Revised Cumulation (3 Volumes).* Detroit: Gale Research, 1985.

572. Shaw, Arnold. *Black Popular Music In America: From The Spirituals, Minstrels, And Ragtime To Soul, Disco, And Hip-Hop.* New York: Schirmer Books, 1986.

573. ———. *Honkers And Shouters: The Golden Years Of Rhythm And Blues.* New York: Collier Books, 1978.

574. ———. *The Jazz Age: Popular Music In The 1920s.* New York: Oxford University Press, 1987.

575. ———. *Rock Revolution.* New York: Crowell-Collier Press, 1969.

576. ———. *The Rockin' '50s: The Decade That Transformed The Pop Music Scene.* New York: Hawthorn Books, 1974.

577. ———. *The Rockin' Fifties.* Dobbs Ferry, NY: Da Capo Press, 1987.

578. ———. *The World Of Soul.* New York: Paperback Library, 1971.

579. Shemel, Sidney, and William Krasilovsky. *This Business Of Music: A Practical Guide To The Music Industry For Publishers, Writers, Record Companies, Producers, Artists, And Agents* (5th ed., rev. and enl.). New York: Billboard Books, 1988.

580. Silber, Irwin. *Songs America Voted By.* Harrisburg, PA: Stackpole Books, 1988.

581. ——— (ed.). *Songs America Voted By: With The Words And Music That Won And Lost Elections And Influenced The Democratic Process.* Harrisburg, PA: Stackpole Books, 1971.

582. Silvester, Peter. *A Left Hand Like God.* London: Quartet Books, 1988.

583. Simels, Steve. *Gender Chameleons: Androgeny In Rock 'N' Roll.* New York: Arbor House, 1985.

584. Sinclair, David. *Rock On CD: The Essential Guide.* London: Kyle Cathie, Ltd., 1992.

585. Singleton, Raynoma Gordy. *Berry, Me, And Motown: The Untold Story.* Chicago: Contemporary Books, 1990.

586. Small, Christopher. *Music Of The Common Tongue: Survival And Celebration In Afro-American Music.* New York: River-Run Press, 1987.

587. Smart, Ted, and David Gibbon. *Rock And Pop Superstars.* New York: Crescent Books, 1983.

588. Smith, Jazzer. *The Book Of Australian Country Music.* Gordon, NSW, Australia: Berghouse Floyd Tuckey, 1984.

589. Smith, Joe (edited by Mitchell Fink). *Off The Record: An Oral History Of Popular Music.* New York: Warner Books, 1988.

590. Smith, Richard R. *Rickenbacker Guitar: The History.* Fullerton, CA: Centerstream Press, 1988.

591. Smith, Wes. *The Pied Pipers Of Rock 'N' Roll: Radio Deejays Of The '50s And '60s.* Marietta, GA: Longstreet Press, 1989.

592. Stallings, Penny. *Rock 'N' Roll Confidential.* Boston: Little, Brown and Company, 1984.

593. Stambler, Irwin. *The Encyclopedia Of Pop, Rock, And Soul* (rev. ed.). New York: St. Martin's Press, 1989.

594. ———— (comp.). *Encyclopedia Of Pop, Rock, And Soul.* New York: St. Martin's Press, 1974.

595. ———— (comp.). *Encyclopedia Of Popular Music.* New York: St. Martin's Press, 1965.

596. ————. *Guitar Years: Pop Music From Country And Western To Hard Rock.* Garden City, NY: Doubleday, 1970.

597. Stambler, Irwin, and Grelun Landon (comps.). *The Encyclopedia Of Folk, Country And Western Music* (2nd ed.). New York: St. Martin's Press, 1983.

598. ———— (comps.). *The Encyclopedia Of Folk, Country And Western Music.* New York: St. Martin's Press, 1969.

599. Stecheson, Anthony and Anne (comps.). *The Stecheson Classified Song Directory.* Hollywood, CA: Music Industry Press, 1961.

600. ————. *The Supplement To The Stecheson Classified Song Directory.* Hollywood, CA: Music Industry Press, 1978.

601. Stein, Claudia, Thomas Stein, and Michael Niehaus. *For Musicians Only.* New York: Billboard Books, 1988.

602. Steward, Sue, and Sheryl Garratt. *Signed, Sealed, And Delivered: True Life Stories Of Women In Pop.* Boston: South End Press, 1984.

603. Stidom, Larry (comp.). *Izatso?! Larry Stidom's Rock 'N' Roll Trivia And Fact Book.* Indianapolis, IN: L. Stidom, 1986.

604. *Story Of Rock—The Sound Heard Round The World: Volume Two—Teen Music Takes Over.* New York: Generation Press, 1974.

605. Street, John. *Rebel Rock: The Politics Of Popular Music.* New York: Basil Blackwell, 1986.

606. Stuessy, Joe. *Rock And Roll: Its History And Stylistic Development.* Englewood Cliffs, NJ: Prentice-Hall, 1990.

607. Sugerman, Danny. *Wonderland Avenue: Tales Of Glamour And Excess.* New York: William Morrow, 1989.

608. Suskin, Steven. *Show Tunes, 1905–1985: The Songs, Shows, And Careers Of Broadway's Major Composers.* New York: Dodd, Mead and Company, 1986.

609. Swenson, John (ed.). *The Rolling Stone Jazz Record Guide.* New York: Random House/Rolling Stone Press, 1985.

610. Szatmary, David P. *Rockin' In Time: A Social History Of Rock And Roll.* Englewood Cliffs, NJ: Prentice-Hall, 1987.

611. Szwed, John F. (ed.). *Black America.* New York: Basic Books, 1970.

612. Taft, Michael. *Blues Lyric Poetry: An Anthology.* New York: Garland Publishing, 1983.

613. ————. *Blues Lyric Poetry: A Concordance (3 Vols.).* New York: Garland Publishing, 1984.

614. Tagg, Philip, and David Horn (eds.). *Popular Music Perspectives: Papers From The First International Conference On Popular Music Research.* Exeter, U.K.: International Association for The Study of Popular Music, 1982.

615. Tame, David. *The Secret Power Of Music: The Transforma-*

tion Of Self And Society Through Musical Energy. New York: Inner Tradit, 1984.

616. Taraborrelli, J. Randy. *Motown: Hot Wax, City Cool, And Solid Gold.* Garden City, NY: Doubleday, 1986.

617. Tatham, David. *The Lure Of The Striped Pig: The Illustration Of Popular Music In America, 1820–1870.* Barre, MA: Imprint Society, 1973.

618. Tawa, Nicholas. *A Music For The Millions: Antebellum Democratic Attitudes And The Birth Of American Popular Music.* New York: Pendragon Press, 1984.

619. ———. *Sweet Songs For Gentle Americans: The Parlor Song In America, 1790–1860.* Bowling Green, OH: Bowling Green State University Popular Press, 1980.

620. Taylor, Derek. *It Was Twenty Years Ago Today.* New York: Simon and Schuster, 1987.

621. Taylor, Paul (comp.). *Popular Music Since 1955: A Critical Guide To The Literature.* New York: Mansell Publishing, 1985.

621a. Tharpe, Jac L. (ed.). *Elvis: Images and Fancies.* Jackson, MS: University Press of Mississippi, 1979.

622. Thomas, James L. (ed.). *Nonprint In The Secondary Curriculum: Readings For Reference.* Littleton, CO: Libraries Unlimited, 1982.

623. Thomas, Tony. *That's Dancing: A Glorious Celebration Of Dance In The Hollywood Musical.* New York: Abrams Press, 1984.

624. Thomson, Elizabeth (ed.). *New Women In Rock.* New York: Delilah/Putnam Books, 1982.

625. Thomson, Elizabeth, and David Gutman (eds.) *The Lennon Companion: Twenty-Five Years Of Comment.* New York: Macmillan Books, 1988.

626. Tobler, John, and Pete Frame. *Rock 'N' Roll: The First 25 Years.* New York: Exeter Books, 1980.

627. Tobler, John, and Stuart Grundy. *The Record Producers.* New York: St. Martin's Press, 1982.

628. ————. *The Song Producers.* New York: St. Martin's Press, 1983.

629. Tobler, John, and Alan Jones (comps.). *The Rock Lists Album.* London: Plexus Publishing, 1982.

630. Toop, David. *The Rap Attack: African Jive To New York Hip Hop.* Boston: South End Press, 1984.

631. Tosches, Nick. *Country: Living Legends And Dying Metaphors In America's Biggest Music* (rev. ed.). New York: Charles Scribner's Sons, 1985.

632. ————. *Hellfire: The Jerry Lee Lewis Story.* New York: Dell Publishing, 1982.

633. ————. *Unsung Heroes Of Rock 'N' Roll: The Birth Of Rock 'N' Roll In The Dark and Wild Years Before Elvis.* New York: Charles Scribner's Sons, 1984.

634. Tracy, Steven C. *Langston Hughes And The Blues.* Urbana, IL: University of Illinois Press, 1988.

635. Tudor, Dean (comp.). *Popular Music: An Annotated Guide To Recordings.* Littleton, CO: Libraries Unlimited, 1983.

636. Tunzi, Joseph A. *The First Elvis Video Price And Reference Guide.* Chicago: J.A.T., 1988.

637. Turner, Steve. *Hungry for Heaven: Rock 'N' Roll and the Search for Redemption.* London: Virgin, 1988.

638. Umphred, Neal (comp.). *Goldmine's Price Guide To Collectible Record Albums. Discographies And Prices For Pop And Rock Albums.* Iola, WI: Krause Publications, 1989.

639. ——— (comp.). *Goldmine's Rock 'N' Roll 45 R.P.M. Record Price Guide.* Iola, WI: Krause Publications, 1990.

640. Uslan, Michael, and Bruce Solomon. *Dick Clark's The First 25 Years Of Rock And Roll.* New York: Dell Publishing, 1981.

641. Van Der Merwe, Peter. *Origins Of The Popular Style: The Antecedents Of Twentieth-Century Popular Music.* Oxford, U.K.: Clarendon Press, 1989.

642. Vaughan, Andrew. *Who's Who In New Country Music.* New York: St. Martin's Press, 1990.

643. Ventura, Michael. *Shadow Dancing In The U.S.A.* Los Angeles: Jeremy P. Tarcher, 1985.

644. Vulliamy, Graham, and Ed Lee (eds.). *Pop Music In School* (rev. ed.). Cambridge, U.K.: Cambridge University Press, 1980.

645. ———. *Pop, Rock And Ethnic Music In School.* Cambridge, U.K.: Cambridge University Press, 1982.

646. ———. *Popular Music: A Teacher's Guide.* London: Routledge and Kegan Paul, 1982.

647. Walker, Clinton (ed.). *The Next Thing: Contemporary Australian Rock.* Kenthurst, Australia: Kangaroo Press, 1984.

648. Walker, John A. *Cross-Overs: Art Into Pop/Pop Into Art.* London: Comedia/Methuen Books, 1987.

649. Waller, Don. *The Motown Story: The Inside Story Of America's Most Popular Music.* New York: Charles Scribner's Sons, 1985.

650. Walters, David. *The Children Of Nuggets: The Definitive Guide To "Psychedelic Sixties" Punk Rock On Compilation Albums.* Ann Arbor, Michigan: Popular Culture, Ink., 1990.

651. Ward, Ed, Geoffrey Stokes, and Ken Tucker. *Rock Of Ages: The Rolling Stone History Of Rock And Roll.* New York: Rolling Stone/Summit Books, 1986.

652. Webb, Colin David. *Captain Beefheart: The Man & His Music.* Millbrook, Cornwall, U.K.: C. D. Webb, 1989.

653. Webber, Graeme. *Australian Rock Folio: Music Industry Photos.* Burwood, Australia: Pentacle Press, 1976.

654. Weinberg, Max, with Robert Santelli. *The Big Beat: Conversations With Rock's Great Drummers.* Chicago: Contemporary Books, 1984.

655. Wells, Dicky. *The Night People.* Boston: Crescendo, 1971.

656. Wenner, Hilda E., and Elizabeth Freilicher (comps.). *Here's To The Women: 100 Songs For And About American Women.* Syracuse, NY: Syracuse University Press, 1987.

657. Wenner, Jann S. *20 Years Of Rolling Stone: What A Long, Strange Trip It's Been.* New York: Friendly Press, 1987.

658. Wenzel, Lynn, and Carol J. Binkowski. *I Hear America Singing: A Nostalgic Tour Of Popular Sheet Music.* New York: Crown Publishers, 1989.

659. Whetmore, Edward Jay. *Mediamerica: Form, Content, And Consequence Of Mass Communication* (Updated 3rd ed.). Belmont, CA: Wadsworth Publishing, 1987.

660. ————. *Mediamerica: Form, Content, And Consequence Of Mass Communication* (3rd ed.). Belmont, CA: Wadsworth Publishing, 1985.

661. Whitburn, Joel (comp.). *The Billboard Book Of Top 40 Albums: The Complete Chart Guide To Every Album In The Top 40 Since 1955.* New York: Billboard Books, 1987.

662. ———— (comp.). *The Billboard Book Of Top 40 Hits* (3rd. ed.). New York: Billboard Books, 1987.

663. ————. *The Billboard Hot 100 Charts: The Seventies.* Menomonee Falls, WI: Record Research, 1990.

664. ————. *The Billboard Hot 100 Charts: The Sixties.* Menomonee Falls, WI: Record Research, 1989.

665. ———— (comp.). *Billboard Top 1,000 Singles, 1955–1986: The 1,000 Biggest Hits Of The Rock Era.* Milwaukee, WI: Hal Leonard Books, 1986.

666. ———— (comp.). *Billboard's Top 10 Charts: A Week-By-Week History Of The Hottest Of The Hot 100, 1958–1988.* Menomonee Falls, WI: Record Research, 1989.

667. ———— (comp.). *Billboard's Top 2,000, 1955–1985: The 2,000 Biggest Hits Of The Rock Era.* Menomonee Falls, WI: Record Research, 1985.

668. ———— (comp.). *Billboard's Top 3,000 Plus, 1955–1987: A Ranking Of Every Top 10 Hit Of The Rock Era.* Menomonee Falls, WI: Record Research, 1988.

669. ———— (comp.). *Daily #1 Hits: A Day By Day Listing Of The #1 Pop Records Of The Past Fifty Years, 1940–1989.* Menomonee Falls, WI: Record Research, 1990.

670. ———— (comp.). *Music Yearbook 1985.* Menomonee Falls, WI: Record Research, 1986.

671. ———— (comp.). *Music Yearbook 1986.* Menomonee Falls, WI: Record Research, 1987.

672. ———— (comp.). *Music And Video Yearbook 1987.* Menomonee Falls, WI: Record Research, 1988.

673. ———— (comp.). *1988 Music And Video Yearbook.* Menomonee Falls, WI: Record Research, 1989.

674. ———— (comp.). *1989 Music And Video Yearbook.* Menomonee Falls, WI: Record Research, 1990.

675. ———— (comp.). *Pop Memories, 1890–1954: The History Of American Popular Music.* Menomonee Falls, WI: Record Research, 1986.

676. ———— (comp.). *Pop Singles Annual, 1955–1986.* Menomonee Falls, WI: Record Research, 1987.

677. ————. *Top Country Singles, 1944–1988.* Menomonee Falls, WI: Record Research, 1989.

678. ———— (comp.). *Top Pop Albums, 1955–1985.* Menomonee Falls, WI: Record Research, 1985.

679. ———— (comp.). *Top Pop Singles, 1955–1986.* Menomonee Falls, WI: Record Research, 1987.

680. ———— (comp.). *Top Rhythm And Blues Singles, 1942–1988.* Menomonee Falls, WI: Record Research, 1988.

681. Whitcomb, Ian. *Rock Odyssey: A Musician's Guide To The Sixties.* Garden City, NY: Dolphin Books, 1983.

682. ———— (comp.). *Whole Lotta Shakin': A Rock 'N' Roll Scrapbook.* London: Arrow Books/ EMI Music, 1982.

683. White, Avron Levine (ed.). *Lost In Music: Culture, Style, And The Musical Event.* London: Routledge and Kegan Paul, 1987.

684. White, Timothy. *Catch A Fire: The Life of Bob Marley.* (Rev. ed.). New York: Henry Holt, 1989.

685. ————. *Rock Stars.* New York: Stewart, Tabori, and Chang, 1984.

686. Wicke, Peter (translated by Rachel Fogg). *Rock Music: Culture, Aesthetics, And Sociology.* Cambridge, U.K.: Cambridge University Press, 1987.

687. Widgery, David. *Beating Time: Riot 'N' Race 'N' Rock 'N' Roll.* London: Chatto and Windus/Tigerstripe Books, 1986.

688. Wiegand, Wayne A. (ed.). *Popular Culture And The Library: Current Issues Symposium II.* Lexington, KY: University of Kentucky, 1978.

689. Wildbihler, Hubert, and Sonja Volklein (comps.). *The Musical: An International Annotated Bibliography.* Munich, Germany: K.G. Saur, 1986.

690. Williams, Brett. *John Henry: A Bio-Bibliography.* Westport, CT: Greenwood Press, 1983.

691. Williams, Paul. *The Map: Rediscovering Rock And Roll—A Journey.* South Bend, IN: And Books, 1988.

692. Williamson, Bill. *The Temper Of The Times: British Society Since World War II.* Oxford, U.K.: Basil Blackwell, 1990.

693. Willoughby, Larry. *Texas Rhythm/Texas Rhyme: A Pictorial History Of Texas Music.* Austin, TX: Texas Monthly Press, Inc., 1984.

694. Wilson, Mary. *How To Make It In The Music Business.* London: Columbus Books, 1987.

695. Woliver, Robbie. *Bringing It All Back Home: 25 Years Of American Music At Folk City.* New York: Pantheon Books, 1986.

696. Wootton, Richard. *Honky Tonkin': A Travel Guide To American Music.* Charlotte, NC: East Woods Press, 1980.

697. Worth, Fred L. *Rock Facts.* New York: Facts On File, 1986.

698. Yorke, Ritchie. *Axes, Chops, And Hot Licks: The Canadian Rock Music Scene.* Edmonton, Alberta, Canada: M.G. Hurtig, 1971.

699. Zalkind, Ronald (comp.). *Contemporary Music Almanac 1980/81.* New York: Schirmer Books, 1980.

APPENDIX B: A BASIC COLLECTION OF ESSENTIAL ROCK RECORDINGS

Introductory Comments

This compilation of 100 titles (some of which consist of two or more discs) attempts to include virtually all stylistic facets of rock history. It is *not* a listing of either the best (artistically speaking) or most popular recordings. These criteria, however, constitute key considerations for inclusion, along with (1) representativeness, (2) historical value, and (3) availability (as of early 1991) in the compact disc format. Most are also available in the cassette and vinyl configurations, often on multiple labels. It should be noted that a few of the titles are available only as imports; the greed of many American record companies, as reflected in their inclination to release only those recordings likely to sell huge quantities (the likelihood of a modest profit—which you can be sure that the import labels are making—does not appear to be sufficient motivation to them), is largely responsible for the need to include foreign releases. Nevertheless, many specialty record/tape stores can easily order them, albeit at a higher price (generally 25 to 50% more) than domestic retail rates.

Those users interested in a more comprehensive stock list might consider looking at the discographical listing from the second installment of *The Literature of Rock II,* covering the period 1954–1983.

The entries are arranged alphabetically under artist name; multiple-artist compilations are listed by title. The entries also include album title, year of initial release (although material included might have been recorded at an earlier date), and name of the compact disc label on which the title is most readily available (any domestic version takes precedence).

The Listing

Anderson, Laurie—*Home of the Brave.* Warner Brothers. 1986.
Art of Noise—*The Ambient Collection.* 1990.
The Band—*The Band.* Capitol. 1969.
Be Bop Deluxe—*Modern Music.* EMI/Harvest. 1976.
The Beach Boys—*Little Deuce Coupe/All Summer Long.* Capitol. 1963/1964.
The Beach Boys—*Pet Sounds.* Capitol. 1966.
The Beatles—*Meet the Beatles.* Capitol. 1964.
The Beatles—*Rubber Soul.* Capitol. 1965.
The Beatles—*Revolver.* Capitol. 1966.
The Beatles—*Sgt. Pepper's Lonely Hearts Club Band.* Capitol. 1967.
The Beatles—*The Beatles.* Capitol. 1968. (2 discs)
The Beatles—*Abbey Road.* Capitol. 1969.
The Bee Gees—*1st.* RSO/PolyGram. 1967.
The Bee Gees—*Bee Gees Greatest.* RSO/PolyGram. 1975–1980. (2)
Berry, Chuck—*The Chess Box.* MCA. 1955–1972. (3)
Big Brother and the Holding Company—*Cheap Thrills.* Columbia. 1968.
Blood, Sweat and Tears—*Blood, Sweat and Tears.* Columbia. 1969.
Blue Oyster Cult—*Blue Oyster Cult.* Columbia. 1972.
Bowie, David—*The Rise and Fall of Ziggy Stardust and the Spiders from Mars.* Ryko. 1972.
The Byrds—*Legacy.* Columbia. 1965–1972. (4)
Cabaret Voltaire—*Listen Up With Cabaret Voltaire.* Restless. 1980–1990. (2)
Can—*Future Days.* Restless Retro. 1973.
Canned Heat—*Living the Blues.* See for Miles. 1969.
The Clash—*London Calling.* Columbia. 1980. (2)
The Clash—*Sandanista.* Columbia. 1982. (3)

Classic Rock. Various Artists. Time/Life Music. 1964–1969. Includes one-disc greatest hits compilations by Creedence Clearwater Revival and Diana Ross and the Supremes. (30)

Country Joe and the Fish—*I-Feel-Like-I'm-Fixin'-to-Die.* Vanguard. 1968.

Cream—*Wheels of Fire.* Atco. 1968. (2)

The Cure—*Disintegration.* 1989.

Davis, Miles—*Bitches Brew.* Columbia. 1970. (2)

Dax, Danielle—*Dark Adapted Eye.* Sire. 1988.

The Dead Kennedys—*Frankenchrist.*

Deep Purple—*In Rock.* Warner Brothers. 1970.

Depeche Mode—*Violator.* Sire/Reprise. 1990.

The Doors—*The Doors.* Elektra. 1967.

The Doors—*Strange Days.* Elektra. 1967.

Duran Duran—*Rio.* Capitol. 1982.

Dylan, Bob—*Biograph.* Columbia. 1961–1985. (4)

Dylan, Bob—*Highway 61 Revisited.* Columbia. 1965.

The Eagles—*One of These Nights.* Geffen. 1975.

Eno—*Apollo: Atmospheres & Soundtracks.* Jem. 1983.

Fairport Convention—*Full House.* Island. 1970.

The Flamin' Groovies—*Teenage Head.* 1971.

The Four Seasons (featuring Frankie Valli)—*25th Anniversary Collection.* Rhino. 1962–1978. (3)

Free—*Fire and Water.* A & M. 1970.

Grateful Dead—*Live/Dead.* Warner Brothers. 1970.

Hagen, Nina—*Ecstasy.* 1984.

Hammer, M.C.—*Please Hammer Don't Hurt 'Em.* Capitol. 1990.

Hendrix, Jimi, Experience—*Electric Ladyland.* Polydor. 1968.

Holly, Buddy—*The Original Master Tapes.* 1956–1959.

Husker Du—*Zen Arcade.* SST. 1987. (2)

Jefferson Airplane—*2400 Fulton Street.* RCA. 1966–1970. (2)

Killing Joke—*Night Time.* EG. 1985.

King Crimson—*Lizard.* EG. 1971.

Led Zeppelin—*Led Zeppelin IV.* Atlantic. 1971.

Love and Rockets—*Earth Sun Moon.* Big Time/Beggars Banquet. 1987.

The Lovin' Spoonful—*Do You Believe in Magic/Anything Playing.* Castle Communications. 1965/1967. (2)

The Mamas and the Papas—*If You Can Believe Your Eyes and Ears.* MCA. 1966.

Marley, Bob, and the Wailers—*Natty Dread.* Island. 1974.
Miller, Steve, Band—*Italian X Rays.* Mercury. 1984.
Moby Grape—*Wow/Grape Jam.* 1968.
The Moody Blues—*Days of Future Passed.* 1967.
Morrison, Van—*Moondance.* Warner Brothers. 1870.
The Mothers of Invention. See: Frank Zappa.
New Order—*Substance.* Qwest. 1987. (2)
Newman, Randy—*Sail Away.* Warner Brothers. 1973.
Orchestral Manoeuvres in the Dark—*Dazzle Ships.* 1982.
Peter, Paul and Mary—*Peter, Paul and Mary.* Warner Brothers. 1962.
Presley, Elvis—*The Sun Sessions CD.* RCA. 1954–1955.
Prince—*1999.* Warner Brothers. 1984.
Procol Harum—*Procol Harum* (also titled as: *A Whiter Shade of Pale*).
    1967.
Propaganda—*A Secret Wish.* ZTT. 1985.
Quicksilver Messenger Service—*Happy Trails.* Capitol. 1969.
The Raspberries—*The Very Best of the Raspberries.* Zap! 1972–1974.
The Replacements—*Let It Be.* Twin Tone. 1984.
The Righteous Brothers—*The Righteous Brothers' Greatest Hits.* Verve.
    1964–1966.
The Rock'n' Roll Era. Various Artists. Time/Life Music. 1954–1964.
    Includes one-disc greatest hits compilations by the Everly
    Brothers, Rick Nelson and Elvis Presley. (40)
The Rolling Stones—*The London Years.* 1964–1970. (3)
Roxy Music—*Country Life.* 1975.
Rundgren, Todd—*Something/Anything?* Rhino. 1972. (2)
Santana—*Abraxas.* Columbia. 1971.
The Sex Pistols—*Never Mind the Bollocks, Here's the Sex Pistols.* 1976.
Sounds of the Seventies. Various Artists. Time/Life Music. (In progress)
Spirit—*The Family That Plays Together.* 1969.
Stewart, Rod—*Every Picture Tells a Story.* Mercury/PolyGram. 1971.
The Stone Roses—*The Stone Roses.* 1989.
T. Rex. See: Tyrannosaurus Rex.
The Teardrop Explodes—*Kilimanjaro.* 1982.
The Temptations—*Anthology.* Motown. (2)
The Thompson Twins—*In the Name of Love.* 1982.
Traffic—*Mr. Fantasy.* 1967.
2 Live Crew—*As Nasty as They Wanna Be.* 1989.
Tyrannosaurus Rex—*Unicorn/A Beard of Stars.* Castle Communica-
    tions. 1970/1971. (2)

The Who—*Tommy*. MCA. 1969. (2)

Wonder, Stevie—*Fulfillingness First Finale*. Tamla. 1974.

The Wonder Stuff—*The Eight-Legged Groove Machine*. Polydor. 1988.

The Yardbirds—*The Yardbirds' Greatest Hits, Volume One, 1964-1966*. Rhino. 1964–1966.

Yes—*Close to the Edge*. Atlantic. 1972.

Young, Neil, and Crazy Horse—*Everybody Knows This is Nowhere*. Warner Brothers/Reprise. 1970.

ZZ Top—*Deguello*. 1979.

Zappa, Frank, and the Mothers of Invention—*We're Only in It for the Money/Lumpy Gravy*. Ryko. 1968/1969. (2)

Zappa, Frank, and the Mothers of Invention—*Uncle Meat*. Ryko. 1970. (2)

APPENDIX C: JOURNALS INCLUDED IN THE INDEX

APRA Journal. Australia: Australasian Performing Rights Association, 1969– . Quarterly. Jim Bradley, ed. Free to members.

ARSC Journal. Silver Spring, Maryland: Association for Recorded Sound Collections, 1969– . Semiannual. Ted Sheldon, ed.

ASCAP in Action. New York, NY: American Society of Composers, Authors and Publishers, 1967– . Karen Sherry, ed. Free to members.

American Music. Champaign, IL: University of Illinois Press, 1982– . Quarterly. John Graziano, ed.

BMI: The Many Worlds of Music. New York, NY: Broadcast Music, Inc., 1962– . Monthly. Howard Colson, ed. Free to members.

Backstage Magazine. Biweekly.

The Baltimore Sun. Baltimore, MD: 19—. Daily.

Billboard. Los Angeles, CA: Billboard Publications, Inc., 1894– . Weekly. Gerry Wood and Kip Kirby, eds.

Blue Suede News. Duvall, WA: Blue Suede News, 1986. Bimonthly. Marc Bristol, ed.

Buddy: The Original Texas Music Magazine. Dallas, TX: Buddy, Inc., 1973– . Monthly. Louis Solganick, ed.

Business Week. New York, N.Y.: McGraw-Hill Publications, Co., 1929– . Weekly. Lewis H. Young, ed.

Buzz. Minneapolis, MN: City Pages, Inc., 1985– . Monthly. Steve Perry, ed.

Cadence. Redwood, NY: Cadence Press, 1976– . Monthly. Robert Rusch, ed.

Canadian Composer. Toronto, Ontario: Canadian Composer, n.d. Monthly. Richard Flohil, ed.

Canadian Musician. Toronto, Ontario: Morris Publications, 1979– . Bimonthly. Karen Whitney, ed.

Cash Box. Los Angeles, CA: Cash Box Publishing Co., Inc., 1942– . George Albert, president and publisher.

Cat Tales. Sterling, VA: G. Milewski, 1989– . Bimonthly. Greg Milewski, ed.

Choice. Chicago: American Library Association, 1954– . Monthly.

Christian Century. Chicago, IL: Christian Century Foundation, 1884– . Weekly. James M. Wall, ed.

Christianity Today. Carol Stream, IL: Christianity Today, Inc., 1956– . Monthly. Kenneth Kantzer, ed.

Cosmopolitan. New York, NY: Hearst Magazines, 1901– . Monthly. Helen Gurley Brown, ed.

Creem. Birmingham, MI: Creem Magazine, Inc., 1969– . Monthly. Barry D. Kramer, ed.

Detroit Free Press. Detroit, MI: Rider Newspapers, Inc., 1831– . Daily. Joe H. Stroud, ed.

DISCoveries. Port Townsend, WA: Jerry P. Osborne, 1988– . Monthly. Jon E. Johnson, ed.

Down Beat. Chicago, IL: Maher Publications, Inc., 1934–. Monthly. Jack Maher, ed.

Down Home Music Newsletter. El Cerrito, CA: Down Home Music, Inc., 1980– . 5x/year. Frank Scott, ed.

Ear, Magazine of New Music. New York, NY: New Wilderness Fdtn., 1976– . 10x/year. David L. Laskin, managing ed.

Ebony. Chicago, IL: Johnson Publishing Co., Inc., 1945– . Monthly. Herbert Nipson, ed.

Electronic Musician. Monthly.

Elvis Monthly. Leicester, UK: Albert Hand Publications, 1959– . Monthly. Todd Slaughter, ed.

Esquire. New York, NY: Esquire Publishing, Inc., 1933– . Monthly. Phillip Moffitt, ed.

Flipside Fanzine. Whittier, CA: n.d. Bimonthly.

Folk Roots. Farnham, Surrey, UK: Folk Roots, 1979– .
Monthly. Ian A. Anderson, ed.

Forbes. New York, NY: Forbes, Inc., 1917– . Biweekly. James
Michaels, ed.

The Golden Age. Corby, Northants, UK: Squirrel Publishing,
1986– . Quarterly. Joan Gray, ed.

Goldmine. Iola, WI: Krause Publications, 1974– . Biweekly.
Jeff Tamarkin, ed.

Guitar for the Practicing Musician. Port Chester, NY: Cherry
Lane Music Co., 19—. Monthly. Bruce Pollock and John
Stix, editors-in-chief.

Guitar Player. San Diego, CA: GPI Publications, 1967– .
Monthly. Tom Wheeler, ed.

Guitar World. New York, NY: Harris Publications, Inc.,
1980– . Monthly. Joseph Bosso, editor-in-chief.

Harper's. New York, NY: Harper's Magazine Co., 1850– .
Monthly. Lewis H. Lapham, ed.

Hi-Fi/Musical America. See: *Musical America.*

High Fidelity. New York, NY: ABC Leisure Magazines, Inc.,
1951– . Monthly. Robert Clark, ed.

The History of Rock. London, UK: Orais Publishing, Ltd.,
1982– . Weekly. Ashley Brown, ed.

Hit Parader. Derby, CT: Charlton Publications, 1954– . Bimonthly. Shelton Ivany, ed.

Hot Wax Quarterly. Kitchener, Ontario: Blue Flake Productions, Inc., 1980– . Quarterly. J.C. Costa, ed.

International Journal of Instructional Media. New York, NY: Westwood Press, Inc., 1973– . Quarterly. Phillip J. Sleeman, ed.

International Musician. New York, NY: American Federation of Musicians of the United States and Canada, 1901– . Monthly. Kelly J. Castleberry, II, ed.

Jazz Journal International. London, UK: Pitman Periodicals, Ltd., 1948– . Monthly. Eddie Cook, ed. Formerly: *Jazz & Blues.*

Jazz Podium. Monthly.

Journal of American Culture. Bowling Green, OH: Bowling Green State University Popular Press, 1978– . Quarterly. Pat Browne, ed.

Keyboard. San Francisco, CA: Mill Freeman Publications, 1974– . Monthly. Dominic Milano, ed.

Ladies' Home Journal. New York, NY: Meredith, 1884– . Monthly. Myrna Blyth, editor-in-chief.

Life. Chicago, IL: Time, Inc., 1936–1972; resumed 1978– . Monthly. Richard B. Stolley, ed.

Living Blues. Chicago, IL: Living Blues Publications, 1970– . Quarterly. Jim and Amy O'Neal, eds.

Maclean's. Toronto, Ontario: Maclean-Hunter Ltd., 1905– . Weekly. Peter C. Newman, ed.

Mademoiselle. New York, NY: Conde Nast Publications, Inc., 1935– . Monthly. E.R. Locke, ed.

Maximumrocknroll. Berkeley, CA: n.d. Monthly.

Melody Maker. London, UK: IPC Specialist and Professional Press Ltd., 1926– . Weekly. Ray Coleman, ed.

Michigan Academician. Ann Arbor, MI: Michigan Academy of Science, Arts and Letters, 1968– . Quarterly. Kathleen F. Duke, ed.

Modern Drummer. Clifton, NJ: Modern Drummer Publications, Inc., 19—. Monthly. Ronald Spagnardi, ed.

Music Scene. Toronto, Ontario: Performing Rights Organization of Canada, Ltd., 1967– . Bimonthly. Mrs. Nancy Gyokeres, ed.

Music Week. London: Spotlight Publications, 1959–1981 (*Music and Video Week* after July, 1981) Weekly.

Musical America. Monthly.

Musician. Gloucester, MA: Billboard Publications, Inc., 1976– . Monthly. Bill Flanagan, ed. Formerly: *Musician, Player & Listener.*

NASM. Reston, VA: National Association of Schools of Music, 1968– . Quarterly.

New Musical Express. London, UK: IPC Magazines, Ltd., 1952– . Weekly. Neil Spencer, ed.

New York Times Magazine. New York, NY: Arthur-Ochs Sulzberger Adv., 1851– . Weekly. A.M. Rosenthal, ed.

Newsletter on Intellectual Freedom. Chicago, IL: American Library Association, Office for Intellectual Freedom, 1967– . Monthly.

Newsweek. New York, NY: Newsweek, Inc., 1933– . Weekly. Edward Kosner, ed.

Now Dig This. South Shields, Tyne and Wear, UK: Now Dig Publishers, 1983– . Monthly. Trevor Cajaio, ed.

OneTwoThreeFour: A Rock 'N' Roll Quarterly. Los Angeles, California: Strong Sounding Thought Press, Inc., 1985– . Quarterly. Kevin Barrett, Brenda Johnson-Grau and Glenn Johnson-Grau, eds.

People Weekly. New York: Time, Inc., 1974– . Weekly. London L. Jones, Jr., ed.

Playboy. Chicago, IL: Playboy Enterprises, Inc., 1953– . Monthly. Hugh Hefner, ed.

Popular Music. Cambridge, U. K. Quarterly. David Horn, ed.

Popular Music and Society. Bowling Green, OH: Bowling Green State University Popular Press, 1972– . Quarterly. R. Serge Denisoff, ed.

Progressive. Madison, WI: Progressive, n.d. Monthly.

Public News. Houston, TX: Public News, 1982– . Weekly. Bert Woodall, ed.

R.P.M. Toronto, Ontario: R.P.M. Music Publications, Ltd. Weekly. Walt Grealis, ed.

The Record; a Newsletter from the Parents' Music Resource Center. Arlington, VA: Parents Music Resource Center, 1985– . Monthly.

Record Collector. Ealine, London, UK: Diamond Publishing Group, Ltd., 1978– . Monthly. Peter Doggett, ed.

The Rocket. Seattle, WA: Rocket Towers Press, 1979– . Monthly. Charles R. Cross, ed.

Rockin' 50s. Lubbock, TX: W.F. Griggs, 1986– . Bimonthly. William F. Griggs, ed.

Rolling Stone. New York, NY: Straight Arrow Publishers, Inc., 1967– . Fortnightly. Jann Wenner, ed.

Saturday Review. Columbia, MO: Saturday Review Magazine Company, 1924–82; 198— .

Serious Hip Hop. Philadelphia, PA. Bimonthly.

Social Education. Washington, DC: National Council for the Social Studies, 1937– . 7x/year. Salvatore J. Natoli, ed.

Social Studies. Washington, DC: Heldreff Publications, 1909– . Bimonthly. Helen Kress, managing editor.

Song Hits. Derby, CT: Charlton Publications, 1942– . Bimonthly. Mary Jane Canetti, ed.

Soul Survivor. Toronto, Ontario: Mary Koppel, n.d. Quarterly. Richard Pack, ed.

Sound Choice. 1987– . Quarterly.

Sounds. London, UK: Spotlight Publications Ltd., 1970– . Weekly. Alan Lewis, ed.

Spin. New York, NY: Camouflage Publications, 1985– . Monthly. Bob Guccione, Jr., ed.

Stereo Review. New York, NY: Ziff-Davis Publishing Company, 1958– . Monthly. Bill Livingston, ed.

Super Song Hits. Derby, CT: Charlton Publications, n.d. Bi-monthly.

Symphony. Bi-monthly.

Texas Guitar. 1985– . Quarterly.

Texas Monthly. 197— . Monthly.

Time. New York, NY: Time, Inc., 1923– . Weekly. Ray Cave, ed.

Tracking: Popular Music Studies. Eau Claire, WI: University of Wisconsin at Eau Claire, Journalism Department, 1988– . Semiannual. Steve Jones, ed.

USA Today. Arlington, VA: Gannett Company, Inc. Daily except Saturdays and Sundays. John C. Quinn, ed.

Variety. New York, NY: Variety, Inc., 1905– . Weekly. Syd Silverman, ed.

Video Review. Surrey, UK: IPC Business Press Ltd., 1980– . Monthly.

Village Noize. Bayside, NY: Village Noize Publications. Irregular. Eric Wielander, ed.

Village Voice. New York, NY: Village Voice, Inc., 1955– . Weekly. David Schneiderman, ed.

Wall Street Journal. New York, NY: Dow Jones and Company, 1851– . Daily. Robert Bartley, ed.

Western Folklore. Los Angeles, CA: California Folklore Society, 1942– . Quarterly. William A. Wilson, ed.

INDEX

A & M   833, 856
ABC   563–564
AC/DC   317
A.C. Marias   511
AIDS   770–771
AOR (see also Lee Abrams; Contemporary Hits Radio)   436–452, 829
APB   670
A.R.M.S.   771
ATV Music Corp. (see also The Beatles; Michael Jackson)   821
Abba   364–365
Abbey Road (studio)   856
Abbott, Gregory   598
Abdul, Paula   470
Above the Law   625
Abrams, Lee (see also AOR)   827–828
Acappella   144
Accept   317
Accordians   816
Ace, Johnny   14
Acid House   488–489
Acid Rock   286–288
Ackerman, William   645
Act Fuseli   670
Adam and the Ants/Adam Ant (see also Bow Wow Wow)   564–565
Adams, Bryan (see also Jim Vallance)   217–218
Adams, Faye   15
Adamski (r.n. Adam Tinley)   477
Ade, King Sunny   307
Adeva   490
Adkins, Hasil   49
Adult Contemporary (see also Black Adult Contemporary)   828–829
Adult Net   670
Adventures   671
Advertising (see also The Beatles)   750

Aerosmith (see also Joe Perry)   317–318
Afro-Rock (see also World Beat)   306–308
Age of Chance   478, 671
A-ha   363–364
Air Supply   426–427
Alabama (see Retailing)
Alarm   527–528
Albright, Gerald   351
Album Packaging   754
Alexander, Arthur   15
Alien Sex Fiend   505–506
All About Eve   671
Allen, Donna   471
Alligator (record company)   833
Allman Brothers Band (see also Dickey Betts)   274
Almighty   318
Almond, Marc   575–576
Alomar, Carlos (see also David Bowie)   645
Alone Again Or   671
Alpert, Herb   182
Altamont   785
Alternative Dance   477
Alternative Rock   651–670
Alternative TV   671
Amazulu   471
Ambient (music style)   648–650
Ambient House   493–494
Ambrosia   427
American Bandstand   179
American Renaissance   230–263
Amnesty International   771
Ana   427, 471
And Why Not?   277, 573
Anderson, Laurie   586
Andrews, Lee, and the Hearts   144–145
Angel (City)   215, 318–319
Animal Nightlife   671

Animals, The (*see also* Eric Burdon)   191
Animotion   436, 672
Anka, Paul   179
Answer Songs   185
Answered Questions   598
Anthony and the Camp   471
Anthrax   348
Antilles (record companies)   833
Any Trouble   672
Apollo Theatre   12–13
Apollo Theatre Records   13
Appice, Vinny   865
Apple Mosaic   672
April Wine   218
Arcadia (*see also* Duran Duran)   565
ARChive   750
Archive of Contemporary Music   750
Archives   750–752
Ariola (*see* RCA)
Arista (record company)   834
Aronoff, Kenny   865
Arrows   214
Arsenal   672
Art   751–752
Artist and Repertoire Men   856–857
Artists United Against Apartheid   771–772
Asch, Moe   852
Ashford and Simpson   471
Asphalt Ribbons   672
Assassins   672
Association   420
Astley, Rick   427
Aswad   277
Atco   13
Athens Sound   543–546
Atlantic (record company)   13, 834
Atlantic 252 (Irish radio network)   826
Atwater, Lee (*see also* Blues Revival)   875
Audio Two/MC Lyte   625
Austin, Patti   599
Australia   215–217, 790
Austria   361
Autograph   367
Avalon, Frankie   180
Avant-Garde   586–592
Average White Band   257–258
Awards   752
Aztec Camera   672–673
Azymuth   351

B-52's   543
BET   869

Bacharach, Burt   172
Bacharach, Burt, and Hal David (*see* Brill Building Era)
Bachman-Turner Overdrive (*see also* Guess Who)
Bad Company (*see also* The Firm)   436
Bad English (*see also* Journey)   427
Bad News   319
Badarou, Wally   748
Badfinger   570
Badlands   673
Baez, Joan   186
Bailey, Philip (*see also* Earth, Wind and Fire)   599
Baker, Anita   599
Baker, Arthur   857–858
Baker, LaVern   15
Baker('s), Ginger, Air Force (*see also* Jack Bruce; Eric Clapton)   292
Balaam and the Angel   673
Balancing Act   233
Balin, Marty (*see also* Jefferson Airplane)   427
Ballard, Hank, and the Midnighters   145–146
Baltimora   478
Bananarama (*see also* Shakespeare's Sister)   428, 673
Band Aid   772
Bandera   282
Band of Holy Joy   673
Band of Susans   674
Bang Bang   674
Bangles, The (*see also* Susanna Hoffs)   554–555
Bang Tango   674
Bang the Party   478
Banks, Tony (*see also* Genesis)   296
Barclay James Harvest   292
Bardots   674
Barri, Steve   858
Barry and the Tamerlanes   166
Basia   366
Bastro   674
Batfish Boys   674
Bators, Stiv (*see also* Lords of the New Church)   517
Bay City Rollers   382
Beach Boys (*see also* Parents Music Resource Center; Brian Wilson)   231
Beacon Street Union   274
Bearsville (*see* Rhino)
Beastie Boys   625–626

Beat/English Beat (*see also* General Public; Ranking Roger) 573–574
Beat Era (1956–1958) 108–142
Beat Farmers 555, 651–652
Beat Rodeo 674–675
Beatles, The (*see also* George Harrison; Michael Jackson; John Lennon; Paul McCartney; Ringo Starr) 191–195
Beats International (*see also* Housemartins) 478
Beausoleil 266–267
Beautiful South (*see also* Housemartins) 675
Beauvoir, Jean 319
Beaver Brown Band 436
Beck, Bogart and Appice (*see* Jeff Beck)
Beck, Jeff (*see also* Ron Wood; The Yardbirds) 207–208
Beckett, Barry 866
Bee Gees 208–209
Beefheart, Captain (*see also* Frank Zappa) 586
Bel Canto 648
Belafonte, Harry 187
Belew, Adrian (*See also* Bears; David Bowie; Talking Heads; Frank Zappa) 292–293
Belfegore 362
Belgium 361
Bell, Freddie, and the Bellboys 113
Bell, Maggie 380
Bell Biv DeVoe (*see also* New Edition) 599–600
Belle, Regina 600
Belmonts (*see* Dion)
Beloved 479, 675
Beltane Fire 675
Belvin, Jesse 15–16
Benatar, Pat 436–437
Benitez, "Jellybean" 858
Bennett, Boyd 49
Bennett, Tony 98
Benson, George 351–352
Benton, Brook 98
Berlin 576
Berry, Andrew 737
Berry, Chuck 113–118
Berry, Richard 880
Berwald, David 399
Bettis, John 880
Betts, Dickey (*see also* Allman Brothers Band) 274
Beyond 319
Bible (group) 675
Biff Bang Pow! 675

Big Audio Dynamite (*see also* The Clash; Mick Jones) 652
Big Band Rock 305–306
Big Country 528, 652–653
Big Dipper 653
Big Dish 653
Big Maybelle 16
Big Mouth 627
Big Sound Authority 490
Big Star (*see* Alex Chilton)
Big Stick 676
Big Three 199
Big Trouble 188
Big Wheel 676
Big Youth 676
Birdland 676
Bishop, Stephen 420
Black (*see also* Darling Buds) 676
Black, Bill, Combo (*see also* Elvis Presley) 182
Black, Jay (*see* Jay and the Americans)
Black, Karen 815
Black Adult Contemporary (*see also* Adult Contemporary) 829
Black Box 676
Black Britain 676
Black Contemporary (*see also* Radio) 598–619
Black Flag 511
Black Oak Arkansas (*see* Lord Tracy)
Black Sabbath (*see also* Ozzy Osbourne) 319
Black Tie (*see also* Bread; The Eagles) 437
Black Uhuru 278
Black Velvet Band 237
Blackwell, Bumps 880–881
Blackwell, Otis 111–112
Blades, Ruben 282
Blaine, Hal 866
Blake Babies 677
Blancmange 528
Bland, Billy 16
Bland, Bobby "Blue" 16
Blane, Marcie 180
Blasters (*see also* X) 741
Bliss 677
Blitz (*see* New Romantics)
Blondes (*see also* Platinum Blonde) 219
Blondie 529
Bloodrock 437
Blood, Sweat and Tears (*see also* Lew Soloff) 305
Bloom, Luka 238
Blow, Kurtis 627

Blow Monkeys 677
Blu, Peggi 600
Blue Aeroplanes 653–654, 677
Blue Chip (record company) 835
Blue in Heaven 677
Blue Murder 678
Blue Nile 678
Blue Oyster Cult 320
Blue Pearl 490
Blue Rodeo 219
Blue-Eyed Soul 257–263
Blues Brothers 377
Blues for Salvador 772
Blues Revival 368–377
Blur 320
Bobbettes 16
Bobby Z (see also Prince)
BoDeans 654
Bogmen 678
Bolshoi 654
Bomb Party 678
Bon Ami (record company) 835
Bon Jovi (, Jon) 320–322
Bond, Eddie 49
Bonds, Gary U.S. 181
Bonedaddys 748
Boney M 278, 362
Bongos (see also Individuals) 570
Bonham 322
Bonzo Dog Band 815
Boo, Betty 627
Boo Radleys 524
Boo-Yaa T.R.I.B.E. 627
Boogie Boys 627
Book of Love 678
Booker T and the M.G.s (see also Memphis
    Sound) 182
Boom Boom Boom 678
Boomtown Rats (see also Charity; Bob Gel-
    dof) 529
Boone, Pat 99
Bootlegging (see Counterfeiting)
Boss 678
Boss Hog 679
Bosstown Sound (see Beacon Street Union)
Boston 437
Boulevard 219
Bourgeois Tagg 679
Bow Wow Wow (see also Adam and the Ants)
    565
Bowen, Jimmy 49–50
Box Tops (see Alec Chilton)

Boy George (see also Culture Club) 566–
    567
Boy Meets Girl 679
Boys Don't Cry 438
Bragg, Billy 399–400
Brandos 654
Branigan, Billy 438
Branigan, Laura 428
Brass Construction 306
Bread (see also Black Tie) 420
Breakdancing 470
Breathe 258
Brecker, Michael 352
Brecker, Randy 352
Breeders (see also Pixies; Throwing Muses)
    679
Brensten, Jackie (see also Ike and Tina Turner)
    17
Brickell, Edie, and the New Bohemians
    679
Bride Farmers 555
Bridewell Taxis 555
Brighter Side of Darkness 679
Brill Building Era (1959–1965) 172–188
Brilliant 322, 680
British Folk Rock 237–240
British Invasion 189–229
Britny Fox 322
Britten, Roy 450
Broadcasters 741
Broken Homes 680
Bronski Beat (see also The Communards)
    479
Brooks, Lonnie 369
Bros. 382
Brother Beyond 680
Brown, Bobby (see also New Edition) 600
Brown, Buster 17
Brown, Charles 17
Brown, Chuck 619
Brown, James (see also Rap) 17–20
Brown, Jocelyn 600
Brown, Julie 815–816
Brown, Nappy 20
Brown, Peter 467
Brown, Roy 21
Brown, Ruth 21
Brown, Tim 493
Brown Dots (see also Four Tunes) 146
Browne, Jackson 400
Bruce, Jack 369
Brucken, Claudia 592

Bruford, Bill (*see also* Genesis) 293
Brunswick (record company) 835
Bryant, Boudleaux and Felice 112
Bryant, Sharon (*see also* Atlantic Starr) 601
Bryson, Peabo 601
Bubble Puppy 382
Bubblegum 382–389
Buchanan, Roy 369–370
Buckingham, Lindsey (*see also* Fleetwood Mac) 293–294
Bucks Fizz 363
Buffalo Springfield (*see also* Crosby, Stills and Nash; Loggins and Messina; Neil Young) 234
Buffett, Jimmy 284
Bunchofuckingoofs 506
Burdon, Eric (*see also* The Animals) 199
Burgess, Sonny 50
Burke, Solomon 242
Burlison, Paul (*see also* Sam Phillips and Sun Records; Johnny Burnette) 50
Burnett, T-Bone 294
Burnette, Dorsey (*see also* Johnny Burnette) 50
Burnette, Johnny (*see also* Dorsey Burnette) 50–52
Burtnick, Glen 438
Burton, James (*see also* Rick Nelson) 52, 866
Bush, Kate 401
Butcher, Jon (, Axis) 294
Butler, Jerry (*see also* Curtis Mayfield) 244
Butterfield, Paul 370
Butthole Surfers 506
Buzzcocks 495
Byrds, The 234
Byrne, David (*see also* Talking Heads) 537–538
Byrne, Jerry 52

CBI 680
CBS (record company) 835–836
CBS Compact Disc Club 804
CD-5 800
CD-3 800–801
CD-V 801
CTI (record company) 836
Cabinet Voltaire 594
Cable Television 868–870
Cactus World News 655
Cadets (*see* Jacks)
Cadillacs 146

Cain, Jonathan (*see also* Journey) 443
Cajun Rock 266–267
Cale, John (*see also* Lou Reed; Velvet Underground) 587
California Sound 230–233
Call 655
Calypso (*see* Jamaican Sound)
Cambridge Folk Festival 786
Cameo 453, 601
Campbell, Jo Ann 52
Campbell, Stan 574
Camper Van Beethoven (*see also* Touring) 680
Campi, Ray 53
Canada (Lyrics; Ratings; Stickering) 217–229, 756
Candy 680
Candy Flip 737
Capitol (*see also* Nettwerk Productions) 837
Capris 166
Captain of Industry 681
Captain Sensible 681
Captain and Tennille 429
Car Songs 232
Cara, Irene 601
Caravan 294
Cardenas, Luis 322
Cardiacs 681
Cardinals 147
Carey, Mariah 429
Carey, Tony 681
Carlisle, Belinda (*see also* The Go-Go's) 498
Carlos, Don 278
Carlos, Wendy/Walter Carlos 288
Carlton, Larry 866
Carnes, Kim 429
Carpenters (*see also* Television) 420–421
Cars, The (*see also* Elliot Easton; Benjamin Orr) 529
Carson, Lori 401
Carter, Mel 99
Carter the Unstoppable Sex Machine 489
Case, Peter 401, 681–682
Cash, Johnny 395–396
Cashman, Pistilli and West 429
Cassettes 795–796
Cassidy, David (*see also* Partridge Family) 382–383
Cast of 1000s 682
Caterwaul 546
Caufield, Tom 438
Cavaliere, Felix (*see also* The Rascals) 260

Cave, Nick   655–656
Censorship (*see also* Marc Almond; Audio
    Two; Beastie Boys; Christian Death;
    Johnny Clegg; Cure; Dead Kennedys; A
    Flux of Pink Indians; John Fogerty; Heavy
    Metal; Zodiac Mindwarp; Pretenders;
    Prince; 2 Live Crew; Frank Zappa)   753–
    770
A Certain Ratio   510
Cetera, Peter (*see also* Chicago)   430
Chad and Jeremy   199
Chain Tape   772
Chakk   682
Chamberlains (*see also* Lucy Show)   656
Chameleons (*see also* The Dun and the Moon)
    555
Champaign   430
Champlin, Tamara   401
Chandler, Gene   244
Chandra, Sheila   682
Channels   147
Chapin, Harry   402
Chapman, Tracy   402
Charanga 76   282
Charity (*see also* record companies)   770–
    782
Charlatans (U.K.)   737
Charles, Ray   21–22
Charts   782–783
Chastain, David T.   323
Checker, Chubby   181–182
Cheech and Chong   815
Chenier, Clifton   268
Chequered Past   682
Cher   430
Cherrelle   602
Cherry Bombs   323
Cherry, Neneh   479
Chertoff, Rick   856
Chess   13
Chic   468
Chicago (*see also* Peter Cetera)   306
Chicago Bears' **Super Bowl Shuffle**   780
Chicago Sound   244
Childs, Toni   402
Chi-Lites   244
Chills   555–556
Chilton, Alex   255
Chimes   471, 602
Chordettes   99
Chords   147
Christian Death (group)   506
Christian Rap (genre)   624

Christian Rock (genre)   285
Christianity   756–757
Christians   682
Christie, Lou   173–174
Chrysalis (record company)   837
Church (*see also* Steve Kilbey; Marty Willson-
    Piper)   556–557
Ciani, Suzanne   645–646
Cinderella   323
Cinema   453
Circle Jerks   506–507
Circus Circus Circus   683
Circus X3   683
City   430
Clapton, Eric (*see also* Yardbirds)   209–210
Clark, Dick   179
Clark, Dick, Productions   871
Clark, Petula   199
Clark, Sanford   53
Clarke, Stanley   352
Clarke, Tony (*see also* The Hollies)   430
Clash, The (*see also* Big Audio Dynamite;
    Nick "Topper" Headon; Joe
    Strummer)   495–496
Classic Rock   829–830
Classical Rock (*see* Symphonic Rock)
Claytown Troupe   683
Clean   683
Clegg, Johnny   307
Clement, Jack   53
Clemons, Clarence (*see also* Bruce Spring-
    steen)   378
Click Click   522
Cliff, Jimmy   278
Clifford, Linda   468
Clinton, George (*see also* Funkadelic)   453–
    454
Clocks   683
Clovers   147
Club Nouveau (*see also* Times Social Club)
    602
Clubs and Concert Venues   783–784
Coasters   148
Cochran, Eddie   118–119
Cock Robin   438, 683
Cockburn, Bruce   402–403
Cocker, Joe   380–381
Cocteau Twins   648–649
Cohen, Leonard   403
Coil   522–523
Cold Chillin' (record company)   628, 838
Cole, Jude   403
Cole, Lloyd   403, 683–684

Cole, Nat "King" 99–100
Collins, Albert 370
Collins, Phil (*see also* Genesis; Marilyn Martin) 438–439
Collins Kids 53
Colour Field (*see also* Fun Boy Three) 684
Columbia (record company) 838
Colvin, Shawn 403
Combat (record company) 838
Comic Books 819
Commercial Folk 186–187
Commodores (*see also* Lionel Ritchie) 454
Commonwealth Contributions 215–229
Communards (*see also* Bronski Beat) 480
Communist Bloc Nations 757
Compact Disc Group 798
Compact Disc Jukeboxes 798
Compact Discs (*see also* Digital Audio Tape) 796–806, 808
Comstock, Bobby 119
Concerts, Festivals, Touring 784–788
Concrete Blonde 656
Contemporary Hits Radio (CHR) 830
Cooder, Ry 370
Cooke, Sam 22–24
Cool Down Zone 480
Coolidge, Rita 422
Cooper, Alice 310–311
Cooper, Ray (*see also* Elton John) 212
Cope, Julian (*see also* Teardrop Explodes) 547
Copeland, Ian 852
Copeland, Stewart (*see also* Police) 594–595
Copy Code System 789
Copy Protection (DAT) 807–808
Copyright (*see also* Beastie Boys; Counterfeiting, Bootlegging, etc.; Rap; Bruce Springsteen; Turtles) 788–789
Corea, Chick 352–353
Count Five 285
Counterfeiting, Bootlegging, etc. (*see also* Copyright) 789–790
Country Connection 390–398
Country Crossovers 395–398
Country Joe (and the Fish) 270
Country Rock 390–395
County, Jayne/Wayne County 497
Cousin Brucie 825
Covay, Don 24
Cover Recordings 96–98
Cowboy Junkies 656, 684
Coyne, Kevin 294

Coyote (record company) 838
Cramps 381
Cranes 547
Cray, Robert 370–372
Crazy House 547
Crazyhead 684
Creach, Papa John (*see also* Jefferson Starship) 372
Creaming Jesus 684
Creation (group) 286
Creation (record company) 838
Creatures (*see also* Siouxsie and the Banshees) 511–512
Creedence Clearwater Revival 378
Creepers 685
Crenshaw, Marshall 570
Crests 166
Crew-Cuts (*see also* Cover Recordings) 100
Crewe, Bob 858
Crickets, The (*see also* Buddy Holly) 119–121
Crime and the City Solution 685
Critique (record company) 839
Crosby, Bing 100
Crosby, David (*see also* The Byrds; Crosby, Stills and Nash) 421
Crosby, Gary (*see also* Bing Crosby) 100
Crosby, Stills and Nash/Crosby, Stills, Nash and Young (*see also* Buffalo Springfield; The Byrds; David Crosby; The Hollies; Neil Young) 421, 772
Crowded House (*see also* Split Enz) 570–571
Crowell, Rodney 396
Crows 148
Crudup, Arthur 24–25
Cruise, Julee 649
Cruzados (*see also* Havalinas) 741
Crystals 187
Cucumbers 685
Cult 323–324
Culture Club (*see also* Boy George; Duran Duran) 565–566
Cure 547–549
Curiosity Killed the Cat 685
Currie, Cherie 512
Curry, Mickey 259
Curtis, Sonny 54
Curved Air 288
Cutting Crew 685
Cycle Sluts 686
Cypress (record company) 839

D-Mob   628
dB's   571
DJ Jazzy Jeff and the Fresh Prince   628
DOA   219
D.O.C.   628
DRI   348
Daffodils   686
Daintees   686
Dali's Car   592
Daltrey, Roger (*see also* The Who)   206–207
Damen, Das   349
Damn Yankees (*see also* Night Ranger; Ted Nugent; Styx)   324
Damned   497
Dance Crazes (1960–1964)   181–182
Dance-Oriented Rock   470–477
Dancing Hoods   571
Dane, Dana   628
Daniels, Charlie (*see also* Concerts, Festivals, Touring)   390–391
Danny and the Juniors   167
D'Arby, Terence Trent   459–460
Darin, Bobby   174
Darling Buds (*see also* Black)   686
Dave Clark Five   199
Dave Dee, Dozy, Beaky, Mick and Tich   210
Davies, Ray (*see also* The Kinks)   201
Davis, Clive   853
Davis, Martha (*see also* Motels)   404
Davis, Miles   353
Davis, Sammy, Jr.   425
Dax, Danielle (, and the Lemon Kittens)   549
Day, Bobby   25
Day, Morris (*see also* The Time)   464
Dayne, Taylor   431
Dazz Band   454
De La Soul (*see also* Turtles)   628
Deacon Blue   686–687
Dead Can Dance   289
Dead Kennedys (*see also* Censorship)   507–508
Dead Milkmen   656
     Or Alive   480
  rge   602–603
  rgh, Chris   687
  -Lite   472, 480
  e   603
  Purple (*see also* Whitesnake)   324–325
  , Rick   185–186
  Jam (record company)   839
     Leppard   325

Defunkt   465
Del Amitri   687
Del Conte, Andrea   687
Del Fuegos   742
Del-Lords   742
Del-Vikings   149
Delaney and Bonnie   372
Delfonics   257
Delicious Vinyl (record company)   839
Dells   149
Deltones   687
Demento, Dr.   185
Dene, Terry   189
Denver, John (*see also* Parents Music Resource Center)   422–423
Deodato, Eumir   858
Depeche Mode (*see also* Erasure; Yaz)   576
Des Barres, Michael (*see also* Power Station)   325
Detroit Sound   269–270
Device   220, 439
DeVille, Willy   258
Devo (*see also* Mark Mothersbaugh)   530, 576
Dexy's Midnight Runners   238
Diamond, Neil   431
Diamonds   167
Diddley, Bo   25–27
Diesel Park West   688
Difford, Chris, and Glenn Tilbrook (*see also* Squeeze)   503
Dig   688
Digital Audio Tape (DAT)   806–808
Digital Underground   629
Dillard, Varetta   27
Dinner Ladies   423
Dino, Desi and Billy   383
Dinosaur Jr.   524
Dinosaurs (*see also* Jefferson Airplane; Quick-silver Messenger Service)   270
Dio (, Ronnie James) (*see also* Riverdogs)   326
Dion   167–168
Dire Straits   531
Dirty Dozen Brass Band   264
Disc Jockeys (*see also* Clubs and Concert Venues)   784, 824–826
Disco   467–494
Disco Aid   773
Distant Cousins   737
Divinyls   512
Dixon, Don   274–275
Dixon, Willie   27–28

Doctor and the Medics 557
Dr. Buzzard's Original Savannah Band (*see also* Kid Creole and the Coconuts) 468
Dr. Dre (*see also* N.W.A.) 858
Dr. Hook and the Medicine Show 431
Dr. John 264
Dokken (*see also* Mob Rules) 326–327
Dolby, Thomas 577–578
Dolby's Cube (*see* George Clinton; Thomas Dolby)
Domino, Ana (*see also* Anne Taylor) 587
Domino, Fats 28
Dominoes, The (*see also* Clifton Chenier; The Drifters; Clyde McPhatter; Jackie Wilson) 149
Don and Dewey 28
Don and Juan 29
Donner, Ral 54
Donovan, Jason (*see* Kylie Minogue)
Doors 294–295
Doo-wop (1954–1957) 143–165
Dorman, Harold 55
Dorsey, Lee 264–265
Double Destiny 603
Doug and the Slugs 220
Downing, Big Al 55
Downing, Will 472
Drake, Nick 404
Dread Zeppelin 278–279
Dream Academy 289
Dream Syndicate (*see also* Steve Wynn) 558
Dream Warriors (*see* Krush and Skad)
Dreams So Real 742
Drifters, The (*see also* The Dominoes; Ben E. King; Clyde McPhatter) 150–151
Drugs (*see also* Boy George) 790–791
Drums 816
Dubs 151
Duke, Patty 180
Dunbar, Sly 279
Dunhill 840
Dural, Buckwheat 268
Duran Duran (*see also* Arcadia; Culture Club; Power Station; Andy Taylor) 567–568
Dury, Ian (, and the Blockheads) 531
Dylan, Bob 234

EMI (record company) 840
Eagles, The 391
Earle, Steve 391
Earls 151–152
Earth, Wind and Fire (*see also* Philip Bailey; Maurice White) 454–455

Easterhouse (*see also* Censorship) 688
Easton, Elliot (*see also* The Cars) 530
Easton, Sheena 414
Easybeats 215–216
Eat 742
Echo and the Bunnymen (*see also* Teardrop Explodes) 558–559
Economics and Marketing (*see also* Music Industry) 791–792
Eddie, John 688
Eddie and the Tide 689
Eddy, Duane 182–183
Edge, Graeme (*see also* Moody Blues) 291
Edmunds, Dave (*see also* Fabulous Thunderbirds) 368, 743
Education 792–793
Egan, Mark (*see also* Arcadia; David Sanborn) 353
Ege Bam Yasi 689
Eight Seconds 220
808 State 493–494
Eighth Wonder 689
Einstuerzende Weubauten 595
El Dorados (*see also* Kool Gents) 152
Electribe 101 489
Electric Boys 465
Electric Light Orchestra 289
Electric Morning 689
Electric Prunes 286
Electronic Equipment (*see also* Guitars) 817
Electronic Music 592–594
Elegants 152
Ellis, Jimmy (*see also* Orion) 55
Ely, Joe 391
Emerson, Keith (*see also* Emerson, Lake and Palmer) 290
Emerson, Lake and Palmer/Emerson, Lake and Powell (*see also* Moody Blues; Keith Emerson) 290
Emotional Fish, An 689
En Vogue 188
Enchanters (*see also* Garnet Mimms) 168
Energy Orchard 690
Engineers (studio) (*see* Steve Hodge)
English Rhythm and Blues Revival 380–381
Enigma (record company) 840
Eno (*see also* Roxy Music; Talking Heads) 649
Enuff Z'Nuff 327
Enya 646
Epic (record company) 840
Erasure (*see also* Depeche Mode; Yaz) 578

Erikson, Roky (*see* 13th Floor Elevators)
Ertegun, Nesuhi   14, 853
Escape Club   690
Esquerita   121
Esquires   168
Essex   169
Essex, David   439–440
Estefan, Gloria (*see also* Miami Sound Machine)   284
Etheridge, Melissa   404
Eurogliders   690
European Pop Tradition   93–107
Euro-Pop/Euro-Rock   361–367
Eurythmics   579
Everly Brothers (*see also* John Fogerty)   121–124
Everything But the Girl   354
Exile   396–397
Experimental   594–597
Expose (*see also* Girl Groups)   629
Extreme   327

FM   690
Fabian   180
Fabulous Thunderbirds (*see also* Dave Edmunds; Mason Ruffner; Stevie Ray Vaughan)   372–373
Face to Face   392, 690
Faces (*see also* Jeff Beck; Humble Pie; Ronnie Lane; Rod Stewart)   210
Fairground Attraction   690
Fairport Convention (*see also* Ian Matthews; Richard Thompson)   238
Faith, Adam   190
Faith Brothers   691
Faith No More   465
Faithfull, Marianne   199–200
Falco (*see also* Censorship)   361
Falcons   152
Fall   512
Family   295
Family Stand   603
Fans, Audiences, etc.   793
Fanzines   819
Far Voyagers   559
Farm   513
Farm Aid (*see also* Willie Nelson)   773
Farm Aid II   774
Farm Aid III   774
Farm Aid IV   774
Fashion   793
Fast, Larry   579, 587

Faster Pussycat   691
Fat Boys   629
Fatal Charm   691
Faze One   691
Feathers, Charlie   55–56
Feelies   571
Fela   307
Feliciano, Jose   305
Felt   513, 691
Ferry, Bryan (*see also* Roxy Music)   431
Ferry Aid   774
Fetchin' Bones   275
Fever Tree   286
Fields of the Nephilim   349
Fiestas   152
5th Dimension   421
54–40   220
Films   793–795
Fine Young Cannibals (*see also* Beat/English Beat)   656–657
Fingers Inc.   494
Finland   800
Finn, Tim   216
Fire   691
Fire Next Time   692
Fire Town   657
Firm (*see also* Bad Company)   440
Fish (*see also* Marillion)   692
Fishbone   692–693
Fisher, Climie   657
Fisher, Eddie   101
Fit   603
Five Chances   153
Five Keys   153
5 Royales   153
Five Satins   153
Five Sharps   154
Five Star   693
5TA   693
Five Thirty   480
Fixx   531
Flack, Roberta   242
Flairs   154
Flaming Mussolinis   693
Flamingos   154
Flat Duo Jets   543–544
Fleetwood Mac   211
Flesh   693
Flesh For Lulu   657
Fleshtones   497
Flipper   508
Florida   757

Flotsam and Jetsam   349
Flowered Up   738
Floy Joy   694
Flux of Pink Indians, A   513
Fly (record company)   840
Flying Nun (record company)   841
Focus   363
Foetus, Jim/Scraping Foetus Off the Wheel   523
Fogelberg, Dan   404
Fogerty, John (*see also* Saul Zaentz)   378–379
Foghat   379
Foley, Ellen   404–405
Folk Rock   233–237
Fontaine, Eddie   56
Fontana, D.J. (*see also* Elvis Presley)   56
Force M.D.'s   604, 630
Ford, Baby (*see also* Adamski)   490
Ford, Lita (*see also* Runaways)   327
Fordham, Julie   405
Foreigner   440
Foremost Poets   491
Formats   795–814
Forrest, Jimmy   29
Forty-Five R.P.M. Single   808
Fountainhead   694
Four Blazes   154
Four Buddies   154
Four Coins   155
Four Freshmen   101
Four Lads   101
4 of Us   472
Four Seasons, The   169
Four Tops   246
Four Tunes (*see also* Brown Dots)   155
400 Blows   694
4,000,000 Telephones   694
Fox, Samantha   472
Foxx, John   579
Fra Lippo Lippi   694
Frampton, Peter (*see also* Humble Pie)   211, 440
France   361–362
Francis, Connie   174
Frank, David   354
Frank Chickens   694
Frankie Goes to Hollywood   481–482
Franklin, Aretha   256
Frantz, Chris (*see also* Talking Heads)   538
Frazier Chorus   482
Freddie and the Dreamers   200

Freed, Alan   3–4
Freeez   695
Friction Groove   695
Friday, Gavin, and the Man Seezer (*see also* Virgin Prunes)   695
Friedman, Kinky   392
Friesen, Gil   853
Fripp, Robert (*see also* King Crimson)   587–588
Frith, Fred   588
Front   373
Frozen Ghost   220
Fruits of Passion   695
Fugazi   657
Fugs   235
Full Circle   354
Full Force (*see also* Lisa Lisa)   630
Fulson, Lowell   29
Fun Boy Three   574
Funk   453–466
Funk Metal   465
Funk-Punk   459–464
Funkadelic (*see also* George Clinton)   455
Fuqua, Harvey (*see* The Moonglows; Motown Sound)
Furniture   695
Fury   695
Furys   285
Fuzzbox   696
Fuzztones   559

GRP (record company)   841
GTR   295
Gabriel, Peter (*see also* Genesis)   295–296
Gadd, Steve (*see also* Simon Phillips)   866–867
Galaxie 500   657–658
Gamma   296
Gang Green   513
Gant, Cecil   29
Gap Band   455
Garfunkel, Art (*see also* Simon and Garfunkel)   421
Gavin, Bill   828
Gaye, Marvin   246–247
Gaye Bykers on Acid   509–510
Geffen (*see also* Chrysalis; MCA)   841
Geils, J., Band (*see also* Peter Wolf)   379
Geldof, Bob (*see also* Band Aid; Boomtown Rats; Charity)   696–697
Gene and Eunice   29
Gene Loves Jezebel   549

General Public (*see also* Beat/English Beat;
  Ranking Roger) 532, 697–698
Genesis (*see also* Tony Banks; Phil Collins;
  Peter Gabriel; Steve Hackett; Mike and
  the Mechanics) 296
Gentle Giant (*see also* Derek Shulton) 296
Georgia Satellites 743
Germany 362–363
Germs 508
Gerry and the Pacemakers 200
Getting the Fear 698
Giant (record company) 842
Giant Sand (*see also* Dream Sandworms;
  Green on Red) 698
Gibb, Andy 431
Gibbons, Shannon 698
Gibson, Debbie (*see also* Tiffany) 383
Gill, Johnny (*see also* New Edition) 604
Gilder, Nick 405
Gilkyson, Eliza 405
Giorno, John 588
Gipsy Kings 361–362
Girl Groups 188
Girlschool 327
Giuffria 327–328
Gladiolas 164–165
Glasnost Rock Concert 775
Glass Tiger 221
Glastonbury 786
Glenn, Glen 56–57
Glitter, Gary 311
Glitter Rock 309–314
Globestyle (record company) 842
Glover, Crispin 698
Go-Betweens 699
Go Fundamental 699
Go-Go 619–620
Go-Go's, The (*see also* Belinda Carlisle; Kathy
  Valentine) 497–498
Go West 482
Godfathers 699
Godflesh (*see* Loop)
Godley and Creme (*see also* Charity) 595
Goffin, Gerry, and Carole King (*see also*
  Carole King) 172–173
Goffin, Louise 405
Gold Castle (record company) 841
Golden Horde 700
Golden Palominos (*see also* Syd Straw) 297
Gone 700
Good Question 472
Goodbye Mr. Mackenzie 311, 700
Goodman, Steve 235

Gordon, Roscoe 29
Gordy, Berry (*see also* Motown) 245
Goth Rock 546–554
Gottlieb, Danny 354
Gracie, Charlie 124
Grammys 752
Grandmaster Dee 630
Grandmaster Flash 630
Grant, Eddy 279
Grateful Dead 270–272
Great Divide 700
Great Society (*see also* Jefferson Airplane)
  272
Great Southern (*see* Dickey Betts)
Great White 328
Grebenshikov, Boris 367
Green, Al 255
Green on Red 513–514
Greenhouse of Terror 700
Greenpeace 775
Greenwich, Ellie 173
Gregson, Clive (*see also* Any Trouble; Richard
  Thompson) 392
Grid 494
Grisman, David 354
Groove B Chill 630
Guadalcanal Diary 544
Guess Who 221
Guitar Slim 266
Guitar Synthesizers 817–818
Guitars, Electric 817
Gun Club 514
Guns N' Roses 328–329
Gunter, Hardrock 57
Guthrie, Gwen 604
Guy (group) 630
Gwar 508

Hackett, Steve (*see also* Genesis) 297
Hackford, Taylor, and Joel Sill 859
Hagar, Sammy (*see also* Van Halen) 346
Haircut 100 532
Haley, Bill 5–7
Half Man Half Biscuit 700–701
Hall (, Daryl) and (John) Oates (*see also*
  Mickey Curry) 258–259
Hall, Roy 57
Hamilton, Roy 30
Hammer, Jan 355
Hammer, M.C. 631
Hancock, Herbie 355–356
Hands Across America (*see also* Kenneth
  Kragen) 775–776

Hanoi Rocks (see also Michael Monroe)
329
Happy Mondays   738
Hard Corps   701
Hard Rock Soul Movement   701
Hardcastle, Paul   482–483
Hardcore   505–509
Harding, John Wesley   405
Harper, Roy   297
Harptones   155
Harris, Emmylou   397
Harris, Hugh   405
Harris, Thurston   30
Harris, Wynonie   30
Harrison, George (see also The Beatles)
195–196
Harrison, Jerry   538 (see also Talking Heads)
Harrison, Kodac   406
Harrison, Wilbert   30
Hart, Corey   221–222
Hartman, Dan   859
Hartman, Lisa   414
Hathaway, Donny   242
Havalinas (see also Cruzados)   743
Havens, Richie   235
Hawkins, Dale   57
Hawkins, Ronnie   124–125
Hawkins, Screamin' Jay   31, 124
Hawkwind   287
Hay, James Colin (see also Men At Work)
217
Hayes, Isaac   254
Hayward, Justin (see also Moody Blues)
291
Haywire   222
Haza, Ofra   483
Head, Roy   260
Head of David   701
Headon, Nick "Topper" (see also The Clash)
496
Headpins   222
Healey, Jeff   373
Health   815
Hear 'N' Aid   776
Heart   441
Heart Throbs   701
Hearts and Minds   702
Hearts on Fire   702
Heaven 17 (see also Human League)   579
Heavy Metal (see also Censorship)   314–348,
757
Heavy Shift   631
Hedges, Michael   646

Helix (see also Honeymoon Suite)   223
Helter Skelter   550
Hendricks, Bobby   31
Hendrix, Jimi (Experience)   297–298
Hendryx, Nona (see Melba Moore)   604
Henley, Don (see also The Eagles)   441–442
Herman's Hermits   200
Hewerdine, Boo, and Darden Smith   743
Heyman, Richard X   702
Heyward, Nick   702
Hiatt, John   406
Hickman, Sara   406
Highwaymen   186
Hilltoppers   101
Hilt (see also Skinny Puppy)   526
Himmelman, Peter   406
Hine, Rupert   859
Hip Hop (see Rap)
Hip House   490
Hipsway   702
History (music)   814–815
History Featuring Q-Tie   494
Hit Video   870
Hit-N-Run (record company)   842
Hitchcock, Robyn (, and the Egyptians)
559–560, 658
Hodges, Steve   857
Hoffs, Susanna (see also The Bangles)   702
Holden, Ron   125
Holdsworth, Allan   298
Holland   363
Holland-Dozier-Holland   859
Holland Group (record company)   842
Holliday, Jennifer   604
Hollies, The (see also Crosby, Stills and Nash)
200
Hollow Sunday   703
Holly, Buddy (see also The Crickets)   125–
130
Hollywood Beyond   703
Hollywood Flames (see also Bobby Day)
155–156
Holy Modal Rounders   236
Home Videocassettes   809–810
Honey Smugglers   703
Honeychild   483
Honeydrippers   703
Honeymoon Suite (see also Helix)   223–224
Hoodoo Gurus   658–659
Hook 'N' Pull Gang   703
Hooker, John Lee   31–32
Hooters   703–704
Horne, Lena   32

Hornsby, Bruce (, and the Range) 432
Horse 580
Hothouse Flowers 659
House Music 489–493
House of Freaks 659
House of Love 550
Housemartins 704
Houston, Whitney 605
Howe, Steve (see also Yes) 304
Hue and Cry 704
Hugo Largo 596
Hula 514
Human League (see also Heaven 17) 580
Humble Pie (see also Faces; Peter Frampton) 211
Humor 815–816
Humperdinck, Engelbert 426
Hunter, Ian 298–299
Hunter and Ronson (see also David Bowie; Mott the Hoople) 329
Husker Du (see also Bob Mould) 514–515
Huxley, Parthenon 406
Hypnotics, Thee 704

INXS 483
I Start Counting 705
Ian, Janis 241
Ian and Sylvia 236
Ice-T 631
Icicle Works 532–533
Idle Eyes 224
Idle Race (see also Electric Light Orchestra) 211
Idol, Billy 484–485
Immaculate Fools 705
Impalas 156
Impossibles 705
Incredible String Band 238
Indigo Girls 236
Industrial Dance 526–527
Industrial/Material Music 522–524
Innes, Neil 705
Innocence Mission 705
Insiders 442
Inspiral Carpets 738
Instrumentals 182–185
Instruments 816–818
Into Paradise (see also Blue in Heaven) 706
Iron Maiden 329–330
Isaak, Chris 406–407
Isham, Mark 646
Island (record company) 842
Isle of Man 432

Isley Brothers 32
It Bites 706
It's Immaterial 659

Jack Rubies 706
Jacks 156
Jackson, Bullmoose 32
Jackson, Chuck 242–243
Jackson, Freddie 606
Jackson, Janet 472–473
Jackson, Jermaine (see also Jackson Five) 248
Jackson, Joe 596
Jackson, Michael (see also The Beatles; Charity; Jackson Five; Music Publishers) 248–250
Jackson, Millie 606
Jackson, Wanda 57–58
Jackson Five/Jacksons (see also Jermaine Jackson; Michael Jackson) 247
Jagger, Mick (see also David Bowie; Rolling Stones) 204–205
Jam, The (see also Style Council; Paul Weller) 498–499
Jam, Jimmy, and Terry Lewis (see also Steve Hodge; Human League; Janet Jackson; The Time) 860
Jamaica Boys (see also Miles Davis; Luther Vandross) 606
Jamaican Sound 186–187
James 550, 660
James, Etta 33
James, Rick 460
Jamie Wednesday 706
Jan and Dean 232
Jandek 407
Janes, Roland 58–59
Jane's Addiction 550, 660
Japan 533
Jarre, Jean-Michel 593
Jason and the Scorchers 392
Jay, Michael 881
Jay and the Americans 169
Jazz Butcher 706
Jazz-Rock Fusion 351–360
Jefferson Airplane/Jefferson Starship (see also Dinosaurs; Great Society; KBC Band) 272
Jem (record company) 842–843
Jesters of Destiny 330
Jesus Jones 660
Jesus and Mary Chain 516
Jet Set (see Timex Social Club)

Jethro Tull   299
Jets   606–607
Jett, Joan, and the Blackhearts   499
Jimmy Jimmy   706
Jive (record company)   843
Jive Five   169
Jo Jo and the Real People   706
Joboxers   707
Jobson, Eddie   356
Joel, Billy (see also USA for Africa; "We are the World")   407–408
Johansen, David (see also New York Dolls)   312
John, Elton (see also Ray Cooper; Copyright; Nigel Olsson)   212
John, Lee   707
John, Little Willie   33
Johnnie and Joe   156
John's Children   213
Johnson, Don   442
Johnson, Eric   707, 743–744
Johnson, General   169
Johnson, Henry   356
Johnson, Jesse (see also The Time)   455
Johnson, Marv   33–34
Jomanda   491
Jones, Grace   468
Jones, Howard (see also Thomas Dolby)   580–581
Jones, Joe   265
Jones, Marti   707
Jones, Mick (see also Big Audio Dynamite; The Clash)   652
Jones, Oran "Juice"   607
Jones, Quincy   607
Jones, Rickie Lee   408
Jones, Tom   426
Joneses   608
Joplin, Janis   272–273
Jordan, Louis   34
Jordan, Stanley   356
Jordan, Steve   867
Journalism   819–820
Journey (see also Jonathan Cain; Bad English; Santana)   442
Joy Division (see also New Order)   551
Judas Priest   330
Juju   306
Juncosa, Sylvia   560
Jungklas, Rob   408
Junkanoo   284
Junior   608
Jury   224

K-Tel (record company)   843
KBC Band (see also Jefferson Airplane)   ' 273
K.C. and the Sunshine Band   284
KLF   494
KMC   631
Kaiser, Henry   560
Kajagoogoo/Kaja   707
Kalahari Surfers   707
Kaleidoscope   299
Kamen, Nick   473
Kane, Big Daddy   632
Kane Gang   456, 707
Kansas (see also Steve Morse)   443
Karr, Tim   331
Kasem, Casey   824–825
Kashif (see also Meli'sa Morgan)   608
Katrina and the Waves   708
Keel   331
Keene, Tommy   571–572
Keita, Salif   749
Keith   421
Kelly, Paul   216, 408
Keltner, Jim   867
Kemp, Johnny   456
Kendrick, Eddie (see also Hall and Oates; The Temptations)   251
Kennedy, Brian   708
Kentucky Headhunters   275
Kershaw, Nik   267, 409
Kesler, Stan (see also Sam Phillips and Sun Records)   59
Khan, Chaka   456
Khan, Steve   356
Kid Creole and the Coconuts (see also Dr. Buzzard's Original Savannah Band)   456
Kid Flash   632
Kid 'N Play   632
Kihn, Greg (, Band)   708
Kill Ugly Pop   708
Killdozer   708
Killing Joke   516
Kilzer, John   409
King   473
King, B.B.   374
King, Ben E. (see also The Drifters)   174
King, Carole (see also Gerry Goffin)   173, 409
King, James   709
Kingdom Come   331
Kings of the Sun   331
King's X   332
Kinks, The (see also Ray Davies)   200–201

Kinney, Kevin (see also Drivin' n' Cryin';
  R.E.M.) 709
Kiss 311–312
Kiss That 709
Kissing Bandits 709
Kitaro 646–647
Kitchens of Distinction 709
Kix 332
Klymaxx 457
Knebworth 786
Knight, Gladys 608
Knight, Sonny 34
Knox, Buddy 59
Kool and the Gang 457–458
Kool Gents (see also El Dorados) 156
Kool Rock Jay 632
Kottke, Leo 647
Kraftwerk 593
Kragen, Kenneth (see also Hands Across
  America; U.S.A. For Africa) 776
Kramer, Billy J, and the Dakotas 201
Kramer (, Mark) (see also Shimmy Disc)
  861
Kravitz, Lenny 461
Kreutzmann, Bill, and Mickey Hart (see also
  Grateful Dead) 749
Kristofferson, Kris 392–393
Krokus 332
Krush 491
Krush and Skad 632

L.A.'s 710
LL Cool J 632–634
LaBeef, Sleepy 60
Labeling (see Stickering)
LaBelle, Patti 243, 608–609
Lach 409
Laddins 157
Lady Pank 366
Ladysmith Black Mambazo 308
Laibach 525
Laine, Frankie 101
Lane, Ronnie (see also ARMS; Faces) 210
Lang, K.D. 397
Lanois, Daniel 861
Lanson, Snooky 102
Larks 157
Last Few Days 473, 568
Late Night With David Letterman 872
Latin Quarter (group) 660
Latin Rock 305
Laughing Academy 710

Lauper, Cyndi 710–711
Lavitz, T. 357
Law, Linda 485
Laws and Legislation (see also Maryland;
  Stickering) 757–758
Le Roux 443
Leather Nun 711
Leaves 285
Leaving Trains 517
LeBlance, Keith 526
Led Zeppelin (see also Jimmy Page; Robert
  Plant; The Yardbirds) 332–333
Lee, Brenda 174–175
Lee, Dickey 175
Lee, Johnny 397–398
Lee, Peggy 102
Leiber, Jerry, and Mike Stoller 113
Lemonheads 517
Lennon, John (see also The Beatles) 196–
  197
Lennon, Julian 409–410
Lennon Sisters 102
Les Negresses Vertes 362
Let's Active 544
Level 42 357
Levert 609
Levy, Morris 853–854
Lewis, Gary, and the Playboys 230
Lewis, Huey, and the News 443–444
Lewis, Jerry Lee (see also Little Richard; Sam
  Phillips and Sun Records) 130–134
Lewis, Terry (see Jimmy Jam)
Liberace 102
Liggins, Joe 34
Lightning Seeds (see also Echo and the Bun-
  nymen) 661
Lil Louis 491
Lilac Time 711
Lind, Bob 60
Lindley, David 868
Lipps, Inc. 468
Lisa Lisa and the Cult Jam (With Full Force)
  (see also Full Force) 634
Little Anthony and the Imperials 157
Little Caesar 485
Little Caesar and the Romans 157
Little Feat 233
Little Richard 134–138
Little River Band 216
Live Aid (see also Counterfeiting, Bootleg-
  ging, etc.) 776–778
Living Colour 466

Lloyd, Michael   862
Lofgren, Nils (*see also* Bruce Springsteen)   410
Loggins and Messina (*see also* Buffalo Springfield; Jim Messina)   233
Loggins, Dave   422
Loketo   749
London, Julie   102
London Posse   634
London Quireboys (*see* Quireboys)
Lone Justice (*see also* Maria McKee)   744
Long-Playing Record Album (LP)   808–809
Long Ryders   744–745
Loop (*see also* Sonic Boom; Spacemen 3)   581, 661
Loose Ends   609
Lord Tracy   333
Lords of the New Church (*see also* Stiv Bators)   517
Los Angeles Sound   233
Los Lobos   269
Lost Loved Ones   712
Lou, Bonnie   60
Loud (*see also* New Model Army)   333
Loudness   334
Louisiana (*see also* Stickering)   758
Love   287
Love, Joeski   609
Love, Monie   634
Love and Money   712
Love and Rockets   551
Love Tractor   544
Loverboy   225
Lovich, Lene   533
Lovin' Spoonful   236
Lowe, Nick   572
Lucy Show (*see also* Chamberlains)   661
Luman, Bob   60–61
Lunch, Lydia   500
Lush   649
Luxuria (*see also* Buzzcocks)   662
Lymon, Frankie, and the Teenagers   157–158
Lymon, Lewis, and the Teenchords   158
Lynyrd Skynyrd (*see also* Festivals)   275
Lyres   662
Lyrics, Song (*see also* Censorship; PMRC; Ratings)   758–760, 818–819

M   473
M/A/R/R/S   485

MC 900 Ft. Jesus   634–635
MCA (record company)   843–844
MC5   269
MTV   768–769, 868–870
MacColl, Kirsty   410
Mack, Lonnie (*see also* Stevie Ray Vaughan)   183
Mad Professor   712
Madame   225
Madame X   712
Maddox, Rose   61
Madness   574–575
Madonna (*see also* Dire Straits)   474–476
Magazines, Newsletters, etc.   760, 820–821
Magnum   334
Mahon, Willie   34
Mainframe   712
Makeba, Miriam (*see* Hugh Masekela)
Makin' Time   712
Malaco (record company)   845
Malmsteen, Yngwie   334
Malo-Tones   713
Mamas and the Papas   236
Man   299
Managers (*see also* Drugs)   819
Manchester Sound   737–740
Mancini, Henry   102
Mandela, Nelson, International Tribute Concert   778
Manfred Mann('s Earth Band)   201
Manhattan (*see* EMI)
Manhattan Transfer   170, 357
Manilow, Barry   424–425
Manitoba's Wild Kingdom   500
Mann, Barry, and Cynthia Weil   173
Mann, Carl   61
Mano Negra   362
Mantler, Karen   357
Mantronix   635
Mapfumo, Thomas   308
Marathons (*see also* Olympics)   158
March Violets   713
Marie, Teena   609–610
Marillion (*see also* Fish)   299–300
Markie, Biz   635
Marley, Bob (*see also* Peter Tosh)   279–280
Marley, Ziggy   280
Maroon Town   575
Marsalis, Branford (*see also* Sting)   360
Martha and the Vandellas   250
Martika   410

Martin, Janis   61
Martin, Marilyn (see also Phil Collins)   432,
   444
Martinez, Eddie   867
Martyn, John   238
Marvelettes   250
Marvelows   170
Marx, Richard   432
Mary Jane Girls (see also Rick James)   610
Mary My Hope   713
Maryland (see also Laws and Legislation;
   Stickering)   760–761
Masekela, Hugh   308
Mason Proffit   393
Masquerade   713
Mass Media   819–873
Mathis, Johnny   103
Matthews, Ian/Matthews' Southern Comfort
   (see also Fairport Convention)   238
Mauriat, Paul   425
Max Q (see also INXS)   713
Maxwell, Holly   243
May, Raymond   745
Mayall, John (see also Eric Clapton; Fleetwood
   Mac; The Yardbirds)   375
Mayfield, Curtis (see also Jerry Butler)   244
Maze   458
Mazzy Star   560
McCartney, Paul (see also The Beatles)   197–
   198
McCoy, Van   468
McDaniel, Gene   175
McDowell, Carrie   250
McFadden and Whitehead   610
McFerrin, Bobby   610
McGarrigle Sisters/McGarrigles   225–226
McGhee, Stick   35
McGuire Sisters   103
McKay, Kris (see also Wild Seeds)   713
McKee, Maria (see also Lone Justice)   744
McKinley, Mitchell   35
McLaren, Malcolm (see also Sex Pistols)   749
McLaughlin, John   357–358
McNeely, Big Jay   37
McNichol, Kristy and Jimmy   383
McPhatter, Clyde (see also The Dominoes;
   The Drifters)   35–36,   151
Meat Beat Manifesto   491
Meat Loaf   444
Meat Puppets   349
Megadeth   350
Mekons   662
Mel, Grandmaster Melle   635–636

Mellencamp, John Cougar   444–445
Mello-Kings   159
Melvin, Harold, and the Blue Notes (see also
   Teddy Pendergrass)   257
Membranes   517, 714
Memphis Sound   254–255
Men At Work (see also James Colin Hay)
   216
Men They Couldn't Hang   714
Menudo   383
Mercy Seat   476
Merengue   748
Merry-Go-Round   572
Messina, Jim (see also Loggins and Messina)
   393
Metal Blade   845
Metallica   350
Meters (see Neville Brothers)
Metros   714
Meyers, Augie   269
Miami Bass   636
Miami Sound Machine (see also Gloria
   Estefan)   283–284
Michael, George (see also Wham!)   433
Mickey and Sylvia   36
Microdisney   662–663
Middle-of-the-Road (MOR)   422–425,
   830
Midler, Bette   426
Midnight (record company)   845
Midnight Oil   517–518
Midnight Star   611
Mighty Lemon Drops   714
Mighty Mighty   714
Mike and the Mechanics (see also Genesis;
   Nick Lowe; Paul Young)   300, 445
Milburn, Amos   36–37
Millar, Robin   862
Miller, Mitch   103
Miller, Roger   398
Miller, Steve (, Band)   273
Milli Vanilli   476, 611
Mills, Stephanie   611
Mind, Body & Soul   485
Mind Over Four   715
Mindwarp, Zodiac, and the Love Reaction
   560–561
Ministry   526
Mink DeVille (see Willy DeVille)
Minogue, Kylie   384
Minor Threat   518
Mint Juleps   188
Minutemen   518

Miracle Legion   715
Miro   715
Missing Persons (*see also* Frank Zappa)   533
Mission (U.K.)   334–335
Mr. Big   446
Mr. Mister   446
Mitchell, Guy   61
Mitchell, Joni   411
Mizell, Hank   62
Mob Rules (*see also* Dokken)   335
Mock Turtles   738
Mofungo   715
Moho Pack   508, 715
Monkees, The (*see also* The New Monkees)   384
Monochrome Set   551
Monotones   159
Monroe, Michael (*see also* Hanoi Rocks)   335
Moodists   716
Moody Blues (*see also* Graeme Edge; Justin Hayward)   202, 290–291
Moon, Keith (*see also* The Who)   207
Moonglows   159
Moore, Gary (*see also* Thin Lizzy)   716
Moore, Johnny   37
Moore, Melba   611
Moore, Scotty (*see also* Elvis Presley)   62
Moore, Sparkle   62
Morales, David   825
Morgan, Meli'sa (*see also* Kashif; Chaka Khan)   612
Moroder, Giorgio   469
Morrissey (*see also* Smiths)   551, 666
Morrison, Van   411–412
Morrow, Bruce (*see* Cousin Brucie)
Morse, Steve (*see also* Kansas)   443
Moscow Music Peace Festival   786
Moss, Jerry   854
Motels   551, 716
Mothers   716
Mothers of Invention (*see also* Frank Zappa)   588
Motley Crue   335–336
Motorhead   336–337
Motown (record company) (*see also* Berry Gordy; MCA)   245–246, 845–846
Motown Sound   245–253
Mould, Bob (*see also* Husker Du)   515
Movement 98   647
Moyet, Alison (*see also* Yaz)   585
Mtume (, James)   636
Mulcahy, Russell   811
Mumbles   716

Murphey, Michael Martin   393
Murphy, Eddie   612
Murphy, Peter   552
Murray, Anne   393
Muscle Shoals Sound (*see also* Stax Records)   256–257
Museum of Broadcast Communications   751
Music Machine   286
Music Publishers (*see* ATV Music Corp.)
Music Video   809–814
Musto and Bones   491
Mute Drivers   716
My Bloody Valentine   561
Myles, Alannah   446
Mystics   170

NRBQ   379
N.W.A. (*see also* Censorship)   636
Najee   358
Naked City   358
Nash the Slash   500
Nazz   287
Near, Holly   236
Ned's Atomic Dustbin   717
Nelson, Bill   300
Nelson, Lory   412
Nelson, Rick(y)   180
Nelson, Willie   398
Neo-doo-wop   166–171
Neo-Psychedelia   554–563
Neo-Rockabilly   381
Neon Judgement   593
Nesmith, Mike (*see also* The Monkees)   394
Netherlands   812
Nettwerk Productions (record company)   846
Neurotics   717
Nevil, Robbie   433
Neville Brothers (*see also* Aaron Neville)   265
New Age   644–648
New Edition (*see also* Bell Biv DeVoe; Bobby Brown; Johnny Gill)   612–613
New Kids on the Block   384–385
New Model Army   509
New Monkees, The (*see also* The Monkees)   433
New Music Festival   786
New Order (*see also* Joy Division)   581
New Orleans Sound   264–266
New Romantics/Blitz   563–569
New Wave   495–585

New York Dolls (*see also* David Johansen)
    312
New Zealand   215–217
Newman, Randy   412
Newton-John, Olivia   425
Nexus   226
Night Music   872
Night Ranger   446–447
Night Tracks   872
Nina and the UFO's   717
Nine Inch Nails   523
Nitty Gritty Dirt Band   394
Nitzer Ebb   523
No Sweat   717
Nomads   717
Nomeansno   717
Nonsense Humor   815
Nordoff-Robbins Music Therapy Center
    778
Northern Girls   717
Northside   739
Norway   363–364
Nostalgia (*see also* Radio; Rock and Roll
    Revival)   368–381, 874
Notting Hillbillies (*see also* Dire Straits)   394
Novelty Songs   185–186
Numan, Gary   581–582
Numbers Band   375
Nuns   718
Nutmegs   159–160
Nylons   226

O.A.O.   337
Obey, Chief Ebenezer   308
Ocean, Billy   613
O'Connor, Sinead   718
Octave One   582
Ode (record company)   846
Odyssey   812
O'Hara, Mary Margaret   412
O'Hearn, Patrick   647
Ohio Players   458
Oi   510–511
Oingo Boingo   534
O'Jays   257
Okosuns, Sonny   308
Olatunji, Babatunde   308
Oldfield, Mike   300
Oldies (*see also* Nostalgia)   830–831
Olsson, Nigel (*see also* Elton John)   212
Olympics (*see also* Marathons)   160
Omar and the Howlers (*see* Mason Ruffner)
    380

Omertian, Michael   862
One-Hit Wonders   185
O'Neal, Alexander   613
Onellana, Raul   862
Onionhead   395
Ono, Yoko (*see also* John Lennon)   588–589
Opus   361
Orange Juice   718
Orbison, Roy   175–178
Orchestral Manoeuvres in the Dark/OMD
    582–583
Originals   170
Orioles   160
Orion (*see also* Jimmy Ellis)   62
Orleans   447
Orr, Benjamin (*see also* The Cars)   530
Osbourne, Ozzy (*see also* Black Sabbath)
    337–338
Osmond, Donny (*see also* Osmonds)   385–
    386
Osmond, Marie (*see also* Donny Osmond)
    386
Osmonds/Osmond Brothers (*see also* Donny
    Osmond)   386
Otis, Johnny   37–38
Outfield   572–573
Owens, Robert   492

Packaging (compact discs)   801–803
Page, Jimmy (*see also* Led Zeppelin)   333
Page, Patti   103
Paladins   745
Pandy, Daryl   469
Papa Brittle   485
Papa Dee   637
Paper Lace   433
Parachute Club   226–227
Parent Teacher Association (*see also* Parents
    Music Resource Center; Ratings)   764
Parents Music Resource Center
    (PMRC)   761–764
Parker, Graham   314
Parker, Ray, Jr.   613
Parks, Van Dyke   300
Parr, John   433
Parsons, Alan, Project   301
Parsons, Gram (*see also* The Byrds)   395
Partland Brothers   227
Partridge Family (*see also* David Cassidy)
    386
Pastels   719
Patsy   412
Paul, Les, and Mary Ford   103–104

Pay-for-Play 812–813
Payola (*see also* Radio; Recording Industry) 821–822
Payolas 534
Peaches and Herb 243
Pebbles 614
Peel, John 826
Pendergrass, Teddy (*see also* Harold Melvin) 614
Penguin Cafe Orchestra 589
Penguins 160–161
Penn, Michael 412
Percetto, Jeff 882
Perkins, Carl 62–65
Perry, Joe (*see also* Aerosmith) 318
Personics 877–878
Persuasions 170
Pet Shop Boys 486
Peter and Gordon 202
Pettaway, Bill 881
Petted Lips 719
Petty, Tom (, and the Heartbreakers) 447–448
Phantom Chords (*see also* Damned) 381
Phantom, Rocker and Slick (*see also* David Bowie; John Lennon; Stray Cats; John Waite) 745
Philadelphia Sound, The 257
Phillips, (Little) Esther 38
Phillips, Phil (, and the Twilights) 38
Phillips, Sam (singer/songwriter) 412
Phillips, Sam, and Sun Records 65–68
Phillips, Simon (*see also* The Who) 207
Phranc 719
Piccolo Trumpet 818
Pickett, Wilson 256
Pink Floyd (*see also* Roger Waters) 301–302
Pink Industry 524
Pink Peg Slax 719
Pin-Ups 227
Pirate Stations (*see also* Prince) 827
Pitchford, Dean 882
Pitney, Gene 178
Pittman, Barbara 68
Pixies (*see also* Breeders) 663
Plagiarism (*see also* Stevie Wonder) 790
Plant, Robert (*see also* Led Zeppelin) 333
Platinum Blonde (*see also* Blondes) 227–228
Platters 161–162
Play Dead 719
Playground 719

Playn Jayn 720
Pogues 238–239
Poi Dog Pondering 663
Poindexter, Buster (*see* David Johansen) 434
Pointer Sisters/Pointers 614
Poison 338–339
Poison Girls 720
Poland 366
Police (*see also* Sting) 534–535
Politics (*see also* Billy Bragg; Jackson Browne; Paul Hardcastle; MC5; Bruce Springsteen; U2) 874–875
PolyGram (record company) 847
Ponty, Jean Luc 358
Poovey, Groovey Joe 68
Pop, Iggy (*see also* David Bowie) 312–313, 500
Pop-Rock 426–435
Pop Stylists 425–426
Pop Will Eat Itself 637, 663
Pope, Tim 810
Poppy Family 387
Porter, Royce 68
Portrait (record company) 847
Post-Punk 511–522
Posters (*see also* Art; Record Album Covers) 875
Postmodern 670–736
Power 720
Power, Johnny 69
Power Pop 570–573
Power Station (*see also* Michael Des Barres; Duran Duran; Toby Thompson) 568–569
Precious Metal 339
Prefab Sprout 552
Presley, Elvis (*see also* Sam Phillips and Sun Records; Films) 69–87, 794
Preston, Billy 458
Preston, Johnny 87
Pretenders 535
Pretty Poison 476
Previn, Dory 413
Previte, Franke 882
Price, Lloyd 265
Pricing Policies 792
Primal Scream 518–519
Primevals 720
Primitives 720
Prince (*see also* Levi Seacer; Wendy and Lisa) 461–463
Prine, John 413

Pritchard, Bill   583, 721
Proby, P.J.   213
Producers (studio)   857–864
Professor Griff (see also Public Enemy; 2 Live Crew)   637–638
Profile (record company)   847
Progressive Rock   291–304
Prong   509
Propaganda   649–650
Propaganda Films   813
Protest Songs   240–241
Prunes   721
Psych-Oh Rangers, Das   721
Psyche   524
Psychedelia (see Acid Rock)
Psychedelic Furs   561
Psychic TV   489
Psycho Surgeons   721
Pub Rock (see Graham Parker)
Public Image, Ltd./PiL (see also Sex Pistols)   596–597
Public Relations   876
Pump It Up!   872
Punk   495–505
Punk Rock   285–286
Pursuit of Happiness   721

Quarterflash   448
Queen   339
Queen B   313
Queen Ida   268
Queen Latifah   638
Queensryche   339
Quicksilver (Messenger Service) (see also Dinosaurs)   273
Quireboys   339
Qwest (record company)   847–848

RCA (record company)   848
R.E.M. (see also Michael Stipe)   544–546
REO Speedwagon   448
ROIR (record company)   848
Radiators   266
Radio (see also Lyrics; Rap)   764–765, 823–831
Railway Children   721
Rain Parade   561–562
Raindogs   722
Rainmakers   722
Rainwater, Marvin   87
Raitt, Bonnie   375
Ramone, Phil   863
Ramones   500–501

Rank and File   746
Ranking Roger (see also Beat/English Beat; General Public)   575
Rap/Hip Hop   620–643, 759–760
Rare Earth   260
Rascals, The (see also Felix Cavaliere)   260
Ratings   765
Ratt (see also Motley Crue)   339–340
Raunch Hands   269
Rave-Ups   722
Ravens   162
Ray, Goodman and Brown   614
Ray, Johnnie   104
Raybeats   183–184
Raymonde   722
Razor   340
Razorcuts   722
Rea, Chris   434
Reading '90   787
Ready for the World   614
Rebel MC   486
Reckless Sleepers   723
Record Album Covers   876
Record Companies (see also individual company names)   803, 833
Record Promoters   855
Recording Industry   831–867
Recording Studios   856–857
Red Alert   638
Red Box   723
Red Guitars   723
Red Harvest   723
Red Hot Chili Peppers   519–520
Red Letters Day   520
Red Lorry Yellow Lorry   520
Redd Kross   562
Redding, Otis   254
Reddy, Helen   425
Redskins   723–724
Reed, Dan, Network   466
Reed, Lou (see also John Cale; Velvet Underground)   413–414
Reese, Della   104
Reggae (see also Afro-Rock)   276–281
Reivers   746
Religion   876
Renaissance   291
Renaldo and the Loaf   589
Renegade Soundwave   487
Replacements   520–521
Residents   589
Retailers and Retailing (see also Alabama; CBS Compact Disc Club; Lyrics; Sticker-

ing; Texas)   754, 765–766, 769, 803–
804, 877–878
Revenge (see also Joy Division; New Order)
663
Reverb Brothers   724
Revere, Paul, and the Raiders   230
Revillos   573
Revolting Cocks   511
Rhino (record company)   848–849
Rhythm and Blues   7–43
Rhythm and Blues Foundation   779
Rhythm and Blues Revival (see also British
Rhythm and Blues Revival)   377–380
Rhythm Corps   663
Ribot, Marc   358
Rich, Charlie   87–88
Richards, Keith (see also Rolling Stones)
205
Richie, Lionel (see also Commodores)   614
Richman, Jonathan, and the Modern Lovers
724
Ridgeley, Andrew (see also Wham!)   389
Righteous Brothers   260
Riley, Billy Lee   88
Riley, Teddy   638
Riley, Terry   589
Ritenour, Lee   358
Riverdogs (see also Dio; Whitesnake)   340
Robertson, Robbie   414
Robinson, Smokey   250
Rock Hall of Fame   751
Rock and Hyde   228
Rock and Roll, Stylistic Antecedents of   1–
107
Rock and Roll Hall of Fame   752
Rock and Roll Revival   368
Rock Moments   873
Rock 'N' Roll Evening News   872
Rock Opera   292
Rock Steady (see Jamaican Sound)
Rockabilly   44–93
Rockin' Sidney   267
Rockplace   873
Rodgers, Nile (see also Chic)   863
Roe, Tommy   179
Rolling Stone   820–821
Rolling Stone Annual Music Awards   752
Rolling Stones (see also Mick Jagger; Keith
Richards; Ian Stewart; Ron Wood; Bill
Wyman)   202–204
Romania   366
Romeo's Daughter   724
Ronettes   187

Ronson, Mick (see David Bowie; Ian Hunter)
Ronstadt, Linda   233
Roots Rock   741–747
Rosetta Stone   552
Ross, Diana (see also The Supremes)   251
Rotary Connection   302
Roth, David Lee (see also Van Halen)   346
Roulette (record company)   849
Rounder (record company)   849
Roxanne (rap motif)   639, 790
Roxy Music (see also Bryan Ferry)   313
Royal Court of China   725
Royal Crescent Mob   615
Royals (see Hank Ballard and the Mid-
nighters)
Rubin, Rick   863
Rubin, Trevor   304
Rubinoos   573
Rude Buddha   302
Ruff Justis   639
Ruffin, David (see also Hall and Oates; Eddie
Kendrick; The Temptations)   251
Ruffner, Mason   746
Run-D.M.C.   639
Rundgren, Todd   302
Rush   228–229
Rush, Tom   236
Rushen, Patrice   615
Russell, Brenda   615
Ruthless Rap Assassins   639
Ryan, Charlie   88

SBK (record company)   849
S.O.S. Band   458
SST (record company)   850
Sade   359
St. Etienne   476
Salem 66   521
Salsa   281–284
Salt 'N' Pepa   639
Salvation Sunday   725
Sam and Dave   254–255
Sampling (see also Copyright)   864–865
San Antonio Concerts   769–770
San Francisco Sound   270–274
Sanborn, David   359
Sanity Plexus   593
Santana   305
Satire   815–816
Satriani, Joe   184, 725
Savoy (record company)   850
Saxon, Sky, Blues Band (see The Seeds)
Scaffold   213

Scaggs, Boz   260
Scandal   725
Scarlet Fantastic   725
Schilling, Peter   363
Scott, Jack   89
Scott, Ray   89
Scritti Politti   487
Scruffy the Cat   663, 726
Seacer, Levi (see also Prince)   463
Seals and Crofts   422
See No Evil   521
Seeds, The   286
Seger, Bob   270
Self, Ronnie   89
Self-Aid   779
Sequencers   818
Session Players   865–867
Setzer, Brian   381
Seventh Avenue South (club)   351
Sex Pistols (see also Public Image Ltd./
    PiL)   501
Sexton, Charlie   746
Sha Na Na   171, 368
Shadows   190
Shakespeare, Robbie (see Sly Dunbar)
Shakespear's Sister (see also Bananarama)
    476
Shamen   492
Shankar, Ravi   749
Shannon   615
Shannon, Del   179
Shannon, Scott   826
Sharkey, Feargal   260, 726
She Rockers 18   640
Shear, Jules (see also Reckless Sleepers)
    414
Shiela E.   464
Shelleyan Orphan   291
Shields   162
Shimmy Disc (record company)   850
Shinehead   726
Shirelles   188
Shocked, Michelle   414
Shocking Blue   363
Shotgun   341
Shriekback   535–536
Shrubs   726
Shulman, Derek   857
Siberry, Jane   590
Sigue Sigue Sputnik   569
Silas, Lovil, Jr.   857
Silencers   664
Silhouettes   162–163

Silk Tymes Leather   640
Sill, Joel (see Taylor Hackford)
Silos   664
Silver Bullet   640
Simmons, Gene   90
Simon and Garfunkel   237
Simple Minds   536, 726
Simply Red   261
Simtec and Wylie   243
Sinatra, Frank   104–106
Sinatra, Frank, Jr.   106
Sindecut   640
Singer/Songwriter Tradition   399–419
Sinister Cleaners   726
Sink   510
Siouxsie and the Banshees (see also Creatures)
    521
Sisters of Mercy (see also Sigue Sigue Sputnik)
    521–522
Ska (see Jamaican Sound)
Ska/Bluebeat Revival   573–575
Skid Row   341
Skin Games   727
Skinny Puppy (see also Hilt)   527
Skyliners   163
Slave   615
Slay, Frank   863
Slayer   350
Sleeping Dogs Wake   727
Sleeze Beez   363
Slide   746
Sloan, P.F.   241
Sly and the Family Stone   243, 459
Sly Fox   305
Small Faces (see Faces)
Smash Palace   727
Smile   341
Smith, Huey "Piano"   266
Smith, Patti   501
Smith, Ray   90
Smith, Warren   90
Smithereens   664
Smiths (see also Morrissey)   665–666
Smyth, Patty (see Scandal)
Snapdragons   727
Snow, Phoebe   415
So Good So Far   727
Sobule, Jill   415
Social Distortion   522
Sociology   878–879
Soft Rock   420–435
Solar (record company)   850
Solar Enemy   583

Soloff, Lew (*see also* Blood, Sweat and Tears)
    305
Something Happens   727
Songwriters   880–883
Sonic Boom (*see also* Loop; Spacemen 3)   562
Sonic Youth   525–526
Sopwith Camel   274
Soukous (*see* Loketo)
Soul, David   434
Soul Asylum   522
Soul Music   242–263
Soul II Soul   477, 615
Sound Barrier   341
Soundgarden   341
Soundtracks (*see also* Danny Elfman;
    Prince)   794–795, 873
Sounds of the South   274–276
Soup Dragons   487
South Africa   766
Souther, Richard   647
Southside Johnny and the Asbury Jukes
    261
Soxx, Bob B., and the Blue Jeans   187–188
Space Music   648
Spacemen 3 (*see also* Loop, Sonic Boom)   562
Spaniels   163
Spear of Destiny (*see also* Theatre of Hate)
    666, 727–728
Spector Sound (1958–1966)   187–188
Speed Metal   348–350
Spin (magazine)   821
Spinal Tap   342
Spooky Tooth   213
Spread Eagle   342
Springsteen, Bruce (, and the E Street Band)
    (*see also* Roy Britten; Clarence Clemons;
    Nils Lofgren)   449–450, 779
Squeeze/U.K. Squeeze (*see also* Chris Difford
    and Glenn Tilbrook)   502–503
Stabilizers   583
Stacy Q   616
Stamey, Chris (*see also* Golden Palominos)
    666
Stanford Archive of Recorded Sound   751
Stansfield, Lisa   261–262
Stardust, Alvin   214
Starlighters   163
Starr, Andy   90
Starr, Kay   106
Starr, Ringo (*see also* The Beatles; Rory Storm
    and the Hurricanes)   198
Starship (*see* Jefferson Airplane)
Stasium, Ed   863

Stax Records   254, 850
Steeleye Dan   302–303
Steeleye Span   239
Stern, Leni   359
Stetsasonic   640
Stewart, Ian (*see also* Rolling Stones)   205
Stewart, Mark   728
Stewart, Rod (*see also* Jeff Beck; Faces)   213
Stewart, Scott   415
Stickering (*see also* Louisiana; Lyrics; Ratings;
    Retailers and Retailing)   766–768
Stiff Little Fingers   217
Sting (*see also* Branford Marsalis; Police)
    359
Stipe, Michael (*see also* R.E.M.)   546
Stone Roses   739–740
Storm, Gale   106
Storm, Rory, and the Hurricanes   190
Storm, Warren   267
Strader, David   751
Stranglers   503
Straw, Syd (*see also* Golden Palominos)   297
Stray Cats (*see* Brian Setzer)
Streisand, Barbra   426
Strong, Nolan, and the Diablos   163–164
Strummer, Joe (*see also* The Clash)   496
Stryper   342
Style Council (*see also* The Jam; Paul Weller)
    487
Stylistics   257
Sue (record company)   851
Sugar Hill (record company) (*see also* MCA)
    851
Sugar Hill House Band   640
Sugarcubes   667
Suicidal Tendencies   510
Summer, Donna   469
Summers, Gene   90
Summer, Henry Lee   450
Sun and the Moon (*see also* Chameleons U.K.)
    562
Sun City   779–780
Sun Rhythm Section (*see also* Sam Phillips
    and Sun Records)   91
Sundays   728
Sunset (studio)   856
Sunsonic   487
Supertramp   303
Supremes (*see also* Diana Ross)   251
Surf Sound   230–232
Surface   616
Surf MC's   624
Surfaris   232

Surgin' 342
Survival (record company) 851
Survivor 451
Sutliff, Bobby 415
Sweden 364–365, 813
Sweet, Rachel 503
Sweet F.A. 342
Swing Out Sister 477
Switzerland 365
Sylvester 469
Sylvian, David 415, 647
Symphonic Rock 288–291
Synthesizers 818

T'Pau 365
T. Rex 313–314
TV5 871
Tairrie B. 640
Talking Heads (see also David Byrne; Chris
  Frantz; Jerry Harrison; Tom Tom Club)
  536–537
Tams 171
Tangerine Dream 594
Taxxi 343
Taylor, James 415
Taylor, Livingston 415
Taylor, Steve 285
Teardrop Explodes (see also Julian
  Cope) 562–563
"Tears are not Enough" 780
Tears for Fears 538–539
Techno-Pop/Synth-Pop 575–585
Technotronic 459, 492, 641
Teddy and the Twilights 38
Tee, Willie 171
Teen Idols 179–181
Teen Queens 38
Teenage Fan Club 552
Television (see also Music Video; United
  Kingdom; Tom Verlaine) 539, 768–
  769, 868–873
Temple, Julien 811
Temptations, The (see also Eddie Kendrick;
  David Ruffin) 251
10,000 Maniacs 728–729
Tennessee (see also Lyrics; Stickering) 769
Tepper, Robert 434
Terry, Tony 616
Tesla 343
Testament 343
Tex, Joe 257
Tex-Mex 268–269
Texas 729, 769–770, 826

Textones 539
That Petrol Emotion 552–553
The The 539, 667
Theatre of Hate 553
Thee Hypnotics (see Hypnotics, Thee)
They Might Be Giants 667–668
Thin Lizzy 214
3rd Bass (see also MC Hammer) 641
Third World 280
13th Floor Elevators 287
.38 Special 275–276
This Mortal Coil 650
This Poison! 729
Thomas, Carla 255
Thomas, Chris 375, 746
Thomas, David 597
Thomas, Irma 243
Thomas, Rufus 255
Thompson, Hayden 91
Thompson, Richard (and Linda) (see also Fair-
  port Convention) 239–240
Thompson Twins 583–584
Thornton, Willie Mae 38–39
Thorogood, George (, and the Destroyers)
  375
Thrash 509–510
Thrashing Doves 668
Three Dog Night 422
Three Johns 730
Three O'Clock 563
Thrill Kill Kult 487
Throwing Muses (see also Breeders) 668
Thunder, Shelly 641
Thunderpussy 492
Tiffany 387
Tikaram, Tanita 416
Til, Sonny (see The Orioles)
'Til Tuesday 730
Timbuk 3 668–669
Time, The (see also Morris Day; Jimmy "Jam"
  Harris and Terry Lewis) 464
Times 584
Times Two 477
Timex Social Club (see also Club Nouveau)
  616
Titiyo 492
Toad the Wet Sprocket 730
Toasters 575
Tonio K. 540
Tom Tom Club (see also Talking Heads)
  488
Tommy Boy (record company) 851
Top 40 831

Torres, Liz, and Jesse Jone   492
Tosh, Peter (*see also* Bob Marley)   280–281
Toto   233, 451
Touring   787–788
Townshend, Pete (*see also* The Who)   207
Toy Matinee   731
Toys   792
Tradewinds   232
Traffic (*see also* Steve Winwood)   213
Tragedy   641
Translator   540
Treat Her Right   376
Treniers   39
Tribe   303
Tribe Called Quest, A   641
Tridents Mist   731
Triffids   669
Trio (*see also* Emmylou Harris; Linda Ronstadt)   398
Trip Shakespeare   237
Triumph   343–344
Trouble Funk   620
Trower, Robin (*see also* Procol Harum)   376
True Believers   747
True North   851
True West   731
Tuck and Patti   648
Turbans   164
Turncoats   731
Turner, Ike (*see also* Jackie Brenston; Tina Turner)
Turner, (Big) Joe   39–41
Turner, Tina   616–617
Turtles   237
Twelve-Inch Singles/Extended Play Discs   814
Twisted Sister   344
Twitty, Conway   91–92
2 Live Crew (*see also* Censorship)   642
Two Nations   731
Tyrannosaurus Rex (*see* T. Rex)

U2   540–541
U68 (Television channel)   871
UB40   281
UFO   344–345
UK Subs (*see* Moho Pack)
USA For Africa (*see also* "We are the World")   780–781
U.S.S.R.   367
Ullman, Tracey   434
Ulrich, Peter   732

Ultra Vivid Scene   553
Ultrasonic   492
Ultravox   584
Unforgiven   451, 509
United Kingdom (*see also* Television)   770, 782–783, 805–806, 813, 827, 875, 878, 879
Urban Dance Squad   642
Uriah Heep   345

VH-1 (*see* Video Hits One)
Vai, Steve   867
Valens, Ritchie   138–139
Valentine, Kathy (*see also* The Go-Go's)   498
Vallance, Jim (*see also* Bryan Adams)   882
Valli, Frankie (*see* The Four Seasons)
Van Eaton, James   92
Van Halen (*see also* Sammy Hagar; David Lee Roth)   345–346
Van Story, Marcus   92
Vandross, Luther   617–618
Vangelis   594, 648
Vanity   618
Vannelli, Gino   262
Vaughan, Frankie   190
Vaughan, Sarah   107
Vaughan, Stevie Ray (*see also* Jeff Beck)   376
Vaughn, Robert   452
Vee, Bobby (*see also* The Crickets; Buddy Holly)   181
Vega, Alan   584
Vega, Suzanne   416
Velours   164
Vels   434
Velvet Elvis   669
Velvet Underground (*see also* John Cale; Lou Reed)   590
Venetians   731
Ventures   184
Venus in Furs   732
Vera, Billy   434
Verlaine, Tom (*see also* Television)   541
Vernon, Mike   864
Video Clips   810–814
Video Hits One (VH-1)   870
Video Jukeboxes   813–814
Vincent, Gene   139–142
Vinton, Bobby   179
Violence   732, 883–884
Violent Femmes   669
Visconti, Tony   864

Vixen   346
Voivid   526, 732
Volunteer Jam   787

W.A.S.P.   346–347
Wa Wa Nee   217
Wainwright, Loudon, III   416
Waits, Tom   417
Waldman, Wendy   435
Walkabouts   395
Walker, Joe Louis   377
Walker, Jr., and the All Stars   252
Walker Brothers   262
Wall of Voodoo   542
Wang Chung   488, 732
Ward, Billy (see The Dominoes)
Warner Brothers (record company) (see also
   Cold Chillin')   852
Warnes, Jennifer (see also Leonard Cohen)
   435
Warrant   347
Warren, Dianne   882
Warrior Soul   563
Warwick, Dionne   618
Was (Not Was)   488
Washington, Dinah   107
Washington Squares   237
Waters, Muddy   41
Waters, Roger (see also Pink Floyd)   302
Watley, Jody   619
We are Going to Eat You   522
"We are the World" (see also USA for Africa;
   Counterfeiting, Bootlegging, etc)   781–
   782
We've Got a Fuzzbox and We're Gonna Use
   It   733
Weather Prophets   733
Weather Report (see also Josef Zawinul)
   360
Webb, Jim   883
Wednesday Week   733
Welch, Bob   422
Welk, Lawrence   107
Weller, Paul (see also The Jam; Style Council)
   733–734
Wells, Mary   252
Wendy and Lisa (see also Prince)   464
West Germany   783
Westwood One   826–827
Wet Wet Wet   734
Wexler, Jerry (see also Rhythm and Blues)
   854

Wham! (see also George Michael; Andrew
   Ridgely)   387–389
What Is This   452, 734
What? Noise   740
Whispers   243
White, Alan (see also Yes)   304
White, Andy   734
White, Barry   470
White, Karyn   619
White Lion   347
White Noise (see also Producers)   524–526
White Rope   734
Whitesnake (see also Deep Purple; Riverdogs)
   347
Who, The (see also Roger Daltrey; Keith
   Moon; Simon Phillips; Pete Townsh-
   end)   206
Wiedlin, Jane (see also The Go-Go's)   735
Wigs   735
Wild Cherry   459
Wild Choir   735
Wild Seeds   669
Wilde, Kim   435
Wilder, Webb, and the Beatnecks   395
Williams, Jay   493
Williams, Larry   142
Williams, Lucinda   377, 747
Williams, Maurice, and the Zodiacs   164–
   165
Williams, Otis, and the Charms   165
Williams, Victoria   417
Williams, Wendell, and the Criminal Ele-
   ment Orchestra   643
Willis, Chuck   42
Willows   165
Wilson, Brian (see also Beach Boys)   232
Wilson, Danny   686
Wilson, Jackie (see also The Dominoes)   42–
   43
Wilson, Nancy   107
Wilson, Shanice   619
Wilson Phillips   435
Winchester, Jesse   417
Winger   347
Winwood, Steve (see also Traffic)   262
Wire   504
Wire Train   747
Wizzard (see Roy Wood)
Wolf, Peter (see also J. Geils Band)   380
Wolfhounds   735
Wolfsbane   348
Womack, Bobby   459

Wonder, (Little) Stevie   252–253
Wonder Stuff   563
Wood, Ron (*see also* Jeff Beck Group; Faces;
Rolling Stones)   206
Wood, Roy   303
Wood Children   735
Woodentops   670
Woodstock   787
Working Week   735
World Beat (*see also* Afro-Rock; Junkanoo;
Reggae)   748–749
World Party   736
Wray, Link   184–185
Wright, Betty   244
Wyatt, Robert   303
Wyman, Bill (*see also* Rolling Stones)   206
Wynn, Steve (*see also* Dream Syndicate)   558

X   504–505
XTC   542–543
X-Clan   643
X-Mal Deutschland   554
X-Ray Spex   505
Xymox/Clan of Xymox   554

Y Kant Tori Read   418
Yardbirds, The (*see also* Jeff Beck; Eric Clapton)   207
Yargo   493

Yaz (*see also* Alison Moyet)   584
Yeah Yeah Noh   736
Yello   585
Yellow Balloon   288
Yellow Magic Orchestra/Y.M.O.   585
Yellowman   281
Yelvington, Malcolm   93
Yes (*see also* Steve Howe; Trevor Rubin; Alan
White)   304
Yetnikoff, Walter   854
York, Rusty   93
Young, Neil (*see also* Crosby, Stills and
Nash)   418
Young, Paul   262–263
Young Disciples   493
Young Gods   365
Young MC   643
Young Neal and the Vipers   736

ZZ Top   377
Zaentz, Saul (*see also* John Fogerty)   855
Zapp   459
Zappa, Frank (*see also* Censorship; Mothers of
Invention)   590–592
Zawinul, Josef (*see also* Weather Report)
360
Zevon, Warren   419
Zutaut, Tom   855
Zydeco   268

ABOUT THE AUTHORS

FRANK W. HOFFMANN (B.A., M.L.S., Indiana University; Ph.D., University of Pittsburgh) is Professor of Library Science at Sam Houston State University and has taught at the Graduate Library School of Louisiana State University. He has been a library practitioner at nearly a dozen public, academic, and special libraries. He is Vice President on the Board of Trustees for the Montgomery County (Texas) Library System and is a Voting Representative for the Houston Area Libraries System. In addition to serving on many national and regional professional committees, he regularly evaluates federal grant applications, speaks to libraries and educational groups on various popular culture topics, and edits a quarterly academic journal, *Popular Culture in Libraries* (Haworth Press). He has published numerous articles (including five entries in the recently published *Encyclopedia of Recorded Sound,* Garland Press) and more than a dozen books, most notably the multi-volume sets, *The Encyclopedia of Fads,* the *Cash Box* chart series (Scarecrow Press) and the *Literature of Rock* series (Scarecrow Press).

B. LEE COOPER (B.S., Bowling Green State University; M.A., Michigan State University; Ph.D., Ohio State University) is Academic Vice President and Professor of History at Great Falls (MT) College. An internationally recognized expert on American culture and popular music, Dr. Cooper serves on the editorial advisory boards of three scholarly periodicals—*Popular Culture In*

Libraries, Journal Of American Culture, and *Popular Music And Society.* In addition, he is the author of seven books and more than 250 articles and reviews. In 1983 he received the prestigious ASCAP-Deems Taylor Award For Literary Excellence. Two of Dr. Cooper's recently released Scarecrow Press volumes are *Response Recordings: An Answer Song Discography, 1950–1990* (with Wayne S. Haney) and *Rockabilly: A Bibliographic Resource Guide* (with Wayne S. Haney).